Y0-BWG-564

Principles of

ACCOUNTING

Intermediate

PRENTICE-HALL ACCOUNTING SERIES
H. A. FINNEY, Editor

Prentice-Hall, Inc., Englewood Cliffs, New Jersey

Principles of ACCOUNTING

INTERMEDIATE

by

H. A. FINNEY, Ph.B., C.P.A.

and

HERBERT E. MILLER, Ph.D., C.P.A.

Michigan State University

SIXTH EDITION

LIBRARY OF CONGRESS
CATALOG CARD NO. 65-18498

PRINTED IN THE UNITED STATES OF AMERICA

70285-C

Current printing (last digit):
11 10 9 8

PRENTICE-HALL INTERNATIONAL, INC., *London*
PRENTICE-HALL OF AUSTRALIA, PTY., LTD., *Sydney*
PRENTICE-HALL OF CANADA, LTD., *Toronto*
PRENTICE-HALL OF INDIA (PRIVATE) LTD., *New Delhi*
PRENTICE-HALL OF JAPAN, INC., *Tokyo*

Preface

As in the past, the advice of teachers was sought in the preparation of this, the sixth, edition; helpful suggestions were received. Although the revision is thoroughgoing, responses from teachers indicated that no drastic changes were needed; it is believed that the general approach, the level of presentation, and the objectives that characterized the preceding edition have been maintained.

The authors have continued the practice of quoting abundantly from publications of the American Accounting Association and the American Institute of Certified Public Accountants, including the latter's *Accounting Research Studies,* weaving the quotations and references into the text discussions to acquaint the student with any pronouncements of these organizations relative to the matters under consideration.

In the chapters of this revision, the mechanics of the accounting process have been de-emphasized and the theoretical aspects have been stressed. In general, the character of the assignment material has been modified: fewer working papers are required in solutions and more emphasis has been placed on analysis.

Among the more significant features of the revision, the following may be mentioned. New and simplified working papers have been presented in the "Funds Statements" chapter, and the coverage has been expanded to take cognizance of the recently published Opinion No. 3 of the Accounting Principles Board, which recognizes that funds statements may be prepared for purposes other than to account for changes in working capital. Income tax allocation has been given additional attention, with extended discussion of loss carryback and carryforward. The price-level discussion has been revised and expanded, with special attention to procedural techniques; assignment material has been provided.

As in the preceding edition, the assignment material has been tailor-made to be specifically applicable to, and to thoroughly cover, the related text material. The problems vary widely as to length and difficulty. The workbook accompanying the text provides additional problem material, in objective form, for use as class exercises or as homework.

We are indebted to the companies which permitted us to use statements that appeared in their annual reports and that are reproduced in Chapter 3. They are illustrative of modern trends in corporate reports.

H. A. FINNEY

HERBERT E. MILLER

Contents

CHAPTER

1

Accounting Procedures Reviewed

Accounting defined. An often-quoted definition of accounting is the one formulated by the Committee on Terminology of the American Institute of Certified Public Accountants.

> Accounting is the art of recording, classifying, and summarizing in a significant manner and in terms of money, transactions and events which are, in part at least, of a financial character, and interpreting the results thereof.

The accounting cycle. The principal procedural activities of the accounting process, other than the preparation and checking of business papers, are:

Recording transactions in books of original entry.
Posting to ledger accounts.
Taking a trial balance of the general ledger and seeing that the subsidiary records are in agreement with their controlling accounts.
Making adjustments for such matters as bad debts, depreciation, accruals, and revenue and cost apportionments.
Preparing working papers.
Preparing statements showing the results of business operations and the financial position of the business.
Closing the books.
Possibly reversing some of the adjusting entries.
Taking an after-closing trial balance.

Debit-credit process. The record-keeping part of accounting is based on a fundamental relationship or equation, namely:

ASSETS = LIABILITIES + OWNERS' EQUITY

The elements in the above equation represent broad categories. A business may have anywhere from a few to dozens of different assets, and records must be maintained to show the increases, decreases, and present status of each asset. The same applies to liabilities. And there are numerous causes of increases and decreases in the owners' equity. To record all of the increases and decreases in assets, liabilities, and owners' equity, accounts are maintained.

Increases and decreases are recorded in accounts in the manner shown below.

Asset Accounts	
Increases	Decreases

Liability Accounts	
Decreases	Increases

Owners' Equity Accounts	
Decreases	Increases

Many business transactions result in revenue or expense. Such transactions affect the amount of the owners' equity. It is customary to use revenue and expense accounts to accumulate the results of such transactions. Because revenues increase the owners' equity and expenses reduce the owners' equity, the revenues and expenses are recorded according to the following plan.

Expense Accounts	
(Debited for expenses)	

Revenue Accounts	
	(Credited for revenues)

Kinds of accounting records. In general, business records consist of the following:

Documents, or business papers, such as invoices, credit memorandums, bank checks, insurance policies, freight bills, and promissory notes. These furnish detailed information about business transactions, state the terms of contracts, and serve as evidence of the propriety of accounting entries.

Books of original entry, such as the general journal, sales journal, accounts payable journal, and cash receipts and disbursements journals. These books contain chronological records of business transactions and show, among other facts, the accounts to be debited and credited to record the transactions.

Ledgers—both general and subsidiary. These show in detail or in summarized form the debits and credits to each account.

Registers and other supplementary records, such as the notes receivable register, the notes payable register, and the insurance register. These furnish more detailed information than can conveniently be recorded in the accounts. They may also serve as books of original entry, and may take the place of subsidiary ledgers.

Working papers in which information for the periodical statements is assembled.

Periodical statements, which show the results of operations and the financial position of the business.

Books of original entry. A book of original entry contains a record of transactions in their chronological order, names the accounts to be debited and credited to record each transaction, and states the debit and credit amounts. The recording function is completed by posting the debits and credits shown in the journals to the various accounts.

Ledgers and controlling accounts. A *ledger* is a group of accounts. If a ledger contains accounts (some of which may be controlling accounts rather than detailed accounts) for all of the assets, liabilities, and elements of ownership equity of the business, including revenues and expenses, it is called a *general ledger.*

In a large business there usually are several groups of similar accounts. There may be many accounts receivable and accounts payable; if deposits are kept in several banks, an account must be kept for each bank account; it may be desirable to maintain a separate account for each parcel of land, for each building, and for each security investment; there will be numerous selling expense accounts, and numerous general expense accounts; and there may be other groups of kindred accounts.

If all of these accounts are kept in one ledger, the posting work may be too much for one employee. To provide for a division of labor, the following procedure may be applied:

Keep the several accounts of the group in a subsidiary ledger.
Keep a controlling account in the general ledger. It is debited with totals of the charges to the accounts in the subsidiary ledger; it is credited with totals of the credits to the accounts in the subsidiary ledger; and its balance should be equal to the sum of the balances of the accounts in the subsidiary ledger.

The controlling account and subsidiary ledger device also has the advantage of helping to locate errors by isolating them. If the trial balance of the general ledger shows that the general ledger is in balance, but the sum of the balances in a subsidiary ledger does not agree with the balance in its controlling account, it may be presumed (but not definitely known) that the error is in the subsidiary ledger. If the general ledger is not in balance and the subsidiary ledger is in agreement with its control, it may be presumed (but, again, not definitely known) that the error is in the general ledger—some place other than in the controlling account.

Auxiliary accounts. An auxiliary account is one which is closely related to another (major, or principal) account. Auxiliary accounts are sometimes called *contra,* or *offset,* accounts if the principal account has a debit balance and the auxiliary account has a credit balance, or vice versa. They are sometimes called *adjunct* accounts if the balances of the principal and auxiliary accounts are both debits or both credits.

The Sales Returns and Allowances account is a contra to the Sales account. The Purchase Returns and Allowances account is a contra to, and the Transportation In account is an adjunct to, the Purchases account. The Allowance for Doubtful Accounts and accumulated depreciation accounts are contra accounts.

The general journal. It is theoretically possible, although not often practicable, to use a general journal as the only book of original entry. Entries in a general journal are illustrated below.

JOURNAL

19—						
July	1	Cash	10,000	00		
		Capital stock			10,000	00
		Issuance of 100 shares of stock.				
	2	Purchases	2,500	00		
		Cash			2,500	00
		Purchase of merchandise for cash.				

Accountants have given a great deal of thought to the development of books of original entry that effect a division and saving of labor. Two principal devices have been employed: special-purpose books and special columns. Some illustrations follow.

Special-purpose books of original entry. The following sales journal is a special-purpose book of original entry.

SALES JOURNAL (Page 1)

Date		√	Name	Invoice No.	Debit Accts. Rec. / Credit Sales	
19—						
May	2	√	R. E. West	1	800	00
	7	√	G. O. Davis	2	450	00
	12	√	S. E. Bates	3	600	00
	18	√	R. E. West	4	850	00
	23	√	G. O. Davis	5	280	00
	30	√	R. E. West	6	300	00
					3,280	00
					(10) (40)	

The check marks show that the individual entries have been posted to the customers' accounts in the subsidiary ledger. The number (10) at the foot of the money column shows that the total has been posted to the debit of the Accounts Receivable controlling account. The number (40) shows that the total has been posted as a credit to the Sales account.

Such a journal facilitates a division of labor because one employee can be assigned to recording sales on account. It saves posting work because the column total, instead of the individual entries, is posted to the Sales account.

Some of the other special-purpose books of original entry that may be kept are listed on the following page.

Sales returns and allowances journal.
Accounts payable journal.
Purchase returns and allowances journal.
Cash receipts journal.
Cash disbursements journal.

Special columns. Special columns may be introduced in books of original entry for the following purposes:

For classification of data.
To facilitate recording transactions.
To save labor in posting.

Special columns for these purposes are shown in the cash receipts journal on page 6.

Columns for classification of data are illustrated by the two Sales columns.

The Sales Discounts debit and Interest Earned credit columns are examples of columns to facilitate recording transactions when the entry includes more than one debit or credit. If no special column is provided, entries may be made in the Sundry sections.

Posting labor is saved when there is more than one entry in a column, because the column total, rather than the individual entries, can be posted to the general ledger. For this reason, a special Accounts Receivable controlling account credit column should usually be provided in the cash receipts journal. Postings of totals of special columns are indicated by writing the account numbers below the totals.

Combined books of original entry and subsidiary records. The voucher register is one of the most frequently used records combining the features of a book of original entry and the features of a subsidiary record. Many other such dual-purpose books are used in the accounting systems of large enterprises.

When a voucher system is in use, a formal voucher must be prepared and approved before a cash disbursement can be made. As each liability is processed for payment, information is entered on the voucher by various employees. When the voucher form is complete, it describes the transaction that created the liability and shows the work done in verifying the liability and approving it for payment. Each voucher is recorded in the voucher register; the proper asset, expense, or other account is debited, and the Vouchers Payable account is credited. When the cash disbursement is made (either immediately or at a later date), an entry is made in the cash disbursements journal (sometimes called a *check register*) debiting Vouchers Payable and crediting Cash, and also crediting Purchase Discounts if a discount is taken.

The form of the voucher register is indicated by the very abridged illustration on page 7.

(Left side)

CASH RECEIPTS JOURNAL

Line No.	Date		Explanation	Debits: Cash	Debits: Sales Discounts	Debits: Sundry Accounts: Name	L.F.	Amount
	19—							
1	May	1	Sale	480 00				
2		2	Invoice April 24, less 2%	980 00	20 00			
3		3	Fred White's note	505 00				
4		4	Note discounted at bank	990 00		Interest expense	51	10 00
5								
28		29	Invoice May 21, less 2%	1,470 00	30 00			
29		30	Sales	490 00				
30				29,578 00	298 00			80 00
31				(1)	(47)			

(Right side)

Line No.	Account Credited	Credits: Accounts Receivable: √	Accounts Receivable: Amount	Sales: Dept. A	Sales: Dept. B	Interest Earned	Sundry Accounts: L.F.	Sundry Accounts: Amount
1				280 00	200 00			
2	Frank Brown	√	1,000 00					
3	Notes receivable					5 00	13	500 00
4	Notes payable						28	1.000 00
5								
28	George White	√	1,500 00					
29				315 00	175 00			
30			15,875 00	4,860 00	5,645 00	60 00		3,516 00
31			(10)	(45)	(46)	(50)		

VOUCHER REGISTER

Voucher No.	Date		Payee	Explanation	Terms	Date Paid	Check No.	Credit Vouchers Payable	Debits				
									Purchases	Transportation In	Sundry Accounts		
											Name of Account	L.F.	Amount
7-93	19— July	6	The Osborne Company . .	Invoice, July 3	1/10; n/30			270 00	270 00				

The entry in the voucher register records a debit to Purchases and a credit to Vouchers Payable, which is another name for Accounts Payable. Voucher registers usually contain many debit columns for accounts which are frequently debited. Only three debit columns are shown in the illustration—one for purchases, one for transportation in, and one for accounts for which no special column is provided.

The cash disbursements entry for the payment of The Osborne Company voucher is shown below.

CHECK REGISTER

Check No.	Date		Payee	Voucher No.	Debit Vouchers Payable	Credits	
						Purchase Discounts	Cash
1668	19— July	12	The Osborne Company	7-93	270 00	2 70	267 30

When a voucher is paid, notations are made in the Date Paid and Check Number columns of the voucher register, in the manner illustrated below.

VOUCHER REGISTER

Voucher No.	Date		Payee	Explanation	Terms	Date Paid		Check No.	Credit Vouchers Payable		P
7-93	19— July	6	The Osborne Company . .	Invoice, July 3	1/10; n/30	19— July	12	1668	270	00	

Entries in the voucher register with no notations in the Date Paid and Check Number columns are "open," or unpaid, items. Their total should agree with the balance in the Vouchers Payable controlling account in the general ledger. The voucher register thus serves as a subsidiary record which takes the place of the accounts payable subsidiary ledger.

Posting from documents. One illustration should suffice to show how labor can be saved by posting directly from documents. Instead of recording sales in a sales journal and posting therefrom, carbon copies of all sales invoices can be kept in a binder, which thus serves as a sales journal. The amount of each charge sale can be posted directly from the carbon copy of the invoice to the customer's account in the subsidiary accounts receivable ledger, and the total, shown by an adding-machine tape (retained in the binder), can be posted as a debit to the Accounts Receivable controlling account and as a credit to the Sales account.

The procedures reviewed in this chapter to save labor and to permit the division of labor may need further refinement whenever the volume of transactions is large. The recording process may be expedited by the use of accounting machines or electronic devices. Their use does not alter the basic debit-credit process whereby transaction data are recorded, classified, and summarized into meaningful aggregates; they do nothing more than can be achieved through the use of special journals of the type previously illustrated, but they do offer greater speed and economy.

Trial balance and subsidiary ledger schedules. The general ledger trial balance taken periodically serves as a test of the mechanical accuracy of the bookkeeping procedures (to the extent of establishing the equality of debits and credits) and provides a list of account balances to be used in the preparation of statements. If the general ledger is well organized, the account balances will appear in the trial balance in a sequence similar to that in which they will appear in the statements. However, amounts may appear in the statements although they do not appear in the general ledger trial balance—for instance, the sum of the credit balances in accounts in the subsidiary accounts receivable ledger.

The schedules of the subsidiary ledgers are also a test of mechanical accuracy; they establish the agreement of the subsidiary ledgers with their related controlling accounts.

Cut-off. There must be a correct cut-off at the end of any period for which statements are prepared. That is, the accounts should include entries for all transactions which occurred before the end of the period, and should not include entries for any transactions which occurred after the end of the period. Complete information regarding some transactions may not be available on the last day of the period in which they occurred; for this reason, it often is necessary to wait a few days after the end of the period before completing the recording and posting and taking a trial balance.

Mistakes in the accounts. An accountant not infrequently discovers that mistakes have been made in the accounts. This becomes apparent if the trial balance does not balance, or if the balance in a controlling account is out of agreement with the sum of the account balances in its subsidiary ledger.

If the general ledger trial balance does not balance, the accountant should perform the following operations, in the order indicated:

(1) Refoot the general ledger trial balance.
(2) Compare the balances shown by the trial balance with those shown by the accounts in the general ledger.
(3) Recompute the balances of the general ledger accounts.
(4) Trace the postings to the general ledger.
(5) Refoot the books of original entry.
(6) See whether the sum of the totals of the debit columns is equal to the sum of the totals of the credit columns of each columnar book of original entry; if they are not in balance, refoot each column. If this does not disclose the error, see whether the debits and credits in each entry are equal.

When the general ledger is in balance but a subsidiary ledger is out of agreement with its control, the presumption is that the error or errors causing the disagreement are within the subsidiary ledger. In this case the accountant should:

(1) Refoot the schedule of the subsidiary ledger.
(2) See that the balances were carried correctly from the subsidiary ledger to the schedule.
(3) Recompute the balance of each subsidiary ledger account.
(4) Trace the postings to the subsidiary ledger.

ADJUSTING ENTRIES

Cash and accrual bases of accounting. Because statements of operations and financial position are prepared periodically, it is necessary to determine the accounting period to which revenues, expenses, and losses are applicable.

There are two principal bases for assigning revenues and expenses to accounting periods: the cash basis and the accrual basis.

Cash basis. On a pure cash basis, no income is taken from sales on account until collections are received; purchases are not recorded until payments are made; and no consideration is given to inventories.

Revenue from other sources is regarded as earned in the period in which the cash collection is received. No revenue is regarded as having been earned for services performed unless the cash has been collected; and any cash collections for services to be rendered in the future are regarded as revenue of the period in which the collections are received, even though nothing has been done to earn it.

Expenses are regarded as applicable to the period in which the cash payment is made. No charge for bad debts appears in the operating statement because no earning is taken until the receivable is collected; and there is no charge for depreciation because the entire cost of a fixed asset is regarded as an expense of the period in which the purchase disbursement is made.

It is obvious that such an accounting basis is wholly unsatisfactory for a business with material amounts of expenses accrued or prepaid, revenue accrued or collected in advance, fixed assets, inventories, accounts receivable, or accounts payable.

The so-called cash basis of reporting income for federal income tax purposes, as governed by the law and the regulations, is really a mixed cash-accrual basis. If sales of purchased or manufactured goods are a major source of revenue, recognition must be given to sales on account, purchases on account, and inventories. An expenditure for fixed assets cannot be taken as a deduction wholly in the period in which the purchase disbursement is made; deductions can be taken only for periodical depreciation and amortization. But consideration need not be given to bad debt provisions (since the taxpayer may elect the charge-off basis), nor to accrued or deferred revenue or expense.

Accrual basis. On the accrual basis of accounting, revenue is regarded as earned in the period in which sales are made or the services rendered (regardless of when collected), and expenses are regarded as applicable to the period in which they are incurred (regardless of when paid).

The "matching" of revenues and expenses for the purpose of determining net income on an accrual basis often requires the exercise of trained judgment, and not infrequently involves estimates. But it is fundamental that, if the books are to reflect the results of operations and the financial position on an accrual basis, adjusting entries must be made for bad debts, accruals, and cost and revenue apportionments.

Illustrative adjusting entries. Adjusting entries dealing with matters such as those mentioned in the preceding section are illustrated below. Instead of showing the adjusting journal entries, their effect on the accounts is shown.

Provision for doubtful accounts. The adjusting entry to provide for doubtful accounts debits an expense account and credits an allowance account, which is contra to the accounts receivable.

		Bad Debts		Allowance for Doubtful Accounts	
1965					
Dec. 31	Adjusting entry	1,000			1,000

The debit balance in the Bad Debts account will be shown as an expense in the income statement.

The credit balance in the allowance account will be shown in the balance sheet as a deduction from the accounts receivable.

Cost apportionments—Depreciation and amortization. The cost of a fixed asset should be written off as an expense gradually over the life of the asset. The periodical adjusting entry includes a debit to a depreciation (expense) account and a credit to an accumulated depreciation account.

		Depreciation Expense —Building		Accumulated Depreciation —Building	
1965					
Dec. 31	Balance from prior periods				6,000
31	Adjusting entry	1,500			1,500

The $1,500 debit balance in the Depreciation Expense—Building account will be shown as an expense in the income statement.

The $7,500 credit balance in the Accumulated Depreciation—Building account will be shown in the balance sheet as a deduction from the balance in the Building account.

Cost apportionments—Prepaid expenses. The kind of adjusting entry to be made for the apportionment of an expense prepayment that will benefit more than one period depends on the nature of the account that was charged with the expenditure.

To illustrate, assume that a company paid $300 at the beginning of the year for a three-year insurance policy. The adjusting entry at the end of the year, to show that the insurance expense for the year amounts to $100, will depend on whether the $300 expenditure was charged to an unexpired insurance (asset) account or to an insurance expense account. The two conditions are illustrated below.

Original charge to an asset account: The adjusting entry should transfer the *expired* portion from the asset account to an expense account.

		Unexpired Insurance		Insurance Expense	
1965					
Jan. 2	Original expenditure	300			
Dec. 31	Adjusting entry		100	100	

Original charge to an expense account: The adjusting entry should transfer the *unexpired* portion from the expense account to an asset account.

		Unexpired Insurance		Insurance Expense	
1965					
Jan. 2	Original expenditure			300	
Dec. 31	Adjusting entry	200			200

In either case:

The $200 debit balance in the Unexpired Insurance account should appear as an asset in the balance sheet.

The $100 debit balance in the Insurance Expense account should appear in the income statement.

Revenue apportionments. The kind of adjusting entry to be made for the apportionment of revenue booked in advance and to be earned during more than one period depends on the nature of the account that was originally credited.

To illustrate, assume that a magazine publisher made collections of $100,000 during the year for one-, two-, and three-year subscriptions, and that at the end of the year only $40,000 had been earned by the issuance of magazines. The adjusting entry at the end of the year, to show that $40,000 had been earned, will depend on whether the $100,000 was credited to Subscriptions Collected in Advance (an unearned revenue account) or to Subscriptions Earned. The two conditions are illustrated below.

Original credit to an unearned revenue account: The adjusting entry should transfer the *earned* portion from the unearned revenue account to an earned revenue account.

		Subscriptions Collected in Advance		Subscriptions Earned	
1965					
Various dates	Advance collections		100,000		
Dec. 31	Adjusting entry	40,000			40,000

Original credit to a revenue account: The adjusting entry should transfer the *unearned* portion from the revenue account to an unearned revenue account.

		Subscriptions Collected in Advance		Subscriptions Earned	
1965					
Various dates	Advance collections				100,000
Dec. 31	Adjusting entry		60,000	60,000	

In either case:

The $40,000 credit balance in the Subscriptions Earned account should appear in the income statement.

The $60,000 credit balance in the Subscriptions Collected in Advance account should appear on the liability side of the balance sheet.

Accrued income. Assume that, in addition to $100 of interest collected on notes receivable during the year, uncollected accrued interest at the end of the year amounts to $50. The adjusting entry consists of a debit to an asset account and a credit to an income account.

		Accrued Interest on Notes Receivable		Interest Earned	
1965					
Various dates	Collected				100
Dec. 31	Adjusting entry	50			50

The $50 debit balance in the Accrued Interest on Notes Receivable account should appear in the balance sheet as an asset.

The $150 credit balance in the Interest Earned account should appear in the income statement.

Accrued expenses. Assume that, in addition to $10,000 of wages and salaries paid during the year, accrued and unpaid wages at the end of the year amount to $500. The adjusting entry consists of a debit to an expense account and a credit to an accrued liability account.

		Wages and Salaries		Accrued Wages and Salaries	
1965					
Various dates	Paid	10,000			
Dec. 31	Adjusting entry	500			500

The $10,500 debit balance in the Wages and Salaries account should appear in the income statement.

The $500 credit balance in the Accrued Wages and Salaries account should appear as a liability in the balance sheet.

CHAPTER

2

Working Papers; Closing Procedures

Purpose of working papers. Working papers facilitate the preparation of financial statements by classifying the account balances according to the statements in which they will appear, and the preparation of entries involved in the procedure of adjusting and closing the books. The form in which working papers are prepared depends to some extent on the preference of the accountant. Several illustrations are presented.

MERCANTILE BUSINESS

First illustration—Perpetual inventory maintained. These working papers, shown on page 15 were prepared as follows:

Step 1. The general heading and column headings were entered.
Step 2. The trial balance was entered in the first pair of columns.
Step 3. The following year-end adjustments were entered in the Adjustments columns.

(A) The allowance for doubtful accounts was increased $600.

Bad debts expense	600	
Allowance for doubtful accounts		600

(B) Depreciation of the delivery equipment was computed at 20 per cent of the $4,000 balance in the asset account.

Depreciation—Delivery equipment	800	
Accumulated depreciation—Delivery equipment		800

(C) Interest on the bank loan to maturity, in the amount of $120, was paid and debited to Prepaid Interest. The portion applicable to 1965 was $80.

THE *A* CORPORATION

Working Papers—For the Year Ended December 31, 1965

	Trial Balance		Adjustments		Adjusted Trial Balance		Income Statement		Retained Earnings Statement		Balance Sheet	
Cash	9,730				9,730						9,730	
Accounts receivable	19,500				19,500						20,000	500
Allowance for doubtful accounts		300		A 600		900						900
Notes receivable	5,000				5,000						5,000	
Inventory, December 31, 1965	30,000				30,000						30,000	
Unexpired insurance	375			D 160	215						215	
Prepaid interest	120			C 80	40						40	
Delivery equipment	4,000				4,000						4,000	
Accumulated depreciation—Delivery equipment		1,600		B 800		2,400						2,400
Bank loans		8,000				8,000						8,000
Accounts payable		10,300				10,300						10,300
Delivery fees collected in advance		300	E 200			100						100
Capital stock		25,000				25,000						25,000
Retained earnings, December 31, 1964		9,380				9,380				9,380		
Dividends	2,000				2,000				2,000			
Sales		203,000				203,000		203,000				
Sales returns and allowances	980				980		980					
Sales discounts	1,670				1,670		1,670					
Cost of goods sold	150,000				150,000		150,000					
Salesmen's salaries	12,650		F 500		13,150		13,150					
Rent expense	3,000				3,000		3,000					
Advertising	10,200				10,200		10,200					
Delivery expense	3,275				3,275		3,275					
Miscellaneous selling expenses	860				860		860					
Office salaries	3,260		F 130		3,390		3,390					
Office expense	930				930		930					
Property taxes	190				190		190					
Interest earned		60		G 25		85		85				
Interest expense	200		C 80		280		280					
	257,940	257,940										
Bad debts expense			A 600		600		600					
Depreciation—Delivery equipment			B 800		800		800					
Insurance expense			D 160		160		160					
Delivery earnings				E 200		200		200				
Accrued salaries payable				F 630		630						630
Accrued interest receivable			G 25		25						25	
			2,495	2,495	259,995	259,995	189,485	203,285				
Net income before income tax—down							13,800					
							203,285	203,285				
Net income before income tax—brought down								13,800				
Federal income tax							3,036					3,036
Net income							10,764			10,764		
							13,800	13,800	2,000	20,144		
Retained earnings, December 31, 1965									18,144			18,144
									20,144	20,144	69,010	69,010

Interest expense	80	
Prepaid interest		80

(D) Insurance premiums were debited to Unexpired Insurance. The expired portion, $160, was transferred to an expense account.

Insurance expense	160	
Unexpired insurance		160

(E) On November 1, the company collected $300 for services to be rendered in making deliveries for another store during November, December, and January. The credit was made to Delivery Fees Collected in Advance. By the end of the year, $200 was earned; it is transferred to a revenue account.

Delivery fees collected in advance	200	
Delivery earnings		200

(F) Accrued salesmen's salaries amount to $500, and accrued office salaries amount to $130.

Salesmen's salaries	500	
Office salaries	130	
Accrued salaries payable		630

(G) Accrued interest on notes receivable is $25.

Accrued interest receivable	25	
Interest earned		25

Step 4. The Adjustments columns were totaled and the account balances after adjustments were entered in the Adjusted Trial Balance columns. Then these columns were totaled.

Step 5. Each account balance in the Adjusted Trial Balance columns was extended to the appropriate column for the statement in which the balance should appear. Debit balances were extended to debit columns; credit balances were extended to credit columns.

(The amount shown as accounts receivable in the Adjusted Trial Balance column is the balance of the controlling account. The subsidiary ledger contains accounts with debit balances totaling $20,000 and accounts with credit balances totaling $500. These amounts were entered in the Balance Sheet columns.)

Step 6. The Income Statement columns were footed; the net income before income tax was entered as a balancing figure and brought down after again footing the columns.

Step 7. The income tax was computed and entered in the Income Statement debit column, and in the Balance Sheet credit column as a liability. If the federal income tax is not recorded until the net income before tax is computed in the working papers, an additional adjusting entry therefor is required.

If the income tax was recorded in the accounts before the working papers were prepared, Step 6 would consist merely of footing the Income Statement columns, and Step 7 would be omitted.

Step 8. The net income was entered as a balancing figure in the Income Statement debit column and in the Retained Earnings credit column.

Step 9. The Retained Earnings columns were footed; the amount of the retained earnings at the end of the year was entered as a balancing figure in the Retained Earnings debit column and in the Balance Sheet credit column. The Retained Earnings and Balance Sheet columns were footed.

Some accountants make the adjusting entries in the journal and then apply them to the unadjusted balances in the working papers. Other accountants first enter the adjustments in the working papers and do not make the adjusting entries in the journal until later, when they make the entries to close the books.

If statements are prepared monthly but the books are closed only annually, the monthly adjustments may be applied to the working papers only, without making adjusting entries in the books.

Closing entries. After the annual statements have been prepared, it is customary to close the books. This is accomplished by making and posting closing entries. When the closing has been completed, the only accounts showing balances will be the asset, liability, and owners' equity accounts. The revenue, expense, and dividend accounts will be closed; that is, these accounts will have zero balances.

Several illustrations of closing entries are presented in this chapter. The first illustration is based on data in the preceding working papers for The *A* Corporation.

Sales	203,000	
Interest earned	85	
Delivery earnings	200	
Revenue and expense		203,285
To close the accounts with credit balances.		
Revenue and expense	192,521	
Sales returns and allowances		980
Sales discounts		1,670
Cost of goods sold		150,000
Salesmen's salaries		13,150
Rent expense		3,000
Advertising		10,200
Delivery expense		3,275
Miscellaneous selling expenses		860
Office salaries		3,390
Office expense		930
Property taxes		190
Interest expense		280
Bad debts expense		600
Depreciation—Delivery equipment		800
Insurance expense		160
Federal income tax		3,036
To close accounts with debit balances.		

Revenue and expense	10,764	
Retained earnings		10,764
To close the Revenue and Expense account.		
Retained earnings	2,000	
Dividends		2,000
To close the Dividends account.		

The first entry closes all of the accounts whose balances were extended to the Income Statement credit column of the working papers.

The second entry closes all of the accounts whose balances were extended to the Income Statement debit column of the working papers, and also the income tax expense.

The third entry closes the Revenue and Expense account.

The last entry closes the Dividends account.

Second illustration—Periodical inventory method. Illustrative working papers for a company that does not maintain a perpetual inventory are shown on the opposite page. Under such circumstances, the inventory balance shown in the unadjusted trial balance is the beginning inventory. An adjusting entry may be used to determine the cost of goods sold, to remove the beginning inventory from the account balances, and to set up the ending inventory. To simplify the illustration, no other adjusting entries are used.

As indicated by the working papers, the cost of goods sold by The *B* Corporation is $32,000. The following schedule confirms this amount.

THE *B* CORPORATION
Schedule of Cost of Goods Sold
For the Year Ended December 31, 1965

Inventory, December 31, 1964			$ 4,500
Add net cost of purchases:			
Purchases		$30,500	
Add transportation in		1,670	
Total		$32,170	
Deduct:			
Purchase returns and allowances	$770		
Purchase discounts	600	1,370	30,800
Cost of goods available for sale			$35,300
Deduct inventory, December 31, 1965			3,300
Cost of goods sold			$32,000

There is no liability for income taxes because 1965 was an unprofitable year.

Closing entries. Some accountants do not use a Revenue and Expense account. They credit the net income or debit the net loss directly to Retained Earnings. Such a practice is illustrated in the closing entries for The *B* Corporation on page 20.

THE *B* CORPORATION
Working Papers
For the Year Ended December 31, 1965

	Trial Balance		Adjustments		Adjusted Trial Balance		Income Statement		Retained Earnings Statement		Balance Sheet	
Cash	29,090				29,090						29,090	
Inventory	4,500		A 3,300	A 4,500	3,300						3,300	
Accounts payable		2,200				2,200						2,200
Capital stock		25,000				25,000						25,000
Retained earnings, December 31, 1964		8,000				8,000				8,000		
Dividends	2,500				2,500				2,500			
Sales		56,000				56,000		56,000				
Sales returns and allowances	500				500		500					
Sales discounts	710				710		710					
Purchases	30,500			A 30,500								
Transportation in	1,670			A 1,670								
Purchase returns and allowances		770	A 770									
Purchase discounts		600	A 600									
Cost of goods sold			A 32,000		32,000		32,000					
Transportation out	750				750		750					
All other expenses	22,350				22,350		22,350					
	92,570	92,570	36,670	36,670	91,200	91,200	56,310	56,000				
Net loss								310	310			
							56,310	56,310	2,810	8,000		
Retained earnings, December 31, 1965									5,190			5,190
									8,000	8,000	32,390	32,390

Sales	56,000	
Retained earnings	310	
Sales returns and allowances		500
Sales discounts		710
Cost of goods sold		32,000
Transportation out		750
All other expenses		22,350
To close the revenue and expense accounts.		
Retained earnings	2,500	
Dividends		2,500
To close the Dividends account.		

Proprietorship and partnership working papers. Instead of a pair of columns for the Statement of Retained Earnings, the working papers for a proprietorship have a pair of columns headed, for example, *John Smith, Capital.* The balances of the proprietor's capital and drawing accounts and the net income or net loss for the period are extended to these columns, and the balance of the columns is extended to the Balance Sheet credit column.

Working papers for a partnership contain a pair of similar columns for each partner, showing the balances of the capital and drawing accounts and the division of the net income or net loss.

MANUFACTURING BUSINESS

Two types of working papers are illustrated for a manufacturing business:

Pages 22–24. Single set of working papers.

Pages 28–31. Separate working papers for each statement.

The two illustrations are based on the same trial balance and adjustments. The adjusting entries appear below:

(A) Bad debts expense	300	
Allowance for doubtful accounts		300
To add $300 to the allowance account.		
(B) Factory supplies expense	2,070	
Factory supplies		2,070
Supplies used.		
(C) Insurance expense	975	
Unexpired insurance		975
Premium expiration for the year. (Manufacturing, $910; General, $65.)		
(D) Depreciation—Factory buildings	2,600	
Accumulated depreciation—Factory buildings		2,600
Depreciation for the year.		
(E) Depreciation—Machinery and equipment	4,788	
Accumulated depreciation—Machinery and equipment		4,788
Depreciation for the year.		
(F) Depreciation—Office equipment	314	
Accumulated depreciation—Office equipment		314
Depreciation for the year.		
(G) Interest expense—Bonds	250	
Discount on bonds		250
Amortization of discount for the year.		

(H) Rent collected in advance	50	
Rent earned		50
Earned portion of rent collected in advance.		
(I) Accrued interest on notes receivable	45	
Interest earned—Notes receivable		45
Interest accrued on notes.		
(J) Interest expense—Notes payable	20	
Accrued interest on notes payable		20
Interest accrued on notes.		

The end-of-year inventories were: Finished goods, $10,991; goods in process, $13,212; materials, $9,923.

Some expenses cannot be regarded as entirely manufacturing, selling, or general, but should be apportioned to two or more of these groups on some appropriate basis. In this illustration, property taxes and insurance are apportioned 14/15 to manufacturing and 1/15 to general expense, as indicated by the amounts in the Manufacturing and the Income Statement columns. Stationery and printing expense is apportioned 20 per cent to selling expense and 80 per cent to general expense; the apportionment is indicated by the letters *S* and *G* beside the related amounts in the Income Statement debit column.

Single set of working papers. A single set of working papers for a manufacturing business is illustrated on pages 22, 23, and 24. As indicated by the illustration, an accountant need not provide for the adjusted trial balance when setting up the column headings in the working papers.

Closing the books. The closing of the books of a manufacturing business using the periodical inventory procedure involves closing the accounts used in the preparation of the statement of cost of goods manufactured and recording the end-of-period inventories of materials and goods in process; closing the accounts used in the preparation of the income statement and recording the end-of-period inventory of finished goods; and closing any other accounts affecting retained earnings. Entries are shown below. The numbers at the left are for comment reference purposes only.

(1) Manufacturing	174,859	
Goods in process		8,120
Materials		6,325
Purchases—Materials		54,630
Transportation in		1,200
Direct labor		65,805
Indirect labor		14,260
Heat, light, and power—Factory		8,920
Repairs to buildings and machinery		635
Factory supplies expense		2,070
Insurance expense		910
Property taxes		896
Depreciation—Factory buildings		2,600
Depreciation—Machinery and equipment		4,788
Miscellaneous factory expenses		3,700
To close accounts with debit balances.		

(*Continued on page 25.*)

Single set of working papers.

THE INGRAM MANUFACTURING COMPANY
Working Papers
For the Year Ended December 31, 1965

	Trial Balance		Adjustments		Manufacturing		Income Statement		Retained Earnings Statement		Balance Sheet	
Cash	27,600										27,600	
Marketable securities	10,000										10,000	
Accounts receivable	35,365										35,365	
Allowance for doubtful accounts		650		A 300								950
Notes receivable	6,000										6,000	
Inventories:												
Finished goods	12,400						12,400	10,991			10,991	
Goods in process	8,120				8,120	13,212					13,212	
Materials	6,325				6,325	9,923					9,923	
Factory supplies	2,420			B 2,070							350	
Unexpired insurance	1,375			C 975							400	
Stock of Murdock Sales Company	5,000										5,000	
Land	23,000										23,000	
Factory buildings	65,000										65,000	
Accumulated depreciation—Factory buildings		14,500		D 2,600								17,100
Machinery and equipment	53,900										53,900	
Accumulated depreciation—M. & E.		13,600		E 4,788								18,388
Office equipment	3,140										3,140	
Accumulated depreciation—Office equipment		750		F 314								1,064
Discount on bonds	2,500			G 250							2,250	
Accounts payable		4,000										4,000
Notes payable		5,000										5,000
Rent collected in advance		150	H 50									100
Bonds payable		50,000										50,000
Capital stock—Preferred		40,000										40,000
Capital stock—Common		75,000										75,000
Capital in excess of par value—Common stock		7,500										7,500
Retained earnings, December 31, 1964		18,714								18,714		
Dividends—Common	6,000								6,000			
Dividends—Preferred	2,400								2,400			
Sales		238,625						238,625				
Sales returns and allowances	1,315						1,315					
Sales discounts	1,617						1,617					
Totals forward	273,477	468,489	50	11,297	14,445	23,135	15,332	249,616	8,400	18,714	266,131	219,102

THE INGRAM MANUFACTURING COMPANY

Working Papers (Continued)

For the Year Ended December 31, 1965

	Trial Balance		Adjustments		Manufacturing		Income Statement		Retained Earnings Statement		Balance Sheet	
Totals brought forward	273,477	468,489	50	11,297	14,445	23,135	15,332	249,616	8,400	18,714	266,131	219,102
Purchases—Materials	54,630				54,630							
Purchase returns and allowances		425				425						
Purchase discounts		675				675						
Transportation in	1,200				1,200							
Direct labor	65,805				65,805							
Indirect labor	14,260				14,260							
Heat, light, and power—Factory	8,920				8,920							
Repairs to buildings and machinery	635				635							
Property taxes	960				896		64					
Miscellaneous factory expenses	3,700				3,700							
Advertising	7,320						7,320					
Salesmen's salaries	8,000						8,000					
Salesmen's traveling expenses	4,100						4,100					
Transportation out	850						850					
Miscellaneous selling expenses	875						875					
Officers' salaries	16,500						16,500					
Office salaries	4,200						4,200					
Office supplies expense	312						312					
Stationery and printing expense	415						{ 83 S { 332 G					
Miscellaneous general expenses	561						561					
Interest earned—Notes receivable		141		I 45				186				
Dividends on Murdock stock		400						400				
Interest expense—Bonds	3,000		G 250				3,250					
Interest expense—Notes payable	410		J 20				430					
	470,130	470,130										
Bad debts expense			A 300				300					
Factory supplies expense			B 2,070		2,070							
Insurance expense			C 975		910		65					
Depreciation:												
Factory buildings			D 2,600		2,600							
Machinery and equipment			E 4,788		4,788							
Office equipment			F 314				314					
Rent earned				H 50				50				
Totals forward			11,367	11,392	174,859	24,235	62,888	250,252	8,400	18,714	266,131	219,102

THE INGRAM MANUFACTURING COMPANY

Working Papers (Concluded)

For the Year Ended December 31, 1965

	Trial Balance		Adjustments		Manufacturing		Income Statement		Retained Earnings Statement		Balance Sheet	
Totals brought forward			11,367	11,392	174,859	24,235	62,888	250,252	8,400	18,714	266,131	219,102
Accrued interest on notes receivable			I 45								45	
Accrued interest on notes payable				J 20								20
			11,412	11,412	174,859	24,235						
Cost of goods manufactured						150,624	150,624					
					174,859	174,859	213,512	250,252				
Net income before income tax—down							36,740					
							250,252	250,252				
Net income before income tax—brought down								36,740				
Federal income tax							11,135					11,135
Net income							25,605			25,605		
							36,740	36,740	8,400	44,319		
Retained earnings, December 31, 1965									35,919			35,919
									44,319	44,319	266,176	266,176

		Debit	Credit
(2)	Purchase returns and allowances	425	
	Purchase discounts	675	
	Goods in process	13,212	
	Materials	9,923	
	Manufacturing		24,235
	To close accounts with credit balances and record end-of-year inventories.		
(3)	Revenue and expense	150,624	
	Manufacturing		150,624
	To transfer the cost of goods manufactured to the Revenue and Expense account.		

Entries 1 and 2 may be combined, with a net debit of $150,624 to Manufacturing.

Entries 1, 2, and 3 may be combined, with a net debit of $150,624 to Revenue and Expense, thus eliminating the Manufacturing account.

		Debit	Credit
(4)	Sales	238,625	
	Interest earned—Notes receivable	186	
	Dividends on Murdock stock	400	
	Rent earned	50	
	Finished goods	10,991	
	Revenue and expense		250,252
	To close accounts with credit balances and record end-of-year inventory of finished goods.		
(5)	Revenue and expense	74,023	
	Finished goods		12,400
	Sales returns and allowances		1,315
	Sales discounts		1,617
	Advertising		7,320
	Salesmen's salaries		8,000
	Salesmen's traveling expenses		4,100
	Transportation out		850
	Miscellaneous selling expenses		875
	Officers' salaries		16,500
	Office salaries		4,200
	Office supplies expense		312
	Stationery and printing expense		415
	Bad debts expense		300
	Insurance expense		65
	Depreciation—Office equipment		314
	Property taxes		64
	Miscellaneous general expenses		561
	Interest expense—Bonds		3,250
	Interest expense—Notes payable		430
	Federal income tax		11,135
	To close accounts with debit balances.		
(6)	Revenue and expense	25,605	
	Retained earnings		25,605
	To transfer the net income to Retained Earnings.		

Entries 4 and 5 may be combined, with a net credit of $176,229 to Revenue and Expense.

Entry 3 may be omitted and the $150,624 credit to Manufacturing may be included in entry 5. If that is done, the net credit to Revenue and Expense in an entry combining 4 and 5 will be $25,605, the amount of the net income. The Revenue and Expense account can be eliminated by crediting Retained Earnings with the $25,605 net income.

Entries 1, 2, 4, and 5 may be combined, eliminating all debits and credits to Manufacturing and Revenue and Expense in those entries, and having one net credit of $25,605 to Revenue and Expense or to Retained Earnings.

(7) Retained earnings	8,400	
Dividends—Common		6,000
Dividends—Preferred		2,400
To close the dividends accounts.		

Separate working papers for each statement. If the general ledger trial balance is very long, some accountants prefer to make a separate work sheet for each statement. This practice has the advantage of classifying the data so that each statement can be prepared from its own working papers.

The forms are illustrated on pages 28 through 31. Observe that accounts that have no balances but that are affected by adjusting entries are entered in the working papers in their proper sequence, with no amounts in the Trial Balance columns. This can be easily accomplished by listing the account titles shown by a chart of accounts and then entering the account balances. The same procedure could have been followed in the preceding illustration.

Separate working papers are prepared for the following statements: statement of cost of goods sold (sometimes called the "statement of cost of goods manufactured and sold"); income statement; statement of retained earnings; balance sheet. Observe the following matters with respect to these working papers:

The working papers for each statement contain the trial balance items and all of the adjustments applicable to that statement.

Totals of the Trial Balance and Adjustments columns are forwarded:

From the cost of goods sold papers to the income statement papers.

From the income statement papers to the retained earnings papers.

From the retained earnings papers to the balance sheet papers.

Balancing figures are forwarded as follows:

The cost of goods sold is forwarded from the cost of goods sold papers to the income statement papers.

The net income is forwarded from the income statement papers to the retained earnings papers.

The amount of the retained earnings at the end of the year is forwarded from the retained earnings papers to the balance sheet papers.

End-of-year inventories and balances brought forward from preceding papers are entered in the positions in which they will appear in the statements.

The income tax expense for 1965 and the related liability are entered in the income statement papers and the balance sheet papers by adjusting entry K.

It will be remembered that, in the preceding illustration, insurance and property taxes were apportioned between manufacturing and general expenses, and stationery and printing was apportioned between selling and general expenses. In the preceding working papers, the apportionments were made as follows:

A portion of the insurance expense was extended to the Manufacturing debit column and the remainder was extended to the Income Statement debit column.

The apportionment of the property taxes was accomplished in the same manner.

The apportionment of the stationery and printing expense was indicated by extending the two portions of the balance of the account to the Income Statement debit column, with identifying letters *S* and *G*.

In the working papers in this illustration, no new problem is presented with respect to showing the apportionment of stationery and printing, because the selling and general expenses appear in the same working papers. The apportionment is indicated in the same manner as in the preceding illustration.

The apportionments of insurance and property taxes are dealt with as follows:

Insurance:

Insurance premiums had been charged to Unexpired Insurance and an adjusting entry (C) was made as follows:

Insurance expense	975	
Unexpired insurance		975
Premium expiration for the year. (Manufacturing, $910; General, $65.)		

The $910 is entered in the debit Adjustments column of the cost of goods sold papers, and the $65 is entered in the debit Adjustments column of the income statement papers.

Property taxes:

There is no adjusting entry for property taxes. Since the major portion of the tax is classified as manufacturing expense, the balance of the property tax account is shown in the Trial Balance debit column of the cost of goods sold working papers, and a transfer of the $64 portion to be included in general expenses is made by a credit in the Adjustments columns of the cost of goods sold papers and a debit in the Adjustments columns of the income statement papers. The transfer is identified by a lower-case letter (*a*) to distinguish it from ordinary adjusting entries, which are identified by capital letters.

Second set of working papers.

THE INGRAM MANUFACTURING COMPANY

Statement of Cost of Goods Sold Working Papers

For the Year Ended December 31, 1965

	Trial Balance		Adjustments		Statement of Cost of Goods Sold	
Cost of goods manufactured:						
Materials:						
Purchases	54,630					54,630
Deduct:						
Purchase returns and allowances		425			425	
Purchase discounts		675			675	1,100
Net						53,530
Transportation in	1,200					1,200
Total						54,730
Deduct increase in materials inventory:						
December 31, 1965					9,923	
December 31, 1964	6,325				6,325	3,598
Materials used						51,132
Direct labor	65,805					65,805
Manufacturing overhead:						
Indirect labor	14,260				14,260	
Heat, light, and power—Factory	8,920				8,920	
Repairs to buildings and machinery	635				635	
Factory supplies expense			B 2,070		2,070	
Insurance expense			C 910		910	
Property taxes	960			a 64	896	
Depreciation—Factory buildings			D 2,600		2,600	
Depreciation—Machinery and equipment			E 4,788		4,788	
Miscellaneous factory expenses	3,700				3,700	38,779
Total manufacturing cost						155,716
Deduct increase in goods in process inventory:						
December 31, 1965					13,212	
December 31, 1964	8,120				8,120	5,092
Cost of goods manufactured						150,624
Add decrease in finished goods inventory:						
December 31, 1964	12,400				12,400	
December 31, 1965					10,991	1,409
Cost of goods sold—forward						152,033
Totals forward	176,955	1,100	10,368	64		

THE INGRAM MANUFACTURING COMPANY

Income Statement Working Papers
For the Year Ended December 31, 1965

	Trial Balance		Adjustments		Income Statement	
Totals brought forward	176,955	1,100	10,368	64		
Sales		238,625				238,625
Sales returns and allowances	1,315				1,315	
Sales discounts	1,617				1,617	2,932
Net sales						235,693
Cost of goods sold—brought forward						152,033
Gross profit on sales						83,660
Operating expenses:						
Advertising	7,320				7,320	
Salesmen's salaries	8,000				8,000	
Salesmen's traveling expenses	4,100				4,100	
Transportation out	850				850	
Stationery and printing expense	415				{ 83 S { 332 G	
Miscellaneous selling expenses	875				875	
Officers' salaries	16,500				16,500	
Office salaries	4,200				4,200	
Office supplies expense	312				312	
Bad debts expense			A 300		300	
Insurance expense			C 65		65	
Depreciation—Office equipment			F 314		314	
Property taxes			a 64		64	
Miscellaneous general expenses	561				561	43,876
Net operating income						39,784
Other revenue:						
Dividends on Murdock stock		400				400
Interest earned—Notes receivable		141		I 45		186
Rent earned				H 50		50
Total						40,420
Other expenses:						
Interest expense—Bonds	3,000		G 250		3,250	
Interest expense—Notes payable	410		J 20		430	3,680
Net income before income tax						36,740
Federal income tax			K 11,135			11,135
Net income—forward						25,605
Totals forward	226,430	240,266	22,516	159		

THE INGRAM MANUFACTURING COMPANY
Statement of Retained Earnings Working Papers
For the Year Ended December 31, 1965

	Trial Balance		Adjustments		Statement of Retained Earnings	
Totals brought forward	226,430	240,266	22,516	159		
Retained earnings, December 31, 1964		18,714				18,714
Add net income—brought forward						25,605
Total						44,319
Deduct:						
Dividends—Common	6,000				6,000	
Dividends—Preferred	2,400				2,400	8,400
Retained earnings, December 31, 1965—forward						35,919
Totals forward	234,830	258,980	22,516	159		

THE INGRAM MANUFACTURING COMPANY
Balance Sheet Working Papers
December 31, 1965

	Trial Balance		Adjustments		Balance Sheet	
Totals brought forward	234,830	258,980	22,516	159		
Assets						
Current assets:						
Cash	27,600					27,600
Marketable securities	10,000					10,000
Accounts receivable	35,365				35,365	
Allowance for doubtful accounts		650		A 300	950	34,415
Notes receivable	6,000					6,000
Accrued interest on notes receivable			I 45			45
Inventories:						
Finished goods					10,991	
Goods in process					13,212	
Materials					9,923	34,126
Factory supplies	2,420			B 2,070		350
Unexpired insurance	1,375			C 975		400
Total current assets						112,936

Stock of Murdock Sales Company	5,000					5,000
Fixed assets:						
Land	23,000					23,000
Factory buildings	65,000				65,000	
Accumulated depreciation—Factory buildings		14,500		D 2,600	17,100	47,900
Machinery and equipment	53,900				53,900	
Accumulated depreciation—Machinery and equipment		13,600		E 4,788	18,388	35,512
Office equipment	3,140				3,140	
Accumulated depreciation—Office equipment		750		F 314	1,064	2,076
Total fixed assets						108,488
Deferred charges:						
Discount on bonds	2,500			G 250		2,250
						228,674
Liabilities and Stockholders' Equity						
Current liabilities:						
Accounts payable		4,000			4,000	
Notes payable		5,000			5,000	
Federal income tax payable				K 11,135	11,135	
Accrued interest on notes payable				J 20	20	
Rent collected in advance		150	H 50		100	20,255
Long-term liabilities:						
Bonds payable		50,000				50,000
Stockholders' equity:						
Capital stock—Preferred		40,000			40,000	
Capital stock—Common		75,000			75,000	
Capital in excess of par value—Common stock		7,500			7,500	122,500
Retained earnings—brought forward						35,919
	470,130	470,130	22,611	22,611		228,674

REVERSING ENTRIES

Adjusting entries made at the end of a period are sometimes reversed at the beginning of the next period. This matter is discussed in the remainder of this chapter.

Bad debts and depreciation. Adjusting entries for bad debts and depreciation are not reversed. The Allowance for Doubtful Accounts and accumulated depreciation accounts are contra to the related asset accounts. Together they show the net book values of the assets.

Cost apportionments—Prepaid expenses. Page 11, Chapter 1, shows how accounts are adjusted for the apportionment of a prepaid expense. The accounts are repeated below, with the addition of the closing entry.

Original charge to an asset account:

		Unexpired Insurance		Insurance Expense	
1965					
Jan. 2	Original expenditure	300			
Dec. 31	Adjusting entry		100	100	
31	Closing entry				100

A reversing entry debiting Unexpired Insurance and crediting Insurance Expense would be improper. The $200 balance of the Unexpired Insurance account is the correct amount of the remaining asset.

Original charge to an expense account:

		Unexpired Insurance		Insurance Expense	
1965					
Jan. 2	Original expenditure			300	
Dec. 31	Adjusting entry	200			200
31	Closing entry				100

In this case, a reversing entry is desirable.

		Unexpired Insurance		Insurance Expense	
1965					
Jan. 2	Original expenditure			300	
Dec. 31	Adjusting entry	200			200
31	Closing entry				100
1966					
Jan. 1	Reversing entry		200	200	

The desirability of the reversing entry becomes apparent if we assume that no reversing entry is made, and that an additional premium of $175 is paid and charged (in accordance with the company's previous procedure) to Insurance Expense.

		Unexpired Insurance		Insurance Expense	
1965					
Jan. 2	Original expenditure			300	
Dec. 31	Adjusting entry	200			200
31	Closing entry				100
1966					
Feb. 1	Additional premium			175	

An undesirable situation is produced. At the end of 1966, when it came time to make the annual adjusting entry, part of the apportionable costs would be in the Unexpired Insurance account and part would be in the Insurance Expense account. This would be a confusing situation, which the reversing entry avoids.

If an expense prepayment will benefit more than one period, it is advisable to charge the expenditure to an asset account because a reversal of the adjusting entry will thus be avoided.

Revenue apportionments. As shown by the Subscriptions Collected in Advance illustration on page 12 of Chapter 1, prospective revenue booked in advance may be credited to:

An unearned revenue account:
The adjusting entry will transfer the earned portion to a revenue account and no reversing entry need be made.

A revenue account:
The adjusting entry will transfer the unearned portion to an unearned revenue account and a reversing entry will be desirable.

If prospective revenue booked in advance will be earned during more than one period, it is advisable to credit an unearned revenue account because a reversing entry will thus be avoided.

Accrued income. Page 13 of Chapter 1 shows how accounts are adjusted for accrued income. The accounts are repeated below, with the addition of the closing entry. It was assumed that, in addition to the $100 collected on notes receivable during the year, uncollected accrued interest at the end of the year amounted to $50.

		Accrued Interest on Notes Receivable		Interest Earned	
1965					
Various dates	Collected on matured notes				100
Dec. 31	Adjusting entry	50			50
31	Closing entry			150	

If the adjusting entry is reversed and interest in the amount of $75 is collected at maturity, the accounts will appear as follows:

Date		Accrued Interest on Notes Receivable		Interest Earned	
1965					
Various dates	Collected on matured notes				100
Dec. 31	Adjusting entry	50			50
31	Closing entry			150	
1966					
Jan. 1	Reversing entry		50	50	
?	Collected				75

The $25 credit balance in the Interest Earned account is the amount earned in 1966.

If the $50 accrued at the end of 1965 was all applicable to one note, there would be little advantage in the reversing entry. The collection of the note and interest could be recorded as follows:

Cash	5,075	
Notes receivable		5,000
Accrued interest on notes receivable		50
Interest earned		25

But if the $50 was applicable to several notes and no reversing entry was made, it would be necessary, each time an interest collection was received, to determine what portion thereof should be credited to Accrued Interest on Notes Receivable and what portion should be credited to Interest Earned. To illustrate, assume the following facts with respect to interest on notes receivable:

	Accrued December 31, 1965	Collected During 1966	Earned During 1966
Note A	$20	$30	$10
Note B	30	45	15
	$50	$75	$25

The reversing entry simplifies the recording of interest collections, as shown below:

Date		Accrued Interest on Notes Receivable		Interest Earned	
1965					
Various dates	Collected on matured notes				100
Dec. 31	Adjusting entry	50			50
31	Closing entry			150	
1966					
Jan. 1	Reversing entry		50	50	
?	Collection of interest on Note A				30
?	Collection of interest on Note B				45

The $25 credit balance in the Interest Earned account is the amount earned in 1966.

As indicated by this illustration, a reversing entry, although not necessary, is desirable because it simplifies the subsequent recording of collections.

Because reversing entries for accrued income are desirable in many instances, and because it is advisable to establish a uniform policy, many accountants reverse all adjusting entries for accrued income.

Accrued expense. Page 13 of Chapter 1 shows how accounts are adjusted for accrued expenses. The illustration is repeated below, with the addition of the closing entry.

		Wages and Salaries		Accrued Wages and Salaries	
1965					
Various dates	Paid	10,000			
Dec. 31	Adjusting entry	500			500
31	Closing entry		10,500		

If wages and salaries are payable on the same future date, a reversing entry is not important. But if they are payable on different dates, it may be advisable to reverse the adjusting entry, so that, when payments are made, it will not be necessary to determine how much of the $500 accrual was for wages and how much was for salaries. The illustration is continued by showing the reversing entry and the payments.

		Wages and Salaries		Accrued Wages and Salaries	
1965					
Various dates	Paid	10,000			
Dec. 31	Adjusting entry	500			500
31	Closing entry		10,500		
1966					
Jan. 1	Reversing entry		500	500	
8	Wages paid	1,200			
10	Salaries paid	1,800			

The $2,500 debit balance in the wages and salaries expense account is the portion of the January payments that is a January expense.

For the reasons stated at the end of the discussion of accrued income, it may be desirable to establish a policy of reversing all adjusting entries for accrued expenses.

Adjusting and reversing entries for The Ingram Manufacturing Company. The adjusting entries of The Ingram Manufacturing Company, shown on page 20 of this chapter, are restated below. Related reversing entries are indicated in a parallel column. It is customary to date reversing entries as of the first business day of the new accounting period.

Adjusting Entries			Reversing Entries		
Bad debts expense	300				
Allowance for doubtful accounts		300			
Factory supplies expense	2,070				
Factory supplies		2,070			
Insurance expense	975				
Unexpired insurance		975			
Depreciation—Factory buildings	2,600				
Accumulated depreciation—Factory buildings		2,600			
Depreciation—Machinery and equipment	4,788				
Accumulated depreciation—Machinery and equipment		4,788			
Depreciation—Office equipment	314				
Accumulated depreciation—Office equipment		314			
Interest expense—Bonds	250				
Discount on bonds		250			
Rent collected in advance	50				
Rent earned		50			
Accrued interest on notes receivable	45		Interest earned—Notes receivable	45	
Interest earned—Notes receivable		45	Accrued interest on notes receivable		45
Interest expense—Notes payable	20		Accrued interest on notes payable	20	
Accrued interest on notes payable		20	Interest expense—Notes payable		20
Federal income tax	11,135				
Federal income tax payable		11,135			

The reasons why some of the adjusting entries are not reversed are:

Bad debts and depreciation:

Because the Allowance for Doubtful Accounts and the accumulated depreciation accounts are contras to the related asset accounts, the adjusting entries for bad debts and depreciation are not reversed.

Other cost apportionments—Factory supplies used, expired insurance, and bond discount amortized:

Because the original charges were made to asset or deferred charge accounts, the adjusting entries are not reversed.

Revenue apportionment—Rent collected in advance:

Because the original credit was made to an unearned revenue account, the adjusting entry is not reversed.

Accrued federal income tax:

Because the liability account is customarily debited when the tax is paid, the adjusting entry is not reversed.

CHAPTER

3

Financial Statements

The statements in this chapter are based on the working papers of The Ingram Manufacturing Company in Chapter 2.

THE INGRAM MANUFACTURING COMPANY — Exhibit D

Statement of Cost of Goods Manufactured
For the Year Ended December 31, 1965

Materials:			
Inventory, December 31, 1964			$ 6,325
Cost of purchases:			
Purchases		$54,630	
Purchase returns and allowances	$425		
Purchase discounts	675	1,100	
Net		$53,530	
Transportation in		1,200	54,730
Total inventory and purchases			$ 61,055
Inventory, December 31, 1965			9,923
Materials used			$ 51,132
Direct labor			65,805
Manufacturing overhead:			
Indirect labor		$14,260	
Heat, light, and power—Factory		8,920	
Repairs to buildings and machinery		635	
Factory supplies expense		2,070	
Insurance expense		910	
Property taxes		896	
Depreciation—Factory buildings		2,600	
Depreciation—Machinery and equipment		4,788	
Miscellaneous factory expenses		3,700	38,779
Total manufacturing cost			$155,716
Add goods in process, December 31, 1964			8,120
Total			$163,836
Deduct goods in process, December 31, 1965			13,212
Cost of goods manufactured			$150,624

THE INGRAM MANUFACTURING COMPANY Exhibit C

Income Statement

For the Year Ended December 31, 1965

Gross sales			$238,625
Sales returns and allowances		$ 1,315	
Sales discounts		1,617	2,932
Net sales			$235,693
Cost of goods sold:			
Finished goods inventory, December 31, 1964		$ 12,400	
Cost of goods manufactured—Exhibit D		150,624	
Total		$163,024	
Finished goods inventory, December 31, 1965		10,991	152,033
Gross profit on sales			$ 83,660
Operating expenses:			
Selling expenses:			
Advertising	$ 7,320		
Salesmen's salaries	8,000		
Salesmen's traveling expenses	4,100		
Transportation out	850		
Stationery and printing expense	83		
Miscellaneous selling expenses	875	$ 21,228	
General expenses:			
Officers' salaries	$16,500		
Office salaries	4,200		
Office supplies expense	312		
Stationery and printing expense	332		
Bad debts expense	300		
Insurance expense	65		
Depreciation—Office equipment	314		
Property taxes	64		
Miscellaneous general expenses	561	22,648	43,876
Net operating income			$ 39,784
Other expenses:			
Interest expense—Bonds	$ 3,250		
Interest expense—Notes payable	430	$ 3,680	
Other revenue:			
Dividends on Murdock stock	$ 400		
Interest earned—Notes receivable	186		
Rent earned	50	636	3,044
Net income before income tax			$ 36,740
Federal income tax			11,135
Net income			$ 25,605

THE INGRAM MANUFACTURING COMPANY Exhibit B

Statement of Retained Earnings

For the Year Ended December 31, 1965

Retained earnings, December 31, 1964		$18,714
Add net income for the year—Exhibit C		25,605
Total		$44,319
Deduct dividends:		
Common	$6,000	
Preferred	2,400	8,400
Retained earnings, December 31, 1965		$35,919

THE INGRAM MANUFACTURING COMPANY Exhibit A

Balance Sheet

December 31, 1965

Assets

Current assets:			
Cash		$ 27,600	
Marketable securities—at the lower of cost or market		10,000	
Accounts receivable	$35,365		
Less allowance for doubtful accounts	950	34,415	
Notes receivable		6,000	
Accrued interest on notes receivable		45	
Inventories—at the lower of cost or market:			
Finished goods	$10,991		
Goods in process	13,212		
Materials	9,923	34,126	
Factory supplies		350	
Unexpired insurance		400	
Total current assets			$112,936
Stock of Murdock Sales Company—at cost			5,000
Fixed assets:			
Land—at cost		$ 23,000	
Factory buildings—at cost	$65,000		
Less accumulated depreciation	17,100	47,900	
Machinery and equipment—at cost	$53,900		
Less accumulated depreciation	18,388	35,512	
Office equipment—at cost	$ 3,140		
Less accumulated depreciation	1,064	2,076	
Total fixed assets			108,488
Deferred charges:			
Discount on bonds			2,250
			$228,674

Liabilities and Stockholders' Equity

Current liabilities:			
Accounts payable		$ 4,000	
Notes payable		5,000	
Federal income tax payable		11,135	
Accrued interest on notes payable		20	
Rent collected in advance		100	
Total current liabilities			$ 20,255
Long-term liabilities:			
Real estate mortgage bonds payable—6%—due December 31, 1974			50,000
Total liabilities			$ 70,255
Stockholders' equity:			
Capital stock—$10 par value:			
Preferred—6% cumulative; authorized, 5,000 shares; issued, 4,000 shares	$40,000		
Common—authorized and issued, 7,500 shares	75,000	$115,000	
Capital in excess of par value—Common stock		7,500	
Total		$122,500	
Retained earnings—Exhibit B		35,919	
Total stockholders' equity			158,419
			$228,674

Note: At the balance sheet date the company was contingently liable on notes receivable discounted in the amount of $2,000.

Bases of balance sheet valuations. Many people who have little knowledge of accounting probably think that the amounts shown in a balance sheet are determined with the precision of pure mathematics, on the basis of immediately realizable market values of assets and definitely ascertainable liabilities. Accountants know that such ideas are incorrect; that realizable market value is not, in general, the conventional basis of accounting for assets; and that asset valuations and liability amounts are very often based on estimates.

A few assets are stated in the balance sheet at actual present realizable values. This presumably is the case with cash on hand and in domestic banks, and presumably should be (but not always is) the case with short-term marketable investments when the market value is less than cost.

In a few other cases, assets may be stated at estimated realizable values; for instance, the creation of an allowance for doubtful accounts is presumed to produce such a net valuation in the case of receivables.

Inventories are not valued at actual, or even estimated, realizable values, even when the "cost or market" rule is applied. The cost-or-market rule does give some recognition to market values, but only to decreases therein. Moreover, "market" refers to replacement price and not to selling price. The realizable value of an inventory to a going concern presumably would be more than cost or market, and its realizable value to a concern in liquidation might be less than cost or market, because losses probably could be expected.

Fixed assets, current expense prepayments, and long-term deferred charges usually are carried in the accounts in accordance with accounting principles or conventions, which are not concerned with currently realizable values but are concerned with the equitable absorption of costs by charges to operations over the periods of utilization.

Because the assets are not all valued at actual, or even estimated, realizable values, and because estimates have so much effect on asset and liability accounts, the amount shown in the balance sheet as the owners' equity cannot be regarded as representing "net worth" in the sense of an amount which would be distributable to the owners upon immediate disposal of the assets and payment of the liabilities.

Balance sheet classifications. The classifications used in a balance sheet depend upon the nature of the business and the nature of the items appearing in the balance sheet. The classifications mentioned below and on the following page are typical, but others are sometimes used.

ASSET SIDE

Current assets:

The rules determining the classification of assets as current are stated later in the chapter.

Sundry assets:

Stocks, bonds, and other securities not representing temporary investments properly classified as current assets.

Any assets, such as sinking funds, land held for plant expansion, and abandoned plant held for disposal, which do not fall into the other classifications.

Fixed assets:

Property of a relatively permanent nature, used in the operation of the business and not intended for sale. Tangible and intangible fixed assets may be separately classified.

Deferred charges:

Charges to be included in the determination of net income of subsequent periods covering a time span in excess of an operating cycle—a concept, discussed on page 42, that serves as a major criterion for the classification of assets as current.

LIABILITY AND OWNERS' EQUITY SIDE

Current liabilities:

The rules determining the classification of liabilities as current are stated later in the chapter.

Long-term liabilities:

Bonds, mortgages, and other debts not maturing in the near future.

Deferred credits:

Credits to be included in the determination of net income of subsequent periods covering a time span in excess of an operating cycle.

Owners' equity:

The proprietorship interest.

Current assets and current liabilities. In its Bulletin No. 30, issued in 1947, and with slight revisions in Bulletin No. 43, issued in 1953, the Institute's Committee on Accounting Procedure made some important recommendations with respect to definitions of current assets and current liabilities.* There were three principal reasons why such a bulletin was needed.

First, confusion existed because accountants had been unable to make a unanimous choice betwen the two following conflicting definitions:

Current assets consist of cash and other assets which presumably *will be* converted into cash in the near future (generally regarded as a year) *as a result of* regular operations.

Current assets consist of cash and other assets which presumably *can be* converted into cash in the near future (generally regarded as a year) *without interference with* the regular operations.

* Such bulletins are often referred to as *A.R.B. 30* or *A.R.B. 43,* the initials standing for *Accounting Research Bulletin.*

The second definition was considerably more inclusive than the first. For instance, the cash surrender value of life insurance, although immediately available, was not a current asset under the first definition, because life insurance is not purchased for the purpose of being converted into cash. But the cash surrender value was a current asset under the second definition, because it could be converted into cash without interference with the regular operations.

Second, both of the old definitions were often challenged because current expense prepayments, such as unexpired insurance, were excluded. From the standpoint of a going concern, what essential difference in current position exists on December 31 between a company which used cash in December to buy insurance and another company which will use cash in January for the same purpose? From a liquidating standpoint, to be sure, there is a difference. In the past, when bankers were primarily concerned with the "pounce" possibilities, and were therefore primarily interested in knowing how quickly their loans could be collected from the proceeds of forced liquidation, the liquidating concept strongly influenced accountants in their definition of current assets. But creditors are coming to give more consideration to a debtor's ability to pay as a going concern.

Third, the old one-year rule or convention was somewhat arbitrary and was not consistently applied. It was arbitrary because it gave no consideration to the fact that one concern might convert its merchandise to cash several times a year, whereas another concern might require considerably more than a year to make one such conversion. It was not consistently applied because assets were sometimes included in the current classification although they would not be converted into cash within twelve months. For instance, under the one-year rule, materials should not have been included in current assets unless within a year the materials would be converted into finished goods, the finished goods would be sold, and the resulting receivables would be collected. But accountants sometimes took the inconsistent position of excluding from current assets those receivables which would not mature within a year, while including the total of all inventories in the current assets.

The one-year rule was also arbitrary when applied to liabilities. Just why should a debt which matures in 11½ months be included in current liabilities, and a debt which matures in 12½ months be excluded?

The operating cycle concept. The Institute bulletin recommends that the "operating cycle" be recognized as a concept of major importance in the determination of working capital. Operations consist of a round of conversions—cash to inventories and prepaid expenses, to receivables, to cash. The average time required to complete this round is referred to in the bulletin as the "operating cycle."

Bulletin No. 43 states: "A one-year time period is to be used as a basis for the segregation of current assets in cases where there are several operating cycles occurring within a year. However, where the period of the operating cycle is more than twelve months, as in, for instance, the tobacco, distillery, and lumber businesses, the longer period should be used. Where a particular business has no clearly defined operating cycle, the one-year rule should govern."

What assets are current? The bulletin says that the following assets are properly regarded as current:

Cash available for current operations.
Inventories, including supplies.
Trade receivables.
Receivables from officers, employees, affiliates, and others, if collectible in the ordinary course of business within a year from the balance sheet date.
Installment and deferred receivables, if due in accordance with terms prevailing throughout the industry.
Temporary investments.
Prepaid current expenses.

The bulletin mentions the following as items that should not be regarded as current assets:

Cash not available for current operations because segregated or required for the acquisition of noncurrent assets or the payment of noncurrent debts.
Long-term investments or advances.
Receivables arising from nonoperating transactions and not expected to be collected within 12 months.
Cash surrender value of life insurance.
Fixed assets.
Long-term deferred charges, such as bond discount.

What liabilities are current? The bulletin states:

The term *current liabilities* is used principally to designate obligations whose liquidation is reasonably expected to require the use of existing resources properly classifiable as current assets, or the creation of other current liabilities. As a balance-sheet category, the classification is intended to include obligations for items which have entered into the operating cycle, such as payables incurred in the acquisition of materials and supplies to be used in the production of goods or in providing services to be offered for sale; collections received in advance of the delivery of goods or performance of services; and debts which arise from operations directly related to the operating cycle, such as accruals for wages, salaries, commissions, rentals, royalties, and income and other taxes. Other liabilities whose regular and ordinary liquidation is expected to occur within a relatively short period of time, usually twelve months, are also intended for inclusion, such as short-term debts arising from the acquisition of capital assets, serial maturities of long-term obligations, amounts required to be expended within one year under sinking fund provisions, and agency obligations arising from the collection or acceptance of cash or other assets for the account of third persons.

This concept of current liabilities would include estimated or accrued amounts which are expected to be required to cover expenditures within the year for known obligations (a) the amount of which can be determined only approximately (as in the case of provisions for accruing bonus payments) or (b) where the specific person or persons to whom payment will be made cannot as yet be designated (as in the case of estimated costs to be incurred in connection with guaranteed servicing or repair of products already sold). The current liability classification, however, is not intended to include a contractual obligation falling due at an early date which is expected to be refunded, or debts to be liquidated by funds which have been accumulated in accounts of a type not properly classified as current assets, or long-term obligations incurred to provide increased amounts of working capital for long periods. . . .

ALTERNATE STATEMENT FORMS

The following statement is based on the working papers on page 28.

THE INGRAM MANUFACTURING COMPANY — Exhibit D

Statement of Cost of Goods Sold
For the Year Ended December 31, 1965

Cost of goods manufactured:		
Materials:		
Cost of purchases:		
Purchases		$ 54,630
Purchase returns and allowances	$ 425	
Purchase discounts	675	1,100
Net		$ 53,530
Transportation in		1,200
Total		$ 54,730
Deduct increase in materials inventory:		
December 31, 1965	$ 9,923	
December 31, 1964	6,325	3,598
Materials used		$ 51,132
Direct labor		65,805
Manufacturing overhead:		
Indirect labor	$14,260	
Heat, light, and power—Factory	8,920	
Repairs to buildings and machinery	635	
Factory supplies expense	2,070	
Insurance expense	910	
Property taxes	896	
Depreciation—Factory buildings	2,600	
Depreciation—Machinery and equipment	4,788	
Miscellaneous factory expenses	3,700	
Total manufacturing overhead		38,779
Total manufacturing cost		$155,716
Deduct increase in goods in process inventory:		
December 31, 1965	$13,212	
December 31, 1964	8,120	5,092
Cost of goods manufactured		$150,624
Add decrease in finished goods inventory:		
December 31, 1964	$12,400	
December 31, 1965	10,991	1,409
Cost of goods sold		$152,033

Condensed statements. Condensed statements can be prepared showing totals of related items, supported by schedules, as illustrated on page 45.

Exhibit C

THE INGRAM MANUFACTURING COMPANY
Income Statement
For the Year Ended December 31, 1965

Gross sales		$238,625
Sales returns and allowances	$ 1,315	
Sales discounts	1,617	2,932
Net sales		$235,693
Cost of goods sold—Exhibit D (Page 44)		152,033
Gross profit on sales		$ 83,660
Operating expenses—Schedule 1:		
Selling	$21,228	
General	22,648	43,876
Net operating income		$ 39,784
Deduct other expense and revenue—net—Schedule 2		3,044
Net income before income tax		$ 36,740
Federal income tax		11,135
Net income		$ 25,605

Exhibit C
Schedule 1

THE INGRAM MANUFACTURING COMPANY
Schedule of Selling and General Expenses
For the Year Ended December 31, 1965

Selling expenses:	
Advertising	$ 7,320
Salesmen's salaries	8,000
Salesmen's traveling expenses	4,100
Transportation out	850
Stationery and printing expense	83
Miscellaneous selling expenses	875
Total	$21,228
General expenses:	
Officers' salaries	$16,500
Office salaries	4,200
Office supplies expense	312
Stationery and printing expense	332
Bad debts expense	300
Insurance expense	65
Property taxes	64
Depreciation—Office equipment	314
Miscellaneous general expenses	561
Total	$22,648

Exhibit C
Schedule 2

THE INGRAM MANUFACTURING COMPANY
Schedule of Other Revenue and Expense
For the Year Ended December 31, 1965

Expense:		
Bond interest, including amortization of discount	$3,250	
Interest on notes payable	430	
Total		$3,680
Revenue:		
Dividends on Murdock stock	$ 400	
Interest earned—Notes receivable	186	
Rent earned	50	
Total		636
Net expense		$3,044

Combined statement of income and retained earnings. To show all of the causes of the change in retained earnings during the period in one statement, a combined statement of income and retained earnings may be prepared. The income statement items may be shown in detail, as on page 38, or condensed, as below, or as on page 45.

THE INGRAM MANUFACTURING COMPANY

Statement of Income and Retained Earnings
For the Year Ended December 31, 1965

Net sales		$235,693
Cost of goods sold—Exhibit D (Page 44)	$152,033	
Operating expenses—Schedule 1	43,876	195,909
Net operating income		$ 39,784
Deduct other expense and revenue—net—Schedule 2		3,044
Net income before income tax		$ 36,740
Federal income tax		11,135
Net income		$ 25,605
Retained earnings, December 31, 1964		18,714
Total		$ 44,319
Dividends:		
Common	$ 6,000	
Preferred	2,400	8,400
Retained earnings, December 31, 1965		$ 35,919

ALTERNATIVE TREATMENT OF CERTAIN STATEMENT ITEMS

There have been some differences of opinion about the proper location of certain items in the operating statements. These are discussed below and on the next two pages.

Purchase discounts. Traditionally, cash discounts on purchases were shown in the income statement as an item of other income. Current practice generally recognizes that, from the standpoint of accounting theory, cash discounts on purchases should be deducted from purchases to arrive at cost. It is a basic principle of accounting that profits are not made on purchases. A company cannot earn income merely by making purchases and taking the discounts, without making a sale.

The nature of purchase discounts as related to cost rather than as an earning would be more obvious if it were customary to invoice goods at the net price, with an addition representing a supplementary charge or penalty for late payment. A purchase would then be recorded by a debit to Purchases and a credit to an account payable at the net price; if payment was made within the nonpenalty period, the payment would be recorded by a debit to the account payable and a credit to Cash. If payment was made after the nonpenalty period, it would be recorded by a debit to the account payable, a debit to some account such as Discounts Lost, or Late Payment Penalties, and a credit to Cash. Accounts are sometimes kept in this way, even with the present system of billing. If they are kept in the customary manner, it is still possible to show the balance of the Purchase Discounts account as a deduction from purchases in the operating statement.

However, there is a matter of expediency to consider. If purchase discounts are shown in the operating statement as a deduction from purchases, complete consistency would require that perpetual or physical inventories be priced at the net amounts after deduction of discounts. This immediately raises a question of accounting expediency. Assume that 1,000 articles are purchased at $.69 each, or a total of $690, subject to a cash discount of 1½%; this would make the net price of the invoice $679.65, and the unit price $.67965. But the use of such net prices for all inventory items would add materially to the work of the accounting department. It would be necessary to compute the net price of every item on every invoice subject to a cash discount, and perpetual or physical inventory computations would have to be made at prices carried to extended decimal fractions of a cent.

The pricing of inventories at gross unit prices, in order to avoid this work, must be recognized as a departure from accounting principles because income is anticipated to the extent of the discounts on goods in the inventory; but the violation of principle can probably be considered of minor consequence. So far as the operating statement is concerned, the anticipations of income at the beginning and end of the period tend to offset each other, and the net income for the period is misstated to only a minor degree. The departure from principle has a greater effect on the balance sheet; but, considering the low rates of cash discount usually offered, the overstatement of the inventory can perhaps be regarded as of insufficient consequence to justify insistence upon the accounting principle at the expense of inconvenience and added work.

Cash discounts on sales. Cash discounts on sales are sometimes shown in the operating statement as miscellaneous expense, and sometimes as direct deductions from sales. The effect on income is the same, and the only accounting principle involved is the principle of consistency. If discounts on purchases are shown as a deduction from purchases, discounts on sales should be shown as deductions from sales. If discounts on purchases are shown as miscellaneous income, discounts on sales should be shown as miscellaneous expense.

Transportation charges on purchases. Transportation charges on purchases are undoubtedly an addition to the cost of purchases, and they should be so shown in statements. To be consistent, it would be necessary to include the transportation cost in the inventory valuation. But, because often it is difficult to apportion transportation costs to various items in the inventory, the transportation costs frequently are excluded from the inventory valuation although they are added to the purchases in the operating statements. However, if freight charges are a substantial portion of the cost incurred in acquiring inventoriable goods, such as coal and steel, the accountant presumably will insist on the inclusion of freight charges in the determination of cost for inventory purposes.

Transportation charges on sales. Different opinions are held regarding this item, as follows:

(1) Such charges are a selling expense because they are an expense incident to the disposal of goods.

(2) Transportation charges on sales, like sales returns and allowances, should be deducted from gross sales in the determination of net sales. Those who hold this view maintain that, if it is a regular practice of the seller to pay the transportation charges, the price is raised sufficiently to include them; hence they should be deducted from the sales to determine the price received for the merchandise. On the other hand, if it is not the custom of the seller to pay the transportation charges, any concessions on this point to a few customers or in a few instances are virtually a reduction of the sales price.

It seems to the authors that the first opinion is the better, and that transportation out should be considered a selling expense. The fact that the price should be high enough to include such charges does not seem a conclusive argument for deducting them from the sales, because the selling price should be high enough to cover all expenses. If occasional concessions are given, transportation out seems to be all the more clearly a selling expense. Of course, if the price quoted on shipments f.o.b. destination is higher than that on shipments f.o.b. shipping point, transportation out is a logical deduction from sales.

Bad debts. The following opinions are held with respect to the classification of bad debts:

(1) Bad debts are a selling expense because they result from sales.

(2) Bad debts are a general or administrative expense because the granting of credit is usually a function of the administrative department of the business.

(3) Bad debts are a direct deduction from sales.

It has long been the custom to show bad debts in the income statement as an expense rather than as a direct deduction from sales. If they are to be so treated, it seems to the authors that they should be charged to the department which supervises the granting of credit. If the sales department passes on credit, bad debt losses should be considered a selling expense. If the general administrative department supervises credit, the loss should be classified as a general expense.

Some accountants have advocated showing bad debts as a direct deduction from sales, on the theory that such losses represent revenues which did not materialize rather than expense outlays.

Importance of disclosure. Increasing emphasis is being placed on the importance of full disclosure of significant information. This is a logical development, in view of the increasing use being made of financial statements for investment, regulatory, and other business purposes.

The capital of corporations is now provided, in large measure, by stockholders who take no active part in the management of the business and who are not intimately acquainted with its affairs. Therefore, published financial statements should provide the stockholders with the information they need in order to arrive at an informed opinion about the conduct of the business by the management to which they have delegated authority and entrusted their investments. A stockholder should be able to rely on such reports in reaching a decision as to whether he will keep his stock or sell it; and a person who is considering purchasing the stock of a company should be able to rely on its reports in making his decision. For these reasons, it is important that accountants make clear and complete disclosure of significant information.

Article (5) of the Rules of Professional Conduct of The American Institute of Certified Public Accountants has the following to say with respect to disclosure:

> In expressing an opinion on representations in financial statements which he has examined, a member may be held guilty of an act discreditable to the profession if
>
> (a) he fails to disclose a material fact known to him which is not disclosed in the financial statements but disclosure of which is necessary to make the financial statements not misleading; or
>
> (b) he fails to report any material misstatement known to him to appear in the financial statement; or
>
> . . . .
>
> (e) he fails to direct attention to any material departure from generally accepted accounting principles or to disclose any material omission of generally accepted auditing procedure applicable in the circumstances.

The Securities and Exchange Commission also is insistent upon adequate disclosure of material and significant information, and numerous deficiencies have been cited by the Commission because of failure to make disclosure or because disclosure was inadequate.

The matters which may require disclosure can be classified into two general groups:

(1) Facts applicable to the statements showing the results of operations during a period and the financial position at the end of a period.

(2) Information relative to subsequent events or prospective events.

Some of these matters are mentioned in the following paragraphs. It is not always practicable to make disclosure in the body of a statement; in such cases, disclosure may be made in footnotes appended to the statements or in comments accompanying the statements in an audit report.

Matters applicable to the statements. Bare-bone statements consisting merely of account titles and balances will rarely give a clear and complete picture of the results of operations during a period and the financial position at the end thereof. Some matters which may require disclosure, either in the body of the statement or in the accompanying opinion, footnotes, or comments, are mentioned below:

If there has been any departure from consistency in the accounting principles applied, the nature of the inconsistency should be clearly stated, as well as the dollar effect thereof on the statements, if the effect is material and determinable.

If changes in classifications may result in misleading comparisons of current and preceding statements, the changes should be disclosed if the effect is consequential. If comparative statements are prepared, reclassifications should be made in the prior statements to conform with the current classifications, or the inconsistency should be disclosed.

There should be disclosure of mortgaged, or otherwise pledged, assets and the liabilities secured thereby.

Any cash not subject to unrestricted withdrawal should be separately stated.

Receivables from stockholders, directors, officers, and employees should be separately stated, unless they arose from ordinary trade transactions and are collectible in accordance with the customary trade terms; even in that case, it is preferable to distinguish them from accounts with ordinary trade debtors, if they are of material amount.

Receivables from subsidiaries or other affiliated companies should be shown separately even though they arose from trade transactions.

Deposits as security or guarantees, and advances to suppliers for future delivery of merchandise, should be separately shown.

Notes and accounts receivable maturing later than one year from the balance sheet date, including installment receivables, should be segregated unless such a treatment is impracticable or contrary to trade practice.

Inventories should be detailed, and the bases of valuation (such as *at the lower of cost or market,* or *cost on a first-in, first-out basis*) should be stated.

The valuation basis of securities owned should be disclosed. If the securities represent temporary investments of funds and are therefore classified as current assets, they are traditionally shown in the balance sheet at market value if market is lower than cost. If market is higher than cost, parenthetical disclosure of the current market value is quite generally favored. If they represent long-term investments, they may be carried in the accounts and shown in the balance sheet at cost, regardless of minor decreases in market value; but if the market value is materially less than cost, with a probable inability to recover the cost of the investments, the asset may be written down. The decision whether to write down the asset will be influenced by such factors as (a) the seriousness of the market decline and (b) the reason for holding the investment—for instance, if the investment consists of stock acquired for the purpose of maintaining a desirable material purchase or finished goods sale relationship, there seems to be no necessity for anticipating a loss that there is no prospect of incurring. When a write-down is not made, the market value should be disclosed.

Fixed assets should be detailed. The basis of valuation (cost, cost less depreciation, appraisal value, or other) should be indicated. If the fixed assets are shown at appraised values, the basis of the appraisal (such as replacement cost new less depreciation thereon) and the date thereof should be stated. It is also desirable to tell who made the appraisal, as an indication of the independence and reliability of the appraisers.

Intangible fixed assets, such as patents, franchises, and goodwill, should be detailed.

Prepayments of current expenses should be distinguished from long-term deferred charges, and amortization procedures applicable to deferred charges should be described unless they are obvious.

Current liabilities payable to affiliated companies, as well as those payable to stockholders, directors, officers, and employees, should be set out separately if material in amount.

If estimates of liabilities are subject to considerable uncertainty, the amount stated should be indicated to be an estimate. If the amount of a tax or other liability is in dispute, adequate provision should be made or the facts should be stated in a footnote.

Currently maturing installments of long-term liabilities should be included in current liabilities. If the entire amount of a long-term liability is due within a year, it should be included in current liabilities unless a program of refunding is in prospect; in that case, the reason for excluding the debt from current liabilities should be stated.

It is not sufficient to show merely the amounts of long-term debts. There should also be disclosure of any bonds or other evidences of indebtedness authorized but not issued, the interest rate, the maturity, whether in installments or otherwise, and any sinking fund or other requirements for debt retirement. There should be disclosure of any defaults in interest, principal, or sinking fund payments.

Each class of capital stock should be shown separately. There should be disclosure of the par value per share, or, in the case of no-par stock, the stated or assigned value, if any. There should also be disclosure of the numbers of shares authorized, issued, in treasury, and outstanding. The preferred dividend rate, cumulative and participating rights, and redemption and liquidating prices should be shown. If there are any outstanding purchase options or warrants, or if one class of stock is convertible into another class, or if any class of stock is callable, these facts should be disclosed.

Treasury stock should be shown in the Stockholders' Equity section of the balance sheet as a deduction from capital stock, from retained earnings, or from the total thereof, as the laws of the state of incorporation or other considerations may indicate to be proper.

The balance sheet should state separately any (a) retained earnings, (b) capital in excess of par or stated value (paid-in surplus), and (c) unrealized increments in asset values shown by recorded appraisals. The changes in the various elements of stockholders' equity during the period should be accounted for. If any stock dividends have been distributed during the period, this fact should be clearly stated. There should be a disclosure of any restrictions on retained earnings, such as those in state laws which limit dividend payments to the amount of retained earnings in excess of the cost of treasury stock, or those which arise from agreements made in connection with the incurring of liabilities.

There should be an adequate description of any significant contingent liabilities not covered by insurance or provided for in the accounts, such as judgments and pending law suits, notes receivable discounted, and claims for damages. There should be disclosure of any preferred dividends in arrears; any commitments for purchases if the amounts thereof are significant or if there is a prospect that the market price may decline, after the balance sheet date, below the commitment price; any contracts for the construction or acquisition of fixed assets; and any commitments on long-term leases. There should be a statement of the date to which federal income tax returns have been examined.

The income statement should show the gross, or at least the net, sales. The statement should indicate whether profits on installment sales are taken into income in the period of sale, or proportionately to collections. It is desirable to show the amounts of depreciation, depletion, and amortization for the period, and any extraordinary expenses of material amount charged to operations.

Subsequent events and prospects. The primary function of accounting statements is to report the results of operations during a period and the financial position at the end of a period. The accountant is not a prophet, and he should never assume the position of forecasting the future. But, at the same time, he must recognize that the statements he renders are likely to be used as indications of probable future earnings and probable future financial position. He is under certain obligation, therefore, to disclose matters occurring after the balance sheet date but before the year-end statements are completed and released which materially affect the operating results or financial position portrayed by the financial statements. Such matters might include:

The purchase, sale, or destruction of a plant, or the destruction of inventories.

A material decline in the market value of inventories or investments.

The expiration of a patent which had given the company a virtual monopoly in the sale of one of its principal products.

The settlement of income tax liabilities of prior periods.
The settlement of a law suit, adversely or favorably, which was pending at the balance sheet date.
The institution of important legal proceedings by or against the company.
A material change in the capital structure resulting from an issuance, retirement, or conversion of stock, a stock split-up, or a stock dividend.

The accountant may also be under obligation to disclose contemplated actions which might have a material effect on the financial position or the profitability of operations, such as a proposed reorganization, refinancing, or change in plant, product, or management. But in this realm of the possible, the accountant should tread cautiously. The mere fact that an action is under consideration is rarely sufficient reason for disclosure; contemplation must usually have reached the point of decision.

ILLUSTRATIONS OF PUBLISHED STATEMENTS

Importance of clarity in published statements. Financial statements are receiving increasing attention from management, credit grantors, stockholders, governmental agencies, and the general public. They provide a basis for the formulation of many business decisions. Financial statements also serve as a device by which management reports on its accountability for, or stewardship of, the properties placed under its control.

With regard to published statements—those released to stockholders and the general public—the accountant is naturally interested in designing statements which will minimize misunderstanding by persons or groups of persons who are entitled to receive the statements and who make a sincere effort to understand them. This concern on the part of the accountant has caused him to consider whether the use of technical accounting terminology may cause misunderstanding, particularly in those cases in which accounting has adopted terms found in our general vocabulary and has attached special meanings to them. The words *reserve* and *surplus* are cases in point.

Similarly, accountants recognize the possibility that conventional statement forms, although logical to a trained accountant, may not be as effective as less conventional forms in giving the nonaccountant information about the financial position of a business and the results of its operations.

These considerations have led many corporations to experiment with alternative statements and alternative terminology. Some of these alternatives are illustrated in the remainder of this chapter.

Notes accompanying the published statements shown in this chapter have been omitted because the objective is merely to illustrate statement forms.

Single-step income statements. The income statements previously shown are multiple-step statements—so-called because costs and expenses are deducted, and certain income items are added, in such a manner as to show remainders such as gross profit on sales, net operating income, and net income. The single-step statement presents all items of revenue and income at the top, with a total thereof; all costs and expenses are then shown, and their total is deducted to determine the net income. No intermediate balances, such as gross profit, are shown. An illustration of a single-step statement, from the annual report of Kern County Land Company, appears below.

CONSOLIDATED STATEMENTS OF EARNINGS

EARNINGS FOR THE YEAR

	YEAR ENDED DECEMBER 31	
	1963	1962
Revenues		
Sales	$ 96,681,307	$ 82,502,878
Royalties and Rents	34,043,448	34,214,308
Interest and Other	1,149,852	1,069,834
Total	131,874,607	117,787,020
Expenses		
Costs and Operating Expenses	91,683,425	79,030,175
Oil and Mineral Exploration and Development	5,630,059	4,768,723
Selling, Administration and General	7,599,338	6,655,596
Federal and State Income and Franchise Taxes	9,612,115	9,845,345
Total	114,524,937	100,299,839
Net Earnings for the Year	$ 17,349,670	$ 17,487,181

The advocates of the single-step statement present the following arguments in its favor:

The multiple-step statement implies that some costs and expenses take precedence over others as deductions from revenues, and that "profits" remain after each deduction. This implication, they maintain, is fallacious; all costs and expenses rank alike as deductions from income, and there is no "profit" until all costs and expenses have been deducted.

By listing miscellaneous income after the deduction of selling and general expenses, the statement carries the erroneous implication that such income is earned without the incurring of any expense.

The subtotals and titles in the multiple-step statement have no universally recognized meaning.

The single-step statement is simple and easy to understand.

Combined single-step income and retained earnings statement. The following statement of Caterpillar Tractor Co. is an illustration of a combined single-step income statement and statement of retained earnings.

Consolidated Results of Operations Year 1963

Sales		**$966,135,837**
Costs:		
Inventories brought forward from previous year	$ 238,282,120	
Materials, supplies, services purchased, etc.	491,736,308	
Wages, salaries and contributions for employee benefits	280,952,412	
Portion of original cost of buildings, machinery and equipment allocated to operations (depreciation)	41,213,723	
Interest on borrowed funds	6,795,548	
United States and foreign taxes based on income	81,629,643	
	1,140,609,754	
Deduct: Inventories carried forward to following year	251,205,453	
Costs allocated to year		889,404,301
		76,731,536
Profit of Caterpillar Credit Corporation		542,480
Profit for year—consolidated		**77,274,016**
Add:		
Profit employed in the business at beginning of year		258,918,013
		336,192,029
Deduct:		
Dividends paid in cash during year—$1.15 per share		31,365,677
Profit employed in the business at end of year		$304,826,352

Showing the working capital. The statement of financial position of King-Seeley Thermos Co. illustrates a form in which the current liabilities are deducted from the current assets, thus giving some emphasis to the working capital position of the company.

Simplified statements. Some companies present simplified or informal versions of their financial statements in addition, or as supplements, to the

KING-SEELEY THERMOS CO. ILLUSTRATION

CONSOLIDATED STATEMENT OF FINANCIAL CONDITION

	July 31 1963	July 31 1962
CURRENT ASSETS:		
Cash	$ 3,705,791	$ 4,093,592
U. S. Government securities	6,522,816	7,895,008
Accounts receivable, less $210,000 for doubtful accounts	9,992,420	8,547,439
Cost of dies collectible from customers	592,233	250,443
Inventories, at lower of cost (first-in, first-out) or market	14,585,069	12,604,724
Prepaid insurance and other expenses	287,064	370,948
TOTAL CURRENT ASSETS	$35,685,393	$33,762,154
LESS—CURRENT LIABILITIES:		
Notes payable	$ —	$ 123,749
Accounts payable	2,802,440	3,089,777
Accrued payrolls, taxes and other items	3,611,705	2,676,873
Estimated liability for income taxes	5,319,629	3,843,870
TOTAL CURRENT LIABILITIES	$11,733,774	$ 9,734,269
WORKING CAPITAL	$23,951,619	$24,027,885
PROPERTY ACCOUNTS, less depreciation and amortization	15,110,572	15,751,273
PATENTS AND TRADEMARKS, at cost less amortization of $479,172 (1963) and $356,961 (1962)	935,723	415,806
	$39,997,914	$40,194,964
LONG-TERM LIABILITIES, less amounts payable within one year	—	(3,640,000)
DEFERRED INVESTMENT CREDIT AND CANADIAN INCOME TAXES	(203,862)	(136,734)
NET ASSETS	$39,794,052	$36,418,230
DERIVED FROM:		
Common stock, $1 par value Authorized 2,000,000 shares Issued 1,665,710 shares (1963) and 1,656,505 shares (1962)	$ 1,665,710	$ 1,656,505
Capital surplus	8,210,497	8,095,043
Income retained for use in the business	29,917,845	26,666,682
	$39,794,052	$36,418,230

conventional variety. The following examples are typical of this practice. The first example was included in the 1963 report of Chain Belt Company; the second was taken from the report of Parke, Davis & Company for the same year.

simplified statements for 1963

results of operations

	amount	per $100 of sales
THE COMPANY RECEIVED from customers	**$90,823,675**	**$100.00**
THIS MONEY WAS USED FOR: Wages, salaries and employee benefits	$36,451,972	$ 40.13
Materials, supplies and services, and depreciation	45,146,344	49.71
Costs applicable to operations for the year	81,598,316	89.84
Estimated federal and state income taxes	5,185,000	5.71
Dividends paid to shareholders	2,314,187	2.55
Retained for use in the business	1,726,172	1.90
	$90,823,675	**$100.00**

financial condition

	amount	per share
As a result of these operations, the financial statement at October 31, 1963, showed the company:		
Owned cash and U.S. Government securities of	$11,802,992	$ 9.40
Was owed by customers and subsidiaries	11,492,225	9.15
Had raw materials, products being manufactured and products ready for sale of	24,277,062	19.34
Had paid in advance for insurance and other expenses	1,179,005	.94
Amounting to total current assets of	48,751,284	38.83
Against this the company owed:		
To employees for wages and salaries, to suppliers for materials, to shareholders for dividends, etc.	5,673,119	4.52
To federal and state governments for income taxes	3,662,234	2.92
Leaving working capital of	39,415,931	31.39
To this add the buildings, machinery, tools and land of	21,642,790	17.24
And other assets of	4,037,826	3.22
Making a total of	65,096,547	51.85
From this deduct the long-term debt and deferred federal taxes on income of	12,640,000	10.07
This is the shareholders' investment in the company	**$52,456,547**	**$ 41.78**

SUMMARY OF OPERATIONS 1963

	YEAR 1963	PER CENT OF RECEIPTS 1963	PER CENT OF RECEIPTS 1962
WE RECEIVED:			
From sale of products	$189,183,584	98.2	98.5
From royalties, interest earned, etc.	3,546,738	1.8	1.5
Total receipts	$192,730,322	100.0	100.0
WE PAID OUT OR PROVIDED:			
For wages and salaries, including employee benefit plans and payroll taxes	$ 66,613,018	34.6	35.2
For materials, services, supplies, and other expenses	80,126,422	41.6	42.1
For depreciation and obsolescence	6,923,803	3.6	3.6
For taxes other than payroll taxes	16,867,363	8.7	8.7
For minority interest in consolidated subsidiaries	35,223	—	.1
Total costs	$170,565,829	88.5	89.7
WE HAD LEFT:			
In net earnings	$ 22,164,493	11.5	10.3
WHICH WAS USED:			
For dividends to stockholders	$ 14,865,930	7.7	8.0
For continuing needs of the business	7,298,563	3.8	2.3
	$ 22,164,493	11.5	10.3

HOW WE STAND ON DECEMBER 31, 1963

	DECEMBER 31, 1963	INVESTMENT PER EMPLOYEE 1963	INVESTMENT PER EMPLOYEE 1962
WHAT WE OWN:			
Cash and marketable securities needed for prompt payment of current obligations and to provide for future expansion programs	$ 55,989,424	$ 4,626	$ 3,360
Receivables due from customers for merchandise delivered	33,964,616	2,806	2,578
Claims for recoverable excise taxes	713,654	59	81
Inventories and supplies for servicing customer needs	42,419,313	3,505	3,444
Taxes, insurance, and other expenses paid in advance	3,618,225	299	291
Investment in unconsolidated subsidiaries	3,858,707	319	159
Land, buildings, and equipment which originally cost $136,729,927 and against which depreciation in the amount of $53,601,643 has been provided	83,128,284	6,868	6,856
Sundry other assets	1,083,165	89	178
Deferred pension plan costs	2,338,411	193	271
	$227,113,799	$18,764	$17,218
WHAT WE OWE:			
Obligations to employees for wages, salaries, and commissions; to manufacturers for materials purchased; to various governments for taxes other than taxes on income; and to stockholders for dividends	$ 23,799,334	$ 1,966	$ 1,829
Taxes on income to United States and other countries	17,796,705	1,470	1,512
Money borrowed to provide for current requirements in other countries	17,084,486	1,412	671
Minority interest in consolidated subsidiaries	1,025,285	85	148
	$ 59,705,810	$ 4,933	$ 4,160
STOCKHOLDERS' INVESTMENT AND SAVINGS:			
Amounts owned less amounts owed, representing the value of the original investment made by stockholders plus accumulated savings	$167,407,989	$13,831	$13,058

Graphic presentations. Many companies, in their annual reports, make good use of graphic material as part of their public relations programs.

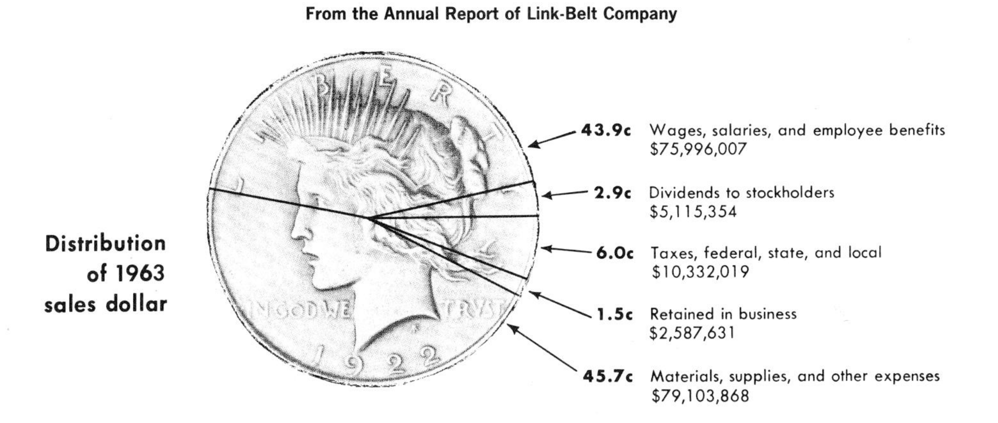

Conclusion. If there is any likelihood that the end product of the accounting process is subject to misunderstanding, accountants should be encouraged to explore all possible avenues to avoid such an undesirable condition. However, it may be relevant to note that the desirable policy of avoiding, in published financial statements, terms subject to misunderstanding by members of the general public should not necessarily require that those terms be discarded from the accountant's vocabulary. For instance, it may be sensible to avoid the term *surplus* in published financial statements, but it need not follow that accountants should forever strike *surplus* from their technical terminology.

Much the same position can be taken regarding financial statements. It would seem unwise to take a negative attitude toward nonconventional statement forms. If there is any evidence suggesting that conventional forms do not communicate information regarding financial position and results of operations in an effective manner, then alternative forms should be given a fair trial. However, it should be recognized that there are certain groups of people who will not adequately understand financial information no matter what form is selected for presentation. In some instances, this may be attributed to a lack of familiarity with business and financial matters generally. In some cases, perhaps, an individual's bias will not enable him to interpret fairly the information presented in financial statements.

There is merit, of course, in conventional forms of financial statements in that they are reasonably uniform and thus enable a statement user to compare them with the statements of other companies in the same industry or trade. It would be unfortunate if our interest in presenting information in a readily understandable form resulted in a loss of basic uniformity.

CHAPTER

4

Net Income Concepts and Corrections of Prior Years' Earnings

NET INCOME CONCEPTS

A basic problem. In the preparation of financial statements, the accountant may encounter unusual, and presumably nonrecurring, gains and losses and may have to do something about errors made during prior periods which caused the net income of such prior periods to be incorrectly reported. How should these items be dealt with in the financial statements, keeping in mind that the objective of the accountant is always to present meaningful and useful financial statements?

The problem narrows down to the basic question of *what* is properly includible in the computation of net income *for the period?* For instance, is the net income for the period affected by unusual, extraneous, and nonrecurring gains and losses, such as an uninsured flood loss? Is the net income for the current period affected by corrections of income-computation errors of prior periods?

The current operating concept of net income and the all-inclusive (clean surplus) theory. For many years accountants adhered to the current operating concept of net income, believing that corrections of the net income of prior years and unusual, extraneous, and nonrecurring items of income and expense (such as gains and losses resulting from disposals of fixed assets) should be shown in the statement of retained earnings (also called the *earned surplus statement*). The procedure of showing all such items in the statement of retained earnings was considered desirable because the income statement then showed the results of *regular operations* for the *current period,* unaffected by unusual, extraordinary, or extraneous transactions or by corrections of the income statements of prior years.

The concept described in the preceding paragraph has been challenged. A considerable number of accountants question the propriety, or at least the advisability, of showing extraneous gains and losses and corrections of prior years' earnings in the statement of retained earnings. They adhere to the clean surplus theory. They believe that, as a matter of pure theory, such items are related to income determination, and that net income for the period would be misstated if they were excluded.

The clean surplus theory. The advocates of this concept maintain that all items of revenue, expense, gain, or loss are necessary factors in determining net income. They believe, and in fact urge, that extraordinary and correction items should be included (properly described and segregated) in the income statement. They contend that mere size, unusualness, or timing does not convert what would otherwise be an item of revenue, expense, gain, or loss into something else. Some of the additional arguments presented by the advocates of this school of thought are stated below.

The total of the amounts shown as net income in the statements for a series of years should be the aggregate net income for those years. This will not be the case if corrections of net income of prior years are shown in the retained earnings statement rather than the income statement. Incidentally, including corrections of prior years' net income in the income statement calls attention to the tentative and estimated nature of the income statement.

When an accountant charges retained earnings with a loss because he considers it extraordinary or extraneous, he implies that it is nonrecurring. But a study of business history indicates that, over a period of years, such losses do recur, and that the retained earnings charges tend to exceed the retained earnings credits, with the result that the income statements for a series of years give an exaggerated impression of a company's earning power.

The line of demarcation between operating items and extraordinary or extraneous items is not clear cut and is often a matter of opinion. There are many borderline cases. For instance, assume that a department was closed during the year, and that severe losses were incurred in the disposal of the inventories. Does the fact that this department's operations were a part of the regular operations in the past require that the liquidation loss be charged to operations? Or do the department's activities become extraneous to operations when the decision to discontinue its operations is reached?

The Securities and Exchange Commission has cited numerous deficiencies because, in its opinion, retained earnings have been charged with losses which should have been charged to income.

Studies of annual reports have shown many inconsistencies in classifications between the income statement and the statement of retained earnings made by different companies, and by the same company in different years. Wide variations in net income and in earnings per share can be caused by such inconsistencies.

Many so-called extraordinary or extraneous charges and credits are closely related to operations—not to the operations of a single year, but to those of a series of years.

They may be regarded as corrections of the stated net income of a number of past years. For instance, a gain or loss on the disposal of a fixed asset may be regarded as a correction of prior years' income charges for depreciation, which were misstated because of an error in estimating the effect of use or obsolescence on the useful life of the asset, or because of an inability to foresee the effect of changing price levels on the residual value of the property.

Or extraordinary charges may relieve future operations of charges which would otherwise be made against them. This is the case when fixed assets are written off or written down and future years are thereby relieved of depreciation and amortization charges.

Permitting charges and credits to retained earnings thus creates an opportunity for manipulation in the determination of stated net income, because charges and credits to retained earnings may be made to take the place of income charges and credits properly applicable to the operations of past or future periods.

Many people who are not trained accountants but have occasion to rely on accountants' statements do not realize that the income statement does not always tell the complete story about the year's activities, and that the statement of retained earnings should also be scrutinized. They are probably somewhat influenced by the practice of financial reporting services in reporting earnings per share based on the net income shown by the income statement.

The current operating concept of net income. The opposing school of thought holds that the income statement should be concerned only with items of revenue and expense that are applicable to the *regular operations* of the *current period.* The proponents of the current operating concept of net income support their position by the following arguments:

Investors and prospective investors are more interested in the net income of a business than in any other one figure shown by the annual statements. And the net income in which they are most interested is that produced by the normal operating activities of the business during the year. Although the net income of one or more years is only one of numerous factors which should be considered in the formation of opinions about prospective earning power, the stated net income should reflect, as nearly as possible, what happened during the year as the result of normal operating transactions. Otherwise, it is difficult to determine the trend of a company's operations and to compare the results of operations of one company with those of other companies.

If the stated net income of one year is affected by a material correction of the net income of a prior year, there is a distortion. The error is compounded, because the current year's net income is overstated or understated to the extent that the net income of the past was understated or overstated. Indicated trends are therefore misleading. When an accountant renders an opinion with respect to the net income *for a year,* he indulges in an obvious contradiction if the amount of net income he shows in the statement includes a correction of the net income of some other year.

If the stated net income includes extraordinary and extraneous items not likely to recur, the reader of the statement is left to make his own decisions regarding the items which should be excluded to determine the results of normal operations. Although it is often difficult to draw a clear and definite line of demarcation between operating and extraordinary items, management and the trained accountant, familiar with the facts, are in a better position to do so than outsiders can possibly be.

There should be full disclosure of all material extraneous and extraordinary items and corrections of earnings of prior years; such disclosure should be made in a way which will avoid any possible distortion and any confusion in the mind of the reader of the statements regarding the results of the regular operations of the business during the year.

The Institute opinion. It is apparent that accountants differ on a very fundamental and important issue: What classes of items should be included in the computation of net income? The continuing shift in emphasis during the last 20 to 30 years from the balance sheet to the income statement has increased the importance of the issue.

The position of the Committee on Accounting Procedure of the American Institute of Certified Public Accountants, as expressed in Bulletin 43, is set forth below:

> . . . it is the opinion of the committee that there should be a general presumption that all items of profit and loss recognized during the period are to be used in determining the figure reported as net income. The only possible exception to this presumption relates to items which in the aggregate are material in relation to the company's net income and are clearly not identifiable with or do not result from the usual or typical business operations of the period. Thus, only extraordinary items such as the following may be excluded from the determination of net income for the year, and they should be excluded when their inclusion would impair the significance of net income so that misleading inferences might be drawn therefrom:
>
> (a) Material charges or credits (other than ordinary adjustments of a recurring nature) specifically related to operations of prior years, such as the elimina-

tion of unused reserves provided in prior years and adjustments of income taxes of prior years;
(b) Material charges or credits resulting from unusual sales of assets not acquired for resale and not of the type in which the company generally deals;
(c) Material losses of a type not usually insured against, such as those resulting from wars, riots, earthquakes, and similar calamities or catastrophes except where such losses are a recurrent hazard of the business;
(d) The write-off of a material amount of intangibles;
(e) The write-off of material amounts of unamortized bond discount or premium and bond issue expenses at the time of the retirement or refunding of the debt before maturity.

Net of tax. Whenever unusual and nonrecurring items affect a company's income tax liability by being includible or deductible in the computation of taxable income, a related question arises concerning the appropriate accounting for such "added tax" or "tax savings," as the case may be. It is acceptable, and preferred, practice to associate the tax effect with the unusual or nonrecurring item. For example, assume that an unusual gain of $100,000 causes a company's income tax to increase by $25,000. Actually, the net result of the assumed unusual item is a net gain of $75,000—$100,000 less the tax increase of $25,000. It is considered more informative to report unusual and nonrecurring items on a net-of-tax basis. That is, such items should be reported in a way that will disclose the net, or after-tax, results. To illustrate, let us assume that the all-inclusive concept of reporting is being followed by State Company, and that the company experiences the unusual gain mentioned above. Notice how the $25,000 added tax is associated with the unusual gain in the following income statement.

Illustration of application of all-inclusive concept.

STATE COMPANY
Income Statement
For the Year Ended December 31, 1965

Net sales		$1,000,000
Cost of goods sold	$600,000	
Operating expenses	200,000	800,000
Net operating income		$ 200,000
Income tax thereon		100,000
Net income before unusual gain		$ 100,000
Unusual gain (a more complete description would be given)	$100,000	
Less income tax associated with unusual gain	25,000	75,000
Net income		$ 175,000

The income tax liability shown in the December 31, 1965 balance sheet of State Company would amount to $125,000: $100,000 + $25,000.

Should State Company apply the current operating concept, the final figure in its 1965 income statement would be $100,000, and the statement of retained earnings would appear as follows:

Illustration of application of current operating concept.

STATE COMPANY
Statement of Retained Earnings
For the Year Ended December 31, 1965

Retained earnings, December 31, 1964		$800,000
Add:		
Net income for the year—per income statement		100,000
Unusual gain	$100,000	
Less income tax associated with unusual gain	25,000	75,000
Total		$975,000
Dividends		60,000
Retained earnings, December 31, 1965		$915,000

Combined income and retained earnings statement. The combined statement of income and retained earnings is sometimes described as a compromise between the current operating and clean surplus concepts of net income. It is not such a compromise. The net income may be computed in accordance with either concept. The purpose is to combine in one statement all elements affecting the retained earnings during the period, so that none will be overlooked.

Concluding note. The proper concept of net income remains unsettled. It is an important issue, and an accounting student should be thoroughly familiar with the points of view discussed and be able to follow alternative approaches, as directed. Until the issue is more clearly resolved, an instructor is justified in suggesting the adoption of a single point of view, if for no other reason than to achieve class uniformity.

CORRECTIONS OF PRIOR YEARS' EARNINGS

Description of errors. The accounting problems created by the necessary correction of errors that affected prior financial statements are not limited to matters of statement location and disclosure; the accounting techniques involved warrant explanation and illustration.

Many mistakes affecting financial statements are merely classification errors; loans to officers recorded or classified as trade accounts receivable, or salesmen's salaries charged to Office Salaries, are examples. Mistakes of a more significant nature result in incorrect net income amounts. Of course, such mistakes also affect the balance sheet. If the net income is overstated as a result of accounting errors, the retained earnings are overstated on the companion balance sheet. If retained earnings are overstated, the net assets are overstated—by overstatement of assets, understatement of liabilities, or a combination thereof. An understatement of net income and retained earnings is accompanied by a balance sheet understatement of net assets.

Errors affecting net income. Errors that affect the income statement for a period and the balance sheet at the end of the period are of two kinds.

(1) Errors that overstate (or understate) the net income of one period and correspondingly understate (or overstate) the net income of the following period. These are *counterbalancing* errors; although the net income for each period and the balance sheet at the end of the first period are incorrect, the net income for the two periods combined is correct, and the balance sheet at the end of the second period is correct. This assumes that the same income tax rates will prevail in both periods.

For an example of a counterbalancing error, assume that an accountant overlooks the accrual of $1,000 of interest expense as of December 31, 1964. In 1965 the interest applicable to 1964 is paid and charged to Interest Expense. The net income before income tax for 1964 is overstated $1,000 and the net income before income tax for 1965 is understated $1,000. By the end of 1965 the error has been counterbalanced; the total net income for the two years is unaffected (unless different income tax rates are applicable), and the balance sheet at the end of 1965 is correct. The following income statement data illustrate the counterbalancing produced by the above oversight.

	With Counterbalancing Errors ($1,000 of 1964 Interest Expense Recorded in 1965)			Without Errors		
	1964	1965	Total	1964	1965	Total
Net income before interest and income tax	$8,000	$8,000		$8,000	$8,000	
Interest expense	2,000	4,000		3,000	3,000	
Net income before income tax	$6,000	$4,000		$5,000	$5,000	
Income tax—25% assumed for both years	1,500	1,000		1,250	1,250	
Net income	$4,500 +	$3,000 =	$7,500	$3,750 +	$3,750 =	$7,500

(2) Errors that overstate or understate the net income of one period and are not counterbalanced by a corresponding understatement or overstatement of the net income of the succeeding period. Such errors leave the retained earnings and one or more asset or liability accounts inaccurate until an entry is made to correct the errors, or, in the case of fixed assets, until they are disposed of or become fully depreciated—either of which removes the effects of the error from the account balances.

For example, assume that the depreciation charged to operations and credited to an accumulated depreciation account in 1964 was too small. As a result, the net income for 1964 was overstated; this error will not be automatically counterbalanced by any corresponding understatement of net income in 1965. Therefore, retained earnings will remain overstated and the accumulated depreciation will remain understated until a correcting entry is made or until the asset involved is disposed of or becomes fully depreciated.

Alternative procedures for dealing with errors. The accountant, concerned with the importance of presenting meaningful and useful financial statements, must decide on the best reporting procedure for dealing with errors that have caused misstatements of the net income of prior periods.

He has the following choices:

If the errors are not material in amount, they may be absorbed in the income statement of the year of discovery without disclosure. This procedure is permissible if the current income statement will not thereby be appreciably distorted. However, it should be noted that several immaterial errors may produce material consequences.

If the errors are material in amount, the accountant has three alternatives:

The errors may be disclosed in the income statement for the year of discovery.

The errors may be disclosed in the statement of retained earnings for the year of discovery.

Revised statements for prior years may be prepared.

The choice of procedure is important, because an unwise selection of a method of dealing with the corrections may have the unfortunate effect of causing the statement user to misunderstand or overlook the correction.

Illustrations of the four methods mentioned above are shown in the remainder of this chapter. In order to facilitate concentration on the correction problem, income taxes are ignored. However, it should be recognized that a tax refund or deficiency can result from the discovery of certain kinds of errors.

Basis of illustrations. Assume that The A. B. Company found it necessary to replace its accountant at the end of 1966, before the financial statements had been prepared. The new accountant was informed that the company follows the accrual basis of accounting, and he determined that adjusting entries were required to give recognition to depreciation ($2,200), accrued wages ($250), and office supplies on hand ($400). After recording the above adjustments, the new accountant prepared the adjusted trial balance on page 68.

At this point the accountant discovers that his predecessor had committed several errors in the preparation of financial statements for previous years. He had (1) failed to make adjusting entries for accrued wages and office supplies on hand; (2) miscomputed depreciation for 1963 and 1964; and (3) made clerical errors in computing the inventories as of December 31, 1964 and 1965.

THE A. B. COMPANY
Adjusted Trial Balance
December 31, 1966

Cash	17,615	
Inventory, end of year	16,200	
Office supplies on hand	400	
Furniture and fixtures	28,300	
Accumulated depreciation		12,305
Accounts payable		11,390
Accrued wages payable		250
Capital stock		30,000
Retained earnings		6,650
Dividends	6,000	
Sales		124,000
Cost of goods sold	90,550	
Wages	15,280	
Office supplies expense	1,375	
Depreciation	2,200	
Other expense	6,675	
	184,595	184,595

In order to determine the effects of these mistakes, the accountant develops the following information.

Accrued wages of prior periods:

No entries for accrued wages were made at the end of 1963, 1964, or 1965; such wages were charged to the wages expense account in the following year, when they were paid. The overlooked accruals amounted to:

December 31:	
1963	$175
1964	215
1965	230

The counterbalancing effects on net income as a result of failing to adjust for accrued wages are shown by the following schedule:

	December 31, 1963 Retained Earnings Were Overstated	Net Income Was Overstated-Understated*		1966 Net Income Will Be Understated*
		1964	1965	
Failure to adjust for accrued wages:				
December 31, 1963	175	175*		
December 31, 1964		215	215*	
December 31, 1965			230	230*
Net overstatement		40	15	

The foregoing schedule reveals that, as a result of the failure to make adjusting entries for accrued wages, the December 31, 1963 retained earnings were overstated $175, the 1964 reported net income was overstated $40, the 1965 reported net income was overstated $15, and (unless a correction is made) the current year's net income will be understated $230 as a result of the accrued wages as of December 31, 1965, being charged to the 1966 wages expense account.

Office supplies on hand:

No recognition was given to the amount of office supplies on hand at the end of 1963, 1964, or 1965. As a result, all purchases of office supplies were treated as an expense in the year of purchase, whether or not they were used in that period. The overlooked amounts on hand were:

December 31:	
1963	$365
1964	415
1965	505

The counterbalancing effects are shown below.

	December 31, 1963 Retained Earnings Were Understated*	Net Income Was Overstated-Understated*		1966 Net Income Will Be Overstated
		1964	1965	
Failure to inventory office supplies:				
December 31, 1963	365*	365		
December 31, 1964		415*	415	
December 31, 1965			505*	505
Net understatement*		50*	90*	

Merchandise inventories:

Year-end inventories were understated and overstated as follows:

December 31:	
1964—understated	$1,390
1965—overstated	615

The counterbalancing effects are shown below.

	Cost of Goods Sold Was Overstated-Understated*		Net Income Was Overstated-Understated*		1966 Net Income Will Be Understated*
	1964	1965	1964	1965	
Error in computing merchandise inventory:					
December 31, 1964—understated	1,390	1,390*	1,390*	1,390	
December 31, 1965—overstated		615*		615	615*
Net overstatement-understatement*	1,390	2,005*	1,390*	2,005	

As the above schedule reveals, an understated ending inventory will understate earnings for the current period and overstate earnings for the following period, and vice versa.

Depreciation:

Depreciation for 1963 was overstated $160.
Depreciation for 1964 was understated $200.
Depreciation for 1965 was correct.

The effects of depreciation errors on net income work themselves out only when the depreciating asset is disposed of or becomes fully depreciated. In the case of The A. B. Company, no assets subject to depreciation have been disposed of or become fully depreciated during the 1963–1966 period. As a result, the depreciation errors have had the following effects:

	December 31, 1963 Retained Earnings Were Understated*	Net Income Was Overstated-Understated*		December 31, 1966 Accumulated Depreciation Will Be Understated*
		1964	1965	
Error in computing depreciation:				
1963–depreciation overstated	160*			40*
1964–depreciation understated ...		200		

In order to determine the net effect of all of the errors on the financial statements, a work sheet similar to the example on page 71 may be prepared.

Such a work sheet is useful for two purposes: It shows whether the net effect of the errors is sufficiently material to require disclosure; and it assembles the information required for statement-correction purposes. In this instance, the work sheet shows that:

(1) By the end of 1965, all errors except the following were counterbalanced:

December 31, 1965 wage accrual ignored—$230.
December 31, 1965 office supplies on hand omitted—$505.
December 31, 1965 inventory overstated—$615.
1963 depreciation overstated—$160.
1964 depreciation understated—$200.

(2) By the end of 1966, all errors except the depreciation misstatements will have been counterbalanced. However, the net income for 1966 will be understated by $340 as a result of the 1965 errors relating to wages, office supplies, and the merchandise inventory.

Procedure If Corrections Are to Be Absorbed in the Current Year's Income Statement Without Disclosure

Assume that the errors of prior years are not considered sufficiently material to require disclosure, and that those not already counterbalanced will be allowed to affect the 1966 income statement, without listing or otherwise disclosing them. Therefore, only the depreciation errors will need correcting; the other errors have been counterbalanced or will be counterbalanced in 1966 by the operation of normal accounting procedures.

The following correcting entry will be required:

Depreciation		40	
Accumulated depreciation			40
To correct for:			
Underdepreciation in 1964	$200		
Overdepreciation in 1963	160		
Net........	$ 40		

The small letters appearing in the work sheet are key references used later in the chapter in illustrative working papers.

THE A. B. COMPANY
Work Sheet to Determine Effect of Errors
On Prior and Current Years' Financial Statements
Overstatement-Understatement*

	References	Prior Years' Financial Statements			1966 Financial Statements If No Corrections Are Made		
		Retained Earnings December 31, 1963	Net Income		Income Statement	Balance Sheet	
			1964	1965	Net Income	Accumulated Depreciation	Retained Earnings
Failure to adjust for accrued wages:							
December 31, 1963	a	175	175*				
December 31, 1964	b		215	215*			
December 31, 1965	c			230	230*		
Failure to inventory office supplies:							
December 31, 1963	d	365*	365				
December 31, 1964	e		415*	415			
December 31, 1965	f			505*	505		
Errors in computing merchandise inventory:							
December 31, 1964—understated	g		1,390*	1,390			
December 31, 1965—overstated	h			615	615*		
Errors in computing depreciation:							
1963—depreciation overstated	i	160*				} 40*	40
1964—depreciation understated	j		200				
Net overstatement—understatement*		350*	1,200*	1,930	340*	40*	40

The income statement and retained earnings statement for 1966 shown below are based on the adjusted trial balance given on page 68, as modified by the depreciation correction. Balance sheets are not presented in the examples in this chapter because there are no special features to illustrate.

THE A. B. COMPANY
Income Statement
For the Year Ended December 31, 1966

Sales		$124,000
Cost of goods sold		90,550
Gross profit on sales		$ 33,450
Expenses:		
Wages	$15,280	
Office supplies expense	1,375	
Depreciation	2,240	
Other expense	6,675	25,570
Net income		$ 7,880

THE A. B. COMPANY
Statement of Retained Earnings
For the Year Ended December 31, 1966

Retained earnings, December 31, 1965	$ 6,650
Net income—per income statement	7,880
Total	$14,530
Dividends	6,000
Retained earnings, December 31, 1966	$ 8,530

Procedure If Errors Are to Be Disclosed in the Current Income Statement

If the accountant prefers to *disclose* the correction of prior years' earnings in the income statement, he will make correcting entries for *all* of the errors not counterbalanced at the beginning of 1966.

	Dr.	Cr.
Correction of prior years' earnings—1965 wage accrual	230	
Wages		230
To remove wages applicable to 1965.		
Office supplies expense	505	
Correction of prior years' earnings—Office supplies improperly expensed in 1965		505
Supplies on hand at beginning of year.		
Correction of prior years' earnings—Inventory overstatement—December 31, 1965	615	
Cost of goods sold		615
To correct the cost of goods sold because of the error in the beginning inventory.		
Correction of prior years' earnings—Depreciation errors	40	
Accumulated depreciation		40
To correct Accumulated Depreciation account for errors made in computing depreciation for 1963 and 1964.		

Working papers showing such corrections appear on the opposite page. The income statement prepared from these working papers is presented on page 74.

THE A. B. COMPANY
Working Papers
For the Year Ended December 31, 1966

	Adjusted Trial Balance		Corrections		Income Statement		Statement of Retained Earnings		Balance Sheet	
Cash	17,615								17,615	
Inventory, end of year	16,200								16,200	
Office supplies on hand	400								400	
Furniture and fixtures	28,300								28,300	
Accumulated depreciation		12,305		i–j 40						12,345
Accounts payable		11,390								11,390
Accrued wages payable		250								250
Capital stock		30,000								30,000
Retained earnings		6,650						6,650		
Dividends	6,000						6,000			
Sales		124,000				124,000				
Cost of goods sold	90,550			h 615	89,935					
Wages	15,280			c 230	15,050					
Office supplies expense	1,375		f 505		1,880					
Depreciation	2,200				2,200					
Other expense	6,675				6,675					
	184,595	184,595								
Correction of prior years' earnings:										
1965 wage accrual			c 230		230					
Office supplies improperly expensed in 1965				f 505		505				
Inventory overstatement, December 31, 1965			h 615		615					
Depreciation errors			i–j 40		40					
			1,390	1,390	116,625	124,505				
Net income					7,880			7,880		
					124,505	124,505	6,000	14,530		
Retained earnings, December 31, 1966							8,530			8,530
							14,530	14,530	62,515	62,515

THE A. B. COMPANY
Income Statement
For the Year Ended December 31, 1966

Sales			$124,000
Cost of goods sold			89,935
Gross profit on sales			$ 34,065
Expenses:			
Wages		$15,050	
Office supplies expense		1,880	
Depreciation		2,200	
Other expense		6,675	25,805
Net income before correction of prior years' earnings			$ 8,260
Correction of prior years' earnings:			
Add office supplies improperly expensed in 1965			505
Total			$ 8,765
Deduct:			
1965 wage accrual		$ 230	
Inventory overstatement		615	
Depreciation:			
Insufficient provision in 1964	$200		
Excess provision in 1963	160	40	885
Net income			$ 7,880

The statement of retained earnings for 1966 would be the same as the one presented on page 72.

Procedure If Errors Are Disclosed in the Retained Earnings Statement

If the accountant prefers to show the correction of errors affecting prior years' earnings in the statement of retained earnings, the working papers would be the same as those in the immediately preceding illustration, except that the correction entries at the bottom of the working papers would be extended to the Retained Earnings columns instead of to the Income Statement columns, and the net income amounts would be different because of the difference in the treatment of the correction items.

Under the procedure being illustrated, there would be nothing unusual in either the form or the content of the income statement. The statement of retained earnings, however, would appear as follows:

THE A. B. COMPANY
Statement of Retained Earnings
For the Year Ended December 31, 1966

Retained earnings, December 31, 1965:	
Per books	$ 6,650
Corrections of prior years' earnings:	
Add:	
Office supplies improperly expensed in 1965	505
Total	$ 7,155

Deduct:			
1965 wage accrual		$230	
Inventory overstatement, December 31, 1965		615	
Depreciation:			
Insufficient provision in 1964	$200		
Excess provision in 1963	160	40	885
As adjusted			$ 6,270
Net income—per income statement			8,260
Total			$14,530
Dividends			6,000
Retained earnings, December 31, 1966			$ 8,530

Closing entries. When the correction items are shown in the statement of retained earnings, the revenue and expense accounts and the Revenue and Expense account will be closed in the usual manner. The correction accounts will be closed to Retained Earnings, as follows:

Retained earnings	380	
Correction of prior years' earnings—Office supplies improperly expensed	505	
Correction of prior years' earnings—1965 wage accrual		230
Correction of prior years' earnings—Inventory overstatement, December 31, 1965		615
Correction of prior years' earnings—Depreciation errors		40
To close correction-of-prior-years'-earnings accounts.		

For 1966, the Retained Earnings account would show the following amounts:

Retained Earnings

1966			1966		
12/31	Correction accounts	380	1/ 2	Balance	6,650
12/31	Dividends	6,000	12/31	From Revenue and Expense	8,260

The year-end account balance is $8,530, which agrees with the statement of retained earnings.

Procedure If Statements for Prior Years Are to Be Revised

When errors are discovered that caused prior years' financial statements to be incorrect, revised financial statements for such prior periods may be prepared. As a practical matter, this is done only if the earlier statements are materially in error and therefore possibly misleading, or if the company is faced with the task of submitting current and prior years' financial statements to prospective investors in connection with an issuance of bonds or stocks. Waiving the question whether the errors illustrated are significant, The A. B. Company case will be used to show how revised statements may be prepared. Although some of the errors affected the 1963 statements, we shall assume (in order to shorten the illustration somewhat) that 1964 is the first year for which revised statements are to be presented. The working papers used in the preparation of revised statements for 1964 are presented on page 76.

THE A. B. COMPANY
Working Papers to Revise Financial Statements
For the Year Ended December 31, 1964

	Per Statements		Corrections		Revised Statements	
Income Statement						
Sales		114,500				114,500
Cost of goods sold	84,100			g 1,390	82,710	
Expenses:						
Wages	13,200		b 215	a 175	13,240	
Office supplies expense	1,620		d 365	e 415	1,570	
Depreciation	1,745		j 200		1,945	
Other expense	7,035				7,035	
	107,700	114,500			106,500	114,500
Net income—down	6,800				8,000	
	114,500	114,500			114,500	114,500
Statement of Retained Earnings						
Retained earnings, beginning of year		5,000	a 175	d 365 i 160		5,350
Net income—brought down		6,800				8,000
Dividends	6,000				6,000	
	6,000	11,800			6,000	13,350
Retained earnings, end of year—down	5,800				7,350	
	11,800	11,800			13,350	13,350
Balance Sheet						
Cash	12,545				12,545	
Inventory, end of year	15,700		g 1,390		17,090	
Office supplies on hand			e 415		415	
Furniture and fixtures	27,000				27,000	
Accumulated depreciation		7,945	i 160	j 200		7,985
Accounts payable		11,500				11,500
Accrued wages payable				b 215		215
Capital stock		30,000				30,000
Retained earnings—brought down		5,800				7,350
	55,245	55,245	2,920	2,920	57,050	57,050

Note the following about the working papers.

(1) The amounts shown in the first two money columns were copied from the financial statements prepared before the discovery of the errors in the statements of prior years.

(2) The corrections were taken from the work sheet prepared by the new accountant to determine the effects of the errors he discovered. (See page 71.) The key references refer to that work sheet. The necessary corrections are repeated here to make it easier to follow the working papers.

- a, b } Corrections required because of failure to adjust for accrued wages.
- d, e } Corrections required because of failure to give recognition to office supplies on hand.
- g Correction required because of clerical error in computing merchandise inventory.
- i, j } Correction required because of errors in computing depreciation provisions.

(3) The three errors affecting the December 31, 1963 retained earnings are applied to the December 31, 1963 retained earnings figure of $5,000 (corrections a, d, and i). All other errors affect 1964 income statement or balance sheet accounts.

Working papers to revise the 1965 financial statements are presented on page 78. In connection with these working papers, note that when the beginning-of-year retained earnings has been properly corrected, the revised amount, $7,350, agrees with the end-of-year revised retained earnings figure shown in the working papers to revise the financial statements for the year ended December 31, 1964 (page 76).

If revised statements are prepared for 1964 and 1965, the prior years' errors need not appear in the 1966 financial statements. The four correction amounts shown in the Corrections columns in the working papers on page 73, under the side caption "Correction of prior years' earnings," are applied to the retained earnings balance of $6,650, thus producing a corrected balance of $6,270. Working papers following the above suggestion appear on page 79. They agree with the working papers on page 73, except for the location of the prior years' corrections which affected the December 31, 1965 balance of retained earnings. As adjusted, the December 31, 1965 balance of retained earnings is $6,270, which agrees with the amount that would be reported in the revised statements for 1965. (See the working papers on page 78.)

The correction entries would be made directly to Retained Earnings.

THE A. B. COMPANY

Working Papers to Revise Financial Statements
For the Year Ended December 31, 1965

	Per Statements		Corrections		Revised Statements	
Income Statement						
Sales		116,000				116,000
Cost of goods sold	85,050		g 1,390 h 615		87,055	
Expenses:						
Wages	14,100		c 230	b 215	14,115	
Office supplies expense	1,715		e 415	f 505	1,625	
Depreciation	2,160				2,160	
Other expense	6,125				6,125	
	109,150	116,000			111,080	116,000
Net income—down	6,850				4,920	
	116,000	116,000			116,000	116,000
Statement of Retained Earnings						
Retained earnings, beginning of year		5,800	i–j 40 b 215	e 415 g 1,390		7,350
Net income—brought down		6,850				4,920
Dividends	6,000				6,000	
	6,000	12,650			6,000	12,270
Retained earnings, end of year—down	6,650				6,270	
	12,650	12,650			12,270	12,270
Balance Sheet						
Cash	15,455				15,455	
Inventory, end of year	16,100			h 615	15,485	
Office supplies on hand			f 505		505	
Furniture and fixtures	28,000				28,000	
Accumulated depreciation		10,105		i–j 40		10,145
Accounts payable		12,800				12,800
Accrued wages payable				c 230		230
Capital stock		30,000				30,000
Retained earnings—brought down		6,650				6,270
	59,555	59,555	3,410	3,410	59,445	59,445

THE A. B. COMPANY
Working Papers
For the Year Ended December 31, 1966

	Adjusted Trial Balance		Corrections		Income Statement		Statement of Retained Earnings		Balance Sheet	
Cash	17,615								17,615	
Inventory, end of year	16,200								16,200	
Office supplies on hand	400								400	
Furniture and fixtures	28,300								28,300	
Accumulated depreciation		12,305		i–j 40						12,345
Accounts payable		11,390								11,390
Accrued wages payable		250								250
Capital stock		30,000								30,000
Retained earnings		6,650	c 230 h 615 i–j 40	f 505				6,270		
Dividends	6,000						6,000			
Sales		124,000				124,000				
Cost of goods sold	90,550			h 615	89,935					
Wages	15,280			c 230	15,050					
Office supplies expense	1,375		f 505		1,880					
Depreciation	2,200				2,200					
Other expense	6,675				6,675					
	184,595	184,595	1,390	1,390	115,740	124,000				
Net income					8,260			8,260		
					124,000	124,000	6,000	14,530		
Retained earnings, December 31, 1966							8,530			8,530
							14,530	14,530	62,515	62,515

Corrections

c—Corrections for 1965 wage accrual.
f—Correction for office supplies improperly expensed.
h—Correction for beginning inventory overstatement.
i–j—Correction for depreciation errors.

The 1966 statement of retained earnings will show a beginning-of-year balance of $6,270, as in the following statement.

THE A. B. COMPANY
Statement of Retained Earnings
For the Year Ended December 31, 1966

Retained earnings, December 31, 1965—per revised statements	$ 6,270
Net income—per income statement	8,260
Total	$14,530
Dividends	6,000
Retained earnings, December 31, 1966	$ 8,530

It is also acceptable to include the correction items in the above statement. If this is done, the statement will be the same as the statement of retained earnings illustrated on page 74.

Summary. To indicate clearly how the four methods of dealing with corrections of errors affecting prior years' earnings differ, the income statements and statements of retained earnings of The A. B. Company for 1966, prepared by the four methods, are compared on page 81. Balance sheets are not shown; they would all be alike.

The first method (absorbing the corrections in the current income statement without disclosure) should be used only if the errors are not material in amount. What is material is a matter of judgment. It is probably desirable for the accounting student to treat all errors as material.

The second method (disclosing the errors in the current income statement) and the third method (disclosing the errors in the current statement of retained earnings) are the methods most commonly used. As noted earlier in this chapter, accountants differ as to which is the preferable practice.

The fourth method (preparing revised statements) is not often used, for several reasons: errors may apply to a number of prior periods, and numerous prior statements would have to be revised; the counterbalancing effects of certain types of accounting errors tend to make the net result thereof in any one year insignificant; it is not always possible to determine the year to which the correction should apply—for instance, the allowance for doubtful accounts at the end of some year might be discovered to be too great or too small, but there might be great difficulty in apportioning the correction over prior years; the revised statements give corrected figures, but do not show the amounts of the corrections—they can be determined only by comparisons with the original statements; furthermore, it is probably true that most statement users are not greatly interested in historical information—their interest is primarily in current and prospective earnings.

Loss carryback-carryforward. Corporations engaged in a trade or business are permitted by the federal income tax law to carry back and carry forward losses. Losses may be carried back and deducted from the earnings of the three preceding years. Thus, a 1964 loss of $50,000 can be carried back to

THE A. B. COMPANY

Comparison of Results of the Four Methods of Dealing With Errors in Statements of Prior Years

1966

Income Statement	Errors Absorbed in Current Income Statement Without Disclosure	Errors Disclosed in Current Income Statement	Errors Disclosed in Current Statement of Retained Earnings	Statements for Prior Years Revised
Sales	$124,000	$124,000	$124,000	$124,000
Cost of goods sold	90,550	89,935	89,935	89,935
Gross profit on sales	$ 33,450	$ 34,065	$ 34,065	$ 34,065
Expenses:				
Wages	$ 15,280	$ 15,050	$ 15,050	$ 15,050
Office supplies expense	1,375	1,880	1,880	1,880
Depreciation	2,240	2,200	2,200	2,200
Other expense	6,675	6,675	6,675	6,675
Total expenses	$ 25,570	$ 25,805	$ 25,805	$ 25,805
Net income before corrections of prior years' earnings		$ 8,260		
Add (Deduct*) corrections of prior years' earnings:				
Office supplies improperly expensed in 1965		$ 505		
1965 wage accrual		230*		
Inventory overstated—December 31, 1965		615*		
Underdepreciation—1964		200*		
Overdepreciation—1963		160		
Total corrections		$ 380*		
Net income	$ 7,880	$ 7,880	$ 8,260	$ 8,260
Statement of Retained Earnings				
Retained earnings, December 31, 1965-per books	$ 6,650	$ 6,650	$ 6,650	
Add (Deduct*) corrections of prior years' earnings:				
Office supplies improperly expensed in 1965			$ 505	
1965 wage accrual			230*	
Inventory overstatement—December 31, 1965			615*	
Underdepreciation—1964			200*	
Overdepreciation—1963			160	
Total corrections			$ 380*	
As adjusted			$ 6,270	$ 6,270
Net income—per above	7,880	7,880	8,260	8,260
Total	$ 14,530	$ 14,530	$ 14,530	$ 14,530
Dividends	6,000	6,000	6,000	6,000
Retained earnings, December 31, 1966	$ 8,530	$ 8,530	$ 8,530	$ 8,530

1961 and deducted from the earnings of that year. The 1961 income tax is refigured and the difference between the tax paid and the revised tax for 1961 is refunded. If the 1964 loss is greater than the 1961 income, the unused portion of the loss is applied to the income of 1962 and 1963, in that order, and taxes are refigured to determine the amount to be refunded. Should the 1964 loss exceed the earnings of the three preceding years, any unused loss may then be carried forward and deducted from earnings of the next five years. Thus, whenever a company's losses exceed the earnings of the three preceding years, with the result that the company has a loss carryforward, future earnings equal to the loss carryforward are tax-free if they occur within the five-year limitation.

The operation of the carryback-carryforward provisions is illustrated in the following table, in which a company that was profitable during the years 1961 through 1963 turns unprofitable for 1964 and 1965.

	1961	1962	1963	1964	1965
Net income (loss*) before income taxes	$5,000	$15,000	$10,000	$50,000*	$ 5,000*
Loss carryback	(5,000)	(15,000)	(10,000)	30,000	
Loss carryforward (cumulative)				$20,000*	$25,000*

With an assumed income tax rate of 25 per cent, the company is entitled to a tax refund of $7,500 as a result of the 1964 loss [25% of ($5,000 + $15,000 + $10,000)]. If the company should earn $25,000 during, say, 1966, 1967, and 1968, there would be no income tax on the earnings because of the carryforward privilege.

The question is, how should the tax refund from the use of a loss carryback and the tax reduction from the use of a loss carryforward be reported in the financial statements?

Carryback case. Using the data in the above illustration, the December 31, 1964 balance sheet should include among the current assets a $7,500 claim for tax refund. Presumably, the handling of the resulting credit will depend on which income concept has been adopted by the company. If the company uses the all-inclusive approach, then the $7,500 credit should be included in the 1964 income statement and the net loss for the year will be reported as $42,500 ($50,000 minus the $7,500 tax refund). This position has the support of A.R.B. (*Accounting Research Bulletin*) No. 43, which states that: ". . . amounts of income taxes paid in prior years which are refundable to the taxpayer as the result of the carry-back of losses . . . ordinarily should be included in the income statement of the year in which the loss occurs . . . ."

On the other hand, if the company uses the current operating concept, the credit for the refund would be shown in the statement of retained earnings. Apparently, support for this alternative can also be found in A.R.B. No. 43. Note the reference to "adjustments of income taxes of prior years" in paragraph (a) of the quotation from the bulletin on page 63.

Carryforward case. As a general rule, accountants do not assign any value to the loss carryforward privilege. Thus, if a corporation has incurred losses that can be carried forward and used to reduce future taxes, the benefit is accounted for when the tax reduction is taken. The following two methods of reporting earnings when a carryforward privilege has been utilized to reduce taxes have the support of practice:

(1) Show as an expense in the income statement the income taxes actually payable.
(2) Show as an expense in the income statement the income taxes that would have been payable without the use of the carryforward privilege and show as a credit in the statement of retained earnings the tax reduction attributable to the carryforward privilege.

The consequences from the application of the above alternatives can be noted by returning to the data set forth to illustrate the operation of the carryback-carryforward provisions. The illustration stopped at the end of 1965 with a $25,000 loss carryforward. Assume that the company earns $25,000 in 1966. Because this equals the loss carryforward, there is no liability for an income tax on the 1966 earnings. A tax benefit of $6,250 (25% of $25,000) has been realized. Under alternative (1), the net income would be shown as $25,000. Suitable disclosure is required to explain the absence of income taxes. Under alternative (2), the net income would be shown as $18,750 and a credit of $6,250, equal to the tax reduction, would be included in the statement of retained earnings. Thus, the tax reduction which materialized in 1966 is classified as a correction of prior years' losses; the losses were in fact $6,250 less than reported in the prior income statements.

Some accountants, including the authors, question the fairness of reporting earnings subsequent to loss-carryforward years as though such earnings were tax free. They believe that such a practice overstates both the net loss and the subsequent net income, as in the following example, in which it is assumed that the company has used up its carryback privileges and can only carryforward its 1965 net loss.

	1965	1966
Net income (loss*)	$20,000*	$20,000

Because there is no income tax liability from the 1966 earnings, such earnings appear much better merely because they follow a loss year. In order to counteract such distortion, the setting up of a noncurrent asset in the loss year for the potential tax benefit is advocated. The noncurrent asset indicates the amount that can be used during the next five years to reduce any future liability for income taxes. In the example under consideration, such a noncurrent asset would be set up as of December 31, 1965, in the amount of $5,000 (25% of the $20,000 loss), and credited as of December 31, 1966, when used to reduce the income tax liability on the 1966 earnings. The following income statement portrayal would result.

	1965	1966
Net income (loss*) before income tax	$20,000*	$20,000
Loss-carryforward credit	5,000	
Provision for income tax		5,000
Net income (loss*)	$15,000*	$15,000

When an asset is set up for the potential tax benefit and the benefit lapses because earnings fail to materialize within the five-year carryforward period, then the asset should be written off as an additional loss of the year in which the carryforward privilege lapses.

CHAPTER

5

Capital Stock

Objectives in accounting for stockholders' investments. Corporate accounts need not differ from the accounts of other types of business organization except in the manner of reflecting the elements of the owners' equity. In accounting for the elements of owners' equity in a corporation, the emphasis is placed on *source*. How much of the owners' equity was produced by stockholders' capital contributions? How much consists of retained earnings? How much, if any, was produced in other ways?

Proper accounting for the elements of stockholders' equity according to their source requires a knowledge of the nature of capital stock and of the various classes of surplus.* These matters are discussed in this and subsequent chapters.

Par and no-par stock. Prior to 1912, it was required that the capital stocks of all corporations in the United States have a par value. In that year, the first American law permitting the issuance of stock without par value was enacted in New York. Other states have since passed similar laws, but, unfortunately, the laws of the several states are not uniform.

Generally, the organizers of a corporation, if they choose to use par value stock, may select the amount for par. Thus, par value may be $1,000, $100, $25, $7.50, $1, $.50, or any other dollar amount.

Rights inherent in stock. The capital stock of a corporation is divided into shares which entitle their holders to some or all of certain basic rights, the most important of which are mentioned below and on page 86.

(1) The right to vote at stockholders' meetings, and thus to participate in the management.

* The American Institute of Certified Public Accountants has recommended the discontinuance of the use of the word *surplus* in account titles, and compliance with the recommendation has been widespread; however, the word is still in general use by accountants as a technical term in discussions and writings.

(2) The right to share in the earnings; that is, to receive dividends when they are declared by the directors.
(3) The right to participate in any additional issues of stock of the class owned, ratably to their holdings at the date of the additional issue (known as the "pre-emptive right"). This right is often abridged or withheld.
(4) The right to share in the distribution of the assets of the corporation upon dissolution.

If there is only one class of stock, these rights are enjoyed proportionately, share and share alike, by all stockholders. If there are two or more classes of stock, one class may enjoy more or less than its proportionate share of certain rights.

Common stock and preferred stock. The two principal classes of stock are common and preferred. Holders of preferred shares have one or more "preferences" over the common stockholders. Thus, preferred stockholders may enjoy certain preferential rights in the sharing of earnings or in the distribution of assets in liquidation. On the other hand, preferred stockholders may have no rights, or only limited rights, to vote.

Stock preferred as to dividends. Stock that is preferred as to dividends entitles its holders to a dividend at a specified rate on par (or of a specified amount per share, in the case of no-par stock) before dividends are paid on the common stock.

A preference as to dividends is not an assurance that dividends will be paid. No stockholder, whether holding preferred or common shares, has an unconditional right to receive a dividend, for two reasons. First, the payment of dividends on stock of any class depends upon whether the corporation has a legal right to pay a dividend. Second, even though the corporation has a legal right to pay a dividend, the directors, after giving due consideration to matters of corporate policy and cash requirements, may decide that it would be inexpedient to distribute funds to the stockholders. In general, the stockholders' only remedy is to bring an action in a court of equity, and undertake to present evidence to prove that dividends have been unjustifiably withheld. This has not proved to be much of a remedy, because courts have shown a reluctance to order dividend payments. For this reason, dividends should not be regarded as accruing.

A company cannot *guarantee* the payment of dividends on its preferred stock. However, dividends on the stocks of one company are sometimes guaranteed by another company; for instance, Company *A*, in connection with a lease of facilities of Company *B*, may guarantee the payment of dividends on Company *B*'s stock.

Cumulative and noncumulative stock. If preferred stock is cumulative, any preferred dividends in arrears must be paid in the future before any dividends can be paid on the common stock. If a partial dividend is paid, the unpaid portion accumulates. If preferred stock is noncumulative, a dividend lost in one year is lost forever.

Participating and nonparticipating stock. Preferred stock may be participating or nonparticipating. Participating preferred stock shares with the common stock in any dividends paid after the common has received a dividend at the preference rate. That is, if the preferred is entitled to dividends of 6% on par, and if both preferred and common have received 6% dividends, an additional payment on the common stock would require an additional payment on the preferred stock. Preferred stock may be fully participating (that is, entitled to dividends at a rate on par value, or in an amount per share on no-par stock, equal to that paid on the common stock); it may be partially participating (that is, a maximum may be placed on the total dividends which may be paid annually on the preferred stock); or it may be nonparticipating. If preferred stock is nonparticipating, its holders are entitled to dividends at the preference rate (par value stock) or amount (no-par stock) and no more, regardless of the rate at which dividends are paid on the common stock.

Cumulative or participating rights not stated. If preferred stock is issued without a specific statement as to its cumulative or participating rights, what is its status with respect to such rights? This is a question to which no general answer can be given, as there is no uniformity of law in the various states.

Stock preferred as to assets. Stock that is preferred as to assets entitles its holders to payment in liquidation before any payments are made to the common stockholders. The fact that stock is preferred as to dividends does not make it also preferred as to assets; this preference must be specifically stated.

Some stock that is preferred as to assets in liquidation is preferred not only to the extent of par, or a stated liquidation value in the case of no-par stock, but also with respect to cumulative dividends in arrears. Therefore, in the event of liquidation, the holders of such preferred stock are entitled to a distribution equal to such dividends even though the company has no surplus.

Special features of preferred stock. Various classes of preferred stock may be issued. If there are first and second preferred stocks, the rights of the second preferred are subject to the rights of the first preferred, although the rights of all preferred stockholders are superior, in certain particulars, to the rights of common stockholders.

Corporations sometimes obtain an authorization of a certain number of shares of preferred stock with the right to issue portions thereof from time to time with different features—for instance, with different dividend rates. Thus, a company may obtain an authorization for the issuance of 10,000 shares of $100 par value preferred stock; it may immediately issue 4,000 shares designated as 5% series; later it may issue 4,000 shares designated as 6% series; and still later it may issue the remaining 2,000 shares designated as 5½% series.

As the right to vote is one of the basic rights of stockholders, preferred stock carries this right unless it is specifically withheld. Corporations organized in certain states cannot withhold the right to vote.

Preferred stock sometimes carries the right of conversion into bonds or common stock. This right is intended to make the investment an attractive one. For instance, if the stock is cumulative and participating, the holder has the chance of sharing in the earnings of a successful business, but his dividend income is dependent upon earnings, and he has no security for his principal; if earnings prove to be small, the privilege of conversion into bonds allows him to obtain a security that makes his income independent of earnings and affords greater safety as the principal. Or, if the preferred stock is nonparticipating, and earnings prove to be good, the right to convert into common stock allows the holder to switch to a type of investment having full participation in the larger earnings.

Preferred stock may be subject to gradual retirement through the operation of a redemption fund (frequently called a *sinking fund*) or otherwise. Or it may be redeemable at the option of the corporation; in other words, the stock may be made callable after a certain date and at a stipulated or determinable price. If called, all dividends in arrears must usually be paid if the stock is cumulative, and the right to redeem cannot be exercised if creditors' rights would thereby be jeopardized. Charter clauses that provide for redemption of stock should be made permissive and not obligatory, because a corporation cannot enter into an unconditional contract to pay off its stockholders.

The terms of issuance of preferred stocks frequently contain provisions intended to safeguard the interests of the preferred stockholders. For instance, the consent of the preferred stockholders may be required before the management can participate in a merger or change the nature of the company's operations. The most customary restrictive provisions have to do with the payment of cash dividends on common stock or the retirement of common shares or their acquisition as treasury stock. The restrictions take various forms. For instance, the payment of common dividends or reductions of outstanding common shares may not be permissible if contributions to preferred stock retirement funds are in arrears; or if the working capital is less than a stated amount or less than a certain number of times the preferred dividend requirements; or if the net tangible assets are less than a certain number of times the liquidating value of the preferred stock; or if the surplus available for dividends is less than a stipulated amount. This last restriction often takes the form of "freezing" the surplus at the date of issuance of the preferred stock, by providing that dividend payments on, and retirements of, common shares or their acquisition as treasury stock can be made only to the extent of the increase in retained earnings since that date.

Common stock. The term *common stock* is applicable to corporate shares which have no preferences. If all of the stock is of one class, there obviously are no preferences, and all of the shares are common.

Stated capital. In addition to the emphasis on source, which, as noted earlier, is a primary consideration in the accounting for stockholders' equity, there is the matter of stated capital to consider.

Among the advantages of the corporate form of business organization is that of limited liability, which means that the stockholders normally cannot be held personally liable for the debts of the corporation. Because the law gives stockholders this immunity, it is only fair that creditors should be given some assurance that the corporation will not be permitted to make payments or distributions to its stockholders which will reduce the stockholders' equity below a stipulated amount known as *stated capital.* In the absence of any restriction on the amount of assets that can be returned to shareholders, the directors of a corporation in financial difficulty could strip the corporation of most of its assets by declaring dividends or by using company funds to purchase or retire the corporation's capital stock, to the benefit of shareholders and to the detriment of creditors. In general, there is less risk associated with a creditor's claim if there is a prescribed amount of stockholders' equity that cannot be reduced by payments or distributions to the shareholders.

The amount of the stated capital is determined by the law of the state in which the corporation is organized. Because there is considerable variation in the state laws on this matter, only the more common definitions are mentioned below:

In the case of par value shares, stated capital is usually defined as an amount equal to the aggregate par value of the shares issued.

In the case of no-par shares, stated capital is the aggregate credited to the capital stock accounts. The amounts thus credited may equal

(1) the total received for the shares issued, or

(2) an amount based on a stated value per share.

Generally the board of directors has the right to designate a stated value per share; in some states the amount which the directors elect to establish as stated value per share cannot be less than a minimum set forth in the law, for example, $5 per share.

Amounts received in excess of stated capital may be credited to paid-in surplus accounts with titles clearly indicating the nature of the credits. Thus, if $25 par value common shares are issued for $28 per share, $3 per share may be credited to Capital in Excess of Par Value—Common Stock Issuances. Similarly, if no-par common shares having a stated value of $10 per share are issued for $12 per share, $2 per share may be credited to Capital in Excess of Stated Value—Common Stock Issuances.

Stated capital can be reduced (provided that the action complies with the provisions of the state corporation act) by a reduction in the number of issued shares or in their par or stated value; by changing par value shares to no-par shares with a lower stated value than the former par; or by changing no-par shares to par shares with a par less than the former stated value.

It should be noted that the existence of legal provisions regarding stated capital reduces, but does not eliminate, the risk of loss by creditors. Stated capital can be impaired by unprofitable operations. Also, some of the assets may not be available to satisfy the claims of general creditors, because the directors of the corporation may have mortgaged or otherwise pledged them as security for specific obligations.

Because stated capital is a legal concept, and because there is considerable variation in the state laws, it is impracticable to deal exhaustively with the subject in an accounting text; it must suffice to call attention to the fact that the treatment of matters related to stated capital is governed by the law of the state in which the company is incorporated.

Accounts used to show stockholders' investment. The following types of accounts are used in connection with investments by stockholders.

Capital stock accounts. A separate account is set up in the ledger for each class of stock authorized. The account title should be broadly descriptive of the stock. The number of shares authorized and pertinent details regarding the stock are indicated by a memorandum notation in the account. Thus, if a corporation is authorized to issue 10,000 shares of $25 par value, 5% cumulative preferred stock and 50,000 shares of no-par common stock with a stated value of $10 per share, the ledger accounts would be set up as shown below.

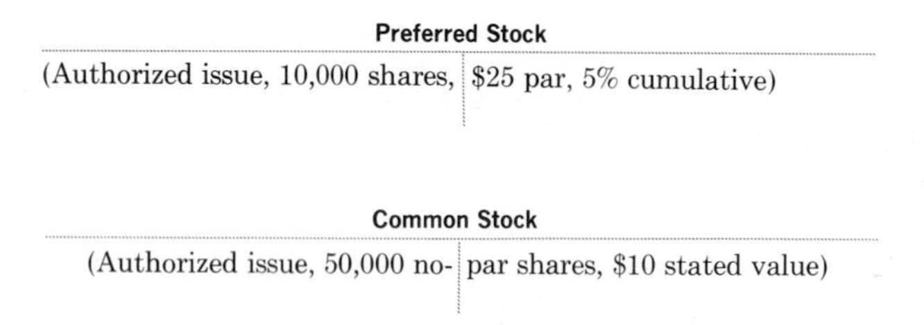

Preferred Stock

(Authorized issue, 10,000 shares, $25 par, 5% cumulative)

Common Stock

(Authorized issue, 50,000 no-par shares, $10 stated value)

Capital stock accounts are credited when the stock certificates are issued to the stockholders; the accounts are credited with the par or stated value of the shares issued or, in the case of no-par stock without stated value, the aggregate price paid for the shares issued.

Paid-in surplus accounts. Amounts received in excess of the par or stated value of shares are credited to paid-in surplus accounts, the titles of such accounts indicating the source of the credits. Thus, if par value preferred shares are issued at a premium, Capital in Excess of Par Value—Preferred Stock Issuances would be a suitable account title. If no-par common shares are issued at a price in excess of their stated value, the account credited for the excess could be described as Capital in Excess of Stated Value—Common Stock Issuances.

Stock issued for less than par value. Stock is rarely issued for less than its par value for two reasons:

(1) In many states it is illegal to do so.
(2) In states where it is legal, stockholders to whom the stock was issued at a discount generally face a contingent liability; should the corporation become insolvent, they may be held personally liable to the corporation's creditors for amounts equal to such deficiency. As a general rule, the contingent liability does not pass to a subsequent holder unless he had notice of the discount or should have known about it.

If capital stock is issued for less than par value, the discount should be debited to a separate account (the word "discount" and the class of stock involved should appear in the account title) and shown as a deduction in the Stockholders' Equity section of the balance sheet.

Interval between receipt and collection of subscriptions. Time may elapse between the date when subscriptions for stock are received and the date when they are collected and the stock is issued. Under such circumstances, there is need for accounts to show the amount receivable from the subscribers and the shares that have been subscribed for but as yet are unissued. The accounts to be used under such circumstances are described below.

Subscriptions Receivable:
When subscriptions are received, this account is debited with the aggregate price of shares subscribed.
As collections are received from subscribers, the account is credited.

Common (or Preferred) Stock Subscribed:
When subscriptions are received, this account is credited with the par or stated value or, in the case of no-par stock without stated value, the subscription price of the shares subscribed.
When stock certificates are issued, this account is debited and Common (or Preferred) Stock is credited.
The credit balance in this account shows the par or stated value or subscription price, as the case may be, of the shares subscribed for but not issued.
The account is shown in the Stockholders' Equity section below the presentation for the stock issued.

Common (or Preferred) Stock:
When certificates are issued, this account is credited with the par or stated value or aggregate subscription price of the shares represented by the certificates. In other words, whatever amount was credited to the stock subscribed account when the shares were subscribed for is credited to the Common (or Preferred) Stock account when the shares are issued.

Illustration. Subscriptions are received for 200 shares of no-par common stock with a stated value of $10 per share. The subscription price is $12 per share.

Subscriptions receivable	2,400	
Common stock subscribed		2,000
Capital in excess of stated value—Common stock issuances		400
Subscriptions for 200 shares at $12 per share.		

Each subscriber pays one-third of the subscription price.

Cash	800	
Subscriptions receivable		800
Partial collection of subscriptions receivable.		

Each subscriber pays the balance of the subscription price.

Cash	1,600	
Subscriptions receivable		1,600
Collection of balance of subscriptions receivable.		
Common stock subscribed	2,000	
Common stock		2,000
Issuance of 200 shares after collection of subscriptions in full.		

A corporation may issue stock before the subscriber has paid in full for the subscribed shares. A variety of terms or conditions may be set forth in subscription agreements concerning the requirements that must be satisfied before the shares are issued. Whatever the conditions, whenever they are satisfied and the shares are issued, the stock subscribed account is debited and the capital stock account is credited.

Balance sheet presentation. The balance sheet should show, with respect to each class of stock:

(1) The par value, if any, or the fact that the stock is without par value, in which case the stated value, if any, should be shown.
(2) The special rights appertaining to any class of stock.
(3) The number of shares authorized; the number issued and outstanding (which will differ from the number issued if there is any treasury stock—that is, stock that has been issued and reacquired); and the number, if any, subscribed for but not issued.
(4) The capital in excess of par or stated value, if any, applicable to each class of stock.
(5) The balances of any subscriptions receivable.

Where should uncollected subscriptions receivable be shown? If it is expected that the subscriptions will be collected, they can be shown on the asset side of the balance sheet. If collection is expected in the relatively near future, it is customary to show the subscriptions receivable as a current asset, but they should be clearly shown as subscriptions to capital stock, and not as ordinary accounts receivable. If there is no immediate intention to call upon the subscribers for the uncollected balances of their subscriptions, the subscriptions may still be shown on the asset side of the balance sheet, but not as a current asset.

However, if there is some question whether the uncollected balances will ever be called, or whether they are collectible, it is preferable to exclude them from the assets and show them as a deduction in the Stockholders' Equity section, in some manner similar to the following:

Stockholders' equity:		
Capital stock:		
Preferred—6% cumulative, participating; par value, $100; authorized, 1,000 shares; issued and outstanding, 750 shares	$75,000	
Less uncollected subscriptions	15,000	$ 60,000
Common—No par value; authorized, 5,000 shares; issued and outstanding, 3,100 shares, at stated value of $50		155,000
Total		$215,000
Capital in excess of stated value—Common stock issuances		31,000
Total		$246,000

Forfeited subscriptions. A subscriber may fail to pay his subscription in full. The accounting procedure depends upon the law of the state of incorporation. To illustrate, assume that the following transactions occur:

A. B. Jones subscribes at par for 5 common shares with an aggregate par value of $500.
He pays $200 and defaults.
The shares are issued to another for $480.
The expenses incurred as a result of the default are $30.

In some states the subscriber is allowed a specified time to complete his payments; if he remains delinquent at the close of that period, he is entitled to no refund, whether or not the shares are issued to another. Under these conditions the entries would be:

Subscriptions receivable	500	
Common stock subscribed		500
Subscription of A. B. Jones.		
Cash	200	
Subscriptions receivable		200
Collection from Jones.		
Common stock subscribed	500	
Subscriptions receivable		300
Capital in excess of par—Forfeited subscriptions to common stock		200
Forfeiture of subscription.		
Cash	480	
Capital in excess of par—Forfeited subscriptions to common stock	20	
Common stock		500
Issuance of stock to another.		
Capital in excess of par—Forfeited subscriptions to common stock	30	
Cash		30
Expense incurred as a result of default by subscriber.		

In other states, an effort must be made to find another subscriber for the forfeited shares. If the corporation is successful, the amount received from the original subscriber, minus any discount and expense incurred as a result of the default, must be refunded to him.

Account	Debit	Credit
Subscriptions receivable	500	
Common stock subscribed		500
Subscription from A. B. Jones.		
Cash	200	
Subscriptions receivable		200
Collection from Jones.		
Common stock subscribed	500	
Subscriptions receivable		300
Liability to defaulted subscriber		200
Default by stock subscriber.		
Cash	480	
Liability to defaulted subscriber	20	
Common stock		500
Stock issued to another.		
Liability to defaulted subscriber	30	
Cash		30
Expense incurred as a result of default by subscriber.		
Liability to defaulted subscriber	150	
Cash		150
Refund to Jones.		

There is also the possibility that the defaulting subscriber may be entitled to receive the number of shares which his partial payments will pay for in full. Referring to the preceding illustration, the subscriber would receive shares with a par value of $200 and the following entry would be made:

Account	Debit	Credit
Common stock subscribed	500	
Subscriptions receivable		300
Common stock		200
Issuance of shares and cancellation of balance of defaulted subscription.		

But assume that Jones had paid $230 on his subscription. The immediately preceding entry would become:

Account	Debit	Credit
Common stock subscribed	500	
Subscriptions receivable		270
Common stock		200
?		30

If the law required that Jones be reimbursed for the $30, a liability account (or Cash) would be credited with the $30. If the $30 was forfeited by Jones, a capital-in-excess account would be credited.

Stock issued for property. When stock is issued for noncash assets, a valuation problem may arise. If a valuation is placed on the property in an arm's-length transaction, and if related facts do not make the valuation questionable, it may be accepted for purposes of determining the entry to be made to record the transaction. In other cases the valuation may be based on the fair market value of the property or the fair market value of the stock, whichever is more readily determinable. The price at which other shares of the same class were issued for cash (or were the subject of a stock exchange transaction) at about the time when stock was issued for property may be a good evidence of fair value. Such evidence is not conclusive, however; instances have been known in which a few shares have been issued for cash at a price in excess of fair value, in a transaction not at arm's length, for the very purpose of attempting to establish an inflated stock valuation to support an inflated asset valuation.

The existence of a par value for stock and the accounting necessity for balancing the books have been responsible for much inflation in the recorded valuations of assets acquired by issuance of stock. If the property acquired is not worth the par of the stock, a discount on stock account should appear on the books; such an account is not likely to appear, however, because directors are disposed to value the property at the par of the stock. The law allows directors great latitude in exercising their discretion as to the value of property taken for stock. The general rule of law has been that courts will not overrule the directors' valuation even when creditors are trying to prove that par value stock was in reality issued at a discount, unless valuations have been grossly excessive and unless fraud is apparent. There is, however, a growing tendency for courts to scrutinize the valuations of assets taken for stock when creditors are attempting to prove that stock was issued for property at a discount.

The Securities and Exchange Commission has taken a more positive attitude and has frequently found that statements were misleading when property taken for stock was set up at arbitrary and inflated values. This attitude has strengthened the position of the accountant, even in cases outside the jurisdiction of the Commission. Although it may still be impossible for an accountant to insist on the recording of noncash assets at a fair cash value lower than the directors' valuation thereof, an independent public accountant should give serious consideration to the advisability of mentioning the facts in his report, particularly in view of the increasing degree of responsibility which governmental agencies and the public are expecting him to assume.

Stock issued for services. What should be the basis of valuation for stock given to an employee for services? Should it be the par or stated value, the market value, the book value, the cost to the company (if treasury stock is used), or the fair value of the services?

The fair value of the services is the most logical basis, but the market value of the stock is presumptive evidence of the value of the services, because the corporation foregoes the opportunity to sell the stock at the market price. In other words, the issuance of stock to the employee seems tantamount to issuing the stock for cash and giving the cash to the employee.

For income tax purposes, the fair value of the stock at the date of receipt is income to the recipient. Consistency would presumably require that this be recognized by the corporation as the cost of the services. However, the market value at the date when the contract was made is a more logical basis; cost to a subscriber paying in installments of cash would be the cost at the date of the subscription, and there seems to be no difference between a cost payable in installments of cash and a cost payable in installments of services.

Income (or perhaps Retained Earnings, if the stock was issued for services in prior periods) should be charged with the determined value of the services or stock; a capital stock account should be credited with the par or stated value of the stock; and a paid-in surplus ("excess") account should be credited with any excess of the total charge for the services over the amount credited to capital stock. A paid-in surplus account should be credited just as it would be with any excess of cash received for stock over its par or stated value.

The cost of treasury stock given for services is not a proper basis for a charge to income unless this cost happens to represent the fair value of the services.

Bonus stock. To make a preferred stock issue or a bond issue more attractive to an investor, common stock is sometimes offered as a bonus. When par value stock is issued as a bonus, the entire par value of the bonus stock may be charged to a bonus account. For instance, if one share of common stock, par value $100, is given as a bonus with ten shares of preferred stock of the same par value per share, the entry may be:

Cash	1,000	
Common stock bonus to preferred stockholders	100	
Preferred stock		1,000
Common stock		100

The objection to such an entry is that is does not face squarely the fact that there is an element of discount, on the preferred stock or the common stock or both, which should be recognized. If it is possible to determine the price at which either the preferred stock or the common stock could be sold alone, recognition can be given to the discount. For instance, referring to the foregoing illustration, assume that it is known that the preferred stock could be sold at 95 without the bonus; the transaction could be recorded as follows:

Cash	1,000	
Discount on preferred stock	50	
Discount on common stock	50	
Preferred stock		1,000
Common stock		100

The same theory applies to transactions in which stock is given as a bonus to the purchasers of bonds. Theoretically, the discount should be apportioned between the bonds and the stock on the basis of the market prices of the two securities if issued separately. However, if the corporation issuing the bonus stock was organized in a state where stock discount is illegal, the management probably would want the records to indicate that the stock was issued at par and that the bonds were issued at a discount.

As a practical matter, bonus transactions usually are managed in some manner that will avoid any debit to either a bonus account or a discount account. Corporations naturally seek to avoid having such accounts on their books, and investors who are aware of the law do not care to risk a stock discount liability. To avoid bonus and discount accounts, corporations sometimes obtain donations of stock from their stockholders; because such treasury shares are acquired at no cost, no debit to Treasury Stock is required when they are received by the corporation; therefore, no credit to Treasury Stock is required when they are reissued as a bonus; and, because no credit to Treasury Stock is required, no debit to a bonus or discount account is required.

Stock rights or warrants. Stock warrants, or rights to acquire stock at a stated price during a specified period, may be issued by a corporation:

(1) After a decision to issue additional shares. The holders of shares of the same class may have a pre-emptive right to subscribe to the new shares, and warrants may be issued to them as evidence of this right.
(2) Concurrently with the issuance of securities of a class other than those obtainable by exercise of the rights. For instance, bonds may be issued with rights to purchase stock; or stock of one class may be issued with rights to acquire stock of another class.
(3) To personnel in connection with employment contracts.

If a corporation has outstanding stock rights, its balance sheet should indicate the number of shares of stock reserved to meet the issuance requirements to which it is committed by the rights.

Some accounting problems incident to the issuance and redemption of stock warrants are discussed below.

(1) Pre-emptive rights. No entry need be made upon the issuance of warrants evidencing the pre-emptive right of stockholders to acquire additional shares, of the same class held by them, about to be issued. Nor are any special entries required upon the issuance of the shares when the warrants are exercised if par value shares are paid for by the stockholders at par or more, or if no-par shares are paid for at an amount at least equal to the stated value. But assume that the rights entitle the stockholders to acquire, at $25 per share, no-par stock to be set up at a stated value of $30; upon issuance of the shares, a transfer from retained earnings to capital stock of $5 per share would be required, regardless of the market price of the stock at the time of issuance.

(2) Stock rights issued with other securities. To illustrate transactions of this type, let us assume that a corporation issues 1,000 shares of preferred stock at $100 per share, with warrants entitling the holders to acquire 1,000 shares of common stock of no par or stated value at $25 per share. The customary method of recording such a transaction is to debit Cash and credit the Preferred Stock account at par; no entries are made with respect to the rights. If 1,000 shares of common stock are subsequently issued, the entry is simply:

Cash	25,000	
Common stock—No par value		25,000

Stock warrants may have a separate market value at the time of their issuance. For example, let us assume that the purchase rights are detachable and can be sold separately from the preferred stock, and that the market value of the common stock at the date of the issuance of the rights is $27 per share. Because the rights entitle the holder or a transferee to acquire common shares at $25 each, the rights apparently have a value of $2 each. Entries for the issuance of the preferred stock and the rights, giving recognition to the $2 valuation of the rights, could be made as follows:

Cash	100,000	
Discount on preferred stock	2,000	
Preferred stock		100,000
Common stock warrants outstanding		2,000

Such an entry gives recognition to the economic fact of inferential discount logically assignable to the preferred stock. If entries are made in this manner, the subsequent issuance of 1,000 shares of common stock at $25 would be recorded as follows:

Cash	25,000	
Common stock warrants outstanding	2,000	
Common stock—No par value		27,000

However, a corporation issuing rights with other securities is not required to give recognition in the accounts to their separate market value.

(3) Employee stock option plans. Stock option plans may be adopted by corporations whereby employees meeting the stated requirements are granted options to purchase a given number of shares of the company's capital stock during some specified time period at stated prices. Sometimes such a plan is used as a means of raising additional capital, but it is used more often as an incentive or as a device to obtain a more widespread ownership of the corporation's stock by its employees with a consequent increased employee interest in the corporation's activities. If the market value of the corporation's stock should increase above the purchase price set forth in the option, those holding options would be in the attractive position of being able to invest in the corporation's stock at less than the currently prevailing market price.

For many years now the federal income tax laws have included provisions relating to employee stock option plans. Such provisions were necessary in order to set forth the tax consequences that follow from the sale of shares of stock acquired through a stock option plan. The tax consequences depended on how the gain or loss should be figured and whether all or some portion thereof was a capital gain or loss.

In order to avoid income tax consequences unfavorable to employees, the stock option plans are usually designed to comply with the income tax provisions. Some idea of such provisions can be gained from the following reference to the income tax law enacted in 1964 (the current law at the time of this writing), which makes provisions for two classes of employee stock option plans.

(1) Qualified stock option plans, which provide for the granting of options to key employees. If the option price is inadvertently set at less than the market value of the stock when the option is granted, or if the stock is held for less than three years, or if the option remains exercisable after five years, a less favorable tax treatment results. In general, a smaller portion of the gain is treated as capital gain.

(2) Employee stock purchase plans, which cover stock options granted to employees on a nondiscriminatory basis. The option price can be as low as 85 per cent of the market value when the option is granted or when the option is exercised. If the option price is lower than 85 per cent, or if the stock is held for less than six months, or if the combined holding period of the option and the stock is less than two years, a less favorable tax treatment results.

According to generally accepted accounting principles, expense to the corporation arises in the case of option plans restricted to key officers and executives if the option price is less than the market value of the stock on the date the option is granted. As an illustration, consider the following facts:

Market value per share on date option is granted	$20
Price stated in option at which holder is permitted to purchase a specified number of shares within a stated period	18
Market value per share when option is exercised	30

The expense to the corporation would amount to $2 per share. However, as long as the provisions in the 1964 act are applicable, it is unlikely that any need will arise to apply the above principle because corporations can be expected to refrain from granting options to key employees in which the option price is below market value at the date the option is granted.

Assessments on stockholders. Under certain circumstances a corporation may make an assessment against its stockholders. The method of recording the collection of assessments paid by stockholders depends upon whether the stock was originally issued at a discount. If it was not issued at a discount, the amount received should be credited to a paid-in surplus account with some title such as "Donated Capital—Stockholders' Assessments." If the stock was originally issued at a discount, a portion of the assessment equal to the discount should be credited to the discount account, and only the remainder, if any, should be credited to donated capital.

Change from par to no par. Most state laws permit corporations with par value stock outstanding to change to a no-par basis, or vice versa.

If a change from a par to a no-par basis consists merely of calling in shares which had been issued at par and issuing an equal number of no-par shares with a stated value equal to the par value of the old shares, the only entry required is one closing out the par value stock account and opening a new account with the same balance. For instance, assume that a company's authorized issue consists of 1,000 shares of common stock of $100 par value, and that 600 shares were issued at par and are outstanding; assume also that the charter is amended to cancel the old par value shares and authorize the issuance of 1,000 shares of no par value; assume further that the directors assign a stated value of $100 per share to the no-par stock. The only entry required is:

Common stock	60,000	
Common stock		60,000

The old and new Common Stock accounts appear as follows:

Common Stock

(Authorized issue, 1,000 shares, $100 par value)

Date	600 shares converted to shares of no par value	60,000	Date	600 shares issued	60,000

Common Stock

(Authorized issue, 1,000 no-par shares, $100 stated value)

			Date	600 shares issued	60,000

Assume that 2,000 no-par shares were authorized and that they were given a stated value of $50 per share. The journal entry to record the conversion would be the same as that shown above. The 2,000 shares of no-par stock authorized and the 1,200 shares issued would be shown in the new Common Stock account.

If a company changing from a par to a no-par basis has any surplus accounts resulting either from operations or from transactions in the stock which is being converted to a no-par basis, the balances of these accounts should not be transferred, in whole or in part, to capital stock unless the directors authorize such a transfer entry or take some formal action which is equivalent to authorizing such an entry. Any such transfers usually would be made first from any capital-in-excess or other paid-in surplus accounts resulting from transactions in the par value shares which are being converted to a no-par basis; the remainder should be transferred from Retained Earnings. To illustrate, assume that a company has the following accounts:

Common stock (1,000 shares of $100 par value)	100,000
Capital in excess of par—Common stock issuances	25,000
Retained earnings	40,000

Assume also that the par value shares are called in and that 3,000 shares of no-par common stock are issued with a stated value, established by resolution of the directors, of $50 per share. This would mean a declaration of $150,000 as stated capital. The entry for the conversion would be:

Common stock	100,000	
Capital in excess of par—Common stock issuances	25,000	
Retained earnings	25,000	
Common stock		150,000

After a change from a par basis to a no-par basis has been recorded, any balance remaining in a capital-in-excess account or any other paid-in surplus account related to the par value shares converted should be transferred to new accounts, because the reference in the old account titles to a kind of stock no longer outstanding would be confusing.

If a company with par value stock and an accumulated deficit from operations changes its capital structure to no-par stock with a stated value less than the par value of the stock previously outstanding, thus creating a paid-in surplus, the law may permit the elimination of the deficit by charge to such paid-in surplus. If the par value stock was issued at a discount, the permission to change to a no-par basis might carry an implied permission to eliminate the discount account; this is a matter of law.

Convertible stocks and bonds. Some stocks and bonds are convertible into other securities of the issuing corporation at the option of the holder. The specified conversion ratios will affect the accounting for the conversion. For instance, a $1,000 bond may provide that it can be converted into common stock at a conversion price of $20 per share. In effect, such a bond can be used to buy 50 shares of common stock. At the time of the bond issuance, the market price of the common stock will presumably be below $20 per share. Should the issuing company prosper and the market value of its shares increase, a bondholder may find it attractive to convert his investment into common stock.

The following generalizations suggest the framework within which the accountant approaches the recording of conversions.

Conversions should not result in an increase in retained earnings.

All amounts related to the securities being converted must be transferred to accounts associated with the new securities issued at conversion.

The examples below indicate the application of the above requirements.

Example—Convertible bonds.

Facts: Each $1,000 bond may be exchanged at any interest date for 30 shares of the company's no-par, $20 stated value, common stock.

Ten bonds are presented for conversion when the company's accounts show the following information relating to the bonds:

Bonds payable	$500,000
Discount on bonds	5,000

Entries for conversion:

Bonds payable	10,000	
Discount on bonds		100
Common stock		6,000
Capital in excess of stated value—Common stock issuances		3,900

Issuance of 300 shares of no-par common in exchange for ten bonds, per conversion terms.

Example—Convertible preferred stock.

Facts: Each share of $50 par value preferred stock may be exchanged for four shares of no-par (no stated value) common stock.

Four hundred shares are presented for conversion when the company's accounts show the following information relating to the outstanding preferred stock:

Preferred stock	$200,000
Capital in excess of par value—Preferred stock issuances	10,000

Entries for conversion:

Preferred stock	20,000	
Capital in excess of par value—Preferred stock issuances	1,000	
Common stock		21,000
Issuance of 1,600 shares of no-par common in exchange for 400 shares of preferred (one-tenth of the outstanding shares), per conversion terms.		

If one class of a company's stock is convertible at the holder's option into shares of another class, the balance sheet (or a footnote appended thereto) should state the number of authorized but unissued shares of stock which have been reserved to meet the conversion requirements.

CHAPTER

6

Surplus and Dividends

Terminology. Formerly it was the custom to use only one Surplus account, and it was credited with such diverse elements as earnings, portions of contributed capital, and unrealized increases in the valuation of assets shown by appraisals or market values.

During the quarter-century following World War I, much thought was given to the desirability of classifying the elements of surplus according to their *source,* and the adoption of appropriate distinguishing terminology. As a consequence, the terms *earned surplus, capital surplus, paid-in surplus,* and *appraisal surplus* came into use.

In more recent years accountants have become concerned about the term *surplus* as a potential source of misunderstanding by users of financial statements. In 1948 the American Accounting Association dropped the term *surplus* from its statement of accounting concepts and standards. In 1949 the Institute's Committee on Accounting Procedure authorized the publication, as Bulletin 39, of a report of its Subcommittee on Terminology, in which the discontinuance of the use of the term *surplus* was recommended. The subcommittee noted the misleading connotations associated with the term *surplus,* such as excess, overplus, residue, or "that which remains when use or need is satisfied"—meanings which are not intended in its accounting usage. Words indicating source, such as *retained income, retained earnings,* or *accumulated earnings,* were suggested as suitable replacements for *earned surplus.* Over the years, *retained earnings* has gained general acceptance. In place of *paid-in surplus,* the words *capital contributed for shares in excess of par (or stated value)* were proposed. *Excess of appraised or fair value of fixed assets over cost* or *appreciation of fixed assets* was recommended in place of *appraisal surplus.*

The positions noted above were reiterated in *Accounting Terminology Bulletin* No. 1, issued in 1953, and in the 1957 revision of accounting concepts and standards, prepared by a committee of the American Accounting

Association. With regard to the term *earned surplus,* these recommendations have had a significant impact on the terminology of financial statements.

In this text, the term *surplus* has not been discarded completely. In illustrations of financial statements, the more modern terminology has been favored. But in discussions, terms are used interchangeably—as they are in practice. However, the term *capital surplus* is not used because it does not have a definite and generally recognized meaning. It has not been authoritatively defined, nor has it been uniformly used by accountants. There is considerable agreement that it should not be used as the title of an account, but should be regarded merely as a generic term to be applied to a class of accounts. However, accountants are not in agreement as to the accounts which should be regarded as belonging to the capital surplus class. But such uncertainties are of slight significance, because the term is rapidly being discarded.

Paid-in surplus. Paid-in surplus includes the following:

(A) Surplus resulting from transactions in the company's own stock:
- (1) Premiums on par value stock.
- (2) Excess of amounts received for no-par stock over amounts set up as stated values thereof.
- (3) Forfeited part payments on stock subscriptions.
- (4) Surplus resulting from miscellaneous stock transactions and changes:
  - (a) Reissuance of treasury stock at more than the amount at which it is carried in the accounts.
  - (b) Retirement of stock by an expenditure less than the amount set up as stated capital.
  - (c) Conversion of stock of one kind into a smaller amount of stock of another kind.
  - (d) Reduction of stated capital.

(B) Surplus resulting from stockholders' contributions:
- (1) Donations by stockholders, including gifts and forgiveness of indebtedness.
- (2) Assessments on stockholders.

(C) Surplus resulting from contributions by outsiders, including gifts of assets (such as a plant given to induce a company to locate in the donor city) and forgiveness of indebtedness.

(D) Surplus resulting from distributions of stock dividends and similar actions ordered by the board of directors by which some portion of retained earnings is reclassified as part of the capital of the corporation and thus credited to the capital stock and paid-in surplus accounts.

Although all of these elements may be regarded as paid-in surplus, the reader is aware that they should not all be recorded in a single paid-in surplus account. To so record them would result in an inadequate classification of paid-in surplus according to source and a failure to maintain the detailed record necessary for proper accounting and statement-preparation purposes.

One reason for keeping separate accounts with the various elements of paid-in surplus is that certain elements of paid-in surplus may be available for dividends whereas other elements are not.

Writers have frequently expressed the opinion that dividends should not be charged to paid-in surplus. Such statements are likely to be misleading, because they may create the impression that paid-in surplus is not legally available for dividends. Paid-in surplus may or may not be available for dividends, depending upon how the paid-in surplus arose and upon the law of the state in which the company was incorporated. In many states there seems to be little or no restriction against the payment of dividends from paid-in surplus. It probably would be better to state that stockholders should have the right to assume that dividends come from earnings unless they are informed to the contrary, and that, if dividends are charged against paid-in surplus, disclosure of that fact will be made to them.

What, if any, charges can with propriety be made against paid-in surplus accounts? Paid-in surplus accounts can properly be reduced by certain direct opposites of proper credits thereto. For instance, a paid-in surplus resulting from the issuance of stock at a premium can properly be charged with a premium paid on the retirement of stock *of the same class*. But if preferred stock is issued at par and common stock is issued at a premium of, say, $40,000, and if the preferred stock is subsequently retired at a premium of $15,000, the Securities and Exchange Commission refuses to sanction charging the premium on retirement of the preferred stock against the paid-in surplus resulting from the issuance of the common stock at a premium. And most accountants appear to recognize the propriety of the refusal.

If stock was issued for property valued at an amount in excess of the par or stated value of the stock issued, with a consequent credit to a paid-in surplus ("excess") account, and if the property is subsequently found to be overvalued, can the book value of the property be reduced by a debit to the paid-in surplus account which was credited when the property was acquired? To do so does not seem to be a defensible procedure unless the property was overvalued when it was received. But even in such a case it may be argued that a charge to the paid-in surplus account is improper because, after a company has once made an avowal as to the valuation of the property and established its depreciation accounting on the basis thereof, it is bound to abide thereafter by that avowal. It is not bound to retain the overvaluation in the asset account, but it is restrained from recording a reduction in the valuation in any way which would relieve retained earnings of proper direct charges thereto or of indirect charges which would result from periodical depreciation provisions.

As to asset write-downs and losses generally, the basic principle was stated in *A.R.B.* No. 1, issued in 1939, which took the position that paid-in surplus, however created, should not be used to relieve the income statement of the current or future years of charges which should be included in the determination of net income. This is in conformity with a 1937 opinion of Carman G. Blough, then chief accountant of the Securities and Exchange Commission, reported in the S.E.C.'s *Accounting Series Release* No. 1. It was his conviction that paid-in surplus should "under no circumstances be used to write off losses which, if currently recognized, would have been chargeable against income." A similar position was taken as early as 1936 by the American Accounting Association.

The basic principle is somewhat modified to permit a company to utilize paid-in surplus to absorb a debit balance in the Retained Earnings account which may have been caused in whole or in part by a write-down or write-off of assets, if this is done in connection with a quasi-reorganization. This matter is discussed in a later chapter.

Retained earnings. Retained earnings represent the retained portion of current and prior years' net income, plus or minus the cumulative effect of unusual and nonrecurring gains or losses or other credits and charges assigned directly to retained earnings.

Under certain circumstances, retained earnings may be transferred to other accounts within the stockholders' equity group. Some such transfers reduce the retained earnings legally; this can be achieved by suitable action on the part of the board of directors, with the result that some designated amount of retained earnings is changed into stated capital. As an example, suppose that a corporation's capital stock consists of $10 par value stock which was issued at par, that there was no paid-in surplus, and that the board of directors, after complying with the applicable legal requirements, changed the par value stock to no-par with a stated value of $15 per share. Thus, for each share of outstanding stock, $5 of retained earnings would be capitalized.

It is possible for retained earnings to be a negative quantity, in which case it is customarily described as a deficit.

Appraisal increments. *Accounting Research Bulletin* No. 5, issued in 1940, contained the following statement: "Accounting for fixed assets should normally be based on cost, and any attempt to make property accounts in general reflect current values is both impracticable and inexpedient." Nevertheless, the accounts of some businesses have been adjusted to reflect fixed asset valuations based upon appraisals; and, when such asset revaluations have been upward, credits have not infrequently been made to accounts with titles such as "Appraisal Surplus" and "Appreciation Surplus." As previously stated, it seems undesirable to use the word *surplus* in the title of an account unless its balance represents an increment which has been realized. Therefore, a title such as "Unrealized Increment in Valuation of Fixed Assets" seems preferable.

If an unrealized increment in value is recorded in the accounts, what disposition should be made of the resulting credit-balance account when the written-up assets have been fully depreciated or sold? The answer is not settled, but there is support for treating the credit item as part of permanent capital. The board of directors could formalize the treatment by issuing additional shares of stock to the stockholders, debiting the unrealized increment account for the amount thereby capitalized and considered to be a part of permanent capital. An alternative approach is to transfer the unrealized increment to retained earnings when the asset is disposed of or written off as fully depreciated. This matter and other accounting problems incident to appraisals are discussed at some length in Chapter 18.

Dividend restrictions. Restrictions on the payment of dividends may result from:

(A) Contracts:
- (1) With creditors. For instance, bond indentures, in addition to requiring the establishment of a sinking fund for the payment of the bonds, may place a limitation on the amount of dividends that may be paid; the purpose is to prevent the impairment of working capital that might result from cash deposits in the sinking fund and cash disbursements for dividends.
- (2) With preferred stockholders. Retirable preferred stock is sometimes issued; a restriction on dividend payments to common stockholders may be imposed to preserve funds to meet the stock-retirement commitment with the preferred stockholders.

(B) Law. The statutes of many states prescribe that dividend payments and disbursements for the acquisition of treasury shares must not impair the stated capital.

(C) Voluntary action of the directors:
- (1) To indicate that dividends will be limited in order to accumulate funds for plant expansion or other purposes.
- (2) To indicate the existence of a contingency that may result in a loss but a contingency so problematical that a charge to current revenue would not be justified.

In the past, and sometimes even yet, such dividend restrictions have been recorded by debiting Retained Earnings and crediting surplus reserves. It should be understood that neither the retained earnings nor the stockholders' equity is reduced by the creation of surplus reserves. They should be shown in the Stockholders' Equity section of the balance sheet in the manner illustrated below:

Retained earnings:		
Appropriated:		
Sinking fund reserve	$ 60,000	
Reserve for retirement of preferred stock	50,000	
Reserve for plant expansion	75,000	
Reserve for contingencies	10,000	
Total	$195,000	
Free	115,000	
Total retained earnings		$310,000

When the conditions that prompted the creation of a surplus reserve no longer exist, the account should be closed by a reversing entry returning its balance to Retained Earnings. In fact, the only proper debit to a surplus reserve is for its return to retained earnings. Surplus reserves are not set up to take debits that are properly chargeable to expense or loss accounts or directly to retained earnings.

It is probably true that many nonaccountants misunderstand the nature of surplus reserve accounts. Because the primary purpose of surplus reserves is to inform the statement user of contingencies or that certain amounts of surplus are restricted and not available as a basis for dividends, there is merit in the alternative of using one or more footnotes to communicate such information. It seems reasonable to believe that footnotes to financial statements are less likely to confuse the reader. An example follows:

Retained earnings (See Note A) $700,000

Note A:

In view of the extensive addition to the company's manufacturing facilities now being planned, the directors have earmarked $300,000 of the retained earnings as not available for dividend purposes.

A serious problem associated with setting up such surplus reserves is the difficulty of getting rid of them. If a reserve for plant expansion is established, it cannot be charged with the cost of any additional plant acquired; the new plant must be charged to the asset accounts. A reserve for advertising, created as an appropriation of retained earnings to disclose a special advertising program, cannot be charged with advertising expenditures; these must be charged to the expense accounts. Therefore, setting up surplus reserves to reduce retained earnings to the amount which the directors feel may be distributed in dividends has its disadvantages. Setting up such reserves merely temporizes with the situation, because there is no way of getting rid of the reserves except by returning them to retained earnings. Furthermore, the appropriation of retained earnings for purposes other than dividend payments, if carried to its logical conclusion, could result in the complete disappearance of the retained earnings account from the balance sheet. All earnings retained in the business are presumably retained for one purpose or another; if one purpose is to be indicated by an appropriation of retained earnings, why should not all purposes be similarly indicated? For instance, if funds are retained for additional working capital, why not have a reserve for working capital?

When a significant portion of the funds provided by past earnings has been permanently committed to the business by being invested in fixed assets or required inventories, management sometimes declares a stock dividend. In effect, such action transfers a portion of retained earnings to capital stock and possibly paid-in surplus, and thereby gives explicit recognition to the fact that a portion of past earnings is not subject to distribution as dividends.

Reserves for self-insurance. If a company has tangible assets distributed in relatively small amounts in a large number of locations, it may decide

108 – 110

upon a policy of self-insurance; no insurance is carried, and the company must stand all losses suffered. Under these circumstances, businesses sometimes establish a reserve for self-insurance by charges to expense, the reserve account being charged with the losses if and when they occur. In this way, losses may be spread more evenly over successive fiscal periods. Accountants are not in agreement whether this type of reserve procedure is acceptable.

Some accountants maintain that such a reserve should not be established by charges to operations. They argue that no expense is incurred unless and until a loss is sustained; until this occurs the assets are still in existence, no loss or expense has been incurred, the stockholders' equity has not been diminished, and the reserve is actually a part of retained earnings, set aside as a provision for a contingency. Sir A. Lowes Dickinson took this position when he wrote that "provisions for insurance against future possible losses from fire and other insurable risks [are] mere allocations of surplus." Following this line of reasoning, if reserves for self-insurance are established, they should be created by charges to Retained Earnings, and they should not be used to absorb charges for expenses or losses arising from the failure to carry insurance.

On the other hand, it is sometimes argued that, if a company practices so-called self-insurance, it should charge operations and credit a reserve with an amount which it would otherwise pay for insurance premiums, in order to put its accounts on a basis comparable with that of other companies and to avoid the distorting effects of unusual or nonrecurring losses attributable to the self-insurance program. The answer to this argument seems to be that a company on a self-insurance program is different from companies carrying insurance; why should accounting attempt to cover up this difference by hypothetical entries for insurance expense? A company which pays insurance premiums incurs an operating expense; a company which does not pay such premiums does not incur a premium expense, and no loss is incurred unless a fire or accident occurs.

The following statements summarize the prevailing alternative methods of dealing with reserves for self-insurance:

Alternative 1. Reserves for self-insurance may be created by charges to Retained Earnings as a method of disclosing the contingency that losses may arise from an election to self-insure.

Such reserves, being surplus reserves, should not be used to absorb any expenses or losses.

Expenses or losses arising from an election to self-insure should be recorded and reported as though no reserve for self-insurance existed.

Alternative 2. Reserves for self-insurance may be created by periodic charges to operating expense.

Reserves of this origin may absorb expenses and losses arising from an election to self-insure.

Reserves of this origin, not having been created by charges to Retained Earnings, should not be classified in the Stockholders' Equity category.

From the preceding discussion it may be readily seen why it is often difficult to decide whether a reserve intended to even out expenses and losses by years should be condemned as a device to equalize reported earnings or accepted as a sensible procedure to determine more accurately the periodic net income. It is generally agreed that, whenever reserves of this type develop relatively large balances, they probably are, in fact, profit-equalization reserves.

Liquidating value of stock. In the event of liquidation, the preferred stockholders may be entitled to receive, in addition to cumulative dividends in arrears, an amount in excess of the valuation at which the stock is shown in the balance sheet. For instance, the stock may have a par value of $100 per share, but carry a preference right to $110 per share in liquidation; or no-par stock carried in the balance sheet at $50 per share may have a liquidating value of $60 per share.

When preferred stock has a liquidating value greater than the amount at which it is shown in the balance sheet, a clear disclosure of that fact should be made in the balance sheet, or in a footnote appended thereto. Disclosure (parenthetically in the balance sheet or by footnote) may be made by stating the total dollar amount of the liquidating value; or by stating the excess of the total liquidating value over the total par or other amount at which the stock is shown in the balance sheet; or by stating the number of shares outstanding and the liquidating value per share.

If the aggregate liquidating value of the preferred stock, plus any preferred dividends in arrears, exceeds the par or stated value of the junior stocks and the total surplus (so that the holders of such junior stocks have no liquidating equity in the company), this fact should be clearly disclosed.

There may be a dividend restriction on surplus in an amount equal to the excess of the liquidating value of the preferred stock over its par or stated value. For instance, assume that the outstanding preferred stock has a par value of $100,000 and a liquidating value of $110,000, and that the company has retained earnings of $25,000. There may be a $10,000 restriction on the retained earnings, so that dividends of only $15,000 can be paid. The balance sheet or an appended footnote should so state if such a restriction exists. If the company has a paid-in surplus which was created by transactions in the preferred stock, such paid-in surplus may reduce the restriction on retained earnings.

If there are more than two classes of stock, two of the classes may have liquidating values in excess of the amounts at which they are shown in the balance sheet. Disclosures such as those mentioned above should then be made with respect to both such classes of stock.

Surplus availability for dividends. Although it is sometimes necessary for the accountant to disclose surplus restrictions or appropriations, it should be emphasized that the objective is to make the financial statements more useful and informative. It is not the accountant's responsibility to determine amounts legally available for dividends; this is a matter of law, and availability differs in various states.

Accountants are primarily interested in a classification of surplus according to *source*. Source is determined by the facts and not by the law, and therefore is not affected by jurisdictional differences; moreover, the determination of source is properly within the province of the accountant. Although the determination of the amount of surplus available for dividends is not the function of the accountant, the classification of surplus according to source provides information which may be essential to a legal determination of the amount available for dividends.

Dividends. Dividends distributed by corporations to their stockholders may be classified as follows:

(A) Dividends which reduce retained earnings or paid-in surplus legally available for dividends:

(1) Decreasing stockholders' equity:

(a) Cash dividends.

(b) Dividends paid in noncash assets. For example, a company holding securities may distribute these securities among its stockholders as a dividend.

Although dividends received in property other than cash generally are taxable to the recipients at the fair market value thereof, the corporation paying the dividend should ordinarily give no recognition to such market value, but should record the distribution at the book value of the assets distributed. A peculiar problem may arise if a company has participating preferred stock and common stock and pays a property dividend on one class of shares and a cash dividend on the other class. For instance, assume that a company has outstanding $100,000 par value of common stock and participating preferred stock of an equal par value; that it distributes as a dividend to the common stockholders certain investment securities carried at $6,000 but having a fair market value of $10,000; and that a matching cash dividend is to be paid to the preferred stockholders. Because equity would require that the preferred stockholders receive a cash dividend of $10,000, and because the accounts should show that the two classes of stock participated equally in the dividends, it probably would be desirable to write up the securities to their market value before distributing them as a dividend to the common stockholders.

(c) Liability dividends. Dividends may be distributed in the form of bonds, notes, or scrip. Bonds or notes so issued usually have a definite maturity and bear interest; scrip dividends may or may not have a definite maturity, and may or may not bear interest. When scrip or some other evidence of short-term indebtedness is issued as a dividend, it is usually done for the purpose of maintaining the appearance of a regular dividend when cash is temporarily not available for payment. The issuance of long-term securities as a dividend is not common; such securities occasionally are issued to convert surplus available for dividends into funded debt. The issuance of evidences of indebtedness as a dividend may require the authorization of the stockholders.

(2) Not decreasing stockholders' equity:

This classification covers stock dividends. A stock dividend does not change the amount of the stockholders' equity of a corporation; it merely changes the portions of stockholders' equity represented by surplus and by capital stock. If all of a corporation's stock is of one class, a stock dividend does not change the individual stockholder's interest in the stockholders' equity; it merely increases the number of shares by which his interest is represented. If a company has more than one class of stock, the issuance of a stock dividend to shareholders of one class may alter the stockholders' interests, particularly if the dividend is paid in shares of another class.

(B) Dividends out of capital. Such dividends return to the stockholders a portion or all of the capital. They may be classified as follows:

(1) Intentional liquidating dividends, intended to return all of the capital to the stockholders because the company is discontinuing operations, or to return a portion thereof to the stockholders because the scope of the business is being reduced and the total capital is no longer required. If a liquidating dividend is paid, stockholders should be informed of its nature. It is desirable to set up a special account to show the amount of capital returned by liquidating dividends. In the balance sheet it can be shown in the Stockholders' Equity section contra to the accounts credited with the capital invested by the stockholders.

(2) Unintentional returns of capital resulting from the payment of dividends that, although intended to be dividends out of surplus, are in reality partly out of capital. The payment of such dividends may result from accounting errors which have overstated earnings.

Dividends on par value stock are usually stated as a per cent of par. Dividends on no-par stock must be stated in terms of dollars or cents per share, because the stock does not have a par value on which a per cent can be based.

Stock split-up. A split-up should be distinguished from a stock dividend; a stock split-up is a transaction in which the outstanding shares are called in and replaced by a larger number, the larger number being a multiple of the number of previously outstanding shares. To be properly classified as a split-up, the transaction should not be accompanied by any change in the dollar amount representing the stockholders' equity or, as a general rule, in the subtotals of the paid-in capital and retained earnings elements thereof. A split-up may involve a reduction in the par or stated value of the shares, or a change from par to no-par stock or vice versa, but, as just noted, as a general rule this will not result in any change in the aggregate amount shown in the accounts as paid-in capital.

Split-ups frequently occur when a corporation's stock has so high a market value as to interfere with trading. If, for example, a corporation's stock has a market value of $500 per share, the market at such a price may be limited. To increase the market, the corporation may call in its outstanding shares and issue new shares at the rate of five for one. As a consequence, the market price will probably be reduced to approximately $100 per share, and public trading may be facilitated.

Legality of dividends. In general it may be said that:

The laws seek to prohibit the impairment of stated capital by the payment of dividends.

The legality of a dividend declaration may depend upon current earnings, retained earnings, or the satisfaction of certain conditions relating to aggregate stockholders' equity, or it may be determined by other statutory provisions, such as that the fair value of the assets must exceed the liabilities of the corporation. The legality of a dividend is not dependent upon the amount of the corporation's cash. The adequacy of the cash balance has a bearing on the financial expediency of paying a dividend, but not upon the legal right to declare one.

Gains from extraneous transactions are generally included with earnings from regular operations for purposes of determining availability for dividends.

Aside from the foregoing, few rules applicable to the country as a whole can be stated.

Current net income is the normal source of dividends. Retained earnings are generally acceptable as a basis for dividends, subject, however, to certain limitations and modifications, among which may be mentioned the following:

(1) In some states, dividends may be paid if there are sufficient earnings, before a discount on the issuance of stock has been written off; in

other states, dividends can be paid only to the extent that surplus has been accumulated in excess of the discount.

(2) In most states, dividends can be paid in an amount equal to the sum of the surplus and the depletion provisions; in some states, this is prohibited if the rights of creditors are jeopardized; and, in a few states, the rights of preferred stockholders are similarly safeguarded.

(3) If losses have impaired the stated capital, most states prohibit the payment of dividends. The impairment of stated capital may be remedied by profitable operations and abstaining from the payment of dividends, or by taking the proper legal action to reduce the stated capital. A few states permit the payment of dividends equal to current earnings, regardless of the existence of an accumulated deficit. Dividends can ordinarily be paid if surplus has been accumulated in the past, even though a loss has been incurred during the current period.

(4) Some states make the legality of a dividend dependent upon the solvency of the corporation; that is, no dividend can be paid if the corporation is insolvent or if the payment of the dividend would render it insolvent. This seems clearly to mean that the value of the assets must be in excess of the liabilities; however, there seems to be an uncertainty as to whether, under such statutes, the assets should be valued on a cost basis or on a current market basis. In one state, no dividends may be paid if the liabilities exceed two-thirds of the assets.

(5) Surplus which normally would be available for dividends may become temporarily or permanently not so available. Such restrictions may be imposed by law or may result from contracts. A legal restriction results in many states from the acquisition of treasury stock; this matter will be discussed later in connection with treasury stock. A sinking fund reserve is an illustration of surplus temporarily not available for dividends because of a contract with creditors.

We now turn to the question of the availability of paid-in surplus as a source of dividends, and here we face a great diversity of laws. Some states prohibit charging any dividends to paid-in surplus; in other states, preferred dividends can be charged to it. Most states appear to permit charging dividends against premiums on par value stock. Some states require that the entire amount received for no-par shares shall be regarded as stated capital; however, many states permit a portion of the amount received to be credited to paid-in surplus and make such surplus available for dividends.

In some states, a reduction of capital stock or stated capital does not produce a surplus available for dividends; in other states, a dividend may be charged to surplus thus produced; and, in at least one state, a reduction in the common stock may create a surplus available for dividend payments on the preferred stock.

Although appreciation "surplus" is unrealized and is therefore regarded by accountants as a dubious, if not improper, source of dividends, the laws of the various states do not uniformly prohibit its use for that purpose. Some states prohibit the payment of any dividends from unrealized appreciation of assets; others permit the distribution of stock dividends from unrealized appreciation; and some permit the distribution of either cash or stock dividends from such a source. The trend of recent legislation seems to be in the direction of explicitly prohibiting the payment of cash dividends (but not always stock dividends) by charge to unrealized appreciation; such a provision is incorporated in the Uniform Business Corporation Act which was recommended to state legislatures in 1928. Although the act has not been widely adopted, the trend of legislation seems to indicate that its provisions with respect to unrealized appreciation have had considerable influence on the state legislatures.

A good many writers on accounting have said that dividends should be paid from retained earnings only. If they mean that dividends from other sources are illegal, the statement is subject to contradiction; if an action is permitted by law, accountants can interpose no effective "should not" deterrent. However, because it is quite possible that stockholders may be uninformed as to the law and may assume that all dividends received represent distributions of retained earnings, the ethics of business management may properly require that, if a dividend is paid from any source other than retained earnings, the stockholders be informed of the source.

Because of the diversities in corporation laws, accountants can scarcely hope, without making an intensive study of the laws, to master more than the general principles underlying the legality of dividends. The determination of the legality of a dividend should be understood to lie within the province of the attorney. An accountant should not state in a balance sheet the amount which is legally available for dividends, unless his statement is based on an attorney's opinion. Even so, such a statement is not customary.

Preferred dividends in arrears. If dividends on cumulative preferred stock are in arrears, the balance sheet should disclose the fact, because common stockholders are entitled to know the prior claims of preferred stockholders against the surplus. Disclosure is usually made by a footnote, with some wording similar to the following: "On (the balance sheet date) dividends on the preferred stock were in arrears since (date)"; or, "No dividends have been paid on the preferred stock since (date)"; or, "On (the balance sheet date) dividends on the preferred stock were in arrears in the amount of $ ______." If the company has retained earnings which exceed the preferred dividend arrearage, disclosure may be made as follows:

Retained earnings:		
Equal to dividends in arrears on preferred stock	$12,000	
Remainder	35,000	$47,000

In this connection it may be noted that partial dividends may be paid on preferred stock.

Declared dividends a liability. The notice of the declaration of a dividend should state the date of the declaration, the date on which the stock records will be closed to determine the stockholders of record, and the date on which the dividend will be paid.

After a cash dividend has been legally declared and notice of the declaration has been given to the stockholders, the unpaid dividend ranks as a liability and should be shown as such in the balance sheet. A declared but unpaid dividend is a current liability if it is payable in cash, in short-term scrip or notes, or in property classified as a current asset.

The declaration of a dividend can be rescinded by the directors if no one but the directors has knowledge of the declaration. It can be rescinded by the stockholders at any time before the date of payment.

The fact that cash has been deposited with a trustee or fiscal agent for the payment of a dividend does not justify the omission of the liability from the balance sheet. The depositary is the agent of the company, not of the stockholders; a deposit with the company's agent does not constitute payment to the stockholders. This rule applies to the total dividend prior to the payment date, and any unpaid dividends thereafter.

If a corporation becomes insolvent before the payment of a legally declared dividend of which the stockholders had notice, the stockholders will be entitled to share pro rata with unsecured creditors in the payment of declared dividends and debts. For instance, if there are unpaid dividends of $5,000, other liabilities of $45,000, and assets of $40,000, distribution should be made as follows:

To stockholders:	4/5 of $ 5,000, or $ 4,000
To creditors:	4/5 of $45,000, or $36,000

But this rule will not hold if the corporation was insolvent when the dividend was declared, or if the dividend was illegal, or if notice of the declaration was not given to the stockholders until after the company became insolvent.

If, when the corporation is solvent, a fund is set aside for the payment of a declared dividend, and if the company becomes insolvent before the fund is used for the designated purpose, the fund will be considered a trust fund for the stockholders, and will not be available for payments to general creditors.

Stock dividends. The principal question which accountants face in connection with stock dividends is the determination of the amount or amounts which should be transferred from certain stockholders' equity accounts to other stockholders' equity accounts. The laws differ in their requirements. In some cases, stock dividends are intended merely to convert paid-in surplus into capital stock; such dividends have no effect on retained earnings, and no accounting problems arise in recording them.

We are here concerned with the important problems which arise in connection with the issuance of stock dividends which are presumed to constitute a capitalization of retained earnings. In such cases the laws usually specify a minimum amount which must be transferred from retained earnings to stated capital. With respect to par value stock, the legal minimum usually is par. With respect to no-par stock, the legal minimum may be the minimum amount at which the stock could be issued, or the stated value per share of the stock of the same class previously outstanding. In the case of preferred stock, it is often the liquidating value.

But the minimum transfers required by law are not always regarded by accountants as sufficient to meet the requirements of proper accounting. Corporate practice has varied as to the amount of retained earnings capitalized in connection with such stock dividends, and accountants have held different opinions as to the amount which should be capitalized. Following are some of the bases which accountants have advocated for determining the amount per share of dividend stock to be transferred from retained earnings:

The amount credited to the capital stock account for shares previously outstanding, divided by the number of shares outstanding.

The total amount received for shares previously outstanding (whether credited to capital stock or paid-in surplus accounts) divided by the number of shares outstanding.

The total amount received for shares previously issued plus any other paid-in surplus applicable to the shares, divided by the number of shares previously issued.

The per-share fair value of the additional shares issued. This is the procedure advocated in *A.R.B.* 43, which is discussed below.

In its treatment of this matter, the Committee on Accounting Procedure concerned itself only with the most frequently encountered type of stock dividend, namely, common shares issued as a dividend to common shareholders. The committee placed considerable weight on a belief that "many recipients of stock dividends look upon them as distributions of corporate earnings and usually in an amount equivalent to the fair value of the additional shares received. Furthermore, it is to be presumed that such views of recipients are materially strengthened in those instances, which are by far the most numerous, where the issuances are so small in comparison with the shares previously outstanding that they do not have any apparent effect upon the share market price and, consequently, the market value of the shares previously held remains substantially unchanged." In other words, the recipients do not view stock dividends as mere capitalizations of retained earnings, but consider them as a distribution of earnings much like ordinary dividends except that shares of stock are received in place of cash.

The committee therefore recommended that "where these circumstances exist the corporation should in the public interest account for the transaction by transferring from earned surplus to the category of permanent capitalization (represented by the capital stock and capital surplus accounts) an amount equal to the fair value of the additional shares issued."

In reaching the above position, considerable weight was attached to the expectation that the additional shares issued as a stock dividend have no influence on the market value of the stock. This expectation was believed to be likely if the additional shares issued were "less than, say, 20% or 25% of the number previously outstanding. . . ."

In a following paragraph the committee commented that "where the number of additional shares issued as a stock dividend is so great that it has, or may reasonably be expected to have, the effect of materially reducing the share market value, . . . the transaction clearly partakes of the nature of a stock split-up [and] under such circumstances there is no need to capitalize earned surplus, other than to the extent occasioned by legal requirements."

To illustrate the accounting entries under the above approach, assume that a company has 10,000 authorized shares of common stock of $10 par value, of which 6,000 shares are outstanding; also assume that a 10% stock dividend (600 shares) is declared and immediately issued. Assuming that the shares issued in this illustration have a fair value of $12 each, the entry to record the distribution of the stock dividend is:

Stock dividends (to be closed to Retained Earnings)	7,200	
Common stock		6,000
Capital in excess of par value—From stock dividends		1,200
Issuance of a 10% dividend: 600 shares of $10 par value stock having a fair value of $12 each.		

Assume that the stock was without par value and that it had been given a stated value of $7.50 per share; the entry would be:

Stock dividends	7,200	
Common stock		4,500
Capital in excess of par value—From stock dividends		2,700
Issuance of a 10% dividend: 600 shares of no-par stock (stated value, $7.50 per share) having a fair value of $12 each.		

If time intervenes between the declaration and issuance of the stock dividend, the entries (for the dividend on par value stock, for instance) should be:

At date of declaration:

Stock dividends	7,200	
Stock dividend payable		6,000
Capital in excess of par value—From stock dividends		1,200
Declaration of 10% stock dividend to stockholders of record on December 31, 1964; shares to be issued February 1, 1965.		

At date of issuance:

Stock dividend payable	6,000	
Common stock		6,000
Issuance of 600 shares as a stock dividend.		

If a balance sheet is prepared between the date of declaration and the date of distribution of a stock dividend, the Stockholders' Equity section should appear as follows:

Stockholders' equity:			
Common stock—$10 par value; authorized, 10,000 shares.			
Issued, 6,000 shares	$60,000		
To be issued February 1, 1965, as a stock dividend —600 shares	6,000	$66,000	
Capital in excess of par value—From stock dividends		1,200	
Retained earnings		11,000	$78,200

There is merit to one of the suggestions made in an earlier bulletin (Number 11) on this topic to the effect that: "In the case of any stock dividend, the issuing corporation should inform its stockholders, by notice at the time of issuance, as to the amount capitalized per share and the aggregate amount thereof, as well as to the account or accounts to which such aggregate has been charged and credited, whether or not such notification is required by statute or regulation."

The committee made no reference to the date, period of time, or sources of information that should be used in determining the fair value per share. Presumably this is a matter requiring the exercise of professional judgment. Certainly, recent market prices and trends would be important factors to consider. However, it would seem desirable to eliminate the influence of temporary conditions that may have distorted the current values of corporate shares.

Fractional shares. When stock dividends are issued, it usually is impossible to issue full shares to all of the stockholders. For instance, if a stock dividend of one share for each ten shares outstanding is to be issued, the holder of three shares could not receive a full share, and the holder of 25 shares would be entitled to receive two full shares and a fractional (½) share. Sometimes corporations will pay cash to the stockholders in lieu of fractional shares. Or they may issue special certificates for the fractional shares. Such special certificates customarily provide that no voting or dividend rights attach to the fractional shares. Often corporations sponsor an arrangement which will enable the recipients of fractional shares to sell them, or to buy the needed additional fractional interest to obtain full shares.

Returning to the last preceding illustration, assume that, although the dividend declaration contemplated the issuance of 600 dividend shares, it was necessary to issue special fractional share certificates equivalent to 60 shares. The entry for the distribution of the full shares and the special certificates for fractional shares should be:

Stock dividend payable	6,000	
Common stock		5,400
Fractional share certificates—Common		600
Issuance, as a stock dividend, of 540 full shares and special certificates for fractional shares equivalent to 60 shares.		

When any of the stockholders have acquired special certificates aggregating full shares, they can be presented to the corporation in exchange for regular stock certificates. Entries similar to the following should be made for such exchanges.

Fractional share certificates—Common	100	
Common stock		100
Issuance of 10 shares in exchange for special certificates covering that number of full shares.		

The right to exchange the special certificates for full shares may expire at a specified date. Returning to the foregoing illustration, assume that special certificates amounting to five shares, issued with the dividend shares, expire. A $50 balance remains in the Fractional Share Certificates —Common account. What disposition should be made of it? The declaration of a stock dividend capitalizes a portion of the retained earnings. If, under the law of the state of incorporation, the declaration of the dividend cannot be in part rescinded, the aggregate amount of retained earnings to be capitalized (in part by credit to Common Stock and in part by credit to Capital in Excess of Par Value—From Stock Dividends) is irrevocably determined. If the amount credited to common stock is reduced because of the expiration of fractional share certificates, the amount credited to paid-in surplus should be correspondingly increased. The entry to clear the Fractional Share Certificates—Common account would then be:

Fractional share certificates—Common	50	
Capital in excess of par value—From stock dividends		50
Lapse of fractional share certificates covering 5 full shares of common stock.		

If it is legally possible for the directors to rescind the dividend to the extent of the full shares not issued, and this is done, the following entry would be in order:

Fractional share certificates—Common	50	
Capital in excess of par value—From stock dividends	10	
Retained earnings		60
Return to Retained Earnings of amount of stock dividend related to lapsed fractional share certificates.		

Restoration of retained earnings after a stock dividend. Assume that a company has issued shares as a stock dividend; that it has subsequently incurred losses which have created a deficit in its Retained Earnings account; and that it proposes to reduce its stated capital by reducing the number of shares outstanding, or the par or stated value of the shares. Can retained earnings be restored to the extent of the amount debited to Retained Earnings when the dividend shares were issued? Accountants generally agree that this would be improper.

CHAPTER

7

Miscellaneous Topics Relating to Stockholders' Equity

Treasury stock. Treasury stock is a corporation's own stock, once issued and later reacquired but not cancelled. Technically it is still classed as issued stock, although no longer outstanding. It will be noted that there are three important elements in this definition:

(1) Treasury stock must be the company's own stock; holdings of stock of other companies should not be called "treasury stock."

(2) The stock must have been issued; unissued stock should not be called "treasury stock." There are several reasons why a distinction should be maintained between unissued stock and treasury stock: Stockholders' pre-emptive rights do not apply to treasury stock; treasury shares may be returned to an outstanding status without stockholders' authorization; treasury stock and unissued stock have wholly different relations to stated capital (as discussed hereafter); and, if treasury stock was fully paid when originally issued, it can be reissued at a discount without imposing any discount liability on the new owner.

(3) The stock must not have been cancelled. Cancellation is effected by procedures specified by the law. In some cases cancellation may result in reducing the authorized issue of stock; in other cases the shares remain authorized, the only reduction being in the issued shares, which constitute the stated capital of the corporation.

Treasury stock may be acquired by donation, by purchase, or in settlement of a debt. Stockholders may donate stock to the corporation which it may sell to obtain working capital, or they may donate stock to be given as a bonus to the purchasers of other securities or for other reasons. It may be purchased to buy out a stockholder, to reduce the total capital, or to acquire shares needed for profit-sharing or employee-pension programs.

Treasury stock is not an asset. Although treasury stock is occasionally shown in balance sheets as an asset (sometimes even combined with securities which are assets, under such conglomerate title as "Government bonds and other securities"), it is generally recognized that the purchase of treasury stock does not result in the acquisition of an asset, but causes a reduction in the stockholders' equity. Treasury shares may have a ready marketability and may be reissued, just as unissued shares may be issued; and it seems obvious that treasury stock, like unissued stock, is not an asset but is merely a possible source of additional funds. A corporation which acquires its own stock obviously cannot acquire the basic rights inherent in stock ownership: the right to vote, the right to participate in dividend distributions, the pre-emptive right, and the right to receive a proportionate share of the corporation's assets in the event of liquidation.

As a general rule, it is clear that treasury stock is not an asset. There are cases, however, where the merits of the general rule seem less obvious to some. For example, companies may acquire treasury shares for the purpose of reissuing them to employees. This is done to encourage employee interest and support in the affairs of the company; the price of the shares to the employees may be slightly below current market price, and the company may help the employees by using some sort of installment plan to spread the payment of the shares over a period of time. The accounts of the company may show a long history with such a plan and a steady turnover of the treasury shares. Under these circumstances, are the treasury shares assets? The answer is still no.

However, there are occasional circumstances that *may* warrant some modification of the above position. Suppose that a corporation has a bonus agreement with its officers and employees which provides that the bonus liability, after being determined, must be satisfied by distributing shares of the company's stock to those who have earned a bonus. Under these circumstances, assuming that the corporation had no unissued shares or that it preferred not to increase the number of shares outstanding, the bonus liability would be satisfied in two steps: cash would be used to acquire treasury shares; then treasury shares would be transferred to those entitled to a bonus, thus satisfying the liability. As a practical matter, there would probably be a time interval between the acquisition and disposition of the treasury shares. Under the circumstances described above, the treasury shares have the capacity to satisfy or remove, directly, a liability—which is a characteristic associated with certain kinds of assets, for instance, cash. Perhaps it would be reasonable to permit a company to show as an asset treasury shares (at cost) equal to the amount of liability that will be settled in the near future by transfer of treasury shares to officers and employees.

Although such cases are rare and do not significantly detract from the generalization that treasury stock is not an asset, it may be this sort of situation that influenced the Committee on Accounting Procedure, in its Bulletin No. 43, to state: "While it is perhaps in some circumstances permissible to show stock of a corporation held in its own treasury as an asset, if adequately disclosed, the dividends on stock so held should not be treated as a credit to the income account of the company."

Treasury stock and stated capital. As mentioned in Chapter 5, stated capital is a measure of creditor protection; it is intended to give the creditors assurance that a minimum capital will be maintained as a safeguard for the payment of liabilities, subject, of course, to the risk that unprofitable operations could impair the minimum capital as well as cause a weakening of financial position that could make it difficult for the company to meet its obligations. If the intended protection for creditors is to be effective, it is necessary to limit the amount which can be paid out to stockholders. Therefore, the laws which establish and define stated capital have usually placed a limitation on the combined disbursements for dividends and acquisitions of treasury shares. In a large majority of the states, the limitation is related to surplus —a restriction which is often referred to as the "surplus rule." In some states, acquisitions of treasury stock can be made only to the extent of the earned surplus; in other states, they can be made to the extent of all classes of surplus available for dividends.

The differing effects of a dividend and a treasury stock acquisition on the surplus of a corporation chartered in a state which has the surplus rule regarding treasury stock should be noted. Assume that a company has retained earnings of $25,000 and pays a $12,000 dividend; the retained earnings are reduced to $13,000. If, on the other hand, it pays $12,000 for treasury stock, the retained earnings are still $25,000, but $12,000 thereof is restricted and cannot be used for dividends or additional treasury stock acquisitions. It is possible to remove the restriction by either disposing of the treasury shares or cancelling them (restoring them to the status of unissued shares) and thereby reducing the stated capital; a corporation may effect a reduction of stated capital by filing with the proper state authorities a certificate of reduction or otherwise complying with the statutory requirements.

Treasury stock transactions: Terminology. It has long been customary to speak of *purchases* and *sales* of treasury stock. However, because treasury stock is not an asset, there is a certain inappropriateness in the use of these words in connection with treasury stock. Some effort has been made to substitute other terminology, such as *contraction of capital* for *purchase,* and *reissue* for *sale.* If a disposal of treasury stock is called a "reissue" instead of a "sale," the words *gain* and *loss* seem equally inappropriate as labels for the difference between "cost" and "selling price" of treasury shares. Efforts to introduce substitute terminology have not been very successful. Custom and habit are powerful forces.

Balance sheet presentation of treasury stock. The history of the development of procedures for recording treasury stock transactions and for showing treasury stock in the balance sheet is an interesting one. It has been affected by the enactment of laws permitting the issuance of no-par stock, by the split-up of the old general surplus account into retained earnings and paid-in surplus accounts, and by the enactment of laws relative to stated capital.

The old par value procedure. In the old days when all stock had a par value, it was customary, in the balance sheet, to deduct the par value of the treasury stock from the par value of the issued stock to show the par value of the stock outstanding. To facilitate this procedure, it was customary to debit the Treasury Stock account with the par value of stock acquired, and to record any difference between the par value and the acquisition price in the general surplus account.

Early no-par procedure. When laws were passed permitting the issuance of stock without par value, it was natural to attempt to apply the methods which had been found suitable for use with par value stock. No difficulty was encountered if, at the time of the issuance of the shares, the Capital Stock account was credited with the same amount per share for all shares issued.

This was the case if all shares were issued at one price and the Capital Stock account was credited with the issuance price. The Treasury Stock account could be debited with this issuance price, as it had formerly been debited with par. In the balance sheet, the debit balance in the Treasury Stock account could be deducted from the credit balance in the Capital Stock account so that the issuance price of the shares outstanding would be shown.

It was also the case if, regardless of different issuance prices, the Capital Stock account was credited with a uniform amount per share and excesses of issuance prices over this uniform amount were credited to a paid-in surplus account. The Treasury Stock account could be debited with the uniform amount previously credited to Capital Stock. The debit balance in the Treasury Stock account could be deducted in the balance sheet from the credit balance in the Capital Stock account to show the amount credited to Capital Stock when the remaining outstanding shares were issued.

Difficulties were encountered, however, if the Capital Stock account had been credited with differing amounts per share of stock issued. These difficulties were met in two ways:

Some accountants advocated debiting the Treasury Stock account with the amount credited to Capital Stock when the specific shares being acquired were issued.

Because of the difficulty frequently encountered in attempting to determine the original issuance price of the specific shares being acquired, most accountants considered it satisfactory to debit the Treasury Stock account with the *average* amount which had been credited to Capital Stock for all shares of the class issued.

Effect of laws relative to stated capital. All of the foregoing procedures were based on the assumption that the balance in a Treasury Stock account should be deducted in the balance sheet from the balance in the related Capital Stock account, so that a net balance would be shown representing, in the case of par value stock, the par value of the shares outstanding, and, in the case of no-par stock, the original (actual or average) credit to Capital Stock for the shares still remaining outstanding.

The enactment of laws relative to stated capital, and the restriction of surplus as a result of treasury stock purchases, made the balance sheet presentations of treasury stock described above inappropriate or inadequate in certain cases.

They would be *inappropriate* for corporations organized in states in which the stated capital is based on the shares issued, because the treasury shares are still issued shares, and the acquisition of treasury stock does not reduce the stated capital. To deduct the treasury stock from the capital stock issued would therefore leave a balance sheet remainder which would be less than the stated capital.

The described balance sheet procedures would be *inadequate* if the law placed a restriction on surplus as a result of the treasury stock acquisition, because the surplus restriction would not be disclosed.

There has been some difference of opinion among accountants regarding the most desirable balance sheet presentation when the acquisition of treasury stock does not reduce the stated capital and when it places a restriction on surplus. All agree, however, that in such cases the balance sheet presentation of treasury stock should be such as to indicate that the stated capital has not been reduced, but that the surplus has become restricted.

To illustrate some of the procedures which have been used, assume that a company's accounts contain the following balances:

Common stock (representing 1,000 shares of $100 par value)	$100,000
Capital in excess of par value—Common stock issuances	15,000
Retained earnings	25,000

and that the company purchases 100 shares for $12,000.

Most accountants believe that the cost of the treasury stock should be deducted from the total issued stock, paid-in surplus, and retained earnings. They differ as to the method of disclosing the surplus restriction. Three acceptable procedures are illustrated.

(1) The surplus restriction may be disclosed parenthetically:

Stockholders' equity:	
Common stock–authorized and issued, 1,000 shares of $100 par value, of which 100 shares are in the treasury	$100,000
Capital in excess of par value–Common stock issuances	15,000
Retained earnings (of which $12,000, the cost of treasury stock, is restricted)	25,000
Total	$140,000
Less cost of treasury stock	12,000
Stockholders' equity	$128,000

(2) The surplus restriction may be indicated by dividing the retained earnings into two parts:

Stockholders' equity:		
Common stock–authorized and issued, 1,000 shares of $100 par value, of which 100 shares are in the treasury		$100,000
Capital in excess of par value–Common stock issuances		15,000
Retained earnings:		
Restricted–equal to cost of treasury stock	$12,000	
Free	13,000	25,000
Total		$140,000
Less cost of treasury stock		12,000
Stockholders' equity		$128,000

(3) The surplus restriction may be indicated by a footnote—a method increasing in popularity:

Stockholders' equity:	
Common stock–authorized and issued, 1,000 shares of $100 par value, of which 100 shares are in the treasury	$100,000
Capital in excess of par value–Common stock issuances	15,000
Retained earnings (See note)	25,000
Total	$140,000
Less cost of treasury stock	12,000
Stockholders' equity	$128,000

Note. Dividends and treasury stock acquisitions are restricted to the amount of the retained earnings less the cost of treasury stock held.

A few accountants have advocated deducting the cost of the treasury stock from the retained earnings, thus:

Stockholders' equity:		
Common stock–authorized and issued, 1,000 shares of $100 par value, of which 100 shares are in the treasury		$100,000
Capital in excess of par value–Common stock issuances		15,000
Retained earnings	$25,000	
Less portion applied to purchase of treasury stock	12,000	13,000
Stockholders' equity		$128,000

This procedure has met with objection on the ground that it suggests an actual reduction in the retained earnings instead of merely a restriction. The company still has retained earnings of $25,000, but $12,000 of it is restricted.

Recording treasury stock transactions—cost basis. In all of the foregoing balance sheet presentations, there was a deduction of treasury stock *at cost.* Although the procedures illustrated are particularly applicable to companies subject to laws relative to stated capital and surplus restrictions resulting from treasury stock purchases, most accountants seem to believe that companies not subject to such laws can also show treasury stock properly as a deduction at cost in the Stockholders' Equity section of the balance sheet. For this reason it has become a rather general custom to carry treasury stock in the accounts at cost.

Entries for acquisitions. The accounting for treasury stock acquisitions on the cost basis is, of course, very simple. Assume that 100 shares of treasury stock of $100 par value were acquired at $85 per share. Regardless of whether the stock has or has not a par value, and regardless of the amount received for the stock when it was issued and the amount credited to the capital stock account at that time, the entry for the purchase is merely:

Treasury stock	8,500	
Cash		8,500
Acquisition of 100 treasury shares.		

Of course, the treasury stock account title should indicate the class of stock if more than one class has been issued. Thus, the account title might be: "Treasury Stock—Preferred," or "Treasury Stock—Common," or "Treasury Stock—Common—No Par Value."

Entries for reissuances. The entries for reissuances of treasury stock will depend upon whether the stock is reissued at the price at which it was acquired, at a price above cost, or at a price less than cost.

Reissuance at cost. Assume that the shares mentioned above were reissued at $85 per share. The entry is:

Cash	8,500	
Treasury stock		8,500
Reissuance of 100 treasury shares, at cost.		

Reissuance at a price in excess of cost. There is a general agreement among accountants that any gain on the reissuance of treasury stock should be recorded in a paid-in surplus account clearly described as to source. Assume that the shares mentioned above were reissued at $90 per share. The reissuance might be recorded as follows:

Cash	9,000	
Treasury stock		8,500
Capital in excess of par value—From treasury stock transactions		500
Reissuance of 100 treasury shares at $90 per share.		

Reissuance at a price less than cost. In practice, the accounts charged with losses on reissuances of treasury shares depend on the law of the state of incorporation and the kinds of surplus accounts on the company's books. Although a logical case can be made in favor of charging losses from treasury stock transactions first to any paid-in surplus resulting from previous treasury stock transactions and next to retained earnings, it is well established that such losses may be charged to any other paid-in surplus related to the same class of stock as the treasury shares, provided that such paid-in surplus is available for dividends and therefore is not a part of legal capital. The latter condition is pertinent because the amount of legal capital is governed by statute and not necessarily by the results of treasury stock transactions.

If paid-in surplus is not a part of legal capital under the law of the state of incorporation, and if a company has paid-in surplus resulting from the issuance of shares of the same class or resulting from other transactions in shares of that class, it is customary to assign treasury stock losses in the sequence shown below:

If there is paid-in surplus resulting from previous treasury stock transactions in the same class of shares, losses are first charged thereto until it is exhausted.

If there is other paid-in surplus applicable to the same class of shares, and not a part of legal capital, losses may be charged thereto until it is exhausted.

In the absence or inadequacy of suitable paid-in surplus, losses are chargeable to retained earnings.

Three cases are presented to illustrate the accounting for losses from treasury stock transactions.

	Case		
	1	2	3
Stockholder's equity accounts:			
Common stock, 10,000 shares issued, $10 stated value	$100,000	$100,000	$100,000
Capital in excess of stated value—From common stock issuances	10,000	60,000	1,000
Capital in excess of stated value—From treasury stock transactions	2,000	None	None
Retained earnings	38,000	10,000	49,000
Treasury stock, 100 shares, at cost	2,500	1,500	2,400

Case 1: Treasury shares are reissued at $23 per share.

Cash	2,300	
Capital in excess of stated value—From treasury stock transactions	200	
Treasury stock		2,500
Reissuance of 100 shares of treasury stock at $23 per share.		

Case 2: Treasury shares are reissued at $12 per share.

Cash	1,200	
Capital in excess of stated value—From common stock issuances	300	
Treasury stock		1,500
Reissuance of 100 shares of treasury stock at $12 per share.		

Case 3: Treasury shares are reissued at $10 per share.

Cash	1,000	
Capital in excess of stated value—From common stock issuances	1,000	
Retained earnings	400	
Treasury stock		2,400
Reissuance of 100 shares of treasury stock at $10 per share.		

The basic objectives that govern the accounting for treasury stock transactions may be summarized as follows:

Retained earnings are not to be increased as a result of treasury stock transactions.
Retained earnings are to be decreased as a result of treasury stock transactions only in the absence of available paid-in surplus applicable to the same class of shares.

Retirement of treasury shares. If a corporation complies with the required legal formalities and cancels any reacquired shares, the capital stock account should be debited for the amount credited thereto when such shares were issued, except that, in the case of no-par stock without a stated value, an average issuance price is acceptable unless the shares being cancelled can be traced to a specific issuance, in which case the issuance price should be used to record the cancellation.

It is also necessary to debit any related paid-in surplus accounts for any amount specifically traceable to the shares being cancelled; or, in those cases in which it is impossible or impracticable to make such an identification, it is acceptable to debit the related paid-in surplus accounts for the pro-rata portions thereof applicable to the shares being cancelled. To balance the entry, the Retained Earnings account is charged, or, if a credit is needed to balance the entry, a special paid-in surplus account is used. In any event, it is unacceptable to handle the cancellation of shares in a fashion that would increase retained earnings.

The following entries record the cancellation of the treasury shares shown under each of the three assumed fact situations presented on page 128.

Case 1.

Common stock	1,000	
Capital in excess of stated value—From treasury stock transactions	20	
Capital in excess of stated value—From common stock issuances	100	
Retained earnings	1,380	
Treasury stock		2,500
Cancellation of 100 shares of treasury stock acquired at $25 per share.		

Case 2.

Common stock	1,000	
Capital in excess of stated value—From common stock issuances	600	
Treasury stock		1,500
Capital in excess of stated value—From common stock retirements		100
Cancellation of 100 shares of treasury stock acquired at $15 per share.		

Case 3.

Common stock	1,000	
Capital in excess of stated value—From common stock issuances	10	
Retained earnings	1,390	
Treasury stock		2,400
Cancellation of 100 shares of treasury stock acquired at $24 per share.		

Donated stock. If treasury stock is recorded at cost, it is obvious that no debit to a treasury stock account can be made for donated stock. However, a memorandum notation of the number of shares acquired should be made in that account.

The *usual* methods of recording reissuances are stated below:

If the treasury shares consist wholly of donated stock, the entire proceeds of reissue are credited to a paid-in surplus account.

If purchased and donated shares are held and the shares reissued are specifically identified as donated shares, the entire proceeds are credited to paid-in surplus. If the shares reissued are not specifically identified as donated shares, paid-in surplus can be credited with the excess of the reissuance price over a cost computed on the first-in, first-out basis or on an average basis.

The word *usual* was included in the above statement to provide for a possible exception. Stock is sometimes issued to the organizers of a corporation for noncash assets, and a portion of the stock is then donated to the company to be reissued to provide working capital. This procedure was often used by mining and other speculative companies before the introduction of no-par stock made the expedient unnecessary. If such a company undertook to issue par value stock to the public, the stock usually had to be offered at a discount to make it attractive. But if unissued stock were issued at a discount, the purchasers might be liable for the discount, and this contingency might detract from the marketability of the stock. Such companies therefore resorted to the "treasury stock subterfuge." By issuing all of the stock for the mine or other property and reacquiring part of it as treasury stock, the reacquired stock became, theoretically at least, fully paid treasury stock which could be reissued at a discount. To credit paid-in surplus with the proceeds of the reissuance of such donated stock is of doubtful propriety. The financial position of the business would doubtless be more truly reflected if the proceeds of the reissuance were credited to the account with the property which was received when the stock was originally issued, because the property was obviously overvalued.

Recommended departure from the cost basis. The American Accounting Association has not favored the cost basis for treasury stock transactions. The 1957 revision, "Accounting and Reporting Standards for Corporate Financial Statements," covered the matter as follows:

> The acquisition of its own shares by a corporation represents a contraction of its capital structure. However, statutory requirements are particularly restrictive in this area of corporate activity and, to an important degree, are controlling in the reporting of such transactions. Preferably, the outlay by a corporation for its own shares is reflected as a reduction of the aggregate of contributed capital, and any excess of outlay over the pro-rata portion of contributed capital as a distribution of retained earnings. The issuance of reacquired shares should be accounted for in the same way as the issuance of previously unissued shares, that is, the entire proceeds should be credited to contributed capital.

To illustrate the procedure recommended by the above revision, assume that a company's stock was originally issued at $80 per share, of which $75, the stated value per share, was credited to Common Stock and $5 was credited to Capital in Excess of Stated Value—From Common Stock Issuances. If 100 shares were acquired at $85 per share, the entry, according to the method described above, would be:

Treasury stock	7,500	
Capital in excess of stated value—From common stock issuances ($5 × 100)	500	
Retained earnings	500	
Cash		8,500
Acquisition of 100 treasury shares.		

The recommendation that the issuance of treasury shares should be accounted for in the same way as the issuance of previously unissued shares is not as definite as might be desired.

If the treasury stock mentioned above is reissued for $9,000, the entry undoubtedly would be:

Cash	9,000	
Treasury stock		7,500
Capital in excess of stated value—From treasury stock transactions		1,500

But if the treasury stock is reissued at $7,000, we face a problem which does not arise in connection with an original issue: What should be done with the excess of the carrying value of the treasury stock over the reissue price? Presumably it would be debited to an account with some clearly descriptive title, such as "Excess of Par (or Stated) Value of Treasury Stock over Proceeds of Reissue."

Watered stock. Stock is said to be *watered* when the stockholders' equity is overstated in the balance sheet. The overstatement of stockholders' equity may be accompanied by an understatement of liabilities, but is usually accompanied by an overstatement of assets.

The water may be eliminated by any procedure which eliminates the overstatement of stockholders' equity and net assets. It may be eliminated by a scaling down of the outstanding stock (which may be accomplished by reduction of either the number of shares or the par or stated value) and a corresponding reduction of the book values of the overstated assets. If each stockholder suffers a pro-rata reduction, his proportionate interest in the corporation is not affected. Or stock may be donated and reissued, thus increasing the assets without increasing the outstanding stock, but the credit for the proceeds of the donated stock should be made in the overvalued asset accounts rather than in paid-in surplus, or the asset overvaluation and the water in the stock will not be eliminated. The water may be eliminated by writing down the overvalued assets. Or capital expenditures may be charged to expense. This method is not to be recommended, because it corrects one error by committing another, namely, the misstatement of operating income.

Book value per share of stock. The following describes the approach ordinarily used by accountants in computing book value per share: What would the stockholders receive on a per-share basis if the company were liquidated without gains, losses, or expenses; in other words, if the cash available for distribution, after the payment of all liabilities, were exactly equal to the stockholders' equity shown by the balance sheet?

Computations of book value per share must give consideration to the rights of various classes of stockholders. It is impracticable to give more than a few typical illustrations—enough to indicate the nature of the problems involved.

If there is only one class of stock, the book value per share is computed by dividing the total stockholders' equity (or book value of all of the stock) by the number of shares outstanding. The total book value of all the shares should include any reserves which are mere appropriations of surplus.

Assume that the stockholders' equity of a corporation includes the following:

Common stock—2,000 shares outstanding	$200,000
Capital in excess of par value—From common stock issuances	50,000
Sinking fund reserve	60,000
Reserve for contingencies	25,000
Retained earnings	65,000
Total	$400,000

The book value per share is $400,000 ÷ 2,000, or $200.

The computation is not so simple if there are common and preferred shares outstanding. It is then necessary to determine the portion of the stockholders' equity, or aggregate book value, applicable to the preferred stock, divide this amount by the number of shares of preferred stock outstanding to determine the book value per share of the preferred, and divide the remainder of the stockholders' equity by the number of common shares outstanding to determine the book value per share of the common.

The determination of the portion of stockholders' equity applicable to the preferred stock consists of a computation of the amount which the preferred stockholders would be entitled to receive if the company were liquidated without gain or loss. This involves consideration of the following questions:

What preference rights do the preferred stockholders have with respect to dividends? Is the preferred stock cumulative or noncumulative? If it is cumulative, are there any dividends in arrears? If there are dividends in arrears, is there any surplus from which they can be paid? Is the preferred stock participating or nonparticipating?

What preference rights do the preferred stockholders have with respect to assets in liquidation?

There are so many combinations of conditions, and consequently so many answers to these questions, that it is impracticable to illustrate them all. The following illustrations may suffice.

First illustration. The stockholders' equity of a company on June 30, 1965, consisted of the following:

Preferred stock—6% cumulative, nonparticipating; $100 par value; 1,000 shares outstanding	$100,000
Common stock—$100 par value; 1,000 shares outstanding	100,000
Retained earnings	50,000
Total	$250,000

Preferred dividends have been paid to December 31, 1964.

Under the terms of issuance of the preferred stock, it can be called at 105; but in the event of liquidation it is entitled only to par and unpaid cumulative dividends. Some accountants believe that the book value per share of preferred should be based on the call price plus the unpaid dividends. If this procedure is adopted, the book values per share will be computed as follows:

Total stockholders' equity		$250,000
Portion applicable to preferred stock:		
Call price	$105,000	
Unpaid dividends for six months	3,000	
Total		108,000
(Book value per share = $108,000 ÷ 1,000 = $108)		
Remainder applicable to common stock		$142,000
(Book value per share = $142,000 ÷ 1,000 = $142)		

But a call price does not seem appropriate. A call price for preferred stock is applicable when the preferred stock is to be retired but the common stock is to remain outstanding. Therefore, it seems preferable to ignore call prices and make the computations as follows:

Total stockholders' equity		$250,000
Portion applicable to preferred stock:		
Par value	$100,000	
Unpaid dividends for six months	3,000	
Total		103,000
(Book value per share = $103,000 ÷ 1,000 = $103)		
Remainder applicable to common stock		$147,000
(Book value per share = $147,000 ÷ 1,000 = $147)		

A call price should be distinguished from a liquidating value. If the preferred stockholders in the foregoing illustration were entitled to receive $105 per share in the event of liquidation, this valuation should be used in the computation.

Second illustration. The stockholders' equity of a company on December 31, 1965, consisted of the items listed below:

Preferred stock—6% cumulative, participating; $100 par value; 1,000 shares outstanding	$100,000
Common—No par value; stated value, $50 per share; 3,000 shares outstanding	150,000
Retained earnings	50,000
Total	$300,000

After 6% dividends are paid on the preferred stock, the common stockholders are entitled to receive $3 per share; thereafter, the two classes of stock are entitled to participate in dividends in the ratio of $2 per preferred share to $1 per common share; because there are 1,000 shares of preferred and 3,000 shares of common outstanding, the participation ratio is $2,000 to $3,000, or ⅖ to the preferred and ⅗ to the common. Dividends for the first six months of 1965 have been paid on the preferred stock; no dividends have been paid for 1965 on the common stock. The computations are made as follows:

		Preferred	Common
Par or stated value		$100,000	$150,000
Retained earnings:			
Total	$50,000		
Amount required for preferred dividend for second six months of 1965	3,000*	3,000	
Portion required for dividends on common stock for year	9,000*		9,000
Remainder—divisible ⅖ and ⅗	$38,000	15,200	22,800
Total		$118,200	$181,800
Shares outstanding		1,000	3,000
Book value per share		$ 118.20	$ 60.60

* Deduction.

Third illustration. Assume the same facts as in the second illustration except that the retained earnings are only $7,000. The computations would then be made as follows:

		Preferred	Common
Par or stated value		$100,000	$150,000
Retained earnings:			
Total	$7,000		
Deduct amount required for preferred dividend for second six months of 1965	3,000	3,000	
Remainder	$4,000		
Because the common stockholders are entitled to receive dividends of $3 per share before any participating dividends are paid on the preferred stock, and because the remaining $4,000 of retained earnings is not sufficient to pay such a dividend on the common stock, the entire remaining $4,000 is applicable to the common stock			4,000
Total		$103,000	$154,000
Shares outstanding		1,000	3,000
Book value per share		$ 103.00	$ 51.33

Fourth illustration. The stockholders' equity of a company on December 31, 1965, consisted of the following:

Preferred stock—6% cumulative, nonparticipating; no par value; stated value, $50 per share; 1,000 shares outstanding	$ 50,000
Common stock—No par value; stated value, $10 per share; 10,000 shares outstanding	100,000
Deficit	20,000*
Total	$130,000

* Deduction.

Dividends of $25,000 are in arrears on the preferred stock.

Before book values per share can be computed, it is necessary to know whether the preferred stockholders are entitled, in the event of liquidation, to the dividends in arrears notwithstanding the existence of the deficit.

If they are entitled to the dividends in arrears, the book values should be computed as follows:

Total stockholders' equity		$130,000
Portion applicable to preferred stock:		
$50 × 1,000	$50,000	
Dividends in arrears	25,000	
Total		75,000
(Book value per share = $75,000 ÷ 1,000 = $75)		
Remainder applicable to common stock		$ 55,000
(Book value per share = $55,000 ÷ 10,000 = $5.50)		

If the preferred stockholders are not entitled to the dividends in arrears, the book values should be computed as follows:

Total stockholders' equity	$130,000
Portion applicable to the preferred stock:	
$50 × 1,000	50,000
(Book value per share = $50,000 ÷ 1,000 = $50)	
Remainder applicable to common stock	$ 80,000
(Book value per share = $80,000 ÷ 10,000 = $8)	

Significance of book value per share. Unfortunately, book values per share are more likely to be misunderstood than understood. This condition is attributable, in part at least, to the fact that book-value-per-share computations are made on the basis of a liquidating concept, although the balance sheet amounts used in the computation are based on a going-concern concept. Because "value" may be misinterpreted as synonymous with "worth," the term *book equity per share* might be preferable because it is less likely to be misunderstood.

It is obvious that accounting errors or improprieties will affect the book value per share. Recognition of this fact is given in the definition in the Institute's *Accounting Terminology Bulletin* No. 3:

> *Book value* is the amount shown on accounting records or related financial statements at or as of the date when the determination is made, after adjustments necessary to reflect (1) corrections of errors, and (2) the application of accounting practices which have been consistently followed.

Comprehensive illustration of a Stockholders' Equity section. The following illustration shows the balance sheet treatment of various matters affecting the stockholders' equity.

Stockholders' equity:		
Capital stock:		
Preferred stock—6% participating, cumulative; par value, $100; authorized and issued, 1,000 shares	$100,000	
Common stock—No par value; stated value, $10; authorized and issued, 10,000 shares, of which 500 shares are in the treasury	100,000	$200,000
Capital in excess of par or stated value:		
From preferred stock issuances	$ 5,000	
From common stock issuances	27,000	
From treasury stock transactions—Common	2,000	
From stock dividends	4,000	38,000
Retained earnings:		
Appropriated:		
Reserve for contingencies	$ 25,000	
Reserve for plant extensions	15,000	
Not available for dividends—Equal to cost of treasury stock	7,500	
Total	$ 47,500	
Free	132,000	179,500
Total		$417,500
Deduct cost of treasury stock—Common		7,500
Stockholders' equity		$410,000

In published financial statements it is often necessary to combine or group some of the related stockholders' equity accounts. This is acceptable provided that the subtotals for paid-in surplus and retained earnings are clearly set forth and that any restrictions or appropriations of surplus are disclosed. If there are any accounts showing unrealized increments in asset amounts, they should be clearly labeled and presented below the subtotal for retained earnings and above any treasury shares. Such accounts are rarely found because it is considered unacceptable to write up assets to reflect current values.

Secret reserves. A secret reserve exists whenever the stockholders' equity shown in the balance sheet is understated. It is, in a sense, the exact opposite of water in the stock. A secret reserve may be created by any device which understates assets or overstates liabilities. Capital expenditures may be charged to expense, income may be credited to the asset which produced the income, excessive depreciation or bad debt provisions may be made, liabilities may be overstated, assets may be written off, and a great variety of other devices may be employed.

The creation of secret reserves is not so common now as it was before the income tax rendered inexpedient the misstatement of income. In the old days, corporations frequently wrote down assets arbitrarily, defending the procedure on the grounds of conservatism, and directors often deliberately created secret reserves because such reserves made it possible to equalize earnings and thus to maintain an appearance of uniformity and stability which was considered advantageous to the corporation.

The theory and operation of the secret reserve were somewhat as follows: In a prosperous year, when income was above normal, it was wise to conceal the company's prosperity, partly to avoid attracting competition and partly to avoid creating in the stockholders' minds an expectation of similarly abnormal earnings in the future. The directors, therefore, charged excessive depreciation or resorted to some other method of overstating the expenses. In a subsequent year, when earnings were subnormal, and when a disclosure of this fact might adversely affect the standing and stability of the corporation, expenses were understated.

Secret reserves may be deliberate or unintentional. Provisions for depletion, depreciation, bad debts, and certain other expenses are necessarily based on estimates. If the estimate is excessive, the expenses are overstated, the earnings and stockholders' equity are understated, and a secret reserve is thereby created. Even when estimates are made in the most careful manner possible, secret reserves may develop. But when discovered, the secret reserve, whether the result of deliberate or inadvertent actions, should be eliminated by a proper correction of the accounts.

Voting trusts and stock pools. Because stockholders are entitled to votes in proportion to the stock they hold, the control of a corporation lies with the majority stockholders. For the protection of the minority holders, the device of pooling a portion of the stock is sometimes used. Assume that *A*, *B*, and *C*, formerly in partnership, form a corporation, the shares being issued as follows: to *A*, 105 shares; to *B*, 55 shares; and to *C*, 40 shares. In order to protect *B* and *C* against *A*, and also give all stockholders equal shares in the management, *A* and *B* may place all of their shares in excess of 40 (the number held by *C*) in the hands of a trustee, the terms of the trust or pool requiring that the trustee shall vote the stock so held as directed by a majority (or two-thirds, or three-fourths, or unanimous, or any other specified) vote of the unpooled stock. The condition would then be:

Stockholder	Shares Owned	Shares Pooled	Shares Not Pooled
A	105	65	40
B	55	15	40
C	40	0	40
Total	200	80	120

If the pooled stock can be voted at the direction of a two-thirds vote of the unpooled stock, any two stockholders can control the company. If the pooled stock can be voted only at the direction of a three-fourths vote of the unpooled stock, no action can be taken without the consent of all stockholders.

A stock pool or trust may also be used to effect a distribution of profits in a ratio other than the ratio of stockholdings. For instance, assume that *A*, *B*, and *C*, in the preceding illustration, had previously been partners with differing capital interests but sharing profits equally. If it is desired to continue the equal interests in profits notwithstanding the differing capital interests, the numbers of shares shown above as pooled might be placed in trust, under an agreement providing that dividends on the shares in trust should be paid to the trustees and distributed by them in equal amounts to *A*, *B*, and *C*.

Before the merger and holding company devices attained their present popularity as methods of combining corporations, the stock pool or trust was frequently resorted to. In such cases all of, or a controlling interest in, the stock of each affected company was placed in trust to be voted by trustees. Although each company retained its separate legal entity, the activities of all companies were subjected to a unified control by the trustees.

Because, in the early days of corporate combinations, trusts of this nature were frequently established, large businesses generally came to be known as *trusts,* but this is loose terminology.

CHAPTER

8

Generally Accepted Accounting Principles

Introduction. It is generally agreed that the primary function of accounting is to accumulate information about the financial activities of a business entity in a manner that will permit its meaningful summarization in the form of financial statements. It is agreed, also, that there can be no widespread understanding of, and reliance on, accounting statements unless they have been prepared in conformity with a body of generally accepted rules or conventions. The necessity of some common agreement on accounting matters becomes apparent when we contemplate the chaotic condition that would prevail if every businessman or every accountant could follow his own notions about the measurement of revenue and expense.

The nature of prevailing accounting rules. It would be incorrect to suggest that the rules which establish whether a given accounting procedure is acceptable or unacceptable are in the nature of principles like those found in physics or chemistry. Accounting principles are more properly associated with such terms as *concepts, conventions,* and *standards.* It is important to remember that accounting principles are man-made, in contrast to natural law.

It is also important to remember that accounting principles are not rigid. They are constantly evolving, being influenced by business practices; the needs of statement users; legislative and governmental regulation; the opinions and actions of stockholders, creditors, labor unions, and management; and the reasoning and experience of accountants. Such influences affect the definitions, assumptions, and procedures that form the content of generally accepted accounting. In final analysis, accounting must serve the needs of society; it must be reasonably sensitive to changes in the economic system.

Although professional accountants pretty clearly understand the concepts, standards, and conventions (no single word seems quite adequate) to which they should conform, there is no comprehensive *authoritative* compilation or code of accounting principles. Principles cannot be established in accounting, as they are in the realm of natural sciences, by experimentation; nor have they been determined, as in the law, by authoritative pronouncement, although the accounting procedures of railroads, utilities, and certain other lines of business have been standardized by governmental regulation. The Securities and Exchange Commission has issued rules and regulations which touch the realm of accounting principles; these are binding only on those persons who are subject to the authority of the Commission, but they have exercised a profound influence on the practice of accounting generally. The American Institute of Certified Public Accountants, through its Committee on Accounting Procedure and, more recently, its Accounting Principles Board, has issued numerous bulletins and pronouncements dealing with matters which may be regarded as accounting principles, but no authoritative status is claimed for such issuances. Whether they acquire any authoritative force depends upon the general acceptability of the opinions which they set forth. The American Accounting Association has also done commendable work in formulating a statement of accounting standards, but the pronouncements of the Association, as well as those of the Institute, have not been greeted with unanimous acceptance.

In the final analysis, the subject matter of accounting represents the cumulative results of years of experience with the intricate problems of providing a record of business transactions and measuring and reporting on the position and progress of business enterprises. In recent decades there has been a widespread interest in periodic income results. As a consequence, the income statement has received more attention than the balance sheet. To some extent, the balance sheet is becoming a statement of residuals; that is, the balances shown therein are the result of the application of procedures considered proper to account for revenue and expense.

Some underlying assumptions. The accounting process is based on an assumption that the business involved is going to continue operations indefinitely. This "going concern" assumption makes it unnecessary for the accountant to place any particular emphasis on forced-sale or liquidation values. In fact, the accounting process cannot be characterized as being predominantly a "valuation" process. It is primarily a process of income determination; attention is directed to revenue realization and cost expiration. For a going concern that intends to continue using a particular combination of assets for business purposes, the objective is one of spreading their cost over the periods benefited by their use in the conduct of business operations.

Another basic assumption is that fluctuations in the purchasing power of the dollar will be insignificant and hence may be ignored. During certain periods this assumption has squared substantially with reality. But it is also true that during other periods the purchasing power of the dollar has changed significantly. In spite of such changes, accounting has continued to treat all dollars as equal, whether the dollar amounts in the accounts represent 1939 dollars or 1949 dollars or current dollars. Such accounting could result in misleading financial statements.

Although the assumption regarding the stability of the dollar is an assumption contrary to fact, to date the majority of accountants have felt no compulsion to modify accounting methods or procedures in an attempt to make allowance for such variation in the unit of measurement. Such reluctance is hardly the result of an unawareness on the part of accountants that prices change. It is more likely attributable to a belief that changes in the value of money, during most periods, have been so gradual as not materially to undermine the validity of the assumption. Another reason is that cost is a determinable fact. Financial accounting in terms of cost outlays does provide a meaningful accountability of management's utilization of the resources at its disposal. There is also considerable apprehension that procedures directed toward modifying the financial statements so that all amounts would be stated in dollars of the same size could lead to more, instead of less, misunderstanding and confusion.

Some basic accounting concepts. Although the accounting profession has never adopted a comprehensive code of accounting principles, as noted earlier, the following may be considered to have fundamental importance:

(1) The accounts and statements should give expression, as far as possible, to facts evidenced by completed transactions and supportable by objective data.

(2) Cost is the proper basis for the accounting for assets and asset expirations, subject to downward modification in those instances in which there is convincing evidence that cost cannot be recovered, through either use or sale.

(3) Conservatism, although generally desirable, is not a justification for the understatement of the owners' equity or the misstatement of periodic net income.

(4) Consistency should be maintained between the statements prepared at the end of one period, and between the statements of successive periods. However, a proper regard for consistency need not preclude a desirable change in procedure. If a change of material consequence is made, the fact should be mentioned and the effect thereof on the statements should be indicated, if determinable.

(5) The determination of net income requires a proper matching of revenues and expenses.

 (a) Revenues should not be regarded as earned until an increment has been realized, or until its realization is reasonably assured.

 (b) Expenses are expired costs.

(6) Statements should not be misleading, and should make full disclosure of significant information. This was discussed in Chapter 3.

Objectivity. Contrary to a belief held by some nonaccountants, accounting statements are not entirely factual. Judgment, opinion, and estimate enter into the accounting process. This is necessarily so, but it does not follow from the above observation that it would be desirable if accounting were completely discretionary in nature. To the extent practicable, the accounting process is based on bargained transactions where the money amounts represent prices determined in the market place as opposed to amounts based on opinion. The accountant prefers amounts that can be verified by reference to business documents originating outside of the enterprise. Such support lends validity to accounting data.

The criterion of realization is another example of preference for objectivity. Informed opinion or even price increases are not considered to be sufficiently objective to warrant revenue recognition. There must be a transfer or exchange, a business agreement, or some ascertainable change in an asset or liability to remove or minimize what might be described as the "flaw of indefiniteness."

The cost principle. Accounting literature has had much to say about the "cost principle," which may be stated as follows: Subject to generally recognized exceptions, and excluding cash and receivables, cost is the proper basis of accounting for assets and expenses, and accounting records should reflect acquisition costs and the transformation, flow, and expiration of these costs.

The cost basis for recording and reporting is sometimes criticized by people who believe that reports would be more informative if all assets were stated on the basis of realizable values or replacement costs at the date of the report. It is questionable whether a value basis would be more significant than the cost basis. The use of realizable values for inventories could result in the anticipation of profit and possibly the distortion of profit should the volume of production exceed the volume of sales. Usually there is no intention to convert fixed assets into cash immediately; therefore, information relative to their market or realizable values is not of great importance, except perhaps to certain creditors, and the information can be given parenthetically in the balance sheet or in supplementary schedules without abandoning the cost basis in the records themselves. The relevance of the replacement cost of an asset is also open to question. Quite often management would not be interested in replacing an asset with another of its kind, possibly because of technological change. It should also be recognized that the computation of replacement costs involves the use of assumptions about such key factors as overhead costs and volume of production. Furthermore, cost to replace is often a poor indicator of value. More definite and objective evidence is available for the determination of cost than for the determination of realizable values and replacement costs, which in many instances would be matters of pure conjecture. Less use of cost would certainly make accounting more subjective in character.

Conservatism. In the past, accountants were primarily concerned with presenting a conservative picture of the financial condition of a business in its balance sheet. They regarded the balance sheet as of primary, and the income statement as of secondary, importance. Moreover, they were inclined to assume that a conservative balance sheet was a good balance sheet for all purposes, and that balance sheet conservatism automatically resulted in a proper and conservative income statement.

The emphasis upon the balance sheet and upon conservative asset valuations and liability and loss provisions doubtless resulted from the fact that, in the early days of the development of accounting, the services of public accountants were required principally for the preparation of reports for bankers and other grantors of short-term credit who were primarily concerned with the question of the margin of security. For many years, bankers and other short-term creditors were much more interested in the balance sheet than in the income statement, and they were naturally disposed to regard balance sheet conservatism as a safeguard and hence a basic virtue. Accountants naturally were influenced by their attitude.

Although balance sheet conservatism is still regarded as an accounting virtue, the time-honored emphasis upon the balance sheet and upon conservatism in asset valuations has been subjected to critical reconsideration. One reason for this is the recognition that, with the increase in the number of corporate stockholders who are not active in the management, accounting reports must serve the requirements of investors as well as of short-term creditors. Ultraconservatism may be prejudicial to the interests of stockholders or other security holders who, having been led to believe that the company in which they have made investments is less prosperous than it really is, may sell their securities for less than they are really worth.

Also, with the income statement now receiving the emphasis formerly accorded the balance sheet, accountants have become increasingly aware that adherence to a doctrine of balance sheet conservatism may result in incorrect, and even unconservative, income statements. If an expenditure or a cost which can be presumed to be essential or beneficial to the operations of more than one period is charged either to surplus or to current income in one period—a procedure which may be conservative from the balance sheet standpoint—the income statements for all periods are distorted, and the income statements for the periods which are relieved of their just portions of the cost are the opposite of conservative.

At the present time, conservatism is a less potent force. However, it continues to be a factor when matters of opinion or estimate are involved, accountants believing that it is commendable, in instances of doubt, to understate net income and owners' equity rather than to overstate them. The consequences of an understatement of assets and net income do not seem as serious as the opposite. However, conservatism can scarcely be regarded as a virtue if, as its consequence, balance sheets and income statements do not fairly present the financial position and the results of operations.

Consistency. The accountant, perhaps more than any other person, is aware of the influence that estimates and policy decisions have on periodic net income determinations and of the fact that such estimates and policy decisions cannot be eliminated from the accounting process. However, it would be most unfortunate if the stated net income of a business could be determined by the whim or fancy, and particularly by the changing whim or fancy, of those directing its affairs.

There are many areas of accounting in which different procedures may be acceptable from the standpoint of approved current practice. The accountant should seek to apply the method best suited to each particular case, but it is important that the method selected be applied consistently year after year. Inconsistency destroys comparability; it has the potential of misleading users of financial statements. For example, by changing depreciation or inventory methods, it is possible to increase or decrease the net income for the current period, perhaps significantly. A statement user might be misled and think that the increase or decrease was the result of a change in business conditions or management effectiveness, whereas in reality it was the result of a change in an accounting method. Changes in net income reported in successive statements should be traceable to things more fundamental than mere changes in accounting methods.

Whenever financial statements are audited by a certified public accountant, it is customary for the auditor to issue an accompanying opinion or certificate so that statement users may know that there has been an audit by an independent professional accountant. Consistency has come to be regarded as of such primary importance that a declaration with respect thereto can be found in the typical auditor's opinion. The last paragraph of the opinion is customarily worded somewhat as follows:

> In our opinion, the accompanying balance sheet and statement(s) of income and retained earnings present fairly the financial position of X Company on December 31, 19–, and the results of its operations for the year then ended, in conformity with generally accepted accounting principles applied on a basis consistent with that of the preceding year.

A proper regard for consistency need not preclude a desirable change in procedure. But if a change is made, the fact should be mentioned and the dollar effect thereof on the statements should be disclosed, if determinable.

Income determination. Because the majority of accountants probably would agree that the accountant faces his greatest challenge when he undertakes the determination of net income, and because income determination is a factor to be considered in the discussion of most accounting matters, and hence is frequently referred to throughout this text, it may prove helpful to devote the balance of this chapter to a brief digest of the topic.

A preliminary consideration concerns terminology. The terminology of accounting is not crystallized and precise, and it therefore is advisable to indicate the senses in which certain words are used in the following discussion and generally throughout the text.

We shall consider the word *revenue* to mean an inflow of assets,* but it must be recognized that there are inflows of assets which are not revenue. Obviously, an inflow of capital funds from stockholders is not revenue to a corporation, nor should a business regard as revenue an inflow of assets which is offset by an increase in liabilities. Increases in the value of assets resulting from growth, natural increase, or a rise in market prices are not generally regarded as revenue. Revenue consists of an inflow of assets from customers and clients, and is related to sales and the rendering of services. The 1957 revision, *Accounting and Reporting Standards for Corporate Financial Statements,* published by the American Accounting Association, states that revenue is "the monetary expression of the aggregate of products or services transferred by an enterprise to its customers during a period of time."

The term *revenue* has sometimes been used by accountants to mean the *gross* proceeds from operating activities such as sales and the rendering of services, and to mean, in the case of incidental transactions consummated at a gain, only the *net* proceeds after deduction of the related costs. For example, if investment securities carried on the books at cost, $10,000, are sold for $12,000, some accountants think that it would be misleading to treat the gross proceeds of $12,000 as revenue because such transactions are incidental to the primary operating activities of the typical business. Such considerations may have influenced an earlier committee of the American Accounting Association, for, in *Accounting Concepts and Standards Underlying Corporate Financial Statements,* its definition of *revenue* applies the gross proceeds concept in the case of sales and services and the net concept in the case of incidental transactions. The definition of *revenue* is stated as embracing:

> (a) the amount of assets received or liabilities liquidated in the sale of the products or services of an enterprise, (b) the gain from sales or exchanges of assets other than stock in trade, and (c) the gain from advantageous settlements of liabilities.

As a general rule, the text will use the term *revenue* in its gross sense.

Revenue may be received before it is earned, as in the case of rent collected in advance. Because there may be a lapse of time between the date when revenue is received and the date when, in accordance with accepted accounting procedures, it is regarded as earned, there may be *unearned revenues* and *earned revenues.*

---

* Revenues sometimes take the form of a decrease in liabilities—a variation from normal which could be recognized by saying "an inflow of net assets," but which is ignored here for purposes of simplicity of statement.

The word *cost* is related to expenditure. An expenditure is a payment, in cash or otherwise, or the incurring of an obligation to make a future payment, for a benefit received. *Cost* is the measure of the expenditure. But when used without modifying words, *cost* does not always have a sufficiently definite and refined meaning. For precision of expression, we shall use several terms.

The expression *cost outlay* will be used with reference to expenditures and acquisitions, regardless of whether the benefit received is chargeable to an asset or an expense account.

The term *cost transformation* refers to such changes as the conversion of material, labor, and overhead costs into finished goods costs.

Expired costs are those which no longer have any asset status. Expired costs are of two classes: *utilized costs* and *lost costs. Utilized costs* include the cost of merchandise sold and the costs of services, utilities, and other benefits used for the purpose of producing revenue. *Lost costs* are costs which have expired without utilization or without contributing to the production of revenue. A *cost residue* is the unexpired portion of a cost outlay; it may properly appear on the asset side of the balance sheet of a going concern.

The income-determination process in accounting is a matter of matching, or associating, revenues with related expenses (and, occasionally, lost costs). Thus, revenue is a gross concept, whereas income is a net or resultant amount. If revenues exceed expenses, the business earns income, the dollar amount thereof being shown in the income statement usually as "net income." If expenses exceed revenues, a loss results. Whether or not all items affecting income given recognition during a period should be included in the determination of periodic net income is a matter on which accountants do not agree, as indicated by the discussion of the all-inclusive and current operating concepts in Chapter 4.

Most businesses can be characterized as being engaged in a continuing "stream" of activity. Not until a business has ceased to function as a going concern and has disposed of its assets is it possible to compute with absolute accuracy the net income earned or the loss sustained. But it obviously would be impractical to make no computations of net income until the business completes its life span. Unless interim computations are made, no adequate basis exists for reporting on the success of a business, because it is the net income figure, more than any other bit of information, that provides a means of comparing the operations of a business during different periods, or of comparing the results of operations of different businesses. But it must be recognized that, in the whole history of the operations of a business, the income statement for a period is merely a chapter—subject to possible revision.

When is revenue realized? Business operations customarily involve a long series of activities: The purchase of materials, the fabrication of product, the sale of the product, the collection of the proceeds of the sale, and sometimes the subsequent rendering of service or fulfilment of guarantees. All of these activities are conducted for the purpose of earning revenue. At what point in the series should the revenue be regarded as earned?

The point of sale. The sale is the step in the series of activities at which revenue generally is regarded as realized. Realization of revenue does not necessarily require a collection in cash, because a valid receivable from a solvent debtor is an asset in as good standing as cash.

The point of sale is generally regarded as the point of revenue realization because (1) it is the point at which a conversion takes place—an exchange of one asset for another—and conversion is regarded as evidence of realization; and (2) it is the point at which the amount of the revenue is, in the normal case, objectively determinable from a sale price acceptable to both parties.

The legal rules governing the passing of title determine when a sale is made, but these rules are complex and full of technicalities. Delivery to the vendee or his agent is a general test of the passing of title, and for general accounting purposes throughout the period it is advisable, for convenience, to regard a sale as having been made when the goods are invoiced and delivery or shipment is made to a purchaser. (Delivery alone is not a sufficient test because delivery may be made on consignment.) At the close of the accounting period it may be necessary to consider the legal aspects of title-passing more closely and to exclude from realized revenue the billed price of goods which have been delivered without passing of title, and to include in realized revenue the billable price of goods which have not been delivered but the title to which has passed. Even such end-of-period adjustments are usually ignored if the amounts are small.

It must be recognized that even after the date of sale, events may occur which will modify the amounts of revenue and income on the sale transaction. Merchandise may be returned, allowances may be given to customers, service expenses may be incurred, and losses may arise from uncollectible accounts. However, these possibilities are usually not regarded as of sufficient importance to serve as a deterrent to the adoption of the sales basis for recognizing revenue realization; business experience may indicate that the revenue deductions and costs arising from these sources are so inconsequential in amount that they can be ignored, or that they can be forecast with reasonable accuracy and provided for during the period of sale by the use of allowance accounts.

Recognizing revenue as earned before the point of sale. Adopting the point of sale as the point of recognition of revenue realization, although appropriate and recommended for most revenue transactions, is not followed in all cases. Under certain conditions it is considered both acceptable and advisable to recognize revenues as earned before all the requirements of a completed sale have been met. Some of these special situations are mentioned on the following page.

If goods are being manufactured under a cost-plus contract and the amounts of revenue applicable to completed portions of the contract are determinable and the collection of revenue is reasonably assured, there is little to recommend postponing the recognition of revenue until delivery and transfer of title. There is some reluctance on the part of the accountant to recognize revenue on fixed-price contracts in process because the ultimate outcome (whether the contract will prove to be profitable or unprofitable) is much less predictable. However, when the execution of a contract extends into two or more accounting periods, there may be a question as to whether the income statements fairly reflect the results of operations during these periods if the entire revenue is reported in the period of completion, particularly if the major portion of the work was done prior to the period of completion. If a portion of the contract price on contracts in process is recognized as earned, it should be evident that the reported income may be based to a greater degree on estimate and opinion than the accountant would prefer. However, this disadvantage should be weighed against the alternative of the less informative and less equitable income statement which might result from deferring the matching of revenue and expense on fixed-price contracts until their completion.

The mining industry provides another case where more equitable and informative accounting may result if revenue recognition is not delayed until the point of sale. In the case of certain metals, a mining company can dispose of all it can mine at an established price with no selling effort. Delivery and transfer of title are mere formalities and under the circumstances would not provide as meaningful a basis for revenue recognition as production. Agricultural products provide an analogous case. With government-supported prices for farm products, delaying revenue recognition until delivery and transfer of title would seem somewhat artificial.

When recognition is given to revenue before the point of sale, a basis other than cost has to be used for inventory valuation. Net realizable value has the most support as an alternative basis. In some industries, such as mining and agriculture, net realizable values can be determined with greater assurance than can cost; and, when this condition exists, there is additional justification for the recognition of revenue before the point of sale.

Recognition of revenue after the date of sale. The practice of postponing the recognition of revenue as earned until some time after delivery and transfer of title is considered appropriate in the case of installment sales. The collection hazards and the considerable collection expenses incurred in periods subsequent to the period of sale justify delaying recognition of revenue realization. Whenever the collection of the receivable is not reasonably assured, the accountant prefers to take a cautious position and not treat the revenue as realized until collection is made or until it is reasonably apparent that collection will be made in the due course of business.

It is generally recognized that accountants must give consideration to the substantive aspects of transactions as well as to their legal form. Misleading accounting might result if accountants were committed to giving recognition to revenue every time there was compliance with the legal requirements for a sale. To take an extreme case, suppose that articles sold were repurchased at their selling price; if consideration was given only to matters of legal form, overstatement of revenue, profit, and assets would result. Or suppose that a seller has granted a concurrent loan to the purchaser equal, or almost equal, to the selling price. Under such circumstances, the deferment of revenue would bring the accounting more in line with the facts.

Unrealized appreciation. Is unrealized appreciation revenue? Let us consider this question first with respect to marketable securities, where it is possible to make the strongest case for an affirmative answer. If marketable securities were purchased for $50,000, were worth $60,000 at the end of the year of purchase, and were sold for $70,000 during the following year, was there a $20,000 gain in the second year or a $10,000 gain in each year? Although a $10,000 gain could have been realized the first year, realization did not occur until the second year. The requirements of realization were not met during the first year, because the management elected not to sell but preferred to take the hazards of market fluctuation, and thus there was no realization nor any reasonable assurance that any revenue would ever be realized.

If increases in the value of readily marketable securities cannot properly be counted as revenue, although a gain could be immediately realized by a sale at the prevailing market price, attributing revenue to the valuation of inventories at market prices in excess of cost is, under ordinary conditions, even less proper. For one thing, a rise in market selling prices usually is not immediately realizable, for it is rarely possible, and it presumably would be inexpedient even if it were possible, to sell the total inventory at the end of the period, as could be done with marketable securities. If it is considered improper as a general rule to regard any revenue as being earned by manufacturing or by any other operating activities prior to sale, it certainly is much less proper to take up as realized revenue mere increases in value resulting from rises in market prices.

Turning to the field of fixed assets, if it is improper to take up as realized revenue an increase in the market value of current assets which presumably will soon be realized through sales, there is even less reason for considering that any revenue has resulted from an increase in the disposal value of fixed assets which the business, as a going concern, presumably must retain.

Very plausible arguments have been advanced for taking increments in asset values into the accounts prior to sale if the production process consists of a natural increase during two or more accounting periods. Such conditions exist in the case of growing crops, timber, and livestock, and in the case of some inventories, such as wines and liquors, which increase in value as a result of aging. Although such increments in value are in certain instances recognized as income for tax purposes, the accountant is disinclined to report such increments as revenue because there is no certainty that the items will ever be sold or that market prices will remain at prevailing levels.

Revenue from services. When should revenue from services, as distinguished from sales of merchandise, be regarded as earned? The logical answer probably is: When the service is rendered. However, the taking up of revenue from services frequently is postponed until the service is completed and billed, because of uncertainty as to the amount to be charged; or until the cash is received, because of uncertainty regarding collection. If expenses are incurred in performing the service in a period prior to that in which the revenue is recognized, consistency requires that such expenses be deferred until the period in which the revenue is taken up, unless, of course, it appears that the revenue being postponed will not be collected, in which case it may never be recognized. The related expenses under these circumstances should be regarded as lost costs and be written off.

The dollar amount of realized revenue. Having considered the question of *when* revenue should be regarded as realized, we turn to the question of the *dollar valuation* that should be placed on the revenue.

Most revenues arise from bargained transactions, and the price agreed upon by the parties to the transaction is an appropriate measure of the resulting revenue. Thus, if goods costing $100 are sold at a cash price of $150, the selling price is the measure of the revenue resulting from the sale. The same measure is appropriate for sales on account, because there is an expectation that cash will be received in due course.

More difficult problems may arise when noncash assets are traded, no transaction price being established in terms of money. Bases for the determination of the revenue, if any, to be recognized in trades are discussed below.

If a business trades articles it normally sells, accepting in exchange assets other than cash, the accountant would be justified in most cases in using the selling price of the product normally sold as the measure of revenue. But if there were any unusual features surrounding the trade transaction (for instance, if an unusually large quantity of the product was involved), due allowance for such features should be made in measuring the resulting revenue. In some circumstances where stock in trade is exchanged for other property, the accountant would be justified in using the market value of the assets received as the measure of revenue. This would be an appropriate procedure where the articles received had a more well-established market price than the articles disposed of. For example, suppose a real estate dealer sold a plot of land for 10,000 bushels of wheat. Because the value of wheat is readily determinable by reference to market quotations on any organized grain exchange, the prevailing price of wheat might be the more objective measure of revenue.

If the trade involves assets not held for sale, the accountant would be justified in using the market value of the asset being traded or the market value of the asset being acquired, whichever value could be determined with the greater assurance. In the rare instances when neither the asset traded nor the asset received has a reasonably determinable market value, the accountant is justified in bringing the acquired asset onto the books at the carrying value of the asset traded off. In this case, although there is an inflow of assets, the valuation problem is so subjective as to justify no recognition of revenue.

Cost outlays. Because business management does not ordinarily toss dollars to the wind, accounting is based on the assumption that all cost outlays result in the acquisition of something of value to the business—something tangible like merchandise or fixed assets, or something intangible like insurance protection or the right to occupy and use certain premises. It may therefore be said that, in a broad sense, all cost outlays result in the acquisition of assets. It does not follow, however, that all cost outlays must necessarily be charged to asset accounts when the outlays are made.

Classification of cost outlays. If it is known at the time of making a cost outlay that the benefit derived will not extend beyond the current accounting period (as when a month's rent is paid at the beginning of the month), it is customary and expedient to charge the cost immediately to an expense account. Although the cost may not have expired at the time of the outlay, the accounting entries are reduced by making an immediate charge to an expense account rather than charging an asset account and subsequently making a transfer from the asset account to an expense account.

If a cost outlay will presumably benefit more than one period, but only a few periods (as in the case of insurance costs), accounting procedures differ; sometimes the outlay is charged to an asset account (such as Unexpired Insurance) and the expired portions of cost are transferred periodically to an expense account (such as Insurance Expense). Sometimes the cost outlay is charged to an expense account and cost residues are transferred periodically to an asset account.

If a cost outlay results in the acquisition of an asset which presumably will benefit a considerable number of periods (as in the case of the acquisition of a fixed asset), the cost should be charged to an asset account and the periodical cost expirations should be charged to expense.

Some of the most difficult problems of classification of cost outlays at the time when the outlays are made arise in connection with fixed assets. These problems are discussed in Chapter 16, which comprehensively differentiates capital and revenue expenditures.

Cost apportionments. When assets of several classes are acquired at a lump-sum cost, an apportionment of the cost outlay should be made, so that there will be a basis for subsequent entries recording cost transformations, cost expirations, and cost residues applicable to the various assets. Such apportionments may be made on the basis of appraisals, market quotations, or proposed selling prices.

Cost transformations and allocations. Between the time when a cost outlay is made and the time when the cost expires, many transformations may take place. In manufacturing operations cost outlays are made for materials, labor, and factory overhead; by the transformations of the manufacturing process, these costs become merged into costs of goods in process and finished goods. It therefore becomes essential to trace the initial costs through the processes of transformation and to allocate them, as accurately as possible, to the products. This is the function of cost accounting, which cannot be discussed at length here. However, two matters of fundamental importance require mention.

First, a distinction must be maintained between transformed costs and expired costs. Use does not necessarily mean expiration of cost. If gasoline is used in a truck with which merchandise deliveries are made, its cost expires with use. But if gasoline is used in an engine which furnishes power for manufacturing purposes, its cost becomes transformed into the cost of the product.

Second, in the allocation of costs to various products, including fixed assets constructed, no special favors or cost exemptions should be granted.

Cost expirations. Expired costs are of two kinds: utilized costs and lost costs. Although it is important to distinguish between transformed costs and expired costs, it is not usually considered important to distinguish in the income statement between expired costs which have been utilized and expired costs which have been merely lost. Some accountants do undertake to make such a distinction in the income statement, and classify as losses those cost expirations which have no traceable association with the production of revenue. Thus, rent for a building used in current operations would be classified in the income statement as an expense, whereas rent for premises not in use and hence not contributing to the generation of revenue would be classified in the statement as a loss. Similarly, the undepreciated portion of the cost of plant being discarded would be classified as a loss.

Although the above distinction is commonly found in accounting literature, income statements which reflect such a distinction may be misunderstood unless it is recognized that lost costs are a type of expense, peculiar only in that there is no traceable association between them and the production of revenue. And, even if the distinction were important, it often would be difficult to make, because the decision as to whether there is a traceable relationship between the cost expiration and the production of revenue is frequently a matter of opinion.

The American Accounting Association's *Accounting Concepts and Standards Underlying Corporate Financial Statements* mentions three categories of expired costs. It states that costs should be regarded as expiring in the period in which there is:

(a) a direct identification or association with the revenue of the period, as in the case of merchandise delivered to customers;

(b) an indirect association with the revenue of the period, as in the case of office salaries or rent; or

(c) a measurable expiration of asset costs even though not associated with the production of revenue for the current period, as in the case of losses from flood or fire.

Cost expirations and cost residues. The end-of-period determination of cost expirations for income statement purposes is, of course, directly associated with the determination of asset valuations for balance sheet purposes. In a sense, an expense calculation is at the same time an asset valuation procedure, and vice versa.

In some situations the accountant approaches the problem of measuring expenses by determining the portion of the cost outlay that may fairly be assignable to future periods. Under this general approach, the expense figure is derived incidentally as a consequence of an asset calculation. Such asset computations may be made by taking an inventory of the items on hand and unused, or by relying on their estimated use-life as a basis, or by estimating the recoverable value of the particular asset.

In other situations, the accountant approaches the problem of expense measurement by computing the amount of cost outlay that has expired during the current period and that will have no usefulness or benefit to future periods, the amount carried forward being the residue to be assigned to future periods. The accountant will follow the approach most likely to produce a reasonably conclusive answer.

An illustration of each approach follows:

(1) Expense measurement approached from the point of view of asset valuation.

> An example would be the acceptable accounting practice of taking an inventory of tools on hand and reducing the fixed asset account balance to reflect the inventory; the amount written off is the expense for the period.

(2) Expense measurement approached from the point of view of expense computation.

> Accounting for the purchase and use of coal by a public utility or large industrial plant provides an example of this approach. As coal is acquired and dumped on the coal pile, an asset account is charged. As the coal is consumed, its quantity is determined and the cost is assigned to expense; the asset balance is the cost residue assignable to future periods.

Irrespective of the measurement approach, the accountant will disapprove carrying forward cost residues if there is no reasonable likelihood that they can be recovered, either through use or by sale. To illustrate, if significant in amount, the undepreciated cost of idle, excess plant should be written down to a figure reflecting an amount fairly assignable to future periods. Or the valuation of temporary investments should be reduced below cost if there is evidence that the amount invested cannot be recovered. Such considerations are always being weighed by the accountant.

In some cases it is practically impossible to arrive at a conclusive figure for the current period's cost expiration or for the residue to be carried forward for assignment to expense in future periods. Depreciation of fixed assets is an excellent example. There often is no way to be certain that the current charge for depreciation or the asset amount carried forward will prove to be even a reasonably correct approximation. The amortization of many intangibles is similarly subject to approximations that may prove to be substantially inaccurate.

"Anticipate no profit and provide for all possible losses." The accounting student of three decades ago was taught to apply to all questions involving income determination and asset valuation the precept, "Anticipate no profit and provide for all possible losses." It was the expression of the doctrine of conservatism—a doctrine which was given the position of greatest importance. In the matter of income recognition, the accountant took the position that, no matter how sure the businessman might be of capturing the bird in the bush, he, the accountant, must see it in the hand. And in the matter of loss recognition, the accountant again resisted optimism; loss recognition must not be postponed to the point of certainty. Moreover, he refused to accept actual realization of a loss as a necessary prerequisite to loss recognition, because this would have enabled management to postpone loss recognition by postponing asset disposals.

As noted earlier, conservatism is now regarded as a matter of lessened importance. Accountants no longer feel that they can merely say: It is conservative to provide for *all possible* losses; therefore, we will provide for them. They are coming more and more to apply certain criteria to the determination of the propriety of a loss provision. Among these criteria are the following:

(1) The loss should relate to assets owned or on order.
(2) The actual realization of the loss must be reasonably certain to occur within the foreseeable future.
(3) The prospect of loss should be such that a reasonable approximation of the amount can be made.

Savings versus income. A saving, but not income, results from manufacturing a thing at a price less than that at which it could be purchased.

Companies sometimes construct their own fixed assets, and when this is done at a cost lower than the price at which these could be purchased, there is often an inclination to value the fixed assets at a theoretical purchase price and to take up a "profit." There is a subtle semblance of fairness in such a procedure. Why should a company utilize its manufacturing facilities to make fixed assets for its own use and thus forego the opportunity of manufacturing merchandise that could be sold at a profit? The answer is that, even if the manufacture of fixed assets curtailed the manufacture of merchandise (which would be unlikely), the income statement should show what really happened instead of what might have happened. The manufacture of fixed assets may increase future net income by reducing depreciation charges, but a present saving with a prospect of increased future net income must not be confused with a present, realized gain.

Manufacturing merchandise at a cost lower than the price at which it could be purchased, or purchasing merchandise at a cost which is less than the normal market price, should not be regarded as producing income. Such an action may ultimately increase net income, but such an increase should be recognized as resulting from a reduction in the cost of goods sold rather than an increase in revenue; moreover, whether or not the gross profit will be increased is a problematical matter not determinable at the time of making the cost outlay.

The accounting procedure, sometimes adopted, of passing inventories from one stage of production to another at a market valuation in excess of cost (whether for the purpose of determining the "profit" resulting from manufacturing instead of buying or for the purpose of better measuring departmental performance) may provide management with information it believes useful and, of course, may properly be developed for internal uses but not for use in a company's financial statements.

Matching revenues and related expenses. In the determination of periodic net income, it is imperative that revenues and related expenses be reported in the same period. Thus, if revenue is deferred because it is regarded as not yet earned, all elements of expense related to such deferred revenue must be deferred also, in order to achieve the matching of revenue and expense which is essential to a proper determination of net income.

As a simple illustration, assume that commissions are paid to salesmen when orders are received for future delivery; to obtain a proper matching, the commissions should not be reported as an expense until the period in which the sales are reported as revenue.

In cases where a "future" expense is associated with current revenue, provisions for such future outlays should be made by charges to expense in the period when the related revenue is earned. Companies sometimes sell equipment or other merchandise with agreements to provide service for a period of time without cost to the purchaser; goods are sold with guarantees; a lessee may agree to return the leased property to the lessor at the end of the lease period in the condition in which it existed at the beginning of the lease; cemetery companies sell lots with agreements to provide perpetual care; pension systems are in operation; premium coupons redeemable in merchandise are issued. As a result of these and similar transactions and contracts, revenue may be earned in one period and expense payments applicable thereto may be made in subsequent periods. Such conditions may properly be, and frequently are, dealt with by taking revenues into income in the period in which they are earned and providing for the estimated future expense payments in the same period, by charges to operations. Any estimates so recorded should usually be shown with the liabilities because they generally are established to reflect obligations.

Another peculiar problem sometimes arises when some of the cost expenditures are applicable to future production. To illustrate, assume that the estimated cost of a logging railroad, adequate to meet the requirements of an entire timber tract, is $18,000; this cost should be spread equitably over all of the timber cut from the tract. A railroad from the waterfront one-half the distance to the back of the tract has been completed.

Assume that it is considered equitable to allocate half of the $18,000 total estimated cost to each half of the tract. If the first half of the road cost $12,000, only $9,000 of this cost should be charged against the product of the front half of the tract and $3,000 should be deferred. This deferred cost, plus the $6,000 completion cost, will produce a charge of $9,000 against the back half.

A concluding note. One should not attribute too much precision to the income-determination process. An income figure is an approximation, partly the product of facts objectively determined, partly the product of accounting policy decisions, and partly the product of judgment and estimate.

The lack of unanimity that exists regarding the inclusion or exclusion of certain items in the process of income determination is a serious matter. If the current operating concept of income determination has been applied, the reported income figures may be construed as those that may normally be expected in the future, provided that the currently prevailing business conditions and volume levels continue, because extraneous, extraordinary, and nonrecurring items do not affect the reported income. Obviously, income figures thus determined are more affected by judgment decisions than are those arrived at by following the all-inclusive concept of income determination. However, it may be relevant to observe that the actual position and earnings of a business are not altered by the income concept adopted; only the "appearance" is affected.

If the all-inclusive approach is used, the interpretation to place on income figures should be modified accordingly. Under this approach, the income statement becomes more of a report of accountability and less of an attempt at measuring normal earning power. Less judgment is required of the accountant because he does not have to decide whether some element of revenue or cost expiration is normal or is extraneous, extraordinary, or nonrecurring.

There can be no doubt that income figures are misunderstood and misinterpreted by many persons who have an interest in business earnings. Accountants cannot entirely escape responsibility for some of this lack of understanding. The variety of acceptable alternatives and the changes that occur within the area of acceptable practices are bound to be confusing to the nonaccountant. But it would be unrealistic to expect accounting to be static. Change is an inevitable feature of accounting in a relatively free economy. This characteristic was nicely described by Marquis G. Eaton, when he was president of the American Institute of Certified Public Accountants, in the following words:

> What is happening, in fact, is a never-ending search for better and more refined methods of reporting the truth about the financial affairs of corporations. But these affairs grow more and more complex, the truth is not clear and simple, and as a matter of fact there is no ultimate truth in the practical affairs of man. As George O. May once said, "Accounting can rise no higher in the scale of certainty than the events which it reflects."
>
> In this search for improved methods there are bound to be differences of opinion, at any given moment of time, as to which method among two or more alternatives, all supportable in theory and in logic, would yield the result most useful to all concerned. Experience alone reveals which one is superior, and that method eventually becomes generally adopted. Meanwhile, however, there are variations in practice.

Although accountants have expressed great interest in narrowing the areas of difference and accelerating the process whereby the superiority of one method over alternatives becomes known, very little "narrowing" has occurred. In the final analysis, the usefulness of financial statements is enhanced if they permit the making of meaningful comparisons between companies. Regrettably, the area of acceptable alternatives is so extensive at present that efforts to make comparisons will as likely prove misleading as informative.

CHAPTER

9

Cash

What is cash? Cash consists of legal tender, checks, bank drafts, money orders, and demand deposits in banks. In general, nothing should be considered unrestricted cash unless it is available to the management for disbursements of any nature.

Monies advanced to salesmen or other representatives for traveling and other expense disbursements have ceased to be under the control of the management for immediate disbursement for other purposes, and are therefore properly shown in the balance sheet as prepaid expense or receivables from employees.

Some concerns make a practice of allowing customers ordering goods by mail to make payment in postage stamps; such remittances should not be recorded as cash, but should be recorded as postage inventory.

The practice of carrying due bills or I.O.U.'s in the cash in place of money advanced to individuals should be discouraged. If they are found in the cash, they should be shown in the balance sheet as amounts receivable from officers, employees, and so forth, and not as cash.

Although checks payable to a company are usually included in its cash, there are some exceptions. If a check credited to a customer's account and sent to the bank for deposit is returned by the bank because of insufficient funds, the entry crediting the customer should be reversed. (A reversing entry is not necessary if the check is returned for lack of endorsement.) Postdated checks should not be recorded until the date when they can be deposited. Company officials and others in a position to do so sometimes "pay" the debit balance in their accounts by checks which it is understood will not be deposited; obviously, if there is any restriction upon the deposit or cashing of a check, the check is not an available source of current funds; any statement prepared while such a check is held should show the amount thereof as a receivable.

Deposits in savings accounts are usually classified in the balance sheet as cash, notwithstanding the legal right of the bank to demand a certain notice before withdrawal; the classification of such balances as cash appears to be justified, because the bank's right to demand notice is rarely exercised. Demand certificates of deposit may be classified as cash, but time certificates should not be so classified. A portion of the balance on deposit in an ordinary commercial checking account may not be subject to immediate withdrawal because, under the terms of a bank loan, the depositor is obligated to maintain a minimum or compensating balance; notwithstanding such restrictions, it is customary to include the entire bank balance as current cash.

Deposits in closed banks should not be regarded as current cash, nor should balances in foreign banks be so considered if they are subject to any restrictions. If the deposits in foreign banks are available for unrestricted withdrawal, they may be classified as current cash at an amount determined by conversion at the current exchange rate.

Cash deposits made in connection with contract or other bids, or deposits made in connection with purchase contracts, should be shown as deposits on contract bids or as advances against purchases, rather than as cash, even though the deposits are returnable in cash under certain circumstances.

A distinction should be made in the balance sheet between cash available for general operating purposes and cash tied up in special-purpose funds. If a fund is to be used for the payment of a current liability, as is the case with money deposited with a trustee for the payment of mortgage interest and taxes on mortgaged property, it should not be merged with the general cash. However, because the debt is a current liability, the special fund can properly be classified under the Current Assets caption, with a statement of the purpose for which it is available. Special funds not available for current purposes, such as a sinking fund for the payment of the principal of a long-term debt, a fund for the retirement of capital stock, or the proceeds of a construction mortgage which are impounded and available for disbursement only for construction work, should not be shown under the Current Assets caption.

Whether notes and acceptances endorsed to a bank should be shown in the balance sheet as cash or as receivables depends on whether the bank took the paper as deposits or merely for collection. If the bank credited the depositor's account with the paper, the item may properly be included in the cash; otherwise not.

Bank overdrafts. There is some difference of opinion among accountants as to the proper balance sheet treatment of overdrafts.

If there is only one bank account and this account is overdrawn, the amount of the overdraft must be shown as a liability.

If there are several bank accounts, one or more with overdrafts and one or more with available balances, and if the available balances are in excess of the overdrafts, it has until recently been regarded as permissible to show on the asset side of the balance sheet the excess of the available bank balances over the overdrafts, particularly if it is the company's practice to transfer funds from bank to bank as required. However, this opinion is no longer generally held, and it is now considered better practice to show the bank balances on the asset side and the overdrafts on the liability side. Some accountants still consider it permissible merely to show on the asset side the net available bank funds, provided that reference is made to the overdrafts by the use of some clearly descriptive balance sheet title, such as "Cash in Banks—Net of Overdrafts."

Some accountants have taken the position that, if the company's books show an overdraft, whereas the bank statement shows an available balance (the difference being represented by outstanding checks), such an overdraft may be offset against balances in other banks without disclosure in the balance sheet, disclosure being necessary only if the bank statement shows an overdraft. Such a distinction scarcely seems logical. If the checks are outstanding, the issuing company has no control over them and, so far as available funds are concerned, an overdraft in fact exists. Of course, if the checks have been merely drawn and recorded but have not been issued, and are therefore under the company's control, adjusting entries should be made to restore the amounts thereof to the bank balance and to the accounts payable.

Distorted cash balances. To make a better showing in its balance sheet, a company may resort to the practice of holding its cash book open for a few days after the close of the period and recording as of the last day of the period remittances received after the close of the period. Such a procedure has the effect of overstating the most current asset, cash, by correspondingly understating the less current asset of accounts receivable.

The company may then go one step further by drawing checks after the close of the period for payment of current liabilities, and recording such payments as of the last day of the period.

To illustrate the effect of this practice upon the current position shown by the balance sheet, let us assume that a company holds its cash book open for collections of receivables amounting to $25,000, and for payments totaling $20,000 on current liabilities. The true current position and the distorted position are shown below:

	Correct		Incorrect	
	Amount	Per Cent of Total Current Assets	Amount	Per Cent of Total Current Assets
Current assets:				
Cash	$ 5,000	5.88%	$10,000	15.38%
Accounts receivable	50,000	58.82	25,000	38.46
Inventories	30,000	35.30	30,000	46.16
Total current assets	$85,000	100.00%	$65,000	100.00%
Current liabilities:				
Accounts payable	50,000	58.82	30,000	46.16
Net current assets	$35,000	41.18%	$35,000	53.84%
Dollars of current assets per dollar of current liabilities	$1.70		$2.17	

By this artifice, the company shows a working capital ratio of 2.17 to 1 instead of 1.70 to 1, and considerably overstates its cash balance and the ratio of cash to total current assets, thus overstating the liquidity of its position.

Internal control. A system of internal control consists of a division and integration of procedures to such an extent that the activities of various members of an organization are so interrelated that accounting errors and omissions presumably will be detected automatically and the perpetration and concealment of fraud will require collusion.

An adequate system of internal control to safeguard the cash requires a control over both receipts and disbursements. The methods of effecting this control vary greatly; the system described below should be understood to be indicative of the objectives to be attained rather than a procedure to be invariably followed.

The danger of misappropriation of cash is reduced if collusion is made necessary to conceal an abstraction of cash receipts; it is therefore desirable to divide the work of handling cash receipts among several people, whose records must agree. One method of providing such an internal control is indicated below.

(1) All mail receipts and the totals of cash register tapes should be listed and totaled by a trusted employee who is neither the cashier nor a bookkeeper; the letter or other evidence of remittance accompanying each mail receipt should be marked by this employee with the amount of the remittance, initialed by him, and turned over to the accounts receivable bookkeeper, who should also be given duplicates of prenumbered receipts issued to customers for any cash received on account and rung up on the cash register. The cash should be turned in to the cashier, and a copy of the list mentioned above should be given to the general ledger bookkeeper.

(2) All cash received should be deposited daily. The cashier, after making up the deposit, should submit the deposit slip to the employee mentioned in (1), who should compare the amount of the deposit with the amount of cash received, as shown by his list; if the deposit slip and the list of receipts are in agreement, this employee should initial the deposit slip. When the bank's monthly statement is received, it should be checked by the general ledger bookkeeper, and the deposits shown by it should be compared by the employee mentioned in (1) with the daily lists prepared by him.

(3) The cashier, the general ledger bookkeeper, and the accounts receivable bookkeeper should be different persons.

(4) An added safeguard may be introduced by having a fifth individual reconcile the bank account.

With such a system of internal control, fraud with respect to collections from debtors cannot be practiced and concealed even for a day without collusion. The first employee has no access to the books and cannot falsify the records to conceal a misappropriation; he cannot expect to withhold funds received from debtors without detection because the debtors will receive statements or letters from the credit department and will report their remittances. If the cashier withholds any cash, his daily deposit will not agree with the first employee's list or with the general ledger bookkeeper's cash receipts record made from the list of receipts. The general ledger and accounts receivable ledger bookkeepers, having no access to the cash, have no opportunity to misappropriate any of it, and, therefore, have no incentive to falsify their records unless they are parties to collusion.

The bank should be instructed to cash no checks of outsiders payable to the company but should accept them only for deposit. Checks drawn by the company itself for petty cash or other requirements may be cashed.

Because all receipts are deposited daily in the bank, all disbursements (except from petty cash) must be made by check. Disbursements from petty cash should be approved by someone in authority, and periodical totals thereof should be represented by replenishing checks. The person authorized to sign checks should have no authority to make entries in any of the books; thus, a fraudulent disbursement by check could not be concealed without the collusion of two persons. A file of approved invoices, expense bills, and other documents evidencing the propriety of the disbursements should be maintained.

The collusion of a third person in the falsification of disbursements can be made necessary:

(1) Either by requiring that all checks shall be signed by one person and countersigned by another, or
(2) By allowing checks to be signed by one person, but only upon authorization by another person, evidenced by approved invoices, expense bills, and so forth. The documents presented to the authorizing person as evidence of the propriety of the disbursement should be initialed or otherwise marked by him to prevent their use a second time.

All checks should be prenumbered. All spoiled, mutilated, or voided checks should be preserved. Some companies even go so far as to require that such checks be recorded in their proper sequence in the cash disbursements record, without entry in the money column but with a notation to the effect that the check is void.

It is advisable to review the system of internal control from time to time to see whether any revisions are desirable as a result of changed operating conditions, and also to determine whether the system of internal control is actually being operated as planned or whether deviations or omissions have been allowed to impair the system.

Cash over and short account. As a part of the system of internal control, frequent and unannounced cash counts should be made by the internal auditing department. Any unlocated differences between the balance per books and the cash on hand and in bank, whether discovered by the accounting staff or by the internal auditing staff, may be set up in a Cash Over and Short account. If all reasonable efforts fail to disclose the cause of the shortage or overage, the account may be closed to Revenue and Expense.

Cash Over and Short should not be charged with an ascertained defalcation; the amount of a defalcation should be charged to a special account, which should be written off only in the event of failure to collect from the party responsible therefor or from a bonding company.

Imprest cash. In the discussion of internal control it was stated that all disbursements should be made by check. Petty expenditures not made by checks can nevertheless be represented by checks through the operation of an imprest cash, or petty cash, fund. A check is drawn for an amount which will provide for petty expenditures for a reasonable time, and cashed. The cash is held in the office. The drawing of the check is recorded by a debit to Petty Cash and a credit to the general Cash account. As expenditures are made from the petty cash fund, receipts and other memoranda are retained to evidence the nature and propriety of the disbursements. A petty cash book may be kept with a number of columns in which to classify the disbursements, or the classification may be made from the memoranda when the fund is replenished. When the fund is nearly exhausted, another check is cashed for the amount of the expenditures, thus restoring the fund to its original amount; this check is recorded by a credit to the general Cash account and debits to various expense or other accounts properly chargeable with the disbursements.

The petty cash fund should be replenished or increased only by check, and never from undeposited cash receipts. The fund should be replenished at the end of each accounting period, even though it is not depleted to the customary replenishing point, so that the disbursements will be recorded in the proper period. If the issuance of a replenishing check is overlooked at the end of the period, an adjusting journal entry may be made debiting the proper expense or other accounts and crediting Petty Cash; when a replenishing check is issued in a subsequent period, the Petty Cash account should be debited with the amount with which it was credited in the adjusting entry, and other accounts should be debited with the remainder of the replenishing check. Except for such possible credits and debits, no entries should be made in the Petty Cash account other than the original debit unless the established amount is increased or decreased.

When the petty cashier requests a replenishing check, he should submit a report of his disbursements, accompanied by receipts or other evidences of the authenticity of the disbursements. This report should be audited, and all of the supporting documents should be initialed, or otherwise marked, by the person who audits the report, so that the petty cashier cannot subsequently use the supporting receipts or other vouchers to obtain a check to which he is not entitled. The internal control over the petty cash fund is also improved by unexpected counts thereof made by the internal auditing staff.

The imprest system can be applied to the control of funds of small or large amounts required at factories, branches, or offices located at a distance from the main office.

Lapping. Lapping is a device for concealing a shortage; it consists of a series of postponements of entries for collections of receivables. Lapping would be difficult if not impossible without collusion in an office where the previously described system of internal control is in operation, but it would be possible if the cashier were also the bookkeeper.

To illustrate, assume that $100 in currency is received from *A* on account. The cashier pockets the money and makes no entry. But it is dangerous to leave *A*'s account uncredited for any length of time, because *A* may receive a statement and make a protest, which will bring the facts to light. Therefore, within a day or two, when $110 is collected from *B*, the cashier turns in $100 of the cash, debits Cash and credits *A* with $100, and pockets the extra $10. This process may be carried on indefinitely, the cashier being short all the time, but the credit to each customer's account being delayed only a few days.

If customers remit only by check, and no currency is received from other sources, a lapping of receipts will require the forging of endorsements, unless lax procedures enable the cashier to obtain funds on checks payable to the company. But if currency is received from cash sales or other sources, lapping can be carried on even though all remittances from debtors are received in the form of checks. For instance, assume the following chain of events:

Monday—A check for $100 is received from *X*, and $150 is received for cash sales. The cashier takes $100 of currency, deposits the remaining $50 of currency and *X*'s check, and makes the following entry:

Cash	150	
Sales		150

The shortage is $100, the amount of the unrecorded credit to *X*.

Tuesday—A check for $125 is received from *Y*, and $165 is received for cash sales. The cashier takes $25 of currency, deposits the remaining $140 of currency and *Y*'s check, and makes the following entry:

Cash	265	
X		100
Sales		165

The shortage is now $125, the amount of the unrecorded credit to *Y*.

(*Continued on page 165.*)

Wednesday—A check for $115 is received from *Z*, and $130 is received for cash sales. The cashier deposits the $115 check, the $130 of currency, and $10 from his pocket, and makes the following entry:

Cash	255	
Y		125
Sales		130

The shortage is now $115, the amount of the unrecorded credit to *Z*.

Noncash credits to customers. Another method of covering a shortage consists of taking money received from a customer and passing a noncash credit through the books, usually for some item such as returns and allowances. The system of safeguarding receipts already discussed will make this practice difficult; but, in addition, it is desirable to have all noncash credits supported by duplicate credit memorandums, which should be initialed by someone in authority other than the cashier.

Reconciliation of the bank account. The balance at the end of the month shown by the bank statement rarely agrees with the balance shown by the depositor's books.

Very frequently there are items on the depositor's books which do not appear on the bank statement. For instance, there may be outstanding checks (checks written by the depositor that have not as yet been presented to the bank for payment), and deposits mailed toward the end of the month may not reach the bank and be recorded on its books until the next month.

Less frequently there are items on the bank statement which do not appear on the depositor's books. For instance, the bank may have made collection or other charges which the depositor may not know about and record until the bank statement is received; or the bank may have credited the depositor with the proceeds of paper left with it for collection and the notice of collection may not have been received by the depositor before the end of the month.

The purpose of a bank reconciliation is to establish that reconciling items such as those just mentioned are the reason for the difference between the balance per bank statement and the balance per books and, thus, that there is agreement between the bank's records and the depositor's records.

First illustration. In this illustration, the reconciling items are:

A deposit in transit.
The outstanding checks.

These are items recorded on the books of the depositor but not as yet entered on the bank's records.

The bank charges.
The proceeds from a collection made by the bank for the depositor.

These are items recorded by the bank but not as yet recorded by the depositor.

The bank reconciliation appears below:

A B C **CORPORATION**

Bank Reconciliation—The City National Bank

December 31, 1965

Balance per bank statement			$10,361.51
Add:			
Deposit in transit—mailed December 31			9,849.83
Bank's charges:			
Telegram		$ 1.80	
Collection charges		1.17	2.97
Total			$20,214.31
Deduct:			
Outstanding checks:			
No. 1264	$1,000.00		
1329	52.80		
1499	84.70		
1510	108.07		
1511	2,500.00		
1512	3,281.70		
1513	3,370.91		
1514	100.80	$10,498.98	
Proceeds of draft on J. C. White collected by bank		500.00	10,998.98
Balance per books			$ 9,215.33

The company should make entries (equivalent to the one below) to record the items appearing on the bank statement but not on the books.

Cash	497.03	
Telephone and telegraph	1.80	
Collection and exchange	1.17	
Accounts receivable (J. C. White)		500.00

Second illustration. This illustration is based on the assumed facts of the first illustration, with some additional information, stated below.

Reconciliation—November 30, 1965—before the recording of items which were on the bank statement but not on the books:

Balance per bank statement	$11,216.22
Add: Deposit in transit	7,216.85
Bank's charges	3.15
Total	$18,436.22
Deduct outstanding checks	6,215.30
Balance per books	$12,220.92

Reconciliation—November 30, 1965—after recording items on the bank statement but not on the books:

Balance per bank statement	$11,216.22
Add deposit in transit	7,216.85
Total	$18,433.07
Deduct outstanding checks	6,215.30
Balance per books	$12,217.77

Summary of the depositor's books for December:

Balance in bank, November 30, 1965	$12,217.77
Add cash receipts—all deposited	47,763.78
Total	$59,981.55
Deduct disbursements—all by check	50,766.22
Balance in bank, December 31, 1965	$ 9,215.33

Summary of the bank statement for December:

Balance, November 30, 1965	$11,216.22
Credits for deposits	45,630.80
Total	$56,847.02
Charges for checks, et cetera	46,485.51
Balance, December 31, 1965	$10,361.51

The $45,630.80 total of deposits was determined by running an adding-machine tape of the deposits shown on the bank statement.

The $46,485.51 total of checks paid and other charges was determined by running an adding-machine tape of them, or by the following computation:

Balance, November 30, 1965, per bank statement	$11,216.22
Credits for deposits	45,630.80
Total	$56,847.02
Balance, December 31, 1965, per bank statement	10,361.51
Checks and other charges	$46,485.51

The reconciling items on December 31, 1965, as in the preceding illustration, were:

Deposit in transit	$ 9,849.83
Outstanding checks	10,498.98
Bank charges	2.97
Credit for collection made by bank	500.00

The reconciliation procedure described below is more than a bank reconciliation. It consists of three reconciliations:

(1) It is assumed that, in accordance with good internal control procedure, all cash receipts are deposited in the bank. The receipts by the bank, as shown by its statement, are reconciled with the receipts shown by the books.

(2) It is also assumed that all disbursements are made by check. The bank's disbursements and other charges are reconciled with the disbursements shown by the books.

(3) The balance shown by the bank statement is reconciled with the balance shown by the books.

The reconciliation statement is started as shown on page 168.

Observe that the first line consists of a summary of the bank statement for December. The first column shows the bank reconciliation on November 30, 1965, after the company recorded the items which were on the bank

ABC CORPORATION
Reconciliation of Receipts, Disbursements, and Bank Account
The City National Bank
For the Month of December, 1965

	Balance, Nov. 30, 1965	Add Receipts	Deduct Disbursements	Balance, Dec. 31, 1965
Per bank	$11,216.22	$45,630.80	$46,485.51	$10,361.51
Deposits in transit:				
November 30	7,216.85			
Outstanding checks:				
November 30	6,215.30*			
Per books	$12,217.77	$47,763.78	$50,766.22	$ 9,215.33

* Deduction.

statement for November but which had not been recorded before the bank statement was received. The last line is a summary of the depositor's cash records for December. The complete reconciliation statement is on page 169. The three reconciliations are made as follows:

(1) Reconciliation of receipts per bank statement ($45,630.80) with receipts per books ($47,763.78):

The $7,216.85 deposit in transit on November 30 was included in the receipts per books in November; therefore, it is deducted from the receipts per bank for December to reconcile with the receipts per books.

The $9,849.83 deposit in transit on December 31 is added to the receipts per bank to reconcile with the receipts per books.

The $500 collected by the bank for the depositor appeared on the bank statement but was not recorded on the books; therefore, it is deducted from the receipts per bank to reconcile with the receipts per books.

(2) Reconciliation of the disbursements per bank statement ($46,485.51) with the disbursements per books ($50,766.22):

The $6,215.30 of checks outstanding on November 30 were recorded on the books as disbursements prior to December; therefore, they are deducted from the December disbursements per bank to reconcile with the December disbursements per books.

The $10,498.98 of checks outstanding on December 31 are added to the disbursements per bank to reconcile with the disbursements per books.

The $2.97 of bank charges are not included in the disbursements per books; therefore, they are deducted from the disbursements per bank.

(3) The items in the bank reconciliation (last column) are the same as those in the first illustration.

The completed reconciliation appears below:

ABC **CORPORATION**

Reconciliation of Receipts, Disbursements, and Bank Account
The City National Bank
For the Month of December, 1965

	Balance, Nov. 30, 1965	Add Receipts	Deduct Disburse-ments	Balance Dec. 31, 1965
Per bank	$11,216.22	$45,630.80	$46,485.51	$10,361.51
Deposits in transit:				
November 30	7,216.85	7,216.85*		
December 31		9,849.83		9,849.83
Outstanding checks:				
November 30	6,215.30*		6,215.30*	
December 31			10,498.98	10,498.98*
Bank's charges			2.97*	2.97
Proceeds of draft collected by bank		500.00*		500.00*
Per books	$12,217.77	$47,763.78	$50,766.22	$ 9,215.33

* Deduction.

The treatment of the checks outstanding at the beginning and end of December does not mean that all of the checks which were outstanding on November 30 had cleared the bank in December, and that all of the checks which were outstanding on December 31 had been issued in December. Let us assume that, of the checks outstanding on December 31, check No. 1264 for $1,000.00 was issued in November. The outstanding checks *could have been shown* in the reconciliation statement as follows:

	Balance, Nov. 30, 1965	Add Receipts	Deduct Disburse-ments	Balance, Dec. 31, 1965
Outstanding checks:				
Issued prior to December	6,215.30*		5,215.30*	1,000.00*
Issued in December			9,498.98	9,498.98*

Using the standard procedure shown in the reconciliation statement, there is a net addition of $4,283.68 (the difference between $6,215.30 and $10,498.98) in the Disbursements column; in the alternative procedure, there is also a net addition of $4,283.68 (the difference between $5,215.30 and $9,498.98). And, by both procedures, the outstanding checks shown in the last column total $10,498.98.

In addition to reconciling the recorded receipts with the bank's credits, and reconciling the disbursements per books with the bank's charges, this procedure has the advantage of localizing errors. If there is an error in the cash receipts records (and there are no errors elsewhere), the Receipts column and the Balance (bank reconciliation) column will be "out" the same amount. The error is thus localized, and only the amounts in the Receipts column need be checked.

Third illustration. In all of the preceding illustrations, we have reconciled the balance per bank to the balance per books. But if there are items on the books which do not appear on the bank statement *and also* items on the bank statement which do not appear on the books, neither the balance per bank nor the balance per books is the true balance. In such cases it is advisable to reconcile the balance per bank and the balance per books to the correct, or adjusted balance. To illustrate, using the data in the preceding illustration, the reconciliation statement may be prepared as follows:

ABC CORPORATION
Bank Reconciliation—The City National Bank
December 31, 1965

Balance per bank statement	$10,361.51
Add deposit in transit	9,849.83
Total	$20,211.34
Deduct outstanding checks	10,498.98
Adjusted balance	$ 9,712.36
Balance per books	$ 9,215.33
Add proceeds of draft collected by bank	500.00
Total	$ 9,715.33
Deduct bank charges	2.97
Adjusted balance	$ 9,712.36

Fourth illustration. The following reconciliation of the bank account of Bailey Transformer Company includes several reconciling items not previously mentioned.

BAILEY TRANSFORMER COMPANY
Bank Reconciliation—The First National Bank
September 30, 1965

Balance per bank statement		$5,215.60
Add: Deposit in transit		723.90
Check of Bailey Transit Company charged to our account		350.00
Check of Henry Bigley returned for endorsement		216.50
Total		$6,506.00
Deduct outstanding checks:		
No. 2345	$115.21	
2347	579.99	
2362—Certified—$300.00		695.20
Adjusted balance		$5,810.80
Balance per books		$5,900.05
Add error in recording check No. 2357 as $297.20 instead of as $279.20, the amount for which it was drawn		18.00
Total		$5,918.05
Deduct: N.S.F. check—H. E. Gates	$ 75.50	
Check No. 132 issued in 1962, restored to cash balance in May, 1965, but now cleared	25.00	
Monthly service charge	6.75	107.25
Adjusted balance		$5,810.80

The items included in this reconciliation are:

The books of Bailey Transformer Company showed a balance of $5,900.05

in The First National Bank on September 30, 1965. There was a deposit of $723.90 in transit. The following checks had not cleared:

No. 2345	$115.21
2347	579.99
2362	300.00

Although check No. 2362 had not cleared, a memo accompanying the bank statement reported that the check had been certified, and consequently charged to the company's account. A check for $350.00 drawn by Bailey Transit Company was improperly charged to Bailey Transformer Company. Check No. 132 for $25.00 was issued in 1962; it was restored to the bank balance in May, 1965, as it was believed at that time that, having been outstanding so long, it would not be presented; the entry made in May was a debit to Cash and a credit to Miscellaneous Income. This check was paid by the bank in September with the approval of Bailey Transformer Company. Two checks deposited on September 29 were returned: One was a check for $75.50 received from H. E. Gates to apply on account, and returned because there were insufficient funds in the drawer's account to provide for payment of the check; the other was a check for $216.50 received from Henry Bigley, which was returned because it had not been endorsed by Bailey Transformer Company. The latter check was endorsed and redeposited on October 1. Check No. 2357 for $279.20 was improperly recorded as $297.20; the offsetting debit was to Purchases. The bank's service charge for September was $6.75.

Although check No. 2362 has not cleared the bank, it was certified and charged by the bank to the company's account; therefore, it is not shown as a reconciling item.

The check returned by the bank because of insufficient funds is shown as a deduction from the balance per books, because the check is not good and should be charged back to the maker.

The check returned for endorsement is added to the balance per bank because the check was immediately endorsed and redeposited.

The following entries should be made.

	Debit	Credit
Cash	18.00	
Purchases		18.00
To correct error in recording Check No. 2357 as $297.20 instead of $279.20.		
Accounts receivable (H. E. Gates)	75.50	
Cash		75.50
To charge Gates with check returned N.S.F.		
Bank service charges	6.75	
Cash		6.75
Charges for September.		
Miscellaneous income	25.00	
Cash		25.00
To reverse entry made in May, 1965, eliminating Check No. 132 from outstanding checks; it has now cleared.		

Estimating the cash position. For various reasons it may be desired to estimate the probable cash position during some future period. For instance, assume that a company wishes to obtain a loan at the bank, and the bank requests a statement showing the probable date when the loan can be repaid. On June 30, 1965, the company had the current assets and liabilities shown below.

Cash	$ 3,000
Accounts receivable	8,000
Merchandise	10,000
Accounts payable and accruals	7,000

Some of the merchandise in which the company deals is obtainable only in the summer months, and purchases are therefore high from June to September. The prospective purchases for the next six months are:

July	$10,000
August	9,000
September	8,000
October	6,000
November	5,000
December	4,000

The company wishes to borrow $5,000 on August 1, and assures the bank that the loan can be repaid at the end of December. The bank asks for a cash forecast, which appears on page 173. The forecast is based on the following facts and assumptions: The company's sales are fairly uniform through the year, averaging about $8,000 a month; they are made at an average gross profit of 25 per cent. Expenses paid immediately in cash average about $600 per month. It is assumed that liabilities for purchases and expenses will be paid in the month following that in which they are incurred, and that accounts receivable will be collected in the month following the month of sale.

Forecast of Cash and Current Position
For the Six Months Ending December 31, 1965

	Cash	Accounts Receivable	Merchandise	Accounts Payable and Accruals	Bank Loan
June 30:					
Balances	$ 3,000	$8,000	$10,000	$ 7,000	
July:					
Collections	8,000	8,000*			
Payments	7,000*			7,000*	
Sales		8,000	6,000*		
Purchases			10,000	10,000	
Expenses				600	
Balances	$ 4,000	$8,000	$14,000	$10,600	
August:					
Bank loan	5,000				$5,000
Collections	8,000	8,000*			
Payments	10,600*			10,600*	
Sales		8,000	6,000*		
Purchases			9,000	9,000	
Expenses				600	
Balances	$ 6,400	$8,000	$17,000	$ 9,600	$5,000
September:					
Collections	8,000	8,000*			
Payments	9,600*			9,600*	
Sales		8,000	6,000*		
Purchases			8,000	8,000	
Expenses				600	
Balances	$ 4,800	$8,000	$19,000	$ 8,600	$5,000
October:					
Collections	8,000	8,000*			
Payments	8,600*			8,600*	
Sales		8,000	6,000*		
Purchases			6,000	6,000	
Expenses				600	
Balances	$ 4,200	$8,000	$19,000	$ 6,600	$5,000
November:					
Collections	8,000	8,000*			
Payments	6,600*			6,600*	
Sales		8,000	6,000*		
Purchases			5,000	5,000	
Expenses				600	
Balances	$ 5,600	$8,000	$18,000	$ 5,600	$5,000
December:					
Collections	8,000	8,000*			
Payments	5,600*			5,600*	
Sales		8,000	6,000*		
Purchases			4,000	4,000	
Expenses				600	
Bank loan paid	5,000*				5,000*
Balances	$ 3,000	$8,000	$16,000	$ 4,600	$ –

* Deduction.

CHAPTER

10

Receivables

ACCOUNTS RECEIVABLE

Classification. Because accounts receivable are classed as current assets in the balance sheet, no balances (with a few exceptions mentioned later) should appear as accounts receivable unless they presumably will be converted into cash during the operating cycle.

Amounts receivable from officers, directors, and stockholders, except in instances where goods have been sold to them on account for collection in accordance with the regular credit terms, are not likely to be collected with any promptness and should be shown under some noncurrent caption.

Accounts for advances to stockholders, officers, and directors are often found on the books of close corporations, particularly if the business was previously conducted as a partnership. The former partners, having become accustomed to taking drawings, continue to do so, not realizing that, whereas partners are allowed to take drawings in any free and easy manner they desire, the profits of a corporation can be legally divided only by the formal declaration of a dividend. Until a dividend is declared, these advances are in the nature of loans, recoverable by creditors in case the corporation is unable to pay its debts.

Although advances to subsidiary companies are, in a sense, accounts receivable, they should not be included with customers' accounts in the balance sheet. Advances are usually of a more permanent nature and are not current. To show them in the balance sheet as accounts receivable is likely to be misleading: The casual reader of the balance sheet will probably obtain too favorable an impression of the financial position because of the overstatement of current assets and working capital. On the other hand, a more penetrating reader may compute the ratio of receivables to sales and may gain the unwarranted and unfavorable impression that too great a percentage of the period's sales remains uncollected, and that the receivables are therefore of dubious value.

Receivables resulting from sales to subsidiaries, collectible currently, can be included in accounts receivable under the Current Assets caption.

It has often been said that the term *accounts receivable* is too inclusive and that it should therefore be abandoned. The term *customers' accounts* has been suggested to take its place. *Trade debtors* has also been suggested as an even better term, because it corresponds with the similar term *trade creditors*.

A distinction should be made between the words *receivable* and *due*. An account receivable is a claim against a debtor. A receivable which is due is a claim which the creditor has a right to collect at the present time. Accounts receivable may be due, or not yet due. Hence, it is undesirable to speak of the total accounts receivable as "receivables due from customers" or by any other expression in which "due" is used improperly.

In most businesses, the terms of sale require payment within 30, 60, or 90 days, but in some types of business the accounts receivable are due in installments over a long period of time. It was formerly considered improper to include among current assets any receivables due beyond one year from the balance sheet date; Institute Bulletin No. 43 sanctions including in the current assets any "installment or deferred accounts and notes receivable if they conform generally to normal trade practices and terms within the business."

If special deposits made in connection with contract bids or for other purposes are likely to remain outstanding for considerable periods of time, they should not be classed as current assets.

Some receivables which can properly be classified as current assets should nevertheless be segregated from the receivables from customers. Some of these are: debit balances in suppliers' accounts; claims against railroads and other common carriers for damages to goods in transit; uncollected stock subscriptions; currently recoverable deposits made against contract bids; claims for cash refunds; declared dividends receivable on stock investments; insurance claims receivable; and advances on purchases. If the circumstances of a particular case indicate that collection will not be received currently, the item should not be classified under the current caption.

If contingent receivables such as claims under guarantees and amounts thought to be recoverable in litigation are placed on the books as a matter of record, proper consideration should be given to both the question of valuation and the question of classification in the balance sheet. The degree of probability of collection will determine the advisability of establishing an allowance account; the date of probable collection will determine the current or noncurrent classification.

Memorandum charges to consignees for goods shipped on consignment should not be included in accounts receivable because title to the merchandise has not passed to the consignee and there is no valid claim against him.

Receivables from consignees arise only upon the sales of the consigned goods.

Valuation. In the valuation of the total of customers' accounts, consideration should be given to certain possible deductions. These deductions are for:

Uncollectible accounts.
Freight.
Returns and allowances.
Discounts.

The deduction for uncollectible accounts is almost invariably applicable; the deductions for freight, returns and allowances, and discounts are applicable only under special circumstances.

Allowance for doubtful accounts. The creation of an allowance for doubtful accounts is intended to accomplish two results, namely:

To charge the loss by the sale of goods to customers whose accounts prove to be uncollectible against the period that caused the loss.
To show the estimated realizable value of the customers' accounts.

It is not always possible, however, to accomplish both of these results, as will be shown in the following discussion of methods of estimating the amounts to be credited to the allowance account.

The three customary procedures for computing the periodical credits to the allowance account are indicated below:

(1) Adjusting the allowance account to the amount of loss estimated by aging the accounts receivable and considering supplementary data.
(2) Adjusting the allowance account to a percentage of the accounts open at the end of the period.
(3) Increasing the allowance account by a percentage of the sales for the period.

The per cents used in the second and third methods are usually determined from the loss experience of prior periods. However, full consideration should be given to changes in economic conditions or in the credit policy of the company, because such changes may cause the losses to differ materially from those of the past.

Aging accounts. When this method is used, a list of all accounts may be made on working papers, with columns with various headings such as "Not due," "1 to 30 days past due," "31 to 60 days past due," and so forth. All accounts in the subsidiary ledger are then listed, and the component elements of the balances are classified in the proper columns.

An accounts receivable aging schedule, summarizing the data assembled in the working papers, is illustrated at the top of page 177.

The amount of the allowance account is then determined on the basis of the age of the past-due accounts. Supplementary information must also be considered, because it may be known that some accounts not past due are doubtful, whereas others long past due may be collectible. In this connec-

Age of Accounts Receivable
December 31, 1965 and 1964

	December 31, 1965		December 31, 1964	
	Amount	Per Cent of Total	Amount	Per Cent of Total
Not due	$15,000	30.93%	$20,000	41.67%
1 to 30 days past due	12,000	24.74	16,000	33.33
31 to 60 days past due	8,000	16.50	5,000	10.42
61 to 90 days past due	6,000	12.37	4,500	9.38
91 to 120 days past due	4,000	8.25	1,000	2.08
More than 120 days past due	2,000	4.12	1,000	2.08
Bankrupt or with attorneys	1,500	3.09	500	1.04
Total	$48,500	100.00%	$48,000	100.00%

tion, the credit terms must, of course, be taken into consideration, for the terms will determine when an account is past due.

This method has the advantage of accomplishing the second of the two objectives stated above, because it results in a fairly accurate valuation of the accounts on the books. However, it may easily result in a failure to distribute losses to the periods during which they were caused. Bad debt losses are caused by making sales to customers who do not pay their accounts. Theoretically, therefore, provision for the loss should be made in the period in which the sales were made. But, if the aging method is used, accounts may not appear to be uncollectible until a date subsequent to the period of sale; in that case the loss, or the provision therefor, will not be charged to income until a period subsequent to that of the sale. Thus, one period will get the credit for the income and a later period will get the charge for the loss.

Percentage of open accounts. If a company's experience indicates that a certain per cent of the accounts open at any date will ultimately prove uncollectible, the total allowance requirement at any date can be estimated by multiplying the open account balances by the loss experience per cent. The allowance account is then credited with an amount sufficient to increase the existing balance to the estimated required balance. The theory of this method is the same as the theory of the preceding method; the difference lies in the procedure of estimating the total allowance requirement. It is not a method to be recommended; it is subject to the disadvantage pointed out in connection with the aging method, and it is difficult to obtain experience data from which to make a reliable estimate of the per cent to be applied.

Percentage of sales. The best matching of revenues and expenses (or losses) for a period is usually made by crediting the allowance account at the end of the period with a percentage of the sales of the period. The rate is computed on the basis of the statistics of sales and bad debt losses of the past periods. Theoretically, the rate should be computed by dividing the losses of past periods by the charge sales of past periods, not by the total sales. The rate thus ascertained should be applied to the charge sales for the current period. But, practically, it makes very little difference whether or not this distinction is made. By using the total sales to compute the rate, a per cent is obtained lower than that which results from dividing losses by credit sales. This lower rate is then applied to the total sales for the period instead of to the credit sales.

If statements are prepared monthly, it is important that allowance provisions be made monthly rather than annually; otherwise, the monthly balance sheets may show very inaccurate net valuations of the receivables. Assume that balance sheets are prepared monthly, but no provision for losses on the year's sales is made until the end of the year. Obviously, in all balance sheets prepared before the close of the year, the receivables will be shown without provision for losses on receivables which arose from sales during the year—presumably, the major portion of the receivables. On the other hand, if an adequate allowance account exists throughout the year by reason of provisions in prior years, the year-end provision based on the total sales for the year will produce an excessive allowance account.

When the credit to the allowance account is computed as a percentage of sales, there is some danger that the account balance may become excessive or may prove to be inadequate, regardless of whether provisions are made monthly or annually. For this reason, the accounts receivable should be reviewed from time to time for the purpose of estimating probable losses, the amount of which can be compared with the existing allowance account balance. If it is excessive or inadequate, the per cent applied to sales should be revised accordingly.

Recoveries. If a collection is made on an account once charged off as uncollectible, the customer's account should be recharged with the amount collected, and possibly with the entire amount previously written off if it is now expected that collection will be received in full. The collection should then be credited to the customer's account. These entries are made in the customer's account so that it will show that the debtor has attempted to re-establish his credit by the payment.

What account should be credited when the customer's account is recharged? From the standpoint of theory, the following may be said:

It is conservative to credit recoveries to the allowance account if the credits to it were determined by multiplying the sales by a per cent representing the relation of net bad debt losses (losses less recoveries) to sales. It is not correct if the per cent used in computing the provision represents the relation of gross write-offs to sales; in this case, recoveries should be credited to an income account.

If the allowance account was credited on a valuation basis (by aging the accounts or using a per cent representing the relation of losses to account balances), it makes no difference, from a theoretical standpoint, whether recoveries are credited to the allowance account, to the Bad Debts expense account, or to an income account, as the allowance account balance and likewise the net income will be the same in any

> case. For, if a recovery is credited to the allowance account, the amount to be charged to expense at the end of the period to raise the allowance account to its required balance will be reduced by the amount of the recovery; if the recovery is credited to the Bad Debts expense account or to an income account, the charge for the current provision will be correspondingly increased; the net income will be the same by either method.

From a practical standpoint, the choice of methods is usually of no serious consequence, because the loss reserve and the net operating charge for bad debts are usually matters of estimate; the theoretical considerations, therefore, seem to be of no great practical importance unless recoveries are of abnormally large amounts.

Freight. Merchants sometimes sell goods f.o.b. destination but ship the goods "freight collect," with an understanding that the purchaser will pay the freight charges to the transportation company and deduct the amount thereof in making his remittance. In such instances, any freight to be deducted in the settlement of accounts which are open at the end of the period should be deducted from the accounts receivable by setting up a contra account with the offsetting debit to the expense account for freight charges.

In this connection it is worth noting that the customer is entitled to discount on the full amount of the invoice, and not on the amount of the invoice less the freight. If the shipper paid the freight, the invoice would not be subject to a freight deduction, and discount would probably be taken on the whole amount of the invoice. The purchaser should not suffer a loss of discount merely because he pays the freight for the seller.

Returns and allowances. Should a contra account be set up to provide for the probable allowances to be credited to customers on accounts open at the end of the period, and for losses represented by the difference between probable credits for returns and the valuation which can properly be placed on the goods returned to inventory? Theoretically, yes, because otherwise the realizable value of the accounts receivable, as well as the net sales, would be overstated. In practice the provision is rarely made.

Provision for discounts. From a theoretical standpoint, a contra account should be set up for the discounts which will probably be taken on the accounts receivable; otherwise, the net realizable value of the receivables presumably will be overstated. However, the creation of such a contra account is not customary, and the charge to income to set up such an account is not deductible for federal income tax purposes.

Discounts on returned sales. Assume that a customer buys goods invoiced at $1,000, subject to a 2% discount, and that he pays the invoice within the discount period with a check for $980. Subsequently he returns one-tenth of the goods, which had been billed to him at $100 and which were paid for at the net amount of $98. What credit should he receive? Although this is largely a matter of policy, it would seem that the credit should be $98 if the customer is to be reimbursed in cash, and $100 if the credit is to be traded out. The reason behind this conclusion may be made clearer by assuming that the entire invoice is returned. If a credit of $1,000 were allowed, to be paid in cash, the discount privilege could be abused, for the customer who paid $980 could obtain $1,000 in cash; on the other hand, if a credit of only $980 were allowed, payable in merchandise, the customer would lose the benefit of having paid his bill within the discount period.

Credit balances. If the subsidiary accounts receivable ledger contains accounts with credit balances, the balance of the controlling account will be the difference between the total of the debit balances and the total of the credit balances in the subsidiary ledger. At what figure should the accounts receivable be shown in the balance sheet? The accounts receivable should be shown at the total of the debit balances, and the credit balances should be shown on the liability side of the balance sheet, as a separate item: Credit balances of customers' accounts.

Accounts receivable financing. Some businesses, usually because they are not sufficiently established to obtain an assurance of funds from a bank, finance their current operations to some extent by utilizing their accounts receivable. The procedures are of two kinds: open accounts receivable financing and factoring.

Open accounts receivable financing. Under this procedure an agreement is made with a finance company to advance funds against accounts receivable for a definite period of time, usually a year, with a provision that the contract can be terminated by written notice by either the client or the finance company six months prior to the termination date stated in the contract. The contract states the percentage of the accounts which the finance company will advance. The rate ranges from 75% to 90%, depending on the quality of the accounts and their average size, as well as the financial status of the client. An 80% rate is normal.

The client usually pledges the receivables as collateral to the obligation for the funds advanced, with full recourse to the client if an account is not collected when due.

Such financing usually is done on a nonnotification basis; that is, the client's customer is not informed that his account has been assigned to a finance company. The client makes the collections and agrees to transmit them, in the form in which received, to the finance company, which deposits them. The finance company makes arrangements with its bank to use a code endorsement, so that the checks returned to the customers will bear no evidence that the accounts have been financed.

Because the amount received from the finance company at the time of the financing is less than the amount of the receivables, the client retains an equity in the accounts, which the finance company credits to the client. Any returns, allowances, and discounts reduce the equity. If the equity is exhausted or reduced to an amount which the finance company regards as an inadequate cushion of protection, the client sends the finance company a check in an amount sufficient to create an acceptable equity. When accounts are collected, the related equity may be paid to the client immediately or periodically.

The finance company's charges consist of interest, usually at a daily rate of 1/30 of 1% applied

Sometimes to the daily uncollected balances of the accounts; for instance, if the uncollected balances on a certain day totaled $75,000, the interest charge for the day would be 1/30 of 1% of $75,000, or $25.

Sometimes to the cash-advanced element of the daily uncollected balances; for instance, if the amount originally advanced was 80% of the accounts, the interest charge for the day would be 1/30 of 1% of ($75,000 × 80%), or $20.

Because of the contingent liability which the client assumes in open accounts receivable financing, the transaction is similar in nature to the discounting of notes receivable and may be similarly recorded. To illustrate, assume that $10,000 of accounts receivable were financed and that $8,000 in cash was advanced to the client. The entry to record the financing would be:

Cash	8,000	
Equity in assigned accounts	2,000	
Accounts receivable assigned		10,000

The ledger should indicate the accounts that have been assigned.

The balance sheet presentation at this point, assuming that the company has $20,000 of unassigned accounts, would be:

Current assets:		
Accounts receivable	$20,000	
Equity in assigned accounts	2,000	$22,000

The balance sheet should disclose, preferably by a footnote, the contingent liability on the financed accounts. This is always the total of the uncollected balances of the assigned accounts, minus the equity. The footnote might state:

> On December 31, 19–, the company was contingently liable in the amount of $8,000 on accounts receivable financed.

Assume a return or an allowance of $175; the following entries would be required:

Sales returns and allowances	175	
Equity in assigned accounts		175
Accounts receivable assigned	175	
Accounts receivable		175

No entries to cash should be made for collections on assigned accounts; they do not belong to the company but must be forwarded to the finance company. However, they should be recorded in the company's books to show the reduction in the accounts receivable assigned and in the contingent liability. If a $2,000 account is collected, with or without a deduction for discount, the entry should be:

Accounts receivable assigned	2,000	
Accounts receivable		2,000
(Details should be posted to the accounts receivable ledger.)		

Assuming that a $40 discount was taken, the following additional entry would be required:

Sales discounts	40	
Equity in assigned accounts		40

The contingent liability to be shown in a balance sheet footnote at this point is computed as follows:

Uncollected balances of assigned accounts:			
Original amount		$10,000	
Deduct:			
Collections—including cash discounts	$2,000		
Returns and allowances	175	2,175	$7,825
Deduct equity:			
Original amount		$ 2,000	
Deduct:			
Returns and allowances	$ 175		
Cash discounts	40	215	1,785
Contingent liability			$6,040

The finance company's interest charges are reported to the client monthly and are payable in cash.

The above discussion is descriptive of usual procedures, but there are some variations among finance companies.

Factoring. Factoring is the outright purchase of receivables by a factor. The purchase is made on a notification basis, and the customer makes his remittances direct to the factor, who assumes the responsibility of keeping the receivable records and collecting delinquent accounts.

Before merchandise is shipped to a customer, the client requests the factor's credit approval. If it is obtained, the account is sold to the factor immediately after shipment of the goods. The factor credits the client's account for the amount of the invoice less the amount of the permitted cash discount, and less the factor's commission and a holdback intended primarily to absorb charges for returns and allowances. The per cent of holdback (applied to the face of the account minus cash discount and commission) is a matter of agreement, but is normally about 20%. After there is no further prospect of returns and allowances or anything else that reduces the amount of the receivable, any remaining balance in the holdback is returned to the client. The client assumes no responsibility for loss.

The factor's compensation consists of:

Commission, which is a percentage of the net amount of the invoice—the gross amount minus available cash discount. The commission is a charge for the service of passing on credits, assuming all credit risks, and keeping the accounts. It usually varies from 1%, or somewhat less, to 2% or more, depending upon the amount of work and risk involved. Customary rates are 1⅛% or 1¼%.

Interest, which is computed—usually at 6% per annum or at an equivalent daily rate—on amounts withdrawn by the client before the due date. Withdrawals can be made on the due date interest free. After the due date, interest (also usually at 6%) accrues to the client on any amounts not withdrawn.

The "due date" of a single invoice is ten days after the date on which the discount period expires. Clients frequently sell several invoices to a factor at the same time. It then becomes necessary to compute the average due date. This is done as follows:

(1) Select an arbitrary "focal date"; the most convenient focal date is the last day of the month preceding the earliest due date of any of the invoices.
(2) Determine, for each invoice, the number of days between the focal date and the date on which the discount period expires.
(3) Multiply the net amount (gross amount minus available discount) of each invoice by the number of days between the focal date and the date when the discount period expires, to determine an amount called *dollar-days.*
(4) Add the net invoice amounts.
(5) Add the dollar-days amounts.
(6) Divide the dollar-days total by the net invoice total. The quotient is the number of days between the focal date and the average discount period expiration date.
(7) Add ten days to this quotient to determine the average "due date."

To illustrate, assume that four invoices, all subject to 2% discount if paid within ten days, are sold to a factor on August 28. The computation (using August 31 as the focal date) of the average due date is shown below.

Invoice Date	Latest Discount Date	Invoice Amount Gross	Invoice Amount Net	Days Between Focal Date and Latest Discount Date	Dollar-Days
Aug. 28	Sept. 7	$1,000	$ 980	7	6,860
26	5	1,500	1,470	5	7,350
25	4	2,500	2,450	4	9,800
30	9	3,000	2,940	9	26,460
		$8,000	$7,840		50,470

50,470 ÷ 7,840 = 6.4 (rounded off to 6) Days from focal date to average discount period expiration date.
September 6 + 10 = September 16, the average "due date."

Assuming that the commission rate is 1¼% and that the holdback rate is 20%, the client's entry to record the factoring will be:

Sales discounts (2% of $8,000)	160.00	
Factoring commission (1¼% of $7,840)	98.00	
Factor's holdback [20% of ($8,000 − $258)]	1,548.40	
Factor	6,193.60	
Accounts receivable		8,000.00

As with accounts receivable financing, it should be observed that factors' procedures are not entirely uniform.

NOTES AND ACCEPTANCES RECEIVABLE

Definitions. A *note* is defined by the Uniform Negotiable Instruments Law as follows:

> A negotiable promissory note within the meaning of this act is an unconditional promise in writing made by one person to another, signed by the maker, engaging to pay on demand or at a fixed or determinable future time a sum certain in money to order or to bearer.

A *bill of exchange* is defined by the same law as follows:

> A bill of exchange is an unconditional order in writing addressed by one person to another, signed by the person giving it, requiring the person to whom it is addressed to pay on demand or at a fixed or determinable future time a sum certain in money to order or to bearer.

After a bill of exchange has been accepted by the drawee, it becomes an acceptance.

A *trade acceptance,* as defined by the Federal Reserve Board, is a "bill of exchange, drawn by the seller on the purchaser, of goods sold, and accepted by such purchaser."

Terminology. Because bills of exchange instead of notes have been commonly used in England, the terms *bills receivable* and *bills payable* found their way into American terminology. However, the terms *notes receivable* and *notes payable* have now come into general use as more exactly indicative of the form of paper most in use here. If the bulk of a company's paper is in the form of notes, there is no serious objection to recording a few acceptances in the note accounts. But if acceptances are frequently used, it may be desirable to distinguish between the two classes of paper in the accounts by the terms *notes receivable* and *acceptances receivable,* and *notes payable* and *acceptances payable.*

Advantages of trade acceptances. Banks usually prefer to discount a customer's trade acceptance receivable rather than to discount his own note payable—for two reasons. First, the acceptance is two-name paper, a primary liability of the acceptor and a secondary liability of the drawer. Second, it is "self-liquidating"; because the acceptance arose out of a purchase of goods, it is assumed that sales will provide the funds with which to pay the paper.

From the standpoint of the selling merchant, the trade acceptance is preferable to the open account because (1) it is a written promise to pay a stated amount at an agreed date; (2) it relieves the seller of the financial burden of tying up a considerable portion of his capital in customers' accounts, because acceptances can be discounted at the bank more readily and more cheaply than accounts receivable can be assigned; and (3) it may reduce losses from bad debts.

Because trade acceptances are assumed to have a better credit standing than notes receivable, because the nature of their origin makes them presumably self-liquidating, it may be advisable to show them as separate items in the balance sheet if they are of any considerable amount.

Dishonored notes. When a note has reached its maturity and been presented to the maker without being collected, it is said to have been *dishonored.* It should then be taken out of the Notes Receivable account and transferred to the customer's account by the following entry:

Accounts receivable (John Doe)	500	
Notes receivable		500
To charge Doe's dishonored note back to his account. (The purpose of this entry is to show the dishonor of the note in Doe's account for purposes of credit information.)		

If the dishonored note bore interest, the Interest Earned account should be credited and the maker of the note should be debited. This should be done in order to maintain a record of the interest earned and the total amount receivable from the debtor. If any protest fees were paid, they should be charged to the maker. Any amount regarded as uncollectible should be written off.

It has been suggested that dishonored notes be passed on to a Dishonored Notes Receivable account, thus:

Dishonored notes receivable	500	
Accounts receivable (John Doe)		500
To transfer the note to a dishonored notes account.		

This entry takes the item out of the accounts receivable, which are assumed to be current and collectible, and shows its true nature as a past-due note.

Credit limit on notes and accounts. When the credit department fixes a maximum credit limit for a customer, and when customers settle their accounts by notes, it may be desirable to keep the records in such a way as to show the combined liability of each customer on notes and on account. This purpose can be accomplished by providing customers' accounts with two debit and two credit columns, the inner columns to be used as memorandum note columns. When a customer is credited with a note in the outer credit column, he is also charged in the inner, or memorandum, debit column. When he pays the note, Notes Receivable is credited and a memorandum entry is made in the inner credit column of the customer's personal account. Thus, the balance of the outer columns will show the customer's liability on open account, and the balance of the inner columns will show his liability on notes.

Valuation of, and losses on, notes. Notes receivable, whether interest-bearing or without interest, are stated in the accounts and the balance sheet at their face. Because noninterest-bearing notes are not worth their face until maturity, it would be theoretically correct to reduce their gross valuation by the deduction of discount to maturity. Such an accounting refinement is not, however, recognized in practice.

If ample provision is made in the allowance account (reserve for bad debts) for losses on notes as well as on accounts, note losses should be charged to the allowance account. If the provisions made to the allowance account are not intended to be sufficient to cover losses on both classes of receivables, the note losses should be charged to an expense account.

When estimating the amount required for possible losses on notes, it may be advisable to determine whether the notes were received in the regular course of trade and in accordance with settlement terms made at the time of sale, or were taken from debtors whose accounts had become old and were not immediately collectible. Notes of the latter class are obviously less likely to be collected than those of the former class.

Bank discount. The bank discount and the proceeds of a note or acceptance discounted at a bank are computed as follows:

Compute the value of the note at maturity.
- The value of a noninterest-bearing note is its face.
- The value of an interest-bearing note is its face plus interest, at the rate stated by the note, for the full term of the note.

Compute the bank discount; this is equivalent to interest, on the value at maturity and at the discount rate, for the discount period.

Deduct the discount from the value at maturity.

Three illustrations are given below. In each case the principal of the note is $600, its date is June 15, it is due in 60 days, and it is discounted on June 27. The discount period, therefore, is 48 days. The discount rate is 6%. The first column shows the computation if the note does not bear interest; the second column shows the computation if the note bears 4% interest; the third column shows the computation if the note bears 7%.

	No Interest	4% Interest	7% Interest
Value at maturity:			
Face of note	$600.00	$600.00	$600.00
Interest on face for term of note:			
None			
At 4% for 60 days		4.00	
At 7% for 60 days			7.00
Value at maturity	$600.00	$604.00	$607.00
Bank discount at 6% for 48 days:			
On $600	4.80		
On $604		4.83	
On $607			4.86
Proceeds	$595.20	$599.17	$602.14

Notes receivable discounted. When a note or an acceptance receivable is discounted, the credit should be made to Notes Receivable Discounted or Acceptances Receivable Discounted, to show the contingent liability resulting from the endorsement.

The traditional method of recording the discounting of a note or an acceptance receivable involved a debit to Interest Expense or a credit to Interest Earned for the difference between the face of the paper and the proceeds. Entries made in this manner, based on the foregoing illustrations, are shown below:

Cash	595.20	
Interest expense	4.80	
Notes receivable discounted		600.00
Cash	599.17	
Interest expense	.83	
Notes receivable discounted		600.00
Cash	602.14	
Interest earned		2.14
Notes receivable discounted		600.00

Such entries do not appear to give adequate expression to the facts if the paper is interest-bearing. They ignore the interest earned between the date of the note and the date of discounting. They also ignore the fact that we are parting with two assets (the note and the accrued interest) and that there is a loss or gain equal to the difference between the total amount of these assets and the proceeds of the note.

Referring to the 4% note, the facts are:

Assets parted with:	
Face of note	$600.00
Accrued interest on $600 for 12 days at 4%	.80
Total	$600.80
Proceeds	599.17
Loss	$ 1.63

and the following entries would appear desirable:

Accrued interest receivable	.80	
Interest earned		.80
Cash	599.17	
Loss on discounting notes receivable	1.63	
Accrued interest receivable		.80
Notes receivable discounted		600.00

Referring to the 7% note, the facts are:

Proceeds		$602.14
Assets parted with:		
Face of note	$600.00	
Accrued interest at 7% for 12 days	1.40	
Total		601.40
Gain		$ .74

and the entries shown on the top of page 188 should be made:

Accrued interest receivable	1.40	
Interest earned		1.40
Cash	602.14	
Accrued interest receivable		1.40
Notes receivable discounted		600.00
Gain on discounting notes receivable		.74

If an Accrued Interest Receivable account stands debited with an interest accrual applicable to the note being discounted, recorded by an adjusting entry at the close of a prior period, the amount of the credit to Accrued Interest Receivable in the entry to record the discounting should be the sum of the prior accrual and the interest accrued since the date of the adjusting entry.

Contingent liability in the balance sheet. It was formerly the custom to indicate the contingent liability on discounted paper by a deduction in the balance sheet, thus:

Current assets:		
Notes receivable	$5,000	
Less notes receivable discounted	1,000	
Notes receivable on hand		$4,000

Modern practice appears to favor the method of showing on the asset side only the notes receivable on hand, with a footnote indicating the contingent liability, thus:

Current assets:	
Notes receivable	$4,000

Note. The company was contingently liable on December 31, 1965, in the amount of $1,000 on customers' notes discounted.

Payment by maker. If a discounted note is paid by the maker, the contingent liability should disappear from the endorser's books. This is accomplished by debiting Notes Receivable Discounted and crediting Notes Receivable.

Because notice of dishonor must be given to the endorser promptly in order to hold him, the endorser may safely assume that a discounted note has been paid at maturity unless he receives notice to the contrary within a few days after the maturity of the paper.

Payment by endorser. Assume that the $600 note, bearing 7% interest, the proceeds of which were computed on page 186, could not be collected from the maker, and that the bank obtained collection from the endorser. Assume that the total collected included the face, the $7 interest payable on the note, and protest fees of $4.30. The endorser's entries are:

Accounts receivable (maker)	611.30	
Cash		611.30
Payment of note discounted June 27, and interest and protest fees.		
Notes receivable discounted	600.00	
Notes receivable		600.00
To eliminate the note and the contingent liability from the accounts.		

Endorsement without recourse. According to the Uniform Negotiable Instruments Law:

> Every person negotiating an instrument by delivery or by a qualified indorsement, warrants:
> (1) That the instrument is genuine and in all respects what it purports to be;
> (2) That he has a good title to it;
> (3) That all prior parties had capacity to contract;
> (4) That he has no knowledge of any fact which would impair the validity of the instrument or render it valueless.

As compared with the contingent liability arising from an unqualified endorsement, these warranties implied by an endorsement without recourse impose so slight a liability that it is usually ignored, and notes transferred by such endorsements are credited to Notes Receivable instead of to Notes Receivable Discounted.

CHAPTER

11

Inventories

Introductory note. Inventories are a source of some of the most difficult accounting problems, both theoretical and practical. Although there is much settled opinion relating to the subject of inventories, there are many points on which there is a noticeable absence of settled opinion. Accountants, individually and collectively, have given, and continue to give, considerable thought to inventory matters, and fresh areas of theory seem to be constantly opening up. To some extent, this condition will remain as long as businesses continue to expand and become more complex and as long as commodity prices continue to change. A dynamic business economy is not conducive to static accounting theory.

Classes of inventories. The inventory of a concern that buys its goods in condition for sale is usually called a *merchandise inventory*. Merchandise inventories are found in wholesale and retail businesses. These businesses do not alter the form of the goods purchased for sale.

Manufacturing concerns have the following classes of inventories:

Finished goods.
Goods in process.
Materials.
Manufacturing supplies.

Finished goods consist of manufactured articles which are ready for sale.

Goods in process consist of partially manufactured goods, and their cost includes the material, labor, and manufacturing overhead applicable to them.

Materials consist of articles purchased for use in manufacture but on which no work has been done by the concern inventorying them. Work may have been done on them by the concern from which they were purchased. Thus, things which are finished goods for one concern may be materials for another. If parts are manufactured before they are required, and are held for future use in manufacturing, they may be classed as finished parts, but they are usually included in the materials inventory.

Manufacturing supplies are distinguished from materials in the manner stated below.

Materials can be directly associated with, and become a part of, the finished product; and they are used in sufficient amounts to make it practicable to allocate their costs to the product.

Some manufacturing supplies, like lubricants, are used indirectly in the process of manufacture and do not become part of the finished product. Some other things classified as manufacturing supplies, like paint and nails, do become part of the finished product, but the amounts involved are so insignificant that it is impracticable to attempt to allocate their costs directly to the product; however, they find their way into the product cost as part of the manufacturing overhead.

The inventories discussed thus far may be listed under the Inventories caption in the current asset group. Because the expenditures for both manufacturing supplies and materials are made for the purpose of producing merchantable goods, there seems to be no theoretical necessity for considering supplies to be less current than materials; both will enter into the cost of manufacture and will be converted into cash by the sale of the product.

Supplies which will be charged to selling and general expense are of a somewhat different nature. Shipping supplies and office supplies are examples. These are more appropriately classified as prepaid expenses but they may be shown under the Current Assets caption.

Some companies classify under the Inventories caption of the balance sheet any advances made to vendors against purchase commitments. This seems to be of doubtful propriety, because the company does not have title to the related merchandise. Such advances should probably appear in the balance sheet after the inventories. Current assets, with the exception of prepaid expenses, are usually marshalled under the current caption in the order of their liquidity—cash, receivables, and inventories. Advances on purchase commitments are less current than goods on hand. Wherever the advances appear, they should be clearly distinguished from debit balances in suppliers' accounts resulting from merchandise returns, overpayments, and other similar causes. Prepaid expenses are shown as the last item under the current caption.

Inventory all goods owned. What should be included in the inventory, and what should be excluded therefrom? The general rule is that the inventory should include all goods for which the company holds title, wherever they may be.

If goods sold under contract or ordered by customers for future delivery are being held in stock, it is important to determine whether title has passed. The mere fact that the goods have been segregated from other merchandise may or may not mean that title has passed to the vendee. If title has passed, the goods should be excluded from the inventory; if title has not passed, they should be included.

On the other hand, goods which have been ordered but not received at the balance sheet date may properly belong in the inventory. If the goods are in transit, the general rule as to passing of title is as follows: If the goods were shipped f.o.b. shipping point, they belong to the purchaser; if they were shipped f.o.b. destination and have not arrived at the destination, they belong to the seller. If merchandise purchases are in transit and title has passed, it is advisable to postpone the completion of the inventory tabulation until the merchandise has been received and checked into stock; this procedure will avoid inventory errors arising from differences between merchandise merely invoiced to the company and merchandise received in good condition. Because the completion of the inventory-taking normally requires some time, the checking of the receipt of merchandise in transit will not ordinarily cause any delay.

Two types of errors may result from a failure to include all owned goods in the inventory.

First, the purchase may be recorded, and the goods may be omitted from the inventory. This omission, of course, results in an understatement of net income.

Second, no entry may be made for the purchase, and the goods may be omitted from the inventory. This omission does not result in an understatement of net income, because the purchases and the closing inventory are equally understated. The practice is to be condemned, however, because it results in an incorrect showing of purchases and inventory in the income statement, and also because it understates the current assets and current liabilities in the balance sheet. Thus, the current financial position appears more favorable than the facts really warrant, partly because the working capital ratio is overstated, and partly because, in many instances, the accounts payable will have to be paid before the merchandise is sold and converted into cash.

Inventory pricing. There are a number of acceptable bases for pricing inventories. Some are considered acceptable only under special circumstances, whereas others are widely applicable. In matters relating to inventory pricing, consistency of method is of prime importance. The principal pricing bases may be listed as follows:

(1) Cost.
(2) Cost or market, whichever is lower.
(3) Selling price.

In this chapter we shall deal with matters related to inventory pricing on a cost basis. Pricing on a cost-or-market basis is discussed in Chapter 12.

Incidental costs. Cost includes not only the purchase price but also any additional costs necessary to placing the goods on the shelves. These incidental costs include duties, freight or other transportation costs, storage, insurance while the goods are being transported or stored, and expenses incurred during any aging period. The total of these items is clearly an addition to the total purchase price of all goods; it is not a simple matter, however, to apply the incidental costs to individual purchases and to determine what portion of the total incidental costs is applicable to the goods in the inventory. Some incidental costs may be easily applied to the particular goods on which the costs were incurred. Other costs may be prorated on a percentage basis; such a distribution is not likely to be strictly accurate, because the incidental costs are not usually incurred in amounts exactly proportionate to the cost of the merchandise. Greater accuracy may be obtained by an attempt to apply each expense bill to its corresponding invoice, but this procedure usually involves more labor and expense than are warranted by the slightly greater degree of accuracy.

Theoretically, there is some justification for regarding the cost of operating the purchasing department as a part of the cost of the merchandise acquired and including an element of such cost in the inventory valuations. However, such a procedure is not usually regarded as practicable or advisable. In the first place, it involves the allocation of general overhead to the purchasing department and thus raises questions as to an equitable determination of the cost of operating the department. In the second place, such a procedure necessitates the apportioning of the purchasing department cost to the various purchases during the period and to the various classes of goods in the inventory at the end of the period, and questions arise as to an appropriate basis for the apportionment of such costs.

If the incidental costs are immaterial, the accountant will consent to either their inclusion or their exclusion for inventory-pricing purposes, on a consistent basis. This does not mean that all incidental costs must be treated alike; for instance, it is acceptable to include freight and exclude storage costs, or vice versa. And it does not follow that, if freight charges are included in computing one section of the inventory, they must be included in computing the other sections of the inventory; but if freight charges are included in pricing an inventory or any section of an inventory, then that practice should be consistently followed over the years.

Manufacturing costs. The purchase price of materials and merchandise bought can, of course, be determined from invoices. But the cost of goods in process and the cost of finished goods can be determined only by keeping accurate cost records showing costs of materials, labor, and overhead assignable to the product.

Some companies have followed the practice of omitting manufacturing overhead from the inventory valuation, on the theory that this is a conservative procedure. There seems to be no more propriety in omitting the overhead element of manufacturing cost than in omitting the material or labor cost.

A similar conclusion seems justified in the case of a fairly recent proposal favoring a procedure known as *direct costing*. Advocates of direct costing contend that manufacturing costs should be divided into two main categories, variable and fixed, and that no portion of the latter should be assigned to inventories or used in computing the inventory valuation. Following this plan, fixed manufacturing costs (those that do not vary with changes in the volume of output) would be treated as expenses of the period, as selling and administrative expenses are treated; only variable costs would be considered when determining cost for inventory purposes. Those arguing in favor of direct costing point out that the plan minimizes the problem of overhead application (which, in practice, is often arbitrary and questionable) because fewer costs are subject to allocation. It is also mentioned that direct costing lends itself to more meaningful cost analyses. For example, changes in the volume of output usually result in considerable fluctuations in unit costs. This effect is primarily attributable to the impact of fixed costs, which are mostly beyond the control of management, at least in the short run. As a consequence, the usefulness of unit cost data is impaired because management is not able to determine readily whether a change in unit cost is the result of a change in volume or the result of poor control over those costs that are subject to management's control. On the other hand, variations in unit costs under direct costing would signal cost variations presumably subject to managerial control, because fixed costs would be expensed and not included in unit cost data. But the point remains that under direct costing a portion of the costs of manufacturing would be ignored for inventory-valuation purposes—which is not a commendable result, considering the effects on financial statements.

The allocation of the total production costs during a period to those goods which have been completed and to those which remain in process is admittedly a difficult problem. Elaborate cost records may be used for this purpose. In the absence of such records, it may be necessary to compute unit costs, for purposes of inventory pricing, from general accounting and production data. If there was work in process at the beginning and/or the end of the period, and if there was any change in the quantity or stage of completion of the work in process at the two dates, unit costs of goods completed during the period cannot be computed by dividing the total manufacturing costs for the period by the number of units of product completed during the period. Consideration must be given to the inventories of work in process at the beginning and end of the period, and to the stages of completion thereof. To illustrate, assume the facts at the top of page 195.

The amounts shown in the 1965 Costs column cannot be divided by the 9,800 units completed in 1965 to obtain unit costs, for two reasons: (1) some of these costs were incurred to complete the work in process on December 31, 1964, and (2) some of the costs were incurred on the work still in process on December 31, 1965.

	Work in Process—Stage of Completion	1965 Costs
Work in process—December 31, 1964—400 units:		
Materials	75%	
Direct labor	50	
1965 cost and production data:		
Cost of material placed in production		$30,000
Direct labor cost		39,600
Overhead (125% of direct labor)		49,500
Units completed—9,800.		
Work in process—December 31, 1965—500 units:		
Materials	100%	
Direct labor	60	

If we take into consideration the work done on the beginning and ending inventories, we can compute the *equivalent production* for the period. This information will enable us to arrive at unit costs for inventory-pricing purposes. The computation of equivalent production is illustrated below:

Computation of Equivalent Quantities Produced—1965

	Materials	Direct Labor
Units completed in 1965	9,800	9,800
Work in process—December 31, 1964—400 units:		
75% of the material was put into process in 1964; hence, 300 units (75%) must be deducted as applicable to 1964	300	
50% of the labor was performed in 1964; hence, 200 units (50%) must be deducted as applicable to 1964		200
Remainder	9,500	9,600
Work in process—December 31, 1965—500 units:		
100% of the material was put into process; hence, 500 units must be added to production quantity	500	
60% of the labor was performed; hence, 300 units must be added to production quantity		300
Equivalent production—1965	10,000	9,900

We can now compute the unit costs applicable to the 1965 ending inventories of finished goods and work in process, as follows:

Unit costs:		
Materials	$30,000 ÷ 10,000	$ 3
Direct labor	$39,600 ÷ 9,900	4
Overhead	125% of direct labor	5
Total		$12

The inventory computations are shown on page 196. Quantity and stage-of-completion data were previously given for the work in process. It is assumed that 1,000 units of finished goods are on hand at the end of 1965.

Cost of finished goods on hand, December 31, 1965:		
Finished goods	1,000 units at $12	$12,000
Cost of work in process, December 31, 1965:		
Materials	500 units 100% complete at $3	$ 1,500
Direct labor	500 units 60% complete at $4	1,200
Overhead	125% of direct labor	1,500
Total		$ 4,200

The foregoing does not constitute a discussion of cost accounting. Its purpose is merely to indicate some of the difficulties involved in the ascertainment of costs in manufacturing concerns.

Standard costs. It is not uncommon for manufacturing concerns to price their work in process and finished goods inventories by using standard costs. There are several varieties of standard costs; they may be developed by relying on time and motion studies, past costs and manufacturing performances, expected costs and manufacturing performance, theoretical costs, or some combination thereof. They may be described as predetermined costs or estimated costs.

To illustrate, the material requirements for a given product are computed and the quantity required to complete one unit of product is priced, perhaps at current purchase prices or at expected purchase prices. Labor cost per unit of product is similarly developed, perhaps by reference to production studies or past performance. And finally, estimated overhead is allocated on the basis of an expected or average volume of production.

As products are completed, the finished goods are charged to the inventory account on the basis of their standard costs. Actual costs probably will differ from predetermined costs, with the result that cost-variance balances will develop in the accounts. These variances are commonly closed to Cost of Sales. For inventory-pricing purposes, it is desirable to review standard costs periodically to see that they do not deviate significantly from actual costs.

Relation of purchase discounts to cost. From a theoretical standpoint, purchase discounts are unquestionably cost reductions. However, because of the amount of work involved, it does not seem reasonable for accountants to insist that they be so treated in the accounts.

If purchase discounts are considered in the computation of cost for purposes of inventory pricing, they should be classified in the income statement in the cost of sales section. If purchase discounts are ignored for inventory-pricing purposes, it might seem to follow that they should be treated in the income statement as financial income. However, there appears to be no objection to classifying purchase discounts as a deduction from purchases in the cost of sales section of the income statement even though they are ignored in the development of cost figures for inventory purposes.

Apportioned costs. A special problem arises when a whole, acquired at a lump price, is divided into parts which, because of differences in nature or in quality, are to be sold at different prices. To determine a cost for the parts sold and a cost for the parts remaining in the inventory, it is necessary to make an apportionment of the lump-sum price.

To illustrate, assume that land is purchased, developed, and subdivided into cemetery lots. The total cost, assumed to be $60,000, may be apportioned to individual lots in the ratio of selling price, thus:

Selling Price Per Lot	Number of Lots	Product	Per Cent of Total	Apportioned Cost Total	Apportioned Cost Per Lot
$200	40	$ 8,000	8%	$ 4,800	$120
500	60	30,000	30	18,000	300
600	80	48,000	48	28,800	360
700	20	14,000	14	8,400	420
Total		$100,000	100%	$60,000	

Lost costs. Cost for inventory purposes may be less than the total original cost because, under some circumstances, it may be apparent that the costs invested in the inventory may not be fully recoverable. This condition may be the result of style changes, technological improvements, deterioration, spoilage, or damage attributable to storm or fire. Whatever the cause, the implication is the same: All or a portion of a cost outlay for merchandise or goods on hand has been lost.

A strict cost basis would be unrealistic if it required all items in the inventory to be priced at full cost irrespective of their potential realizable value. To avoid stating a current asset at an amount in excess of its realizable value, it is customary, even though the basis is described as a cost basis, to price inventory items below cost whenever it is apparent that the cost outlay cannot be recovered through sale in the ordinary course of business.

If an item has once been priced in an inventory below cost, the lower amount becomes a "new" cost for accounting purposes. Items once reduced for inventory purposes should not be reinstated to their original cost in a subsequent period.

COST SELECTION FOR INVENTORY PRICING

Identical goods may be purchased or produced at different costs. Consequently, accountants are faced with the problem of determining which costs apply to the goods that have been sold and which costs apply to the goods that remain in the inventory. Most of the acceptable methods of selecting the costs to be regarded as applicable to the inventory are based on an assumption regarding either:

The flow of goods—for example, an assumption that goods are sold in the order in which they are purchased or produced; or

The flow of costs—for example, an assumption that the most recent costs are applicable to the goods sold, and that the earlier costs are applicable to the goods on hand.

Several methods of selecting the costs which are to be regarded as applicable to the inventory are discussed in the following sections.

For purposes of illustration, assume that the inventory and purchases data are as shown below:

Beginning inventory:	100 units at $1.00	$100
First purchase:	200 units at 1.10	220
Second purchase:	250 units at 1.20	300
Third purchase:	100 units at 1.25	125
Fourth purchase:	150 units at 1.30	195
Total	800	$940

There are 200 units in the ending inventory.

Specific identification. If the goods on hand can be identified as pertaining to specific purchases or specific production orders, they may be inventoried at the costs shown by the invoices or the cost records. Specific identification requires the keeping of records by which goods can be definitely identified and their costs determined.

Although this method appears to have an excellent logical foundation, it is often impossible or impracticable to apply.

Last invoice price. Under this method, the cost applicable to the last purchase transaction is used to price the entire inventory quantity. In other words, $1.30 would be applied to the 200 units in the inventory. If there is a rapid physical turnover of the inventory in the normal course of the business, and the goods are sold in approximately the same order in which they are acquired, the last invoice price may closely approximate the results produced by the use of the specific-identification method, with much less clerical effort.

Simple-average method. The simple arithmetical average of the unit prices is determined by adding the unit costs of the beginning inventory and all purchases and dividing by the number of purchases plus one (for the beginning inventory). Using the foregoing data, the simple average unit cost and the inventory valuation are computed as follows:

$$\text{Unit cost} = \frac{\$1.00 + \$1.10 + \$1.20 + \$1.25 + \$1.30}{5} = \$1.17$$

$$\text{Inventory valuation} = \$1.17 \times 200 = \$234$$

This is a rather illogical method, because the unit prices applicable to large and small purchases are given the same weight in the computation.

Weighted-average method. The cost of the purchases plus the beginning inventory is divided by the total units purchased plus those in the beginning inventory, and a weighted-average unit cost is thus determined. Applied to the foregoing data, this method produces an inventory valuation computed as follows:

Total cost—$940
Total units—800

Unit cost = \$940 ÷ 800 = \$1.175
Inventory valuation = \$1.175 × 200 = \$235

This method is theoretically illogical because it is based on an assumption that all sales are made proportionately from all acquisitions, and that inventories will forever contain some goods of the earliest acquisitions—assumptions which are contrary to ordinary merchandising procedure.

Because the costs determined by the weighted-average method are affected by purchases early in the period as well as those toward the end of the period, there may be a considerable lag between purchase costs and inventory valuations. Thus, on a rising market the weighted-average costs will be less than current costs, and on a falling market the weighted-average costs will be in excess of the current costs.

Moving-average method. This method may be used when perpetual inventories are kept, new unit average costs being computed after each purchase. Assume that the purchases stated in the preceding illustration and the sales were made in the sequence set forth in the following tabulation, which shows how the moving-average unit costs are computed. Each sale is costed out at the latest computed moving-average cost, and the resulting inventory valuation is on the moving-average unit-cost basis.

	Units	Unit Cost	Amount	Moving-Average Cost
Beginning inventory	100	\$1.00	\$100.00	\$1.00
First purchase	200	1.10	220.00	
Inventory	300		\$320.00	1.0666
First sale	175	1.0666	186.67	
Inventory	125		\$133.33	
Second purchase	250	1.20	300.00	
Inventory	375		\$433.33	1.1555
Second sale	275	1.1555	317.78	
Inventory	100		\$115.55	
Third purchase	100	1.25	125.00	
Inventory	200		\$240.55	1.2028
Third sale	50	1.2028	60.14	
Inventory	150		\$180.41	
Fourth sale	100	1.2028	120.28	
Inventory	50		\$ 60.13	
Fourth purchase	150	1.30	195.00	
Inventory	200		\$255.13	1.27565

This method is subject to the same theoretical objection as applied to the weighted-average method. There is implicit in the method an assumption that each sale consists in part of merchandise from each preceding purchase, which is contrary to general merchandising procedure. Moreover, because the cost applied to the inventory is affected to some extent by the cost of all purchases, there is (as in the weighted-average method) a lag between market prices and inventory valuations. However, the lag is less pronounced in the moving-average method than in the weighted-average method.

Widely fluctuating costs. A modification of the moving-average cost computation is peculiarly suited for the determining of monthly inventory valuations when unit costs vary widely from month to month because of differences in the quantity of production. To illustrate, let us assume that a company manufactures a product which sells heavily in warm months and poorly in cold months, and that its production fluctuates with sales. The following are the quantities and the monthly costs of production during two years:

	1964			1965		
	Units Produced	Total Cost	Unit Cost	Units Produced	Total Cost	Unit Cost
January	100	$ 1,660	$16.600	90	$ 1,705	$18.944
February	115	1,738	15.113	75	1,688	22.507
March	220	2,232	10.145	250	2,195	8.780
April	3,200	8,745	2.733	3,720	10,503	2.823
May	4,600	11,935	2.595	4,360	11,700	2.683
June	5,950	13,665	2.297	6,325	15,260	2.413
July	6,300	15,060	2.390	6,720	16,800	2.500
August	6,750	15,855	2.349	7,310	18,215	2.492
September	5,200	13,470	2.590	6,205	16,225	2.615
October	850	4,170	4.906	960	4,515	4.703
November	300	2,475	8.250	412	2,925	7.100
December	140	1,940	13.857	125	2,025	16.200
Totals and averages	33,725	$92,945	2.756	36,552	$103,756	2.839

High unit costs appear in the months of low production because a large fixed overhead is distributed over a small number of units.

The inventories at the close of the year can be valued at the average costs for the year: $2.756 at the end of 1964, and $2.839 at the close of 1965. But what basis can be used for the valuation of monthly inventories, if monthly statements are desired? Obviously, the monthly unit costs would not be appropriate, because of their wide fluctuation. Nor would it be entirely correct to use, in the 1965 monthly statements, the average cost for 1964 ($2.756), because 1965 costs appear to be on a higher level, as evidenced by the higher average for the year ($2.839).

A moving-average cost, computed in the manner illustrated below, appears suitable for such a situation.

	Units			Cost			
	This Year (Add)	Last Year (Deduct)	Twelve Months	This Year (Add)	Last Year (Deduct)	Twelve Months	Moving Average
Year 1964			33,725			$ 92,945	$2.756
Year 1965:							
January	90	100	33,715	$ 1,705	$ 1,660	92,990	2.758
February	75	115	33,675	1,688	1,738	92,940	2.760
March	250	220	33,705	2,195	2,232	92,903	2.756
April	3,720	3,200	34,225	10,503	8,745	94,661	2.766
May	4,360	4,600	33,985	11,700	11,935	94,426	2.778
June	6,325	5,950	34,360	15,260	13,665	96,021	2.795

	Units			Cost			
	This Year (Add)	Last Year (Deduct)	Twelve Months	This Year (Add)	Last Year (Deduct)	Twelve Months	Moving Average
July	6,720	6,300	34,780	16,800	15,060	97,761	2.811
August	7,310	6,750	35,340	18,215	15,855	100,121	2.833
September	6,205	5,200	36,345	16,225	13,470	102,876	2.831
October	960	850	36,455	4,515	4,170	103,221	2.831
November	412	300	36,567	2,925	2,475	103,671	2.835
December	125	140	36,552	2,025	1,940	103,756	2.839

The moving-average cost (using January as an example) is computed as follows:

	Units	Cost
Total—Twelve months ended December 31, 1964	33,725	$92,945
Add amounts for January, 1965	90	1,705
Total	33,815	$94,650
Deduct amounts for January, 1964	100	1,660
Total—Twelve months ended January 31, 1965	33,715	$92,990

$92,990 ÷ 33,715 = $2.758.

The use of such a moving-average cost eliminates the irrational fluctuations in inventory values that would result from pricing the monthly inventories at the widely varying unit costs of production during the busy and slack seasons. The moving-average costs are preferable to the average cost of the preceding year, because the moving averages are affected by the factors that increased the average yearly unit costs from $2.756 in 1964 to $2.839 in 1965.

In the application of this moving-average cost theory, the sales each month, as well as the inventory at the end of the month, should be costed on the moving-average basis. This method will result in overabsorptions and underabsorptions of cost in the monthly statements, and will probably require an adjustment at the end of the year for the net overabsorption or underabsorption. For example, the underabsorption for January 1965 (costing the opening inventory at the $2.756 average for 1964, and the sales and the January 31 inventory at the January average of $2.758) would be determined as follows:

Inventory, December 31, 1964	1,200 units at $2.756	$3,307.20
January production	90 units at actual cost	1,705.00
Total	1,290 units	$5,012.20
January sales	120 units at $2.758	$ 330.96
Inventory, January 31, 1965	1,170 units at 2.758	3,226.86
Total		$3,557.82
Underabsorption of costs		$1,454.38

The cumulative underabsorptions and overabsorptions of cost during the year, computed similarly, are shown on page 202.

	Underabsorption-Overabsorption*
End of:	
January	$ 1,454.38
February	2,933.04
March	4,443.56
April	4,651.80
May	4,231.09
June	1,799.21
July	301.50*
August	2,820.76*
September	4,159.78*
October	2,362.54*
November	611.94*
December	1,051.46

The cumulative adjustment for the year, $1,051.46, is only slightly more than 1% of the actual costs for the year.

First-in, first-out (*fifo*) method. This method is based on an assumption regarding the flow of goods: The goods on hand are considered to be those most recently purchased. Using the data on page 199, the inventory is assumed to be composed of goods:

From the fourth purchase: 150 units at $1.30	$195.00
From the third purchase: 50 units at 1.25	62.50
Total	$257.50

The assumption that the older stock is usually the first to be disposed of is generally in accordance with good merchandising policy. There are, of course, exceptions in practice; for instance, the first coal dumped on a dealer's pile will be the last sold. This method has also been considered desirable because it produces an inventory valuation which is in conformity with price trends; because the inventory is priced at the most recent costs, the pricings follow the trend of the market.

A perpetual inventory record maintained on the first-in, first-out basis appears below:

Perpetual Inventory—First-in, First-out Basis

	Quantity			Cost		
Date	Into Stock	Out of Stock	Balance	Into Stock	Out of Stock	Balance
June 1			100			$100.00
5	200		300	$220.00		320.00
8		175	125		$182.50	137.50
13	250		375	300.00		437.50
18		275	100		317.50	120.00
23	100		200	125.00		245.00
25		50	150		60.00	185.00
26		100	50		122.50	62.50
29	150		200	195.00		257.50

The first sale consisted of:

100 units at a cost of $1.00 each (beginning inventory)	$100.00
75 units at a cost of 1.10 each (first purchase)	82.50
Total	$182.50

The inventory after the first sale consisted of 125 units at a cost of $1.10 each.

The second sale consisted of:

125 units at a cost of $1.10 each (first purchase)	$137.50
150 units at a cost of 1.20 each (second purchase)	180.00
Total	$317.50

The inventory after the second sale consisted of 100 units at a cost of $1.20.

The third sale consisted of:

50 units at a cost of $1.20 (second purchase)	$ 60.00

The inventory after the third sale consisted of:

50 units at $1.20 (second purchase)	$ 60.00
100 units at 1.25 (third purchase)	125.00
Total	$185.00

The same computational procedure would be applied to the fourth sale and fourth purchase for the month.

The first-in, first-out method can be applied without great difficulty even though perpetual inventories are not maintained; it is necessary only to determine prices shown by the most recent invoices for quantities sufficient to equal the number of units in the inventory.

Last-in, first-out (*lifo*) method. This method, based on an assumption regarding a flow of costs, is discussed in Chapter 13.

Gross profit method. The gross profit method of approximating an inventory is based on the assumption that the per cent of gross profit should be approximately the same in successive periods. This does not mean that the amount of gross profit should be the same, because the amount of profit will depend upon the volume of sales; it means only that the rate of gross profit on sales is assumed to be uniform. If, for instance, the rate of gross profit has been uniformly about 25% of the sales for a number of past years, it is assumed that the rate was 25% during the current period. If this assumption is in reasonable conformity with the facts, then it should be possible to approximate, with a fair degree of accuracy, the inventory at the end of the current period.

To illustrate, assume the following data:

Inventory—January 1	$ 10,000
Purchases for the year	94,000
Net sales for the year	124,000

Average rate of gross profit in recent years, 25% of sales.

What should be the approximate inventory on December 31?

Inventory—January 1		$ 10,000
Purchases		94,000
Total		$104,000
Deduct approximate cost of goods sold:		
Sales—net	$124,000	
Less estimated gross profit:		
25% of $124,000	31,000	93,000
Approximate inventory—December 31		$ 11,000

If the rate of gross profit is a composite produced by selling several types or classes of merchandise at different gross profit rates, sales and purchases data must be classified by gross profit classes. The gross profit method is applied to each inventory class. To illustrate, assume the following:

Article *A* is marked to produce a gross profit of 20%.
Article *B* is marked to produce a gross profit of 40%.
Last year's gross profit on all sales was 25%.

Computation of Inventories—Gross Profit Method
Current Year

	A	*B*	Total
Inventory—January 1	$15,000	$ 25,000	$ 40,000
Purchases for the year	80,000	120,000	200,000
Total	$95,000	$145,000	$240,000
Deduct approximate cost of goods sold:			
Sales—net	$90,000	$210,000	$300,000
Less estimated gross profit:			
20% of $90,000	18,000		18,000
40% of $210,000		84,000	84,000
Approximate cost of goods sold	$72,000	$126,000	$198,000
Approximate inventory—December 31	$23,000	$ 19,000	$ 42,000

If the data had not been classified by commodity, the combined inventory would have been estimated at $15,000, as illustrated below:

		Combined
Inventory—January 1 ($15,000 plus $25,000)		$ 40,000
Purchases for the year ($80,000 plus $120,000)		200,000
Total		$240,000
Deduct approximate cost of goods sold:		
Sales ($90,000 plus $210,000)—net	$300,000	
Less estimated gross profit:		
25% of $300,000	75,000	225,000
Approximate inventory—December 31		$ 15,000

In the above illustration, the average rate of gross profit of the business as a whole for the preceding year was an unreliable measure to apply in approximating inventories for the current year because of the significant change that occurred in the average rate of gross profit. Last year's gross profit margin on all sales was 25%, whereas the gross profit margin on all sales for the current year is probably in the neighborhood of 34%. This is evident from the following computation.

Sales, current year—net	$300,000	100%
Approximate cost of goods sold ($72,000 + $126,000)	198,000	
Approximate gross profit	$102,000	34%

If there are any conditions present in the current year that would result in a change in the rate of gross profit, the gross profit method, being based on prior gross margin data, will not produce reliable inventory approximations.

Uses of gross profit method. The gross profit method may be used by an auditor as one of the means of verifying an inventory; for instance, referring to the illustration on page 204, if the December 31 inventory submitted to the auditor was $25,000, whereas the gross profit method indicated that the inventory should be approximately $11,000, either a satisfactory explanation of the increase in the rate of gross profit would have to be forthcoming, or the auditor would have reason to believe that the inventory was overstated. An ending inventory of $25,000 would imply that the gross profit margin had increased to 36% in contrast to the 25% rate which had prevailed in past periods. The gross profit method may also be used to approximate the cost of an inventory which has been destroyed by fire or lost through theft.

Merchandise turnovers based on the average of the inventories at the beginning and the end of the year will be inaccurate if the year-end inventories differ materially in amount from those carried during the year. This error will be avoided if the average of monthly inventories is used. If such inventories are not available, they may be estimated by the gross profit method.

Long-term contracts. A special inventory-valuation problem arises for businesses engaged in the construction of bridges, ships, dams, and similar assets which generally require more than one annual accounting period for their completion. There are two generally accepted accounting methods for dealing with such contracts:

The completed-contract method—No income is taken up until the contract is completed; hence, cost is the valuation basis for any work in process.

The percentage-of-completion method—Income is taken up as the work progresses; hence, the asset accounts will include an increment above cost for the amount of income taken up.

Completed-contract method. Under this method the balance sheet will show, usually as a current asset, the costs incurred to date less progress billings. Businesses engaged in construction work are often able to identify some of their general and administrative expenses as being incurred in direct support of particular construction jobs. Thus, it may be appropriate to include some of the general and administrative expenses with the more direct construction costs being accumulated in the accounts, rather than to regard them entirely as period costs; this procedure may result in a better matching of revenue and expense, particularly in a year in which no contracts were completed.

If progress billings exceed the accumulated contract costs, the excess should be shown as a contra account deducted from the receivables arising from the progress billings.

This method has the advantage of minimizing guesswork, which is more or less inherent in the percentage-of-completion method. Its disadvantage lies in the fact that, because income is taken up in the year of completion, the amounts reported as net income for several successive years may vary widely although operations were fairly uniform through the years.

Although income is not taken up under this method before completion, if a loss appears to be in prospect, provision should be made for it in the accounts.

Percentage-of-completion method. Under this method income is taken up as work is performed. Long-term contracts generally specify the timing and amounts of bills that may be submitted to the customer as the work progresses. Such progress billings do not, as a rule, provide a reasonable basis on which to take up income. The percentage of completion, which is used as the basis for income recognition, is generally determined by one of the following methods:

(1) By a comparison of costs incurred to date with total estimated costs for the entire contract.
(2) By a study of engineering data pertinent for a determination of stage of completion for the project.

An example of income determination based on a study of accumulated costs and estimated future costs is set forth below.

Contract Data

Work under the contract was started in year 1 and completed in year 3.

Contract price	$500,000	
Estimated contract costs:		
At start of project	$400,000	
At end of year 1	400,000	
At end of year 2	420,000	
(Notice that the contract cost estimates are subject to change as the work progresses.)		
Actual costs to complete contract:		
Incurred in year 1	$100,000	
Incurred in year 2	194,000	
Incurred in year 3	121,000	$415,000
Progress billings:		
Annually for 90% of contract value of work completed		

Income Determination

	Year					
	1		2		3	
Contract price		$500,000		$500,000		$500,000
Deduct:						
Accumulated contract costs	$100,000		$294,000		$415,000	
Estimated cost to complete contract	300,000	400,000	126,000	420,000	-0-	415,000
Total income from contract (estimated in years 1 and 2)		$100,000		$ 80,000		$ 85,000
Per cent complete (Accumulated costs ÷ Total estimated costs):						
Year 1—$100,000 ÷ $400,000		25%				
Year 2—$294,000 ÷ $420,000				70%		
Year 3—Contract complete						100%
Income from contract—earned to date		$ 25,000		$ 56,000		$ 85,000
Income assigned to prior periods				25,000		56,000
Periodic income from contract		$ 25,000		$ 31,000		$ 29,000

The following accounts may be used in the accounting for the long-term contract:

Account Title	*Comment*
Cost of Contract Work	Debited with costs identified with the performance of the contract.
Revenue from Contract Work	Credited for amounts of revenue earned.
Contract Value of Work in Process Unbilled	Debited for amounts of revenue earned. Credited for progress billings.
Accounts Receivable	Debited for progress billings.

Data needed for the above accounts in connection with the assumed contract are determined as follows:

Reference to Illustrative Journal Entries on page 208		Year 1	Year 2	Year 3
(1)	Cost of contract work—data given	$100,000	$194,000	$121,000
(2)	Revenue earned—based on percentage of completion computed above:			
	25% of $500,000	125,000		
	(70%–25%) of $500,000		225,000	
	(100%–70%) of $500,000			150,000
(3)	Progress billings—90% of contract value of work completed—90% of revenue earned	112,500	202,500	135,000
(4)	Final billing—cumulative 10% "hold back" billed when contract completed			50,000

Summary journal entries for the contract data shown above are on the following page.

	Year 1		Year 2		Year 3	
(1)						
Cost of contract work	100,000		194,000		121,000	
Cash (or other asset accounts such as Materials and Supplies)		100,000		194,000		121,000
(2)						
Contract value of work in process unbilled	125,000		225,000		150,000	
Revenue from contract work		125,000		225,000		150,000
(3)						
Accounts receivable	112,500		202,500		135,000	
Contract value of work in process unbilled		112,500		202,500		135,000
(4)						
Accounts receivable					50,000	
Contract value of work in process unbilled						50,000

The income statement results are indicated by the following tabulation.

Income Statement Data

	Year 1	Year 2	Year 3
Revenue from construction work	$125,000	$225,000	$150,000
Cost of construction work	100,000	194,000	121,000
Income from construction contracts	$ 25,000	$ 31,000	$ 29,000
Deduct:			
Selling and administrative expenses not identifiable with contract	$ xxx	$ xxx	$ xxx
Income taxes	xx	xx	xx
Net income	$ xx	$ xx	$ xx

If a loss on a contract is in prospect, provision should be made for the total loss, not for portions thereof computed on a percentage-of-completion basis.

General matters. Some contracts provide for cash advances from the customer before any work is performed under the contract. Such advances should be shown among the liabilities on the contractor's books. Each time a progress billing is made, the advances account would be reduced. Accounts Receivable would be debited for the difference between the billable revenue and the applicable portion of the advance. Thus, if an advance was received equal to 20% of the contract price, the contract advances account would be debited subsequently for 20% of each progress billing. For example, assume that a 20% advance in the amount of $5,000 is received. A subsequent progress billing covering $10,000 of work would be recorded as follows:

Accounts receivable	8,000	
Contract advances (20% of $10,000)	2,000	
Contract value of work in process		10,000

If a contract is on a cost-plus basis, there is no hazard in taking up income on an uncompleted contract; but if a contract is on a flat-price basis, there is usually an element of hazard in doing so because of the possibility that unforeseen costs may turn a prospective profit into a smaller profit or into a loss.

The hazards of taking up income on uncompleted contracts may, of course, be eliminated or minimized if the work to be done, or the product to be delivered, is divisible into identifiable units to which portions of the total contract price are definitely applicable. Thus, if a contract calls for the manufacture and delivery of 1,000 units of a certain commodity, there is no lack of conservatism in taking up the earnings applicable to the completed and accepted units. In some such cases, completion alone may provide a sufficient basis for income recognition, particularly if acceptance is reasonably assured and delivery is merely a routine operation. If the contract calls for the construction and delivery of a single unit, such as a ship, the contract may call for inspections by the customer as the work progresses, with reports of any exceptions, and may provide for progress payments at certain stated completion stages; in such instances, the hazards of taking up income as the work progresses are somewhat minimized.

Although, from the standpoint of a going concern, it is always conservative to defer the taking of any income until the contract is completed, consideration should be given to the fact that such conservatism may work an injustice on partners or stockholders. If a partner is to retire before the completion of a contract, and is to sell his interest to the remaining partners, he should, in fairness, receive some benefit for the income reasonably to be regarded as applicable to work done up to the date of his retirement. Because stockholders of a corporation may change before the completion of a long contract, there may also be a responsibility on the part of the corporate management to recognize the question of fairness involved.

Rigid adherence to a policy of taking up no income from contracts until they are completed not only may impose unreasonable hardships on partners or stockholders, but may result in the showing of income from period to period quite at variance with the operating facts. For instance, if we assume that a company is engaged throughout one year on a single contract which was uncompleted at the end of the year, the taking of no income at the end of the year would result in showing a loss if administrative overhead expenses were charged off. The income statement of the succeeding period would also show a distorted picture because it would include income resulting largely from the activities of the prior period. The assumed conditions of this illustration have been made somewhat extreme to emphasize the point; the fact that the distortion may be concealed because other contracts are being carried on concurrently only emphasizes the necessity of recognizing the conditions.

CHAPTER

12

Inventories (Continued)

Chapter 11 dealt principally with matters related to the determination of cost for inventory-pricing purposes. We now turn to matters related to the so-called "cost or market" rule.

What is "market"? "Market" may be determined on one of the following bases, depending on the type of inventory involved.

Purchase or replacement basis:

This basis applies to purchased merchandise or materials. It has been defined by the Treasury Department for tax purposes as follows: "Upon ordinary circumstances and for normal goods in an inventory, 'market' means the current bid price prevailing at the date of the inventory for the particular merchandise in the volume in which usually purchased by the taxpayer." The restriction concerning quantity is important; if it were omitted, inapplicable market values might be used.

Replacement is probably a better word than *purchase,* as it is broad enough to include the incidental acquisition costs, such as freight and duties, which are properly included with the purchase price in the inventory computation.

Reproduction basis:

This basis applies to manufactured goods and goods in process. It is determined on the basis of market prices for materials, prevailing labor rates, and current overhead.

Realization basis:

For some items in the inventory, such as obsolete or repossessed merchandise, a purchase or reproduction market value may not be determinable, and it may be necessary to accept, as an estimate of market value, the prospective selling price minus all prospective costs to be incurred in conditioning and selling the goods, and minus a reasonable profit.

Limits on usable market prices. Current accounting practice has sanctioned certain limits on the application of market values for inventory purposes. These limits have been stated by the Committee on Accounting Procedure in Bulletin 43 as follows:

> As used in the phrase *lower of cost or market* the term *market* means current replacement cost (by purchase or by reproduction, as the case may be) except that:
>
> (1) Market should not exceed the net realizable value (i.e., estimated selling price in the ordinary course of business less reasonably predictable costs of completion and disposal); and
>
> (2) Market should not be less than net realizable value reduced by an allowance for an approximately normal profit margin.

To illustrate the application of the above refinement of the "market" concept, the following table shows relevant prices for five different inventory items. The underlined prices are those to be used for inventory purposes if the definition of "market" set forth in Bulletin 43 is followed.

	1	2	3	4	5
(a) Cost	**.72**	.85	.85	**.68**	.84
(b) Market—cost to replace at inventory date	.76	**.80**	.70	.65	.83
(c) Selling price less estimated cost to complete and sell	.82	.82	.82	.82	**.82**
(d) Selling price less estimated cost to complete and sell and normal profit margin	.73	.73	**.73**	.73	.73
	Cost is used because it is lower than market.	Market is used because it is lower than cost, not greater than (c), and not less than (d).	Market is less than cost, but it is not used because it is lower than (d). Price (d) is used because it measures the limit of reduction.	Market is lower than cost; it is not used because it is less than (d). But, because cost is less than (d), cost is used.	Market is lower than cost, but it is higher than (c); therefore, (c) is used.

Exception (2) is a specific instance of the growing practice of not reducing cost except to the extent of a clearly apparent loss.

Normal profit. The quotation in the preceding subsection from Bulletin 43 refers to "an approximately normal profit margin." This expression is used in the statement that, if market is lower than cost, in no event should the figure used for inventory pricing be less than net realizable value (estimated selling price less reasonably predictable costs of completion and disposal) reduced by an allowance for an approximately normal profit margin.

The use of a normal profit concept seems somewhat unfortunate. How is a "normal" profit determined? By whom? What is the normal profit margin for General Motors Corporation? Can an estimate of a normal profit margin be more than a matter of individual opinion?

There is an additional troublesome feature in the use of normal profit. If an inventory is reduced to "net realizable value reduced by an allowance for an approximately normal profit margin," then in the period of sale a normal profit will be reported, if the sales price is correctly forecast. Such results, however, may be somewhat misleading, because they are attributable to a method of inventory pricing. It seems logical to price the inventory at less than cost if it is clearly apparent that the investment in inventory cannot be recovered. But why adopt an accounting procedure which reduces an inventory figure to such an extent that a profit will likely be reported in the subsequent period?

If December 31 was the close of the accounting period and the goods in question had been sold on December 29, a loss would have been reported. If the goods are priced in the inventory to permit a normal profit when sold, and they are sold on January 5, a profit is reported. The close of an accounting period and the application of an accounting convention have thus made a loss transaction appear to be profitable. By understating profits or overstating losses in one year, a larger profit can be reported in a subsequent year.

It may be relevant to note that this result would arise only if market were below net realizable value. If market is above net realizable value, then cost is reduced to net realizable value without further reduction to provide for an approximately normal profit. The goods thus reduced would be sold at no loss in the period of sale. Only when market is below net realizable value will the inventory be reduced to produce a subsequent accounting profit.

Application of cost or market. Three ways of applying the cost-or-market method are illustrated below and on page 213.

(1) By comparing the cost and market for each item in the inventory, and using the lower figure.

Determination of Lower of Cost or Market—Item-by-Item Method

	Quantity	Unit Price Cost	Unit Price Market	Extended Cost	Extended Market	Lower of Cost or Market
Men's clothing:						
Suits	200	$40	$37			$ 7,400
Coats	100	35	31			3,100
Jackets	50	15	17			750
Hats	80	5	6			400
Ladies' clothing:						
Dresses	300	10	12			3,000
Suits	100	40	38			3,800
Coats	80	30	32			2,400
Robes	60	5	5			300
Inventory at lower of cost or market						$21,150

(2) By comparing the total cost and market for major inventory categories, and using the lower figure.

Determination of Lower of Cost or Market—Category Method

	Quantity	Unit Price Cost	Unit Price Market	Extended Cost	Extended Market	Lower of Cost or Market
Men's clothing:						
Suits	200	$40	$37	$ 8,000	$ 7,400	
Coats	100	35	31	3,500	3,100	
Jackets	50	15	17	750	850	
Hats	80	5	6	400	480	
Total				$12,650	$11,830	$11,830
Ladies' clothing:						
Dresses	300	10	12	$ 3,000	$ 3,600	
Suits	100	40	38	4,000	3,800	
Coats	80	30	32	2,400	2,560	
Robes	60	5	5	300	300	
Total				$ 9,700	$10,260	9,700
Inventory at lower of cost or market						$21,530

(3) By comparing the total cost and market for the entire inventory, and using the lower figure.

Determination of Lower of Cost or Market—Total Inventory Method

	Quantity	Unit Price Cost	Unit Price Market	Extended Cost	Extended Market	Lower of Cost or Market
Men's clothing:						
Suits	200	$40	$37	$ 8,000	$ 7,400	
Coats	100	35	31	3,500	3,100	
Jackets	50	15	17	750	850	
Hats	80	5	6	400	480	
Ladies' clothing:						
Dresses	300	10	12	3,000	3,600	
Suits	100	40	38	4,000	3,800	
Coats	80	30	32	2,400	2,560	
Robes	60	5	5	300	300	
Total				$22,350	$22,090	$22,090

General discussion of cost or market. The cost-or-market basis of inventory pricing conforms with an old rule of accounting conservatism often stated as follows: Anticipate no profit and provide for all possible losses. If market purchase prices decline, it is assumed that selling prices will decline with them; reducing the inventory valuation to market purchase price reduces the profit of the period when the cost price decline took place and transfers the goods to the next period at a price which will presumably permit the earning of a normal gross profit on their sale. If the market purchase price increases, the inventory is valued at cost, so that a profit will not be anticipated.

The cost-or-market basis has been, in the past, one of the most generally accepted applications of conservative accounting principles. It was developed and widely accepted during the long period when bankers and other creditors were primarily concerned with the balance sheet and when relatively little consideration was given to the income statement. With the emphasis thus placed on the balance sheet, the primary essential was a conservative valuation of the assets shown therein. The valuation of the inventory at the lower of cost or market is unquestionably conservative from the balance sheet standpoint.

To obtain this balance sheet conservatism, all other considerations were ignored or their importance was minimized. It was recognized that the cost-or-market approach was subject to question on the ground of consistency; to absorb against current gross profits an unrealized and even problematical loss on unsold merchandise, while ignoring an unrealized potential increase in gross profit which might result from a rising market, was recognized as inconsistent; but such an inconsistency was regarded as of no concern when questions of conservatism were at issue. It was recognized that, even from the balance sheet standpoint, the cost-or-market rule resulted in inconsistencies and in valuations which were not comparable. Different items in an inventory might be priced on different bases—some at cost and some at market; the inventories of the same concern at two dates might be priced on different bases—at cost on a rising market and at market on a falling market—and a comparison of the balance sheet valuations might therefore lead to incorrect interpretations; the inventories of two concerns might be priced on different bases, because acquired at different dates, and therefore not be comparable. But all inconsistencies of this nature were considered unimportant in comparison with considerations of conservatism in the valuation of each inventory.

However, income performance has become increasingly recognized as a significant measure of debt-paying ability and investment desirability. As a consequence, bankers, other creditors, business management, and stockholders are becoming increasingly concerned with the income statement—and not only with the income statement for a single period, but with the trend of earnings as shown by a series of income statements. For this reason the propriety of the cost-or-market approach is becoming a subject of question.

Accountants are now raising the question as to whether, giving consideration to the income statements for a series of periods, the cost-or-market rule is as conservative as it formerly seemed to be. If, at the close of one period, the market value of the inventory is less than its cost, the reduction of the inventory valuation to market undoubtedly produces a conservative balance sheet valuation and a conservative computation of income in the statements for that period. But what is the effect on the income statement of the subsequent period? The effect may be so great a distortion of stated earnings of successive periods as to render a series of income statements definitely misleading.

To illustrate, assume that, at the beginning of January, merchandise was purchased at a cost of $100,000; that half of the goods were sold in January for $75,000; that the remaining half were sold in February for $73,000; and that the inventory at the end of January, which cost $50,000, had a market value (replacement cost) of $40,000. The statement below shows:

In the first column, the computation of gross profits for the two months under the cost-or-market rule.

In the second column, the computation of gross profits for the two months with the inventory valued at cost.

	With Inventory Valued At	
	Cost or Market	Cost
January:		
Sales	$75,000	$75,000
Cost of goods sold ($100,000 of purchases, minus the inventory)	60,000	50,000
Gross profit	$15,000	$25,000
February:		
Sales	$73,000	$73,000
Cost of goods sold (consisting of the opening inventory)	40,000	50,000
Gross profit	$33,000	$23,000

The balance sheet valuation of the inventory at the end of January on the cost-or-market basis instead of on the cost basis ($40,000 instead of $50,000), and the resulting statement of gross profit for January ($15,000 instead of $25,000), may be accepted as conservative. But is the February income statement on the cost-or-market basis (showing $33,000 of gross profit instead of $23,000) conservative? And would not the statements for the two months on the cost-or-market basis give a misleading impression as to the trend of operations to anyone who did not realize that the increase in profit shown by the statements was caused by the write-down of the inventory and the consequent transfer of profits from January to February?

The cost-or-market inventory-pricing basis is founded on the assumption that a decrease in market purchase costs will be accompanied by a similar decrease in selling prices before the disposal of the inventory. This was not the case in the foregoing illustration, and in the actual conduct of business affairs it frequently is not the case. Therefore, there is a trend toward the opinion that it is not necessary or desirable to reduce the inventory valuation to market if there is no probability that sales prices will also decrease; there is also some trend of opinion in favor of the idea that reduction to market is unnecessary if, even though some decline in selling prices has occurred or can be expected, the inventory can probably be disposed of at a selling price which will include the cost and some profit. And there is even some opinion that reduction to market is unnecessary if the inventory can probably be disposed of without loss.

Some accountants, therefore, believe that, instead of assuming that a decrease in selling prices will promptly follow a decrease in cost, consideration should be given to the trend in selling prices, and that the inventory valuation should not be reduced unless selling prices have decreased at the balance sheet date or unless it is expected that they will decrease sufficiently after that date and before the disposal of the inventory to cause a loss.

If a decrease in the realizable value of the inventory is in prospect, balance sheet conservatism undoubtedly requires a reduction in the inventory valuation; however, bearing in mind the importance of the income statement, there still remains the question as to whether the customary procedure of reducing the inventory valuation by an accounting method which also reduces the gross profit of the period in which market costs declined is desirable. The question of distortion of profits between periods still remains. To illustrate, let us return to the foregoing case in which the inventory at the end of January cost $50,000 and had a market cost value of $40,000. In that illustration it was assumed that the selling prices in February were depressed only $2,000 in spite of the $10,000 decrease in replacement costs. Let us now assume that the selling prices decreased $10,000—an amount equal to the decrease in inventory valuation. Statements are presented below:

	With Inventory Valued At	
	Cost or Market	Cost
January:		
Sales	$75,000	$75,000
Cost of goods sold	60,000	50,000
Gross profit	$15,000	$25,000
February:		
Sales	$65,000	$65,000
Cost of goods sold	40,000	50,000
Gross profit	$25,000	$15,000

The figures in the "Cost" column seem to reflect the facts more truly: The company made less profit in February than in January because of the decrease in selling prices. The "Cost or Market" column tells a very strange story: The company made more profit in February than in January, notwithstanding the decrease in selling prices which occurred in February.

It seems to the authors that accountants might expect that the shift in emphasis from the balance sheet to the income statement would produce a similar shift in emphasis in the accounting approach to inventory pricing. When the emphasis was on reporting financial position, the approach to the inventory problem was one of valuation for purposes of properly reflecting financial position. Under these conditions cost or market, whichever is lower, seemed well suited. With the emphasis currently on the measurement of net income, the accountant logically gives pre-eminent consideration to those procedures associated with the assignment or "matching" of costs against related revenues. With the emphasis on a matching of costs and revenues, it would seem that the approach should be shifted to one of determining the portion of the total merchandise cost outlay for a period that should be charged against current revenues and the portion that should be assigned to future periods. The emphasis, thus, would not be one of inventory "valuation," but of cost assignment, the residue being carried forward to apply to future periods.

To some extent, this shift in approach to inventory pricing has occurred. Cost or market, whichever is lower, is receiving less support from accountants and is being refined in a number of ways, all in the direction of not reducing the cost figure unless a loss on the inventory investment is clearly in prospect.

Disclosing market losses. When a business has suffered a significant loss on its investment in inventory because of a decline in market prices, the income statement is made more informative by setting forth the loss as a separate item. Otherwise, the loss is included with the cost of goods sold, which in effect tends to bury the loss rather than disclose it.

To indicate the merits of separate disclosure, consider the following case in which a business using the cost-or-market inventory method has suffered a $10,000 loss because of falling market prices.

Cost of goods available for sale	$100,000	
Ending inventory:		
At cost	50,000	$10,000 loss
At lower of cost or market	40,000	
Sales	80,000	
Operating expenses and income taxes	16,000	

If separate disclosure is not made, the income statement will appear as follows:

Sales	$80,000
Cost of goods sold	60,000
Gross profit	$20,000
Operating expenses and income taxes	16,000
Net income	$ 4,000

The inventory loss of $10,000 is merged with the cost of goods sold. This procedure, although correctly stating the net income, gives a misleading impression of the cost of goods sold and gross profit. With separate disclosure, the income statement will appear as follows:

Sales	$80,000
Cost of goods sold	50,000
Gross profit	$30,000
Loss on reduction of inventory to lower of cost or market	10,000
Gross profit less inventory loss	$20,000
Operating expenses and income taxes	16,000
Net income	$ 4,000

A contra-inventory account may be used in conjunction with the practice of giving separate disclosure to inventory losses. In order to illustrate such a balance sheet account, assume that a perpetual inventory record was maintained in the case just cited. The relevant accounts, in summary form, would appear as follows at year end.

Inventory

Beginning inventory plus purchases (goods available for sale)—debits totaling 100,000	Cost of goods sold—credits totaling 50,000

Cost of Goods Sold

Goods sold—debits totaling 50,000	

When a contra-account procedure is used, the inventory account is maintained at cost, and the reduction to market is achieved by the contra account, thus:

Loss on reduction of inventory to lower of cost or market	10,000	
Reduction of inventory to lower of cost or market		10,000

The income statement would be prepared in the manner illustrated above, in which the loss is set forth separately. In the balance sheet the inventory would be shown at cost, and the reduction would be subtracted therefrom, as follows:

Inventory, at cost	$50,000	
Less reduction of inventory to lower of cost or market	10,000	$40,000

The contra-asset account remains open and its balance is carried forward.

In order to carry the illustration forward, assume that the following data relate to the next year:

Beginning inventory—at cost	$ 50,000
Purchases	70,000
Cost of goods available for sale	$120,000
Ending inventory:	
At cost	60,000
At lower of cost or market	52,500
Sales	96,000
Operating expenses and income taxes	28,500

As indicated, the difference at the end of the second year between cost ($60,000) and the lower of cost or market ($52,500) is $7,500. The contra account, however, would continue to show the $10,000 credit balance carried forward from the previous year. Accordingly, the following entry is required to reduce the contra account balance to $7,500.

Reduction of inventory to lower of cost or market	2,500	
Reduction in inventory valuation account		2,500

The income statement for the second year is presented on the next page. As in the income statement for the preceding year, the cost of goods sold is stated at cost, with the effect of the cost-or-market inventory valuation method disclosed separately. In this instance, the $2,500 decrease in the reduction account would be added to the gross profit.

Sales	$96,000
Cost of goods sold	60,000
Gross profit	$36,000
Reduction in inventory valuation account	2,500
Total	$38,500
Operating expenses and income taxes	28,500
Net income	$10,000

The inventory would be set forth in the companion balance sheet as follows:

Inventory, at cost	$60,000	
Less reduction of inventory to lower of cost or market	7,500	$52,500

The use of inventory loss and inventory contra accounts in conjunction with the cost-or-market inventory method will have no effect on net income. Such accounts offer the following advantages:

The difference, if any, between the inventory at cost and the lower of cost or market is disclosed in the balance sheet.

The effect of market price declines is shown as a separate item in the income statement.

The cost of goods sold and the gross profit are stated on a cost basis.

Obsolete and depreciated merchandise. Regardless of the inventory-pricing basis adopted, merchandise which has become obsolete or has depreciated because of shopwear or damage should be excluded entirely from the inventory if it is unsalable or cannot be utilized in production. If it can be sold at a reduced price, a conservative estimate of realizable value may be assigned to it. The loss on goods which have been damaged or have become obsolete should be taken in the period when the loss developed.

The question of the proper treatment of write-downs for losses on obsolete, shopworn, or otherwise damaged goods requires some consideration. If write-downs are required as a result of shopwear, style changes, or other operating causes, they should be treated as a charge against income, either by a reduction of gross profit or as a special income deduction. However, extraordinary losses, such as those caused by fire or flood, should be set out as extraneous losses.

Goods repossessed in a worn or damaged condition should be priced for inventory purposes at an amount not in excess of the net realizable value (estimated selling price in the ordinary course of business less reasonably predictable costs of reconditioning and disposal). It is also acceptable, and logically justifiable, to reduce the net realizable value by an allowance for an approximately normal profit margin. That procedure would place the repossessed merchandise on a basis comparable with that of new merchandise.

Scrap. The valuation of scrap material presents some special problems. If the scrap cannot be sold or used, it should, of course, be given no inventory value. If it can be sold, it can be priced for inventory purposes on a net realization basis.

If the scrap is used in the manufacture of a by-product, the entire original cost of the material may be charged to the main product; in that case, the cost of the by-product will be computed without the inclusion of any charge for scrap material used, and no valuation should be placed on the scrap for inventory purposes; or the original cost of the material may be charged in part to the main product and in part to the by-product; in that case, the scrap can be given an inventory value. It is important that consistency be maintained, and that the error of charging the main product with the entire cost of the material and also placing a valuation on the scrap in the inventory be not committed; such a procedure obviously would result in an inflation of asset values and profits to the extent of the valuation placed on the scrap.

Goods in foreign countries. If a company operates a branch or factory in a foreign country, the problems of inventory pricing already discussed are applicable, and, in addition, the company must meet the problem of converting values stated in a foreign currency to values stated in domestic currency.

In general, it may be said that the conversion should be made by applying to the foreign currency valuation the exchange rate current on the balance sheet date. This general rule requires some modification. Some companies keep the accounts of foreign branches in such a manner as to show the dollar cost of the foreign money used for the payment of manufacturing costs.

Inventory valuation based on selling price. In some lines of industry, such as meat packing, in which material costs cannot be specifically allocated to joint products, practical considerations may make it advisable or even necessary to determine the inventory valuation on the basis of the relative selling prices of the various commodities. Although selling prices in such cases serve as a convenient basis for the determination of inventory valuations, conservatism requires at least the deduction of a sufficient allowance for marketing and transportation charges to be incurred; and, to avoid an anticipation of profits, the deductions from selling prices should include a provision for profits.

Valuation of the inventory at selling prices less a provision for disposal costs is often regarded as acceptable practice if production costs are difficult to determine and the product has a ready marketability. This condition is recognized as prevailing in farming. It is therefore considered acceptable practice to value crops and livestock on the basis of selling prices less estimated selling and other disposal costs. Any other procedure might involve practical impossibilities of inventory valuation, and might result in imposing the burden of production on one period while waiting until a succeeding period to take the related income.

Unrealized profits in inventories. When the process of manufacturing involves the transfer of work in process from one department to another, the transfer value is sometimes based on the price at which products at that stage of completion could be obtained from outside suppliers. This value may be used for the purpose of comparing manufacturing costs with a presumptive acquisition cost to see whether a manufacturing department is an advantageous or "profitable" one to maintain. A system of bonus payments may be in effect, the bonuses being determined by the difference between manufacturing costs and suppliers' prices. Although such a basis for pricing interdepartmental transfers may be desirable for purposes of management, all such unrealized profits should be excluded from the inventory valuation for balance sheet and income statement purposes.

Variations in inventory pricings and the principle of consistency. We have seen that there are various acceptable methods of inventory pricing. Inventories may be priced at cost, at the lower of cost or market, at cost or less, or on a basis of selling prices. The cost figures may be affected by such matters as the treatment of freight, purchase discounts, and incidental expenditures, and by the choice of the method to be used in the selection of costs for inventory purposes. The lower of cost or market may be determined on a basis of individual items, inventory categories, or inventory totals.

Although the amount of permissible variation in inventory pricing by different companies is somewhat disturbing, the matter is not so serious as it might seem, because the principle of consistency requires that the basis and method of inventory pricing adopted by each company be consistently applied by it over the years, or that the effect of any departure from consistency, if material, be disclosed. The principle of consistency thus reduces the troublesome consequences that might otherwise develop from having a variety of acceptable inventory procedures.

Reserve for possible future market declines. The valuation account discussed on pages 217–219 gave recognition to market declines which had occurred prior to the balance sheet date. Such an account is properly set up by a charge to current income, so that net income will be computed in accordance with the cost-or-market basis of inventory valuation. The valuation account should not be created by a direct charge to Retained Earnings; it is a contra account and should be deducted from the balance in the Inventory account.

A valuation account for price declines that have already taken place must be distinguished from an account set up to reflect anticipated, prospective, or possible inventory price declines. Regarding the latter type of reserve, the Committee on Accounting Procedure made a comment in Bulletin 43 that is quoted below:

> It has been argued with respect to inventories that losses which will have to be taken in periods of receding price levels have their origins in periods of rising prices, and that therefore reserves to provide for future price declines should be created in periods of rising prices by charges against the operations of those periods. Reserves of this kind involve assumptions as to what future price levels will be, what inventory quantities will be on hand if and when a major price decline takes place, and finally whether loss to the business will be measured by the amount

of the decline in prices. The bases for such assumptions are so uncertain that any conclusions drawn from them would generally seem to be speculative guesses rather than informed judgments. When estimates of this character are included in current costs, amounts representing mere conjecture are combined with others representing reasonable approximations.

The same statement would be equally true with respect to estimates of possible price declines made during periods of declining prices. Such estimates are necessarily based on assumptions regarding the extent of the decline, its duration, the inventory quantity affected, and the response of selling prices to the decline.

If a reserve for possible future market declines is set up, it should be created by a debit to Retained Earnings and a credit to an account with some title such as "Reserve for Possible Future Inventory Losses." The reserve is a part of the stockholders' equity and should be shown as such in the balance sheet.

What disposition should be made of the reserve thus created? It should be returned to Retained Earnings whether or not the declines occur. If they do not occur, the reserve is thus proved to have been unnecessary. But if they do occur, the loss should be charged against the operations of the period during which the market decline took place.

Thus, if a concern values its inventory at the lower of cost or market, and if, at the end of 1965, the cost of the inventory is $50,000 and the market value is $40,000, the books should be closed and the income for 1965 ascertained on the basis of an inventory valuation of $40,000. If there is a prospect of additional market declines, a reserve may be set up out of Retained Earnings. But this reserve should be returned to Retained Earnings during, or at the end of, 1966.

Retail method. The so-called "retail" method of inventory pricing is frequently used in department and other retail stores; it is suitable for use by wholesalers also. It is not suitable, however, for manufacturing businesses, because the articles purchased are not immediately priced for resale.

With records showing the opening inventory and purchases at both cost and retail, it is possible to determine a ratio of cost to retail, the uses of which are described below:

(1) To estimate the inventory at any time without taking a physical inventory; the procedure is as follows:

	Cost	Retail
Inventory at beginning of period	$ 10,000	$ 15,000
Purchases during the period	110,000	185,000
Totals	$120,000	$200,000
(Ratio of cost to retail—60%)		
Sales		180,000
Estimated inventory at retail		$ 20,000

Inventory computation—60% of $20,000 = $12,000.

The retail method makes it possible to prepare monthly, weekly, or even daily estimates of the inventory. Such estimates may be useful for purposes of inventory control and formulating purchasing policy.

(2) To permit pricing a physical inventory at marked selling prices and reducing the selling price valuation by applying to it the ratio of cost to retail.

Using retail prices eliminates the necessity of marking costs on the merchandise, referring to invoices, and dealing with the problem of identical merchandise acquired at different costs.

Physical inventories, priced by the retail method, should be taken from time to time as a check on the accuracy of the estimated inventories determined by the procedure described under (1) above. If the inventory determined by procedure (2) is less than the amount estimated by procedure (1), the difference may be attributable to "shrinkages" resulting from theft, breakage, or other causes. However, the difference may be attributable in part to errors in the retail inventory records or in the physical inventory priced at retail.

Terminology. The foregoing illustration ignores the problem created whenever changes are made in selling prices after the original selling prices have been placed on the goods. The fact that businessmen do revise or modify prices of goods on hand necessitates an understanding of the following terms:

Original retail is the price at which the goods are first offered for sale.

Markups are additions that raise the selling price above the original retail.

Markdowns are deductions that lower the price below the original retail.

Markup cancellations are deductions that do not decrease the selling price below the original retail.

Markdown cancellations are additions that do not increase the selling price above the original retail.

To illustrate, assume the following:

The goods cost $100.	
The original retail price was	$140
There was a markup of	20
Which advanced the selling price to	$160
There was a markup cancellation of	5
Which reduced the selling price to	$155
The selling price was further reduced $30:	
This included a markup cancellation of	15
Which reduced the selling price to original retail	$140
It also included a markdown of	15
Which reduced the selling price to	$125
There was a markdown cancellation of	5
Which increased the selling price to	$130

Markups minus markup cancellations may be referred to as *net markup;* markdowns minus markdown cancellations may be referred to as *net markdown.*

A clear understanding of markups, markup cancellations, markdowns, and markdown cancellations, and a careful differentiation thereof in the records are necessary because, in determining the ratio of cost to retail, it is customary to include markups and markup cancellations, but to ignore markdowns and markdown cancellations. To illustrate, assume the following:

	Cost	Retail
Inventory at beginning of period	$20,000	$ 30,000
Purchases	80,000	120,000
Markups		10,000
Markup cancellations		2,000*
Markdowns		7,000*
Markdown cancellations		1,000

The per cent to be used in computing the inventory by the retail method (including net markups and excluding net markdowns) is determined as follows:

	Cost	Retail
Inventory at beginning of period	$ 20,000	$ 30,000
Purchases	80,000	120,000
Markups		10,000
Markup cancellations		2,000*
Totals	$100,000	$158,000

(Ratio of cost to retail: 63.29%)

Markon is the difference between the cost and the original retail plus net markups. In the above example, the markon is $58,000; the per cent of markon is 36.71% ($58,000 ÷ $158,000); and the ratio of cost to retail is the complement of this per cent, or 63.29%. This rate is used in the following inventory computation.

	Cost	Retail
Inventory at beginning of period	$ 20,000	$ 30,000
Purchases	80,000	120,000
Markups		10,000
Markup cancellations		2,000*
Totals (Cost ratio, 63.29%)	$100,000	$158,000
Markdowns		7,000*
Markdown cancellations		1,000
Remainder		$152,000
Sales		120,000
Estimated inventory at retail		$ 32,000

Inventory computation: 63.29% of $32,000, or $20,253.

Why markdowns are ignored in the computation of cost ratio. The intent of the retail inventory method, as conventionally applied, is so to compute the inventory that its sale at prevailing prices will yield at least the normal or prevailing rate of gross profit. The dollar amounts thus determined are intended to conform generally to the cost-or-market rule.

* Starred items throughout this discussion are deductions from retail prices.

Referring to the preceding illustration, let us compute by four different methods the per cents that might be applied to the inventory at selling price, and note which method produces an inventory figure that conforms most nearly to the lower of cost or market.

	Use Markups and Markdowns	Use Markups but Not Markdowns (as above)	Use Markdowns but Not Markups	Use Neither Markups Nor Markdowns
Original retail:				
Inventory	$ 30,000	$ 30,000	$ 30,000	$ 30,000
Purchases	120,000	120,000	120,000	120,000
Markups—net	8,000	8,000		
Markdowns—net	6,000*		6,000*	
Totals	$152,000	$158,000	$144,000	$150,000
Cost	100,000	100,000	100,000	100,000
Cost ratio	65.79%	63.29%	69.44%	66.67%
Inventory at retail	$ 32,000	$ 32,000	$ 32,000	$ 32,000
Computed inventory	21,053	20,253	22,221	21,334

It is obvious that the lowest inventory figure is obtained by the second method, in which net markups are used and net markdowns are ignored in the computation of the cost ratio. But is such a procedure merely conservative without being logical? Two illustrations bearing on this question are presented.

Illustration with markups. Markups in retail prices are presumably related to market increases in wholesale prices; the inventory should, therefore, be priced at cost. In the following illustration it is assumed that half of the merchandise was sold.

	Cost	Retail
Opening inventory and purchases	$60,000	$ 90,000
(Cost ratio, ignoring markups = 66⅔%)		
Markups—net		10,000
Total		$100,000
(Cost ratio, including markups = 60%)		
Sales		50,000
Estimated inventory at retail		$ 50,000

Inventory figure:
At rate ignoring markups: 66⅔% of $50,000 = $33,333.
At rate including markups: 60% of $50,000 = $30,000.

The $33,333 figure is affected by the rise in market prices and is incorrect; the $30,000 figure is on a cost basis, and is correct because cost is lower than market. Therefore markups should be used in the determination of the cost ratio.

Illustration with markdowns. Markdowns may be necessitated by market decreases in wholesale prices; if such a situation exists, the inventory (if it is to conform to cost or market, whichever is lower) should be reduced to market.

	Cost	Retail
Opening inventory and purchases	$60,000	$90,000
(Cost ratio, ignoring markdowns = 66⅔%)		
Markdowns—net		10,000
Remainder		$80,000
(Cost ratio, including markdowns = 75%)		
Sales		40,000
Estimated inventory at retail		$40,000

Inventory figure:
At rate ignoring markdowns: 66⅔% of $40,000 = $26,667.
At rate including markdowns: 75% of $40,000 = $30,000.

The $26,667 figure was affected by the decrease in market value, and is appropriate in view of the fact that the traditional objective of the retail method is to approximate the results produced by the cost-or-market, whichever-is-lower, method. It therefore appears that markdowns should not be used in determining the cost ratio.

Retail method is based on averages. The retail inventory method is based on the assumption that an average cost ratio can appropriately be applied to the selling price of the inventory. Some factors which might tend to make the assumption unwarranted are discussed in the following paragraphs.

Departmental rates. The first point to be considered is the possible effect of differences in departmental rates of markon. The retail inventory method assumes that high-cost-ratio goods and low-cost-ratio goods will be found in the same proportions in the final inventory as in the total of goods offered for sale. But let us assume the following conditions:

	Department *A* 50%-Cost-Ratio Merchandise		Department *B* 80%-Cost-Ratio Merchandise		Total 72.5% Average Cost Ratio	
	Cost	Retail	Cost	Retail	Cost	Retail
Opening inventory and purchases (or total offered for sale)	$25,000	$50,000	$120,000	$150,000	$145,000	$200,000
Sales		45,000		105,000		150,000
Estimated inventory at retail		$ 5,000		$ 45,000		$ 50,000

It will be noted that the proportions of high-cost-ratio goods and low-cost-ratio goods are not the same in the closing inventory as in the total goods offered for sale. Instead, the proportions are those shown below.

	50% Cost Ratio	80% Cost Ratio
Offered for sale:		
Amounts—at selling price	$50,000	$150,000
Per cents	25%	75%
Final inventory:		
Amounts—at selling price	$ 5,000	$ 45,000
Per cents	10%	90%

Under such circumstances it is desirable to keep departmental records, in order that a separate computation can be made for the inventory of each department, thus:

Department A inventory: 50% of \$ 5,000 = \$ 2,500.
Department B inventory: 80% of \$45,000 = \$36,000.

Without the necessary departmental records, the inventory figure would be misstated, thus:

72.5% (average cost ratio) of \$50,000 = \$36,250.

Special-sale merchandise. Special sales of merchandise carrying low rates of markon may distort the average. To illustrate, assume the conditions shown below.

	Merchandise At Normal Cost Ratio—50%		Special-Sale Merchandise 90% Cost Ratio		Total (58% Average Cost Ratio)	
	Cost	Retail	Cost	Retail	Cost	Retail
Opening inventory and purchases	$40,000	$80,000	$18,000	$20,000	$58,000	$100,000
Sales		61,000		19,000		80,000
Estimated inventory at retail		$19,000		$ 1,000		$ 20,000

Again we find that the proportions of high-cost-ratio and low-cost-ratio merchandise in the inventory and in the total of goods offered for sale are not the same, but are as follows:

	50% Cost Ratio	90% Cost Ratio
Offered for sale:		
Amounts—at selling price	$80,000	$20,000
Per cents	80%	20%
Final inventory:		
Amounts—at selling price	$19,000	$ 1,000
Per cents	95%	5%

An attempt to compute the inventory by use of the average cost ratio of 58% would produce erroneous results, as shown below:

Using average rate:		
58% of $20,000		$11,600
Using separate rates:		
50% of $19,000	$9,500	
90% of $ 1,000	900	
Total		$10,400

Under such circumstances it is usually considered desirable to set up separate records, and to make a separate inventory computation, for special-sale merchandise as if such special merchandise constituted a department by itself.

Sales of marked-up and marked-down goods. Let us assume that, after all of the merchandise of a department is marked at a uniform original retail, half of the merchandise is given an additional markup and the other half is marked down; let us also assume that 70% of the sales are made from marked-down merchandise and only 30% from marked-up merchandise. Obviously, under such circumstances, it is fallacious to assume that high-cost-ratio goods and low-cost-ratio goods will be found in the same proportions in the final inventory as in the total of goods offered for sale; and the retail method in such instances would give fallacious results.

Period covered by computation. A year is too long a period to embrace in the inventory computation unless approximately the same rate of markon prevails throughout the year. This situation will not exist if, for example, different rates of gross profit are made on spring- and fall-season sales, or if extensive markdowns are made during one period of the year whereas extensive markups are made during another season.

The illustration below indicates the desirability of making interim inventory computations if the rate of markon is not fairly uniform throughout the year.

If the inventory is computed semiannually:

	Cost	Retail
First Six Months:		
Opening inventory	$100,000	$150,000
Purchases	300,000	450,000
Totals	$400,000	$600,000
(Cost ratio: 66⅔%)		
Markdowns		20,000
Remainder		$580,000
Sales		500,000
Estimated inventory at retail		$ 80,000

Inventory computation, June 30: 66⅔% of $80,000 = $53,333.

	Cost	Retail
Second Six Months:		
Opening inventory	$ 53,333	$ 80,000
Purchases	400,000	500,000
Markups		25,000
Totals	$453,333	$605,000
(Cost ratio: 74.9311%)		
Sales		385,000
Estimated inventory at retail		$220,000

Inventory computation, December 31: 74.9311% of $220,000 = $164,848.

If the inventory is computed annually:

	Cost	Retail
Opening inventory	$100,000	$ 150,000
Purchases	700,000	950,000
Markups		25,000
Totals	$800,000	$1,125,000
(Cost ratio: 71.1111%)		
Markdowns		20,000
Remainder		$1,105,000
Sales		885,000
Estimated inventory at retail		$ 220,000

Inventory computation, 71.1111% of $220,000 = $156,444.

The inventory figure of $156,444, obtained by the foregoing computations covering the full year, is erroneous. Although the average cost ratio during the whole year was about 71%, the cost ratio for the second half of the year was about 75%.

It is apparent that, in this instance, the use of a cost ratio applicable to only the last half of the year will result in the determination of an inventory valuation more nearly approximating the lower of cost or market at the end of the year. By the application of the average cost ratio, 71%, the December 31 inventory computation is unjustifiably affected by the low cost ratio of the first half-year.

If the rates of markon vary during the year, it is obvious that monthly, or even more frequent, inventory computations will produce more correct results than can be obtained by annual computations.

Extended illustration. The following statement shows the treatment of various elements in the computation of inventory by the retail method:

		Cost	Retail
Opening inventory		$ 65,000	$100,000
Purchases		350,000	520,000
Returned purchases		10,000*	14,800*
Transportation in		2,500	
Markups			12,500
Markup cancellations			3,000*
Totals		$407,500	$614,700
(Cost ratio—66.2925%)			
Deductions:			
Sales	$511,000		
Less returned sales	7,000		$504,000
Markdowns	$ 5,000		
Less markdown cancellations	1,500		3,500
Total deductions			$507,500
Estimated inventory at retail			$107,200

Inventory computation: 66.2925% of $107,200 = $71,066.

* Deduction.

Freight, discounts, returns. Transportation and other charges which, in accordance with good accounting theory, are proper additions to merchandise costs, should be added to purchase costs in the retail records. If cash discounts are regarded as deductions from purchases, the purchases should be shown net in the retail inventory records. If such discounts are regarded as financial income, they should not be included in the retail inventory computations.

Purchases should be entered at cost and at retail in the inventory computation; returned purchases should be similarly shown. Returned sales should be deducted from sales to obtain a net sales figure for use in the computation.

CHAPTER

13

Inventories (Concluded)

Last-in, first-out (*lifo*) method. This method assumes that the most recent goods received are the first ones sold. Thus, to price an ending inventory, the accountant refers to the cost data applicable to the beginning inventory, and uses cost data applicable to purchases of the current year only in case the ending inventory is larger than the beginning inventory.

Consider the following facts:

	Quantity	Cost	Total
Beginning inventory	1,000	$ 8	$8,000
Purchases during the current period:			
First purchase	250	9	2,250
Second purchase	300	10	3,000
Third purchase	100	13	1,300
Fourth purchase	200	14	2,800

The following illustrates the approach used under the last-in, first-out method if the ending inventory consists of 1,300 units.

	Quantity	Cost	Total
The beginning inventory	1,000	$ 8	$ 8,000
The first purchase	250	9	2,250
Part of the second purchase	50	10	500
Total			$10,750

An ending inventory of 900 units would be priced at $8 per unit.

In the minds of the advocates of the *lifo* method, the expression "last-in, first-out" does not refer to an assumption regarding the flow of goods, but rather to an assumption regarding the flow of costs. The advocates of the method maintain that during periods of changing costs and prices, more meaningful income statements are produced if "current" costs are applied to current sales, thus achieving a better matching of expense and revenue. To illustrate the point by a simple, and rather arbitrary, example, let us assume that a company sells one unit of a commodity each year. At the beginning of the first year it bought one unit for $1 and marked it to sell for $1.50, as a gross margin of $.50 was considered necessary to cover expenses and leave the desired profit. Before any sale was made, the company purchased another unit for $1.05, and raised the selling price to $1.55. It then sold one unit for $1.55.

By the *fifo* method the gross profit would be computed thus:

Sale	$1.55
Cost of unit sold	1.00
Gross profit	$ .55

And the inventory would be priced at a cost of $1.05.

By the *lifo* method the gross profit would be computed thus:

Sale	$1.55
Current cost of unit sold	1.05
Gross profit	$ .50

And the inventory would be priced at a cost of $1.00.

The purchase and sale operations for a period of eight years are tabulated below; the period embraces a cycle in which costs went from $1.00 to $1.50 and back to $1. The goods were always sold at a price $.50 above the cost of the most recent purchase. The tabulation also shows the gross profit on the *fifo* and *lifo* bases. (The costs applied against the sales are indicated by letters in the "Purchases" and "Gross Profit" columns.)

				Gross Profit			
Year	Purchases		Sales	*Fifo* Basis		*Lifo* Basis	
1	A	$1.00					
	B	1.05	$1.55	A	$0.55	B	$0.50
2	C	1.15	1.65	B	0.60	C	0.50
3	D	1.30	1.80	C	0.65	D	0.50
4	E	1.50	2.00	D	0.70	E	0.50
5	F	1.30	1.80	E	0.30	F	0.50
6	G	1.15	1.65	F	0.35	G	0.50
7	H	1.05	1.55	G	0.40	H	0.50
8	I	1.00	1.50	H	0.45	I	0.50
					$4.00		$4.00

The aggregate gross profits for the eight years were the same in this instance because the first and the last purchase costs were the same.

It will be observed that the *fifo* method resulted in the showing of widely fluctuating gross profits although the company continually adjusted its selling prices to keep them closely related to current purchase costs. The advocates of the *lifo* method would say that it is unrealistic, when the quantity of yearly sales is uniform and sales prices are adjusted in conformity with cost changes, to show annual gross profits varying as widely as 70 and 30. The opponents of the *lifo* method would say that it is unrealistic to price a commodity in the inventory, for balance sheet purposes, at a remote cost not representative of current costs. For instance, at the end of the fourth year in the illustration, the inventory valuation under *lifo* would be $1.00, whereas under the *fifo* method the same inventory would be shown at a 50% higher valuation, or $1.50, which would be a more current, meaningful representation of the investment in the inventory.

Another reason advanced in support of the *lifo* method is that, on a rising market, a portion of the net income shown under the *fifo* method is necessarily plowed back into the inventory, and, although such net income amounts are legally available for dividends, it may be inexpedient, from the working capital standpoint, to distribute them. The *lifo* method tends to keep out of the stated net income any amounts which are not realized in the sense of being represented by a net increase in current assets other than merchandise. To make this point clear, let us refer to the foregoing illustration and assume that the company whose purchases and sales are stated there began its life with the balance sheet shown below.

Cash	$2.00	Capital stock	$2.00

After the first purchase, its balance sheet appears as follows:

Cash	$1.00	Capital stock	$2.00
Inventory	1.00		
	$2.00		$2.00

By the end of the fourth year, the company has made additional purchases totaling $5 and sales totaling $7. Assume, to simplify the case, that it has incurred no expenses and paid no dividends; therefore, its cash has increased $2, and it has a cash balance of $3. Under the *fifo* method its net income for the four years will amount to $2.50, and its balance sheet will be as follows:

Cash	$3.00	Capital stock	$2.00
Inventory	1.50	Retained earnings	2.50
	$4.50		$4.50

If cash in the amount of the entire retained earnings is now distributed as a dividend, the balance sheet will be:

Cash	$ .50	Capital stock	$2.00
Inventory	1.50		
	$2.00		$2.00

After the first purchase, the company had one unit in its inventory and $1 in cash; it now has one unit of inventory and 50 cents in cash. It is not inconceivable that the continuance of such a procedure might result in leaving the company with inadequate cash to carry on successful operations. Of course, the company could limit its dividends to $2, but are not the stockholders perhaps justified in feeling that there is something deficient or peculiar in a situation in which reported earnings cannot be distributed without risking the impairment of working funds?

Under the *lifo* method, the earnings for the four years are shown at $2, the inventory is valued at $1, and the balance sheet appears as follows:

Cash	$3.00	Capital stock	$2.00
Inventory	1.00	Retained earnings	2.00
	$4.00		$4.00

The company can now pay out its entire stated earnings and be in the same asset position as it was after the first purchase—with one unit of merchandise and $1 in cash.

Income taxes should be included in any consideration of *lifo* and *fifo*. And an assumption that a period of increasing prices is followed by a period of relative price stability (and not by a period of declining prices, as was assumed in the preceding example) would be more realistic. Under such conditions, the *fifo* method will result in the reporting of larger earnings and the payment of more income taxes over the years than if the *lifo* method were adopted. These are important considerations for management to weigh, but they should not be the determinants of what constitutes good accounting theory.

Unsettled *lifo* problems. The argument between *lifo* and *fifo* seems to boil down to a question of whether current costs should be regarded as applicable to the inventory to be shown in the balance sheet (*fifo* method) or be matched against current revenue in the income statement (*lifo* method).

The *lifo* method places the emphasis on the income statement, but its effect on the balance sheet, and particularly on the working capital shown therein, should not be overlooked.

If a sustained price rise follows an adoption of the *lifo* method, the dollar balance reported for inventories among the current assets will be substantially less than current costs. Although the *lifo* advocates contend that achieving a more appropriate matching of expense against revenue is such an important objective that it offsets the "incorrect" balance sheet results, the fact remains that, conceivably, inventory quantities might eventually be priced at such "old" costs as to produce a misstatement of working capital position that would be seriously misleading. To some extent, this could be remedied by disclosing current costs for the inventory parenthetically or in a footnote to the balance sheet. This proposal is resisted in some quarters because of the clerical burden it would impose in computing the inventory on two bases. It would be possible to avoid this burden by permitting the use of estimates for purposes of parenthetical disclosure of current costs for the inventory.

In discussions of *lifo,* there seems to be a tacit assumption that a company will adopt the *lifo* method when prices are relatively low though rising. But suppose a company adopts *lifo* when the price level is not at a low point. Under these conditions, it is conceivable that subsequent price declines might bring the replacement costs below the cost level prevailing at the time the company adopted the *lifo* method. In this event, should the *lifo* costs be used for inventory pricing, or should those costs be reduced to coincide with the newer and lower replacement costs? A strict application of the *lifo* method would preclude such a reduction because the matching of current costs against current revenues would thereby be disturbed. However, there is reason to expect that, as with all so-called cost bases of inventory pricing, accountants would sanction a reduction in *lifo* costs when it was apparent that the valuation of a current asset would otherwise be overstated.

A disturbing problem arises whenever a company using the *lifo* method fails, for some reason, to maintain its usual inventory position. If the inventory quantity is drawn down after a significant price rise, a strict application of the *lifo* method would result in matching some old, low costs against current revenues produced by selling goods at current prices. To illustrate, let us assume the following conditions:

Inventory, January 1–1,000 units priced on the *lifo* basis at $100 each	$ 100,000
Purchases during the year–10,000 units at an average cost of $150 each	1,500,000
Sales during the year–10,300 units at an average selling price of $175 each	1,802,500
Inventory, December 31–700 units priced on the *lifo* basis at $100 each	70,000

We here face a situation in which current revenues may be charged with some current costs and with some old costs, as shown below:

Sales–10,300 units		$1,802,500
Cost of sales:		
10,000 units at current costs–$150 each	$1,500,000	
300 units at old costs –$100 each	30,000	1,530,000
Gross profit		$ 272,500

This partial matching of old costs against current revenue would cause some distortion in the net income of the period in which the inventory reduction occurred, because current revenue would not be entirely matched with current costs. Moreover, if the inventory reduction was only temporary and the inventory was replenished in the near future at current costs, a comparison of the replenished inventory with the prior inventory might create a misleading impression, for an equal inventory quantity would be set forth in the accounts at a higher dollar figure–15% higher in the illustration being developed here. This is demonstrated by the following computation, based on the assumption that the inventory was replenished by the purchase of 300 units at $150 each.

Inventory before temporary reduction:		
1,000 units at $100 each		$100,000
Inventory after replenishment:		
700 units at $100 each	$70,000	
300 units at $150 each	45,000	115,000

In some instances an inventory reduction, or "liquidation," may be involuntary, resulting from such uncontrollable causes as shortage of supply or delivery delays due to strikes. In other instances, the quantity reduction may be voluntary, management expecting more favorable purchase prices in the near future. In either case, the inventory quantity impairment could very likely be temporary; and it would seem to be regrettable if income statement and balance sheet distortions were to result from the mere fact that inventory quantities happened to be temporarily low at the end of the accounting period.

Adherents of *lifo* accounting, concentrating on the fundamental objective of matching current costs with current revenues, advocate dealing with such a situation by charging Cost of Sales with current costs, even though some of the goods sold were carried in the accounts at old, lower costs. Referring to the preceding illustration, they would make an entry similar to the following:

Cost of sales (10,300 units at $150 each)	1,545,000	
Inventory (to reduce balance in this account to *lifo* cost of 700 units at $100 each)		30,000
Excess of replacement cost over *lifo* cost of basic inventory temporarily liquidated ($50 × 300)		15,000
Purchases		1,500,000

When the inventory was replenished by the purchase of 300 units, at the current price of $150 per unit, the entry would be:

Inventory (300 units at $100—*lifo* cost)	30,000	
Excess of replacement cost over *lifo* cost of basic inventory temporarily liquidated	15,000	
Cash		45,000

The income statement would then show the following:

Sales—10,300 units	$1,802,500
Cost of goods sold—10,300 units at current cost of $150 each	1,545,000
Gross profit	$ 257,500

The consequences of making entries of the nature indicated above can be shown by a comparison of the results produced without making the foregoing entries and the results obtained by making the entries:

	Without Suggested Entries	With Suggested Entries
Sales	$1,802,500	$1,802,500
Cost of goods sold	1,530,000	1,545,000
Gross profit	$ 272,500	$ 257,500
Inventory before replenishment	$ 70,000	$ 70,000
Excess replacement cost reserve		15,000
Inventory after replenishment	115,000	100,000

The account Excess of Replacement Cost Over *Lifo* Cost of Basic Inventory Temporarily Liquidated would be shown in the balance sheet among the current liabilities.

Adopting *lifo*. If a company changes its inventory pricing method, the resulting effect on net income should be computed and disclosed in the financial statements for the year in which the change was made. This requirement makes it necessary to compute the ending inventory by both the old method and the new method. Thus, if a company decides to abandon *fifo* and adopt *lifo* as of December 31, 1965, it will be necessary to calculate the December 31, 1965 inventory by both the *fifo* and *lifo* methods.

Having made the decision to adopt *lifo* as of December 31, 1965, how are *lifo* costs computed? An acceptable method is to refer to the beginning inventory (December 31, 1964) for this information. The cost figures used there are assumed to be the appropriate costs to apply in pricing the ending inventory quantities not in excess of the December 31, 1964 inventory quantity. In other words, the beginning inventory of the year in which *lifo* is adopted is used as the *lifo* base inventory. For reasons of expediency, the beginning (December 31, 1964) inventory unit costs are averaged in order to arrive at uniform unit-cost data. For example, assume the facts shown below and on the following page in connection with an abandonment of first-in, first-out and the adoption of the last-in, first-out inventory method for 1965 and subsequent years.

December, 31, 1964 inventory (fifo):

Article		Quantity	Unit Costs	Total	Average Unit Costs
A		1,000	$ 9	$ 9,000	
		500	10	5,000	
		500	12	6,000	
	Total—A	2,000		$20,000	$10
B		800	24	$19,200	
		400	27	10,800	
	Total—B	1,200		$30,000	25
	Total			$50,000	

1965 purchases:

	Quantity A	Quantity B	Cost A	Cost B	Total
February 1	1,000		$11		$ 11,000
March 1		600		$28	16,800
June 15	4,000		12		48,000
August 20		1,500		29	43,500
November 25	1,500		13		19,500
December 10		1,200		30	36,000
Total purchases					$174,800

December 31, 1965 inventory:

Quantity: 2,100 units of A
1,100 units of B

Pricing on Last-In, First-Out Basis

Article	Explanation	Quantity	Inventory Price	Total
A	*Lifo* base quantity at established *lifo* cost	2,000	$10	$20,000
	From February 1 purchase	100	11	1,100
	Total—A	2,100		$21,100

Article	Explanation	Quantity	Inventory Price	Total
A	Total (brought forward)			$21,100
B	*Lifo* base quantity is not exceeded, so entire December 31, 1965 quantity is priced at established *lifo* cost	1,100	25	27,500
	Total			$48,600

Pricing on First-In, First-Out Basis

Article	Explanation	Quantity	Inventory Price	Total
A	From November 25 purchase	1,500	$13	$19,500
	From June 15 purchase	600	12	7,200
	Total—A	2,100		$26,700
B	From December 10 purchase	1,100	30	33,000
	Total			$59,700

Computation of effect of change in inventory method on 1965 net income before income taxes:

Inventory, December 31, 1965, first-in, first-out	$59,700
Inventory, December 31, 1965, last-in, first-out	48,600
Net effect—decrease in net income before income taxes	$11,100

The effect on net income (either before or after income taxes) produced by a change in inventory method is generally disclosed by a footnote to the financial statements.

***Lifo* layers.** The technique of inventory valuation applying the *lifo* method can perhaps be best indicated by a graphic presentation of the inventory base and layers at successive dates, as shown on page 238.

We shall assume that the *lifo* base inventory consisted of 1,000 units acquired at an average cost of $10 per unit.

On December 31, 1962, one year later, the inventory consisted of 1,800 units: the 1961 base of 1,000 units, and the 1962 incremental layer of 800 units priced at 1962 costs.

On December 31, 1963, there were 2,400 units in the inventory, consisting of the 1961 base, the 1962 layer, and a 600-unit layer priced at 1963 *lifo* cost.

On December 31, 1964, the inventory had decreased. On the last-in, first-out basis, the decrease came out of the 1963 layer, reducing that layer to 300 units.

On December 31, 1965, the inventory had further decreased. The 1963 layer was gone, and only 500 units of the 1962 layer remained.

On December 31, 1966, the inventory had again decreased, and consisted only of 900 units of the 1961 base.

On December 31, 1967, the inventory had increased 2,000 units. This 2,000-unit increment must be regarded as a new layer, to be priced at 1967 *lifo* cost.

1961
- 1961 Base: 1,000 units at $10

1962
- 1962 Layer: 800 units at $11
- 1961 Base: 1,000 units at $10

1963
- 1963 Layer: 600 units at $12
- 1962 Layer: 800 units at $11
- 1961 Base: 1,000 units at $10

1964
- 1963 Layer: 300 units at $12
- 1962 Layer: 800 units at $11
- 1961 Base: 1,000 units at $10

1965
- 1962 Layer: 500 units at $11
- 1961 Base: 1,000 units at $10

1966
- 1961 Base: 900 units at $10

1967
- 1967 Layer: 2,000 units at $15
- 1961 Base: 900 units at $10

INVENTORY LAYERS AND *LIFO* COSTS AT ENDS OF STATED YEARS

How to price *lifo* layers. Three alternatives are acceptable in pricing an incremental layer. The following data are used to illustrate the application of the alternatives.

Current year's purchases:

Date	Quantity	Cost	Total
January 10	250	$ 9	$2,250
May 15	300	10	3,000
September 20	100	13	1,300
December 27	200	14	2,800
Total	850		$9,350

Average cost—$9,350 ÷ 850 = $11.

Current year's inventory increase (layer)—300 units.

Alternatives:

(1) The incremental quantity is assumed to relate to the first acquisitions of the current year.

Amount to be used in computing new layer of *lifo* inventory:

250 × $ 9 =	$2,250
50 × $10 =	500
Lifo cost	$2,750

(2) Average costs for the current year may be used.

Amount to be used in computing new layer of *lifo* inventory:

300 × $11 = $3,300

(3) The incremental quantity is assumed to relate to the last acquisitions of the current year.

Amount to be used in computing new layer of *lifo* inventory:

200 × $14 =	$2,800
100 × $13 =	1,300
Lifo cost	$4,100

Alternative (1) seems to be the most logical, because it follows the last-in, first-out assumption. However, all three alternatives are acceptable for federal income tax purposes; as a result, all three methods are used in practice.

Once the aggregate dollar amount for any given layer has been determined, it remains unchanged until all or some portion of the layer is sold or utilized.

Dollar-value *lifo*. In the preceding illustration showing how the base inventory and subsequent layers are separated in *lifo* inventory accounting, quantity on hand was the basis used to determine the increments or reductions in the *lifo* inventory. This requires considerable clerical detail, because increments and reductions must be determined for each item in the inventory. Thus, if a business stocks 100 different articles, a record of base and layer quantities must be maintained for each article. To avoid this handicap, dollars may be used as a measure of increments or reductions in a *lifo* inventory.

For example, assuming no change in the price level during the current year, if last year's inventory was $1,000 (at cost) and this year's inventory was $1,100 (at cost), it can be inferred that the inventory has increased 10%. Under *lifo* this would mean that we have an additional layer to deal with. In a sense, this approach views an inventory as a pool or aggregate, in contrast to an item-by-item approach. In practice, the inventory would likely be divided by broad product categories or by departments, with separate *lifo* bases and layers for each grouping.

Of course, the price level changes. So, before we can compare the dollar amount of a current inventory with the dollar amount of a previous inventory to determine whether there has been an increase or decrease, the two inventories being compared must be stated in dollars "of the same size." This could be done by the use of index numbers which measure the extent of changes in the price level. For instance, if it were known that the prices of goods purchased for resale had increased 10% during the current year, an inventory of $11,550, priced by using the current year's costs, could be converted to last year's price level by dividing by 1.10; thus, $11,550 ÷ 1.10 = $10,500.

If last year's inventory amounted to $10,000, the comparison between the $10,500 amount and the $10,000 amount would indicate that the inventory had increased 5%, or by $500 in terms of last year's prices. For purposes of determining the *lifo* inventory, this layer should be stated in terms of the current year's price level, or $550, which is computed by multiplying $500 by 1.10.

Because price index numbers are not available for many industries or lines of business, some alternative device for measuring price change as it affects the inventory of a particular business must be applied. The approach used is to compute an inventory first in terms of current costs and second in terms of the costs prevailing when *lifo* was adopted.

For example, if the current inventory amounts to $110,000 at current costs and to $100,000 in terms of costs prevailing when the *lifo* method was adopted (see below), it can be concluded that as far as this company is concerned, prices of inventory items have gone up 10%.

Inventory

		Unit Costs		Total	
Description	Current Quantity	Current Period	Prevailing When *Lifo* Was Adopted	At Current Costs	At Costs Prevailing When *Lifo* Was Adopted
A	80	$3.00	$2.75	$ 240	$ 220
B	100	2.45	2.25	245	225
C	200	5.50	5.00	1,100	1,000
~~					
				$110,000	$100,000

In the previous paragraph it was stated that each inventory is computed twice—once using current year's costs and again using costs prevailing when the *lifo* method was adopted. It should be pointed out that only a representative sample of the inventory need be thus double-priced, because the purpose of the extra computation is to obtain an index or measure of price change. It should also be mentioned that, as a practical matter, some provision must be made for the effects of discontinued and new products in developing a measure of price change.

The basic techniques of dollar-value *lifo* are illustrated below. Zero is used to designate the year when *lifo* was adopted.

	Inventory of Year			
	0	1	2	3
Priced by using costs of year 0	$10,000			
Priced by using costs of year 1		$10,710		
Priced by using costs of year 2			$11,340	
Priced by using costs of year 3				$11,880
Priced by using costs of year 0	$10,000	$10,500	$10,800	$10,800
Index of price change since year 0, when *lifo* was adopted:				
$10,710 ÷ $10,500		102		
$11,340 ÷ $10,800			105	
$11,880 ÷ $10,800				110

Inventory—*lifo* cost:

Year 0	$10,000

Year 1:

By comparing the year 1 inventory with the year 0 inventory, both stated in dollars of the same price level (year 0), it is seen that there has been an increment to the inventory. This layer amounts to $500 ($10,500 − $10,000) in terms of the price level at year 0. But a new layer must be computed in terms of the current price level, or $500 × 1.02.

Year 1 layer	$ 510
Base	10,000
Inventory—*lifo* cost	$10,510

Year 2:

By comparing year 2 and year 1 inventories, both stated in dollars of the same price level (year 0), it is seen that there has been a further increment to the *lifo* inventory. The year 2 layer amounts to $300 ($10,800 − $10,500) in terms of the price level when *lifo* was adopted. To convert to the year 2 price level, the $300 is multiplied by 1.05.

Year 2 layer ($300 × 1.05)	$ 315
Year 1 layer	510
Base	10,000
Inventory—*lifo* cost	$10,825

Year 3:

By comparing year 3 and year 2 inventories, both stated in dollars of the same price level (year 0), it is seen that there has been no change in the aggregate inventory ($10,800 − $10,800). Therefore, the *lifo* inventory for year 3 is the same as for year 2.

Inventory—*lifo* cost	$10,825

Inventory reductions. Reductions in *lifo* inventories are subtracted first from the most recent layer (or layers, depending on the extent of the reduction), and, after all layers have been utilized, then from the base inventory. To show how a reduction is handled under dollar-value *lifo,* continue the illustration for an additional year and assume that the inventory for year 4 is as follows:

Priced using costs of year 4	$11,770
Priced using costs of year 0	$10,700

By comparing year 4 and year 3 inventories, both stated in dollars of the same price level (year 0), it is seen that there has been a reduction of $100 ($10,800 – $10,700). This reduction is taken from the year 2 layer, as follows:

Year 2 layer stated in terms of year 0 prices	$300	
Reduction occurring during year 4	100	
Remaining layer	$200	
Price index for year 2	1.05	
Remainder of year 2 layer in terms of *lifo* cost	$210	
Inventory—*lifo* cost:		
Year 4:		
Year 2 layer		$ 210
Year 1 layer		510
Base		10,000
Inventory—*lifo* cost		$10,720

Effect of *lifo* on the gross profit method. If a company is using the *lifo* inventory method, the gross profit method for approximating an ending inventory in terms of *lifo* costs can be used only with extreme caution. This situation is attributable to the fact that typically the relation of *lifo* inventory costs to selling prices is considerably at variance with the relation of recent purchase prices to selling prices. Suppose that a company establishes a pricing policy of selling, for $10 each, articles that currently cost $6 to acquire at wholesale. If the company has been on a *lifo* basis for a considerable period of time, the articles might conceivably be carried in the beginning inventory at $3 each. If it should develop in any given year that more items were sold than were purchased, the resulting net reduction in the inventory would produce a distortion in the actual gross profit margin, because some of the goods sold would have been assigned to cost of sales at $3 each, thus inflating the gross profit margin.

For example, assume the following case, in which goods are sold for $10 each and the gross profit rate for several preceding periods was 40%:

Sales, at $10 each, 6,000 units		$60,000
Cost of goods sold:		
Inventory, January 1, 2,000 units at $3 each	$ 6,000	
Purchases for the year at $6 each, 5,000 units	30,000	
Total	$36,000	
Inventory, December 31, 1,000 units at $3 each	3,000	33,000
Gross profit on sales		$27,000

The gross profit rate indicated by the above is 45%. If this distorted gross profit per cent were used in the following period to estimate the inventory by the gross profit method, the results would be unreliable. To illustrate, assume that 5,000 units were sold during the following year, and that sufficient units were purchased to cover the quantity sold. An estimate of the ending inventory by the gross profit method would indicate an inventory of $5,500, whereas in fact the inventory would be $3,000, an error of 83⅓%.

Inventory, January 1, 1,000 units at $3 each		$ 3,000
Purchases for the year at $6 each, 5,000 units		30,000
Total		$33,000
Deduct approximate cost of goods sold:		
Sales, at $10 each, 5,000 units	$50,000	
Less estimated gross profit of 45%	22,500	27,500
Approximate inventory, December 31		$ 5,500

Under *lifo* procedures, the ending inventory would be priced as follows:

Inventory, December 31, 1,000 units (see computation below) at $3 each	$3,000

Computation of Inventory Quantity

	Units
Inventory, January 1	1,000
Purchases for the year	5,000
Total	6,000
Sales	5,000
Inventory, December 31	1,000

Incidentally, the accountant should realize that with the *lifo* method management can intentionally distort gross profit and net income by deliberately curtailing purchases and thereby "dipping into" the *lifo* base quantity.

***Lifo* and the retail method.** When an accountant applies the *lifo* concept to the retail method, he must use procedures which are somewhat different from those used under the conventional retail method.

First difference:

Include markdowns as well as markups in the determination of the cost ratio.

As previously stated, the conventional retail method produces an inventory valuation which closely approximates the amount which would be obtained by taking a physical inventory and pricing the goods at the lower of cost or market. *Lifo,* on the other hand, is a cost method. It is possible to modify the retail method to produce results reasonably conforming to a cost basis by *including markdowns* as well as markups in the determination of the cost ratio.

Second difference:

Ignore the beginning inventory in the determination of the cost ratio.

After the *lifo* method has been in use for a period of time, the difference between current costs and the "old" costs that are considered by the *lifo* method to be applicable to the inventory becomes quite significant. Because the cost ratio is intended to indicate the current relationship between costs and selling prices, the beginning inventory data are not used in the computation of the cost ratio because their inclusion could have a distorting effect on the cost ratio.

The contrasting procedures under the conventional retail method (intended to produce an inventory valuation on the basis of the lower of cost or market) and under the *lifo* method (intended to produce an inventory valuation on a cost basis) are illustrated below.

	Conventional Retail		*Lifo* Retail	
	Cost	Retail	Cost	Retail
→ Inventory—beginning of year	$ 3,200	$ 5,500	Omitted from cost ratio	
Purchases	15,600	24,500	$15,600	$24,500
Transportation in	400		400	
Markups		2,000		2,000
Total	$19,200	$32,000		$26,500
Conventional cost ratio: $19,200 ÷ $32,000	(60%)			
Markdowns		2,500		2,500
Remainder			$16,000	$24,000
Lifo cost ratio: $16,000 ÷ $24,000			(66⅔%)	
→ Inventory—beginning of year				5,500
Total goods, at retail		$29,500		$29,500
Sales		23,500		23,500
Inventory at retail—end of year		$ 6,000		$ 6,000
Applicable cost ratio		60%		66⅔%
Inventory valuation		$ 3,600		$ 4,000

It will be noted that the markups and markdowns were applied, in the foregoing computation of the *lifo* cost ratio, to the selling price of the goods purchased, although they presumably applied in part to the opening inventory. Obviously, this is not strictly correct; however, the slight theoretical impropriety usually is ignored.

The practice of disregarding the beginning inventory when computing the cost ratio is a feature of the *lifo* retail method and, therefore, is followed in all subsequent years and not confined merely to the computation of the base or beginning *lifo* inventory.

Changing from conventional to *lifo* retail. If a conventional retail procedure has been in operation and a decision is reached to change to a *lifo* retail procedure, the following requirements must be observed.

(1) The inventory selected for the *lifo* base, usually the beginning inventory of the year in which the change to *lifo* is made, must be restated on a cost basis by the application of the retail method as

modified by the *lifo* procedures illustrated in the preceding paragraph.

The preceding illustration demonstrates the application of this requirement; if the data pertain to the year prior to that in which the switch-over was made, then the ending inventory of the prior year and, consequently, the opening or base inventory of the year of change would be $4,000.

(2) The effect of the change in inventory methods on net income should be computed and disclosed in the financial statements for the year in which the change was made.

As noted earlier, this requirement is applicable whenever inventory methods are changed.

Subsequent inventories—no changes in the price level. The basic operational features of *lifo* are not affected by the retail-method application. Distinctions must be maintained between the base inventory and any subsequent layers or increments to the inventory. The cost ratio of a particular period is used only to convert the layer of that period to cost. If there is no increase in the inventory in a given year, the cost ratio of that year is not used in converting the inventory from retail to cost.

The following schedule, covering a six-year period after the adoption of *lifo,* illustrates the application of *lifo* procedures to the retail inventory method.

Year	Cost Ratio For Year	Inventory at Retail	Base-Period Inventory at Retail	Increments at Retail (Reference to Year)	Applicable Cost Ratio	*Lifo* Cost: Layers	*Lifo* Cost: Base	Inventory Total
Base	66⅔%	$ 6,000	$6,000		66⅔%		$4,000	$4,000
1	70	8,000	6,000	$2,000 (1)	70	$1,400	4,000	5,400
2	75	9,000	6,000	2,000 (1)	70	1,400		
				1,000 (2)	75	750	4,000	6,150
3	80	12,000	6,000	2,000 (1)	70	1,400		
				1,000 (2)	75	750		
				3,000 (3)	80	2,400	4,000	8,550
4	78	10,000	6,000	2,000 (1)	70	1,400		
				1,000 (2)	75	750		
				1,000 (3)	80	800	4,000	6,950
5	73	7,000	6,000	1,000 (1)	70	700	4,000	4,700
6	69	4,800	6,000					
			1,200*					
			4,800		66⅔		3,200	3,200

* Reduction of base.

Because the inventory at retail is now smaller than the inventory at retail when the *lifo* method was established, the 66⅔% cost ratio prevailing at that time is applicable, and the inventory at the end of the sixth period is stated at a *lifo* cost of 66⅔% of $4,800, or $3,200.

Subsequent inventories—changes in the level of selling prices. In the preceding illustration it was assumed that the level of retail selling prices remained unchanged during the entire period. When retail prices are not stable, it is necessary to make use of retail price indices to adjust the inventory to a retail valuation which would have been shown by the retail records if there had been no change in selling prices.

To illustrate, assume that the retail records of a store showed the following:

	Cost	Retail	Cost Ratio
Purchases	$21,000	$28,000	75%
Base inventory, December 31, 1964	4,000	6,000	
Total		$34,000	
Sales		25,200	
Inventory at retail, December 31, 1965		$ 8,800	

Assume, also, that the retail index applicable to this business was 100 for 1964 and 110 for 1965.

We first reduce the December 31, 1965 inventory at retail to the basis of 1964 selling prices:	
$8,800 ÷ 1.10	$8,000
And then deduct the December 31, 1964 inventory at retail	6,000
To determine the inventory increment in terms of 1964 selling prices	$2,000
The inventory increment in terms of 1965 selling prices was $2,000 × 1.10, or	$2,200

The December 31, 1965 inventory priced at $8,800 retail can now be reduced to *lifo* cost as follows:

	Lifo Cost	Retail
Segment equal to base inventory:		
On 1964 price basis		$6,000
Old cost	$4,000	
Price inflation		600
Incremental segment:		
At retail		2,200
At *lifo* cost—determined by applying the cost ratio of the period—75% of $2,200	1,650	
Total	$5,650	$8,800

Extended illustration. The AB Store adopts the retail inventory method and *lifo* in 1965. Its December 31, 1964 inventory was $80,000 at cost and $130,000 at retail. Inventory computations at three subsequent dates are shown below. The illustration has been simplified by omitting some of the items usually found with the retail method, such as transportation in and markups and markdowns. Applicable index numbers were as follows:

1964	100	1966	110
1965	104	1967	105

	Cost	Retail	Cost Ratio
Data for 1965:			
Purchases	$240,000	$400,000	60%
Inventory—beginning of year (which is the base inventory)	80,000	130,000	
Total		$530,000	
Sales		389,600	
Inventory—end of year		$140,400	

	Cost	Retail	Cost Ratio
Reduction to *lifo* cost:			
1965 inventory in terms of 1964 prices—$140,400 ÷ 1.04		$135,000	
1964 inventory (base)	$ 80,000	130,000	
Increment in inventory:			
In terms of 1964 prices		$ 5,000	
In terms of 1965 prices—$5,000 × 1.04		$ 5,200	
At *lifo* cost—60% of $5,200	3,120		
1965 inventory at *lifo* cost	$ 83,120		
Data for 1966:			
Purchases	$260,400	$420,000	62%
Inventory—beginning of year	83,120	140,400	
Total		$560,400	
Sales		408,600	
Inventory—end of year		$151,800	
Reduction to *lifo* cost:			
1966 inventory in terms of 1964 prices—$151,800 ÷ 1.10		$138,000	
1964 inventory (base)	$ 80,000	130,000	
Increment over 1964 inventory		$ 8,000	
Portion of increment arising in 1965 (see above)	3,120	5,000	
Portion of increment arising in 1966:			
In terms of 1964 prices		$ 3,000	
In terms of 1966 prices—$3,000 × 1.10		$ 3,300	
At *lifo* cost—62% of $3,300	2,046		
1966 inventory at *lifo* cost	$ 85,166		
Data for 1967:			
Purchases	$292,500	$450,000	65%
Inventory—beginning of year	85,166	151,800	
Total		$601,800	
Sales		463,200	
Inventory—end of year		$138,600	
Reduction to *lifo* cost:			
1967 inventory in terms of 1964 prices—$138,600 ÷ 1.05		$132,000	
1964 inventory (base)	$ 80,000	130,000	
Increment over 1964 inventory—regarded under *lifo* theory as acquired in 1965:			
In terms of 1964 prices		$ 2,000	
In terms of 1965 prices—computed by using 1965 price index—$2,000 × 1.04		$ 2,080	
At *lifo* cost—reduced by using 1965 cost ratio—60% of $2,080	1,248		
1967 inventory at *lifo* cost	$ 81,248		

"Nifo." *Nifo* is an abbreviation for "next-in, first-out." Thus far, *nifo* has not attained a status of acceptability as an inventory-pricing method. As the expression indicates, under this approach cost of sales would be computed by using replacement costs. As a result, income would be measured by matching current revenues and the replacement costs of the goods sold.

The argument for *nifo* is founded on reasoning that can be summarized in the following manner. Assume that a merchant has on hand an article that cost $10. Suppose that it is sold for $15. If the merchant is going to continue in business, he must replace the article sold. Assume that the replacement cost is $12. Under these conditions, a proponent of *nifo* would argue that conventional accounting misstates gross profit by reporting it as $5 (because $2 of the $5 reported gross profit is needed to maintain the inventory), and that gross profit and net income would be more truthfully reported if the article sold were "costed" at the $12 replacement cost. The $3 gross profit thus reported under the *nifo* method would measure the real gain produced by the sale, because of the elimination of the "fictitious" profit element that would have to be used merely to maintain a normal inventory.

Base-stock method. The base-stock (sometimes called "normal stock") method is founded on a theory which may be indicated as follows: If a company considers that its inventory of a certain commodity should never normally fall below 100 units, the 100 units are the base stock, and no increase in the market replacement cost of this base stock should be regarded as realized income because, like fixed assets, the base stock cannot be disposed of if the business is to continue operations. To avoid the taking of any profit on such "unrealized" market increases, the base-stock quantities should be priced for inventory purposes at not more than the lowest cost experienced. It should be noted that the base quantity is the minimum quantity a given business needs to carry on normal operations, not an average inventory quantity.

Units sold or issued for manufacture are priced out at the most recent acquisition cost; in this regard, the base-stock method is similar to the last-in, first-out method, because current costs are matched against current revenues. For this reason, the base-stock method (which was developed before the last-in, first-out method) is sometimes regarded as the precursor of the *lifo* method.

The operation of the base-stock method may be illustrated as follows:

	Units	Unit Price	Amount
First purchase (and base-stock quantity)	100	$1.00	$100.00
Second purchase	200	1.10	220.00
Total	300		$320.00
First sale	175	1.10	192.50
Inventory	125		$127.50
Third purchase	250	1.20	300.00
Total	375		$427.50
Second sale	275	1.20	330.00
Inventory	100		$ 97.50
Fourth purchase	100	1.25	125.00
Total	200		$222.50
Third sale	50	1.25	62.50
Inventory	150		$160.00

Observe that, after the second sale, and as a result of costing out 275 units at the most recent unit cost of $1.20, although only 250 units were purchased at so high a cost, the inventory of 100 units—the base quantity—is priced at less than the original base cost of $100.

The results disclosed above are those which would result from a perpetual inventory record. The perpetual inventory record would be adjusted from time to time, at least annually, to conform to the results of a physical inventory, for which the pricing procedure usually adopted is as follows:

If quantities are in excess of base stock:

Base-stock quantities at base price.
Plus excess quantities at current cost.

For instance, if there are 150 units in the inventory, the valuation would be determined as follows:

100 units at $1.00	$100.00
50 units at 1.25	62.50
150	$162.50

If quantities are less than base stock:

Base-stock quantities at base price.
Less deficient quantities at current cost.

For instance, if there are 95 units in the inventory, the valuation would be determined as follows:

100 units at $1.00	$100.00
5 units at 1.25	6.25
95	$ 93.75

The above computations disclose the primary contrasting feature of the base-stock method and the *lifo* method. Under *lifo* procedures, if the ending-inventory quantity is less than the beginning-inventory quantity, the entire quantity is priced by using the *lifo* unit costs used in the beginning inventory. No use is made of current costs or costs applicable to recent purchases.

Because the base price should be the lowest cost experienced, a reduction of market costs below the originally adopted base price should result in the adoption of the new and lower cost as the base price.

The base-stock method is not in general use and is not acceptable for income tax purposes.

Under the base-stock method, the prices used are ordinarily lower—often substantially lower—than current market costs. As a consequence, the inventory shown in the balance sheet may be misleading. This is also typical of *lifo*. It would seem equally appropriate, as suggested in the case of *lifo,* to disclose by footnote the approximate difference between the amount shown and the valuation on a current-cost basis, or by stating parenthetically the inventory on a current-cost basis. Such disclosure is not required by present reporting standards.

CHAPTER 14

Investments

Types of securities. The two principal classes of securities are stocks and bonds. There are so many varieties of each of these two classes that it is impossible to give a complete list of the various types; the following outline includes some of them.

(A) Stocks:
- (1) Common.
- (2) Preferred:
  - (a) As to dividends.
    - Cumulative or noncumulative.
    - Participating or nonparticipating.
  - (b) As to assets.

The characteristics of stocks are described in Chapter 5.

(B) Bonds:
- (1) Classification as to nature of business or obligor:
  - (a) Governments.
  - (b) Municipals: cities and other governmental subdivisions.
  - (c) Public utilities: gas and electric companies, city bus lines, and so forth.
  - (d) Railroads.
  - (e) Industrials: manufacturing and trading concerns.
  - (f) Real estate: apartments, hotels, office buildings, and so forth.
- (2) Classification as to nature of obligation:
  - (a) Mortgage bonds.
  - (b) Collateral trust bonds.
  - (c) Guaranteed bonds.
  - (d) Debenture bonds.
  - (e) Income bonds.

(f) Participating bonds.
(g) Convertible bonds.
(3) Classification as to evidence of ownership and method of collecting interest:
(a) Registered bonds.
(b) Coupon bonds.

Mortgage bonds. There are so many kinds of bonds, carrying so many different kinds of rights, that a general definition can be stated only in the broadest terms. A bond is a promise to pay the principal of and interest on a loan. It differs from a note in that it is more formal and is under seal. In corporate financing, notes are usually given for short-time loans, and bonds for long-time loans; this is a matter of expediency and is not a necessary characteristic of a note or a bond.

A mortgage is a transfer of title to property, usually made by a borrower to a lender, subject to the condition that, upon due payment of the debt, the title to the property is to revest in the borrower. Formerly, a mortgage was considered an actual, although conditional, conveyance of title to the property; if the debt was not paid, the title to the mortgaged property then vested in the mortgagee absolutely.

The modern theory of a mortgage is that it is primarily a security device. Although the mortgage deed does purport to convey to the mortgagee title to the pledged property, actually it serves only to create a lien on the property.

Mortgages may be used with either notes or bonds. If the borrower is able to find a person who is willing to loan the entire amount desired, the note and mortgage may be used; the note recites the terms of the obligation, and the mortgage serves as the security.

If it is necessary to borrow the money from a number of persons, the bond and trust deed are used. The bond issue creates a number of obligations, all of equal rank and all equally secured. However, because there are a number of lenders, because these lenders are not known when the bond issue is being arranged, and because the lenders will change with each transfer of a bond, a mortgage cannot name the lenders personally as the transferees of the pledged property. Therefore, a trust deed, rather than a mortgage deed, is used. Corporations, when borrowing funds on long-time bond issues, generally use the trust deed. By such a deed the corporation conveys the property to a third person, usually a bank or a trust company, as trustee. Upon final payment of the bonds by the corporation, the trustee executes and delivers to the corporation a release deed, whereby the lien on the corporate property created by the trust deed is removed. In the event of a default in payment of the bonds, the trustee may commence foreclosure proceedings for the benefit of the bondholders. It should be understood, therefore, that the issuance of bonds secured by a trust deed is, for all practical purposes, a mortgage transaction and is so considered by law.

Bonds may be secured by first, second, third, and even more mortgages. If the obligations are not met and foreclosure ensues, the proceeds of the property must go first to the satisfaction of the first-mortgage bondholders, any residue to the satisfaction of the second-mortgage bondholders, and so on. Bonds secured by prior liens are called *underlying bonds;* the others are called *junior bonds.*

The mere fact that a bond is called a *first-mortgage bond* does not necessarily mean that it has a lien prior to all others. To illustrate, assume that each of three companies, *A*, *B*, and *C*, has two mortgages on its property. A consolidation is effected by which the three companies are combined, and a new issue of bonds is marketed, secured by a mortgage on all of the property. This issue might be called *First Consolidated Bonds,* but it is really secured by a third mortgage. On the other hand, assume that first-, second-, and third-mortgage bonds have been issued, and that the first and second have been paid; the third-mortgage bonds really have a first lien on the pledged property.

Collateral trust bonds. Collateral trust bonds are similar to collateral notes in that they are secured by pledged collateral. To illustrate, assume that a corporation holds stocks and bonds of several subsidiaries. The tangible property of the holding company and the subsidiaries may be mortgaged to the point where junior mortgage issues cannot be marketed; therefore, the holding company issues its own bonds and places the stocks and bonds of the subsidiaries in the hands of a trustee as collateral.

Guaranteed bonds. A corporation obligates itself to pay the principal of and interest on its bonds, but it cannot guarantee to do so. If a guarantee is made, it must be made by a third party. Sometimes a holding company will guarantee the principal and interest of the bonds of its subsidiaries, and sometimes a company leasing the property of another company will guarantee the bonds of that company.

Debenture bonds. A debenture bond, or debenture, is merely an unsecured bond. It is similar to an unsecured note, in that it rests on the general credit of the debtor. It may or may not be a safe investment, depending upon the financial condition of the issuing company.

Income bonds. The peculiar feature of an income bond is that the payment of interest is conditional upon the earning of income. If the debtor company's income is not sufficient to pay the interest, there is no obligation to pay interest. The bond may be cumulative or noncumulative. If cumulative, any interest not paid in one year becomes a lien against future earnings; if noncumulative, any interest lost in one year is lost forever. The principal may or may not be secured.

Such bonds are sometimes used in reorganizations, in which a scaling down of interests results in security holders taking a less desirable form of security than the one formerly held.

Participating bonds. These are sometimes called "profit-sharing bonds" because, in addition to assuring the holder a definite rate of return regardless of operating results, they entitle him to participate with the stockholders in the earnings of the company. The participation may be pro rata or limited.

Convertible bonds. A convertible bond gives its holder the right to exchange the bond for some other security, usually common stock, of the issuing company. The bond stipulates the terms on which the transfer can be made: that is, par for par; or par for the bond and book value for the stock; or par and accrued interest for the bond and par and "accrued" dividends for the stock; or any other arrangement.

Such bonds give the holder a more assured income and secured principal during the development period of the issuing company than he might have as a stockholder, with a right to become a stockholder if the company is successful.

Registered and coupon bonds. Bonds may be divided into three general types, on the basis of registry:

(1) Registered both as to principal and as to interest.
The name of the owner of the bond is registered on the books of the issuing company or its fiscal agent, and interest is paid by check, drawn to the order of the bondholder. This method has the advantage of safeguarding the owner against loss or theft, because the transfer of a stolen bond could be accomplished only by a forgery. On the other hand, a sale and transfer can be made only by assignment and registry, instead of by delivery.

(2) Registered as to principal only.
If the bond is registered as to principal only, and coupons for the interest are attached, the owner is safeguarded against loss or theft of principal, while the debtor company is relieved of the burden of issuing interest checks.

(3) No registration.
Such a bond is transferable by delivery, without endorsement; interest is collected by clipping coupons and presenting them to a bank for deposit or collection.

GENERAL MATTERS RELATIVE TO INVESTMENTS

Costs of investments. The cost of an investment includes brokerage, taxes, and other expenditures incident to acquisition.

If securities are purchased through a broker on margin account, the books and the balance sheet should reflect as an asset the full cost of the securities and not merely the margin deposit, and the unpaid balance should be shown as a liability. Similarly, if securities are purchased on an installment contract, it is important to set up as an asset the full cost of the securities.

If two or more classes of securities are purchased for a single lump-sum payment, market values may be used for the purpose of apportioning the cost. For example, if 100 shares of common stock and 100 shares of preferred stock of a company are bought at a lump price at a time when the preferred stock has a market value of $105 per share and the common stock has a market value of $140 per share, the total purchase cost may be apportioned in the ratio of 105/245 to the preferred stock and 140/245 to the common stock. If only one of the classes of securities acquired has an ascertainable market value, the lump price may be apportioned by allocating the known market value to the one class of securities, and the remainder of the price to the securities with no ascertainable market value. If neither of the securities has a known market value, it may be necessary to postpone any apportionment of the purchase price until at least one market value can be established.

Exchanges. In accordance with the terms of issuance, securities of one class may be convertible at the option of the holder into other securities of the same company. Accountants are in agreement that, if no fair market value at the date of conversion is determinable for either class of securities, the securities received should be recorded at the cost or carrying value of the securities parted with.

There appears to be no unanimity of opinion regarding the proper method of recording an exchange if there is an ascertainable market value for one or the other class of securities. Suppose that a company owns 100 shares of convertible preferred stock of *X* Company which it acquired and is carrying at a cost of $100 per share, or a total of $10,000, and that this stock is exchanged for 100 shares of common stock of the same company with a market value of $125 per share. The decision to convert probably results in some changes in the rights of the investor. The position of a common stockholder relative to voting, dividends, and such matters is generally different from that of a preferred stockholder. Accordingly, there is some justification for the opinion that a new basis of accountability should be established for the investment at conversion by recording the common stock at its fair market value of $12,500 and taking up a gain of $2,500. On the other hand, and probably with greater justification and more widespread support, the transaction may be regarded as a purchase of the common stock, to be recorded at the $10,000 cost of the consideration initially given.

In reorganizations and mergers in which the exchange of securities is not made at the option of the holder as the exercise of a privilege granted under the terms of issuance of the securities held, the entry for the exchange of the securities will depend primarily upon whether the holder remains in essentially the same position with respect to his equities after the exchange as before. If his status remains practically unchanged, the security received can be put on the books at the cost or carrying value of the security relinquished, and no gain or loss need be recognized. If, however, the holder's status is materially affected, by reason of a change in the number or nature of the securities held before and after the transaction, the newly acquired securities should be put on the books at their fair market value, and the difference between this value and the carrying value of the old securities should be recorded as a gain or loss.

Sales: costs, gains, and losses. If several purchases of the same security are made at different prices, a question may arise concerning the gain or loss on the sale of a portion of the holdings. To illustrate, assume that 20 shares of *X* Company stock were purchased at $100 per share; another 20 shares were subsequently purchased at $125; and 10 shares were later sold at $110. Did the sale produce a gain of $10 per share (the difference between the selling price and the cost of the first shares purchased), or a loss of $15 per share (the difference between the selling price and the cost of the second shares purchased), or a loss of $2.50 per share (the difference between the selling price and the average cost)?

For tax purposes, average costs are not recognized. If the shares sold can be identified as pertaining to the first lot purchased, the transaction can be regarded as producing a gain of $10 per share. If they can be identified as belonging to the second lot purchased, a loss of $15 per share may be reported. If they cannot be identified as pertaining to either lot (which would be the case if the certificates for the two purchases had been converted into a single certificate for all of the shares), the shares sold should be regarded as pertaining to the first lot purchased.

This rule, which is obligatory for tax purposes, appears to be reasonable for general accounting purposes. However, average costs are also recognized from the standpoint of general accounting theory.

Valuation of securities. The rules for the valuation of securities in the accounts and on the balance sheet, and the methods of accounting for investments, depend to some extent on whether the investment is to be held for a short period or for a long period. The following classification reflects this distinction:

(1) Temporary investments:
- (a) Merchandise of a dealer in securities.
- (b) Speculative holdings.
- (c) Investments of surplus funds, forming part of the working capital. Such temporary investments are usually found in industries doing a seasonal business; the excess funds not needed during a slack period are invested temporarily to obtain the income.
- (d) Securities taken on account.

(2) Long-term investments:
- (a) Stock interests in subsidiaries.
- (b) Small holdings maintained for the purpose of establishing business connections.
- (c) Sinking funds and other funds.

Temporary investments. Investments may be classified as current assets if they are of a temporary nature, if it is the owner's intention to convert them into cash to meet cash requirements during the operating cycle, and if there is a ready market for them either on a securities exchange or elsewhere. The mere fact that a security is readily marketable is not sufficient justification for marshalling it among the current assets; the nature of the business of the owning company and the nature and purpose of the investment should be such as to make the current disposal of the security probable. Unless this rule is rigidly adhered to, there is a danger of overstating the working capital by including among current assets securities which, though having a ready market, are really long-term investments.

Because temporary investments in securities are current assets, the traditional view holds that they should be valued at the lower of cost or market for balance sheet purposes. It is not customary to apply the cost-or-market rule to investments by taking the lower value for each item; it is considered sufficient to determine the total valuation of the portfolio at cost and at market and to use the lower of these totals.

Investors cannot take losses from market declines as a tax deduction, but can take gains and losses only upon disposal, the gain or loss being the difference between cost and sales price; therefore, a record of the cost of the securities should be maintained, and any write-downs to market values are preferably made by credit to a contra account rather than to the asset account. The offsetting charge should be made against income.

When the lower-of-cost-or-market rule is applied, the account balance may not always be indicative of the cash potential of this particular current asset because any appreciation in the value of the investments would not be recorded. If current market value could be adopted as the valuation method in place of the lower of cost or market, the cash potential of the temporary investments would be shown at each balance sheet date, which some contend would improve the informative quality of the Current Assets section of the balance sheet. But because such an alternative method could result in writing up an asset above cost, it is not generally accepted. Thus far, the accountant's reliance on realization as a condition precedent to revenue or gain and his inclination to be conservative have worked against asset write-ups. However, accountants do not object to the parenthetical disclosure of current market values which are above cost, and when the amount temporarily invested in marketable securities is material and when the current market value is significantly above cost, such disclosure is recommended.

Long-term investments. Minor declines in the market value of long-term investments in stocks or bonds need not be reflected by entries in the accounts; the market may recover before the investments are realized. But serious declines in the market values of long-term investments should be reflected in the accounts, particularly if there is a probable inability to recover cost; the credit to record the decrease in valuation should be made in a contra account rather than in the asset account, so as to preserve a record of costs for tax purposes. Here is the journal entry that seems desirable when market value decreases:

Market loss on securities	20,000	
Allowance to reduce securities to market		20,000
Provision for decline in market value.		

The investment may be shown on the asset side of the balance sheet, thus:

Stocks owned:		
Cost	$100,000	
Less reduction to market	20,000	$80,000

or merely thus:

Stocks owned—at market, which is lower than cost	$80,000

However, the American Institute's 1962 edition of *Accounting Trends and Techniques* states: "... marketable securities, when shown in the noncurrent asset sections of the balance sheet ... are invariably valued at cost."

If, for any reason, declines in the market value of long-term or temporary investments in securities are not recorded in the accounts, and the securities are stated in the balance sheet at a value other than market, it is important to state the market value parenthetically.

Subsequent adjustments of valuation accounts. If a contra account has been set up to reflect the decline in the market value of temporary or long-term investments, and the market further declines, the contra account can be increased by an additional charge against income.

If, after a contra account has been set up, the market value increases, it has been generally regarded as acceptable to reduce the valuation account in order to reflect the new market value. If such an adjustment is made, it should be recorded as a correction of prior years' earnings. However, there is a respected school of thought which maintains that, although the reduction in the carrying value of the investment is justified on the ground of conservatism, a subsequent credit to income or retained earnings prior to sale would be unjustified because of the absence of realization.

MATTERS RELATIVE TO INVESTMENTS IN STOCKS

Adjustments of cost. After stock investments are made, any subsequent assessments paid or any contributions made for the purpose of eliminating a deficit or for other reasons should be added to the original cost; and any receipts from the issuing corporation representing a return of capital should be deducted from the original cost.

Dividends on stock investments. Dividends are usually declared on one day, payable on a subsequent day, to stockholders of record at some intermediate date. At which of these dates should the dividends be recorded as income to the stockholder? Income should not be taken up until the date of record because the stock may be sold before that date and the right to receive the dividend be thereby lost. At the date of record an entry can be made debiting Dividends Receivable and crediting Dividend Income. When the dividend is collected, the entry is: debit Cash and credit Dividends Receivable.

Dividends received in property should be recorded at the fair market value of the property received. Dividends received from companies engaged in the exploitation of assets subject to depletion may consist partly of income and partly of a return of capital. The portion representing a liquidating dividend should be so designated by the corporation and should be recorded by the recipient as a reduction of the cost of the stock investment.

Stock received as a dividend. Stockholders may receive additional shares as a result of a stock dividend. As a general rule, stock dividends are not income to the recipients from either the general accounting or the income tax standpoint. There is no distribution of assets of the corporation, but merely a change in the component elements of the stockholders' equity; far from being a distribution from retained earnings, a stock dividend constitutes a notice to stockholders that a portion of the retained earnings will not thereafter be available for asset distribution.

If a person owns 100 shares out of a total of 1,000 outstanding shares, and if the corporation issues a 25% stock dividend, the stockholder's shares are increased to 125 and the total outstanding shares are increased to 1,250; but, so far as the stockholder is concerned, he still has a 10% interest in the corporation and the only effect of the stock dividend is an increase in the number of shares by which his equity is represented. Therefore, the receipt of a stock dividend should not be recorded by any entry increasing the carrying value of the investment or taking up income. The only necessary record of the dividend received is a notation in the investment account indicating the increase in the number of shares held.

If stock is acquired at various times and at different prices, if some of the shares are sold, and if the shares sold cannot be identified as pertaining to any particular lot, the cost of the shares sold can be determined, for purposes of computing gain or loss, on the first-in, first-out theory. How should stock received as a dividend be dealt with in applying this theory? If 100 shares were purchased in 1963 at $100 each, another 100 shares were purchased in 1964 at $125 each, another 100 shares were acquired in 1965 at a cost of $150 per share, and a 25% stock dividend was received in 1966, the 75 shares received as a dividend should not be regarded as having been acquired in 1966; they should be associated with the shares on which they were received as a dividend. Thus, the three purchases should now be regarded as follows:

Date	Shares Purchased	Cost	Shares Owned	Adjusted Cost per Share
1963	100	$10,000	125	$ 80
1964	100	12,500	125	100
1965	100	15,000	125	120

If bonds or other similar evidences of indebtedness are received as a dividend, proper accounting and the tax regulations require that they be taken up as assets and income at their fair market value.

Dividends payable in stock or in cash at the option of the stockholder, and taken in stock at his option, are regarded as taxable income.

Likewise, a stock dividend is taxable to the extent that it is distributed in discharge of preference dividends for the distributing corporation's current or preceding tax year.

Stock rights, or warrants. A legal right to purchase stock at a stated price during a specified period may be granted in the form of a stock-purchase warrant or a stock right. Such warrants or rights are issued by corporations and are generally transferable and thus may be purchased or sold by investors as are shares of stock.

The words *warrants* and *rights* are often used interchangeably. The term *warrants* is generally used when the privilege of purchasing shares of common stock, at a price that is potentially attractive, is issued with some other form of security, such as a bond or preferred stock. For example, each bond issued by a corporation may have a warrant attached which enables the holder of the warrant to purchase a specified number of shares of the company's common stock at a stated price during a period of time. Initially, the stated purchase price may be above the prevailing market price of the stock, in which case the warrants probably will have no immediate value. The warrants will become valuable should the market price of the common stock increase and exceed the purchase price stated in the warrants. However, if the warrants have a market value when acquired, the cost of the "investment package" should be allocated between the security acquired (the bond or the preferred stock, as the case may be) and the warrant, following the approach discussed on page 254 of this chapter under the heading "Costs of investments." When warrants are purchased separately in the securities market, their cost is debited to a suitably described asset account. The asset is accounted for as are other investments. A gain or loss may result from their subsequent sale. The warrants account is credited, as is cash, when the warrants are used to purchase from the corporation the common stock described in the warrants.

The entries below, related to the assumed facts, illustrate the proper accounting for stock warrants purchased in a securities market.

Cost of warrants purchased—$1,000.
200 warrants permitting purchase of 400 shares of common stock for $20 per share.

Cost of stock warrants	1,000	
Cash		1,000

Sale of 100 warrants—$600.

Cash	600	
Cost of stock warrants		500
Gain on sale of stock warrants		100

Use of remaining 100 warrants to purchase 200 shares of stock for $4,000.

Investment in common stock	4,500	
Cost of stock warrants		500
Cash		4,000

Stock rights are issued to existing stockholders, giving them the privilege of subscribing for additional shares of the same class of stock held. A corporation would not issue stock rights to its shareholders unless it wished to secure additional capital. As noted earlier, rights are generally transferable; thus, a person need not be a stockholder of a corporation to hold or exercise its rights. Stock rights are usually valuable because the price at which the stock is offered to the rightholders is generally below the price prevailing for such shares in the securities market.

A stockholder receives one right for each share owned; if he owns 50 shares of stock, he will receive 50 rights. The rights will specify the "quantity" of stock that may be purchased with each right. More than one right may be required to purchase one additional share of stock. For example, five rights may be needed to purchase one share of stock.

The announcement of the granting of the rights states the date when the stock records will be closed to determine the stockholders of record to whom the warrants will be issued, and also the later date when subscriptions will be payable. Between the date of the announcement and the date of the issuing of the warrants, the stock and the rights are inseparable, and the stock is dealt in "rights-on." After the warrants are issued, the stock is dealt in "ex-rights," and the rights are dealt in separately. During the period in which the stock is selling rights-on, no special problems arise, because any transactions involve the stock and the rights as a unit. After the warrants are issued and the stock is selling ex-rights, problems arise which require an apportionment of the cost of the originally acquired stock between the stock and the rights; this is done on the basis of the market value of the right and the market value of the share ex-rights at the time of the issuance of the rights. For instance, assume that an investor owns 10 shares of stock for which he paid a total of $1,200.

Cost of share of stock owned	$120
Market values on date of issuance of rights:	
Right	30
Stock	150
Apportionment of $120 cost:	
Right—30/180 of $120	20
Stock—150/180 of $120	100
Apportioned cost of 10 rights	200

When the apportioned cost of the rights is ascertained, it is advisable to make an entry setting up a Cost of Stock Rights account, thus:

Cost of stock rights	200	
Investment in stock of *X* Company		200
Receipt of stock rights.		

The Investment in Stock of *X* Company account and the Cost of Stock Rights account will then appear as follows:

Investment in Stock of *X* Company

Cost of 10 shares	1,200	Apportioned cost of rights	200

Cost of Stock Rights	
Apportioned cost of rights 200	

Assume that each right entitled the holder to purchase one share of stock for $120, and that he exercised the rights. The cost of the new shares should be regarded as including the disbursement made to the issuing corporation therefor and the $200 apportioned cost of the rights. The entry for the acquisition of the 10 new shares is:

Investment in stock of *X* Company	1,400	
Cost of stock rights		200
Cash		1,200
Purchase of stock for cash and rights.		

The first shares of stock acquired are now regarded as having a cost of $100 each, and the new shares acquired are regarded as having a cost of $140 each.

Assume that, instead of using the rights, the holder sold them at their market value of $30 each. The entry would be:

Cash	300	
Cost of stock rights		200
Gain on sale of stock rights		100
Sale of stock rights.		

If the holder of rights is careless enough to neither use them nor sell them but allows them to lapse, the apportioned cost of the rights should be written off as a loss.

As stated above, the right appertaining to each share may entitle the holder to purchase only a fraction of a share; for instance, each right may entitle the holder to purchase one-tenth of a share. The holder of four shares would, in such a case, receive warrants entitling him to purchase four-tenths of one share. The cost to be assigned to each right would be determined in the manner illustrated above. The holder of the rights may:

Buy additional rights to enable him to buy a full share; the cost of the new share will include the apportioned cost of his rights for four-tenths of a share, plus the cost of the rights for six-tenths of a share, plus the subscription price.

Sell his rights for four-tenths of a share, in which case he should compute his gain or loss and make an entry for the sale of the rights in the manner illustrated above.

MATTERS RELATIVE TO INVESTMENTS IN BONDS

Accrued interest at date of purchase. When bonds are acquired between interest dates, the purchase price normally includes the accrued interest. In the entry to record the acquisition of the bonds, the accrued interest should be charged to Accrued Interest Receivable, and only the remainder of the purchase price should be charged to the bond investment account.

Amortization of bond premium and discount. If a bond is purchased at a cost (including incidental costs such as brokerage) in excess of par, the purchase is made "at a premium." The value of the bond tends to decrease to par as its maturity approaches; therefore, for balance sheet purposes, it appears proper to amortize the premium over the life of the bond, and thus gradually to reduce its carrying value to par.* Moreover, the net income on a bond purchased at a premium, held to maturity and collected at par, is the total of the interest collections minus the premium lost; therefore, it appears proper to charge a portion of the premium periodically against the income from interest.

Similarly, the value of a bond of a solvent debtor purchased at a discount tends to increase to par as the maturity approaches; hence, for balance sheet purposes, it appears proper to amortize the discount over the life of the bond, thus gradually increasing its carrying value to par. Moreover, the total income earned on a bond purchased at a discount, held to maturity and collected at par, is the total of the interest collections plus the discount; therefore, it appears proper to regard a portion of the discount as earned periodically.

If bonds are purchased at a premium or a discount, the bond investment account is usually charged with the cost; amortizations (sometimes called *accumulations*) of discount are then charged to the account and amortizations of premium are credited to it. Some accountants prefer to charge the bond investment account with par, and to set up a premium or discount account. The former method is preferable. But if bonds are issued at a premium or a discount, it is better to credit the bond account with par and to set up a separate account with the bond premium or the bond discount.

Amortizations of bond premium and discount may be made by straight-line methods or by scientific effective-interest methods. Straight-line methods are discussed in this chapter; effective-interest-rate methods are discussed in the *Advanced* text.

Amortization of premium—straight-line method. Assume that a $1,000 bond, bearing 6% interest payable semiannually on January 1 and July 1, and due in four years, is purchased on January 1, 1965 for $1,035.85. Although coupons of $30 will be collected each six months, this amount cannot all be considered income; a portion of each coupon must be considered a partial repayment of the premium. Because there are eight interest periods, the premium may be written off by eight semiannual entries of $35.85 ÷ 8, or $4.48 (really seven entries of $4.48 and one of $4.49). Using the straight-line method, the entry to be made at each interest date except the last would be a debit to Cash and credits to Interest Earned and to Investment in Bonds (for the amount of premium amortization).

* For tax purposes the regulations should be consulted, as they are complicated and not entirely in conformity with the procedures discussed in this chapter, which are regarded as acceptable from the standpoint of accounting theory.

Cash	30.00	
Interest earned		25.52
Investment in bonds (for premium amortized)		4.48

The amortization may be scheduled as follows:

Schedule of Amortization
Four-Year 6% Bond Bought for $1,035.85

Date	Debit Cash	Credit Interest Earned	Credit Investment in Bonds	Carrying Value
Jan. 1, 1965				$1,035.85
July 1	$ 30.00	$ 25.52	$ 4.48	1,031.37
Jan. 1, 1966	30.00	25.52	4.48	1,026.89
July 1	30.00	25.52	4.48	1,022.41
Jan. 1, 1967	30.00	25.52	4.48	1,017.93
July 1	30.00	25.52	4.48	1,013.45
Jan. 1, 1968	30.00	25.52	4.48	1,008.97
July 1	30.00	25.52	4.48	1,004.49
Jan. 1, 1969	30.00	25.51	4.49	1,000.00
	$240.00	$204.15	$35.85	

Thus, the amortization of a premium gradually brings the carrying value of the bond down to par, spreading the premium over the life of the bond as a reduction of the bond interest.

Amortization of discount—straight-line method. Assume that a $1,000 bond, bearing 6% interest payable semiannually on January 1 and July 1, and due in four years, is purchased on January 1, 1965 for $965.63. The discount of $34.37 could be spread over the eight periods, in semiannual amounts of $34.37 ÷ 8, or $4.30. (Eight of these amounts would total $34.40 instead of $34.37; hence, three entries must be for $4.29.)

The semiannual entries are indicated by the following amortization schedule:

Schedule of Amortization
Four-Year 6% Bond Bought for $965.63

Date	Debit Cash	Debit Investment in Bonds	Credit Interest Earned	Carrying Value
Jan. 1, 1965				$ 965.63
July 1	$ 30.00	$ 4.30	$ 34.30	969.93
Jan. 1, 1966	30.00	4.30	34.30	974.23
July 1	30.00	4.30	34.30	978.53
Jan. 1, 1967	30.00	4.30	34.30	982.83
July 1	30.00	4.30	34.30	987.13
Jan. 1, 1968	30.00	4.29	34.29	991.42
July 1	30.00	4.29	34.29	995.71
Jan. 1, 1969	30.00	4.29	34.29	1,000.00
	$240.00	$34.37	$274.37	

Thus, the amortization of the discount gradually brings the carrying value of the bond up to par, spreading the discount over the life of the bond as an addition to the bond interest.

Amortization at interim dates. The foregoing illustrations are based on the assumption that an interest date coincides with the close of the fiscal year of the owner of the bonds. Referring to the two schedules above, let us now assume that the investing company closes its books on February 28th.

Entries applicable to the bond purchased at a premium are shown below:

February 28, 1965:		
Accrued interest receivable	10.00	
Investment in bonds (⅓ of $4.48)		1.49
Interest earned		8.51
July 1, 1965:		
Cash	30.00	
Accrued interest receivable		10.00
Investment in bonds ($4.48 − $1.49)		2.99
Interest earned		17.01
January 1, 1966:		
Cash	30.00	
Investment in bonds		4.48
Interest earned		25.52
February 28, 1966:		
Accrued interest receivable	10.00	
Investment in bonds		1.49
Interest earned		8.51

Entries applicable to the bond purchased at a discount are shown below:

February 28, 1965:		
Accrued interest receivable	10.00	
Investment in bonds (⅓ of $4.30)	1.43	
Interest earned		11.43
July 1, 1965:		
Cash	30.00	
Investment in bonds ($4.30 − $1.43)	2.87	
Accrued interest receivable		10.00
Interest earned		22.87
January 1, 1966:		
Cash	30.00	
Investment in bonds	4.30	
Interest earned		34.30
February 28, 1966:		
Accrued interest receivable	10.00	
Investment in bonds	1.43	
Interest earned		11.43

Purchases between interest dates. Assume that a 6% bond due on December 31, 1972 is purchased for $1,051.80 and accrued interest on October 31, 1966, or six years and two months before maturity. Then the premium to be amortized per year on the straight-line basis is $51.80 ÷ 6⅙, or $8.40; the premium to be amortized each six months is $4.20; and the premium to be amortized for the two-months period between the date of purchase and the first interest date, December 31, 1966, is ⅓ of $4.20, or $1.40.

The entry for the purchase is:

October 31, 1966:		
Investment in bonds	1,051.80	
Accrued interest receivable	20.00	
Cash		1,071.80

The entry for the first interest collection is:

December 31, 1966:		
Cash	30.00	
Investment in bonds		1.40
Accrued interest receivable		20.00
Interest earned		8.60

Assume that the bond was bought at a discount of $51.80 instead of at a premium of that amount.

The entry for the purchase is:

October 31, 1966:		
Investment in bonds	948.20	
Accrued interest receivable	20.00	
Cash		968.20

The entry for the first interest collection is:

December 31, 1966:		
Cash	30.00	
Investment in bonds	1.40	
Accrued interest receivable		20.00
Interest earned		11.40

Sales between interest dates. Refer to the first schedule on page 263 showing the amortization of bond premium; observe that the carrying value of the bond on January 1, 1968 was $1,008.97. Assume that the bond was sold on March 1, 1968 for $1,020. A proper accounting for the sale should give recognition to the income from January 1 to March 1, and to the gain or loss. These elements are computed as follows:

Selling price		$1,020.00
Amount received for accrued interest at 6% for two months		10.00
Price received for the bond		$1,010.00
Amortized value of bond at date of sale:		
Carrying value, January 1, 1968	$1,008.97	
Less amortization of premium for two months—⅓ of $4.48 (see amortization schedule)	1.49	1,007.48
Gain on sale		$ 2.52

The entry to record the sale would be:

Cash	1,020.00	
Investment in bonds		1,008.97
Interest earned ($10.00 − $1.49)		8.51
Gain on sale of bond		2.52

Refer to the second schedule on page 263 showing the amortization of bond discount; observe that the carrying value on January 1, 1968 was $991.42. Assume that the bond was sold on March 1, 1968 for $1,000. The computation of the loss on the sale follows.

Selling price		$1,000.00
Amount received for accrued interest at 6% for two months		10.00
Price received for the bond		$ 990.00
Amortized value of bond at date of sale:		
Carrying value, January 1, 1968	$991.42	
Plus amortization of discount for two months—⅓ of $4.29 (see amortization schedule)	1.43	992.85
Loss on sale of bond		$ 2.85

The entry to record the sale would be:

Cash	1,000.00	
Loss on sale of bond	2.85	
Investment in bonds		991.42
Interest earned ($10.00 + $1.43)		11.43

Redemption before maturity. Bonds frequently carry the right of redemption before maturity, usually at a premium. For instance, a bond issued on January 1, 1966 and maturing on January 1, 1986 might be redeemable at the option of the issuing company at premiums as follows:

From January 1, 1976 to January 1, 1982	—at 105
During 1982	—at 104
During 1983	—at 103
During 1984	—at 102
During 1985	—at 101

If such a bond is acquired at a premium greater than the premium at which it can be retired at the next optional retirement date, the premium amortization should be such that the bond will not be carried at any date at an amount greater than the amount at which it can be retired on that date.

If the bond is acquired at a discount, the discount should be amortized in such a manner as to raise the carrying value to par at maturity, without regard for retirement premiums. The retirement privilege may never be exercised, and no redemption premium may be received.

Carrying bond investments at cost. Bond investments may properly be carried at cost if the investments are temporary ones, or if an investment is so small that an amortization procedure is not worth the trouble.

If bonds are purchased at a considerable discount because the issuing company is in a weak financial condition, the collection of par at maturity may be doubtful and the accumulation of the discount may therefore be unjustified.

Bonds purchased with interest in default. In *Accounting Series Release* No. 36, the Chief Accountant of the Securities and Exchange Commission expressed the opinion that, if an investment company acquires bonds with defaulted interest coupons attached, "collections on account of the defaulted interest coupons should be treated not as interest on the sum invested, but rather as repayments thereof. Moreover, in view of the uncertainty of eventually receiving payments in excess of the purchase price,... ordinarily no part of any payment, whether on account of principal or the defaulted interest, should be considered as profit until the full purchase price has been recovered."

Although the opinion is specifically applicable to investment companies, the accounting procedure described seems to be appropriate for use by any investor.

Investments in mortgages. The accounting for investments in individual mortgages does not differ in essence from the accounting for bond investments. Mortgages should be recorded at their cost, and the principles of discount and premium amortization apply to them as well as to bonds.

A special situation arises when property is sold and a mortgage is taken for a portion of the sales price. If the sum of the cash and the mortgage received is in excess of the fair cash value of the property sold, the excess is, in effect, discount on the mortgage. Conservative accounting would require that the mortgage be recorded at a discounted value, determined on the basis of the fair cash value of the property.

Government obligations. No peculiar accounting problems arise in connection with short-term government securities such as the treasury bills, treasury notes, and certificates of indebtedness. Some special problems do arise in connection with the Series E long-term savings bonds.

The Series E bonds are issued at a discount; they yield income at stated annual rates, compounded semiannually, if held to maturity; they are redeemable at the holder's option before maturity at prices stated in a schedule in the bond; but the redemption prices are below par, and therefore the yield rate if the bond is redeemed is less than the rate earned if the bond is held to maturity. Some of the principal characteristics of the Series E bonds are indicated in the following table.

Life	7 years, 9 months
Issuance price per $100 of maturity value	$75
Denominations (maturity value)	$25 $50 $100 $200 $500 $1,000 $10,000
Periodic interest payments	None
Yield rate per annum, compounded semiannually, if held to maturity	3.75%
The bonds may be registered	In the names of natural persons. In the names and titles of the legal representatives of natural persons and of the trustees of a limited class of trusts.

Three methods are used for taking up income on such bonds:

(1) No income is taken until the maturity of the bond. This is probably the method most in use by individual holders of small amounts of such bonds.

(2) Income is taken up over the life of the bond:

(a) By debiting the investment account and crediting income in amounts sufficient to increase the carrying value of the investment to the increasing redemption prices shown in the schedule.

(b) By debiting the investment account and crediting income with amounts computed by applying the yield rate of 3.75% to the increasing carrying value of the investment. This method is probably not widely used, partly because it is more convenient to use method (a), and partly because income may be overstated if the bond is redeemed before maturity.

There is another series of long-term savings bonds (Series H), but they have a number of distinguishing features. The Series H bonds are issued at par in denominations of $500, $1,000, $5,000, and $10,000. The H bonds mature in ten years, but are redeemable at the owner's option at par any time after the first six months. Holders receive semiannual interest payments based on a graduated scale of amounts which have been fixed to result in an investment yield of approximately 3.75% over the ten-year life of the bonds.

CHAPTER

15

Investments (Concluded)

INVESTMENTS IN SUBSIDIARIES

Accounting methods. If a corporation holds more than a 50% interest in the voting stock of another company, the relation of parent and subsidiary exists.

Two radically different procedures have been used by parent companies in accounting for their investments in subsidiaries and their income or loss thereon. They are referred to in this text as the *legal-basis method* and the *economic-basis method.* In the discussion that follows, it will be made apparent that both methods have advantages and both have disadvantages. The legal-basis method is now the generally accepted procedure.

Legal-basis method. From a legal standpoint, a parent and its subsidiary are separate entities; the net income or loss of the subsidiary is not a part of the net income or loss of the parent; dividends received from the subsidiary are income to the parent. If the parent company adopts the legal basis of accounting for its investment in the subsidiary and its income thereon, it will carry the investment at cost and will record dividends as income. To illustrate:

Company *P* organizes a subsidiary, Company *S*, and acquires its entire stock issue by an investment of $100,000.

Investment in stock of Company *S*	100,000	
Cash		100,000
Acquisition of stock of subsidiary.		

During the first year of its operations, the subsidiary earns a net income of $30,000 (for which the parent makes no entry) and pays a dividend of $5,000.

Cash	5,000	
Dividend income		5,000
Dividend from subsidiary.		

The Dividend Income account is closed to Revenue and Expense, and thence to Retained Earnings.

During the second year, the subsidiary loses $15,000 (the parent makes no entry) and pays a dividend of $5,000 from retained earning produced by the earnings of the preceding year.

Cash	5,000	
Dividend income		5,000
Dividend from subsidiary.		

During the third year, the subsidiary loses $12,000. The parent company makes no entry.

The foregoing entries under the legal-basis method are summarized below; starred items are credits.

	Investment	Cash	Dividend Income	Retained Earnings
First year: Investment	$100,000	$100,000*		
Subsidiary net income—no entry.				
Subsidiary dividend		5,000	$5,000*	
Closing entry			5,000	$5,000*
Second year: Subsidiary net loss—no entry.				
Subsidiary dividend		5,000	$5,000*	
Closing entry			5,000	5,000*
Third year: Subsidiary net loss—no entry.				

This accounting procedure conforms strictly to the legal realities of separate corporate entities. However, when this method is used, the balance in the investment account will not reflect the underlying book value of the subsidiary's net assets. The changing amounts of subsidiary net assets and the unchanging balance of the parent's investment account are compared below:

	Net Assets of Subsidiary	Parent's Investment Account
First year:		
Investment by parent	$100,000	$100,000
Increase in subsidiary's net assets resulting from net income	30,000	
Decrease in subsidiary's net assets resulting from payment of dividend	5,000*	
Balance at end of year	$125,000	$100,000
Second year:		
Decrease in subsidiary's net assets resulting from loss	15,000*	
Decrease in subsidiary's net assets resulting from payment of dividend	5,000*	
Balance at end of year	$105,000	$100,000
Third year:		
Decrease in subsidiary's net assets resulting from loss	12,000*	
Balance at end of year	$ 93,000	$100,000

* Deduction.

Of even more consequence is the fact that the dividends taken up by the parent company as income bear no relation to the results of the subsidiary's operations. The parent company is in a position to dictate the dividend policy of the subsidiary; therefore, so long as the subsidiary has a surplus available for dividends, the parent, by determining the dividends to be paid to it, can take into income any amounts which it may desire, instead of taking up the net income or loss resulting from the subsidiary's operations.

Suppose that a company, instead of organizing a subsidiary, purchases the stock of a company that has been in existence for some time. Suppose, also, that the dividends paid by a subsidiary after the acquisition of its stock by the parent company exceed its earnings since that date. How should the parent company record the portion of the dividend which was paid from surplus created prior to acquisition? Although a dividend from surplus created prior to acquisition appears to have a legal status of income to the parent company, accountants are in general agreement that such a dividend should not be recorded as income, but should be regarded as a partial recovery of cost and should be credited to the investment account.

It should be recognized that a parent company may not own all of the outstanding stock of a subsidiary; there may be a minority interest in the subsidiary. Under such circumstances, the parent company will receive only its share of the dividends paid by the subsidiary.

Economic-basis method. The economic-basis method gives recognition to the fact that subsidiary earnings increase the subsidiary net assets which underlie the investment, and subsidiary losses and dividends decrease these net assets. The parent's entries on the economic basis increase and decrease the balance in the investment account in accordance with increases and decreases in the underlying subsidiary net assets. Also, on the economic basis, the amounts shown as income or loss on the investment each year correspond with the amounts shown as income and loss by the subsidiary. To illustrate, assume the same facts as those in the illustration on the legal basis; the entries on the economic basis are indicated below:

	Investment	Cash	Subsidiary Income	Retained Earnings
First year:				
Investment	$100,000	$100,000*		
Subsidiary net income	30,000		$30,000*	
Subsidiary dividend	5,000*	5,000		
Closing entry			30,000	$30,000*
Balance at end of year	$125,000			
Second year:				
Subsidiary net loss	15,000*		$15,000	
Subsidiary dividend	5,000*	5,000		
Closing entry			15,000*	15,000
Balance at end of year	$105,000			
Third year:				
Subsidiary net loss	12,000*		$12,000	
Closing entry			12,000*	12,000
Balance at end of year	$ 93,000			

* Credit.

When entries are made by the parent company in this manner, the changes in the balance of the investment account keep pace with the changes in the net assets of the subsidiary, and the amounts recorded by the parent as income or loss on the investment are in accordance with the income or loss of the subsidiary instead of arbitrary amounts transferred from the subsidiary to the parent as dividends. This accounting procedure undoubtedly reflects the economic realities. The only objection to the economic-basis method (and it is a governing determinant in the choice of method) is that it violates the legal realities, because the parent's Retained Earnings account is affected by subsidiary earnings and losses although it can legally be affected only by subsidiary dividends.

Current practice. As noted, the legal-basis method is now the generally accepted procedure for a parent company to use in recording its relations with a subsidiary; but this is true only because of the restrictions inherent in the legal concept of separate corporate entities. Statements of financial condition and operations prepared from legal-basis records may not constitute adequate disclosure and may be misleading.

To avoid inadequacies of disclosure and misleading inferences, the following procedures have come into somewhat general use:

(a) Statement footnotes or report comments accompanying the parent's legal-basis statements may disclose such matters as the difference between subsidiary dividends received by the parent and the subsidiary's net income or loss for the period.

(b) The legal-basis statements of the parent may be accompanied by statements of the subsidiary. This procedure has merit but it is impracticable if the parent has many subsidiaries.

(c) Consolidated statements may be prepared. They ignore the existence of separate corporate entities and report the financial position and operating results of the group of companies as if they were, essentially, data applicable to a single company.

Consolidated statements, which were dealt with somewhat cursorily in *Principles of Accounting, Introductory,* are dealt with exhaustively in the *Advanced* volume.

FUNDS

Funds and reserves distinguished. Although funds and reserves are wholly different in nature, there seems to be an inclination to confuse them.

Funds are assets, usually set aside for particular purposes. Fund accounts, therefore, always* have debit balances, always represent assets, and always appear on the asset side of the balance sheet.

* This is true so far as general industrial accounting is concerned; terminology is different in municipal and institutional accounting.

Reserves, on the other hand, normally have credit balances and, therefore, never represent assets. At present, it is desired merely to emphasize one fact: namely, fund accounts always represent assets, and reserves never do.

The term *reserve fund* has no well-defined meaning, and its use is not to be recommended.

Classes of funds. Funds may be classified as follows:

(A) As to the use to be made of the assets in the fund:

(1) Payment of an existing liability.
(2) Payment of a contingent liability.
(3) Payment for an asset or a service.
(4) Retirement of capital stock.

(B) As to obligatory or voluntary creation:

(1) Obligatory—required by contract.
(2) Voluntary—created by action of the management.

The classification of funds as obligatory and optional is important because of the bearing it has on the question of the relation existing between the amount of a fund and the amount of a related reserve.

Funds in the balance sheet. Funds should be classified in the balance sheet as current assets if they are created for the payment of current liabilities or for current expenditures. Thus, periodical deposits for the payment of bond interest or for the payment of taxes on property mortgaged as security to a short-term or a long-term liability should properly be shown as current assets.

Funds for the payment of long-term indebtedness should be shown in the balance sheet as a noncurrent account.

It has been suggested that a fund established for plant expansion should be shown under the Fixed Assets caption. This seems unsound because the fund is not being used as a plant asset, and its inclusion under that caption would distort any ratios involving fixed assets. Moreover, funds set aside by the management for plant expansion can be diverted by the management to other purposes. The case is somewhat different with respect to the impounded proceeds of a mortgage issued for construction purposes, but even in such cases the fund should be shown under a special caption rather than under the Fixed Assets caption.

Companies are sometimes required to deposit funds for the payment of current interest on long-term indebtedness and taxes on the mortgaged property, as well as for the repayment of the principal of the indebtedness. In such instances, it seems advisable to divide the fund into two parts for balance sheet presentation, the funds available for current purposes being shown under the Current Assets caption and the remainder being shown under a special caption.

Accounting for funds. The bookkeeping entries required in the operation of funds are usually not complicated. Typical fund transactions may include the following:

(1) The transfer of assets to the fund.
(2) The investment of fund cash in fund securities.
(3) The collection of income on the fund. The entries for this transaction may include the amortization of premium or discount on fund securities.
(4) The payment of expenses incurred in the operation of the fund.
(5) The application of the fund to its intended purpose.

Entries for these transactions are illustrated in the subsequent section devoted to sinking funds.

The discussion in Chapter 14 with respect to the valuation of stocks and bonds held as investments applies equally to securities held in special funds. If a fund is established for the payment of a current liability or for other current expenditures, the principles governing the valuation of temporary investments apply. If securities in a fund are to be held for a considerable period of time, the principles applicable to long-term investments should govern their valuation in the accounts.

Funds for the payment of existing liabilities. Funds may be created for the payment of current liabilities. For example, such funds may be accumulated to meet bond interest requirements or Social Security tax obligations, or for the purchase of savings bonds with monies deducted from employees' pay.

Funds for the payment of long-term liabilities are more common. Funds for the retirement of long-term liabilities may be classified as follows:

(1) Sinking funds.
A sinking fund, strictly defined, consists of assets set aside, together with the accumulated earnings thereon, for the payment of an existing liability at its maturity.
(2) Redemption funds.
A redemption fund consists of assets set aside for the piecemeal retirement of obligations. The resources of the fund may be applied to meet serially maturing obligations or to purchase outstanding obligations of the company.

The distinction between sinking funds and redemption funds is interesting as a matter of precision in terminology. However, usage modifies meanings, and business usage seems to have sanctioned the extension of the term *sinking fund* to include funds used in the periodical retirement of bonds and other obligations and funds for the retirement of capital stock.

Sinking funds are usually administered by a trustee. Sometimes the company itself retains custody and control of the fund, but this plan usually is not entirely satisfactory to the creditors for whose protection the fund is being accumulated.

Sinking fund contributions. The amount of the periodical contribution to the sinking fund is usually stipulated in the trust indenture. The following requirements are typical:

(1) A certain number of cents per unit of output. This method of computing the periodical contributions is often required by the trust indenture when the bonds are secured by a mortgage on wasting assets such as mines and timberlands; the contributions are based on the number of tons mined or of thousand feet of timber cut. Thus, the sinking fund increases as the physical security back of the mortgage decreases. But because operations may not be carried on with sufficient rapidity to provide an adequate fund at the maturity of the bonds, a minimum annual contribution may be required.

(2) A percentage of the annual earnings. This method is frequently used in connection with so-called sinking funds for the retirement of preferred stock. From the standpoint of bondholders, it is not satisfactory to make the provision for the repayment of the bonds conditional upon the uncertain earnings of the business, although in the long run it might be advisable to allow the debtor corporation to make small contributions in poor years with offsetting large contributions in good years; otherwise, the drain upon the working capital when uniform contributions are required even in poor years may handicap the company in its operations and make it impossible for the company to meet its future contribution requirements.

(3) An equal annual amount computed by dividing the total required fund by the number of years of the life of the bonds. For instance, if a fund of $20,000 is to be provided in ten years, the annual addition to the fund will be $2,000. The first year, the contribution out of general cash will be $2,000, but the interest earned on the fund will reduce the subsequent contributions from the general cash.

(4) An equal annual contribution computed on an actuarial basis. The method of computing the periodical contributions required to produce a fund of a given amount is explained in the authors' *Principles of Accounting, Advanced.*

Theoretical accumulation. Often a company will prepare a schedule showing a theoretical accumulation of its sinking fund. Such a schedule is presented on page 276 for a sinking fund to be created by deposits computed on an actuarial basis and intended to accumulate to $20,000 in a ten-year period. It is assumed that all deposits in the fund can be invested in securities on the dates of the deposits, that 5% interest will be earned on all investments from the dates of their acquisition to the date of their disposal at the end of the fund period, and that no gains or losses will be realized when the securities are converted into cash.

Schedule of Accumulation

End of Year	Debit Fund	Credit Cash	Credit Income	Total Fund
1	$ 1,590.09	$ 1,590.09		$ 1,590.09
2	1,669.59	1,590.09	$ 79.50	3,259.68
3	1,753.07	1,590.09	162.98	5,012.75
4	1,840.73	1,590.09	250.64	6,853.48
5	1,932.76	1,590.09	342.67	8,786.24
6	2,029.40	1,590.09	439.31	10,815.64
7	2,130.87	1,590.09	540.78	12,946.51
8	2,237.42	1,590.09	647.33	15,183.93
9	2,349.29	1,590.09	759.20	17,533.22
10	2,466.75	1,590.09	876.66	19,999.97
	$19,999.97	$15,900.90	$4,099.07	

Actual accumulation. Actually, a sinking fund planned as above will not accumulate with any such mathematical exactness. Conditions in the securities markets may delay the prompt investment of sinking fund cash. The fund assets may earn more or less than the expected interest rate. Gains may be realized or losses incurred when the securities in the fund are converted into cash at the end of the fund period. For all these reasons, the actual accumulation of the fund cannot be expected to conform with the theoretical accumulation.

If the sinking fund is required by contract, the contract may call for supplemental contributions whenever the fund is below its scheduled level. If the sinking fund is a voluntary one, the management of the company may make supplemental contributions at its discretion.

Sinking fund entries. The operations of a sinking fund consist of making contributions to the fund, investing in securities, collecting income, paying expenses, disposing of fund securities, and using the cash fund for its intended purpose, such as the retirement of bonded indebtedness. Entries for these transactions, assuming that the fund is being accumulated to pay off bonded indebtedness, are illustrated below:

	Debit	Credit
Contributions of cash:		
Sinking fund cash	xx,xxx.xx	
Cash		xx,xxx.xx
Purchase of securities:		
Sinking fund securities—A B bonds	xx,xxx.xx	
Sinking fund cash		xx,xxx.xx
(Entry if securities are purchased at par and without accrued interest. Purchases at a premium or discount and purchases with accrued interest are considered later.)		
Collection of income:		
Sinking fund cash	xxx.xx	
Sinking fund income		xxx.xx
(Entry for income on securities purchased at par.)		
Payment of expenses:		
Sinking fund expense	xxx.xx	
Sinking fund cash		xxx.xx
(Entry if expenses are paid from fund cash.)		

Sinking fund expense	xxx.xx	
Cash		xxx.xx
(Entry if expenses are paid from general cash.)		
Disposal of sinking fund securities:		
Sinking fund cash	xx,xxx.xx	
Sinking fund securities		xx,xxx.xx
(Entry if securities are sold at carrying value.)		
Sinking fund cash	xx,xxx.xx	
Loss on sinking fund securities	xxx.xx	
Sinking fund securities		xx,xxx.xx
(Entry if securities are sold at a loss.)		
Sinking fund cash	xx,xxx.xx	
Gain on sinking fund securities		xxx.xx
Sinking fund securities		xx,xxx.xx
(Entry if securities are sold at a gain.)		
Cancellation of bonds at maturity:		
Sinking fund cash	x,xxx.xx	
Cash		x,xxx.xx
(Entry if sinking fund cash after disposal of securities is inadequate for retirement of bonds.)		
Bonds payable	xxx,xxx.xx	
Sinking fund cash		xxx,xxx.xx
(Entry for retirement of bonds.)		
Cash	x,xxx.xx	
Sinking fund cash		x,xxx.xx
(Entry if any residue remains in the fund and is returned to general cash.)		

The Sinking Fund Income and Sinking Fund Expense accounts should be closed at the end of each period to Revenue and Expense. Losses or gains on disposals of sinking fund securities should be handled in the same manner as any other extraneous item.

Purchases between interest dates. If securities are purchased for the sinking fund at par plus accrued interest, the following entry is required:

Sinking fund securities	xx,xxx.xx	
Accrued interest on sinking fund securities	xxx.xx	
Sinking fund cash		xx,xxx.xx
(Entry for purchase of sinking fund securities between interest dates.)		

At the date of the first collection of interest, the following entry is made:

Sinking fund cash	xxx.xx	
Accrued interest on sinking fund securities		xxx.xx
Sinking fund income		xx.xx
(Entry for first interest collection when securities were purchased between interest dates.)		

Amortization of premium or discount. If bonds are purchased for the sinking fund at a premium or a discount, the Sinking Fund Securities account should be charged with their cost. Entries for the collection of interest and amortization of premium or discount will be as follows:

Sinking fund cash	x,xxx.xx	
Sinking fund securities		xx.xx
Sinking fund income		x,xxx.xx
(Entry for semiannual interest collection on sinking fund securities purchased at a premium.)		
Sinking fund cash	x,xxx.xx	
Sinking fund securities	xx.xx	
Sinking fund income		x,xxx.xx
(Entry for semiannual interest collection on sinking fund securities purchased at a discount.)		

Cash and accrual basis. If the interest dates on securities purchased for the sinking fund do not coincide with the dates of closing the company's books, adjusting entries may be made for accrued interest. For instance, assuming that interest at 5% on $150,000 of bonds in the fund is due on October 31 and April 30, and that the books are closed on December 31, entries could be made as illustrated below.

December 31:		
Accrued interest receivable—Sinking fund securities	1,250	
Sinking fund income		1,250
(Entry for accrual of interest at closing date.)		
April 30:		
Sinking fund cash	3,750	
Accrued interest receivable—Sinking fund securities		1,250
Sinking fund income		2,500
(Entry for collection of interest.)		

Fund with trustee. If the sinking fund is placed in the hands of a trustee, the company's records generally will not show the individual transactions relating to the purchase and sale of securities and to the earnings and expenses of the fund. The records will show the deposits made with the trustee and summary entries for the earnings and expenses as reported periodically by the trustee.

Own bonds alive in fund. Investments for the sinking fund may be made in the securities of other companies or in the very bonds which the fund is intended to retire. If the sinking fund trustee or manager can obtain the company's own bonds at favorable prices, it is advisable to do so if the company is in a strong financial condition, because the risk associated with an investment in outside securities is thereby eliminated. If the company is not in good financial condition, there is some question regarding the propriety of acquiring the company's own bonds for the fund, because such a transaction may be regarded as giving preference to the bondholders whose bonds are acquired.

If the company's own bonds are purchased, the question arises whether these bonds should be canceled or be "held alive" in the fund.

If the bonds are canceled when purchased, both the fund and the outstanding liability will be reduced, and the entry will be as follows:

Bonds payable	xxx,xxx.xx	
Sinking fund cash		xxx,xxx.xx
(If the bonds are purchased at par.)		

Whenever bonds are purchased and canceled, any unamortized discount or premium on the issuance of these retired bonds should also be written off.

As already pointed out, if the company's own bonds are purchased year by year and immediately canceled, the fund is a redemption fund rather than a true sinking fund. Although questions of terminology are interesting and important, the essential thing is, of course, the fulfillment of the purpose of the fund. If the entire bond issue can be retired by periodical purchases and immediate cancellations, there is no reason why the fund should not be operated on the redemption-fund basis instead of on the sinking-fund basis. But it is necessary to realize that, when the contributions to the fund are computed on the assumption that interest will be earned thereon for the remaining life of the fund, the cancellation of the bonds when purchased will result in a reduction of the interest earned on the fund assets and will make the fund inadequate for the retirement of all of the bonds. This point can be clearly illustrated by referring to the schedule of accumulation on page 276. The contributions out of general cash amount to $15,900.90, and interest is depended upon to make up the remaining $4,099.10. But if the company's own bonds are purchased each year with the contributions out of cash, and if these bonds are canceled, the $4,099.10 interest will not be earned by the fund, the fund will provide for the payment of only $15,900 of bonds, and no provision may be made for the retiring of the remaining $4,100 of bonds.

This condition may not be disadvantageous to the company, or even to the remaining bondholders, because future interest requirements are reduced each time an outstanding bond is acquired and canceled. Even if supplemental contributions to the fund were made necessary because of periodic redemptions of outstanding bonds, the aggregate cash outlay to finance and repay the bond obligation need not be greater, because the cash requirements for bond interest are reduced.

A possible inadequacy in the fund is avoided if the annual contributions are determined on the basis of the third method discussed on page 275. By this method, $2,000 would be provided each year, partly from interest and the balance from general cash. If the securities were canceled and no interest was earned, the entire contribution would have to be made from the general cash, and ten contributions of $2,000 each would provide for the retirement of the entire $20,000 bond issue.

When the company's own bonds are held alive in the sinking fund, they usually have been regarded, for statement purposes, as though they were the bonds of some other company. That is, the balance sheet liability of bonds payable includes those in the sinking fund as well as those in the hands of the public, and the bonds held alive are included in the fund assets. Although this is contrary to the usual rule that a company's own securities should not appear in its balance sheet as an asset, the argument has been presented that the reduction of the sinking fund and the bond liability, by the amount of the bonds held alive, would distort the ratio between the original amount of the bond issue and the funds set aside to date for the retirement of the bonds. The fact that generally a sinking fund is controlled by a trustee rather than by the company itself gives added justification for showing the bonds as assets. Some accountants advocate showing the fund in two parts in the balance sheet: the bonds held alive as a deduction from the liability, and the remainder of the fund as an asset; such a treatment is definitely not customary; if adopted, a cross reference should be made between the two fund amounts in the balance sheet. If bonds held alive are shown as assets, the balance sheet should disclose the fact in some manner, either in the description of the fund or in a footnote.

If the company's own bonds are purchased above or below par and held alive in the sinking fund, the question arises concerning the disposition of the premium or discount on the purchase. This question may be further complicated if there is unamortized discount or premium on the issuance of the bonds. Some accountants prefer to write off immediately the premium or discount on the purchase of such bonds, and also any unamortized issuance premium or discount applicable to these purchased bonds. Although no serious objection can be raised to this procedure, it seems to the authors that if the bonds are still being carried as outstanding liabilities, the discount or premium on issuance should remain on the books; and that, because the securities are being recorded in the fund in the same manner that securities of other companies would be handled, they should be charged to Sinking Fund Securities at cost and the premium or discount on purchase amortized over the period between the date of purchase and the date of maturity.

Following the same line of reasoning, it would be acceptable to continue interest payments on bonds held alive. If the bonds held alive are in the hands of a trustee, it may be legally necessary to continue the interest payments on these bonds. To illustrate the entries to be made if interest payments are continued on bonds held alive, assume that there are $20,000 of 5% bonds in the issue, and that $5,000 of the bonds are being held alive in the sinking fund. The entries for the interest would be:

Bond interest	1,000	
Cash		1,000
For payment of interest on bond issue.		
Sinking fund cash	250	
Sinking fund income (or Bond interest)		250
For collection of interest on securities in fund.		

Bond retirement fund. If a company acquires its own bonds by expenditure of fund cash and retires them instead of holding them as live securities in the fund, the accounting will be somewhat different from that described in the foregoing pages.

Upon purchase and retirement of the bonds, an entry will be made debiting Bonds Payable and crediting Sinking Fund Cash. Any unamortized premium or discount on issuance applicable to the bonds thus retired should be written off when the bonds are canceled.

If the company's own bonds are purchased and canceled, an extraneous loss or gain probably will develop from the transaction. The amount of the loss or gain is the difference between the outlay made to reacquire the bonds and their carrying value on the company's books. The carrying value of bonds outstanding equals their par value plus or minus any unamortized premium or discount.

Sinking funds for principal and interest. Companies are sometimes required to place with a sinking fund trustee monthly deposits for the payment of the semiannual interest as well as the principal of the bonds. In such instances, it should be remembered that making a deposit with a trustee does not constitute payment of the interest any more than it constitutes payment of the principal; the total funds on deposit with the trustee should be shown on the asset side of the balance sheet, and the liability on accrued unpaid interest as well as on principal should be shown on the liability side of the balance sheet. The liability on principal and interest cannot be eliminated from the balance sheet until the trustee has applied the funds to the payment of the liability.

Sinking fund reserves. Indentures executed in connection with long-term debt obligations frequently place a restriction on the payment of dividends. For many years this restriction commonly took the form of a requirement for the creation of a sinking fund reserve in conjunction with a sinking fund; the borrowing company, in addition to being required to deposit cash in the sinking fund, was required to make periodical transfers from Retained Earnings to a reserve. The object was to avoid or minimize the possibility of a working capital impairment which might result from the combined drain upon cash which would be caused by depositing cash in the fund and also paying dividends to the full amount of the current earnings—an impairment which might reduce future earnings and thus lead to a default by the borrowing corporation in its payments to the fund.

If such a sinking fund reserve is required, what should be the amount of the periodical credits to the reserve? The answer to this question is usually found in the indenture. Generally, the prescribed periodical credits are set at a level sufficient to produce in the reserve an increasing balance equal to the amount which would be in the fund if all contributions were made as required and if the actual income accretions to the fund were exactly equal to the anticipated accretions. The balance in the reserve would then show the amount which should be in the fund.

This is true, of course, only with respect to funds and reserves provided for the retirement of obligations at maturity; if bonds are purchased at intervals and canceled, the balance in the fund account will rise and fall, but the balance in the reserve account should continually increase until the last bonds have been retired, because the holder of the last bond to be retired is entitled to all of the protection afforded by the limitation upon dividends measured by the required transfers from Retained Earnings to the restricted surplus reserve.

A sinking fund reserve, being a surplus reserve, is created by charges to Retained Earnings. The reserve should not be charged with expenses incident to the operation of the sinking fund, nor credited with income on the fund assets. After the liability has been paid, the sinking fund reserve may be closed by returning its credit balance to Retained Earnings, thus indicating that the portion of the Retained Earnings once tied up and not available as a basis of dividends has again become free and available for that purpose. Whether or not the company will have the funds with which to pay a dividend is another matter.

Sinking fund reserves have also been required in connection with the periodical retirement of preferred stock.

Sinking fund reserves seem to be going out of use. They are not an entirely satisfactory safeguard against impairment of working capital. If a company is required to deposit $10,000 in a sinking fund, it may not be sufficient merely to require that $10,000 also be transferred from Retained Earnings to a reserve; this requirement may be met, but the borrowing company may still deplete its working capital by paying dividends and charging them to retained earnings accumulated before the long-term debt was incurred. For this reason it is becoming increasingly customary for indentures to provide that the retained earnings at the date of the issuance of the obligations (or a stated portion thereof) shall be "frozen" and shall not be available for charges for dividend payments until the obligations are retired. Such restrictions usually are disclosed, not by a sinking fund reserve, but parenthetically in the balance sheet or by a balance sheet footnote.

Funds for payment of contingent liabilities. Funds for the payment of contingent liabilities are rarely encountered. A deposit by a contractor to guarantee the performance of work in accordance with specifications is an illustration of an obligatory fund for the payment of a contingent liability. A fund for the payment of damages which may result from an adverse decision of a pending patent infringement suit is an illustration of a voluntary fund which may be created for the payment of a contingent liability.

Funds for payment for an asset or a service. Sometimes the directors of a corporation adopt the policy of establishing a fund for the acquisition of plant assets. A Building Fund, Machinery Fund, or similar fund account may then be put on the books.

Funds for the payment of services may be compulsory or voluntary. They are compulsory if the establishment of the fund is based on a contract with outsiders. For example, leases frequently contain clauses requiring the immediate deposit of cash to be applied in payment of rent for subsequent (often the last) years of the lease. Cemeteries frequently sell lots under agreements that a certain portion of the sale price shall be deposited with a trustee as a fund to provide perpetual care.

Funds for future expenditures chargeable to expense accounts may be created voluntarily, by authorization of the management. A fund for research is an example.

It is important that the operation of a fund of the type mentioned here not be confused with the proper measurement of revenue and expense. To illustrate, assume that a company leases property for a period of five years at a rental of $3,000 payable annually, with a further agreement to pay the owners $5,000 at the termination of the lease, to be used in restoring the property to its original condition. Assume also that the contract requires that this $5,000 be provided by the creation of a fund by contributions of $2,000 at the end of the first and second years of the life of the lease and $1,000 at the end of the third year. The amount which should be in the fund at any date is determined by the contract; but the expense element relating to the termination payment accrues at the rate of $1,000 per year, and a liability should be credited (and Rent Expense should be debited) with $1,000 each year, to spread the $5,000 item over the life of the lease.

If this distinction is not clearly recognized, there is danger of assuming that the requirements concerning the fund determine also the charges to expense. But if expense were charged with $2,000 at the end of the first and second years, and with $1,000 at the end of the third year, the operations of the first two years would be burdened with an undue proportion of the expense, and the fourth and fifth years would be relieved of their proper share of the expense.

As another illustration, assume that a cemetery sells lots under an agreement that $50 shall be set aside from the proceeds of the sale of each lot until a fund of $90,000 is accumulated; and that, when all of the lots are sold, the fund shall be turned over to a trustee and the income used to provide perpetual care of the cemetery. Assume that the cemetery contains 3,000 lots having a uniform selling price. The fund should be provided from the sale of the first 1,800 lots, because $\$50 \times 1{,}800 = \$90{,}000$. But each of the 3,000 lots should bear its share of the cost of perpetual care; therefore, the charge to expense should be made at the rate of $\$90{,}000 \div 3{,}000$, or $30 per lot. As each of the first 1,800 lots is sold, entries should be made as follows:

Perpetual care fund	50	
Cash		50
To record the required contribution to the fund.		
Perpetual care expense	30	
Perpetual care liability		30
To charge operations with the pro rata cost of perpetual care of lot sold.		

After 1,800 lots have been sold, the fund should be $90,000 and the liability should be $54,000. No further contributions to the fund need be made, but the $30 expense entry will have to be made when each of the remaining 1,200 lots is sold. When all of the lots have been sold, there will be a $90,000 fund and a $90,000 liability; the fund will have been accumulated in accordance with the contract, and the liability will have been credited in accordance with the expense accrual.

Stock redemption funds. The redemption-fund method has long been used for the retirement of bonds, and is also used for retiring preferred stock. The provisions of the stock issue may require that a definite amount of stock shall be retired annually, but it is doubtful whether this requirement could be enforced against the corporation if earnings were inadequate and creditors' rights were jeopardized. More frequently, the amount of stock to be retired annually is based upon the amount of the net income of the preceding year; it may be a fixed percentage of the net income, or it may be determined by a sliding scale of rates.

Fund arrearages and deposit requirements. If fund deposits required by contract are in arrears, the balance sheet should disclose this fact. It should also disclose the amount, if material, of any deposits required to be made soon after the balance sheet date and which therefore constitute a demand upon the current assets. Footnotes are probably the best device for making such disclosures. Such footnotes might be somewhat as follows: "On (the balance sheet date) the company was in arrears as to sinking fund deposits in the amount of $10,000"; or, "The company is obligated to make a deposit of $15,000 on (a date subsequent to the balance sheet date) in a fund for the retirement of its preferred stock."

Related funds and reserves. In the preceding pages there were occasional references to related funds and reserves, for example, sinking fund and reserve for sinking fund. What relation should exist between the amount of a fund and the amount of an accompanying reserve? Obviously, if either the fund or the reserve is voluntary, no necessary relationship exists, because the voluntary fund or reserve can be created in any desired amount.

If the reserve is required by contract or is used to show a surplus restriction required by law, those considerations govern the dollar amounts. But, as a general rule, the mere fact that a reserve is related to a fund is no basis for assuming that the fund account and reserve account balances must be maintained at identical amounts.

CHAPTER

16

Tangible Fixed Assets

PRINCIPLES OF VALUATION

Fixed assets. Fixed assets are assets of a relatively permanent nature used in the operation of the business and not intended for sale.

A building used as a factory is a fixed asset. It is relatively permanent property; it is used in the operation of the business; and it is not intended for sale.

Land held as a prospective site for a future plant is not a fixed asset. It is permanent property and it is not intended for sale, but it is not used in the operation of the business.

A factory building no longer used in operations is not a fixed asset because it is not used in the operation of the business.

Tangible and intangible fixed assets. The term *tangible* means having bodily substance. An asset is *intangible* if it has no bodily substance and if its value resides only in the rights which its possession confers upon its owner.

Tangible fixed assets include land, buildings, machinery, tools, patterns, delivery equipment, furniture and fixtures, and other similar property having physical substance. Intangible fixed assets include goodwill, patents, copyrights, trademarks, franchises, and other similar assets having no bodily substance but having value because of the rights inherent in them.

Classification of fixed assets. Fixed assets may be classified as follows:

(A) Tangible:
- (1) Plant property.
  - (a) Not subject to depreciation.
    Example: Land.

(b) Subject to depreciation.
Examples: Buildings, machinery, tools and equipment, delivery equipment, furniture and fixtures.
(2) Natural resources, subject to depletion.
Examples: Timber tracts, mines, oil wells.
(B) Intangible:
(1) Normally subject to amortization.
Examples: Patents, copyrights, franchises, leasehold improvements.
(2) Not normally subject to amortization.
Examples: Trademarks, goodwill.

Valuation of fixed assets. Fixed assets usually are carried in the accounts on one of the following bases of valuation:

Cost.
Cost less depreciation, depletion, or amortization.
Appraised value—usually replacement cost new less depreciation thereon. (This basis is not generally recognized as acceptable.)

In this chapter we shall be concerned primarily with matters related to the determination of the cost of tangible fixed assets, which are discussed in the following sequence:

(I) Matters applicable to fixed assets in general:
(A) Capital and revenue expenditures.
(B) Additions, improvements and betterments, replacements, and repairs.
(C) The cost of fixed assets:
(1) Purchased:
(a) For cash.
(b) Subject to a cash discount.
(c) On credit terms.
(d) For securities.
(e) In a mixed acquisition at a lump cost.
(2) Constructed for own use.
(D) Interest during construction.
(E) Valuation of fixed assets received as a gift.
(II) Matters applicable to specific assets.

Capital and revenue expenditures. An expenditure is a payment, or the incurring of an obligation to make a future payment, for a benefit received. Expenditures applicable to fixed assets are of two classes: capital and revenue. Capital expenditures are chargeable to asset accounts or to accumulated depreciation accounts; revenue expenditures are chargeable to expense accounts.

It is not always easy to determine whether an expenditure should be classified as a capital expenditure or as a revenue expenditure. Attempts have been made to state principles or to lay down rules, but the principles and rules are not always susceptible of exact interpretation or application.

Capital expenditures have been defined as those which result in additions or improvements of a permanent character and a substantial amount, and which add value to the property. This is not a wholly satisfactory definition. No fixed asset, with the possible exception of land, is permanent in the sense of having an endless life; permanency is relative. Some expenditures may properly be capitalized even though they are not of substantial amount. And all expenditures, even those for ordinary repairs, are presumed to add some value to the property; otherwise, they would not be made.

Capital expenditures have also been defined as those which should increase net income, either by increasing revenue or by reducing expense. This, also, is not a wholly satisfactory definition. Expenditures which merely keep net income from declining are sometimes properly capitalizable. If this were not so, business management would find itself in the absurd position of being required to make expenditures to keep earnings from decreasing, and at the same time being required to charge the expenditures to expense, thereby reducing the net income.

It has also been said that an expenditure should be charged to expense if it is not expected to benefit any period beyond the one in which it is made, and that an expenditure should be capitalized if it is expected to benefit at least one future period. As George O. May stated clearly and succinctly,* "The distinction . . . between capital and revenue expenditures . . . rests . . . upon the relation of the useful life of the property acquired and the length of the accounting period for which income is being determined. A capital expenditure is one, the usefulness of which is expected to extend over several accounting periods. If the accounting period were increased from the customary year to a decade, most of what is now treated as capital expenditure would become chargeable to income; while if the period were reduced to a day, much of what is now treated as current maintenance would become capital expenditure." This is a helpful criterion but it is not a wholly adequate one; the usefulness of an expenditure for an ordinary repair may extend over more than one period, but the expenditure is not properly capitalizable.

Expenditures for extraordinary repairs which extend the estimated useful life of fixed assets are capital expenditures.

General principles and rules need to be supplemented by a consideration of expenditures of various kinds, such as those for additions, improvements and betterments, replacements, and extraordinary and ordinary repairs. These are discussed in the following sections.

Additions. An addition is something which does not merely replace a thing previously owned. Additions include entirely new units and extensions,

---

* *The Journal of Accountancy,* Vol. LXIII, page 335.

expansions, and enlargements of old units. Thus, an entirely new building is an addition; so, also, is an enlargement of an existing building.

An expenditure for an addition consisting of an entirely new unit presents no accounting problems other than those relative to the determination of cost, which are discussed later. It is a capital expenditure, and the cost of the addition is chargeable to an asset account.

If an addition is an extension, expansion, or enlargement of an old unit, some special problems may arise; for instance, it may be necessary to tear out walls between the old and new portions of the building, or change roof structures, or increase the capacity of water pipes in the old building in order to provide plumbing facilities in the addition. Should the asset accounts be relieved of any of the old costs? The answer is generally in the negative. A negative answer may have some theoretical justification; it may be contended that it is correct to regard all costs, old and new, less salvage from demolished or reconstructed portions of the old structure, as costs of the enlarged building. But it is probable that practical considerations are the usual reason for the negative answer; in most cases it is not feasible to break down the cost of an entire building to determine the cost applicable to some relatively minor portion thereof.

Improvements and betterments. The essential difference between an addition and an improvement or a betterment is that in an addition there is an increase in quantity, whereas in an improvement or a betterment there is a substitution with an increase only in quality. The new thing is better than the old one was when it was acquired. There is an improvement or betterment when a tile roof is substituted for wooden shingles, or shatter-proof glass is substituted for ordinary glass, or high-wattage electric light bulbs are substituted for bulbs of low wattage.

The proper accounting treatment of improvements and betterments depends upon whether they are of a major or a minor nature. Major expenditures, such as those for a better roof or better glass, should be capitalized; minor expenditures, such as those for better light bulbs, should be charged to expense.

In the recording of major improvements, the cost of the thing replaced should be eliminated from the asset account, and the cost of the new property should be charged to it. If the accumulated depreciation on the replaced asset can be determined, it should be eliminated from the accounts. There should be no duplication of capitalized installation costs.

If plant assets are acquired in a run-down condition and rehabilitation expenditures are made, these expenditures result in improvements and are a proper charge to the asset accounts. Even if the expenditures are made over a considerable period of time, it still is proper to capitalize them so long as they result in an improved condition of the property or improved operating effectiveness as compared with the status at the time of acquisition. However, if the rehabilitation program extends over a long period, it is important to distinguish carefully between true rehabilitation costs and repairs. The charges to the property accounts for rehabilitation expenditures should be net of any amount recovered from salvage.

Replacements. A replacement also involves a substitution; but, unlike an improvement or a betterment, the new thing is no better than the old one was when it was acquired. Replacements are of three kinds:

(1) Replacements of whole units.
Amounts related to the old asset are removed from the accounts.
(2) Replacements of parts which may be regarded as ordinary repairs.
These are discussed in the next section.
(3) Extensive replacements of parts which constitute extraordinary repairs.
These also are discussed in the next section.

Repairs. Repairs usually involve replacements of parts, but repairs may be made without replacements. Repairs are of two classes: ordinary and extraordinary.

Ordinary repairs are those frequently encountered or involving relatively small sums of money. They require charges to operations. They may be accounted for in either of two ways.

(1) The expenditures may be charged to expense when made.
This procedure requires no explanation.
(2) A reserve procedure may be used.
Because repair costs vary from year to year, normally increasing with the life of the asset, and also vary from month to month (because repair work may be done during slack operating periods), it may be desirable to equalize the expense over the life of the asset or during a year by the creation of an allowance account. The periodical charge to operations and credit to the allowance account should be determined by estimating the total of such repair expenditures to be made during the entire life of the asset, or during a year, and apportioning the provisions in equal periodical amounts. Although such an apportionment procedure may be desirable for the purpose of equalizing the expense, the charges to operations for the creation of the allowance account are not deductible for income tax purposes. The tax deduction must be based on the actual expenditures charged to the allowance account.

The theoretically ideal method of recording extraordinary repairs is to eliminate the cost of the replaced parts from the asset account, relieve the accumulated depreciation account of the depreciation provided thereon, and charge the asset account with the entire cost of the repairs, including the cost of the new parts. This can be done if the subsidiary records give the necessary information regarding the cost of, and the depreciation provided on, individual parts. In cases in which the necessary information is not available, it has been regarded as acceptable accounting to charge the expenditures to the accumulated depreciation account on the theory that the extraordinary repairs extend the life of the asset beyond the originally estimated period; in other words, the extraordinary repairs make good a portion of the depreciation for which provision has been made in the accumulated depreciation account. When this treatment is accorded to extraordinary repairs, it must be recognized that the procedure is a departure from strict theoretical correctness, because it ignores the difference between the cost of the original asset and the cost of the replacement, does not give consideration to the question of the adequacy of the remaining balance in the accumulated depreciation account as a provision for depreciation to date, and does not squarely face the question of the probable length of the period of extended usefulness and the related question of any necessary revision in the depreciation rate.

Arbitrary classification by dollar amount. Many companies establish a somewhat arbitrary policy of charging expense with all disbursements (except for additions) which are less than a fixed amount, say, $10, $50, or $100. The entries for an expenditure in excess of the fixed amount are determined by the nature of the expenditure.

Repairs and maintenance. A theoretical distinction between repairs and maintenance is sometimes made, maintenance being directed to keeping the assets in good condition and repairs being directed to putting them back into good condition. Maintenance is preventive; repairs are curative. The theoretical distinction usually is difficult to maintain in the accounts.

The term *deferred maintenance* is sometimes encountered, particularly in utility accounting. It means neglected maintenance requirements.

Payment in cash. If fixed assets are purchased for cash, the problem of determining the cost is relatively simple, because no question arises concerning the value of the thing parted with in exchange for the fixed asset. Cost includes the purchase price and all incidental payments such as freight, installation charges, and other items discussed in detail in the sections devoted to specific assets.

Discount on fixed assets. If cash discounts are taken on purchases of fixed assets, should the discount be recorded as financial income or as a reduction of the cost of the property? This is a question on which a considerable difference of opinion has existed. Accountants generally hold to the opinion that purchase discounts of all kinds are theoretically deductions in the determination of cost; that their treatment as financial income is a departure from good accounting principles and is acceptable only for reasons of expediency; but that reasons of expediency generally do not exist with respect to discounts on purchases of fixed assets, and that such discounts should be recorded as cost deductions regardless of the treatment accorded discounts on merchandise purchases.

Purchases on credit terms. If fixed assets are offered at a cash price and at a higher credit price, and are purchased at the credit price, accounting principles dictate that the asset be recorded at the cash price, and that the difference be recorded as interest.

If fixed assets are purchased on the installment plan, and stated amounts of interest are included in the payment, the interest element should be recorded as a financial expense.

In some instances carrying charges may be implicit in the purchase price without being explicitly stated as such. For instance, if an asset is purchased for $2,400 payable in 24 monthly installments of $100 each, no interest is mentioned, but a conservative accounting procedure would require a recognition of the economic reality that the cash cost of the fixed asset is the present value of all of the installments. Although it would be theoretically correct to record the acquisition of the fixed asset at a cost of $2,400 minus some amount charged as interest, this is rarely done—partly because of the necessity of arbitrarily deciding on an interest rate.

Payments in securities. When a corporation acquires fixed assets by issuing its own bonds or stock, there may be some question as to whether or not the securities so issued are worth their par, and whether the cost of the fixed assets is equal to the par value of the securities or is something other than that amount.

If some of the stock or bonds is sold to third parties for cash at approximately the same time that similar securities are issued for other property, the cash price of the securities is indicative of their value, and fixed assets acquired by issuance of securities may be placed on the books at the value thus established.

The words "to third parties" are significant, for, if the same party takes a portion of the stock for cash at par and a very considerable portion of the remaining stock for fixed assets, the two transactions are so closely related as to make the cash sale price a doubtful measure of the real value of the stock. One must consider not only the arm's-length nature of the transaction in which stock is issued for cash, but also the amount of stock sold; otherwise, a small block of stock might be sold to outsiders for cash at par, or even at a premium, but such a transaction might not serve to establish the fair cash value of the stock.

If all of the stock or all of the bonds of a company are issued in payment for fixed assets, there will be no cash sales of the securities to serve as a measure of their cash value. If there is also no appraisal, it may be necessary to value the fixed assets at the par or stated value of the securities issued for them.

The law allows the directors of a corporation a large measure of discretion in valuing property taken in payment for stock. Creditors may, at some later date, attack the values in court in an attempt to show that the stock was really issued at a discount, and that the stockholders are liable for the discount. However, this is a contingency which the company's accountant cannot anticipate by insisting upon a valuation less than that approved by the directors and upon setting up an account with discount on stock.

The public accountant's position is somewhat different. He probably would be considered guilty of misrepresentation if he gave an unqualified opinion regarding financial statements containing gross inflations of asset values. He cannot be expected to assume the responsibility of placing an acceptable valuation on the assets, but he can be expected to qualify his report.

Mixed acquisitions at a lump cost. If several assets are acquired in one purchase at a lump price, it is necessary to apportion the cost to the various assets in order to show costs not subject to depreciation, or subject to depreciation at various rates. The apportionment of cost can be made on the basis of an appraisal by outside appraisers or by company officials. For instance, if land, buildings, and machinery are acquired at a cost of $120,000 and if they are appraised at $15,000, $60,000, and $75,000, respectively, the cost can be apportioned in the ratio of the appraised value of each class of assets to the total appraised value. The computation is shown below:

	Appraisal		Apportioned
Assets	Amount	Per Cent	Cost
Land	$ 15,000	10%	$ 12,000
Buildings	60,000	40	48,000
Machinery	75,000	50	60,000
Total	$150,000	100%	$120,000

Assets constructed. Two matters require consideration with respect to the costs of fixed assets constructed:

(1) The propriety of including manufacturing overhead in the cost.
(2) The construction-period theory.

Overhead as an element of cost. The inclusion of material and labor costs in the cost of fixed assets manufactured by a company for its own use has never been, and should not be, questioned. Over the years, there has been a change in accounting thought relative to the propriety of including factory overhead in the cost of fixed assets manufactured.

It was originally believed that *no overhead should be charged to fixed assets.* This opinion was defended by the following reasoning:

The production of fixed assets presumably will not be allowed to interfere with the manufacture of goods which can be sold, because otherwise any saving on the production of fixed assets would be offset by the loss of profits on finished goods which might have been manufactured and sold.

Therefore, the production of fixed assets will normally occur during periods when the plant facilities will not be required for the manufacture of the salable product; consequently, there will be no increase, or at least no appreciable increase, in the overhead as the result of the production of fixed assets.

To charge fixed assets with part of the normal overhead would result in a corresponding reduction in the overhead charged to the cost of goods manufactured, and a corresponding increase in the profits on merchandise sales.

Because this additional profit would be the result of a charge to the fixed assets for the overhead capitalized, the company would be taking a profit on the manufacture of its fixed assets.

To illustrate the point, let us assume the following facts concerning the costs of manufacturing finished goods during two years and the cost of constructing fixed assets during the second year:

	1964	1965		
	Finished Goods Only	Total	Finished Goods	Fixed Assets
Materials	$ 50,000	$ 75,000	$50,000	$25,000
Direct labor	50,000	75,000	50,000	25,000
Factory overhead	50,000	50,000	?	?
Total	$150,000	$200,000		
Selling price	200,000			
Gross profit	$ 50,000			

Assume that the same quantity of finished goods was manufactured in 1965 as in 1964 and sold at the same price. If we charge part of the factory overhead in 1965 to finished goods and part to fixed assets (on the basis of the direct labor, for instance), we produce the following results:

	1965		
	Total	Finished Goods	Fixed Assets
Materials	$ 75,000	$ 50,000	$25,000
Direct labor	75,000	50,000	25,000
Factory overhead (apportioned on basis of direct labor)	50,000	33,333	16,667
Total	$200,000	$133,333	$66,667
Selling price of finished goods		200,000	
Gross profit		$ 66,667	

The gross profit in 1965 is shown to be $16,667 more than it was in 1964, although the same quantity of merchandise was manufactured, and sales were made at the same price. This $16,667 is the amount of overhead charged to fixed assets. Therefore it was argued that the overhead charged to the fixed assets resulted in an increase in reported net income, and that the company, in effect, was taking a profit on work done for itself.

This illustration is, of course, a simple one because the labor and material costs and the selling prices of finished goods were assumed to be identical during the two years, and because the construction of fixed assets was assumed to cause no increase in overhead. Nonessential variations were purposely eliminated in order to stress the theoretical point.

The next step in the development of thought relative to the inclusion of overhead in the cost of fixed assets manufactured may be stated as follows:

Fixed assets should be charged with overhead specifically incurred in their manufacture. Those who proposed this procedure maintained, and probably rightly so, that the manufacture of fixed assets cannot be carried on without incurring some overhead costs which would not otherwise be incurred. Although there are many fixed charges which would not be increased, there are variable costs which are more or less proportionate to the utilization of the factory facilities. The cost of power is one illustration. It would be improper to load the cost of finished goods with expenses which were not incurred in their manufacture and which would not have been incurred if fixed assets had not been produced.

The now well-established emphasis on the cost principle has resulted in an increasing belief that, in the allocation of costs, no special favors or cost exemptions should be granted, and, therefore, that *overhead should be charged to fixed assets manufactured on the same basis and at the same rate that it is charged to goods manufactured.* This point of view does encounter some resistance from those accountants still influenced by the fetish of conservatism. The increasing recognition of the importance of cost as the basis of accounting has been accompanied by an increasing tendency to sanction the inclusion of overhead in the cost of fixed assets at the same rate as that applied to finished goods, so that there may be no special favors or exemptions resulting in the undercosting of fixed assets and a consequent overcosting of finished goods.

The construction-period theory. The accounting principle which sanctions the capitalization of all expenditures during the construction period applies particularly to buildings. It was at first regarded as applying to a building constructed before the company commenced operations, and it was defended on two grounds: First, if a company was engaged only in the construction of a plant, all of its expenditures (even those which, during operations, would be regarded as administrative expenses) were incurred for the purpose of construction and hence were properly capitalizable; second, a company should not be required to begin operations under the embarrassment of a deficit. The theory is now regarded as also applying to plant additions made while operations are in progress; however, it is not intended that this should result in any favoritism to regular operations.

A period sometimes elapses between the completion of a plant and its occupancy or other utilization as an income-producing factor of the business, and management sometimes desires to capitalize expenses during that period. If operations are being conducted elsewhere, there seems little justification for such a capitalization. If operations have not been commenced, the situation may be somewhat different, and it is sometimes regarded as permissible to capitalize, after completion of construction, some expenditures which normally would be charged to income. For instance, if occupancy of a factory building is necessarily postponed for some time after its completion, capitalizing the carrying charges until the date of occupancy may be sanctioned. However, the construction-period theory should not be abused by capitalizing carrying charges over a long interim period; a long waiting period should probably be recognized as an indication that executive planning was poor, that the building has proved to be a losing venture, and that losses should be taken into the accounts. Even if interim-period expenses appear to be properly capitalizable, it is probably preferable to record them as deferred charges instead of including them in fixed asset costs.

Although a building or other fixed asset may deteriorate to some extent during the construction period, it is customary to ignore such depreciation in the accounts, and to spread the depreciation charges over the period of utilization. There certainly would be no object in making a charge for depreciation during the construction period and recapitalizing such charges by adding them back to the cost of the asset as a construction-period cost.

Interest during construction. Utility commissions permit utility companies to charge the fixed asset accounts with interest costs incurred during the construction period, regardless of whether the construction is done by the company itself or by a contractor. In addition to interest on funds borrowed to finance the new asset, regulatory commissions often approve the capitalization of an interest allowance for the utility's own funds devoted to the construction activity; when permitted, such implicit interest is debited to the asset being constructed and credited to a special income account. Capitalization of interest is permitted because no income is earned by the asset during construction to cover the cost of capital. Because the interest cannot be recovered before the asset is put to use, the utility is permitted to recover it by including it in the investment on which it is permitted to take depreciation and on which its allowed earnings are based.

Although no similar reason exists for allowing nonregulated companies to capitalize interest incurred during the construction period, the sanction of utility commissions has been carried over to such companies without a consideration of the difference in conditions. However, there is this difference: regulated companies have been permitted to capitalize implicit interest (computed on the company's own funds used in construction) as well as interest actually paid; the capitalization of implicit interest by nonregulated companies has not been sanctioned.

Interest paid, by any kind of business, is not a necessary cost of construction; interest could be avoided by the issuance of additional capital stock. Utilities are permitted to capitalize interest in order that rate-fixing bodies will give it proper consideration in determining future rates and earnings; nonregulated businesses do not need to capitalize interest for any such reason, because they are permitted to earn what they can.

Considering interest on indebtedness, incurred by a nonregulated business to obtain funds for construction, as a part of the cost of tangible assets has little justification in theory. Some attempt has been made to justify it under the general theory that all costs during the construction period can be capitalized; but interest is a money cost, not a construction cost, and it can be avoided by an additional investment of equity capital. However, the practice is now so well established that it is rarely challenged.

The issue concerning the propriety of capitalizing interest in the case of nonregulated companies generally arises during the "start-up" period when the new business has construction activity but little, if any, revenue. During such a period, capitalization has some theoretical appeal because it can lead to a better matching of revenue and expense. However, assuming that justification is found to support the capitalization of interest during an organizational period, it would be better if the amount were charged to an intangible asset rather than to a tangible asset as part of its cost.

Donated assets. Corporations sometimes receive gifts of fixed assets, either from their stockholders or from cities which attract industries by providing them with plants or with sites for plants. It has long been established practice to record such assets at their fair value. It has been argued that such accounting is a departure from the cost basis. However, because the purpose of accounting is to reflect accountability, it would seem proper for management to report some value for all assets for which it is accountable. If an asset is acquired by gift, the amount of the accountability seems to be properly measured by the fair value of the property.

Gifts of assets may be unconditional or conditional. If they are unconditional, the recipient obtains immediate title to them, and custom sanctions making entries debiting the asset accounts at appropriate valuations and crediting an account that bears some title such as Donated Capital.

Gifts of fixed assets from a city are frequently subject to some condition, such as continued operations over a stated period of time, or the employment of a certain minimum number of men for a specified number of years. To illustrate, assume that a business is given factory land and buildings on condition that it employ at least 100 men each year for five years. Any entries made to record the contingent gift should clearly indicate that title has not been obtained and that no addition to the owners' equity has been assuredly realized. An entry may be made debiting such accounts as Contingent Asset—Land, and Contingent Asset—Buildings, and crediting an account with some title such as Contingent Donated Capital.

If title is obtained at the end of the five-year period, the balances in the contingent asset accounts should be transferred to the Land and Buildings accounts, and the contingent owners' equity should be transferred to Donated Capital. It would be improper to transfer one-fifth of the contingent equity to Donated Capital annually, because the stipulated conditions must be met during all of the years. Failure to comply with the requirements during any one year will cause a forfeiture.

Fixed assets acquired by gift should be depreciated on the basis of the appraisal values recorded in the accounts. But if the gift is conditional, should depreciation be provided on the assets before the date on which title is obtained? It might be contended that such depreciation should be ignored, because production costs should not be charged with depreciation of assets not owned. On the other hand, if no depreciation is provided during this period, high depreciation charges, sufficient to compensate for the lack of such charges during the period before title was acquired, will be necessary during the period of use following the acquisition of title. These high charges will introduce an element of variation in income charges during two periods of similar operating conditions and will load the total depreciation on the period of ownership rather than on the entire period of use. The authors are, therefore, of the opinion that operations during the period prior to the acquisition of title should be charged with depreciation.

SPECIAL POINTS ON SPECIFIC ASSETS

Real estate. Rights in real estate may be classified as follows:

(1) Freehold estates:
  (a) Estates in fee simple, or estates of inheritance, which descend to one's heirs.
  (b) Estates for life.
(2) Estates less than freeholds:
  These are otherwise known as *leaseholds.*

Only freeholds can properly and legally be considered real property, to be recorded under the heading of "land." Leaseholds are personal property, and are considered later under the classification of intangible assets. Persons holding leaseholds for long periods of time, such as 63, 84, and 99 years, are likely to consider them as freeholds, but the legal distinction should not be lost sight of in the accounts.

Accounts. Land and buildings should not be carried in a single account called "Real Estate." Separate accounts should be opened for the land and the buildings, because land does not depreciate and does not have to be insured, whereas buildings do depreciate and should be insured.

Although land does not decrease in value as a result of use and the passing of years, losses may be incurred as a result of obsolescence or a sort of supersession. Neighborhoods change, and there are consequent declines in income productivity. Although it probably would be improper for a business to make regular provisions for such obsolescence, it might be advisable for management to observe neighborhood changes and give consideration to the possibility that obsolescence is in prospect and make provisions therefor. Any such occurrence would presumably affect the value of the buildings as well as the value of the land.

Land. If any land is held for speculative purposes, or with the intention of using it for future plant extensions, such land should be distinguished in the accounts from land in use as a plant site. The distinction can be made by using such account titles as "Plant Land" and "Nonplant Land." Plant-site land should be shown in the balance sheet under the Fixed Assets caption; land held for speculation or possible plant expansion should be shown under some other caption.

Not only should plant-site and speculative land be separated in the accounts, but various premises should be recorded in separate accounts if there are a considerable number of them. Although one general ledger account for plant land and one for nonplant land may be sufficient, subsidiary records of some kind should be kept, particularly if some of the parcels of land are mortgaged and others are not.

If natural resources are acquired and the land will have a residual value after the wasting asset is exhausted, the portion of the cost applicable to the land itself should be set up in a separate account.

Cost is the generally accepted basis of accounting for land. Cost includes the purchase price, broker's commission, fees for examining and recording title, surveying, draining, clearing (less salvage), and landscaping.

Expenditures for land improvements may be charged to the Land account if the expenditures result in the addition of costs which are not subject to depreciation. If depreciation must be considered in relation to such expenditures, an account with Land Improvements should be opened. Such an account would be charged with expenditures for fences, water systems, and sidewalks and with paving costs.

Assessments for such local benefits as paving and street lighting are often spread so wide geographically that property owners who benefit little, if any, from an improvement are required to contribute to the cost. It would seem that a proper valuation of the land would exclude the cost of such assessments, and that they should be treated as expenses, although for federal income tax purposes special assessments are not recognized as allowable deductions.

Land costs should include any interest, accrued at the date of purchase, on mortgages or other encumbrances on the land, and apportioned to the purchaser.

In the case of land being held for speculation or for future plant-site use, the question arises concerning the treatment of taxes and other carrying charges. It is certainly a conservative procedure to charge off such carrying costs immediately. On the other hand, it may be reasonably contended that, as the purpose of buying such land is either to take advantage of a rising market or to obtain the property when it is available, the carrying charges are proper additions to the cost, particularly because the land produces no income against which the expenses can be charged.

It is often stated that such charges should not be added to the Land account unless the market value is increasing sufficiently to cover both the original cost and the subsequent carrying charges. However, if the land is being held for plant purposes, market values have no bearing on the proper valuation for accounting purposes, because the land may properly be carried at the total of all costs up to the time a plant is constructed on it and occupied. In other words, it is not the liquidating basis of market which governs, but the going-concern basis of cost. If the land is being held for speculation, the eventual gain or loss is the difference between selling price and cost plus carrying charges. If the carrying costs are charged against income from other sources, and if the books show a gain or loss on the sale equal to the difference between purchase and sale prices, both the gain or loss from the speculation and the income from other sources are distorted.

For federal income tax purposes, the taxpayer has the option of capitalizing the carrying charges on vacant land which produces no revenue or treating them as deductible expenses.

Although the accounts with land should reflect cost, the market value of land held for speculation or plant expansion, if substantially below cost, should be shown parenthetically in the balance sheet or be otherwise disclosed. This need not be done in the case of plant land, because, from the going-concern standpoint, market values of fixed assets need not be given recognition.

Buildings. If a building is purchased, cost includes the purchase price plus all repair charges incurred in making good depreciation which occurred before the building was purchased, as well as all costs of alterations and improvements.

If a building is constructed instead of purchased, the cost includes the material, labor and supervision, and other expenses, or the contract price, and a great variety of incidentals, some of which are mentioned below:

(1) If land and an old building which is to be razed are purchased at a flat price, the total cost may be charged to the land. The cost of wrecking, minus any proceeds from the sale of salvage, should be charged to the Land account.

If an old building, formerly occupied by the business, is replaced, the loss on the retirement of the old building should not be capitalized and included in the cost of the new building.

(2) If property is purchased subject to an existing lease, and the building is to be razed to make room for a new structure, any payments made to tenants to induce them to vacate before the expiration of the lease may be included in the cost of the new building.

(3) Costs of excavation should be charged to the building, rather than to the land.

(4) Costs of building permits and licenses may be capitalized.

(5) Costs of temporary buildings used for construction offices or as tool and material sheds may be capitalized, but the cost of temporary buildings used for operations during the construction of the permanent buildings should be absorbed in operations.

(6) Architect's fees and superintendents' salaries are a part of the cost.

(7) The cost of construction of a building can properly include all insurance premiums applicable to the construction period, including premiums on insurance against claims for damages or accidents. If no insurance is carried, any disbursements made in settlement of such claims can be capitalized unless their amount is so excessive as to inflate grossly the valuation of the building.

(8) As indicated on page 294, certain expenditures which ordinarily

would be charged to expense may be capitalized if made during the construction period.

(9) Interest accrued during the construction period on bonds or other obligations assumed or issued to obtain funds for construction purposes may be capitalized; the proportion of bond discount applicable to the construction period may be similarly treated.

Building occupancy account. In Chapter 2 all accounts reflecting costs of building occupancy were closed directly to the Manufacturing account or to the Revenue and Expense account. It may be desirable, under certain circumstances, to close them to intermediate clearing, or assembly, accounts. The purposes for which such procedures are used are discussed below.

To simplify proratings. If building occupancy costs are to be apportioned to several departments (and possibly to functions within departments), it may be desirable to close all accounts reflecting such costs to a Building Occupancy clearing account so that it will be possible to apportion the aggregate amount instead of making apportionments of all of the individual accounts. The clearing account would be closed to Building Occupancy —Manufacturing, Building Occupancy—Selling, and Building Occupancy—General, or to subfunction accounts within the three main classifications.

To compare occupancy costs on ownership or rental bases. If it is desired to assemble, in the accounts, information indicating whether it is more "profitable" to own or to rent, the individual accounts may be closed to two clearing accounts:

Costs Incurred in Lieu of Rent.

This account would be debited with the balances (or portions of the balances) of accounts reflecting costs (such as insurance, taxes, and depreciation) which would not be incurred if the building were rented. After comparing the resulting balance of this account with an amount regarded as a fair rental for the premises, the account is closed to

Building Occupancy.

In addition to the debit mentioned above, this account is charged with transfers to complete the closing of the individual accounts related to occupancy of the building. Its balance will then be the same as that resulting from the procedure described above in the paragraph "To simplify proratings," and the proratings may be made in the same manner.

To determine income from rentals to tenants. If portions of the premises (whether owned or rented) are leased to tenants, the following accounts may be kept:

Rental Activities.

The portions of the individual expense accounts regarded as applicable to space leased to tenants are transferred to this account. It is credited with the rental income and its resulting balance is closed to Revenue and Expense and is shown in the income statement as miscellaneous income or expense.

Building Occupancy.

The remaining expenses, regarded as applicable to the space occupied by the company itself, are transferred from the individual expense accounts to this account. The balance of the account can then be apportioned to departments or subfunctions.

Building expense and income. Concerns owning their own buildings sometimes set up a Building Expense and Income account, charging it with all occupancy costs and crediting it with income, if any, from rents for leased space; the account is also credited, by charge to operations, with an estimated amount representing the cost that would be incurred for space occupied by the company if the premises were leased instead of owned. The balance of the account is then presumed to indicate whether ownership is desirable, and is closed to Revenue and Expense.

It should be noted that, if the theoretical rent for company-occupied space is greater than the actual occupancy cost, the portion of the excess charged to manufacturing overstates the cost of goods manufactured, with an offsetting credit to income. Such offsetting misstatements are undesirable. The situation is made worse if some of the manufactured goods are unsold at the end of the period; in that case, part of the overstated manufacturing cost is lodged in the end-of-period inventory, with a consequent overstatement of net income.

Machinery. The cost of machinery includes the purchase price, freight, duty, and installation costs. If machinery has to be operated for a time for the purpose of breaking it in and testing it, the costs of such necessary preliminary operation may be capitalized.

The records for machinery should be kept in considerable detail, to provide information concerning location, price, and condition for insurance purposes, and to supply information concerning life and repairs for depreciation purposes. Depreciation rates are at best only estimates, which should be revised as the history of the business furnishes statistics on which more accurate estimates may be based. Hence, adequate statistical records should be kept. A subsidiary plant ledger should be maintained, with a page or card for each machine. Punched cards used in connection with tabulating procedures have been found serviceable as subsidiary property records. Each unit of equipment should be tagged or otherwise marked with a number which will definitely identify it, and the same identifying code number should appear in the subsidiary ledger. The subsidiary plant ledger should contain the following information, part of which will be posted from books of original entry and part of which will be recorded merely as memoranda:

Name of machine
Number (to identify the machine)
Location
Manufacturer
Manufacturer's guarantee period

From whom purchased
Date of installation
Purchase price
Cost of installation
Other elements of original cost
(The total of these elements in all subsidiary accounts is controlled by the asset accounts in the general ledger.)
Types of machine tools used with the equipment
Service and depreciation data:
  Estimated life
  Actual life
  Estimated residual value
  Actual residual value
Depreciation rate
Periodical depreciation provision, and accumulated amount provided to date (The total in all subsidiary accounts is controlled by accumulated depreciation accounts in the general ledger.)
Ordinary and extraordinary repairs, with information regarding date, cost, and nature
Information concerning abnormal operating conditions, such as overtime work, affecting depreciation and the operating life of the asset

Such records provide data desirable for insurance purposes and are extremely helpful in proving a claim for loss. The service information is valuable as a guide to future purchases, and the information concerning actual life and actual residual value realized upon the disposal of the asset is helpful in making future estimates of depreciation rates to be applied to similar equipment.

The data concerning total depreciation provided up to any given date are valuable for two reasons:

(1) To avoid overdepreciating any asset. For instance, the general ledger may contain a Machinery account with a debit balance of $50,000, and an Accumulated Depreciation—Machinery account with a credit balance of $20,000. On the average, the machinery is 40% depreciated. But this is an average of old and new machinery. Some of the old machinery may have been fully depreciated; for example, one machine costing $1,000 may have been depreciated at 10% per annum for ten years. Reference to the subsidiary record for this machine will disclose this fact, and no further depreciation will be taken on the machine.

(2) To show the depreciated book value of each unit of machinery, in order that the gain or loss on disposals can be accurately determined.

The subsidiary records should, in some cases, be carried to greater detail than for a single unit of equipment. If the unit of equipment consists of various parts subject to different depreciation rates, and if the costs of the various elements can be ascertained, it is advisable to keep the records in such a way as to show the portions of cost subject to the various depreciation rates. A jet liner is a good illustration of a fixed asset for which subdivided subsidiary records can be kept; the turbines will require replacement before the remainder of the aircraft.

If entries are made in the general ledger to give effect to an appraisal, the subsidiary plant ledger should thereafter be kept on both a cost and an appraisal basis. The cost basis should be retained for income tax purposes, and the appraisal-basis data will be required for purposes of maintaining an agreement between the general ledger controlling accounts and the subsidiary records.

Reinstallation costs. If machinery is rearranged in the factory for the purpose of improving the "routing," and thus reducing the time and cost of production, a question arises with respect to the proper treatment of the reinstallation expense. Presumably the cost of one installation will already have been charged to the Machinery account. Theoretically, therefore, the cost, or the undepreciated remainder of the cost, of the first installation should be removed from the accounts, and the reinstallation cost should be capitalized by charge to the Machinery account.

Tools. Tools may be divided into two classes: machine tools and hand tools. Machine tools are really a part of the machine and may, therefore, be charged to the Machinery account. However, because they usually wear out much more rapidly than the machine, are likely to be lost or stolen, and hence have to be replaced, and because they are similar to hand tools in these respects, it is usually better to carry both classes of tools in the Tools account.

As the element of loss and theft plays a large part in determining the cost of tool replacements, it is usually advisable to abandon the idea of applying a depreciation rate to the tools, and to substitute the physical inventory method. The tools on hand at the close of the period are listed and valued at cost, with an allowance for wear and tear, and the Tools account is written down to the value thus ascertained.

Patterns. Some patterns are used for regular stock work, and thus have a long-term value which can be charged to the asset account and reduced by depreciation charges. Other patterns are made for special jobs and should be charged to the cost of the jobs and not to the Patterns account. Although it may be possible, and even perhaps probable, that orders will be repeated for the special jobs, conservatism requires charging the pattern cost to the first order.

Furniture and fixtures. This account should be charged with the cost of relatively permanent property such as showcases and counters, shelving, display fixtures, safes, and office equipment. It is preferable to have a Store Fixtures account and an Office Fixtures account, in order that the depreciation charges may be properly allocated as selling and administrative expenses. Unless carefully watched, these accounts may become inflated with charges for trivial items and with rearrangement and replacement costs which add no value.

Delivery equipment. What was said with regard to subsidiary records for machinery applies equally to records for delivery equipment. Service records are particularly important in furnishing data on which a per-mile depreciation rate may be based. Parts, such as tires, requiring frequent replacement may be charged off as expenses rather than capitalized and subjected to depreciation.

Containers. Concerns that deliver goods in containers, such as milk bottles, vinegar and oil barrels, cement sacks, steel tanks, drums, carboys, and bakers' baskets, face the problem of accounting for such property.

The record of returnable containers in customers' hands may be kept in a purely memorandum manner without making any charges to the customers' accounts. If, as in the retail milk business, there are no billings to customers and there is a high percentage of loss, the containers may be regarded as operating supplies rather than fixed assets, and the loss thereon should be determined by periodical inventories. If containers not billed to customers are carried in the accounts as fixed assets, a liberal allowance should be set up for the loss incurred from the customers' failure to make returns.

It is not uncommon to bill customers for containers shipped to them, with the understanding that full credit will be granted upon return of the container. The entries below, for a sale and for a return of containers, illustrate such an arrangement.

Accounts receivable	1,075	
Sales		1,000
Allowance for returnable containers		75
To record a sale.		
Allowance for returnable containers	75	
Accounts receivable		75
To record a return of containers.		

The Allowance for Returnable Containers should be deducted in the balance sheet from the receivables for containers.

Customers sometimes pay for and retain the containers billed to them. The entries for such a collection will depend upon whether the billings were at cost or above cost. Referring to the preceding illustration and assuming that the billing was at cost, the entry for a collection for the containers would be:

Cash	75	
Accounts receivable		75
To record the collection.		
Allowance for returnable containers	75	
Containers		75
To relieve the asset account of the cost of containers sold.		

If the billing was above cost (say, $25 above cost), the second entry would be:

Allowance for returnable containers	75	
Containers		50
Income from containers sold		25

It will be noted that there are no debits to an accumulated depreciation account in the foregoing entries relieving the asset account for the containers sold. This is so because containers are usually carried in the fixed asset accounts on an inventory basis; in other words, no accumulated depreciation account is provided, and the asset account is adjusted periodically to a valuation determined by preparing a physical inventory of the containers on hand and those with customers and making an estimate of their condition.

If customers are billed for the containers, their accounts may be kept in such a manner as to distinguish between balances receivable from customers in cash and balances to be settled by the return of containers. It may be convenient also to provide a separate column in the sales journal for charges to customers for containers.

If cash deposits for returnable containers are collected from customers when sales are made, the amount collected should be credited to a liability account, such as Customers' Container Deposits. When the deposit is refunded upon the return of the containers, the Customers' Container Deposits account is debited and Cash is credited.

It may be the company's experience that some containers are never returned, perhaps because of breakage or disappearance while in the customer's possession. Under such circumstances, periodic adjusting entries are required to reduce the liability account and the Containers account. If the required deposit exceeds cost, the difference will be credited to Income from Containers Sold in the adjusting entry. To illustrate such an adjusting entry, assume the following facts:

Cost of containers	\$10 per unit
Cash deposit required of customers	\$15 per unit
Estimated number of containers that will not be returned	100

Customers' container deposits	1,500	
Containers		1,000
Income from containers sold		500
Adjusting entry for estimated nonreturns.		

CHAPTER

17

Tangible Fixed Assets (Continued)

DEPRECIATION

Similarity of fixed assets and prepaid expenses. The cost of a machine which will last twenty years and the cost of a three-year insurance policy on the machine both represent outlays to be charged to expense and recovered, if possible, out of revenue—one during a period of twenty years, the other during a period of three years. The fact that the twenty-year life of the machine is estimated, whereas the three-year life of the insurance policy is definite, should not result in any failure to recognize that the cost exhaustions in both cases represent expenses. The portion of the insurance cost to be absorbed in expense annually is definitely determinable, whereas the portion of the machine cost to be absorbed in expense annually must be estimated; but there is no more justification for preparing a statement of operations in which some amount is shown as net income before depreciation than there would be in preparing an operating statement showing some amount as net income before insurance. Net income is not known until charges have been made for all expirations of costs.

Causes of expiration of plant property costs. The following words are used to denote the causes of the exhaustion or expiration of investments in tangible fixed assets used as plant property:

Depreciation.	Supersession.	Accidents.
Obsolescence.	Inadequacy.	

Obsolescence, supersession, inadequacy, and accidents. Little comment is required with respect to accidents, as the meaning of the word is obvious. In some businesses, accidents, although not occurring with regularity, do occur with sufficient frequency to make them virtually a normal element of operations. In such businesses, it is acceptable accounting to equalize the cost of accidents by establishing a reserve by periodical charges to operations sufficient to absorb the losses which the experience of the business indicates will occur. For federal income tax purposes, accident losses are deductible only in the year in which they are incurred; reserve provisions are not deductible.

Supersession and inadequacy may be regarded as causes of obsolescence. A fixed asset may become obsolete because it is superseded by another fixed asset which operates so much more cheaply or efficiently than the old one that it is profitable to discard the old while it is still usable and install the new. A fixed asset may also become obsolete because its product is superseded by some other article. Thus, if a fixed asset is used in the manufacture or distribution of an article whose sale is dependent on a fad or a fashion, and the fixed asset is capable of use only in connection with this article, the fixed asset will become obsolete if the article is superseded in public favor by some other article. Fixed assets used in the manufacture of player piano rolls suffered obsolescence with the advent of the radio.

Inadequacy usually results from expansion in operations. For instance, a company may begin operations cautiously with equipment capable of small production and find that the sale of the product justifies an increase in production and the utilization of equipment of larger capacity.

Supersession and inadequacy are not the only causes of obsolescence. Any event or condition which renders the continued use of a fixed asset (which is still physically capable of use) inexpedient, impracticable, or impossible is a cause of obsolescence.

Obsolescence may be classified as ordinary or extraordinary. Ordinary obsolescence results from improvements in the arts and from other normal occurrences incident to operations. Extraordinary obsolescence results from causes not normally incident to operations. During World War II, automobile and other factories were converted to war production; at the conclusion of the war, changes in models and in consumer demands caused an extraordinary obsolescence in many fixed assets in use before the war. For tax purposes, ordinary obsolescence may be included in the depreciation provision; extraordinary obsolescence is deductible only when determined.

The necessity of providing for physical deterioration was recognized long before recognition was given to the desirability of making provisions for obsolescence. The increasing inclination of management to include provisions for obsolescence with the provisions for physical deterioration in the periodical charges to income is perhaps due less to considerations of business prudence and sound accounting than to their deductibility for tax purposes.

There is some difference of opinion among accountants regarding the proper accounting procedure to be applied when a fixed asset becomes obsolete. Some maintain that the cost of the asset, minus any accumulated depreciation and obsolescence and minus the proceeds of disposal, should immediately be written off to Retained Earnings; others agree to the advisability of an immediate write-off but say that the charge should be made to current income. If the obsolete asset is not disposed of, accountants are in general agreement that it should not be classified in the balance sheet as a fixed asset; some accountants advocate a reduction in carrying value to a realizable basis; others, while recognizing the theoretical desirability of such a reduction, are influenced by the practical difficulty of estimating a realizable value, and are disposed to adhere to the tax procedure of taking no loss until the period when disposal occurs or the loss is otherwise determined.

Depreciation. Depreciation was formerly rather generally regarded by accountants as the physical deterioration of a tangible asset caused by wear and tear and the action of the elements. The concept of depreciation expressed by the foregoing definition is now regarded by most accountants as unsatisfactory, for two reasons:

First, depreciation, as defined above, has reference only to a physical phenomenon: decay or deterioration. The more modern accounting concept is that depreciation is related to all forces, economic as well as physical, which ultimately terminate the economic usefulness of a fixed asset.

Second, the advocates of the more modern definition believe that, from the accounting standpoint, depreciation should apply to the *investment* in the asset, rather than to the asset itself. Placing the emphasis on exhaustion of the investment rather than on exhaustion of the asset might not satisfy an engineer, who is concerned with depreciation as a physical function, but it is a useful emphasis from the standpoint of the accountant, who is concerned with the erosion of fixed asset costs and their absorption as expenses into the stream of operations. Placing the accounting emphasis on the assignment of cost rather than on physical deterioration gives recognition to the fact that depreciation charges are not intended to parallel physical decline. Depreciation charges are intended to spread the cost of the asset over the years of its usefulness in an equitable manner; this result would not be accomplished if the accumulated depreciation charges followed the curve of physical depreciation. For one reason, physical depreciation usually is less during the early years than during the later years of an asset's life; if the accounting charges followed this curve, the early years would be charged less for the use of the machine than the later years, although a new asset presumably is of more benefit to the business than an old one. For another reason, management often considers it desirable to replace fixed assets before physical depreciation is complete; therefore, if income is to be properly measured, depreciation charged should equal cost less scrap value during the period of useful life.

The more modern concept of depreciation is expressed by the following definition proposed by the Committee on Terminology of the American

Institute of Certified Public Accountants: "*Depreciation accounting* is a system of accounting which aims to distribute the cost or other basic value of tangible capital assets, less salvage (if any), over the estimated useful life of the unit (which may be a group of assets) in a systematic and rational manner. It is a process of allocation, not of valuation. *Depreciation for the year* is the portion of the total charge under such a system that is allocated to the year. Although the allocation may properly take into account occurrences during the year, it is not intended to be a measurement of the effect of all such occurrences."

Depreciation is an expense. Early accountants were confronted with the task of convincing businessmen that depreciation is an expense which must be provided for regardless of the level of earnings; their clients preferred to write off little or no depreciation in years of poor earnings or of losses, and to make large provisions for depreciation in prosperous years. Profits were stated before depreciation was deducted, and the directors then decided how much to credit to the depreciation reserve and how much to pay in dividends.

As accountants began to drive home the argument that depreciation is an expense which must be provided for in bad years as well as in good, they were met by several arguments. One was that depreciation had been offset by an increase in the market value of the property, and that the assets, even after a number of years of use, were worth as much as they cost. Such an argument was unsound because it failed to recognize the fact that, regardless of changes in market values, fixed assets wear out and the resulting cost expiration is an operating expense.

Another argument was that depreciation provisions were unnecessary because repairs kept the asset as good as new. It is difficult to find a better answer to this argument than Professor Hatfield's much-quoted and now almost classic sentence: "All machinery is on an irresistible march to the junk heap, and its progress, while it may be delayed, cannot be prevented by repairs."

The federal income tax law changed the attitude of many businessmen with respect to depreciation. Before the passage of the law, the attitude frequently was: How little depreciation can I take to make as good a profit showing as possible? Since the passage of the law, the attitude in many cases has become: How much depreciation can I take to reduce my taxable income?

Relation of depreciation to dividends. American courts were somewhat slow in recognizing depreciation as an expense to be provided for before the amount available for dividends was determined. There is now, however, a sufficient body of court decisions to establish the fact that the law requires a provision for depreciation, and that the payment of dividends to the full amount of the net income before depreciation would constitute an impairment of capital.

Factors of depreciation. The factors theoretically to be taken into consideration in estimating the amounts to be charged to expense periodically for fixed asset expirations are:

(1) The depreciation base.
(2) Residual or scrap value.
(3) Estimated life.

These factors determine the total depreciation to be provided and the period over which the total depreciation is to be spread. The amount charged to each period depends upon the apportionment method adopted.

The depreciation base. The base generally used for the computation of depreciation is cost, which includes installation and other capitalized incidental expenditures. The base may also include an allowance for removal costs at the expiration of the life of the asset, although it is more customary to apply such costs as a reduction of the realization from salvage.

Replacement or other appraisal values are sometimes used as the depreciation base. The propriety of the use of such bases is discussed in the next chapter.

In the interest of a more exact computation of depreciation provisions, the plant records may be subdivided so that they show, not merely the total cost or other depreciation base of all fixed assets of a certain class, but also the cost or other base of various units having different expected service lives. With such information, various rates can be applied to depreciate different structural elements or subtotals of cost.

Residual or scrap value. The residual or scrap value of an asset is the amount which can be recovered by its disposal when it is taken out of service. The estimated residual value to be used in the computation of depreciation should be net after estimated costs of dismantling and removal are deducted.

Although residual value should theoretically be taken into consideration in determining the total amount of cost expiration to be charged to operations during the life of an asset, it frequently is ignored. This may be justified if the residual value is small, or not subject to reliable estimate, or if the dismantling and removal costs cannot be accurately estimated.

Estimated life. The life of a fixed asset will be affected by repairs, and the repair policy should be taken into consideration when the life is being estimated. Estimated life may be stated in any one of the following ways:

(a) Time periods, as years or months.
(b) Operating periods, or working hours.
(c) Units of output.

Estimating the life of a fixed asset requires consideration of both physical depreciation and obsolescence. In essence, it is the period of expected economic usefulness that governs. Plates used in the printing of a book may be in usable condition long after the sale of the book has ceased, but their cost should be charged to operations during the period when sales are made. Patterns and molds, although physically usable for years, may have a life for production purposes only during the manufacture of one annual model.

Depreciation methods. The following methods of apportioning depreciation by periods are discussed in this chapter:

Straight-line.
Working-hours.
Production.
Reducing-charge. (Accelerated depreciation.)
Inventory.
Income basis.
Retirement basis.

The annuity and sinking fund methods are not discussed in this chapter, as they involve compound interest computations. They are described in *Principles of Accounting, Advanced.*

Symbols. The following symbols are used in the formulas discussed in this chapter:

C = Cost.
S = Scrap or residual value.
n = Estimated life (periods, working hours, or units of product).
r = Rate of depreciation (per period, per working hour, or per unit of product).
D = Depreciation per period.

Basis of illustrations. For purposes of illustration it will be assumed that:

The cost of an asset is \$6,000,
The estimated residual value is \$400, and
The estimated life is eight years (except in two illustrations in which the life is stated in terms of working hours and units of product).

In the illustrations of methods in which the life is expressed in operating hours or units of product, the necessary additional information is furnished.

Straight-line method. This is the simplest and most commonly used method. It results in spreading the total depreciation equally over all periods of life, unless the periodical charge is adjusted because of abnormal operating activities. The formula for computing the periodical depreciation charge is:

$$D = \frac{C - S}{n}$$

Using the assumed facts,

$$\begin{aligned} D &= \frac{\$6{,}000 - \$400}{8} \\ &= \$5{,}600 \div 8 \\ &= \$700 \end{aligned}$$

The following table shows the accumulation of depreciation.

Table of Depreciation—Straight-Line Method

End of Year	Debit Depreciation Expense	Credit Accumulated Depreciation	Total Accumulated Depreciation	Carrying Value
				$6,000
1	$ 700	$ 700	$ 700	5,300
2	700	700	1,400	4,600
3	700	700	2,100	3,900
4	700	700	2,800	3,200
5	700	700	3,500	2,500
6	700	700	4,200	1,800
7	700	700	4,900	1,100
8	700	700	5,600	400
	$5,600	$5,600		

In practical applications of the straight-line method, the residual value usually is ignored and a rate determined from the estimated life of the asset is applied to cost. Thus, in the foregoing illustration, the rate would be 12½% and the annual depreciation would be 12½% of $6,000, or $750.

The straight-line method has the advantage of simplicity. Moreover, because it has been widely used, a considerable body of experience data is available for the determination of straight-line depreciation rates applicable to various classes of tangible fixed assets.

Working-hours method. This method recognizes the fact that property, particularly machinery, depreciates more rapidly if it is used full time or overtime than if it is used part time. Not only is the wear and tear greater, but there is less opportunity for making repairs. Moreover, the full-time and overtime years get more benefit from the asset than do the part-time years. In the application of this method, the total number of working hours of which the machine is capable of operating is estimated, and a charge per hour is determined by the following formula:

$$r = \frac{C - S}{n}$$

If it is assumed that the asset used for illustrative purposes is expected to have an operating life of 22,400 working hours, the depreciation rate per hour of use is computed in the manner illustrated below:

$$r = \frac{\$6{,}000 - \$400}{22{,}400}$$
$$= \$.25$$

The table on the following page shows the number of hours the asset was used during each of eight years, and the depreciation provided on the basis of working hours.

Production method. This method is similar to the working-hours method in that it distributes the depreciation among the periods in proportion to the use made of the asset during each period. The estimated life is stated

Table of Depreciation—Working-Hours Method

Year	Hours Worked	Debit Depreciation Expense	Credit Accumulated Depreciation	Total Accumulated Depreciation	Carrying Value
					$6,000
1	2,600	$ 650	$ 650	$ 650	5,350
2	2,900	725	725	1,375	4,625
3	3,400	850	850	2,225	3,775
4	2,400	600	600	2,825	3,175
5	1,800	450	450	3,275	2,725
6	2,700	675	675	3,950	2,050
7	3,000	750	750	4,700	1,300
8	3,600	900	900	5,600	400
	22,400	$5,600	$5,600		

in units of product or service, and the rate of depreciation is a rate per unit. The figures in the illustration of the working-hours method can serve as an illustration of this method also, if we assume that the estimated life is stated as 22,400 units of product (instead of working hours), and that the figures in the Hours Worked column represent units of finished goods produced. The depreciation rate is then $.25 per unit, and the depreciation each year is computed by multiplying the number of units produced by the rate per unit.

The production method is peculiarly suitable to the depreciation of assets for which the total service units can be rather definitely estimated and when the service is not uniform by periods. The method might, for instance, be appropriately applied in depreciating automobile tires on a mileage basis.

If a fixed asset is subject to obsolescence, the production method appears to be an illogical procedure for establishing a reserve intended to provide for both physical deterioration and obsolescence, because obsolescence presumably develops on a time basis rather than on the basis of units of output. During a period of small production, the depreciation charges might be less than the amount which should be provided for obsolescence on the basis of the lapse of time, and this inadequacy might not be compensated for in periods of larger production.

Reducing-charge methods (accelerated depreciation). A depreciation procedure by which larger charges are made during the early years of the life of a fixed asset than during the later years of its life was originally supported by the following reasoning: The cost of the use of a fixed asset includes depreciation and repairs; the sum of these charges should be a fairly uniform amount year by year; because repairs tend to increase with the age of the asset, the depreciation charge should decrease, so that the increasing repair charges and the decreasing depreciation charges will tend to equalize each other and produce a uniform total charge. This may be good theory, but the plan of making decreasing depreciation charges assumes that repairs will increase in the same amount that the depreciation charges decrease; perhaps they will, but it is likely to be a matter of luck. If it is desirable to equalize the total repair and depreciation charges, it would seem better to create two reserves: one for depreciation and another for repairs. Such a plan is subject to the objection that it may be difficult to estimate accurately the total future repair cost; but with statistics showing past experience, it should be no more difficult to do this than to estimate depreciation. Such a repair reserve would not be deductible for federal income tax purposes.

Diminishing-charge methods were also sometimes advocated on the ground that the large charge in the early part of an asset's life was desirable to correspond with the large initial reduction in value from cost to second-hand market value. This argument seems to be in conflict with the general accounting principle that market values need not be given consideration in the accounting for fixed assets.

A new theory in support of diminishing-charge procedures developed after World War II. It perhaps had its origin in the fact that some companies made large expenditures for fixed assets at postwar prices that were relatively high, with the hope of making large immediate profits by supplying goods to meet the accumulated postwar demand. It was contended that such expenditures would not have been made except for the prospect of such quick profits, and that a proper matching of revenue and costs required making relatively large depreciation charges during this profitable postwar period.

This theory was then expanded until the argument was stated somewhat as follows: Because management cannot foresee the conditions which will exist during the entire physical life of a fixed asset, its decisions regarding the advisability of making large capital expenditures are often determined by the prospects of economic usefulness during a much shorter period; immediate prospects of profits may warrant taking a chance with respect to later periods; larger depreciation charges should be made in the earlier periods than in the later ones, because the expenditures were made with these early periods primarily in mind. George D. Bailey, in an article* quoted in part below, mentions some instances:

> For instance, an entire plant, built in a hurry to take care of the immediate postwar demand for the product, might properly have been amortized in substantial part during the period of immediate heavy and perhaps noncompetitive demand. Another company may have built a store in a high risk location with the belief that the immediate profits would be so good as to offset a loss in value after a short time. Another may have built outlets in highly competitive locations where the future economic risk was high but short-term prospects good. Another may have made a substantial expansion in current facilities merely to get the immediate market, or to keep a competitive position. Others may be influenced by the normal business prudence which can look ahead a few years with confidence but more than that only with some doubt as to type, location, processes, etc.

In depreciation discussions there is increasing emphasis on the theory that, because new assets are generally capable of producing more revenue

* *The Journal of Accountancy,* Vol. 88, page 376.

than old assets, a better matching of revenue and expense is achieved by larger depreciation charges in the early periods when assets have their greatest economic usefulness. Such a depreciation procedure is often referred to as accelerated depreciation, meaning essentially that depreciation charges follow a constantly decreasing pattern although initially greater than those under the straight-line method.

Three methods of providing a diminishing depreciation charge are illustrated in the following sections. These methods are:

(1) Declining-balance.
(2) Sum of years' digits or life periods.
(3) Diminishing rates on cost.

Declining-balance method. Under this method, a fixed or uniform rate is applied to the carrying value of the asset. Theoretically, the depreciation rate to be used in this method is computed by the following formula:

$$\begin{aligned} r &= 1 - \sqrt[n]{S \div C} \\ &= 1 - \sqrt[8]{\$400 \div \$6{,}000} \\ &= 1 - \sqrt[8]{.0666\tfrac{2}{3}} \end{aligned}$$

In extracting the eighth root of .0666⅔, a table of logarithms must be used.

Log .0666⅔	8.8239088	− 10
Add	70	− 70
Divide by 8:	8)78.8239088	− 80
	9.8529886	− 10, which is log .712834

$$\begin{aligned} \text{Then } r &= 1 - .712834 \\ &= .287166 \\ &= 28.7166\% \end{aligned}$$

This rate is applied at the end of the first period to cost, and thereafter to the carrying value at the beginning of each successive period, as shown by the following table. Thus, the depreciation charge the first year is 28.71⅔% of $6,000; the second year, it is 28.71⅔% of $4,277.

Depreciation Table—Uniform Rate on Diminishing Value

Rate: 28.71⅔%

Year	Debit Depreciation Expense	Credit Accumulated Depreciation	Total Accumulated Depreciation	Carrying Value
				$6,000.00
1	$1,723.00	$1,723.00	$1,723.00	4,277.00
2	1,228.21	1,228.21	2,951.21	3,048.79
3	875.51	875.51	3,826.72	2,173.28
4	624.09	624.09	4,450.81	1,549.19
5	444.87	444.87	4,895.68	1,104.32
6	317.12	317.12	5,212.80	787.20
7	226.06	226.06	5,438.86	561.14
8	161.14	161.14	5,600.00	400.00
	$5,600.00	$5,600.00		

The formula requires the use of a residual value. If an asset is assumed to have no residual value, a nominal residual value of $1 can be used.

As a practical matter, the rate used is likely to be based on what is permissible for income tax purposes. The law and regulations in effect at the time of this writing permit, for the declining-balance method, the use of a depreciation rate not exceeding twice that acceptable as a straight-line rate. The regulations also provide that scrap value need not be taken into account. Thus, if it is acceptable for income tax purposes to use 12½% as a straight-line rate (this would agree with the eight-year use life being used in the illustrations), a rate up to 25% is acceptable for the declining-balance method. Assuming that an asset cost $6,000 and that the taxpayer adopted the 25% rate, the depreciation would be

$1,500.00 for the first year—$6,000 × 25%;
$1,125.00 for the second year—$4,500 × 25%;
$ 843.75 for the third year—$3,375 × 25%;

and so on. However, depreciation should not be continued when the result would be to reduce the carrying value below the estimated scrap value. Incidentally, tax rules permit a business to shift to the straight-line method any time after the halfway point in the estimated useful life.

Sum-of-years'-digits method. This method is difficult to reduce to a brief formula; it will be more readily understood if it is stated as follows:

Add the numbers representing the periods of life:
Thus, 1 + 2 + 3 + 4 + 5 + 6 + 7 + 8 = 36
Use the sum thus obtained as a denominator.
Use as numerators the same numbers taken in inverse order:
Thus, 8/36, 7/36, etc.
Multiply the total depreciation ($C - S$) by the fractions thus produced.

Depreciation Table—Sum of Years' Digits

Year	Fraction of $5,600.00	Debit Depreciation Expense	Credit Accumulated Depreciation	Total Accumulated Depreciation	Carrying Value
					$6,000.00
1	8/36	$1,244.45	$1,244.45	$1,244.45	4,755.55
2	7/36	1,088.89	1,088.89	2,333.34	3,666.66
3	6/36	933.33	933.33	3,266.67	2,733.33
4	5/36	777.78	777.78	4,044.45	1,955.55
5	4/36	622.22	622.22	4,666.67	1,333.33
6	3/36	466.67	466.67	5,133.34	866.66
7	2/36	311.11	311.11	5,444.45	555.55
8	1/36	155.55	155.55	5,600.00	400.00
	36/36	$5,600.00	$5,600.00		

The sum of the years' digits can be computed by using the following formula:

$$S = N\left(\frac{N+1}{2}\right)$$

N equals the number of periods of estimated useful life. Applying the formula where the use life is 8 years—

$$S = 8\left(\frac{8+1}{2}\right)$$
$$S = 8(4.5)$$
$$S = 36$$

Diminishing-rates-on-cost method. No formula can be given for determining the rates, as they are chosen arbitrarily when the depreciation program is set up. The following table shows how the method operates, the rate arbitrarily chosen for each year being shown in the table.

Depreciation Table—Diminishing Rates on Cost

Year	Rates	Debit Depreciation Expense	Credit Accumulated Depreciation	Total Accumulated Depreciation	Carrying Value
					$6,000
1	15⅔%	$ 940	$ 940	$ 940	5,060
2	14⅔	880	880	1,820	4,180
3	13	780	780	2,600	3,400
4	12	720	720	3,320	2,680
5	11	660	660	3,980	2,020
6	10	600	600	4,580	1,420
7	9	540	540	5,120	880
8	8	480	480	5,600	400
	93⅓%	$5,600	$5,600		

Fractional-period depreciation under accelerated methods. If an asset to be depreciated by the sum-of-years'-digits method is acquired during the year, it is customary to compute the depreciation applicable to the partial period as follows:

(1) Compute the depreciation for a full year.
(2) Take a fraction thereof, the fraction being representative of the partial year since acquisition.

To illustrate the application of this procedure, assume that the following data relate to a company whose accounting year is the calendar year.

Asset cost	$3,000
Date of acquisition	April 1, 1965
Sum of years' digits (1 + 2 + 3 + 4 + 5)	15
The scrap value is immaterial	-0-

Depreciation for 1965—$750.

Depreciation for first full year:
5⁄15 of $3,000 = $1,000
Portion applicable to 9 months starting April 1, 1965:
9⁄12 of $1,000 = $750

Such fractional-period computations are needed in subsequent years, as is illustrated by computing the depreciation for 1966, the first full calendar year after acquisition.

Depreciation for 1966—$850.

Depreciation for 3 months ending March 31, 1966:		
Depreciation for first full year	$1,000	
Applicable to 1965—above	750	
Applicable to 1966	$ 250	$250
Depreciation for second full year:		
$\frac{4}{15}$ of $3,000 = $800		
Portion applicable to 9 months starting April 1, 1966:		
$\frac{9}{12}$ of $800 =		600
Total		$850

Fractional-period depreciation presents no problem under the declining-balance method. Assume that the applicable rate for the above asset is 20%. The depreciation for the 9 months starting April 1, 1965 is $\frac{9}{12}$ of the amount for the first full year, or $450 [$\frac{9}{12}$ (20% of $3,000)]. For subsequent calendar years, depreciation is computed by applying the rate to the carrying value at the beginning of the calendar year. The following partial table based on the assumed data is illustrative.

Period	Depreciation Expense	Accumulated Depreciation	Carrying Value	Rate = 20%
			$3,000	
April 1–December 31, 1965	$450	$ 450	2,550	
1966	510	960	2,040	
1967	408	1,368	1,632	

Inventory method. When a business owns numerous, relatively inexpensive fixed assets of a given class, such as small tools, a physical-inventory approach to depreciation can be justified on practical grounds. The large number of assets in use, the typical frequent reductions due to breakage and disappearance, and the resulting volume of replacements during each year make it both difficult and expensive to attempt to maintain records of individual units of such property showing accumulated depreciation thereon. As an alternative, periodic inventories are taken to determine the number of usable assets on hand. Next, a valuation formula, devised by the company's accountants and based somewhat on past experience, is applied. The objective of the valuation formula is to produce realistic depreciation charges and carrying values. Valuing the assets at a specific percentage of cost is an example. Or, a more sophisticated plan based on age groupings with varying percentages may be applied. As a general rule, depreciation is recorded by writing down the asset account to its depreciated value. Thus, no use is made of a valuation account for accumulated depreciation.

The valuation formula should not give undue weight to physical deterioration. Likewise, care should be taken to avoid the use of market values, second-hand values, or replacement costs. The objective is to assign cost, on a reasonable basis, to the periods benefited. Showing appraisal valuations or realizable values in the accounts is not the objective of a depreciation method.

This method of computing depreciation is sometimes referred to as the *appraisal* method. This is an unfortunate label, because it implies that depreciation charges are related in some way to what assets are worth. If depreciable assets were stated on the basis of their worth, the method could result in a depreciation charge that was a composite of cost exhaustion and market-value fluctuations. Giving effect, in the computation of income, to unrealized appreciation resulting from market increases is not to be condoned merely because the appreciation is buried in the depreciation provision; the fact that the market fluctuation is netted in the depreciation and the effect thereby obscured makes the practice even more subject to censure.

Depreciation based on income. There still persists, in the management of some businesses, an inclination to determine the amount of the depreciation provision after having ascertained the net income for the period before depreciation. This tendency is possibly a survival from the days when the true nature of depreciation as an expense was not as well recognized as it is now; it possibly also arises from the confused assumption that a credit to an accumulated depreciation account in some way constitutes a provision of funds for asset replacements, and that the amount to be thus provided is a matter of managerial policy to be determined on the basis of the amount of earnings available for that and other purposes; the practice may also stem from the desire of management to use the depreciation provisions as a means of stabilizing the reported net income, a practice which should be recognized as conscious or unconscious deception.

There are, of course, instances in which the relating of depreciation charges to income constitutes a procedure closely akin to the production method. This seems to be true with respect to the computation of depreciation provisions by a public utility on the basis of gross revenue, because gross revenue is presumably very directly related to operating activity and, therefore, to the utilization of the plant assets.

Retirement and replacement systems. The retirement and replacement systems of dealing with depreciation have numerous advocates in the public utility field. In effect, these procedures give no recognition to depreciation until the end of the life of the asset. They are akin to providing no allowance for bad debts and charging ascertained losses to operations.

Under the retirement system, operations are charged with the cost, less salvage, of plant units retired during the period, and new assets acquired are charged to the property accounts at cost. Under the replacement system, operations are charged with the cost of the new assets acquired as replacements, less the salvage recovery on the old assets. Of the two methods, the retirement system is preferable because it produces property account balances which reflect the cost of assets in use rather than the cost of assets replaced.

Retirement or replacement systems are perhaps peculiarly suited to the public utility field because the fixed assets of utilities include large numbers of units of relatively small value in any location (poles, conduits, and so forth), and the distinction between maintenance and replacements is often confused by borderline cases. Such systems probably are also advocated by utilities because property values have a direct bearing upon the rates sanctioned by controlling commissions, and utility companies are indisposed to admit that accumulated depreciation, which may reflect a percentage of depreciation which is acceptable for general accounting purposes but is in excess of the percentage of accrued physical deterioration, is a justifiable deduction from investment for purposes of rate making.

The two principal objections to these procedures are: First, operations are relieved of any charge for the expiration of asset costs until the period of retirement; as a consequence, the operating results of the early periods are relieved of normal charges, and the asset values are stated in the balance sheet without any recognition of accrued depreciation. Second, instead of operations being charged by periods with a uniform cost for the services of the fixed asset, operations become charged with variable amounts determined by the necessity for, or the policy with respect to, replacements.

Lapsing schedules. An often-used device for determining the annual amounts of depreciation and keeping track of the accumulated depreciation is known as a *lapsing schedule.* A common form of lapsing schedule is illustrated on page 321.

The operation of a lapsing schedule is probably self-evident. When an asset is acquired, pertinent facts relating to the asset are entered in the schedule and the depreciation charges for the entire use-life period are extended across the schedule by years. Annual depreciation charges are determined each year by adding the current year's column. If an asset is retired before it has been fully depreciated, the depreciation charges applicable to the remaining estimated useful life are subtracted in the Annual Depreciation columns. This is demonstrated in the illustrative schedule where the Ford truck was traded in on January 3, 1966.

Relating the depreciation charge to use. Because depreciation accounting is intended to charge fixed asset costs to operations over the periods of use, much can be said in favor of making larger charges for depreciation in periods of more-than-average use and smaller charges in periods of less-than-average use. The working-hours and production methods of computing depreciation accomplish this purpose. The straight-line method will not produce this result unless adjustments are made to increase the charge in large-use periods and reduce it in small-use periods.

Accountants generally recognize the propriety of increasing the depreciation in any period in which unusual operating activities (such as excessive overtime, additional shifts, overload, and use by inexperienced operators) tend to decrease the probable useful life of the asset below the original estimate. Management does not seem equally disposed to reduce the depreciation charge when opposite conditions prevail, because it is concerned with the consequent effect upon income taxes.

Delivery Equipment
Lapsing Schedule

Date	Description	Use Life	Depreciable Cost	Annual Depreciation 1963	1964	1965	1966	1967	1968	1974	1975
7/1/63	Ford truck	4 years	2,800	350	700	700	700	350			
1/3/64	Dodge wagon	4 years	3,200		800	800	800	800			
7/2/64	Chevrolet truck	4 years	2,600		325	650	650	650	325		
4/1/65	Plymouth wagon	4 years	2,880			540	720	720	720		
1/3/66	Ford truck traded in—below						700*	350*			
1/3/66	Ford truck	4 years	3,000				750	750	750		
	Total depreciation			350	1,825	2,690	2,920	2,920	1,795		

Although physical deterioration is undoubtedly affected by use, and although it is proper to adjust depreciation charges to give consideration to varying levels of operations, it does not follow that the depreciation charges should be exactly proportionate to use. The normal periodical depreciation charge may include provisions for (a) deterioration caused by wear and tear, (b) deterioration caused by the action of the elements, and (c) obsolescence. If a machine which normally is operated for one eight-hour shift daily is, for some reason, operated on a 24-hour basis, the proper depreciation may be more or less than three times the normal charge. Physical deterioration may be more than tripled, particularly if it is impossible to take care of maintenance and repairs. On the other hand, deterioration caused by the action of the elements will not be tripled, and the hazard of obsolescence is not increased by use.

Depreciation and replacement. People who are not trained in accounting often have the idea that the purpose of accounting for depreciation is to provide funds for the replacement of fixed assets when they wear out. Accountants are perhaps themselves to blame for this confusion because of their use of the expression "*provision* for depreciation." At any rate, there is a prevalent idea that depreciation is an expense for which a cash disbursement will be made in the future when replacement of the asset becomes necessary, and that the "depreciation provision" somehow provides for the expenditure.

From the accounting standpoint, depreciation is an expense for which the cash expenditure was made in the more or less remote past; any future expenditures which may be made to replace the asset will be capital expenditures which will subject the operations to a new series of depreciation expense charges.

Depreciation provisions are in no sense replacement provisions. Writing off the cost of a fixed asset by charges to expense over a 20-year period and writing off the cost of an insurance policy over a three-year period may, by including these elements in the cost of the product, increase the probability of recovering them in the selling price and thus obtaining funds which may be utilized for their replacement. But the entries recording the expiration of plant and insurance costs do not either provide or segregate funds for the replacement of the plant or the insurance.

The segregation of funds for replacement purposes is not customary. Very few industrial concerns create such funds, as it is usually considered that the provision for financing replacements can be postponed until the necessity for, and the cost of, the replacements become definite. In the meantime, it is usually regarded as more advisable to retain the available funds in the working capital with the hope of earning a higher return by their use in operations than could be obtained as income on fund investments.

Income taxes and depreciation methods. It would be unrealistic not to concede that income tax considerations are an important factor in the selection of depreciation methods. In view of the high level of income tax rates, the amount and pattern of depreciation deductions have an important effect on the cash position of a business. With an income tax rate of 50% (which approximates present rates), a method which results in $20,000 greater depreciation in any one year will reduce the cash requirements for income taxes for that year by $10,000. It is very likely that this may not be a permanent saving, because during the life of an asset the depreciation deduction cannot exceed its cost. But for new or expanding businesses particularly, and for all businesses to some extent, a postponement or deferment of income taxes is attractive, because it may permit an earlier retirement of debt created to finance the purchase of the assets being depreciated, or may permit the use of such cash for additional equipment.

Although considerations such as these are primarily financial in character, they can have a significant effect on income measurement. The matter is further complicated if the business wishes to adopt one depreciation method for its tax return and another for its records. Many of the accounting problems caused by income taxes are discussed in Chapter 27. For the moment a tentative opinion is offered: Nonaccounting considerations have had a considerable influence on depreciation accounting, with the inevitable result that the income-determination process is perhaps more subject to the effects of policy decisions than was formerly the case.

Composite life. The composite life of a plant as a whole, sometimes called the *average* or *mean* life, may be computed as in the following illustration.

Asset	Cost	Residual Value	Total Depreciation	Estimated Life	Annual Depreciation (Straight-Line)
A	$20,000	$5,000	$15,000	20 years	$ 750
B	12,000	2,000	10,000	10 years	1,000
C	8,000	2,000	6,000	8 years	750
D	2,100	100	2,000	4 years	500
			$33,000		$3,000

$33,000 ÷ $3,000 = 11, the composite, or average, life.

It is possible to compare the lives of different plants by determining the composite life of each; but because depreciation should be provided on each class of fixed assets on the basis of the life of each class and not on the basis of composite life, accountants are rarely called upon to make composite-life computations. The term is used and the computations are made more frequently by engineers than by accountants.

DEPLETION OF TANGIBLE FIXED ASSETS

The depletion base. Depletion is the exhaustion of the cost or value of a wasting asset, such as a mine, a timber tract, or an oil well, resulting from the conversion of the natural resource into inventories. The depletion base is the total cost or value of the wasting asset to be charged to operations during the period of exploitation of the natural resource. If there is a residual land value, it should be recorded in a separate account.

Development costs, such as those incurred in the removal of surface earth for strip-mining operations, the sinking of shafts, drilling of wells, and timbering of mines, should be set up in the accounts separately from the original cost of the wasting asset. They should be written off in amounts proportionate to the write-offs of the original cost of the wasting asset if the developments will render service throughout the entire life of the wasting asset. They should be written off over a shorter period if their usefulness will expire before the wasting asset is completely depleted.

If development expenditures prove fruitless, as in the case of the drilling of a dry well, they should be written off. It is not acceptable to carry forward any lost costs. However, if a company is engaged more or less continuously in developmental work of the type in which only a fraction of the projects can be expected to be successful, it can be argued that the cost of the unsuccessful projects is a necessary cost to secure the successful projects. Therefore, the cost of fruitless efforts need not be written off immediately but can be assigned to the successful developments, provided that a record exists showing a reasonable number of successes.

If the cutting of a tract of timberland is deferred to obtain the benefit of growth, it is permissible to capitalize the costs of protection, insurance, and administrative expenses incurred in connection with the tract.

Development costs may be incurred after operations begin. Three procedures are used in dealing with such costs. A reserve may be set up for the estimated aggregate development costs to be incurred during the life of the property, so that this aggregate cost will be spread ratably over each unit of product. Or development costs incurred after operations begin can be capitalized when the expenditures are made, and the depletion charge may be adjusted. Or they may be charged to current income.

After operations begin, a careful distinction must be made between operating expenses and expenditures which may be regarded as development costs to be capitalized.

Depletion methods. Depletion is usually computed by dividing the cost or appraised value of the wasting asset by the estimated number of tons, barrels, thousand feet, or other units in the asset, thus determining a unit depletion charge. The total depletion charge for each period is then computed by multiplying the unit charge by the number of units converted during the period from a fixed nature into inventory.

To illustrate, assume that $90,000 is paid for a mine which is estimated to contain 300,000 tons of available deposit. The unit depletion charge is:

$$\$90,000 \div 300,000 = \$.30$$

If 20,000 tons are mined in a given year, the depletion for that year will be $.30 × 20,000, or $6,000.

For purposes of correct income determination, the depletion deduction must be based on the number of units sold. Depletion applicable to the units not sold is included in the cost of the inventory. Amortization of drilling and development costs, as well as the costs associated with the removal of the resource from its natural location to the company's inventory, are also part of inventory cost.

The federal income tax regulations with respect to depletion are too extensive and complex to be discussed here, except to state that, in general, the acceptable depletion bases are: with respect to assets acquired prior to March 1, 1913, cost or fair market value at that date, whichever is higher; with respect to wasting assets acquired as such subsequent to that date, cost; and with respect to certain assets discovered in land purchased without knowledge of the existence of the deposit, discovery value—which means fair market value on the date of discovery or within thirty days thereafter. However, in some instances, depletion need not be based on either cost or discovery value, but can be computed as a percentage of gross income. When this method is used, the depletion charge cannot exceed 50% of the taxable income of the taxpayer from the property, computed without allowance for depletion, but the total depletion charge over the life of the wasting asset may exceed the total cost for income tax purposes.

Wasting-asset write-ups. Writing up wasting assets because of increases in market value is subject to the same objections that apply to writing up other fixed assets for the same reason. However, write-ups to reflect discovery value and accretion are generally regarded as permissible.

Discovery value is a term applicable in situations where property which was acquired at a mere land cost is found to contain deposits of natural resources, or when deposits are found to be more extensive than they were believed to be when purchased.

Accretion is a term particularly applicable to timber tracts. For many years, timber tracts were generally regarded as wasting assets, because it was the custom to cut tracts without reforestation, and the recording of accretion was not considered to be in accordance with good accounting. Now that many companies which are dependent on a constant supply of forest products have adopted a policy of maintaining timber tracts from which successive crops are harvested on a partial and selective basis, timber tracts are no longer always wasting assets. When timber tracts are operated on a crop basis, accountants consider it acceptable accounting to charge the asset account with amounts representing growth accretion.

If wasting assets are written up to reflect discovery value or accretion, the asset write-up should be offset by a credit to an unrealized increment account. Depletion will thereafter be based on the appraised value. There is some opinion to the effect that the credit for the unrealized increment should be considered as part of the permanent capital of the enterprise. The traditional conservative accounting requires that no portion of this credit balance find its way to retained earnings until the depletion charges have accumulated to an amount equal to the cost of the asset; thereafter, transfers may be made from unrealized increment to income or retained earnings in amounts equal to the periodical depletion. It is less conservative, although usually regarded as permissible, after charging operations with depletion on the appraised value, to transfer immediately from the unrealized increment account to income or retained earnings the portion of the periodical depletion charge representing so-called "realized appreciation." Realized appreciation is determined by applying the following formula:

Depletion rate based on appraisal value, minus depletion rate based on cost, times number of units sold.

If the depletion charge based on appraised value is $.08 per unit of ore, and the depletion charge based on cost is $.05 per unit, and 100,000 units are mined, $8,000 of depletion would be charged. If the 100,000 units are sold, a transfer of $3,000 would be made from unrealized increment to income or retained earnings.

In making the entry for realized appreciation, the accountant should give recognition to inventories. For instance, assume that the above data apply to the first year of a company's operations, and that 10,000 units remain in the inventory; the transfer entry would be:

Unrealized appreciation of ore in mine	3,000	
Allowance for unrealized appreciation in inventory		300
Realized appreciation (or Retained earnings)		2,700

If, during the second year of operations, the same quantity is mined but the inventory is reduced to 5,000 units, the transfer entry would be:

Unrealized appreciation of ore in mine	3,000	
Allowance for unrealized appreciation in inventory	150	
Realized appreciation (or Retained earnings)		3,150

Depletion and dividends. Companies operating wasting assets are permitted to pay dividends in amounts equal to the net income plus depletion charges. Corporations paying such dividends should inform their stockholders that the dividends represent a partial return of capital. If such piecemeal capital pay-back could not legally be made to the stockholders during the exploitation of the natural resource, the corporation would be obliged to hold the funds until the exhaustion of the property. This might be advisable if the corporation expected to acquire and operate another similar piece of property, but not otherwise. The law, therefore, allows the corporation to follow the financial policy best suited to its plans, basing this permission on the assumption that the creditors, knowing the nature of the business, are in a position to protect their interests.

Depletion must, of course, be provided as an expense before net income can be known. The fact that dividends can be paid in an amount equal to the net income plus the depletion has given rise to the too-prevalent belief that depletion need not be recognized as an expense for accounting purposes. When it is remembered that the cost of a wasting asset is, in effect, the cost of a long-time supply of raw material, it becomes apparent that the omission of a depletion charge is equivalent to the omission, by a manufacturing company, of a charge for the cost of the materials used.

The fact that companies operating wasting assets can legally pay dividends to the extent of the net income plus the accumulated depletion has given rise to the expression, "dividends paid out of depletion reserves." Such dividends are in no sense paid out of the accumulated depletion account. They may be equal to the depletion charges, but when it is recognized that the accumulated depletion account is a valuation account reflecting a decrease in an asset resulting from operations, it becomes obvious that dividends cannot be paid out of, or charged to, the accumulated depletion account. They should be charged to a special account which will clearly indicate that they represent a distribution of the invested capital.

Ignoring depletion. The sunk cost theory. The estimating of a proper depletion charge is often a very difficult matter. In the first place, it is necessary to have information as to the number of recoverable units. This is not so difficult in the case of surface assets, such as standing timber, or in the case of ores and minerals lying close to the surface. If mining is conducted at low levels, the problem is more difficult and the estimates are frequently a matter of pure conjecture and must be revised as mining proceeds. In the second place, even if the number of units could be determined with absolute accuracy, the proper depletion charge per unit to be extracted could hardly be known without information relative to future selling prices and operating costs. For, if selling prices or costs change to a point where extraction is not profitable, the unextracted units might as well not exist, and the entire cost of the deposit should have been charged to the extracted units. On the other hand, there is the possibility that scientific discoveries or inventions will reduce the cost of extraction to a point where abandoned property can again be profitably operated. In the third place, special hazards, such as floods or other catastrophes, may make a considerable portion of the existing deposit unavailable for extraction. And, in the fourth place, the deposit may be so large that a unit rate based on actual quantity would not provide for the assignment to expense of the balance in the wasting asset account during a period that might be reasonably contemplated as the operating life of a corporation.

Some mining companies consider that the difficulties of estimating depletion justify them in making no depletion charge in their accounts; they defend this procedure on the ground that their stockholders and the public are on notice as to the nature of their investments and operations, and that no charge is preferable to one based on a sheer guess which they cannot support. Some public accountants who specialize in mining accounts appear to feel that this procedure is sometimes justifiable, and that, if any depletion provision is made, the statements should indicate that it is an estimate.

Other corporations deal with the problem by adopting an ultraconservative procedure based on the sunk-cost theory. They regard all capital expenditures for wasting assets and organization and development expenses as costs to be recovered before any earnings are reported. Such a deferment of reporting any earnings, although admittedly conservative, might be grossly unfair to stockholders, particularly those who hold the stock during only the early portion of the corporation's life.

Depreciation of plant. Depreciation must, of course, be provided on buildings and machinery located on a wasting asset. If the life of the wasting asset is estimated to be less than the life of the plant, it is customary to accept the life of the wasting asset as the life of the plant for depreciation purposes. This is done on the theory that the plant will have only a scrap value when it is no longer needed for operations in its present location. As the life of the wasting asset is contingent upon the amount of annual operations, the depreciation of the plant may be computed on the same basis that is used for depletion; that is:

$$\text{Annual depreciation} = (\text{Cost} - \text{Scrap}) \times \frac{\text{Units extracted during year}}{\text{Total estimated units}}$$

CHAPTER 18

Tangible Fixed Assets (Concluded)

DISPOSALS

Disposals of fixed assets. When fixed assets which are subject to depreciation are sold or otherwise disposed of, the property account should be relieved of the cost of the asset. Because most fixed asset disposals occur during, rather than at the end of, the year, we must consider what entries, if any, should be made for depreciation up to the date of disposal, and the amount which should be debited to the accumulated depreciation account to relieve it of the total depreciation provided on the asset. The entries with respect to depreciation at the time of disposal will depend upon the company's depreciation policy with respect to additions and disposals. Four depreciation policies are described below. Entries to be made in each case (by the straight-line method) are based on the following assumed facts:

Asset cost	\$4,000
Scrap value	0
Date of acquisition	April 1, 1965
Annual depreciation rate	20%
Date of disposal	November 15, 1969

(1) Fractional-period depreciation is computed on acquisitions from the date of acquisition to the end of the period. Fractional-period depreciation is computed on disposals from the beginning of the period of disposal to the date of the disposal.

The depreciation provisions to December 31, 1968, would have been:	
1965—9/12 of 20% of $4,000	$ 600
1966	800
1967	800
1968	800
The depreciation to be recorded at the date of disposal would be:	
1969—10½/12 of 20% of $4,000	700
And the amount to be charged to the accumulated depreciation account in the entry for the disposal would be	$3,700

(2) Depreciation is computed at the annual rate on the opening balance in the fixed asset account, plus or minus depreciation at one-half the annual rate on the net additions or deductions during the year. *This is equivalent to computing depreciation on acquisitions and disposals for a half-year, regardless of the date of the acquisition or the disposal.*

The depreciation provisions to December 31, 1968, would have been:	
1965—½ of 20% of $4,000	$ 400
1966	800
1967	800
1968	800
The depreciation to be recorded at the date of disposal would be:	
1969—½ of 20% of $4,000	400
And the amount to be charged to the accumulated depreciation account in the entry for the disposal would be	$3,200

(3) Depreciation is computed at the annual rate on the opening balance in the asset account. *Thus, no depreciation is taken on acquisitions in the year of acquisition, and a full year's depreciation is taken on disposals.*

The depreciation provisions to December 31, 1968, would have been:	
1965	$ 0
1966	800
1967	800
1968	800
The depreciation to be recorded at the date of disposal would be:	
1969	800
And the amount to be charged to the accumulated depreciation account in the entry for the disposal would be	$3,200

(4) Depreciation is computed at the annual rate on the closing balance in the asset account. *This is equivalent to computing depreciation for a full year on acquisitions, regardless of the date of acquisition, and taking no depreciation on disposals in the year of disposal.*

The depreciation provisions to December 31, 1968, would have been:	
1965	$ 800
1966	800
1967	800
1968	800
The depreciation to be recorded at the date of disposal would be:	
1969	0
And the amount to be charged to the accumulated depreciation account in the entry for the disposal would be	$3,200

Whichever method is adopted by a company, it must be followed consistently. The accountant must know which method is in use, in order that overdepreciation or underdepreciation may be avoided and the accumulated depreciation account be relieved of the correct amount of depreciation when fixed assets are disposed of.

It is customary to assume that Method No. 1 is in use in the absence of definite information to the contrary.

At one time it was the general custom to record any loss or gain on the disposal of a fixed asset by a debit or credit to Retained Earnings, on the theory that the loss or gain represented a correction of the depreciation charges of prior periods, or an extraneous item resulting from a price change. Present-day practice generally treats such losses and gains as income statement items. To illustrate, assume that a machine cost $5,000, that depreciation of $3,000 has been provided, and that the machine is sold for $1,500. The entry for the disposal would be:

Cash	1,500	
Accumulated depreciation—Machinery	3,000	
Loss on disposal of machinery	500	
Machinery		5,000
Sale of fixed asset.		

If the asset is sold for $2,300, the entry would be:

Cash	2,300	
Accumulated depreciation—Machinery	3,000	
Machinery		5,000
Gain on disposal of machinery		300
Sale of fixed asset.		

It is only in those cases in which gains or losses arising from fixed asset disposals are so large that their inclusion in the income statement would distort or otherwise impair the significance of the net income amount that accountants consider assigning them directly to retained earnings. Advocates of the all-inclusive income concept would include these gains or losses in the income statement irrespective of size, though properly described and segregated if material.

Disposals of fixed assets are sometimes erroneously recorded by merely debiting Cash and crediting the asset account with the amount received. Adjustments are then required to relieve the asset account of the balance of the cost, to relieve the accumulated depreciation account of the recorded depreciation, and to take up the gain or loss.

Fixed assets are sometimes retired from service without being sold or even removed from the locations where they were formerly used. If they are retained as standby units, the cost and depreciation provisions applicable to them may be retained in the accounts. If, however, their usefulness as operating assets is at an end, their salvage or recovery value should be estimated and set up in an abandoned property account, with appropriate entries to relieve the asset and accumulated depreciation accounts of the cost and recorded depreciation and to record the estimated loss or gain.

Trade-ins. When recording fixed asset trade-ins, what recognition should the accountant give to any gain or loss on the disposal of the old asset, and at what price should he record the new asset? To illustrate, assume the following conditions:

	Case A	Case B
Old asset:		
Cost	$5,000	$5,000
Accumulated depreciation	3,000	3,000
Net book value	2,000	2,000
Second-hand market value	1,800	2,100
Trade-in allowance	2,300	2,300
List price of new asset	6,000	6,000
Cash payment	3,700	3,700

Probably the most theoretically accurate method is to use the second-hand market value (rather than the trade-in allowance) in the computation of any gain or loss on the disposal of the old asset and also in the determination of the price at which the new asset would be recorded. On this basis, the computations would be made as follows:

	Case A	Case B
Loss or gain on disposal of old asset:		
Net book value	$2,000	$2,000
Second-hand market value	1,800	2,100
Loss	$ 200	
Gain		$ 100
Price at which to record new asset:		
Second-hand value of old asset	$1,800	$2,100
Cash payment	3,700	3,700
Total	$5,500	$5,800

The entries are:

	Case A		Case B	
Asset account (new asset)	5,500		5,800	
Accumulated depreciation	3,000		3,000	
Loss on disposal of old asset	200			
Gain on disposal of old asset				100
Asset account (old asset)		5,000		5,000
Cash		3,700		3,700

This method of recording the exchange treats the transaction in effect as the sale of the old asset at its market price and the purchase of the new asset at a cost which includes the market value of the old asset and an additional $3,700.

In Case A the trade-in allowance was $500 in excess of the second-hand market value of the old asset, and in Case B it was $200 in excess of the market value. If the trade-in allowances had been as low as the second-hand values, the cash payments and the total cost of the new asset would have been correspondingly increased. Under such circumstances the cost of the new asset would have been $6,000 in each case and the entries would have been those shown at the top of the following page.

	Case A		Case B	
Asset account (new asset)	6,000		6,000	
Accumulated depreciation	3,000		3,000	
Loss on disposal of old asset	200			
Gain on disposal of old asset				100
Asset account (old asset)		5,000		5,000
Cash		4,200		3,900

Second-hand market values are sometimes ignored and the trade-in allowance is accepted as the basis for measuring the gain or loss on the disposal of the old asset. Referring to the preceding cases, a gain of $300 would in each case be regarded as realized on this basis—this being the excess of the $2,300 trade-in allowance over the net book value. The entry to record the exchange in each case would be:

Asset account	6,000	
Accumulated depreciation	3,000	
Asset account		5,000
Cash		3,700
Gain on disposal of fixed asset		300
New asset acquired for cash plus trade-in.		

Objections may be raised to this procedure on the ground that a gain is taken into the accounts without realization other than by addition to the fixed asset account. When it is remembered that dealers frequently make allowances in excess of market values, the validity of such a gain becomes open to serious question.

As a practical matter, it often is necessary to use the trade-in allowance as the basis for determining the gain or loss on trades because there is no other second-hand market value supportable by objective data.

If the offered trade-in allowance is less than the second-hand market value, the old asset normally will be sold instead of turned in as part payment for the new asset; in such cases, the offered allowance will have no bearing on the entries. For reasons of expediency or because a trade-in is demanded (as frequently happened when automobiles were purchased after World War II), a trade-in allowance lower than market value may be accepted. In such cases, it is customary to use the trade-in allowance as the basis of the entries for the exchange.

For income tax purposes, no gain or loss should be taken on an exchange; the cost of the new asset, for purposes of computing depreciation and the gain or loss on subsequent disposal, should be the sum of the book value of the old asset and the additional expenditure made in the acquisition. On this basis, the entry to record the exchange of assets in the foregoing cases A and B would be:

Asset account	5,700	
Accumulated depreciation	3,000	
Asset account		5,000
Cash		3,700
New asset acquired for cash plus trade-in.		

Fire and casualty losses. To illustrate the accounting procedure applicable to insured losses, let us assume the following facts: A building which cost $100,000, on which depreciation of $30,000 has been provided, and which thus has a book value of $70,000, is insured for $75,000. It is destroyed by fire. A valuation of $77,000 is agreed upon for insurance-settlement purposes, and a check for $75,000, the full amount of the policy, is received.

The entry to record the settlement will include a credit of $100,000 to the asset account, a debit of $30,000 to the accumulated depreciation account, a credit of $5,000 to a special income statement account (or possibly to Retained Earnings if the amount is so large as to distort the net income for the period) for the excess of the settlement price over the carrying value, and a debit of $75,000 to Cash. The $5,000 credit should not be regarded as a gain on the fire; it may be merely an adjustment of the depreciation provisions of prior periods, or a realization of increased market values, or a combination of both.

In fact, the fire may actually have resulted in a loss. In the illustration, this appears to have been the case. Accepting the $77,000 settlement value as a proper market valuation, the $5,000 credit is the net of two amounts: $7,000 representing increase in market value or excessive depreciation provisions, and a $2,000 loss on the fire.

Income tax regulations give relief to taxpayers who realize a nominal or book gain from such events as fires, other casualties, or condemnation proceedings. No taxable income is regarded as resulting from such "involuntary conversions" if the entire amount received as compensation for the converted property is expended in its replacement. If less than the total proceeds is expended in replacement, the book gain is taxable only to the extent of the unexpended funds. Thus, in the foregoing illustration, if $72,000 was expended to replace the destroyed property, $3,000 of the $5,000 book gain would be taxable.

The cost basis of the new property for income tax purposes is actual cost reduced by the amount of the untaxable gain. Thus, in the foregoing illustration the book gain was $5,000, the taxable gain was $3,000, and the untaxable gain was $2,000. The $72,000 cost of the new property is reduced by $2,000 to arrive at the cost basis for income tax purposes.

Assuming that the property was replaced at a cost of $68,000, the entire $5,000 would be taxable gain. Because there would be no untaxable gain, the cost basis of the new property would be the entire $68,000.

A loss is deductible for tax purposes.

Revision of rates. After an asset has been in operation for some time, it may be found that too much or too little depreciation has been provided. Such a condition may be due to an error in estimating the life of the asset or to an incorrect estimate of the residual value.

If an overprovision has been made and is to be corrected in the accounts, the accumulated depreciation account may be charged and a special income statement account (or possibly Retained Earnings) credited; if an underprovision has been made, the correction entry will be just the opposite. The correction should be sufficient to adjust the accumulated depreciation account to the amount which it would have contained if depreciation had originally been based on the estimates which now seem to be correct. After the accumulated depreciation amount has been adjusted, the rate should be revised for subsequent depreciation to prevent a continuation of the overprovision or underprovision.

As an alternative treatment, the undepreciated cost of the asset may be spread over the remaining life of the asset by revised depreciation provisions, without making any adjustment or correction of the current balance in the accumulated depreciation account.

The latter alternative is found more commonly in practice, possibly because it is the procedure permitted for federal income tax purposes.

Fully depreciated assets. If an asset has no salvage value, it is said to be fully depreciated when the credits for accumulated depreciation applicable to it are equal to its cost. If the asset is retired from use, an entry should be made removing the cost and accumulated depreciation from the accounts.

If there is salvage value, an asset is fully depreciated when its related accumulated depreciation plus its realizable salvage value is equal to its cost. In such cases, if the asset is removed from use, the salvage value should be set up in a sundry asset account.

If fully depreciated assets are still in service, it is obvious that their service life was underestimated and the depreciation provisions were excessive. Accountants are not in agreement as to the proper procedure to be applied in such cases.

Some accountants advocate leaving the cost of the property and the accumulated depreciation provisions in the accounts and merely discontinuing the depreciation provisions. Others believe that the asset account and the accumulated depreciation account should be relieved of the cost and the depreciation provisions, so that the property accounts will contain either scrap values or balances which are applicable only to assets still subject to depreciation charges. Under either of these plans there is merit in disclosing, by a balance sheet footnote, the cost of fully depreciated fixed assets still in service.

Other accountants take an entirely different approach. They believe in making a new estimate of the total life of the asset, recomputing the depreciation which would have been provided to date if the new life estimate had been made originally, correcting the accumulated depreciation account to conform to the new estimate, and continuing depreciation provisions, but at a revised rate. This procedure is defended on the ground that depreciation accounting is intended to spread the cost of fixed assets over their useful lives; that the provision of full depreciation at too early a date was an error; and that future periods should not receive service from an asset without bearing a depreciation charge for its use. The reply, but not a conclusive one, to this argument is that, after operations have once been charged with the full cost of an asset, any accounting procedure which produces additional charges against income results in charging the income for the entire period of the asset's life with depreciation in excess of the cost of the asset, and that this is contrary to sound accounting theories relative to depreciation.* Any additional depreciation charges for fully depreciated assets are, of course, not allowable for income tax purposes.

The procedure just discussed would merit attention if the remaining life and depreciation charges, if continued, were significant. However, the accountant might justifiably wonder why such a significant mistake was ignored, perhaps deliberately, until the assets became fully depreciated.

Unit and group bases of depreciation accounting. In the discussion thus far it has been assumed that the accountant, in his attempts to compute and account for depreciation, approaches the problem by considering each asset as a separate unit. Thus, the estimated useful life or depreciation rate selected is one believed to be specifically applicable to the unit of property being depreciated. Accumulated depreciation is related to each unit, and if an asset is retired, the accumulated depreciation related to that particular asset is removed from the accounts when the cost of the asset is removed. It is not uncommon for gains and losses on disposals to arise under this general plan of depreciation accounting.

In contrast, depreciation may be computed on a group basis. Justification for the use of a group basis will not exist unless a business owns a relatively large number of assets that can be identified as belonging to a class. The assets assigned to a class for purposes of depreciation should have similar life expectancies and not widely varying unit costs. Examples of acceptable asset classes include hotel furniture, telephone poles, and typewriters.

The group method may be characterized as an "averaging" procedure. Suppose that a business owns 20 similar machines. The accountant will try to determine the useful life or depreciation rate that on the average best fits the expectancy with respect to such machines when considered as a group. If the machines are depreciated on the basis of a 15-year useful life, it is expected that some of the individual machines may in fact have shorter useful lives and that some may in fact have longer useful lives. It is expected only that, considering the group as a whole, 15 years will work out to be a reasonably close estimate. In fact, prior experience with similar groups of assets, by the company or perhaps by a trade or industry, is generally available to support such an expectation.

Under this plan, accumulated depreciation is not associated with individual assets. When assets are disposed of or retired, the cost less salvage

* The same objection could be raised (with similar inconclusiveness) against reductions of accumulated depreciation such as those discussed on page 334 under the caption "Revision of rates."

is charged against the accumulated depreciation account, and no loss or gain is recognized. This procedure is based on a presumption, which should be supported by past experience, that any underdepreciation on assets retired early will be offset by overprovisions of depreciation on assets which prove to have a longer life than estimated. If disposals or retirements in significant amounts take place for reasons not contemplated when the group depreciation rate was established, with the result that the presumption mentioned above is invalidated, the accumulated depreciation account may be charged with only the depreciation provided at the group rate during the period of use, and a loss or gain may be recognized and recorded.

DEPARTURES FROM THE COST BASIS

Bases of appraisals. Appraisals are sometimes made on the basis of original cost less depreciation. The purpose of such an appraisal is merely to determine whether the asset accounts properly reflect the cost of the plant, and whether the depreciation provisions are justified in the light of events subsequent to acquisition. If the appraiser's estimate of original cost differs from the balance in the asset account, an adjustment of the asset account to conform to the appraisal can be assumed to be an adjustment to a corrected cost basis, and not a departure from the cost basis. If the appraiser's estimate of accrued depreciation differs from the balance in the accumulated depreciation account, it should be remembered that the appraiser's estimate of accrued depreciation may be based on physical deterioration of the plant; that the depreciation provisions in the accounts are intended to absorb the cost of the asset by charges to operations in reasonably equitable periodical amounts; and that the progress of physical deterioration and the accumulation of depreciation in the accounts are not presumed to keep in step. Therefore, a disagreement between the depreciation per books and the depreciation per the appraisal does not necessarily indicate that an adjustment of the accumulated depreciation account should be made. Such an adjustment might be in order if the appraisal indicated that the depreciation provisions had been based on an incorrect estimate of useful life.

Appraisals usually are made for the purpose of determining reproduction cost new and sound value. *Reproduction cost new* is the computed cost of replacing the asset in its present location at current production costs. *Sound value* is reproduction cost new less depreciation to date computed by applying the condition per cent to the reproduction cost new. The determination of reproduction cost new and sound value may be desired for tax, insurance, sale, consolidation, credit, and other purposes.

Recent history of accounting thought. Changes in price levels and the purchasing power of the dollar affect the value of plant assets; values tend to increase during periods of inflation and tend to decrease during periods of deflation. Beginning during World War I and continuing until the late 1920's, there was a period of rising costs, and appraisals showed sound values in excess of depreciated cost. During the great depression of the 1930's, the converse was the case. After World War II, there was another period of inflation.

It seems desirable to consider briefly the development of accounting thought, during this span of years, relative to the propriety of recording appraisals and the propriety of making depreciation provisions on any basis other than cost.

Period of inflation during and after World War I. At the beginning of this period, accountants were generally of the opinion that fixed assets should be carried in the accounts at cost, and that depreciation should be based on cost. But businessmen often thought otherwise. In some cases, business management wanted to write up the fixed assets to appraised values, while continuing to make depreciation charges on the basis of cost. In other cases, they wanted to write up the fixed assets and also base depreciation on replacement value.

Appraised values and the balance sheet. During this period, particularly during the latter part of the 1920's, a great many issues of securities were marketed, and accountants were under pressure, from business management and investment bankers, to show fixed assets in the balance sheet at appraised values. Accountants frequently faced situations such as the following, in which the sound value shown by the appraisal was considerably in excess of the depreciated book value:

	Value Per Appraisal	Value Per Books	Excess Per Appraisal
Cost:			
Reproduction cost new—per appraisal	$140,000		
Original cost—per books		$100,000	
Excess of reproduction cost new over original cost			$40,000
Depreciation:			
On reproduction cost—per appraisal	35,000		
On original cost—per books		25,000	
Excess of depreciation on reproduction cost over depreciation on original cost			10,000
Depreciated value:			
Sound value—per appraisal	$105,000		
Net book value		$ 75,000	
Excess of sound value per appraisal over net book value			$30,000

If a $60,000 mortgage was placed on the property and the accountant insisted upon showing the property in the balance sheet at the net book value of $75,000, without disclosure of the appraised value, a number of statement users probably would have concluded that a liability of $60,000 was secured by property valued at only $75,000. The accountant probably would have been told that his balance sheet was an unfair deterrent to the sale of the securities because it did not indicate the current value of the property serving as security to the mortgage.

To meet such a situation, the accountant might show the facts in the balance sheet thus:

Balance Sheet—December 31, 192—

Asset Side

Machinery (Reproduction cost new, less depreciation, per appraisal by The Blank Appraisal Company, as of December 31, 192—, $105,000):		
Cost	$100,000	
Less depreciation on cost	25,000	$75,000

Liability Side

Mortgage payable		$60,000

But such a balance sheet, in which the appraised value of the fixed assets was merely shown parenthetically, was obviously much less satisfactory, from the standpoint of the company and the investment banker offering securities to the public, than one in which appraised values appeared in the money columns, thus:

Balance Sheet—December 31, 192—

Asset Side

Machinery—per appraisal by The Blank Appraisal Company as of December 31, 192—:		
Reproduction cost new	$140,000	
Less depreciation	35,000	$105,000

Liability Side

Mortgage payable		$ 60,000

Accountants, therefore, reconsidered their position, and practice for a number of years indicated that many accountants had reached the conclusion that appraisals could be recorded in the accounts and reflected in the balance sheet, provided the increase in valuation was not credited to Earned Surplus but was carried to a special account such as Unrealized Increment per Appraisal. The use of such a special account was desirable for two reasons: First, it clearly segregated the appraisal increment from the stockholders' equity which arose from stockholders' investments and from the retention of earnings; second, the laws of most states make such unrealized credits unavailable for the payment of dividends.

Depreciation after recording an appraisal. During the period now under discussion, the recording of increased values disclosed by appraisals usually appealed to management from the balance sheet standpoint only. Management usually desired to continue charging operations with depreciation based on cost.

Some businessmen advanced the idea that depreciation should be based on replacement cost to increase the probability that sales prices would be fixed at a level high enough to provide funds for asset replacements without impairing working capital. They were met with the argument that it should be possible for management to set prices that would meet cash requirements without overstating product costs.

Period of deflation during the depression. During the depression which began in 1929, many concerns adopted the policy of writing down their fixed assets.

In many instances, no doubt, the fixed assets were written down with the idea of more fairly reflecting the financial position of the business. During the depression, the demand for products decreased, production decreased, and prices of products and fixed assets declined. If fixed assets were pledged as security to long-term liabilities, the security behind the liabilities was impaired; moreover, the reduction in asset values affected the proprietorship equity from the standpoint of possible enforced liquidation; information with respect to declines in value was therefore of interest to creditors and stockholders.

But it is probable that most of the asset write-downs during this depression period were made for the purpose of establishing a lower depreciation base, thus reducing the depreciation charges, so that more favorable operating results could be shown in the income statement. Such reductions in depreciation charges may have seemed, at the time, to be justified by a theory which was the converse of that which had previously been used by those who advocated charging operations with depreciation on replacement values which were in excess of cost. If earnings should be reduced by increased depreciation charges to provide for the replacement of fixed assets on a rising market, then earnings might presumably be increased by reducing the depreciation charges if the replacement cost of the fixed assets had decreased.

When fixed assets were written down, the charges were sometimes made to the unrealized increment accounts created by recording former upward appraisals. The write-offs were sometimes made against paid-in surplus, and sometimes against earned surplus. The favorite procedure was the quasi-reorganization, which is discussed in Chapter 26. The quasi-reorganization has come to be regarded as the only procedure, conformable with accepted accounting principles, by which fixed assets can be written down and the future depreciation charges to operations be correspondingly reduced.

Asset write-ups in the present period. The period since World War II can be characterized as one of high and rising prices, with significant inflationary pressure occurring during the years 1945-1949. During the inflation of the 1920's, management was primarily concerned with high replacement costs from the balance sheet standpoint; it desired to write up fixed assets in order to reflect a better financial position and thus increase the marketability of securities. This time, interest centered mainly in the income statement; management would have liked to be able to increase depreciation charges to a basis approximating the replacement cost of the fixed asset.

Although the authors* of *Accounting Research Study* No. 3, published in 1962, offered some theoretical support in favor of the restatement of fixed assets in terms of current replacement costs, the prevailing attitude of most accountants reflects agreement with the position expressed in Institute Bulletin No. 5, issued in 1940, which stated that "accounting for fixed assets should normally be based on cost, and any attempt to make property accounts in general reflect current values is both impracticable and inexpedient. Appreciation normally should not be reflected on the books of account of corporations." However, there has been one significant change in contrast to the 1920's. It is now held that when appreciation has been recorded in the accounts, depreciation should be based on the written-up amounts. As the Committee on Accounting Procedure stated in Bulletin 43, "A company should not at the same time claim larger property valuations in its statement of assets and provide for the amortization of only smaller amounts in its statement of income."

A minority of the committee added the further thought that, "as a matter of consistency, where increased property valuations have been entered on the books the credit item should be treated as permanent capital and would therefore not be available for subsequent transfer to earned surplus as *realized* through depreciation or sale." Although the authors believe there is some merit in the position of the minority, it is probably true that generally accepted accounting would approve of the procedure shown below covering the matter of depreciation and the consequent piecemeal realization of the write-up credit.

Illustrative entries. Presented below are certain account balances after an appraisal was recorded, other assumed facts used in the illustration, and journal entries for depreciation after the appraisal.

Machinery (original cost)	$100,000	
Accumulated depreciation (on cost)		$25,000
When the property was acquired, it was estimated to have a life of 20 years and no residual value. A 5% depreciation rate was therefore adopted. Five years of the estimated life of the asset had expired before the appraisal.		
Machinery (appraisal increase)	40,000	
Accumulated depreciation—Appraisal increase		10,000
Unrealized increment per appraisal		30,000

The periodic entries associated with depreciation are shown below.

Depreciation (chargeable to operations)	7,000	
Accumulated depreciation (on cost)		5,000
Accumulated depreciation—Appraisal increase		2,000
To provide depreciation on the written-up amount.		
Unrealized increment per appraisal	2,000	
Retained earnings		2,000
To transfer the realized appreciation to Retained Earnings.		

The amount of the last entry above is the difference between depreciation based on recorded value and that based on cost. Such periodic entries

* Robert T. Sprouse and Maurice Moonitz.

will, over the remaining life of the asset, transfer the unrealized increment to retained earnings. In lieu of such periodic transfers, a one-time entry transferring the unrealized increment to retained earnings can be made when the asset is disposed of or written off as fully depreciated.

It has been contended that the theory of the quasi-reorganization, which sanctions fixed asset write-downs as an incident to a "fresh start," with subsequent decreased depreciation charges to income, should be extended to permit fixed asset write-ups with increased depreciation charges. Neither the Institute nor the Securities and Exchange Commission has, up to the present time, looked favorably upon such a procedure.

Depreciation in the present period. It has long been a basic theory of accounting that depreciation is concerned merely with the assignment of the cost of a fixed asset to operations during the periods of its useful life. Accountants maintain that the provision for depreciation is not a provision for replacement, and that changes in the purchasing power of the monetary unit should not be given consideration in the determination of periodic depreciation or in the computation of net income.

Admittedly, business management today faces problems of vital importance resulting from inflation and high income taxes, and some businessmen would like to have accounting theories revised in some way so that, in the determination of operating costs and expenses, recognition could be given to the increased cost of plant replacements. One of the chief arguments advanced in support of the proposition that depreciation charges against income must be sufficient to provide for the replacement of plant assets is based on the economic concept of income as distinguished from the monetary concept. The argument goes somewhat as follows: The difference between real and nominal wages (or economic and monetary wages) has long been recognized; the same distinction should be recognized between the economic income and the monetary income of a business enterprise. The economic capital of a business—its capital, not in dollars, but in things—must be maintained before there is any economic income. Accounting concepts relative to depreciation are based on an assumption that fluctuations in the purchasing power of the dollar will be insignificant and hence may be ignored; if this assumption were valid, economic and monetary income would be essentially the same, and depreciation based on cost could result in the maintenance of economic capital. But during some periods the assumption does not square with economic reality, and accountants jeopardize the widespread acceptance of financial statements by insisting that it would be wrong to give recognition to significant changes in the purchasing power of the dollar, and the effects thereof on replacement costs, when such changes occur. Unless the charges to operations for things used up or otherwise disposed of in the process of operations are sufficient to replace these things, there is no economic income, and the real capital is impaired, no matter what the books may show as monetary income.

Although accountants are conscious of the problems of management, they have, up to the time of this writing, stood firm in the position that depreciation accounting is intended only to charge asset costs against operations; they hold that depreciation is one thing, and that the financing of replacements is another.

Accountants object to departures from the cost basis, not only because they believe that the cost basis is theoretically correct, but also because they fear that, if the door is opened, a miscellany of methods may come in, with resulting confusion and uncertainty as to the significance of reported earnings. They feel that such confusion would arise even if depreciation on replacement cost were the only permitted substitute for depreciation on cost. As the Institute's Committee on Accounting Procedure said in a special statement issued in 1947, "It would not increase the usefulness of reported corporate income figures if some companies charged depreciation on appraised values while others adhered to cost. The committee believes, therefore, that consideration of radical changes in accepted accounting procedure should not be undertaken, at least until a stable price level would make it practicable for business as a whole to make the change at the same time."

This general matter is discussed at some length in Chapter 28.

CHAPTER

19

Intangible Fixed Assets

Classification and general principles. Accountants customarily use the categories Type A and Type B to classify intangible fixed assets.

Type A—Those having a limited term of existence, the limitation being a consequence of some law, regulation, or agreement, or the very nature of a given intangible. Examples are patents, copyrights, franchises for limited periods, leaseholds, and leasehold improvements.

Type B—Those having no such limited term of existence. Examples are trademarks, trade names, secret formulas and processes, perpetual franchises, going value, goodwill, and organization costs.

In accordance with the principle that cost is the fundamental basis of accounting, intangible fixed assets should be recorded at their cost. And, in accordance with the generally accepted rule applicable in such cases, the cost of an intangible fixed asset acquired in a noncash transaction can be measured by the fair value of the asset acquired or by the fair value of the consideration given, whichever is the more definitely determinable.

If, in a lump-sum purchase, several intangible assets are acquired, or if intangibles are acquired with other assets, a separate cost should be established for each intangible of Type A, so that the separate costs can be amortized over the respective periods of life. An aggregate cost for all intangibles of Type B may be satisfactory unless there is reason to believe that some of them may immediately or ultimately be subject to amortization, in which event their separate costs will need to be known, in order to establish bases for the amortization.

The cost of a Type A intangible should be amortized by systematic charges in the income statement over the period benefited. It should be understood that the period fixed by law, regulation, or contract is the maximum period, and that the usefulness of such assets may cease prior to the expiration of that period; in such instances, the shorter useful life period should be the period of amortization. As noted by the Committee on Accounting Procedure in Bulletin No. 43, "If it becomes evident that the period benefited will be longer or shorter than originally estimated, recognition thereof may take the form of an appropriate decrease or increase in the rate of amortization or, if such increased charges would result in distortion of income, a partial write-down may be made by a charge to earned surplus."

Intangible fixed assets of Type B may be carried indefinitely at cost if there is no reason to believe that their useful lives will ever terminate. However, although assets of this class are not normally subject to amortization, their amortization or complete write-off may be proper under several conditions. First, at the time of acquisition there may be good reason to fear that the useful life of such an asset will terminate, even though there is no conclusive evidence to that effect; in such instances, periodical amortization charges may be made against income. Second, at some time subsequent to acquisition, conditions may have developed which indicate that the life of the asset will terminate, in such instances, the cost of the asset may be amortized over the estimated remaining life; or, if such charges would result in a material distortion in the income statement, a partial write-off may be made against retained earnings and the remainder of the cost may be amortized. Third, an asset may be found to be valueless; under such circumstances it should be written off. The amount of the write-off should be assigned to the income statement, unless the amount is so large that its effect on net income may give rise to misleading inferences. In that case the write-off should be against retained earnings, but never against any of the paid-in capital accounts.

Many business concerns have written off intangible fixed assets before their useful lives have terminated, or have written them down more rapidly than a normal amortization procedure would require, justifying such action on the grounds of conservatism. There is a growing belief among accountants that conservatism should not be accepted as justification for such arbitrary asset reductions. However, the understatement of intangibles continues to be tolerated in practice. The balance sheets of most companies, particularly those of well-established businesses, show either no value or only a nominal valuation assigned to the intangible assets. This is not a desirable state of affairs; but, on the other hand, the practical difficulties associated with attempts at more meaningful accounting valuations for intangibles must be conceded.

A practice of arbitrarily writing off intangibles upon or immediately after acquisition is improper. It runs counter to the basic accounting assumption that all expenditures result initially in the acquisition of short- or long-term benefits.

Research and development costs. An example of the practical difficulties associated with the accounting for intangibles is provided by research and development costs. Many businesses maintain research departments and make significant expenditures for basic and applied research and for the development of new or improved products or manufacturing processes. Future periods often benefit from such outlays and, if a proper matching of revenue and expense is to be achieved, capitalization and subsequent amortization may be necessary. On the other hand, the accountant must exercise caution and not carry an amount forward as an asset unless there is a reasonable expectation that it will be recoverable from future operations.

The difficulty of accounting for research and development costs is probably apparent. It is not an area in which there is a deficiency of accounting principles. It is the inherent uncertainties and complexities that make it difficult to justify a specific dollar-and-cents answer in most actual cases. Often the problem is centered on the matter of identifying the costs associated with a particular project or a particular achievement. But even when cost identification is possible, uncertainty about the magnitude of the future benefits and the length of time over which such benefits may be expected to be realized lends appeal to the conservative solution of expensing such costs as incurred. As a consequence, most companies do not capitalize any portion of research and development costs. The few companies that do show capitalized amounts for research and development in their balance sheets amortize the asset over relatively short periods.

Although practice has not been able to reach a solution to the intangibles problem that has the support of accounting theory, at least considerable uniformity of treatment has been achieved. However, in developing an understanding of financial statements, it should be noted that outlays for research and development are discretionary in nature. "The management of a company could improve profits by reducing research and development expenditures (with possible future adverse effects), and the stockholders might easily be misled, at least temporarily."*

INTANGIBLE FIXED ASSETS NORMALLY SUBJECT TO AMORTIZATION

Patents. Patents may be productive of earnings through the reduction of manufacturing costs or by the creation of a monopolistic condition which permits the charging of prices favorable to the patent owner. Income may be earned directly from patents through royalties collected under license agreements; some outstanding present examples of this procedure are found in the automobile and television industries.

If a patent is acquired by purchase, its cost is the purchase price. If it is obtained by the inventor, its cost is the total of experimental expense, costs

---

* *Accounting and Reporting Problems of the Accounting Profession* (Arthur Andersen & Co.; 2nd ed., 1962).

of working models, and expenses of obtaining the patent, including drawings, attorneys' fees, and filing fees.

If a company operates a research department for the purpose of developing patentable devices, it is faced with the difficulties mentioned in the above discussion of research and development costs. Three approaches to acceptable solutions are:

(1) Assign the entire cost of the department to the patents obtained, on the theory that all of the research activity was directed to achieving successes and the costs of the research are properly assignable to the successes.

(2) Maintain records so that costs applicable to work which results successfully in a patent can be capitalized and the remaining costs can be charged to expense. (If this method is used, expenditures can be charged initially to an account with some title such as "Unallocated Research Costs" from which transfers can be made to the Patents account or to an expense account when the proper allocation of the costs is ultimately determined.)

(3) Charge all of the research costs to expense as they are incurred, either on the theory that competing concerns presumably are conducting similar research and that such outlays are necessary to keep abreast of the industry, or in recognition of the impracticability of attempting to make cost determinations for specific patents.

A patent has no proven worth until it has stood the test of an infringement suit. The cost of a successful suit may be charged to the Patents account as representing an additional cost of establishing the patent. If litigation costs incurred or other expenditures made in protecting a patent are charged to the Patents account as additions to the cost, the amortization procedure should be such as to insure writing off these additional costs at the expiration of the life of the patent. Although the cost of litigation in successfully defending a patent case seems logically to be a proper addition to the cost of the patent to be set up and amortized over the patent's remaining life, decisions in income tax cases do not so recognize it, but require that it be expensed in the tax year in which it is incurred.

If the suit is unsuccessful and the patent is thereby proved to be worthless, both the cost of the suit and the unamortized cost of the patent should be written off.

Amortizing patents. A patent is issued for 17 years; hence, the cost of the patent should usually be written off during that period. Of course, if a patent is purchased some time after it was granted, the purchaser will have to write it off in less than 17 years.

Protection under the patent starts when the patent is applied for, and runs for 17 years after issuance. Hence, the period of protection may be more than 17 years; but because it is usually difficult to estimate the period that will expire between the date of application and the date of issuance, this additional time prior to actual issuance is usually ignored.

If an additional patent is obtained that is so closely related to a former patent that it in effect extends the life of the basic patent, any unamortized balance of the cost of the old patent remaining in the account at the date of obtaining the new one may be carried forward and written off over the life of the new one. This procedure can properly be adopted only in case there is a reasonable certainty that the productivity of the original patent will continue through the life of the new patent. In the absence of such certainty, the old patent should be amortized over the remainder of its own life.

Although 17 years is the theoretical period for writing off a patent, practical considerations often make it desirable to write off the cost in less than that time. If the patent covers an article which will be marketable only during the period of a fad, it is advisable to write off the patent during the probable continuance of the fad.

If the article patented is subject to the danger of being superseded by some other invention, the element of supersession should be taken into consideration as a probable factor in making the effective life of the patent shorter than its legal life.

If the owner of a patent finds that the product manufactured under it is not in demand and cannot be profitably marketed, the patent is evidently valueless even though its legal life has not expired; in such a case it should be written off.

A patent is sometimes purchased for the purpose of controlling the patent and thus preventing the manufacture of a competing article. Such a patent should be written off over its life unless the sole purpose of the purchase of the patent was to provide additional protection during the remaining life of a patent already owned; in that case, the cost of the new patent should be written off over the remaining life of the old patent.

Assume that several patents with differing remaining lives are purchased at a lump price, and that there is no information by which the cost can be apportioned to the several patents on the basis of prospective profitability. An arithmetical procedure for the computation of amortization of such costs, giving consideration only to the different lives of the patents, is indicated by the following illustration. Assume that three patents are purchased; one has a remaining life of 15 years or 180 months; another, a life of 12 years or 144 months; another, a life of 6 years or 72 months; the total of months is 396. The monthly amortization would be determined by multiplying the cost of the patents by a fraction, the numerator of which is the number of unexpired patents and the denominator of which is the aggregate original number of months of remaining life, in this case 396. The monthly amortization during the first six years would be 3/396 of the total cost. At the end of six years one of the patents will have expired, and the numerator of the fraction will change to 2; the denominator will remain 396.

Copyrights. A copyright gives its owner the exclusive right to produce and sell reading matter and works of art. The fee for obtaining a copyright is only a nominal amount, insufficient to justify an accounting procedure of capitalization and amortization. Costs sufficient in amount to justify such a procedure do arise, however, when copyrights are purchased.

Copyrights are issued for 28 years with a possibility of renewal for an additional 28 years. However, publications rarely have an active market for a period as long as 28 years, and it is usually regarded as advisable to write off the copyright cost against the income from the first printing. The nature of certain publications may justify a less conservative procedure.

Franchises. Franchises should not appear on the books unless a payment, either direct or indirect, was made in obtaining them. Franchises may be perpetual, in which case the cost need not be amortized. They may be granted for a definite period of time, in which case the cost should be systematically written off during that period. They may be revocable at the option of the city or other governmental body that granted them, in which case it is advisable to write them off rapidly, although there is a tendency to look upon such franchises as perpetual and make no provision for amortization of their cost.

Periodical payments made to the governmental unit from which the franchise was obtained are operating expenses.

Leased assets. A lease grants the lessee the right to possession and use of the leased property for a specified period. Leases often carry renewal options, so it is possible to arrange through a lease for the possession and use of property for its entire expected economic life. Thus, leasing provides an alternative to the ownership of assets. To illustrate, assume that a business needs an additional building. Management generally would have, at least, the following alternative courses of action:

Ownership

Build a new building or purchase an existing structure; typically, the acquisition would be financed in part with borrowed funds.

Under this alternative, the following expenses would be incurred:

Interest on the borrowed funds

Depreciation

Taxes, insurance, and maintenance

Long-term lease

Lease a suitable building for its expected economic life.

Under this alternative, the following expenses would be incurred:

Rent

Taxes, insurance, and maintenance

If the lease provides that all or part of the taxes, insurance, and maintenance are to be paid by the lessor (owner), the rent figure will be higher accordingly.

Following are some of the questions that would be considered in making a choice between ownership and leasing:

Which alternative would require the smaller aggregate cash outlay over the period of expected usefulness of the property?
The timing of the disbursements would also be a consideration.
Is there an income tax advantage to one of the alternatives?
How do the alternatives affect the credit standing or borrowing capacity of the business?
A business with considerable debt seems to have less difficulty arranging for a lease of property than for additional financing to acquire a comparable asset. In effect, leasing is a form of financing; through leasing, a business can obtain the services provided by fixed assets which it needs.

The alternatives under discussion are quite different in their legal form but not so different in substance. Under either arrangement, a business acquires the services provided by fixed assets and generally incurs some financial obligation as a consequence. It is often stated that the accountant should look through the legal form of a transaction to its substance. And there is agreement that, if substance is to be given proper weight, it should be recognized that a long-term lease may create a situation that is best portrayed by showing an asset and a related liability in the balance sheet of the lessee, even though legal title remains with the lessor. To do otherwise—to fail to distinguish between form and substance—could result in an unfair portrayal of the financial position of the lessee. But accountants have failed to agree on which terms and conditions in long-term leases justify or require "capitalization," that is, the booking of an asset and a related liability in the accounts of the lessee.

Some accountants contend that the terms and conditions of some long-term leases make the agreement in substance a purchase, and when this is so, favor capitalization. This is the position taken by the Accounting Principles Board in its Opinion No. 5. A purchase interpretation is justified, according to this line of reasoning, when the rental payments, if made as installment payments on a purchase, would have given the purchaser a significant equity in the property. Such a condition would arise whenever the initial term of a lease is less than the expected useful life of the property and the lease grants a renewal option at a nominal price, or whenever the lease gives the lessee the right, at one or more specified dates, to purchase the property for a price substantially below its probable market value at the specified dates. Capitalization is also favored whenever the leased property was acquired by the lessor to meet the special needs of the lessee and will probably be usable only for that purpose.

Other accountants take a different approach and contend that the typical terms and conditions of long-term leases give the lessee a form of property rights, as well as a related financial obligation. The accounting research study by Professor John H. Myers adopts this approach.* The property rights and related financial obligations are found by viewing most long-term leases as variants of the following hypothetical lease.

Terms and conditions of a hypothetical long-term lease

Period—For the entire estimated useful life of the property with no renewal options.

Property costs (taxes, insurance, and maintenance)—Obligation of lessee.

Rights at termination—Lessee may purchase asset for a nominal price.

Rent—Single payment approximating fair value of property.

As observed by Professor Myers: "There probably would be no question as to the proper accounting for such a lease. Cash would be credited and another asset debited. There might be some question as to whether the debit would be classified among the property accounts or among the prepayments. Most accountants probably would classify the asset as 'plant,' in recognition of the property rights acquired."

Advocates of capitalization contend that the variants to the above basic terms and conditions found in most long-term leases are not sufficiently substantive to preclude the finding of property rights and a related financial obligation on the part of the lessee. For instance, suppose that the lease specifies a fixed term shorter than the estimated useful life of the property, but renewal options are granted which would enable the lessee to have use of the property for its entire economic life; or, suppose that, instead of a single payment, the lease specifies that the rent is to be paid in installments, the present value of which approximates the fair value of the property when the lease is negotiated. Those favoring a property-rights approach do not consider such variations sufficiently substantive to eliminate the basis for capitalization.

If capitalization is adopted, the measurement of the asset value and the related liability would involve two steps: (1) the determination of the portion of the rentals which constitutes payment for the property rights (if any part of the rent is intended to reimburse the lessor for his outlays for property taxes or for services supplied to the lessee, such as maintenance, heat, and elevator service, that portion should be excluded), and (2) the reduction of such portion of the future payments to a present value by the use of an appropriate interest rate. In the income statement, the rental payments would be broken down into a depreciation (or amortization) element and an interest element.

If there is merit in having the balance sheet show as assets both those owned and those held under long-term lease, consistency requires that

* John H. Myers, *Reporting of Leases in Financial Statements* (New York: American Institute of Certified Public Accountants, 1962).

leased assets should be removed from the accounts of the lessor and replaced with a receivable account for the valuable claim against the lessee, for future rents, created by the lease agreement.

The controversy about the proper accounting for long-term leases is unresolved at the time of this writing. There is agreement only on the importance of disclosure. The financial statements of lessees should disclose, as a minimum, in a separate schedule or a footnote, the amounts of annual rentals to be paid under long-term leases, not only in the year in which the transaction originates, but also as long thereafter as the amounts involved are material. The authors see merit in capitalization when the provisions of a long-term lease give the lessee the possibility of using the property for its expected useful life and when the lease payments provided for will enable the lessor to recoup his investment.

There is no controversy over short-term leases. An asset would arise only in the event of a prepayment of rent, and a liability would arise only if rent was in arrears. A prepayment of rent applicable to a period shorter than the company's operating cycle would be shown among the current assets. Longer-term prepayments would be treated as intangible assets, possibly described by the account title "Leasehold." It would be unusual for a lessee to make an advance payment of the total rent for the entire period of the lease; frequently, however, leases contain agreements similar to the following: term of lease, 10 years; annual rent, $3,000; advance payment, $10,000; annual payment, $2,000. Under these terms, the Rent Expense account should receive $3,000 of charges during each year of the lease, with offsetting credits of $2,000 to Cash and $1,000 to Leasehold.

Sale and leaseback. By a sale-and-leaseback transaction, a business sells an asset useful in its business operations and retains its use as a lessee under a long-term lease. Such a plan releases capital for other, perhaps more profitable, business uses.

Disclosure of sale-and-leaseback transactions is all that is required of the accountant, although advocates of capitalization for leased assets believe their case is even more convincing when the lease is part of a sale-and-leaseback transaction. It is generally recommended that any gains or losses from the sale of the property leased back be spread over the life of the resulting lease as an adjustment of the rental cost, because the selling price may not be an indication of the value of the asset. However, if it can be established that the property was worth less than its book value when the sale-and-leaseback arrangement was negotiated, such loss should not be deferred.

Leasehold improvements. Leases frequently provide that the lessee shall pay the costs of any alterations or improvements of the leased real estate, such as new fronts, partitions, and built-in shelving. Such alterations and improvements become a part of the real estate and revert to the owner of the real estate at the expiration of the lease. The lessee obtains only the intangible right to benefit by the improvements during the life of the lease.

The lessee should therefore charge such expenditures to a Leasehold Improvements account, which should be amortized over the life of the lease or the useful life of the improvements, whichever is shorter.

Buildings constructed by a lessee on leased land revert to the owner of the fee at the expiration of the lease. The lessee should spread their cost, by proportionate charges, over the life of the lease, unless it is expected that the buildings will become useless before the lease has expired, in which case, the cost should be systematically written off during the estimated life of the buildings.

Although leasehold improvements increase the value of the property of the lessor, it seems advisable for the lessor to postpone making any entries therefor in his accounts until the expiration of the lease. The owner obtains no benefit from the improvements until the expiration of the lease, and may receive no benefit even then because of depreciation, obsolescence, or lack of increase in rent or rentability.

INTANGIBLE FIXED ASSETS NOT NORMALLY SUBJECT TO AMORTIZATION

Trademarks. Trademarks may be registered, but they are valid under the common law without registry if the claimant is able to prove his prior use of the mark. As trademarks do not expire, it is not necessary to write off any cost which may have been incurred in obtaining them.

Trade names, labels, advertised brand names, and secret processes are similar intangibles.

Goodwill. Goodwill exists when the actual or expected earnings produced by the assets of a business, exclusive of goodwill, are in excess of what is considered to be normal, after making allowance for the type of industry, the risk, the state of business conditions, and other relevant alternative investment opportunities. The greater the excess earning power of the assets, the greater is the goodwill. However, there are some complications in the process of determining whether excess earning power exists. To illustrate, consider the following data for corporations *A, B,* and *C*.

	Corporation		
	A	*B*	*C*
Total assets	$100,000	$100,000	$100,000
Current liabilities	$ 20,000	$ 20,000	$ 10,000
Bonds payable—5%	—	40,000	—
Stockholders' equity	80,000	40,000	90,000
	$100,000	$100,000	$100,000
Net income before interest and income taxes	$ 12,000	$ 12,000	$ 18,000
Interest expense (which is deductible for income taxes)	—	2,000	—
Net income before income tax	$ 12,000	$ 10,000	$ 18,000
Income tax—50%	6,000	5,000	9,000
Net income	$ 6,000	$ 5,000	$ 9,000

If the net income data are related to the stockholders' equity, the following earning rates are determined.

	Corporation		
	A	*B*	*C*
Net income to stockholders' equity:			
$6,000 ÷ $80,000	7½%		
$5,000 ÷ $40,000		12½%	
$9,000 ÷ $90,000			10%

Consider first the earnings rates of corporations *A* and *B*. Although *B* has a significantly greater earnings rate on the stockholders' equity, it does not follow that *B*'s assets are worth more than *A*'s assets. Both companies earned 12% on their total assets, before interest and income taxes. It is the greater use of creditor capital and the deductibility of interest for income taxes that cause *B* to have the relatively favorable earnings rate. However, the value of a company's assets is not affected by the form of capitalization. The value of the stockholders' equity is quite a different consideration; it may be influenced by the capital structure of the company and the deductibility of interest. If the objective is to determine whether a particular business has goodwill, care must be exercised to neutralize the effects of the form of financing and the tax benefit produced by interest charges on the earnings data. This can be achieved by

(1) Computing the earnings as though the company had no interest expense;
(2) Relating the earnings thus computed to total assets rather than to stockholders' equity.

This approach is applied to the data given for corporations *A, B,* and *C*.

	Corporation		
	A	*B*	*C*
Net income before interest and income taxes	$12,000	$12,000	$18,000
Provision for income taxes—50%	6,000	6,000	9,000
Net income	$ 6,000	$ 6,000	$ 9,000
Net income to total assets:			
$6,000 ÷ $100,000	6%		
$6,000 ÷ $100,000		6%	
$9,000 ÷ $100,000			9%

Assuming that 8% is generally considered to be the normal or "capital-attracting" rate of return on total assets for the particular industry, only *C* has excess earnings, computed as follows:

Net income	$9,000
Income at "normal" rate on total assets—8%	8,000
Excess earnings	$1,000

The excess earnings of corporation *C* indicate that it has a goodwill; corporations *A* and *B* apparently have none.

The list of sources or causes of goodwill includes everything that could contribute to an attractive earnings result. Some of these sources are: satisfactory customer relations; location; manufacturing efficiency; good employee relations; marketing or production "know-how"; and weak or ineffective competition.

Although businesses customarily spend considerable sums for the purpose of creating goodwill, or at least in the hopes that such expenditures will ultimately result in an advantage to them over their competition, it is generally impossible to establish whether any goodwill was in fact created. Therefore, disbursements made in an attempt to create goodwill are expensed. The only goodwill given recognition in the accounts is that specifically paid for in connection with the purchase of a business, a product line, or some group of assets.

How is the price paid for goodwill determined? To meet the requirements of accounting, the goodwill amount must be the result of a bargained transaction. The figure agreed upon for goodwill may have been selected rather arbitrarily or may have been the result of carefully prepared computations. Some of the factors to be considered in making estimates of goodwill are mentioned in the following paragraphs.

Probable future earnings. When the purchaser of a business pays a price for goodwill, he is not paying for the excess earnings of the past, but for the probable excess earnings of the future. The accomplishments of the past, however, may furnish the best available evidence of the probable accomplishments in the future, and, hence, it is customary to estimate the future earnings on the basis of past net income data. In making a statement of past earnings which is to be used as the basis for computing the goodwill, the following points should be considered:

First: The results of operations for one preceding year are not a sufficient basis for estimating future results of operations, because a statement for one year would not disclose fluctuations in earnings. On the other hand, too many past years should not be included in the base if the earnings of the more remote years were affected by conditions at variance with present conditions or trends.

Second: All extraneous and nonoperating gains and losses should be excluded. If income is earned on investments, such as securities or real estate, the fair market value of the assets should govern their sale price, and the income received from them should be excluded from the net income used in computing the goodwill.

Third: If any known facts point to a possible difference between past and future income results, these facts should be considered.

Have the earnings been derived from sales of articles protected by patents, copyrights, licenses, or royalty agreements? If so, how long will such protection continue in the future? To what extent does the success of the business depend upon its present location, and what tenure of the premises is assured either by ownership or by lease? What is the trend of competition in the field? Are there any prospects of changes in labor conditions?

If management salaries have not been deducted by the vendor, or if the salaries have been merely nominal, deductions should be made for the management salaries to be paid by the purchaser, provided that these salaries are reasonable.

If the success of the business in the past has been due largely to the personality or business ability of the old management, and if those who are responsible for this success are not to go with the business to the new owners, this fact should be considered in estimating future earnings.

If the fixed assets of the business are to be transferred to the purchaser at a higher price than that at which they have been carried on the seller's books, recognition should be given to the fact that higher depreciation charges will be required in the future, and that future net income will be diminished as a consequence.

The effects which the above matters will have on future income taxes should also receive consideration.

Fourth: Consideration should be given to the trend of earnings and perhaps to the trend of some of the important items of revenue and expense. It is unwise to accept the average net income of a number of past years as the basis of a goodwill computation without giving consideration to variations and the trend of earnings. This fact may be shown by the following illustration.

Schedule of Net Income Amounts

	Co. *A*	Co. *B*	Co. *C*	Co. *D*
1960	$ 25,000	$ 19,100	$ 30,000	$ 10,000
1961	40,000	19,800	25,000	15,000
1962	19,000	20,400	20,000	20,000
1963	2,000*	20,200	15,000	25,000
1964	18,000	20,500	10,000	30,000
Total	$100,000	$100,000	$100,000	$100,000
Average	$ 20,000	$ 20,000	$ 20,000	$ 20,000

* Loss.

Although each of these concerns has made an average net income of $20,000 per year, it is evident that it would be unwise to pay the same amount for the goodwill of each business. Company *A*'s earnings show a wide range of fluctuation, from $40,000 net income in 1961 to a loss of $2,000 in 1963. Such a history furnishes very poor evidence of stable earnings in the future.

Company *B*'s earnings, on the other hand, are very uniform year by year and show a slight tendency to increase. Assuming that a net income of $20,000 represents more than a normal return on the assets, it would be reasonable and safe to make a payment for *B*'s goodwill based on an average net income of $20,000.

Company *C* probably has no goodwill, because its earnings are steadily declining, and if the decline continues in the same fashion for two more years, there will be no net income whatever.

Company *D*, on the other hand, probably has the most goodwill of all (assuming equal assets), because its earnings are steadily increasing. In fact, just as it would be unwise for a purchaser to pay for goodwill based on the average of the earnings of Company *C*, which are on the decline, so also would it probably be unfair to the seller to base the goodwill of Company *D* on the average earnings, because the earnings are steadily increasing. The indication is that future earnings will be considerably more than the average.

If an accountant is called upon to prepare a statement of the average net income of a business for purposes of computing goodwill, he should, as a general rule, submit a statement showing the net income of each year as well as the average net income. A statement of only the average is likely to be misleading, because it fails to furnish information concerning the variation and trend of the earnings.

Methods of computation. The price paid for goodwill is usually determined by sheer bargaining; however, the methods of computation illustrated below indicate factors and procedures which may be considered by the purchaser and seller during the negotiations. The illustrations are based on the following assumed facts: The purchaser and the seller of a business have agreed that the assets, other than goodwill, shall be valued at $100,000; the net income figures for the five years next preceding the date of sale were $19,000, $19,500, $19,000, $21,500, and $21,000, or an annual average of $20,000.

(1) Years' purchase of excess earnings. Assume that the goodwill is to be valued at three years' purchase of the past earnings in excess of 12½% of the assets other than goodwill. This may mean net income in excess of 12½% of the assets actually held during each of the three years, or net income in excess of 12½% of the $100,000 price determined as the value of the assets other than goodwill; the latter is the more logical basis. Assuming that the latter basis is agreed upon, the amount to be paid for the goodwill will be computed as follows:

Year Preceding Sale	Net Income	12½% of Assets	Excess
Third	$19,000	$12,500	$ 6,500
Second	21,500	12,500	9,000
First	21,000	12,500	8,500
Total payment for goodwill			$24,000

(2) Years' purchase of average excess earnings. Assume that the goodwill is to be valued at three years' purchase of the average earnings of the past five years in excess of 12½% of the $100,000 agreed value of the assets other than goodwill. This method is similar to the preceding one except that averages are used. The goodwill computation is shown on page 358.

Average earnings of past 5 years	$20,000
Deduct 12½% of $100,000	12,500
Excess	$ 7,500
Multiply by number of years of purchase	3
Goodwill	$22,500

(3) Capitalized earnings, minus assets. Assume that the purchaser and the seller agree upon 12½% as a normal or basic rate, and that they decide to base the valuation of the business upon a capitalization, at that rate, of the average income for the past five years.

The goodwill will be computed as follows:

Capitalized value of average income, or total value of business:	
$20,000 ÷ 12½%	$160,000
Deduct agreed value of net assets other than goodwill	100,000
Goodwill	$ 60,000

(4) Excess earnings capitalized. A serious theoretical objection can be raised to the preceding method. This objection may be made apparent by dividing the total purchase price into two parts and noting what the purchaser of the business obtains in return for his payment.

	Net Assets	Earnings
For the first $100,000 of the purchase price, the purchaser receives:		
Assets other than goodwill	$100,000	
Prospective income of 12½% thereof		$12,500
For the remaining $60,000 of the purchase price, the purchaser receives:		
An intangible asset of goodwill	60,000	
Prospective income of 12½% thereof		7,500

For the first $100,000, the purchaser acquires assets which presumably will have some realizable value even though the prospective earnings fail to materialize; for the $60,000, the purchaser acquires an asset which presumably will have no value if the prospective earnings fail to materialize. It therefore appears that, if 12½% is a fair rate for the capitalization of the first $12,500 of income, a higher rate should be used for the capitalization of the remaining $7,500. The use of two rates is illustrated by the following computation of goodwill; it is assumed that the purchaser and the seller have agreed that 12½% is a fair rate for the capitalization of earnings accompanied by assets other than goodwill, and that the remaining earnings should be capitalized at 25%.

Average earnings of past 5 years	$20,000
Deduct earnings regarded as applicable to assets other than goodwill— 12½% of $100,000	12,500
Remaining earnings, regarded as indicative of goodwill	$ 7,500
Goodwill = $7,500 ÷ 25%	$30,000

Excess earnings may be divided into brackets, and graduated rates may be used in capitalizing them: Earnings at the higher levels are capitalized at a higher rate (and thus given a lower capitalized value) than earnings at lower levels because of the greater danger that they will not continue. This procedure is illustrated below:

Excess earnings regarded as indicative of goodwill (as above)	$ 7,500
Goodwill:	
Capitalization of first $5,000 at 25%	$20,000
Capitalization of remaining $2,500 at 50%	5,000
Total goodwill	$25,000

Assets other than goodwill; normal income rate. If goodwill is to be computed as the capitalized value of earnings in excess of a normal return on the assets other than goodwill, consideration must be given to the valuation of the other assets and a decision must be reached as to what is a normal income rate.

For general accounting purposes, cost (less depreciation, amortization, and so forth) is, in most instances, regarded as the proper basis for the valuation of assets, but this may not be the proper basis when asset valuations are being determined for purposes of goodwill computation. For that purpose, current appraisal values are more appropriate. If they are not used, the difference between the fair present value of the assets and their book value will find its way into the valuation of the goodwill. This can be a matter of considerable importance to the purchaser because the amortization of goodwill is not deductible for income tax purposes.

What is the normal or basic rate of income to be earned before a business can be regarded as having a goodwill? This is purely a matter of opinion. The basic or normal income is, fundamentally, the amount which would attract proprietorship capital equal to the agreed valuation of the assets other than goodwill. It varies with different businesses because of variations in hazards and other conditions peculiar to industries. Moreover, no two investors might hold the same opinion as to the normal rate of income applicable to any one business. The determination of the basic rate applicable to assets other than goodwill, and of the rate to be used in the capitalization of excess earnings, is, therefore, a matter of bargaining between the purchaser and seller.

It should be noted that, if the purchaser is to assume any of the liabilities of the business selling the assets, a deduction therefore is made to arrive at the net payment for the assets.

Justifiable Goodwill account. We have seen that a business possesses a goodwill if it has excess earnings; but even under such a condition a business is not always justified in having a Goodwill account on its books. As noted earlier, a Goodwill account may properly appear on the books of a business only if the goodwill has been paid for in connection with the acquisition of a going and profit-making business, or some segment thereof, and the balance in the Goodwill account cannot properly be more than the amount so paid.

It is often contended that when a concern conducts an extensive advertising campaign for the purpose of developing business, and spends a sum greatly in excess of a normal advertising expenditure, the purpose is to create a goodwill, and the amount by which the cost of the campaign exceeds a normal advertising expenditure can be capitalized as goodwill. Even if such a procedure were theoretically acceptable, the practical difficulties involved in its application are so great as to make it a dangerous one. What will be the normal advertising expenditure necessary to retain the business after the conclusion of the campaign? It is easy to be optimistic about this matter, but there is always a danger that future advertising costs may be much greater than expected. The portion of the expenditure capitalized as goodwill will then be found to be excessive, and the net income of the past will have been overstated. Perhaps the most reasonable compromise is to set up a portion of the campaign cost as a deferred charge to be written off over the periods which the advertising may reasonably be expected to benefit.

Patents and goodwill. A patent may give its owner a monopoly that enables him to develop his business to a point at which, after the expiration of the patent, competitors will find it extremely difficult to enter the field and overcome the handicap. The patent value thus merges into a goodwill value, and it is often argued that, under such circumstances, the patent may be written off to a Goodwill account instead of against income. This practice is considered improper because of the uncertainty of maintaining the monopoly and thereby preserving the goodwill after the expiration of the patent.

Unjustifiable Goodwill account. If the Goodwill account always represented the amount actually paid for goodwill, the account would not be in its present state of disrepute. Unfortunately, the account has been used for all sorts of ulterior purposes, until it is itself so discredited that it is looked upon with little more favor than the stock discount and deficit accounts for which it has often been substituted.

The chief misuse of the Goodwill account has been charging it with discount on stock. Because goodwill is based on earnings, it cannot exist apart from a business; therefore, if stock is issued for cash or for other assets which are not a part of a going business, and if the value of the assets received is less than the par of the stock issued, there is no justification whatever for charging the discount on stock to a Goodwill account. Even when stock is issued in payment for a going business, the Goodwill account may be overstated. For instance, partners who incorporate may issue stock to themselves greatly in excess of the value of the goodwill and other assets transferred to the corporation.

Another abuse of the Goodwill account is charging it with expenses and losses incurred during the early life of the business when it is establishing itself on a paying basis. Under such circumstances the Goodwill account is merely a device for effecting an eventual inflation of the Retained Earnings account by in effect relieving it of the results of charges for expenses and losses.

A company, after years of successful and profitable operation, may feel that it has created a goodwill, and may proceed to put it on the books. Although the company may be entirely correct in maintaining that it has created a goodwill, it is not justified in placing the account on its books by a credit to a surplus account or by any other credit.

Writing up or down. It has already been stated that goodwill should not be placed on the books unless it has been paid for. Having once recorded purchased goodwill at its cost, the balance of the account should not be written up, no matter how much the value of the goodwill may have increased.

Accountants and businessmen sometimes have expressed the belief that, even though excess earnings continue in amounts sufficient to justify the valuation placed on the goodwill at the time of its purchase, it is desirable to write off the Goodwill account by charges to Retained Earnings, because the Goodwill account has been so misused as to make it meaningless and to bring it into disrepute. The write-off is advocated on the ground that it is conservative to "clear the balance sheet of fancy assets." The practice, however, is not wholly commendable. A purchased goodwill represents a part of the investment on which the operations should earn a return. The ratio of earnings to stockholders' equity may appear to be satisfactory only because the stockholders' equity has been reduced by writing off the goodwill element of the investment. Instead of advocating the write-off of a purchased and still-existing goodwill because Goodwill accounts have often been improperly used to absorb stock discount, and otherwise, accountants would render a greater service by bringing the account into good repute by strictly limiting its use to the showing of the cost of goodwill paid for at the time of acquiring a going business, and by educating the business public so that it will come to realize that the Goodwill account shows a purchase cost, but that the value of the goodwill at any time can be ascertained only by a consideration of the assets other than goodwill, the operating results, and the normal or basic rate of income for businesses of the class under consideration.

In the past it has usually been considered proper to carry permanently as an asset the cost of a purchased goodwill, even though the earnings may have declined to a point where goodwill no longer exists. Modern accounting theory, with its emphasis on the recording of costs and cost expirations, seems to be inclining somewhat in the direction of favoring the writing off of the cost of goodwill which has lost its potency as a producer of "better-than-average" earnings. In this connection, the Securities and Exchange Commission appears to incline to the opinion that goodwill is no different from any other asset, and that if its value is permanently impaired, the loss in value should be recognized in the accounts. The Commission has also indicated that a write-off of goodwill against paid-in capital is improper, except, perhaps, in cases where the goodwill was grossly overvalued and the entry originally setting up the Goodwill account carried a credit to a paid-in capital account.

Because the value of the goodwill is dependent upon earnings, and because earnings fluctuate, it follows that the value of the goodwill fluctuates also. However, accountants have never advocated adjusting the balance of the Goodwill account from time to time to reflect the fluctuation in its value resulting from changes in the earnings level. To attempt to do so would require not only consideration of the earnings level at the time of the adjustment, but also an estimate of the immediate and long-time earnings probabilities; the impracticability of such a procedure is obvious.

Goodwill as an asset subject to amortization. All of the foregoing discussion is based on the prevailing concept of goodwill as an asset which is not normally subject to amortization. There are good theoretical reasons for believing that this concept is not entirely justified by the facts.

Methods 3 and 4 on page 358 for the computation of a goodwill valuation have inherent in them the assumption that the excess earnings over a fair return on the tangible net assets will continue in perpetuity—that they will well up forever from inexhaustible springs of profit existing at the time of the transfer of ownership. This assumption is at the bottom of the traditional accounting attitude that purchased goodwill is a permanent asset, the cost of which need not be eliminated from the accounts.

There are many reasons why such an assumption may be false. The vicissitudes of business and the history of individual business enterprises furnish much evidence to nullify such an assumption. There is much reason to believe that the attitude of accountants with respect to goodwill should be revised; that, in any equitable computation of the value of goodwill, recognition should be given to the probability that the profit impetus given to a business by one proprietary management will not continue indefinitely; that the reasonable price to be paid for goodwill should be based on the excess earnings and the number of years during which the momentum given to the business by the vendor management will continue to be reflected in the income statement; and that goodwill should be regarded as an asset subject to amortization.

For instance, referring to Method 4, where excess earnings of $7,500 were used for purposes of illustration, it would be more consistent with the probabilities to base the computation on an assumption that the accumulated momentum may continue to produce excess earnings, not forever, but for a period of, say, five years. If this assumption is accepted as a reasonable basis of computation, the purchaser of the business should pay for the excess earnings for five years.

A further refinement of this theory of goodwill would give recognition to the probable gradual reduction in the momentum and the consequent tapering off of earnings attributable to such momentum. That is, unless the new management continued to supply the factors which produced the excess earnings, the $7,500 annual excess might be reduced year by year.

If businessmen, when computing the valuation of goodwill existing in a business to be transferred, would recognize that excess earnings in perpetuity cannot be acquired by the purchase of goodwill, accountants might more generally question the propriety of accounting procedures applicable to goodwill which are now regarded as acceptable. Instead of regarding the cost of goodwill as something which can be carried indefinitely in the accounts, it would seem necessary to regard goodwill as an intangible subject to amortization—something like bond premiums paid for the right to receive excess interest income during a period. If the purchaser, when buying goodwill, is paying for excess earnings for a specific number of years, it seems reasonable that the payment made for the right to receive these excess earnings should be charged to income, as a cost of the excess earnings purchased, during the period for which the earnings were purchased.

The attitude of the Securities and Exchange Commission on this matter is indicated by the following quotation from Chapter 38 of *Contemporary Accounting,** of which the then Chief Accountant of the Commission was a co-author:

> The Commission has adopted no general rule as to the amortization of goodwill. However, in those cases in which a registrant has retained "goodwill" indefinitely in its accounts, the staff has inquired into the propriety of this accounting treatment. As a result of an analysis of the nature of the account a number of registrants have undertaken programs of amortization which will result in charging the goodwill to income or, in some cases, earned surplus, over a reasonable number of years.

Goodwill in the balance sheet. Goodwill is, in a sense, the most fixed of all assets, because it cannot be sold without selling the business. However, the balance sheet should show the total tangible fixed assets, and the goodwill and other intangibles should be set out separately. The separation may be made as follows:

Fixed assets:			
Land and buildings	$40,000		
Machinery	55,000	$95,000	
Goodwill		15,000	$110,000

The following balance sheet presentation is probably preferable:

Tangible fixed assets:		
Land and buildings	$40,000	
Machinery	55,000	$95,000
Goodwill		15,000

The separation is desirable because tangible and intangible fixed assets are fundamentally different; the bases of valuation applicable to them are

* Thomas W. Leland, editor. Published by the American Institute of Certified Public Accountants, New York, 1945.

different; and ratios of total fixed assets to other amounts shown in the balance sheet or income statement are usually intended to show the relation of only the tangible fixed assets to the other amounts used in the computation.

Organization costs. The traditional attitude of accountants toward organization costs is that they are a sheer loss, and that there is no theoretical justification for any treatment other than writing them off as soon as possible. However, because such a treatment would create a deficit before the company began operations, accountants have sanctioned carrying organization costs as a deferred charge to be written off to Retained Earnings during the early years of the company's life.

There seems to be much theoretical justification for regarding organization expenditures as the cost of an intangible asset not requiring amortization. An immediate write-off to Retained Earnings can be theoretically justified only on the assumption that the business obtained no benefit whatever from the expenditures, which is obviously contrary to fact, because without such expenditures the business could not have been organized and operations could not have been conducted. Writing them off during the early years of a corporation's life can be theoretically justified only on the assumption that the early years are the only ones benefited. Presumably, the benefits will continue through the whole life of the business; for this reason there is theoretical justification for regarding organization expenditures as producing an intangible asset which, although having no disposal value, is a continuing part of the value inherent in the business.

Because accountants are so strongly influenced by considerations of conservatism in balance sheet valuations, it is doubtful whether the profession will accept the theory that organization costs are an intangible asset. However, there seems to be more theoretical justification for regarding organization costs as a continuing asset entitled to a place in the balance sheet than for indefinitely carrying a purchased goodwill which may long since have lost its potency.

CHAPTER

20

Liabilities and Reserves

Nature of accounting problems. One of the chief problems in dealing with liabilities arises from the danger of omissions from the books and the balance sheet at the end of the period. This matter is dealt with at some length in a subsequent section of this chapter.

Problems of valuation of assets arise more frequently than problems of determining the amounts of liabilities. However, not all amounts of liabilities are definitely determinable. It often is necessary to make estimates—particularly in the case of operating reserves set up to obtain a proper matching of revenue and expense.

Security for liabilities. The balance sheet should clearly indicate the nature and amount of the security supporting the liabilities. Some accountants are satisfied to indicate the security on the liability side of the balance sheet, in the description of the liability itself. Other accountants also indicate on the asset side of the balance sheet the amounts of any pledged assets; this procedure seems desirable, because it enables the reader of the balance sheet to identify easily the assets which are pledged and which, therefore, are not available for the payment of unsecured liabilities.

Offsetting liabilities against assets. A relationship frequently exists between an asset and a liability; in such cases, the balance sheet should show the gross amount of the asset and the gross amount of the liability, rather than merely the difference between them. Showing gross amounts is sometimes described as showing the facts "broad"; showing only differences is called stating the facts "net." One of the situations most frequently met is that in which the subsidiary accounts receivable ledger contains accounts with credit balances; it is important that the balance sheet show the gross amount of the debit balances and the total amount of the credit balances, rather than merely the balance of the controlling account. A comparable situation may be found in the accounts payable subsidiary ledger, and a similar treatment should be given it.

Unpaid installments on contracts for the purchase of assets are sometimes omitted from the liabilities, either because they have not been set up on the books or because a deduction on the asset side may be regarded as desirable in order to show the company's equity in the property. Showing the liabilities on the right side of the balance sheet is preferable to showing only net amounts; the relation of the unpaid installments to the carrying value of the assets can be indicated by cross references in the balance sheet.

When securities are purchased from a broker on margin account, the total cost of the securities should be shown as an asset, and the liability to the broker should appear in the balance sheet.

One exception to the rule against offsetting related assets and liabilities is sanctioned in *A. R. B.* No. 43, which states that the deduction of United States Government securities from tax liabilities, "although a deviation from the general rule against offsets, is not so significant a deviation as to call for an exception in an accountant's report on the financial statements."

LONG-TERM LIABILITIES

Nature of long-term liabilities. Long-term liabilities (sometimes called "fixed liabilities") are usually represented by bonds or mortgages. Some of the principal classes of bonds are mentioned in Chapter 14, where they are discussed as investments. Although obligations secured by mortgages are often called *mortgages payable,* the expression is not strictly correct. The obligation is represented by a note, and the mortgage serves as security; a more precise title would therefore be *long-term mortgage notes.* Advances received by one affiliated company from another may be, in effect, long-term liabilities, although represented merely by open accounts.

Recording the bond issue. Bonds may be sold direct by the corporation, or they may be underwritten by an investment banker or a syndicate. Underwriting usually consists of the actual purchase and resale of the bonds by the banker or the syndicate, but it may consist of an agreement by the banker or the syndicate to take over at a certain future time all bonds not sold by the corporation at that time. The method of marketing, however, does not determine the entries; these depend upon whether all or a portion of the authorized bonds are sold, and upon whether they are sold at par, at a premium, or at a discount.

Very frequently an amount of bonds will be authorized larger than that intended for immediate issuance. To illustrate, assume that the fixed property of the corporation is ample in value to secure an issue of $500,000 of first-mortgage bonds. Only $300,000 of funds are now required, but there may be future requirements of $200,000. If the first issue were made for only $300,000, a subsequent issue could be secured by a second mortgage only, which would perhaps necessitate a higher interest rate and might make the marketing of the bonds difficult. By authorizing $500,000 of bonds and issuing $300,000, the corporation is in a position to market the remaining

$200,000 at any future date without incurring the disadvantages incident to a second-mortgage bond issue.

The $200,000 of unissued bonds may be held for use as collateral on short-term note issues. Because these bonds are secured by a first mortgage, they are as good collateral as the bonds of another company would be (assuming equal security behind the bonds), except that the creditor would be able to hold only one debtor instead of two.

If the entire authorized issue is sold at par on the date of issue, the entry is: debit Cash, credit Bonds Payable at par.

If some of the bonds are held unissued, the authorized issue may be shown by a memorandum notation in the Bonds Payable account, which is then credited with the par of the bonds issued. The balance sheet should show, not merely the amount of bonds issued, but also the amount of bonds authorized to be issued under the mortgage. If $500,000 of bonds are authorized under a mortgage on property carried in the balance sheet at $1,000,000, but only $300,000 of the bonds are immediately issued, the holders of the $300,000 of issued bonds should be, and presumably would be, interested in knowing that $200,000 more bonds could be issued under the same mortgage.

If bonds are issued at a price below or above par, the difference between par and selling price should be charged to Discount on Bonds or credited to Premium on Bonds.

If the bonds are issued in payment for property, it is customary to charge the property accounts with the par of the bonds. In reality the bonds may have been issued at a discount, because the vendor may have demanded a larger price payable in bonds than he would have demanded payable in cash. This fact is, of course, difficult to establish unless both a cash price and a bond price were quoted, or unless other bonds of the same issue were marketed for cash at about the same time. If information of this nature is available to indicate that the bonds were really issued at a discount or premium, the discount or premium should be set up.

If the bonds are registered as to principal or interest or both, subsidiary records similar to a stockholders ledger should be kept. If the bonds are not registered, no subsidiary records are necessary.

Bonds in the balance sheet. The reasons for showing unissued bonds have already been discussed. The question remains concerning where such bonds should be shown in the balance sheet. The best practice is to deduct them from the authorized issue on the liability side, carrying out the net amount of bonds outstanding. If any of the unissued bonds have been pledged as collateral, this fact should be shown in the following manner:

Long-term liabilities:			
First-mortgage, 6% bonds payable—due 1985:			
Bonds authorized		$500,000	
Less unissued bonds:			
Pledged as collateral to notes payable	$ 25,000		
In treasury	175,000	200,000	$300,000

Or the same facts may be shown thus:

Long-term liabilities:
First-mortgage, 6% bonds payable—due 1985; authorized, $500,000; unissued, $200,000, of which $25,000 are pledged as collateral to notes payable; outstanding $300,000

Payment of interest. If the bonds are registered as to interest, checks will be mailed to the holders, and interest payments will be recorded by debiting Bond Interest Expense and crediting Cash.

If the bonds are coupon bonds, the interest may be payable by the fiscal agent of the corporation or direct by the corporation. If the interest is payable by a fiscal agent, the corporation will send the agent a check for the full amount of the interest; when recording this deposit with the agent, the accountant should remember that a deposit of cash with the agent does not constitute payment of the liability; if the agent fails to make payment, the company is still liable. To record the facts fully, entries should be made as follows: debit Bond Interest Expense and credit Bond Interest Payable; debit Deposits for Payment of Bond Interest and credit Cash. When the agent reports payment of the interest, debit Bond Interest Payable and credit Deposits for Payment of Bond Interest. Because fiscal agents are usually institutions of unquestioned financial integrity, the possibility of nonpayment by the fiscal agent sometimes is ignored, and no entries are made other than a debit to Bond Interest Expense and a credit to Cash.

If interest on coupon bonds is payable direct, an entry should be made debiting Bond Interest Expense and crediting Bond Interest Payable. As coupons are received and paid, Bond Interest Payable should be debited and Cash credited. Any interest unpaid at a balance sheet date should appear on the balance sheet as a current liability.

There remains for consideration the question of the disposition of the paid coupons. These coupons may be turned over to the trustee under the mortgage, who will destroy them and issue a cremation certificate stating the amount paid and destroyed. Or the paid coupons may be pasted in a register. The register may have a page for each interest date, with spaces numbered to conform with the numbers of the bonds issued. Paid coupons are then pasted in their respective spaces; vacant spaces indicate the numbers of the bonds on which interest due has not been paid. Or the register may have a page for each bond, with a space for the bond itself and a space for each coupon. Paid coupons, and eventually the paid bond, are pasted in their respective spaces.

Amortization of premium and discount. The relation of bond premium and discount to bond interest was discussed in Chapter 14, where bonds were considered from the investment standpoint. The same relation exists with respect to bonds issued. The premium and discount on bonds issued may be amortized by the straight-line, or equal-installment, method, as illustrated in the schedules on page 369; or they may be amortized by the effective-interest method, which is described in the *Advanced* text.

Straight-Line Amortization Schedule
Five-Year 6% $100,000 Bond Issue at a Premium

Period	Debit Bond Interest Expense	Debit Bond Premium	Credit Cash	Unamortized Premium
				$4,376.03
1	$ 2,562.40	$ 437.60	$ 3,000	3,938.43
2	2,562.40	437.60	3,000	3,500.83
3	2,562.40	437.60	3,000	3,063.23
4	2,562.40	437.60	3,000	2,625.63
5	2,562.40	437.60	3,000	2,188.03
6	2,562.40	437.60	3,000	1,750.43
7	2,562.40	437.60	3,000	1,312.83
8	2,562.39	437.61	3,000	875.22
9	2,562.39	437.61	3,000	437.61
10	2,562.39	437.61	3,000	—
	$25,623.97	$4,376.03	$30,000	

Straight-Line Amortization Schedule
Five-Year 4% $100,000 Bond Issue at a Discount

Period	Debit Bond Interest Expense	Credit Cash	Credit Bond Discount	Unamortized Discount
				$4,376.03
1	$ 2,437.60	$ 2,000	$ 437.60	3,938.43
2	2,437.60	2,000	437.60	3,500.83
3	2,437.60	2,000	437.60	3,063.23
4	2,437.60	2,000	437.60	2,625.63
5	2,437.60	2,000	437.60	2,188.03
6	2,437.60	2,000	437.60	1,750.43
7	2,437.60	2,000	437.60	1,312.83
8	2,437.61	2,000	437.61	875.22
9	2,437.61	2,000	437.61	437.61
10	2,437.61	2,000	437.61	—
	$24,376.03	$20,000	$4,376.03	

Some companies have been known to write off bond discount by charge to Retained Earnings at the date of issuance, or shortly thereafter, and have defended this procedure on the ground of conservatism, claiming that it is commendable to eliminate from the balance sheet an element of such intangible value as bond discount. The procedure is not to be commended, partly because the balance sheets thereafter fail to state the true facts relative to the obligation, but primarily because the income statements of subsequent periods are relieved of proper charges for bond interest expense.

A corresponding procedure by which bond premium is immediately credited to Retained Earnings does not even have the justification of conservatism, because it takes up as an immediate credit to Retained Earnings an amount which should be applied gradually over the life of the bonds as a deduction from interest expense.

Premium or discount on convertible or redeemable bonds should be amortized on the basis of the full life of the bonds without consideration of the possible retirement before maturity. Any balance of premium or discount remaining unamortized when the bonds are retired before maturity should be taken into consideration in determining the gain or loss on retirement.

Amortization at interim dates. The foregoing illustrations of the amortization of bond premium and discount are based on the assumption that an interest date coincides with the close of the issuing company's fiscal year. We shall now assume that the bonds were issued on October 31, and that the fiscal year ends on December 31.

Refer to the foregoing schedule of amortization of premium. The semiannual amortization is $437.60, so the amortization for two months would be one-third of $437.60, or $145.87. The bond interest entries are indicated below:

First fiscal year:		
December 31:		
Bond premium	145.87	
Bond interest expense	854.13	
Accrued bond interest payable		1,000.00
Second fiscal year:		
April 30:		
Bond premium	291.73	
Bond interest expense	1,708.27	
Accrued bond interest payable	1,000.00	
Cash		3,000.00
October 31:		
Bond premium	437.60	
Bond interest expense	2,562.40	
Cash		3,000.00
December 31:		
Bond premium	145.87	
Bond interest expense	854.13	
Accrued bond interest payable		1,000.00

Similar procedures would apply to bonds issued at a discount. Refer to the foregoing schedule of amortization of discount. The semiannual amortization is $437.60, so the amortization for two months would be one-third of $437.60, or $145.87.

First fiscal year:		
December 31:		
Bond interest expense	812.54	
Bond discount		145.87
Accrued bond interest payable		666.67
Second fiscal year:		
April 30:		
Bond interest expense	1,625.06	
Accrued bond interest payable	666.67	
Bond discount		291.73
Cash		2,000.00
October 31:		
Bond interest expense	2,437.60	
Bond discount		437.60
Cash		2,000.00

December 31:		
Bond interest expense	812.54	
Bond discount		145.87
Accrued bond interest payable		666.67

Issuances between interest dates. When bonds are issued between interest dates, an Accrued Bond Interest Payable account (or the Bond Interest Expense account) should be credited with the accrued interest to the date of issuance. Assume that $100,000 of 6% bonds due in ten years, dated January 1, 1965, are issued on March 1, 1965 for $108,962.87. The accrued interest for two months is $1,000; the entry to record the issuance may be:

Cash	108,962.87	
Bonds payable		100,000.00
Accrued bond interest payable		1,000.00
Premium on bonds		7,962.87

When the bond interest is paid on July 1, 1965, the entry (exclusive of the premium amortization) will be:

Accrued bond interest payable	1,000.00	
Bond interest expense	2,000.00	
Cash		3,000.00

Or the entries may be:

At time of issuance:		
Cash	108,962.87	
Bonds payable		100,000.00
Bond interest expense		1,000.00
Premium on bonds		7,962.87
At time of payment of interest:		
Bond interest expense	3,000.00	
Cash		3,000.00

The discount or premium on bonds issued subsequent to their date should be amortized over the period between the date of issuance and the date of maturity. In the foregoing illustration, for instance, the $7,962.87 premium should be amortized, not over ten years, but over nine years and ten months.

Bond discount and premium in the balance sheet. It has long been recognized practice to show discount on bonds issued under the Deferred Charges caption of the balance sheet, and premium on bonds issued under the Deferred Credits caption. It has been advocated that discount should be deducted from and premium should be added to the face amount of the bonds on the liability side of the balance sheet. Some of the arguments presented by the proponents of this procedure are discussed below.

With respect to bond discount, one argument runs as follows: Deferred charges are expenses paid in advance; bond discount, although ultimately chargeable to interest expense, is not interest paid in advance at the time of issuance of the bonds, but is unpaid interest; therefore, bond discount is not a deferred charge. This argument seems to depend wholly on an arbitrary definition of deferred charges. If no debit in an account can be regarded as a deferred charge unless the debit was offset by a credit to Cash, bond discount is not a deferred charge. If, however, deferred charges include debits, ultimately chargeable to operations, which were recorded by offsetting credits to liability accounts, bond discount appears to qualify as a true deferred charge. In the past, debits ultimately chargeable to operations have been regarded as deferred charges regardless of whether the offsetting credit was to Cash or to a liability account; to adopt a limited definition of deferred charges in order to defend a method of showing bond discount in the balance sheet does not impress the authors.

With respect to bond premium, the advocates of the proposed balance sheet presentation find themselves unable to advance an argument analogous to that discussed above relative to bond discount. If bonds are issued for cash at a premium, the premium *is* collected in advance. A slightly different argument is therefore advanced, which goes as follows: A deferred credit is an item of income collected in advance; bond premium is not income but is an offset against an expense; therefore, bond premium is not a deferred credit. But must all deferred credits be ultimately applied as credits to income accounts? Credits to expense accounts have an equivalent effect on net income, and it therefore appears that unamortized premium on bonds can properly be regarded as a deferred credit.

A more logical argument, and one which can be applied consistently to both discount and premium, derives by analogy from the long-established practice of carrying bond investments on the asset side of the balance sheet at an amortized valuation. It is advocated that the liability on bonds should be shown in the balance sheet similarly on an amortized basis. This argument is not without merit, although practicing accountants have generally shown no inclination to accept the proposition that amortization methods recognized as applicable to the determination of asset valuations are similarly applicable to the balance sheet presentation of liabilities.

Although the proposed method of showing bond discount and premium on the balance sheet has gained no wide acceptance, it should be recognized that it strikes at an inconsistency which indicates some loose thinking with respect to both current and long-term liability presentation in the balance sheet. For instance, if a $1,000 6% interest-bearing note is issued to mature in one year, the liability will be shown in the balance sheet at the end of three months as follows:

Note payable	$1,000	
Accrued interest	15	$1,015

But if interest for a year is included in the face, the liability will be shown at $1,060 and a prepaid expense of $45 will appear in the balance sheet. Perhaps we should be more concerned with consistency than with arbitrary face values, and show the liability as follows:

Note payable	$1,060	
Less unamortized interest included in face	45	$1,015

The issuance of a note with interest included in the face is, of course, a method of issuing a note at a discount; the immediately preceding case therefore does not differ essentially from the issuance of a $1,000 non-interest note at a $60 discount. Consistency would suggest, therefore, a balance sheet presentation as follows:

Note payable	$1,000	
Less unamortized discount	45	$ 955

And for the same reason of consistency it might be desirable to adopt a similar procedure with respect to unamortized discount on bonds. Perhaps the accounting profession will ultimately change to such a procedure.

The advocates of this procedure make a distinction between bond discount and the expenses of issuance, such as attorneys' fees, printing costs, and marketing expenses. Although they believe that bond discount should be deducted in the balance sheet from the par of the bonds, they consider it proper to classify the issuance expenses as a deferred charge. The expenses, as well as the discount, should, of course, be amortized. When bonds are sold through underwriters who share issuance expenses, and a net amount is received from the underwriters, a difficulty may arise in determining how much of the difference between par and net proceeds to the issuing company should be regarded as discount and how much should be regarded as expense. In such cases it probably would be necessary to regard the entire difference as discount.

Serial bonds. Bonds may be repayable in a series instead of at a single maturity. No special problems are involved in accounting for serial bonds unless they are issued at a premium or a discount. A simple procedure for amortizing premiums and discounts on serial bonds is described below. Amortization procedures using an effective interest rate are described in *Principles of Accounting, Advanced.*

To simplify the illustration by using small numbers, it is assumed that five bonds of $100 par value are issued on January 1, 1965, at a discount of $31.20, or for $468.80. One bond matures on December 31st of each of the years 1970, 1971, 1972, 1973, and 1974.

The amount of discount to be amortized each year is computed in the manner shown below.

Year	Number of Bonds Outstanding	Fraction	Discount Amortization
1965	5	5/40	$ 3.90
1966	5	5/40	3.90
1967	5	5/40	3.90
1968	5	5/40	3.90
1969	5	5/40	3.90
1970	5	5/40	3.90
1971	4	4/40	3.12
1972	3	3/40	2.34
1973	2	2/40	1.56
1974	1	1/40	.78
	40	40/40	$31.20

If a bond is retired before its maturity, the amount of unamortized discount applicable to the bond (to be written off in the entry recording the retirement) may be computed by determining the amount of discount per bond per year, thus:

$$\$31.20 \div 40 = \$.78$$

Now, assume that at the end of 1967 the bond maturing at the end of 1971 is retired—four years before maturity. The unamortized discount is $\$.78 \times 4$, or \$3.12.

Because a bond has been retired, the amounts of discount amortization shown in the foregoing table will have to be revised by deducting \$.78 from the amounts shown for the years 1968 to 1971, inclusive.

Sinking funds and redemption funds. For many years it was common practice to require a company borrowing on bonds to establish a sinking fund which accumulated, as the result of deposits and interest accumulations, until the maturity of the bonds, and which was used at that time for their payment. Bonds to be retired in full at their maturity from such a fund were called *sinking-fund bonds.*

More recently it has become rather general practice to require the borrowing company to make periodical deposits with a trustee to be used for the purpose of making periodical bond retirements. The term *sinking fund* is frequently applied to such funds and the related bonds. Such usage of the term is of somewhat doubtful propriety because, strictly defined, a sinking fund is a fund accumulating at compound interest for the payment of a debt at its maturity. A fund to be used for periodical bond retirements would be more properly called a *bond redemption fund.*

Conversion of bonds to other securities. Bonds sometimes contain a provision entitling their holders to convert them into other securities of the issuing company, such as stock. When such a conversion is made, consideration must be given to the terms of the conversion, any unamortized premium or discount on the bonds, and any accrued interest.

Assume that \$10,000 of bonds are converted into 200 shares of no-par common stock; that there is unamortized discount of \$300 applicable to the bonds converted; that \$15 of this discount should be amortized by charge to operations for the period between the last preceding interest date and the date of conversion; that the accrued interest on the bonds at the date of conversion is \$100; and that the stock is to be set up in the accounts at a stated value of \$40 per share, in accordance with a resolution of the directors. The entry for the conversion is:

	Debit	Credit
Bonds payable	10,000	
Bond interest expense	115	
Bond discount		300
Common stock		8,000
Capital in excess of stated value—Common stock		1,815

The credit to the capital in excess account is based on the theory that, because the cancellation of the liability on the bonds and accrued interest constitutes the payment for the stock, the amount at which the liability is carried in the accounts (par of bonds minus unamortized discount plus accrued interest) is the amount received for the stock. The excess of the amount received over the stated value of the stock is a proper credit to paid-in capital.

If the par or stated value of the stock issued was in excess of the net liability canceled, the account to be charged with the excess would be the same as in the case of the issuance of stock for cash at less than par or stated value. Such a transaction is unlikely.

Redemption of bonds before maturity. Bonds may be retired before maturity either by exercise of a call privilege or by purchase in the market. Assume that bonds of $100,000 par value are outstanding, and that discount of $2,000 remains unamortized at a date when $10,000 of bonds are retired for $10,100. If the bonds are retired by call, the call presumably will be made at an interest date, and it can be assumed that the payment of the interest on the entire $100,000 of bonds and the amortization of the discount applicable to the entire issue will have been recorded. The entry to record the call and retirement of the bonds at 101 will be:

Bonds payable	10,000	
Loss on bond retirement	300	
Bond discount (1/10 of $2,000)		200
Cash		10,100

Assume the same facts as above except that the bonds are purchased in the market two months after an interest date, for $9,500 plus accrued interest at 6%. The accrued interest on the bonds to be retired is, therefore, $100; the price, including interest, is $9,600. The $2,000 of unamortized discount is the balance as of the last interest date, which we shall assume was five years before maturity; the unamortized discount applicable to the bonds purchased is one-tenth of $2,000, or $200; the discount per year is one-fifth of $200, or $40; and the discount applicable to the two months since the last preceding interest date is one-sixth of $40, or $6.67. The entries to record the retirement are:

Bond interest expense	106.67	
Accrued bond interest payable		100.00
Bond discount		6.67
Bonds payable	10,000.00	
Accrued bond interest payable	100.00	
Bond discount ($200.00 − $6.67)		193.33
Cash		9,600.00
Gain on bond retirement		306.67

The gain or loss on retirement may be shown as a nonoperating item in the income statement or, if the amount is so material as to distort net income, it may be shown in the retained earnings statement.

Retirements by exercise of call privileges usually must be made at interest dates; any interest paid in connection with a bond retirement should, of course, be charged to Bond Interest Expense.

Refunding. Matured bonds may be paid from general cash, from a sinking fund, or from funds obtained by a refunding issue of new securities. No peculiar accounting problems arise in connection with such a refunding transaction; entries of the nature previously discussed are made to record the issuance of the new securities and the payment of the old.

Bonds frequently contain a provision giving the issuer an option to retire the bonds before maturity; if interest rates have declined, it may be advantageous to float a new bond issue at the lower rate to obtain funds to pay off the old bonds. Optional retirement provisions usually require the borrower to pay a premium to retire the bonds before maturity, and the proper accounting treatment of such a premium requires consideration. There may also be unamortized discount and expense or unamortized premium on the old bonds.

To illustrate, let us assume that bonds of a par value of $1,000,000 were issued for $950,000, maturing in 20 years, and bearing an interest rate of 5%; after these bonds were outstanding 10 years, it was decided to call them at 106, using for their payment the proceeds of a new issue of $1,000,000 of 4% bonds due in 15 years and sold at par. Of the $50,000 discount on the original issue, $25,000 remains unamortized; what disposition should be made in the accounts of this $25,000 of unamortized discount and of the $60,000 premium paid on the retirement of the old bonds?

Three procedures have been advocated:

(1) Charge the $85,000 to income or retained earnings at the time of the refunding. (This is acceptable procedure from the tax standpoint, because these costs are deductible expenses in the year in which the refunding transaction occurred.)

(2) Amortize the $85,000 by charges to interest expense during the life of the new issue.

(3) Amortize the $85,000 by charges to interest expense during what would have been the remaining life of the old issue.

The first two of these methods were those in most common use prior to 1939, when the Committee on Accounting Procedure of the American Institute issued a pronouncement expressing disapproval of the second method (except for companies subject to regulatory bodies which approve it), giving a somewhat modified sanction to the first method, and stating a definite preference for the third method.

Advocates of the immediate charge to Retained Earnings maintained that the unamortized discount and the retirement premium are costs related solely to the old issue, and that there is no more justification for carrying such costs forward as deferred charges than there would be for capitalizing as part of the cost of a new fixed asset the undepreciated cost of a retired asset and the removal costs. The Institute Committee stated that the immediate write-off was sanctioned because it resulted in a conservative balance sheet from which the intangible of bond discount and retirement premium had been eliminated, but the Committee further stated that the write-off was subject to criticism because it relieved future income statements of charges for costs of borrowed money.

Those who advocated writing off the unamortized discount and call premium on the old issue over the life of the new issue defended the procedure by reasoning which may be summarized somewhat as follows: Assume that *A* gives *B* a 5% note for $1,000 due in 10 years and receives $940 in cash; at the end of the first five years, $30 of the discount has been amortized; at that date *B* (in consideration of $10 received from *A*) consents to extend the note to mature 10 years thereafter; the money cost per year during the first five years (on the basis of the facts known during that period) was $50 interest plus $6 (one-tenth of $60) discount; the money cost during each of the last 10 years was $50 interest plus $3 (one-tenth of $30) discount, plus $1 (one-tenth of the $10 cost incurred to convert a liability maturing in five years into one maturing in 10 years). The reasoning then proceeds as follows: The issuance of bonds and their refunding is essentially analogous to the above-described transaction; in both instances, funds of a certain amount are received, the original borrowing period is extended, the money costs for the entire period include the original discount, the periodical interest, and a cost incurred in postponing the maturity of the obligation; the change in parties, the change in documents, and the change in interest rate incident to a refunding of bonds are immaterial and do not destroy the analogy.

The Institute Committee, in advocating the write-off of the unamortized discount and the call premium over the life of the old issue, reasoned as follows: Charges should not be deferred unless they will benefit future periods, and they should be deferred over only those periods which they can reasonably be assumed to benefit. Referring to our original illustration in which 5% bonds due in 10 years were refunded by the issuance of 4% bonds due in 15 years, the Committee would say that the refunding would obviously be of benefit during the next 10 years (the unexpired life of the old bond issue) by reducing the interest rate from 5% to 4%, but whether or not the refunding transaction would be beneficial during the last five years of the new issue is a matter which cannot be determined at the time of the refunding, because it depends upon the interest rate at which money could be borrowed at the beginning of that five-year period.

The Committee's opinion has not been unanimously accepted. Advocates of the immediate charge to Retained Earnings remain unconvinced by the Committee's reasoning. And the advocates of amortization during the life of the new issue still have spokesmen who reply to the Committee's argument as follows: Refunding is presumably effected with the expectation of benefiting the borrower through the full life of the new issue; otherwise, the refunding would cover only the unexpired period of the old bonds, because a shorter-term financing could presumably be done at a lower rate; the longer period is adopted in order to give the borrower assurance of a satisfactory money cost for the longer period. To say that the unamortized discount and retirement premium "benefit" only the life of the old bonds because it is only that period which can be assured of a saving in money costs distorts the meaning of "benefit" as used in determining the propriety of deferring costs; a cost "benefits" a future period if it gives that period the use of a good or of a service; the unamortized discount and retirement premium are costs incurred for the use of money and should be spread over the full period of use; they benefit the full period of the life of the new bonds because they are part of the cost of giving the borrower the use of funds during that period.

Although the proposal to charge off unamortized discount and retirement premium over the remaining life of the old issue runs counter to tax regulations and is not acceptable to all accountants, there appears to have been some swing in the direction of acceptance of the pronouncement of the Committee of the Institute.*

The foregoing comments are applicable to situations in which bonds were refunded by the issuance of other bonds. The generally accepted idea of the proper treatment of any unamortized discount on bonds retired from the proceeds of the issuance of capital stock was well expressed by the Chief Accountant of the Securities and Exchange Commission in *Accounting Series Release* No. 10, from which the following is quoted:

> While it may be permissible to retain on the books and amortize any balance of discount and expense applicable to bonds refunded by other evidences of indebtedness, similar treatment is not ordinarily acceptable, in my opinion, when funds used to retire the existing bonds are derived from the sale of capital stock. In such cases it is my opinion that, as a general rule, sound and generally accepted accounting principles and practice require that the unamortized balance of the debt discount and expense applicable to the retired bonds should be written off by a charge to earnings or earned surplus, as appropriate, in the accounting period within which the bonds were retired.

Installment contracts. Fixed assets are sometimes purchased on contracts payable in installments over a considerable term of years. The error is sometimes made of charging the fixed asset account with only the installments as paid; and the error is sometimes compounded by charging the fixed asset accounts with the interest payments as well as the payments on principal.

The proper treatment is to set up the total purchase price by a charge to the fixed asset account at the time of acquisition, with an offsetting liability. As periodical payments are made, the amount applicable to principal is charged to the liability account, and the amount applicable to interest is charged as an expense. In the balance sheet, the current installments should be shown as current liabilities, and the noncurrent installments as long-term liabilities.

*See page 390.

Long-term liabilities in the balance sheet. The balance sheet should show, with respect to long-term liabilities, the maturity, the interest rate, the nature of the obligation (such as mortgage bond, or collateral trust bond), and the nature of the underlying security. If there are too many long-term liabilities to permit a detailed description in the balance sheet, the details may be furnished in a supplementary schedule.

With one possible exception, unissued or reacquired bonds should not be shown in the balance sheet as an asset, but should be deducted from the total authorized issue to show the par value of the bonds outstanding.

The one possible exception consists of a company's own bonds, acquired for, and held in, a special-purpose fund, such as a sinking fund. If a company's own bonds are purchased and held by a sinking fund trustee, such purchased bonds are customarily regarded as fund assets to be shown on the asset side of the balance sheet, and as outstanding liabilities to be shown on the liability side. This treatment is, of course, theoretically illogical, but the procedure has long been regarded as acceptable from a practical standpoint, because of the necessity of holding the bonds alive for the purpose of collecting interest in order to safeguard the bondholders who are relying on the fund, and also to indicate the extent of accumulation in the fund on the balance sheet date. If contributions have been made to the fund in accordance with requirements, and if investments of fund cash have been made in the company's own bonds, the elimination of the purchased bonds from the fund and from the liability would distort the ratio between the fund and the liability and would make the balance sheet subject to the possible misinterpretation that the company had not complied with its sinking-fund deposit requirements. However, it would still be possible to conform to good theory by eliminating the treasury bonds from the fund and from the liability, and mentioning the elimination in a footnote.

CURRENT LIABILITIES

Inclusion of all liabilities. Some of the liabilities not infrequently omitted from balance sheets are:

(1) Accounts payable for goods purchased before the close of the accounting period.

In most concerns, it is the custom to record liabilities for purchases when the goods are received. But there is always some delay in getting the record on the books, and goods received during the last few days of the accounting period may not be recorded until the early days of the succeeding period. If the goods are not included in the inventory, the net income is not misstated, because the purchases and the inventory are equally understated. But the assets and liabilities are both understated in the balance sheet, and the ratio of current assets to current liabilities is thus distorted. Moreover, it is a question whether the customary business policy of recording purchases only after the receipt of the goods is sound. A liability exists as soon as title to the goods passes to the purchaser, and, according to the legal rules governing sales, title may pass to the purchaser before he receives the goods. It would seem, therefore, that if the books are to show the facts, entries for purchases should be made when the title passes according to law, which may be before the goods are received.

(2) Miscellaneous liabilities for services rendered the business prior to the close of the accounting period but not billed until the succeeding period.

(3) Accrued liabilities for wages, interest, taxes, employees' bonuses, and so forth.

(4) Liabilities to be liquidated in merchandise, arising from the issuing of due bills, merchandise coupon books, and gift certificates.

(5) Dividends which have been declared and therefore represent a liability, but which have not been recorded.

Classification. Two general problems of classification may be mentioned:

(1) What rule should be followed in differentiating between current and long-term liabilities?

(2) To what extent and in what way should the current liabilities be detailed in the balance sheet?

Concerning the first problem, reference is made to page 43 in Chapter 3, where the portion of Institute Bulletin No. 43 dealing with current liabilities is discussed. In general, it may be said here that, although the bulletin does not entirely abandon the old one-year dividing line between current and long-term liabilities, the basic criterion established by the bulletin is this: Current liabilities are those debts which will be paid from current assets during the operating cycle.

A special problem arises when long-term liabilities approach their maturity and are due within, say, a year. Should they be included among the current liabilities although, in preceding balance sheets, they have been included among the long-term liabilities? The proximity of the maturity date probably should not be the sole determining factor. If bonds maturing in, say, nine months are to be paid by a refinancing program which will involve the issuance of new bonds, the inclusion of the old bonds among the current liabilities would convey the impression that the bonds were to be paid out of current assets, and would so distort the ratio of current assets to current liabilities as to give an entirely erroneous idea of the concern's working capital. It seems, therefore, that all necessary facts would be shown by leaving the bonds among the long-term liabilities, with a statement of the maturity date and a footnote mentioning the contemplated refinancing program.

The situation is different, however, when an installment is shortly to become due on a serial bond issue. The natural assumption is that the installment will be paid out of working capital, and it would seem proper to show the condition as follows:

Balance Sheet—December 31, 1965

Current liabilities:		
Serial bonds payable, due February 10, 1966		$10,000
Long-term liabilities:		
Serial bonds payable	$90,000	
Less bonds due February 10, 1966	10,000	80,000

Current installments need not be classified as current liabilities if they are payable from a fund not classified as a current asset.

With respect to the second problem, that is, the extent to which the current liabilities should be detailed in the balance sheet, it may be said that the answer will properly depend to some extent on the purpose for which the statement is to be used. If a balance sheet is prepared specifically for credit purposes, much more extensive detailing will be required than is expected in an ordinary published balance sheet.

It may be contended that an accountant rendering a balance sheet for publication cannot control its use; but the present attitude is that banks and other creditors or prospective creditors are entitled to much more information than need be given general publicity in the published balance sheet, and that requirements for general balance sheet purposes are satisfied if the current liabilities are detailed as follows:

Accounts payable.
Trade notes payable.
Other notes payable.
Accounts owed to officers, stockholders, and employees.
Notes given to officers, stockholders, and employees.
Accrued liabilities.
Income taxes payable.
Other current liabilities.

The fact that salaries, wages, taxes, or other liabilities may have priority in case of liquidation is given no consideration in the classification of the current liabilities on the balance sheet because the balance sheet is prepared from the standpoint of a going concern.

Theoretically, it is desirable to list the current liabilities in the order of their maturity, but from a practical standpoint this is usually impossible because each class of liability includes debts maturing at different dates.

OPERATING RESERVES, CONTINGENCIES, AND COMMITMENTS

Operating reserves classified as current liabilities. Operating reserves are those which are set up by charges to income to reflect provisions for prospective cash disbursements, the costs of which should be matched against revenues that have been taken into income. If goods are sold with guarantees of performance or with agreements to give free service for a stated period, a proper matching of revenue and expense requires the creation of an operating reserve for the prospective disbursements. Although there may be no present liability to any specific person, and although the amount of the reserve may be an estimate, such reserves are properly shown among the liabilities. The reserve represents a current liability if there is an obligation to make a cash disbursement in the near future.

The word *reserve* has been used above because, although its use in such connections is eschewed for purposes of financial statements, it still is a part of the accountants' working vocabulary.

Liability reserves. It was formerly the custom to use the term *reserve* in a liability account title when the amount of the liability was estimated. Used in this fashion, the word did not imply that the existence of the liability was in any way contingent or unsettled; it merely indicated that the dollar amount of the liability could only be estimated under the existing circumstances.

The account Reserve for Income Tax was an example. There might have been no question about the fact that a given business had an obligation to pay an income tax, but the exact amount of the tax liability might not have been determinable at the time the financial statements were prepared.

As used in this connection, *reserve* was synonymous with *estimate.* It is becoming increasingly common to use the word *estimate* or *estimated* in place of the term *reserve* in all cases where the dollar figure for any liability is an approximation; thus, "Estimated Liability for Federal Income Tax" has been generally substituted for "Reserve for Income Tax."

The term *reserve* was also used when there was an element of uncertainty regarding the existence of a liability. For example, assume that a decision of a lower court resulted in an adverse judgment of a stated amount, thus creating a liability which had to be recognized in the accounts. However, if the case was under appeal at the time the financial statements were prepared, and if there was some prospect that the decision might be reversed or the controversy settled outside of court for a different amount, the term *reserve* was considered appropriate terminology to convey such uncertainty regarding the status of the liability. However, to comply with the recommendation of the Committee on Accounting Procedure that use of reserve terminology be curtailed, some title such as "Judgment Under Appeal" might be used.

Contingent liabilities. A contingent liability exists when there is no present debt but when conditions are such that a liability may develop, usually as the result of an action or default by an outsider. For instance, if a note receivable is discounted, no immediate liability is created, but a contingent liability exists because the maker of the note may default and the endorser may be required to make payment.

The method to be used in reflecting contingent liabilities in the balance sheet depends upon the conditions in each case.

If there is a strong probability that a liability and loss will develop (as might be the case, for instance, if funds are on deposit in a bank in a blocked-exchange country), a loss provision usually would be created by charge to income; accountants who are not advocates of the clean surplus theory might, under some circumstances, consider that a charge to Retained Earnings would be in order. The account thus created might be deducted from the related asset or shown as a liability—usually in the current section.

If the probability of loss is remote but disclosure is nevertheless desirable, the disclosure may be made by the creation of a contingency reserve (appropriation of retained earnings) or by a footnote. The use of footnotes is increasing because the nature and purpose of appropriated surplus reserves are not widely understood and footnotes can be made much more informative.

Some of the more common contingent liabilities, or sources thereof, are mentioned below:

(1) Notes receivable discounted.

The proper procedure for recording the discounting of notes receivable was discussed in Chapter 10. Any estimated liability for prospective payments would be shown under the current classification.

(2) Accounts receivable assigned.

The procedure for recording the assignment of accounts receivable was also discussed in Chapter 10.

(3) Accommodation paper.

A person may become an accommodation party on a promissory note either as a maker or as an endorser. If he signs the note as a maker, he should debit an account with the accommodated party and credit Accommodation Notes Payable. If he signs as an endorser, he should debit an account with the accommodated party and credit Endorser's Liability. These pairs of offsetting accounts should be regarded as memorandum accounts so long as there is no prospect that the accommodating party will have to make payment. If it develops that the accommodating party probably will have to make payment, the credit-balance account should be transferred to a liability account, presumably to be classified as current. If recovery from the accommodated party is a possibility, the debit balance in his account can be shown in the balance sheet as an asset, with an allowance deduction if provision for possible loss should be made.

(4) Lawsuits.

(5) Additional taxes.

No comments in addition to the general introductory remarks in this section seem required in connection with these contingent liabilities.

(6) Guarantees of liabilities of other companies.
One company may guarantee the interest on, or both the principal of and interest on, the bonds of another company, which may or may not be a subsidiary. Any estimated liability set up to reflect prospective payments under the guarantee might be offset by a loss charge, or by a charge to the company whose obligations were assumed.

(7) Mutual insurance.
Although the holders of policies issued by mutual insurance companies are usually subject to assessments, the history of such companies indicates that policyholders are rarely required to pay such assessments; therefore, the contingency is generally regarded by accountants as too remote to require any recognition.

Cumulative preferred dividends in arrears. Arrearages of cumulative preferred dividends are often referred to as contingent liabilities. Strictly speaking, this is a misnomer. Usually, contingent liabilities become real liabilities as the result of an action or default of an outsider; dividend liabilities are created by action of the board of directors. Methods of disclosing preferred dividends in arrears are described in Chapter 6.

Purchase commitments. Losses arising from purchase commitments cannot be ignored in the financial statements. Losses may be forthcoming if prices are declining, although not necessarily, because a business may be protected by hedging operations and contracts to sell products in the future at an established price.

If a loss is clearly in prospect, the amount of the loss should be estimated and deducted in the income statement in arriving at net income. If the amount is significant, it should be separately disclosed in the income statement. The credit offsetting the charge to a loss account is listed among the liabilities under some account title such as "Provision for Losses on Purchase Commitments."

A distinction must be made between losses on purchase commitments which have actually developed and can be measured and mere contingent losses on purchase commitments. The latter may be disclosed, if significant, by mention in a footnote or by setting up a surplus reserve. The surplus thus appropriated should be returned to the Retained Earnings account and may not be used to absorb charges for losses, should they develop.

Contracts for fixed asset acquisitions. If, at the balance sheet date, a company is committed in a material amount on contracts for plant construction or for other fixed asset acquisitions, disclosure should be made in a balance sheet footnote. Although such commitments do not involve prospective losses for which a provision is required, disclosure is important because the use of funds for additions to fixed assets may significantly affect the working capital.

Long-term leases. As noted in the discussion of leased assets in Chapter 19, when rentals on long-term leases are material in amount, disclosure, by supporting schedule or balance sheet footnote, of the annual commitment for rents and the duration of the leases is a minimum requirement. Mention was also made of the case in favor of capitalization for assets held under certain kinds of long-term leases, which would also require the showing of a related liability. To date, however, insufficient support has developed to give this position the general acceptance needed for an accounting principle.

Profit-sharing and pension agreements. The employee profit-sharing and pension plans adopted by business enterprises are too diversified in nature to permit any detailed description of them here. However, two matters require brief consideration.

In order to qualify the plan under the Internal Revenue Code, funds provided by the company and its employees usually are deposited with trustees or paid to insurance companies. The amount of any obligation at the balance sheet date for such deposits or payments should appear in the balance sheet as a liability.

If a pension plan is funded with an insurance company, premiums will be payable to the insurance company annually (or at shorter intervals) in amounts based on the number of employees, their ages, and the amounts of the annuities to be paid to them after retirement. These premiums are chargeable against income in the period in which they accrue, and any premiums accrued at the end of the period should be included in the balance sheet as a liability.

But, in addition, it may be necessary to pay the insurance company the amount of the annuity cost applicable to past services—in other words, an amount in lieu of the premiums which would have been paid to the insurance company from the beginning of each employee's service if the pension plan had been in operation during that period. This past-service annuity cost usually is payable in installments, rather than as a lump sum. In the past, many companies set up a liability account for the full amount of the past-service cost, by charge to Retained Earnings. It was argued that the charge to Retained Earnings was justified as a correction of the earnings of prior periods, on the theory that the past-service annuity cost was an additional cost of services in prior periods. In its Bulletin No. 43, the Institute's Committee on Accounting Procedure said:

> The committee believes that, even though the calculation is based on past service, costs of annuities based on such service are incurred in contemplation of present and future services. . . . The element of past service is one of the important considerations in establishing pension plans, and annuity costs measured by such past service contribute to the benefits gained by the adoption of a plan. . . .
>
> The committee, accordingly, is of the opinion that:
>
> (a) Costs of annuities based on past service should be allocated to current and future periods; however, if they are not sufficiently material in amount

> to distort the results of operations in a single period, they may be absorbed in the current year;
> (b) Costs of annuities based on past service should not be charged to surplus.

The bulletin is silent regarding the number of periods to which the past-service costs should be allocated. In this connection, it is of interest to note that they are deductible for federal income tax purposes over a period of 10 years.

The bulletin is also silent as to whether, when the pension plan is started, an entry should be made debiting a deferred expense account with the full amount of the past-service costs, with an offsetting credit to Cash (if payment is made in full at once) or to a liability account (if payment is to be made in installments). If payment is made in full immediately, such a deferred expense account would seem necessary. If payment is made in installments (the customary procedure), and if each installment is charged to income when payment is made, it might be permissible to omit the deferred expense and liability accounts from the books and the balance sheet, but it would seem essential to make some disclosure of the facts.

General contingency reserves. Reserves for contingencies which are vague, remote, and not susceptible of measurement with respect to the degree of probability that they will ever be required, or with respect to the amount which might ultimately be required, should ordinarily be created, if at all, by appropriations of retained earnings, and not be shown as liabilities.

The Institute's Committee on Accounting Procedure has taken the following position concerning general-purpose contingency reserves:

> General contingency reserves, such as those created:
>
> (a) for general undetermined contingencies, or
> (b) for a wide variety of indefinite possible future losses, or
> (c) without any specific purpose reasonably related to the operations for the current period, or
> (d) in amounts not determined on the basis of any reasonable estimates of costs or losses,
>
> are of such a nature that charges or credits relating to such reserves should not enter into the determination of net income. Hence,
>
> (1) Provisions for such reserves should not be included as charges in determining net income.
> (2) When such a reserve is set up, it should be created preferably by a segregation or appropriation of surplus.
> (3) Costs or losses should not be treated as charges to such reserves, and no part of such a reserve should be transferred to income or in any way used to affect the determination of net income for any year.
> (4) When such a reserve or any part thereof is no longer considered necessary, it should be restored to surplus.

Profit equalization and "budgetary" reserves. Management is sometimes disposed to establish reserves for the purpose of arbitrarily equalizing earnings over a series of years because of a belief that stable earnings add to the attractiveness of a business. Any procedure for arbitrarily and artificially influencing or leveling reported earnings is not acceptable accounting.

The preceding comment relates to annual earnings figures. An accounting procedure adopted to spread an annual expense evenly throughout the year is acceptable without question. Such a procedure is particularly appropriate if monthly or quarterly financial statements are prepared; otherwise, interim income figures would be misleading because certain expenses are not incurred evenly throughout the year. Spreading an annual expense evenly throughout the year may require the use of a "budgetary reserve," the operation of which can be summarized as follows:

(1) An estimate for the year would be made for the particular expense involved in the budgetary reserve procedure.
(2) Each month, one-twelfth of the estimated annual expense would be charged to the appropriate expense account and credited to a budgetary reserve account.
(3) As disbursements were made for the expense involved, they would be charged to the reserve account.
(4) At the end of the year, if the actual expense for the year differed from the estimate, the budgetary reserve account would be adjusted in order that the balance in the expense account would equal the actual expense for the year.

The above procedure can be illustrated by using an example involving vacation pay. Suppose that a company closes its plant for two weeks each August in order that its production employees may take their vacations (with pay) at that time. If the full amount for vacation pay were charged to expense in the month of August, the income statement for that month would be considerably distorted, because payments were made for which services were not received during the month. This distortion can be avoided by making monthly provisions for vacation pay. Assume that the company estimates that the vacation pay will amount to $120,000 for the two-week vacation period. Under these circumstances, the monthly provision would equal $10,000, and the following entry would be appropriate:

Vacation pay expense..	10,000	
Allowance for vacation pay................................		10,000
To set up monthly provision for vacation pay.		

This entry would be repeated each month during the year. Assume further that the disbursement for vacation pay equalled $118,500. This would be recorded as follows:

Allowance for vacation pay....................................	118,500	
Cash		118,500
To record payment of vacation pay allowance.		

At the year-end, because the actual expense was $1,500 less than the estimate, the following adjusting entry would be appropriate:

Allowance for vacation pay	1,500	
Vacation pay expense		1,500
To adjust the budgetary reserve to actual expense.		

On the income statement for the year, Vacation Pay Expense would be reported at $118,500.

The entries for the entire year for the above case are illustrated in the following T-accounts:

Vacation Pay Expense

Debit		Credit	
Jan. Monthly provision	10,000	Dec. Adjustment to bring total of monthly provisions into agreement with actual annual cost for vacation pay	1,500
Feb.	10,000	Dec. Close to Revenue and Expense	118,500
Mar.	10,000		
Apr.	10,000		
May	10,000		
June	10,000		
July	10,000		
Aug.	10,000		
Sept.	10,000		
Oct.	10,000		
Nov.	10,000		
Dec.	10,000		
	120,000		120,000

Allowance for Vacation Pay

Debit		Credit	
Aug. Disbursement	118,500	Jan. Monthly provision	10,000
Dec. Adjustment to bring total of monthly provisions into agreement with actual annual cost for vacation pay	1,500	Feb.	10,000
		Mar.	10,000
		Apr.	10,000
		May	10,000
		June	10,000
		July	10,000
		Aug.	10,000
		Sept.	10,000
		Oct.	10,000
		Nov.	10,000
		Dec.	10,000
	120,000		120,000

Cash

Debit		Credit	
		Aug. Disbursement for vacation pay	118,500

In the above example, notice that during some of the months the Allowance for Vacation Pay account had a debit balance. This is not uncommon. On interim balance sheets, budgetary reserves are presented among the current liabilities if they have credit balances. If they have debit balances, they are presented among the prepaid expenses.

In the preceding example, the objective of the accounting procedure adopted was merely to spread an annual expense evenly throughout the year. A similar procedure is sometimes used in an attempt to achieve more equitable annual charges for certain operating expenses. For example, it may be contended that, if the expense of machinery repairs were spread equally over the years of use, net income would be more precisely measured than if repairs are charged as expense in the years when the repair work is actually performed. This becomes more evident when it is recognized that, typically, repairs are made only when necessary or when the level of operations makes a repair program convenient. Use of a budgetary reserve would avoid the fluctuations that might appear if repair costs were recorded only when repair work was actually undertaken. The use of a budgetary reserve for repairs was discussed on page 289.

Budgetary reserves are acceptable without question when their objective is to spread an annual expense evenly throughout the year. Their use is permitted when the objective, as in the case of a reserve for repairs, is to assign *operating expense charges* to years on a basis that permits more precise income determination than would be achieved under the alternative of recording expense at the time a cash disbursement is made or an obligation is incurred. Their acceptability is questioned by accountants when such reserve techniques are proposed with the intention of equalizing *operating or extraneous losses* by years over a long term. The reason is that reserves of this type are susceptible of becoming, in fact, profit-equalization reserves. The latter are not acceptable, as noted above. But often it is difficult to draw a dividing line between a budgetary reserve and a profit-equalization reserve.

A "Reserves" caption in the balance sheet. The matters discussed in this chapter reveal the difficulties encountered at times in determining the amounts of certain liabilities and in selecting a suitable balance sheet location for some contingent liabilities. A review of published financial statements will show the occasional use of a "Reserves" category located between "Liabilities" and "Stockholders' Equity," and usually comprising contingent-loss provisions. The use of such a category is evidence of the practical difficulty often encountered in determining with reasonable certainty whether some credit-balance accounts represent asset deductions, liabilities, or a part of the stockholders' equity. Practicing accountants not infrequently encounter situations where the probability of a loss is so strong that a stockholders' equity classification of an account provided therefor seems too optimistic; but, on the other hand, no actual impairment of asset values has occurred (so that a deduction from an asset does not seem justified), and no liability exists at the balance sheet date (so that the liability classification does not seem warranted). Under such circumstances, an "in-between" location is sometimes used.

One of the weaknesses associated with the use of a "Reserves" category is that the origin of the reserves located therein is not always clear to the statement user. Furthermore, there is usually no information regarding the nature of the charges that may be made against the reserve accounts thus classified.

Ordinarily the source of a reserve has a direct bearing on its proper location in the balance sheet, as indicated by the following generalizations:

A credit-balance account created by a charge to an expense account should not be classified under "Stockholders' Equity."

Valuation and operating reserves, once having been properly classified, may not be reclassified in subsequent financial statements as part of "Stockholders' Equity." If their credit balances need revision or correction, the necessary adjustment should appear in either the income statement or the statement of retained earnings.

Surplus reserves, once properly classified under "Stockholders' Equity," may not be used to absorb charges for expenses or losses.

Addendum to page 378. The comments on pages 376–378 relative to the treatment, in a refunding transaction, of unamortized discount on refunded bonds and any premium on their retirement, are in accordance with the procedure favored by the Committee on Accounting Procedure as stated in ARB 43, issued in 1953, and in force at the time of publication of this edition. It favored amortization of the above-mentioned costs over the life of the old issue.

In its Opinion 6, issued in October, 1965, the Accounting Principles Board (successor to the Committee) took a different position, stating:

> . . . amortization over the life of the new issue, is appropriate under circumstances where the refunding takes place because of currently lower interest rates or anticipation of higher interest rates in the future. In such circumstances, the expected benefits justify spreading the costs over the life of the new issue, and this method is, therefore, acceptable.

Presumably, if the refinancing took place because of other circumstances, amortization over the life of the old issue would still be preferred.

CHAPTER

21

Interpretation of Accounting Statements

Purpose of interpretation. Accounting statements show the financial position of a business at one or more dates, and the results of its operations for one or more periods. The amount of information that a reader can obtain from such statements depends upon his knowledge of accounting and his training and skills in analyzing and interpreting the statements. This chapter and the two succeeding ones are devoted to developing such skills. The uses of dollar amounts, per cents, and ratios are illustrated.

Vertical analysis—Analytical per cents. Analysis is the process of resolving a thing into its elements, or an examination of the component parts in relation to a whole.

Analytical per cents in a balance sheet may show the relation of each balance sheet item, or significant balance sheet group, to the balance sheet total.

Analytical per cents in an income statement may be based on net sales, as in the following illustration.

THE OSBORNE COMPANY
Income Statement
For the Year Ended December 31, 1965

	Amount	Per Cent of Net Sales
Net sales	$969,065	100.00%
Cost of goods sold	667,940	68.93
Gross profit on sales	$301,125	31.07%
Operating expenses	238,475	24.61
Net operating income	$ 62,650	6.46%
Net financial expense	4,400	.45
Net income before federal income tax	$ 58,250	6.01%
Federal income tax	21,460	2.21
Net income	$ 36,790	3.80%

This statement is an illustration of vertical analysis, which is so called because the per cents are applicable to amounts usually shown in a statement column.

Vertical analysis answers such questions as "Where did the sales dollar go?" About 69 cents went for cost of goods sold, 25 cents for operating expenses, and so on.

Much more information is furnished by vertical analysis of comparative statements.

Comparative statements—Institute's recommendations. Bulletin No. 43 of the Institute's Committee on Accounting Procedure contains the following remarks on the subject of comparative statements:

> 1. The presentation of comparative financial statements in annual and other reports enhances the usefulness of such reports and brings out more clearly the nature and trends of current changes affecting the enterprise. Such presentation emphasizes the fact that statements for a series of periods are far more significant than those for a single period and that the accounts for one period are but an instalment of what is essentially a continuous history.
>
> 2. In any one year it is ordinarily desirable that the balance sheet, the income statement, and the surplus statement be given for one or more preceding years as well as for the current year. Footnotes, explanations, and accountants' qualifications which appeared on the statements for the preceding years should be repeated, or at least referred to, in the comparative statements to the extent that they continue to be of significance. If, because of reclassifications or for other reasons, changes have occurred in the manner of or basis for presenting corresponding items for two or more periods, information should be furnished which will explain the change. This procedure is in conformity with the well recognized principle that any change in practice which affects comparability should be disclosed.

A comparative statement with vertical analysis is shown below.

THE OSBORNE COMPANY
Comparative Income Statement
For the Years Ended December 31, 1965 and 1964

	Year Ended December 31,			
	1965		1964	
	Amount	Per Cent of Net Sales	Amount	Per Cent of Net Sales
Net sales	$969,065	100.00%	$834,880	100.00%
Cost of goods sold	667,940	68.93	553,845	66.34
Gross profit on sales	$301,125	31.07%	$281,035	33.66%
Operating expenses	238,475	24.61	202,235	24.22
Net operating income	$ 62,650	6.46%	$ 78,800	9.44%
Net financial expense	4,400	.45	10,320	1.24
Net income before federal income tax	$ 58,250	6.01%	$ 68,480	8.20%
Federal income tax	21,460	2.21	27,240	3.26
Net income	$ 36,790	3.80%	$ 41,240	4.94%

This statement shows that, although the net sales increased, the cost of goods sold increased from 66.34% of net sales in 1964 to 68.93% in 1965; as a consequence, the rate of gross profit decreased from 33.66% in 1964 to 31.07% in 1965. To make matters worse, the increase in operating expenses was out of proportion to the increase in sales, the operating expenses being 24.61% of net sales in 1965 compared with 24.22% in 1964. The decrease in net financial expense was a helpful change, but it was not enough to prevent a very considerable decrease in the amount of net income before federal income tax and its per cent of net sales.

A comparison of the analytical per cents in a series of statements may be helpful in disclosing trends. However, a word of caution is in order. A change in the per cent of one item to another may be caused by a change in either item or in both. Therefore, before a change in an analytical per cent can be judged to be good or bad, the cause or causes of the change must be known. For instance, the preceding statement showed an increase in the cost of goods sold from 66.34% to 68.93% of net sales; but to what extent was the change in the per cent caused by a change in the sales volume, how much was caused by a change in sales prices, and how much was caused by changes in the unit cost of goods sold?

Horizontal analysis. Horizontal analysis is so called because it deals with relationships between amounts usually shown on the same line of a statement. An illustration appears below. Only a partial income statement is presented; it is sufficient to illustrate the procedure.

THE OSBORNE COMPANY

Partial Comparative Income Statement
For the Years Ended December 31, 1965 and 1964

	Year Ended December 31,		Increase-Decrease*		Ratio 1965-1964
	1965	1964	Amount	Per Cent	
Net sales	$969,065	$834,880	$134,185	16.07%	1.16
Cost of goods sold	667,940	553,845	114,095	20.60	1.21
Gross profit on sales	$301,125	$281,035	$ 20,090	7.15	1.07
Operating expenses	238,475	202,235	36,240	17.92	1.18
Net operating income	$ 62,650	$ 78,800	$ 16,150*	20.49*	.80

Per cents of increase and decrease; ratios. The difference in the procedure of stating per cents of increase-decrease* and ratios is indicated below, using figures not taken from the preceding statement.

Amounts		Increase-Decrease*	Per Cent Increase-Decrease*	Ratio 1965 to 1964
1965	1964			
$ –	$100	$ 100*	100%*	0
125	100	25	25	1.25
60	100	40*	40*	.60
1,500	100	1,400	1,400	15.00

Ratios are less commonly used than per cents of increase and decrease; however, ratios have certain advantages. The Per Cent of Increase-Decrease* column requires the use of red ink for decreases, or the indicating of decreases in some manner such as *100** or (*100*), and the distinction must be constantly recognized. Ratios avoid these disadvantages. Perhaps most important of all, it is difficult for many people to grasp quickly the significance of large per cents, such as a 1,400% increase; it is much easier to understand that one item is 15 times as large as the other item.

Negative amounts—Computing increases and decreases. A negative amount is one which, when appearing in a column of figures, is deducted from the positive items. When negative items appear in a statement, care must be exercised in determining the amount to be shown in the Increase-Decrease* column, and in determining whether this amount should be shown as an increase or a decrease. Some typical cases are illustrated below. Negative amounts are indicated by #.

Item	This Year	Last Year	Increase-Decrease*
A	$3,000	$2,800	$ 200
B	500	800	300*
C	200#	1,000	1,200*
D	200	300#	500
E	1,000#	800#	200*
F	500#	800#	300
Total	$2,000	$2,700	$ 700*

Items shown as increases tend to cause the total of the This Year column to be greater than the total of the Last Year column. Items shown as decreases tend to cause the total of the This Year column to be less than the total of the Last Year column.

Computation of increases, decreases, per cents, and ratios. Following are illustrations of some problems that arise in the determination of increases and decreases, and the computation of related per cents and ratios.

	This Year	Last Year	Increase-Decrease*		Ratio This Year to Last Year
			Amount	Per Cent	
Positive amounts last year:					
A	$1,500	$1,000	$ 500	50%	1.50
B	500	1,000	500*	50*	.50
C	—	1,000	1,000*	100*	0.00
D	500#	1,000	1,500*	150*	—
No amounts last year:					
E	1,500	—	1,500	—	—
F	500#	—	500*	—	—
Negative amounts last year:					
G	1,500#	1,000#	500*	—	—
H	500	1,000#	1,500	—	—
I	—	1,000#	1,000	—	—

The computation of the per cents in A, B, C, and D and the ratios in A, B, and C are obvious; no ratio can be computed for D because there is no ratio relationship between a negative and a positive number. No per cents or ratios can be computed in the second group because no amounts are shown in the Last Year column. And none can be computed for the third group because the Last Year amounts were negative quantities.

Horizontal analysis of more than two statements. If comparative statements show data for more than two periods or at more than two dates, there are two bases for computing increases and decreases.

(1) Comparisons may be made with data for the immediately preceding period or date, thus:

THE A COMPANY

Comparative Income Statement
For the Years Ended December 31, 1965, 1964, and 1963

	Year Ended December 31,			Increase-Decrease*	
	1965	1964	1963	1965-1964	1964-1963
Gross sales	$780,000	$600,000	$800,000	$180,000	$200,000*

(2) Comparisons may be made with data for the earliest date or period, thus:

THE A COMPANY

Comparative Income Statement
For the Years Ended December 31, 1965, 1964, and 1963

	Year Ended December 31,			Increase-Decrease*	
	1965	1964	1963	1965-1963	1964-1963
Gross sales	$780,000	$600,000	$800,000	$20,000*	$200,000*

If price levels have changed materially, the choice of a base date or period too far in the past may distort the comparisons, because changes in amounts may have been caused principally by changes in the purchasing power of the dollar.

If a statement shows dollar increases and decreases based on the data for the immediately preceding date or period, considerations of consistency only would suggest that per cents of increase and decrease or ratios also be based on the data for the immediately preceding date or period, thus:

THE A COMPANY

Comparative Income Statement
For the Years Ended December 31, 1965, 1964, and 1963

				Increase-Decrease*			
				1965-1964		1964-1963	
	Year Ended December 31,				Per		Per
	1965	1964	1963	Amount	Cent	Amount	Cent
Gross sales	$780,000	$600,000	$800,000	$180,000	30%	$200,000*	25%*

But the danger of confusion outweighs the considerations of consistency. The above statement indicates a 25% decrease in sales in 1964 and a 30% increase in 1965. Consideration of these per cents alone would result in an incorrect conclusion that the increase in 1965 had more than offset the decrease in 1964. The confusion arises, of course, from the fact that the per cents are computed on two different bases: the per cent of decrease in 1964 is computed on a base of $800,000, whereas the per cent of increase in 1965 is computed on a base of $600,000.

Therefore, in cases similar to this, it seems desirable to compute the per cents of increase and decrease or the ratios on the basis of data for the earliest date or period, thus:

THE A COMPANY
Comparative Income Statement
For the Years Ended December 31, 1965, 1964, and 1963

	Year Ended December 31,			Increase-Decrease* 1965-1963		1964-1963	
	1965	1964	1963	Amount	Per Cent	Amount	Per Cent
Gross sales	$780,000	$600,000	$800,000	$20,000*	2.5%*	$200,000*	25.0%*

Significance of horizontal analysis. It has been pointed out that vertical-analysis per cents may result in misleading conclusions because the percentage change in an item may be caused by a change in the amount of the item, or by a change in the amount of the base, or by changes in both. Horizontal-analysis per cents and ratios are not subject to this objection because they are affected by changes in the item only.

Horizontal analysis is useful in disclosing balance sheet trends and relationships. For instance, refer to the balance sheet on pages 398 and 399, and observe the per cents of increase, particularly in receivables, inventories, and accounts payable. But also observe the relationship between these per cents and the per cent of increase in net sales shown at the bottom of the balance sheet. The following question immediately arises: With a 16.07% increase in net sales, are a 33.20% increase in accounts receivable, a 19.88% increase in finished goods, and a 9.12% increase in accounts payable indicative of an unfavorable condition and trend?

Horizontal analysis of the income statement is also useful. Refer to the income statement on page 400 and observe that, with a 1.16 ratio of 1965 to 1964 sales, the cost of goods sold ratio is 1.21, with the result that the gross profit ratio is only 1.07. Furthermore, the operating expense ratio is 1.18, with the result that the net operating income ratio is .80.

An increase or decrease cannot be interpreted as desirable or undesirable until its cause is known. An increase in inventories may be advantageous if stocks have previously been inadequate, or if heavy purchases have been made against a rising market or in anticipation of a period when goods will not be available. On the other hand, an increase in inventories may have resulted from unwise purchasing policies or from a decline in sales. An increase in receivables may have resulted from an increase in sales or from an increase in delinquent accounts.

The reliability of horizontal-analysis per cents and ratios may be affected by changes in price levels. For instance, a 19.88% increase in the finished goods inventory does not necessarily mean a 19.88% quantity increase. It may be due wholly to cost increases; in fact, cost increases may more than offset a quantity decrease.

Monthly comparative and cumulative statements. Statements are sometimes prepared for management purposes showing:

The results of operations for the current month, and for the same month of the preceding year;
The results of operations for the year to date, and for the corresponding period of the preceding year.

Such comparisons of operations by months may not be wholly satisfactory because of variations in the calendar; the same months in different years may not be strictly comparable because of differences in the number of Sundays, or because holidays may fall on Sundays in one month and on business days in another, with a consequent difference in the number of business days.

If comparisons are made of the operations of different months in the same year, there is the additional disturbing factor of differences in the number of days in a month.

Comprehensive illustrative statements. The statements on the following pages more fully illustrate the procedures discussed on the preceding pages, and provide data for the subsequent discussion of other methods of statement interpretation.

In the statement of cost of goods manufactured and sold on page 401, the analytical per cents are based on the total cost of manufacturing.

Analytical per cents might have been included in the supporting schedules. The per cents for each schedule usually are computed on the same base used in the statement it supports.

MISCELLANEOUS RATIOS

Equity ratios. Three equity ratios, based on data of The Osborne Company, are computed below:

		December 31,		
		1965	1964	1963
Total assets	(a)	$782,800	$749,790	$789,020
Total liabilities	(b)	273,650	319,030	349,700
Stockholders' equity	(c)	$509,150	$430,760	$439,320
Ratio of total liabilities to total assets (b ÷ a)		.35	.43	.44
Ratio of stockholders' equity to total assets (c ÷ a)		.65	.57	.56
Ratio of stockholders' equity to total liabilities (c ÷ b)		1.86	1.35	1.26

(*Continued on page 403.*)

Exhibit A

THE OSBORNE COMPANY
Balance Sheets
December 31, 1965, 1964, and 1963

Assets	1965			1964			Increase-Decrease* 1965–1964		1963
	Amount	Per Cent of Total	Per Cent of Group	Amount	Per Cent of Total	Per Cent of Group	Amount	Per Cent	
Current assets:									
Cash	$ 22,360	2.85%	5.76%	$ 21,085	2.81%	6.36%	$ 1,275	6.05%	$ 10,740
Accounts receivable	$215,420			$168,845			$ 46,575		$239,240
Less allowance for doubtful accounts	11,065			15,430			4,365*		30,095
Net	$204,355	26.11	52.61	$153,415	20.46	46.27	$ 50,940	33.20	$209,145
Notes receivable	$ 34,050	4.35	8.77	$ 41,600	5.55	12.55	$ 7,550*	18.15*	$ 50,095
Inventories:									
Finished goods	$ 50,710	6.48	13.05	$ 42,300	5.64	12.76	$ 8,410	19.88	$ 37,150
Goods in process	30,260	3.86	7.79	24,860	3.32	7.50	5,400	21.72	17,650
Materials	33,430	4.27	8.61	37,050	4.94	11.17	3,620*	9.77*	25,260
Total	$114,400			$104,210			$ 10,190	9.78	$ 80,060
Supplies	$ 5,995	.77	1.54	$ 4,710	.63	1.42	$ 1,285	27.28	$ 4,280
Unexpired insurance	$ 7,270	.93	1.87	$ 6,540	.87	1.97	$ 730	11.16	$ 6,280
Total current assets	$388,430	49.62%	100.00%	$331,560	44.22%	100.00%	$ 56,870	17.15	$360,600

Fixed assets:									
Land	$ 30,500	3.90%	7.79%	$ 30,500	4.07%	7.36%	$ —	—	$ 30,500
Buildings	$193,000			$193,000			$ —	—	$193,000
Less accumulated depreciation	65,110			59,320			5,790	9.76	53,530
Net	$127,890	16.34	32.68	$133,680	17.83	32.25	$ 5,790*	4.33*	$139,470
Machinery and equipment	$349,680			$349,515			$ 165	.05	$334,790
Less accumulated depreciation	116,700			99,215			17,485	17.62	81,740
Net	$232,980	29.76	59.53	$250,300	33.38	60.39	$ 17,320*	6.92*	$253,050
Total fixed assets	$391,370	50.00%	100.00%	$414,480	55.28%	100.00%	$ 23,110*	5.58*	$423,020
Deferred charges:									
Unamortized bond discount	$ 3,000	.38%		$ 3,750	.50%		$ 750*	20.00*	$ 5,400
	$782,800	100.00%		$749,790	100.00%		$ 33,010	4.40	$789,020
Liabilities and Stockholders' Equity									
Current liabilities:									
Bank loans	$ 30,000	3.83%	24.26%	$ 80,000	10.67%	47.33%	$ 50,000*	62.50%*	$ 85,000
Accounts payable	58,215	7.44	47.08	53,350	7.11	31.56	4,865	9.12	64,210
Accrued taxes and expenses	35,435	4.53	28.66	35,680	4.76	21.11	245*	.69*	20,490
Total current liabilities	$123,650	15.80%	100.00%	$169,030	22.54%	100.00%	$ 45,380*	26.85*	$169,700
First mortgage, 4% bonds	150,000	19.16		150,000	20.01		—		180,000
Total liabilities	$273,650	34.96%		$319,030	42.55%		$ 45,380*	14.22*	$349,700
Stockholders' equity:									
Preferred stock—7%	$ 75,000	9.58%	14.73%	$120,000	16.01%	27.86%	$ 45,000*	37.50*	$140,000
Common stock	375,000	47.90	73.65	200,000	26.67	46.43	175,000	87.50	200,000
Retained earnings	59,150	7.56	11.62	110,760	14.77	25.71	51,610*	46.60*	99,320
Total stockholders' equity	$509,150	65.04%	100.00%	$430,760	57.45%	100.00%	$ 78,390	18.20	$439,320
	$782,800	100.00%		$749,790	100.00%		$ 33,010	4.40	$789,020
Net sales	$969,065			$834,880			$134,185	16.07	

Exhibit B

THE OSBORNE COMPANY

Statement of Income and Retained Earnings

For the Years Ended December 31, 1965, 1964, and 1963

	Year Ended December 31,				1965-1964		Year Ended December 31, 1963
	1965		1964				
	Amount	Per Cent of Net Sales	Amount	Per Cent of Net Sales	Increase-Decrease*	Ratio	
Gross sales	$992,580	102.43%	$853,795	102.27%	$138,785	1.16	$938,055
Deduct:							
Sales returns and allowances	$ 3,280	.34%	$ 3,175	.38%	$ 105	1.03	$ 4,690
Sales discounts	20,235	2.09	15,740	1.89	4,495	1.29	22,360
Total	$ 23,515	2.43%	$ 18,915	2.27%	$ 4,600	1.24	$ 27,050
Net sales	$969,065	100.00%	$834,880	100.00%	$134,185	1.16	$911,005
Deduct cost of goods sold—Exhibit C	667,940	68.93	553,845	66.34	114,095	1.21	612,455
Gross profit on sales	$301,125	31.07%	$281,035	33.66%	$ 20,090	1.07	$298,550
Operating expenses—Schedule 1	238,475	24.61	202,235	24.22	36,240	1.18	245,445
Net operating income	$ 62,650	6.46%	$ 78,800	9.44%	$ 16,150*	.80	$ 53,105
Net financial expense—Schedule 2	4,400	.45	10,320	1.24	5,920*	.43	9,440
Net income before federal income tax	$ 58,250	6.01%	$ 68,480	8.20%	$ 10,230*	.85	$ 43,665
Federal income tax	21,460	2.21	27,240	3.26	5,780*	.79	17,200
Net income	$ 36,790	3.80%	$ 41,240	4.94%	$ 4,450*	.89	$ 26,465
Retained earnings, January 1	110,760		99,320				118,255
Total	$147,550		$140,560				$144,720
Dividends:							
Preferred	$ 8,400		$ 9,800				$ 15,400
Common	80,000		20,000				30,000
Total	$ 88,400		$ 29,800				$ 45,400
Retained earnings, December 31	$ 59,150		$110,760				$ 99,320

Exhibit C

THE OSBORNE COMPANY

Statement of Cost of Goods Manufactured and Sold
For the Years Ended December 31, 1965, 1964, and 1963

	Year Ended December 31,				
	1965		1964		1963
	Amount	Per Cent of Cost of Manufacturing	Amount	Per Cent of Cost of Manufacturing	
Materials:					
Inventory—beginning of year	$ 37,050		$ 25,260		$ 42,750
Purchases	$286,380		$204,960		$184,750
Deduct:					
Purchase returns and allowances	$ 2,960		$ 3,280		$ 2,470
Purchase discounts	7,420		4,400		5,980
Total	$ 10,380		$ 7,680		$ 8,450
Net purchases	$276,000		$197,280		$176,300
Total inventory and purchases	$313,050		$222,540		$219,050
Deduct inventory—end of year	33,430		37,050		25,260
Cost of materials used	$279,620	41.01%	$185,490	32.76%	$193,790
Direct labor	252,170	36.99	254,905	45.02	259,195
Manufacturing overhead—Schedule 1	149,960	22.00	125,810	22.22	136,280
Total cost of manufacturing	$681,750	100.00%	$566,205	100.00%	$589,265
Goods in process—beginning of year	24,860		17,650		28,600
Total	$706,610		$583,855		$617,865
Goods in process—end of year	30,260		24,860		17,650
Cost of goods manufactured	$676,350		$558,995		$600,215
Finished goods—beginning of year	42,300		37,150		49,390
Total	$718,650		$596,145		$649,605
Finished goods—end of year	50,710		42,300		37,150
Cost of goods sold	$667,940		$553,845		$612,455

THE OSBORNE COMPANY
Schedule of Operating Expenses
For the Years Ended December 31, 1965, 1964, and 1963

Exhibit B
Schedule 1

	Year Ended December 31, 1965	1964	1963
Salesmen's salaries	$ 32,465	$ 31,830	$ 39,120
Traveling expense	20,310	14,615	27,095
Advertising	31,375	25,600	34,780
Branch office expense	23,050	21,645	32,610
Dealer service	25,700	24,810	17,065
Transportation out	20,080	15,700	20,810
Officers' salaries	25,000	20,000	20,000
Office salaries	13,750	9,840	12,810
Rent	4,000	4,000	5,000
Stationery and supplies	3,600	2,465	2,800
Telephone and telegraph	4,680	2,910	2,870
Bad debts	8,625	8,295	13,650
Legal and auditing	6,410	3,330	3,650
Miscellaneous	19,430	17,195	13,185
Total	$238,475	$202,235	$245,445

THE OSBORNE COMPANY
Schedule of Net Financial Expense
For the Years Ended December 31, 1965, 1964, and 1963

Exhibit B
Schedule 2

	Year Ended December 31, 1965	1964	1963
Financial expense:			
Bond interest	$ 6,000	$ 7,200	$ 8,000
Amortization of bond discount	750	900	1,000
Other interest	3,075	5,150	5,940
Total	$ 9,825	$ 13,250	$ 14,940
Financial income:			
Interest earned	$ 4,030	$ 2,810	$ 4,160
Miscellaneous	1,395	120	1,340
Total	$ 5,425	$ 2,930	$ 5,500
Net financial expense	$ 4,400	$ 10,320	$ 9,440

THE OSBORNE COMPANY
Schedule of Manufacturing Overhead
For the Years Ended December 31, 1965, 1964, and 1963

Exhibit C
Schedule 1

	Year Ended December 31, 1965	1964	1963
Indirect labor	$ 31,950	$ 23,600	$ 29,310
Superintendence	12,900	7,250	10,840
Heat, light, and power	25,100	15,650	17,150
Repairs and maintenance	21,575	24,700	23,040
Depreciation:			
Buildings	5,790	5,790	5,790
Machinery and equipment	17,485	17,475	16,740
Insurance	4,860	4,255	4,110
Taxes	7,350	6,400	6,500
Supplies	19,260	16,810	16,710
Miscellaneous	3,690	3,880	6,090
Total	$149,960	$125,810	$136,280

These ratios serve as an indication of long-term solvency; the working capital ratio is a measure of short-term solvency.

A low ratio of liabilities to assets, a high ratio of stockholders' equity to assets, and a high ratio of stockholders' equity to total liabilities all express the same condition, namely, a relatively large cushion of security to the creditors, and therefore they are regarded favorably by creditors. From the creditors' standpoint, the changes in the ratios from 1963 to 1965 indicate an improvement.

From the stockholders' standpoint, the changes in the ratios may not be wholly desirable. From the stockholders' standpoint, it is desirable to maintain a sufficient equity to safeguard the company's credit; beyond that point, an increase in the ratio of equity to assets or equity to liabilities may be disadvantageous. Within limits of safety, it is advantageous to the stockholders for a company to "trade on the equity"; in other words, it is advantageous, to the greatest extent practicable, to use interest-free creditors' funds or funds obtained by borrowing at a rate lower than the rate of income which can be earned by the use of the funds. To illustrate: Assume that a company needs $100,000 worth of assets; if the stockholders invest the entire amount and the company earns a net income of $8,000 (after income taxes at an assumed rate of 20%), the income will be 8% of the investment; but if the stockholders invest only $60,000 and the company borrows $40,000 at 5%, the net income will be $6,400, as shown below, and the rate of income on the $60,000 of stockholders' equity will be 10⅔%.

Net income before interest and income taxes	$10,000
Interest expense	2,000
Net income before income taxes	$ 8,000
Income taxes (at the assumed rate of 20%)	1,600
Net income	$ 6,400

Incidentally, the higher the income tax rate, the greater is the leverage effect of borrowing.

If the working capital ratio has improved between two dates, it may be desirable to compare the equity ratios at the two dates. An increase in the working capital ratio may have been caused by profitable operations, which presumably would also cause an improvement in the equity ratios; improvements caused by operations might be expected to continue. But the working capital position might have been improved by converting a portion of the current liabilities into funded debt, which would not cause any improvement in the equity ratios; the question would then naturally arise whether the improved working capital position could be maintained or whether the working capital might again become impaired.

Ratio of security to long-term liabilities. The long-term liabilities are usually secured by mortgages on fixed assets, and the mortgage holders are interested in the ratio of the security to the liability. If obtainable, market values of the mortgaged properties should be used in the computation; if these values are not available, depreciated book values may be used, as in the following computation, which is based on the assumption that the bonds of The Osborne Company are secured by a mortgage on *all of the fixed assets.*

		December 31,		
		1965	1964	1963
Land		$ 30,500	$ 30,500	$ 30,500
Buildings—cost less accumulated depreciation		127,890	133,680	139,470
Machinery and equipment—cost less accumulated depreciation		232,980	250,300	253,050
Total	(a)	$391,370	$414,480	$423,020
Long-term liabilities	(b)	$150,000	$150,000	$180,000
Ratio of security to long-term liabilities (a ÷ b)		2.61	2.76	2.35

The ratio of security to long-term liabilities is significant not only from the standpoint of measuring the protection against the outstanding debt, but also because it is indicative of the available sources of additional funds. If the mortgage obligations are low in relation to fixed assets, additional funds may be obtainable on the same security; on the other hand, if the properties are already mortgaged to their limit, any additional funds required will have to be obtained from other sources.

If a sinking fund is being maintained for the redemption of a long-term liability, the method of computing the ratio of security to debt will depend upon the nature of the sinking fund. To illustrate, assume that a company has a long-term liability of $500,000, a sinking fund of $100,000, and mortgaged fixed assets of $700,000.

If the sinking fund is invested in the company's own bonds, which are being held alive until their maturity, the ratio should be computed as follows:

Fixed assets	(a)	$700,000
Bonds outstanding ($500,000 minus $100,000 in the fund)	(b)	400,000
Ratio of security to bonds outstanding (a ÷ b)		1.75

But if the sinking fund is invested in other securities, the ratio should be computed as follows:

Fixed assets		$700,000
Sinking fund		100,000
Total	(a)	$800,000
Bonds outstanding	(b)	500,000
Ratio of security to bonds outstanding (a ÷ b)		1.60

Income available for bond interest. Bondholders are interested in the debtor company's earnings as well as in the mortgaged security, because current income is the normal source of the funds required for the payment of bond interest. Because the bond interest is a claim against revenue which takes precedence over income taxes, and because the earnings available for bond interest are, of course, the earnings before bond interest, the bond interest and income taxes are added to the net income in the following computation.

		Year Ended December 31,		
		1965	1964	1963
Net income		$36,790	$41,240	$26,465
Add: Bond interest	(a)	6,000	7,200	8,000
Federal income tax		21,460	27,240	17,200
Net income before bond interest and income tax	(b)	$64,250	$75,680	$51,665
Number of times bond interest earned (b ÷ a)		10.71	10.51	6.46

Because all charges against income, including bond interest and income taxes, take precedence over dividends on any class of stock, the relation of earnings to preferred dividend requirements is computed by dividing the net income by the amount required to pay dividends on the preferred stock at the preference rate.

Ratio of stockholders' equity to fixed assets. Is there a tendency toward overinvestment in fixed assets? To obtain a partial answer, we may compute the ratio of stockholders' equity to fixed assets.

		December 31,		
		1965	1964	1963
Stockholders' equity	(a)	$509,150	$430,760	$439,320
Fixed assets less accumulated depreciation	(b)	391,370	414,480	423,020
Ratio of stockholders' equity to fixed assets less accumulated depreciation (a ÷ b)		1.30	1.04	1.04

Ratio of sales to fixed assets. Additional light can be thrown on the question of possible overinvestment in fixed assets by computing the ratio of sales to fixed assets:

		1965	1964	1963
Net sales for the year	(a)	$969,065	$834,880	$911,005
Fixed assets less accumulated depreciation—end of year	(b)	391,370	414,480	423,020
Ratio of net sales to fixed assets less accumulated depreciation (a ÷ b)		2.48	2.01	2.15

Ratio of sales to stockholders' equity. Other things being equal, the higher the ratio of sales to stockholders' equity, the greater the rate of income earned on the stockholders' equity. If, for instance, two concerns have sales of $100,000 and net income of $5,000, while one has a stockholders' equity of $50,000 and the other has a stockholders' equity of $100,000, the ratios are as follows:

		Company *A*	Company *B*
Sales	(a)	$100,000	$100,000
Net income	(b)	5,000	5,000
Stockholders' equity	(c)	100,000	50,000
Ratio of sales to stockholders' equity (a ÷ c)		1 to 1	2 to 1
Ratio of net income to stockholders' equity (b ÷ c)		5%	10%

This illustration makes apparent the fact that high ratios of sales to stockholders' equity tend to increase the rate of income. However, exceptionally high ratios may be undesirable, because they may merely indicate that the company is in an overextended position, doing a larger volume of business than it has the capital to carry safely.

The Osborne Company's ratios are computed below:

		1965	1964	1963
Sales	(a)	$992,580	$853,795	$938,055
Stockholders' equity—end of year	(b)	509,150	430,760	439,320
Ratio of sales to stockholders' equity (a ÷ b)		1.95	1.98	2.14

Ratio of cost of goods manufactured to fixed assets. Ratios of sales to fixed assets are affected by the profit on the sales, an element which should be eliminated in a determination of the relative use made of the fixed assets in production. For this reason, it is preferable to use the cost of goods manufactured instead of the sales. Ratios based on the cost of manufacture will still include the disturbing element of variation in manufacturing costs due to changes in the price level.

		1965	1964	1963
Cost of goods manufactured	(a)	$676,350	$558,995	$600,215
Fixed assets less accumulated depreciation—end of year	(b)	391,370	414,480	423,020
Ratio of cost of goods manufactured to fixed assets less accumulated depreciation (a ÷ b)		1.73	1.35	1.42

The operating ratio. Usually this ratio is computed by dividing the total operating costs by the net sales. Operating costs include the cost of goods sold and selling and administrative expenses; excluded are financial expense, unusual and nonrecurring items, and income taxes.

		1965	1964	1963
Operating costs	(a)	$906,415	$756,080	$857,900
Net sales for the year	(b)	969,065	834,880	911,005
Operating ratio (a ÷ b)		.935	.906	.942

The operating ratio is considered a measure of efficiency: the smaller the ratio, the better; but of most significance is its trend.

Book value per share of stock. An increase in the total capital stock and retained earnings of a company indicates that the aggregate stockholders' equity has increased, but this does not necessarily mean an increase in the book value of the individual stockholdings; the increase in the stockholders' equity may have been caused by the issuance of additional stock. It is therefore desirable to determine the book value of each share of stock.

If there is only one class of stock, the book value per share is computed by dividing the total stockholders' equity (capital stock and retained earnings, including all appropriated surplus reserves) by the number of shares of stock outstanding. If common and preferred stocks are outstanding, the question arises concerning the apportionment of the retained earnings between the two classes of stock. This matter is discussed at length in Chapter 7.

On the assumption that the preferred stock of The Osborne Company is nonparticipating and that no dividends were in arrears, its book value is par, and the book value per share of the common stock is computed as follows:

		December 31,		
		1965	1964	1963
Common stock		$375,000	$200,000	$200,000
Retained earnings		59,150	110,760	99,320
Total	(a)	$434,150	$310,760	$299,320
Number of shares outstanding	(b)	3,750	2,000	2,000
Book value per share (a ÷ b)		$ 115.77	$ 155.38	$ 149.66

It will be noted that, although the total of the common stock and retained earnings increased during 1965, the book value per share of common stock decreased because of the issuance of 1,750 additional shares.

Ratio of net income to stockholders' equity. The computation of the ratio of net income to stockholders' equity follows.

		1965	1964	1963
Stockholders' equity—end of year:				
Capital stock:				
Preferred—7%		$ 75,000	$120,000	$140,000
Common		375,000	200,000	200,000
Retained earnings		59,150	110,760	99,320
Total stockholders' equity	(a)	$509,150	$430,760	$439,320
Net income for the year	(b)	$ 36,790	$ 41,240	$ 26,465
Ratio of net income to stockholders' equity (b ÷ a)		7.23%	9.57%	6.02%

Depending upon the date of issuance of the additional shares, it may be more accurate to determine the ratio of income by using the average stockholders' equity for the year, thus:

		1965	1964	1963
Stockholders' equity:				
Beginning of year		$430,760	$439,320	$488,255
End of year		509,150	430,760	439,320
Average	(a)	$469,955	$435,040	$463,788
Net income	(b)	$ 36,790	$ 41,240	$ 26,465
Ratio of net income to average stockholders' equity (b ÷ a)		7.83%	9.48%	5.71%

If a considerable portion of the capital is invested in securities or other properties not closely associated with operations, it may be desirable to compute two income ratios: First, an over-all ratio of net income to stockholders' equity; second, an operating income ratio computed by dividing net income exclusive of income on nonoperating assets by the stockholders' equity minus investments in nonoperating assets.

Ratio of net income to total assets. Another earnings ratio is computed by dividing the net income by the total assets.

		1965	1964	1963
Net income for the year	(a)	$ 36,790	$ 41,240	$ 26,465
Total assets—end of year	(b)	782,800	749,790	789,020
Ratio of net income to total assets (a ÷ b)		4.70%	5.50%	3.35%

This ratio is useful in comparing businesses with different capital (stock and bond) structures. Also, this ratio may prove informative in preparing historical analyses in those cases where a business has had one or more significant changes in its capital structure, such as bonds converted to stock.

Earnings per share. Earnings-per-share data are frequently included in annual reports to stockholders and are widely circulated through publications dealing with business conditions and the stock market. Ordinarily the data relate to the common shares. Although extensively quoted with reference to market prices of shares of stock, it is a statistic of questionable value.

In computing earnings per share, the amount reported as net income is used, except in cases where deductions therefrom must be made for dividends, paid or cumulative, on preferred shares. As a general rule, the number of common shares outstanding at year end is used; however, if the number of outstanding shares has increased significantly during the year as a result of the raising of additional capital, it is considered preferable to base the computation on a weighted average of the shares outstanding during the period. To illustrate, assume that the 1,750 additional shares of common stock of The Osborne Company were issued for cash on November 1, 1965. The weighted average of outstanding common shares would be computed as follows:

2,000 shares outstanding for 10 months =	20,000
3,750 shares outstanding for 2 months =	7,500
Total	27,500

27,500 ÷ 12 = 2,292 weighted-average number of shares.

The earnings-per-share data for The Osborne Company are shown below:

		1965	1964	1963
Net income for the year		$36,790	$41,240	$26,465
Deduct dividend paid at the 7% preference rate on preferred stock		8,400	9,800	15,400
Net income applicable to common stock	(a)	$28,390	$31,440	$11,065
Shares of common stock outstanding at end of year	(b)		2,000	2,000
Weighted average of shares outstanding during year	(b)	2,292		
Earnings per share (a ÷ b)		$ 12.39	$ 15.72	$ 5.53

When the change in the number of shares outstanding is the result of a stock dividend or a stock split during the year, the computation should be based on the number of shares outstanding at the end of the period.

Distortions in ratios. Comparisons of the ratios of one company with those of another or with composites of numerous companies should be made with great caution. Differences in accounting methods applied by different businesses may cause differences in ratios, and these variations may be more apparent than real. Different classifications of charges to expense accounts, different procedures of providing for depreciation, different bases of inventory and fixed asset valuations, differences in financing methods, arbitrary decisions as to whether distributions to the proprietorship group shall be made in the form of salaries, bonuses, or dividends, and innumerable other possibilities of diverse treatment of similar matters can affect the ratios to an extent that may make any conclusions based upon them very misleading.

To a less extent the same caution is in order with respect to comparing the ratios of the same business for several years. Changes in accounting or administrative policies may affect the ratios, and the basic financial condition or operating results may not be affected to the extent indicated. Moreover, changes in price levels and the purchasing power of the dollar may cause misleading conclusions to be drawn from a comparison of ratios for a series of years.

Income taxes and income ratios. In the computation of the ratios of net income to sales or any other base, should the net income used be the amount after or before the deduction of federal income taxes? Looking at the results of operations for one year only, it seems preferable to use an income figure after the deduction of income taxes, because the remainder is the amount which accrues to the benefit of the stockholders. But because of the wide fluctuation in tax rates over a period of time, it may be preferable in statements showing comparative data for several years to use an income figure computed before the deduction of income taxes; this procedure eliminates the fluctuation in ratios due to tax requirements over which the management has no control, and thus tends to bring out more clearly the fluctuation in ratios resulting from conditions which the management presumably has power to regulate.

STATEMENT OF CHANGE IN STOCKHOLDERS' EQUITY AND NET ASSETS

The following statements co-ordinate information shown by the income and retained earnings statements with information shown by the comparative balance sheet.

First illustration—Increase in stockholders' equity and net assets. The statement on page 410 and its supporting schedules on pages 410 and 411 show an increase in stockholders' equity and net assets.

Second illustration—Decrease in stockholders' equity and net assets. The statement on page 411 shows a decrease in stockholders' equity and net assets. Supporting schedules would be similar in form to those previously illustrated.

Third illustration—Statement covering two years. In a statement covering a series of years, it is not convenient to detail the elements of stockholders' equity in columns at the head of the statement; observe the alternative procedure in the statement on page 412.

Statements for first illustration:

THE OSBORNE COMPANY

Statement Accounting for Increase in Stockholders' Equity and Resulting Increase in Net Assets

Year Ended December 31, 1965

Increase (decrease*) in stockholders' equity:

	Capital Stock		Retained	
	Preferred	Common	Earnings	Total
Changes in capital stock:				
Preferred stock retired	$45,000*			$ 45,000*
Common stock issued for cash		$175,000		175,000
Net income			$ 36,790	36,790
Cash dividends paid:				
Preferred			8,400*	8,400*
Common			80,000*	80,000*
Net increase (decrease*)	$45,000*	$175,000	$ 51,610*	$ 78,390

Resulting increase in net assets:

	December 31,		Increase-
	1965	1964	Decrease*
Assets:			
Current assets—Schedule 1	$388,430	$331,560	$ 56,870
Fixed assets—Schedule 2	391,370	414,480	23,110*
Deferred charges	3,000	3,750	750*
Total assets	$782,800	$749,790	$ 33,010
Liabilities:			
Current liabilities—Schedule 1	$123,650	$169,030	$ 45,380*
First mortgage, 4% bonds	150,000	150,000	—
Total liabilities	$273,650	$319,030	$ 45,380*
Net assets	$509,150	$430,760	$ 78,390

THE OSBORNE COMPANY Schedule 1

Comparative Schedule of Working Capital

December 31, 1965 and 1964

	December 31,		Increase-
	1965	1964	Decrease*
Current assets:			
Cash	$ 22,360	$ 21,085	$ 1,275
Receivables—less allowance	238,405	195,015	43,390
Inventories:			
Finished goods	50,710	42,300	8,410
Goods in process	30,260	24,860	5,400
Materials	33,430	37,050	3,620*
Supplies	5,995	4,710	1,285
Unexpired insurance	7,270	6,540	730
Total current assets	$388,430	$331,560	$ 56,870
Current liabilities:			
Bank loans	$ 30,000	$ 80,000	$ 50,000*
Accounts payable	58,215	53,350	4,865
Accrued taxes and expenses	35,435	35,680	245*
Total current liabilities	$123,650	$169,030	$ 45,380*
Working capital	$264,780	$162,530	$102,250

THE OSBORNE COMPANY Schedule 2

Comparative Schedule of Fixed Assets
December 31, 1965 and 1964

	December 31, 1965	December 31, 1964	Increase-Decrease*
Cost:			
Land	$ 30,500	$ 30,500	$ —
Buildings	193,000	193,000	—
Machinery and equipment	349,680	349,515	165
Total	$573,180	$573,015	$ 165
Depreciation to date:			
Buildings	$ 65,110	$ 59,320	$ 5,790
Machinery and equipment	116,700	99,215	17,485
Total	$181,810	$158,535	$ 23,275
Cost less depreciation	$391,370	$414,480	$ 23,110*

Statement for second illustration:

THE OSBORNE COMPANY

Statement Accounting for Decrease in Stockholders' Equity
and Resulting Decrease in Net Assets
For the Year Ended December 31, 1964

Increase (decrease*) in stockholders' equity:

	Capital Stock Preferred	Capital Stock Common	Retained Earnings	Total
Changes in capital stock:				
Preferred stock retired	$20,000*			$20,000*
Net income			$41,240	41,240
Dividends paid:				
Preferred			9,800*	9,800*
Common			20,000*	20,000*
Net increase (decrease*)	$20,000*	$ —	$11,440	$ 8,560*

Resulting decrease in net assets:

	December 31, 1964	December 31, 1963	Increase-Decrease*
Assets:			
Current assets—Schedule 1	$331,560	$360,600	$29,040*
Fixed assets—Schedule 2	414,480	423,020	8,540*
Deferred charges	3,750	5,400	1,650*
Total assets	$749,790	$789,020	$39,230*
Liabilities:			
Current liabilities—Schedule 1	$169,030	$169,700	$ 670*
First mortgage, 4% bonds	150,000	180,000	30,000*
Total liabilities	$319,030	$349,700	$30,670*
Net assets	$430,760	$439,320	$ 8,560*

Statement for third illustration:

THE OSBORNE COMPANY

Statement Accounting for Changes in Stockholders' Equity and Resulting Changes in Net Assets

Years Ended December 31, 1965 and 1964

	December 31, 1965	Increase-Decrease*	December 31, 1964	Increase-Decrease*	December 31, 1963
Increase (decrease*) in stockholders' equity:					
Capital stock:					
Preferred stock:					
Retired		$ 45,000*		$20,000*	
Common stock:					
Issued for cash		$175,000		$ –	
Retained earnings:					
Net income		$ 36,790		$41,240	
Dividends:					
On preferred		8,400*		9,800*	
On common		80,000*		20,000*	
Total		$ 51,610*		$11,440	
Increase (decrease*) in stockholders' equity		$ 78,390		$ 8,560*	
Increase (decrease*) in net assets:					
Assets:					
Current assets—Schedule 1	$388,430	$ 56,870	$331,560	$29,040*	$360,600
Fixed assets—Schedule 2	391,370	23,110*	414,480	8,540*	423,020
Deferred charges	3,000	750*	3,750	1,650*	5,400
Total assets	$782,800	$ 33,010	$749,790	$39,230*	$789,020
Liabilities:					
Current liabilities—Schedule 1	$123,650	$ 45,380*	$169,030	$ 670*	$169,700
First mortgage, 4% bonds	150,000		150,000	30,000*	180,000
Total liabilities	$273,650	$ 45,380*	$319,030	$30,670*	$349,700
Net assets	$509,150	$ 78,390	$430,760	$ 8,560*	$439,320
Capital structure:					
Capital stock:					
Preferred	$ 75,000	$ 45,000*	$120,000	$20,000*	$140,000
Common	375,000	175,000	200,000	–	200,000
Retained earnings	59,150	51,610*	110,760	11,440	99,320
Total	$509,150	$ 78,390	$430,760	$ 8,560*	$439,320

CHAPTER

22

The Analysis of Working Capital

Working capital schedule. The working capital of The Osborne Company at various dates is shown below:

THE OSBORNE COMPANY
Schedule of Working Capital
December 31, 1965, 1964, and 1963

	December 31,		
	1965	1964	1963
Current assets:			
Cash	$ 22,360	$ 21,085	$ 10,740
Receivables:			
Accounts	$215,420	$168,845	$239,240
Notes	34,050	41,600	50,095
Total receivables	$249,470	$210,445	$289,335
Less allowance for doubtful accounts	11,065	15,430	30,095
Net receivables	$238,405	$195,015	$259,240
Inventories:			
Finished goods	$ 50,710	$ 42,300	$ 37,150
Goods in process	30,260	24,860	17,650
Materials	33,430	37,050	25,260
Total inventories	$114,400	$104,210	$ 80,060
Supplies	$ 5,995	$ 4,710	$ 4,280
Unexpired insurance	7,270	6,540	6,280
Total current assets	$388,430	$331,560	$360,600
Current liabilities:			
Bank loans	$ 30,000	$ 80,000	$ 85,000
Accounts payable	58,215	53,350	64,210
Accrued taxes and expenses	35,435	35,680	20,490
Total current liabilities	$123,650	$169,030	$169,700
Net current assets—working capital	$264,780	$162,530	$190,900

Changes indicated by ratios. The changes in the current assets and current liabilities, over a period of time, may be indicated by a statement similar to that below.

THE OSBORNE COMPANY
Comparative Statement of Working Capital
December 31, 1965, 1964, and 1963

	Amounts—December 31,			Ratios	
	1965	1964	1963	1965 to 1963	1964 to 1963
Current assets:					
Cash	$ 22,360	$ 21,085	$ 10,740	2.08	1.96
Receivables—net	238,405	195,015	259,240	.92	.75
Inventories:					
Finished goods	50,710	42,300	37,150	1.37	1.14
Goods in process	30,260	24,860	17,650	1.71	1.41
Materials	33,430	37,050	25,260	1.32	1.47
Supplies	5,995	4,710	4,280	1.40	1.10
Unexpired insurance	7,270	6,540	6,280	1.16	1.04
Total current assets	$388,430	$331,560	$360,600	1.08	.92
Current liabilities:					
Bank loans	$ 30,000	$ 80,000	$ 85,000	.35	.94
Accounts payable	58,215	53,350	64,210	.91	.83
Accrued taxes and expenses	35,435	35,680	20,490	1.73	1.74
Total current liabilities	$123,650	$169,030	$169,700	.73	1.00
Working capital	$264,780	$162,530	$190,900	1.39	.85
Net sales for the year	$969,065	$834,880	$911,005	1.06	.92

In such a statement it is desirable to show the changes in net sales, as these changes should have a bearing on the changes in current assets and current liabilities. For instance, we find that the sales of 1964 were only .92 of those for 1963; the receivables at the end of 1964 were .75 of those at the end of 1963. These conditions indicate the possibility that the receivables were relatively not so old at the end of 1964 as at the end of 1963. On the other hand, with a decrease in net sales, all of the inventories have increased. Looking at the ratios for 1965, we find that the sales were slightly in excess of those for 1963, as shown by the sales ratio of 1.06; the investments in inventories have increased more rapidly than the sales have increased, thus suggesting a possible overinvestment in inventories.

Working capital ratio. The working capital ratio expresses the relation of the amount of current assets to the amount of current liabilities. For instance, if the current assets are twice the amount of the current liabilities, the working capital ratio is 2 to 1.

Both the amount of working capital and the working capital ratio should be given consideration by anyone who contemplates granting short-term credit to a business. The amount of working capital has a bearing on the *amount* of such credit which may be extended; the working capital ratio is indicative of the *degree of safety* with which short-term credit may be extended, because this ratio reflects the relation of current assets to current debts, and, thus, the per cent of shrinkage in current assets which will not too greatly jeopardize the interests of the current creditors. To illustrate, assume that two companies have the following current assets and current liabilities:

	Company *A*	Company *B*
Total current assets	$200,000	$1,000,000
Total current liabilities	100,000	900,000
Net current assets	$100,000	$ 100,000

Each company has a working capital of $100,000, but Company *A*'s working capital position is relatively more favorable than that of Company *B*, because Company *A* has $2 of current assets per dollar of current liabilities, whereas Company *B* has only $1.11 of current assets per dollar of current liabilities.

The working capital ratios of The Osborne Company are shown below. They were computed by dividing the current assets by the current liabilities.

THE OSBORNE COMPANY
Working Capital Ratios
December 31, 1965, 1964, and 1963

	December 31,		
	1965	1964	1963
Total current assets	$388,430	$331,560	$360,600
Total current liabilities	123,650	169,030	169,700
Working capital	$264,780	$162,530	$190,900
Working capital ratio, or dollars of current assets per dollar of current liabilities	3.14	1.96	2.12

A working capital ratio (sometimes called "current ratio") of at least 2 to 1 was for many years regarded as a standard of satisfactory current position. For reasons discussed in this chapter, analysts are now coming rather generally to recognize that no such arbitrary current-ratio standard can be applied indiscriminately to all types of business (perhaps not even to the same business at different dates during the year), and that the current ratio alone is by no means an adequate measure of the short-term credit position of a business; consideration must also be given to the distribution and movement of the current assets.

Distribution of current assets. The current position of a company is not entirely dependent upon the ratio of current assets to current liabilities but is affected by the kinds of current assets owned. Some current assets are more current than others. Several computations for measuring the distribution of current assets are discussed below.

The acid-test ratio. The inventories are relatively much less current than the cash and receivables. The inventories must be sold before their proceeds can be used for the payment of current liabilities; selling them involves the uncertain factor of the marketability of the inventories, as well as the element of time required for the conversion of raw materials and goods in process into finished goods and for the sale of the finished product.

For these reasons many analysts supplement the working capital ratio by the so-called *acid-test ratio,* sometimes called the "quick current ratio."

The acid-test ratio is sometimes defined as the ratio of cash and receivables (quick current assets) to current liabilities. However, most analysts advocate including among the quick current assets, for purposes of computing the acid-test ratio, not only the cash and current accounts and notes receivable, but also any marketable investments which it is expected will be converted into cash as an incident to the regular operations. This seems to be a justifiable procedure in view of the purpose of the acid-test ratio. However, investments should not be regarded as quick current assets unless (a) they can be disposed of without hampering the operations of the business, (b) there is a ready market for them, and (c) trading is in sufficient volume to reflect a price applicable to the quantity of securities held.

The acid-test ratios of The Osborne Company at various dates are shown below.

THE OSBORNE COMPANY
Acid-Test Ratios
December 31, 1965, 1964, and 1963

	December 31,		
	1965	1964	1963
Quick current assets:			
Cash	$ 22,360	$ 21,085	$ 10,740
Accounts and notes receivable, less allowance for doubtful accounts	238,405	195,015	259,240
Total quick assets	$260,765	$216,100	$269,980
Total current liabilities	123,650	169,030	169,700
Excess of quick current assets over current liabilities	$137,115	$ 47,070	$100,280
Acid-test ratio—dollars of quick current assets per dollar of current liabilities	2.11	1.28	1.59

An acid-test ratio of at least 1 to 1 usually has been regarded as desirable. However, the fact that a company has a 1-to-1 acid-test ratio is no positive evidence that it will be able to pay its current liabilities as they mature. Cash may be required for the payment of operating expenses or for other purposes, and the receivables may not become due before payments of current liabilities must be made.

Percentage distribution of current assets. The distribution of current assets can be shown in greater detail by a percentage distribution statement. Assume the following comparison of a company's current position at two dates:

	December 31,	
	1965	1964
Current assets:		
Cash	$10,000	$30,000
Receivables	20,000	20,000
Inventories	30,000	10,000
Total current assets	$60,000	$60,000
Current liabilities	30,000	30,000
Working capital	$30,000	$30,000

The company had the same working capital ($30,000) and the same working capital ratio (2 to 1) at the two dates. However, its working capital position at the two dates was not the same. From one standpoint, the company's position was much weaker at the end of 1965 than at the end of 1964 because of the shift from the very current asset of cash to the much less current asset of inventories. On the other hand, the amount ultimately to be realized from the current assets may have been increased, because there are larger inventories to be converted at a profit.

Notwithstanding the fact that the current assets at the end of 1965 may have had a greater ultimate realizable value because of the element of prospective profit in the larger inventories, a shift from the more current assets of cash and receivables to the less current asset of inventories is usually regarded as undesirable. To determine whether any such shift is taking place, a statement similar to the following may be prepared.

THE OSBORNE COMPANY
Percentage Distribution of Current Assets
December 31, 1965, 1964, and 1963

	December 31,		
	1965	1964	1963
Cash	5.76%	6.36%	2.98%
Receivables—less allowance	61.38%	58.82%	71.89%
Inventories:			
Finished goods	13.05%	12.76%	10.30%
Goods in process	7.79	7.50	4.89
Materials	8.61	11.17	7.01
Total inventories	29.45%	31.43%	22.20%
Supplies	1.54%	1.42%	1.19%
Unexpired insurance	1.87	1.97	1.74
Total current assets	100.00%	100.00%	100.00%

Breakdown of working capital ratio. Because any considerable shifts from the relatively more current assets to the relatively less current assets, or vice versa, will materially affect a company's ability to pay its current debts promptly, it may be desirable to break down the working capital in a manner which will show whether the current liabilities can be paid from the cash on hand, or whether their payment will require all of the cash and part of the proceeds of the receivables, all of the cash and receivables and part of the proceeds of the finished goods, and so on. The following rather extreme case is used for purposes of an emphatic illustration:

	December 31,		
	1965	1964	1963
Cash	$30,000	$15,000	$ 5,000
Receivables	20,000	10,000	10,000
Finished goods	15,000	20,000	15,000
Goods in process	10,000	30,000	20,000
Materials	5,000	5,000	30,000
Total	$80,000	$80,000	$80,000

The current liabilities at each date were $40,000, and the working capital ratio at each date was, therefore, 2 to 1. However, the company's current position changed materially, as shown by the following summary. The ratios are stated cumulatively; for instance, at the end of 1965, the cash was equal to .75 of the current liabilities; the total cash and receivables were equal to 1.25 times the current liabilities; and so on.

Table Showing Accumulation of Working Capital Ratio

	December 31,		
	1965	1964	1963
Cash	.750	.375	.125
Receivables	1.250	.625	.375
Finished goods	1.625	1.125	.750
Goods in process	1.875	1.875	1.250
Materials	2.000	2.000	2.000

Following is a similar tabulation for The Osborne Company.

THE OSBORNE COMPANY
Table Showing Accumulation of Working Capital Ratio
December 31, 1965, 1964, and 1963

	December 31,		
	1965	1964	1963
Cash	.18	.12	.06
Receivables—less allowance	2.11	1.28	1.59
Finished goods	2.52	1.53	1.81
Goods in process	2.76	1.68	1.91
Materials	3.03	1.89	2.06
Supplies	3.08	1.92	2.09
Unexpired insurance	3.14	1.96	2.12

Movement of current assets. The adequacy of the working capital is dependent, not only on its content, but also on the rapidity with which the noncash current assets move toward cash. Information on this matter can be obtained by determining the turnovers of materials, finished goods, and receivables.

Although the time required for these various operations cannot be determined with absolute accuracy from data furnished by the periodical statements (the statement of cost of goods manufactured and sold, the income statement, and the balance sheet), the methods indicated by the following illustrations are frequently used. The data are those of The Osborne Company.

Materials turnovers. The materials turnovers are computed as follows:

		1965	1964	1963
Cost of materials used (per statement of cost of goods manufactured and sold)	(a)	$279,620	$185,490	$193,790
Materials inventories:				
Beginning of year		$ 37,050	$ 25,260	$ 42,750
End of year		33,430	37,050	25,260
Average	(b)	$ 35,240	$ 31,155	$ 34,005
Number of materials turnovers (a ÷ b)	(c)	7.93	5.95	5.70
Days per turnover (365 ÷ c)		46	61	64

This computation assumes a steady flow of production through the year and no great fluctuations in the inventories during the year. If these conditions do not exist, the turnovers and turnover periods are misstated.

Finished goods turnovers. The following computations also are based on assumptions of uniformity; it is assumed that the cost of sales and the inventories did not fluctuate greatly during the year.

		1965	1964	1963
Cost of goods sold (per income statement)	(a)	$667,940	$553,845	$612,455
Finished goods inventories:				
Beginning of year		$ 42,300	$ 37,150	$ 49,390
End of year		50,710	42,300	37,150
Average	(b)	$ 46,505	$ 39,725	$ 43,270
Finished goods turnovers (a ÷ b)	(c)	14.36	13.94	14.15
Days per turnover (365 ÷ c)		25	26	26

Trade receivables conversion periods. Assuming an even flow of sales and a uniformity of collectibility during the year, the approximate time required for the collection of receivables may be computed as follows:

		1965	1964	1963
Net sales	(a)	$969,065	$834,880	$911,005
Trade receivables at end of year	(b)	249,470	210,445	289,335
Per cent of year's sales uncollected at end of year (b ÷ a)	(c)	25.74%	25.21%	31.76%
Average number of days' sales uncollected (365 × c)		94	92	116

Even though sales and collections may be uniform throughout the year, the average number of days' charge sales uncollected will be misstated if there are large amounts of cash sales, or if a considerable number of the customers pay their accounts within a short discount period.

The foregoing computation should not be understood to mean that at the end of 1965 all of the sales for the last 94 days were uncollected. The probabilities are that some sales during that period have been collected, and that some receivables remain on the books which arose from sales made more than 94 days before the end of the year.

It will be observed that the receivables at the end of the year, not the average receivables at the beginning and end of the year, are used in this computation. The receivables at the beginning of the year have no bearing on the per cent of the year's sales uncollected at the end of the year.

Working capital turnover. It has been suggested that turnover of the working capital as a whole can be used as a reliable measure of movement—instead of, or as a supplement to, inventory turnovers and receivable conversion periods. The so-called "working capital turnover" is computed by dividing the net sales for the period by the average working capital used during the period.

THE OSBORNE COMPANY

Statement of Working Capital Turnover
Years Ended December 31, 1965, 1964, and 1963

	1965	1964	1963
Net current assets:			
End of year	$264,780	$162,530	$190,900
Beginning of year	162,530	190,900	197,395
Average	213,655	176,715	194,148
Net sales for the year	969,065	834,880	911,005
Working capital turnovers	4.54	4.72	4.69

Criticism of working capital turnover. In the authors' opinion, the working capital turnover is of practically no significance.

A turnover is supposed to be a measure of movement. It should indicate *how many times* something happened during a period. And an increase in the turnover should indicate an improvement. But an increase in the turnover may be caused by an increase in the current liabilities, which is not an improvement. To illustrate, let us assume the following:

		1965	1964
Sales	(a)	$500,000	$500,000
Working capital:			
Current assets	(b)	$100,000	$100,000
Current liabilities	(c)	60,000	50,000
Working capital	(d)	$ 40,000	$ 50,000
Working capital ratio (b ÷ c)		1.67	2
Working capital turnover (a ÷ d)		12.5	10

If the increase in the turnover from 10 to 12.5 is considered an indication of improvement, the conclusion is false. The increase in turnover was caused wholly by an increase in current liabilities, which was not an improvement. A much more meaningful analysis can be made by computing two ratios:

(a) The *number* of turnovers based on cost of sales and expenses, which is a measure of the use of the total current assets.

(b) The *rate of income* per turnover of total current assets, which is a measure of the profitability with which the current assets were used.

Let us assume the following facts relative to the cost of sales and expenses and the net income:

	1965	1964
Sales	$500,000	$500,000
Cost of sales and expenses	480,000	450,000
Net income	$ 20,000	$ 50,000

Frequency of Current Asset Turnover

		1965	1964
Cost of sales and expenses	(a)	$480,000	$450,000
Total current assets	(b)	100,000	100,000
Number of current asset turnovers (a ÷ b)	(c)	4.8	4.5

Rate of Net Income Per Current Asset Turnover

		1965	1964
Net income	(d)	$ 20,000	$ 50,000
Ratio of net income to total current assets (d ÷ b)	(e)	20.00%	50.00%
Rate of net income per turnover of total current assets (e ÷ c)		4.17%	11.11%

We now have some really significant information. Instead of assuming that the increase in the working capital turnover from 10 to 12.5 (see above) represented an improvement, which was a false conclusion, we now know that the working capital ratio decreased from 2 to 1.67; the current assets were turned somewhat more frequently—4.8 times instead of 4.5 times; and the turnovers were less profitable—a drop from 11.11% to 4.17%.

Number and profitability of current asset turnovers. The desirability of using the procedures recommended in the preceding section instead of computing a working capital turnover is further indicated by the following illustration, based on data of The Osborne Company presented below:

		Year Ended December 31,		
		1965	1964	1963
Net sales	(a)	$969,065	$834,880	$911,005
Cost of sales and expenses	(b)	932,275	793,640	884,540
Net income	(c)	$ 36,790	$ 41,240	$ 26,465
Current assets:				
Beginning of year	(d)	$331,560	$360,600	$383,705
End of year	(e)	388,430	331,560	360,600
Average	(f)	$359,995	$346,080	$372,153
Current liabilities:				
Beginning of year	(g)	$169,030	$169,700	$186,310
End of year	(h)	123,650	169,030	169,700
Average	(i)	$146,340	$169,365	$178,005
Working capital:				
Beginning of year (d − g)	(j)	$162,530	$190,900	$197,395
End of year (e − h)	(k)	264,780	162,530	190,900
Average	(l)	$213,655	$176,715	$194,148

The following computations make use of yearly averages of current assets, current liabilities, and working capital.

If we were to compute the working capital turnover by using sales and average working capital, thus:

	1965	1964	1963
Working capital turnover (a ÷ 1)	4.54	4.72	4.69

it would look as though things were worse, because the turnover decreased in 1965. But if we make the following computations:

		1965	1964	1963
Turnover of average total current assets (using cost of sales and expenses instead of sales, and using average total current assets instead of average working capital) (b ÷ f)	(m)	2.59	2.29	2.38
Ratio of net income to average total current assets (c ÷ f)	(n)	10.22%	11.92%	7.11%
Rate of net income per turnover of average total current assets (n ÷ m)		3.95%	5.21%	2.99%

we see a different picture. The turnover decreased in 1964, but this decrease was more than offset in 1965. The ratios indicating profitability increased in 1964; although they dropped off in 1965, they were still much higher than in 1963.

A slight theoretical objection can be made to the foregoing computation of current asset turnover. When we divide the cost of sales and expenses by the average current assets, we are attempting to obtain a ratio which will be indicative of the number of times the average current assets were used in the payment of costs and expenses. But the costs and expenses included depreciation charges, which did not involve the use of current assets. This theoretical objection usually is of such slight practical importance that it can be ignored.

Ratio of accounts payable to purchases. It is desirable, if possible, to determine whether the current liabilities are being paid more promptly or less promptly than in the past. Assuming an even flow of purchases and a uniformity of payment policy during the year, some light may be thrown on this question by computing the ratio of accounts payable to purchases; an increase in the ratio indicates that a larger percentage of the accounts payable remains unpaid than in the past, and a decrease in the ratio indicates that a smaller percentage remains unpaid.

	1965	1964	1963
Accounts payable—end of year	$ 58,215	$ 53,350	$ 64,210
Net purchases—Materials	276,000	197,280	176,300
Ratio of accounts payable to purchases	.21	.27	.36

If notes payable and bank loans appear in the balance sheet, the ratio of accounts payable to purchases is not very significant because decreases in the accounts payable may be offset by increases in notes payable and bank loans, and vice versa. Nor is it of great value to determine the ratio of the total accounts payable, notes, and bank loans to purchases, because the notes and loans may have been incurred for the payment of other costs.

The annual cycle. When turnovers, ratios, and per cents are computed by use of the data shown by annual statements, the results obtained can be relied upon only if production, sales, and collections are carried on uniformly through the year.

But in many businesses the sales fluctuate greatly from month to month; production may also vary from month to month, either because of the fluctuations in sales or because raw materials are available at only certain periods of the year.

In all businesses subject to considerable fluctuations in seasonal sales or production, the working capital will vary from month to month. For instance, if we looked at a company's balance sheet a few months after the close of its heavy selling season and before the beginning of a heavy production season, we would probably find the inventories small, the receivables well realized, and the accounts payable and bank loans reduced to a minimum; the working capital ratio would be higher than the average because of the small amount of current liabilities. A few months later, after a heavy production season and before the next heavy selling season, we might find the inventories large in anticipation of the coming business, the receivables small because recent sales have been small, and the accounts payable and bank loans large as the result of large recent production; the working capital ratio would then be relatively low because of the abnormally large current liabilities.

Obviously, no adequate conception of the working capital position of a business can be obtained from an inspection of its balance sheet unless we know whether or not seasonal fluctuations in business cause its working capital position to vary during the year. If such variations are to be expected in the business under consideration, one should know what condition in the cycle the balance sheet depicts.

Illustration. To illustrate the importance of using monthly statements in arriving at conclusions with respect to a company's working capital position, let us compare the results shown by an analysis of annual statements with those shown by an analysis of monthly statements. To simplify the illustration somewhat, data for a trading company will be used instead of data for a manufacturing company.

Working capital ratio. The statement on page 424 shows the working capital of a company at the close of each of 13 successive months. It will be noted that the working capital ratio ranges from 1.60 (December 31, 1964) to 2.81 (April 30, 1965), with variations throughout the year, and, therefore, that the 2.08 ratio at the end of the year is not indicative of conditions throughout the year.

Acid-test ratio. The variation in the acid-test ratio is shown in the following statement.

	Cash and Receivables	Current Liabilities	Ratio
1964—December 31	$78,000	$80,000	.98
1965—January 31	68,000	68,000	1.00
February 28	59,500	53,000	1.12
March 31	51,500	38,000	1.36
April 30	44,000	26,500	1.66
May 31	45,000	27,500	1.64
June 30	55,000	35,500	1.55
July 31	56,000	40,500	1.38
August 31	66,500	61,500	1.08
September 30	61,000	58,500	1.04
October 31	82,000	77,500	1.06
November 30	99,000	80,500	1.23
December 31	89,000	67,000	1.33

Frequency of current asset conversion. The variations in working capital ratios show the changes in the working capital position during the year. The table at the top of page 425 shows the variations in the rapidity with which the current assets are converted at different times during the year. The turnovers are computed by dividing the cost of sales and expenses for the month by the current assets at the beginning of the month; slightly more accurate results might be obtained by using the average current assets for the month.

	Current Assets				Current Liabilities				
	Cash	Accounts Receivable	Inventories	Total	Accounts Payable	Bank Loans	Total	Working Capital	Working Capital Ratio
1964—December 31	$13,000	$65,000	$50,000	$128,000	$60,000	$20,000	$80,000	$48,000	1.60
1965—January 31	15,000	53,000	52,000	120,000	48,000	20,000	68,000	52,000	1.76
February 28	18,500	41,000	46,000	105,500	33,000	20,000	53,000	52,500	1.99
March 31	18,500	33,000	38,500	90,000	28,000	10,000	38,000	52,000	2.37
April 30	18,000	26,000	30,500	74,500	26,500	—	26,500	48,000	2.81
May 31	24,000	21,000	27,000	72,000	27,500	—	27,500	44,500	2.62
June 30	22,000	33,000	24,500	79,500	35,500	—	35,500	44,000	2.24
July 31	24,000	32,000	27,000	83,000	40,500	—	40,500	42,500	2.05
August 31	19,500	47,000	40,000	106,500	61,500	—	61,500	45,000	1.73
September 30	7,000	54,000	46,500	107,500	58,500	—	58,500	49,000	1.84
October 31	11,000	71,000	51,500	133,500	67,500	10,000	77,500	56,000	1.72
November 30	9,000	90,000	49,000	148,000	70,500	10,000	80,500	67,500	1.84
December 31	21,000	68,000	50,500	139,500	57,000	10,000	67,000	72,500	2.08

	Cost of Sales and Expenses	Current Assets Beginning of Month	Turnover for Month	Working Capital Ratio Beginning of Month
January	$37,000	$128,000	.29	1.60
February	29,500	120,000	.25	1.76
March	25,500	105,500	.24	1.99
April	21,500	90,000	.24	2.37
May	18,500	74,500	.25	2.81
June	25,500	72,000	.35	2.62
July	26,500	79,500	.33	2.24
August	37,500	83,000	.45	2.05
September	41,000	106,500	.38	1.73
October	53,000	107,500	.49	1.84
November	63,500	133,500	.48	1.72
December	45,000	148,000	.30	1.84

Merchandise turnover. If the merchandise turnover is computed by using the average of the two December 31 inventories, the computation will be as follows:

Inventory, December 31, 1964	$50,000
Inventory, December 31, 1965	50,500
Average inventory	$50,250

$315,000 (cost of goods sold) ÷ $50,250 = 6.3 turnovers, which is at the average rate of approximately one-half of one turnover per month.

The turnover obtained by this computation is misleading because the December 31 inventories are larger than the average inventories carried during the year. The average of the 13 inventories shown on page 424 is $41,000. On the basis of this average inventory, the turnover is computed thus:

$315,000 ÷ $41,000 = 7.68, which is at the average rate of .64 of one turnover per month.

But the rate of turnover varies radically during the year; interesting information with respect to this variation is obtained from the following statement:

	Inventory at Beginning	Cost of Sales	Fraction Sold
January	$50,000	$28,000	.56
February	52,000	21,000	.40
March	46,000	17,500	.38
April	38,500	14,000	.36
May	30,500	10,500	.34
June	27,000	17,500	.65
July	24,500	17,500	.71
August	27,000	28,000	1.04
September	40,000	31,500	.79
October	46,500	42,000	.90
November	51,500	52,500	1.02
December	49,000	35,000	.71

An analysis of this kind may raise such pertinent questions as the following: If an inventory of $27,000 at the beginning of August was adequate to provide for sales, during that month, of goods which cost $28,000, was an inventory of $50,000 at the beginning of January necessary to provide for sales, during that month, of goods which cost the same amount ($28,000)?

Age of accounts receivable. If we estimate the average age of the receivables by a computation involving the sales for the year and the receivables at the end of the year, thus:

$68,000 (accounts receivable) ÷ $450,000 (sales) = 15.1% (per cent of year's sales uncollected)
365 × 15.1% = 55 (number of day's sales uncollected)

we obtain a misleading result, because the $68,000 balance of accounts receivable at the end of the year is larger than the average balance carried during the year. More meaningful data can be obtained by a computation similar to the following:

	Sales for Month	Receivables at End of Month	Ratio of Receivables to Month's Sales	Days' Sales Uncollected
January	$40,000	$53,000	133%	40
February	30,000	41,000	137	41
March	25,000	33,000	132	40
April	20,000	26,000	130	39
May	15,000	21,000	140	42
June	25,000	33,000	132	40
July	25,000	32,000	128	38
August	40,000	47,000	118	35
September	45,000	54,000	120	36
October	60,000	71,000	118	35
November	75,000	90,000	120	36
December	50,000	68,000	136	41

The figures in the Days' Sales Uncollected column are still slightly misleading, owing to the wide variation in monthly sales. For instance, note the drop in sales from November to December. The large November sales affect the $68,000 balance of receivables at the end of December; as this balance is divided by the December sales only, the decrease in December sales probably accounts to a great extent for the increase in the ratio from 120% to 136% and the increase in the days from 36 to 41. Nevertheless, the figures in the Days' Sales Uncollected column are far more meaningful than the 55 days shown by the computation using the year's sales and the receivables at the end of the year.

The natural business year. Companies whose operations and current position are subject to major fluctuations through the year may advantageously adopt a fiscal year ending on a date immediately subsequent to the low operating period, when the inventories, the receivables, and the payables are reduced to their minimum and the working capital ratio is therefore high.

The presentation in the natural-year-end balance sheet of a favorable working capital position is not the only advantage. The inventory can be more easily taken, partly because of the reduced quantity and partly because in a slack operating period there is less interference with operating activities and more employees are available for the work. Also, the valuation of the inventories and the receivables, which are important assets from a current credit standpoint, necessarily involves the making of estimates, and it is desirable that such estimates apply to the smallest amounts carried at any time during the year.

QUESTIONNAIRE GROUPING OF RATIOS

We may facilitate the interpretation of ratios by assembling them as answers to a questionnaire. When this is done, all ratios should be computed in such a manner that increases in the ratios will be indicative of improvements. The accomplishment of this result may require some modification of the procedures already explained; such a modification is discussed in a note following the tabulation. The ratios are those of The Osborne Company; the numbers in parentheses indicate the pages on which the computations of the ratios are shown.

	1965	1964	1963	(Page)
Is the working capital position improving?				
Working capital ratio—end of year	3.14	1.96	2.12	415
Acid-test ratio	2.11	1.28	1.59	416
Current asset turnovers	2.59	2.29	2.38	421
Materials turnovers	7.93	5.95	5.70	418
Finished goods turnovers	14.36	13.94	14.15	419
Ratio of net sales to gross receivables (See note below)	3.88	3.97	3.15	
Is the stockholders' equity increasing?				
Ratio of stockholders' equity to total debt	1.86	1.35	1.26	397
Book value per share of common stock	$115.77	$155.38	$149.66	407
Is the security for the long-term liabilities increasing?				
Ratio of security to long-term liabilities	2.61	2.76	2.35	404
Is there any tendency toward overinvestment in fixed assets?				
Ratio of stockholders' equity to fixed assets less depreciation	1.30	1.04	1.04	405
Ratio of net sales to fixed assets less depreciation	2.48	2.01	2.15	405
Are the earnings increasing?				
Per cent of net income to stockholders' equity	7.23%	9.57%	6.02%	407
Net income per share of common stock	$ 12.39	$ 15.72	$ 5.53	408
Per cent of net income to sales	3.80%	4.94%	2.91%	400
Per cent of gross profit to sales	31.07%	33.66%	32.77%	400

Note. On page 419 the relative condition of the receivables was determined by computing the following per cents and turnover periods:

	1965	1964	1963
Per cent of year's sales uncollected—at end of year	25.74%	25.21%	31.76%
Average number of days' sales uncollected	94	92	116

Improvements are indicated in the note at the bottom of the preceding page by decreases, as it is better to have only 25.21% of the year's sales uncollected than to have 31.76% uncollected. These per cents were obtained by dividing the receivables by the sales. The ratios (3.88, 3.97, and 3.15) shown in the tabulation on page 427 were obtained by dividing the sales by the receivables, in order that increases in the ratios would indicate improved conditions.

CHAPTER

23

Analysis of Operations

STATEMENT ACCOUNTING FOR VARIATION IN NET INCOME

Causes of variation in net income. The causes of the variation in net income from one period to another may be summarized as follows:

(1) Change in gross profit on sales, due to:
  (a) Change in sales.
  (b) Change in cost of goods sold.
(2) Changes in expenses.
(3) Changes in any other credits and charges to income, such as miscellaneous income, expenses, gains, and losses.

The statement accounting for the variation in net income shows how the net income was affected by these various changes. The statement may be prepared in a very simple manner by the mere assembling of the data shown by a condensed income statement in such a manner as to group the elements which tended to increase the net income and those which tended to decrease the net income; or it may be amplified by inclusion of analytical per cents and comparative per cents or ratios.

Basis of illustrations. The condensed comparative income statement of Company *A* on the following page is used for purposes of illustration.

COMPANY *A*

Condensed Comparative Income Statement
For the Years Ended December 31, 1965 and 1964

	Year Ended December 31, 1965	Year Ended December 31, 1964	Increase-Decrease*
Net sales	$253,000	$200,000	$53,000
Cost of goods sold	181,125	150,000	31,125
Gross profit on sales	$ 71,875	$ 50,000	$21,875
Operating expenses:			
Selling expenses	$ 25,000	$ 20,000	$ 5,000
General expenses	12,000	10,000	2,000
Total operating expenses	$ 37,000	$ 30,000	$ 7,000
Operating income	$ 34,875	$ 20,000	$14,875
Net financial expense	4,000	5,000	1,000*
Net income	$ 30,875	$ 15,000	$15,875

First illustration. The following statement rearranges the income statement figures into two groups: One showing the items tending to increase the net income, and another showing the items tending to decrease the net income.

As there are no per cents or ratios in the statement, it is difficult to see whether the increase in the cost of goods sold and the increases in selling and general expenses were proportionate to the increase in sales.

COMPANY *A*

Statement Accounting for Increase in Net Income
Years 1965 and 1964

Elements tending to increase net income:			
(1) Increase in gross profit on sales, caused by:			
(a) Increase in net sales:			
1965	$253,000		
1964	200,000	$53,000	
(b) Less increase in cost of goods sold:			
1965	$181,125		
1964	150,000	31,125	
Resulting increase in gross profit		$21,875	
(2) Decrease in net financial expense:			
1964	$ 5,000		
1965	4,000	1,000	
Total elements tending to increase net income			$22,875
Elements tending to decrease net income:			
(1) Increase in selling expenses:			
1965	$ 25,000		
1964	20,000	$ 5,000	
(2) Increase in general expenses:			
1965	$ 12,000		
1964	10,000	2,000	
Total elements tending to decrease net income			7,000
Resulting increase in net income:			
1965	$ 30,875		
1964	15,000		$15,875

Second illustration. The statement can be made more informative by the addition of a column showing per cents of various items to net sales, and a column showing the ratio of each 1965 amount to the corresponding 1964 amount. Such a statement is illustrated below:

COMPANY *A*

Statement Accounting for Increase in Net Income
Years 1965 and 1964

	Per Cent of Net Sales	Amounts		Ratio 1965 to 1964
Elements tending to increase net income:				
(1) Increase in gross profit on sales, caused by:				
(a) Increase in net sales:				
1965		$253,000		1.27
1964		200,000		
Increase			$53,000	
(b) Less increase in cost of goods sold:				
1965	71.59%	$181,125		1.21
1964	75.00	150,000		
Increase in amount			31,125	
Decrease in per cent of sales	3.41%			
Resulting increase in gross profit:				
1965	28.41%	$ 71,875		1.44
1964	25.00	50,000		
Increase	3.41%		$21,875	
(2) Decrease in net financial expense:				
1964	2.50%	$ 5,000		
1965	1.58	4,000		.80
Decrease	.92%		1,000	
Total elements tending to increase net income			$22,875	
Elements tending to decrease net income:				
(1) Increase in selling expenses:				
1965	9.88%	$ 25,000		1.25
1964	10.00	20,000		
Increase in amount			$ 5,000	
Decrease in per cent of sales	.12%			
(2) Increase in general expenses:				
1965	4.74%	$ 12,000		1.20
1964	5.00	10,000		
Increase in amount			2,000	
Decrease in per cent of sales	.26%			
Total elements tending to decrease net income			$ 7,000	
Resulting increase in net income:				
1965	12.20%	$ 30,875		2.06
1964	7.50	15,000		
Increase	4.70%		$15,875	

Illustration of decrease in net income. The statement on page 432 accounts for a decrease in net income.

THE Z COMPANY
Statement Accounting for Decrease in Net Income
Years 1965 and 1964

	Per Cent of Net Sales	Amounts		Ratio 1965 to 1964
Elements tending to decrease net income:				
(1) Decrease in gross profit on sales:				
(a) Decrease in net sales:				
1964		$600,000		
1965		513,000		.86
Decrease			$87,000	
(b) Decrease in cost of goods sold:				
1964	75.00%	$450,000		
1965	77.37	396,900		.88
Decrease in amount			53,100	
Increase in per cent of sales	2.37%			
Resulting decrease in gross profit:				
1964	25.00%	$150,000		
1965	22.63	116,100		.77
Decrease	2.37%		$33,900	
Elements tending to increase net income:				
(1) Decrease in selling expenses:				
1964	8.71%	$ 52,280		
1965	9.11	46,735		.89
Decrease in amount			$ 5,545	
Increase in per cent of sales	.40%			
(2) Decrease in general expenses:				
1964	8.99%	$ 53,915		
1965	8.72	44,720		.83
Decrease	.27%		9,195	
(3) Decrease in net financial expense:				
1964	.92%	$ 5,540		
1965	.83	4,235		.76
Decrease	.09%		1,305	
Total elements tending to increase net income			$16,045	
Resulting decrease in net income:				
1964	6.38%	$ 38,265		
1965	3.98	20,410		.53
Decrease	2.40%		$17,855	

This statement shows that the net sales decreased (as shown in the Ratio column) 14% and the cost of goods sold decreased only 12%; because the rate of decrease in the cost of goods sold was less than the rate of decrease in sales, the gross profit rate decreased—from 25.00% to 22.63%.

All of the expenses decreased. The selling expenses decreased only 11% as compared with the 14% decrease in sales; consequently, the ratio of selling expenses to sales increased from 8.71% to 9.11%. The general expenses decreased 17% as compared with the 14% decrease in sales; therefore, the ratio of general expenses to sales decreased from 8.99% to 8.72%.

ACCOUNTING FOR VARIATION IN GROSS PROFIT

The foregoing statements are interesting as far as they go, but they do not go very far in showing the causes of the change in gross profit. The statement on page 431, for instance, shows that the $21,875 increase in gross profit was caused by a $53,000 increase in sales which was partially offset by a $31,125 increase in the cost of goods sold. But this does not get to the root of the matter. It does not answer the following questions:

What caused the increase in sales?
 How much was caused by a change in the quantity volume of goods sold?
 How much was caused by a change in selling prices?
What caused the increase in the cost of goods sold?
 How much was caused by a change in the quantity volume of goods sold?
 How much was caused by a change in unit costs?

Analytical procedures for determining the effects of changes in quantity volume, in selling prices, and in unit costs are discussed in the following sections.

Procedures using detailed statistics—First illustration. The comparative income statement of Company *A* on page 430 shows the following information:

	1965	1964	Increase
Net sales	$253,000	$200,000	$53,000
Cost of goods sold	181,125	150,000	31,125
Gross profit on sales	$ 71,875	$ 50,000	$21,875

Assume that we have the following additional information:

	1965	1964	Increase
Units sold	1,150	1,000	150
Selling price per unit	$220.00	$200.00	$20.00
Unit cost	157.50	150.00	7.50

Causes of the $53,000 increase in sales. With the statistics presented above, we can show the causes of the increase in sales in the following manner:

Quantity factor:		
Amount by which sales would have been increased by the increase in volume if there had been no increase in sales price:		
1964 unit selling price	$ 200	
Multiply by increase in quantity	150	$30,000
Price factor:		
Amount by which sales would have been increased by the increase in sale price if there had been no increase in volume:		
Increase in sale price	$ 20	
Multiply by 1964 quantity volume	1,000	20,000
Quantity-price factor:		
Increase in selling price applied to increase in volume:		
$20 × 150		3,000
Total increase in sales		$53,000

The $30,000 was the result of volume change only, but it was not the total result of the volume change; the $20,000 was the result of price change only, but it was not the total result of the price change; the $3,000 increase was caused partly by the increase in volume and partly by the increase in selling price.

This analysis can perhaps be better explained by use of the following graph, which consists basically of a horizontal axis along which quantities are measured, and a vertical axis along which prices are measured. The 1965 price was greater than the 1964 price, so the 1965 point on the vertical axis is higher than the 1964 point; the 1965 quantity was greater than the 1964 quantity, so the 1965 point on the horizontal axis is to the right of (further away from zero than) the 1964 point.

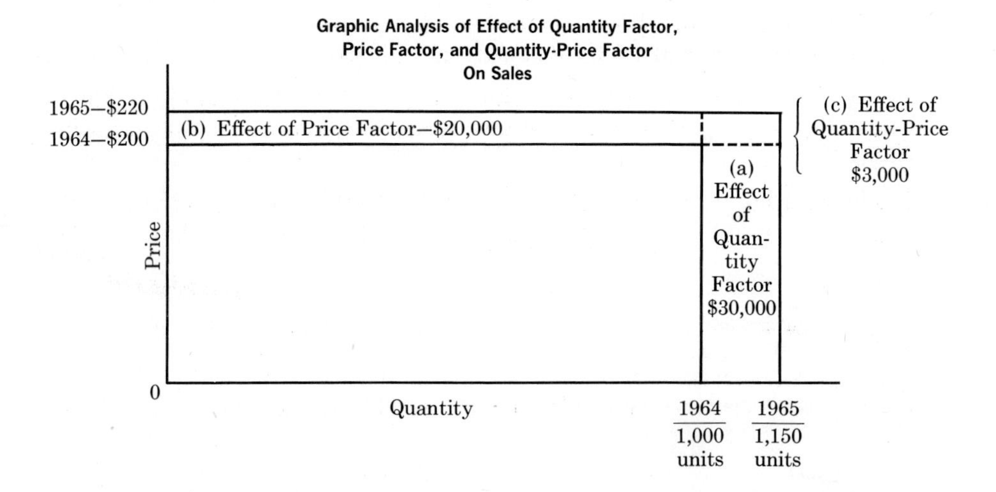

By erecting lines perpendicular to both the horizontal and vertical axes at these points, we can construct two rectangles, one superimposed on the other. The larger rectangle represents the 1965 sales (price times quantity); the smaller rectangle represents the 1964 sales; and the L-shaped margin represents the difference between the two years' sales.

Further analysis discloses that the L-shaped margin (which, as stated above, represents the $53,000 increase in sales) consists of three rectangles. Rectangle (a) obviously represents the effect which the quantity increase would have had on sales *had there been no change in the price;* rectangle (b) represents the effect which the price increase would have had on sales *had there been no change in the quantity;* and the small rectangle (c) in the corner of the L represents the additional effect on sales caused by the simultaneous increase in both price and quantity.

Causes of the $31,125 increase in cost of goods sold. The causes of this increase are determined as follows:

Quantity factor:		
Amount by which the cost of goods sold would have been increased by the increase in volume if there had been no increase in unit costs:		
1964 unit cost	$ 150	
Multiply by increase in quantity	150	$22,500
Cost factor:		
Amount by which the cost of goods sold would have been increased by the increase in unit cost if there had been no increase in volume:		
Increase in unit cost	$7.50	
Multiply by 1964 quantity volume	1,000	7,500
Quantity-cost factor:		
Increase in unit cost applied to increase in volume:		
$7.50 × 150		1,125
Total increase in cost of goods sold		$31,125

The $22,500 was the result of volume change only, but it was not the total effect of the volume change; the $7,500 was the result of cost change only, but it was not the total effect of the cost change; the $1,125 increase was due partly to the increase in volume and partly to the increase in unit cost.

The analyses of the $53,000 increase in sales (page 433) and the $31,125 increase in cost of goods sold (above) may be combined in the manner shown on the following page.

Because it may be presumed that the statement would be prepared for the use of management personnel who would know the nature of the various factors, the statement may be condensed as follows:

COMPANY *A*

Statement Accounting for Changes in Sales, Cost of Goods Sold, and Gross Profit
For the Years Ended December 31, 1965 and 1964

	Sales	Cost of Sales	Gross Profit
Amounts:			
1965	$253,000	$181,125	$71,875
1964	200,000	150,000	50,000
Increases	$ 53,000	$ 31,125	$21,875
Increases (decreases*) caused by:			
Quantity factor	$ 30,000	$ 22,500	$ 7,500
Price factor	20,000		20,000
Cost factor		7,500	7,500*
Quantity-price factor	3,000		3,000
Quantity-cost factor		1,125	1,125*
Totals	$ 53,000	$ 31,125	$21,875

COMPANY *A*

Statement Accounting for Changes in Sales,
Cost of Goods Sold, and Gross Profit
For the Years Ended December 31, 1965 and 1964

	Sales	Cost of Sales	Gross Profit
Amounts:			
1965	$253,000	$181,125	$71,875
1964	200,000	150,000	50,000
Increases	$ 53,000	$ 31,125	$21,875
Increases (decreases*) due to:			
Quantity factor—Amounts by which increased volume would have affected sales and cost of sales if there had been no changes in unit price and cost:			
150 (increase in units sold) multiplied by:			
$200 (1964 sale price)	$ 30,000		$30,000
$150 (1964 unit cost)		$ 22,500	22,500*
Price factor—Amount by which change in unit price would have affected sales if there had been no change in quantity:			
$20 (increase in sale price) multiplied by 1,000 (units sold in 1964)	20,000		20,000
Cost factor—Amount by which change in unit cost would have affected cost of sales if there had been no change in quantity:			
$7.50 (increase in unit cost) multiplied by 1,000 (units sold in 1964)		7,500	7,500*
Quantity-price factor:			
$20 (increase in sale price) multiplied by 150 (increase in units sold)	3,000		3,000
Quantity-cost factor:			
$7.50 (increase in unit cost) multiplied by 150 (increase in units sold)		1,125	1,125*
Totals	$ 53,000	$ 31,125	$21,875

Procedure using detailed statistics—Second illustration. In the preceding illustration, there was an increase in volume, in selling prices, and in unit costs. In this illustration there is a decrease in volume, with increases in selling prices and costs. The illustration shows the opposing effects of increases and decreases. Assume the following facts:

	1965	1964	Increase-Decrease*
Net sales	$183,600	$200,000	$16,400*
Cost of goods sold	140,400	150,000	9,600*
Gross profit on sales	$ 43,200	$ 50,000	$ 6,800*
Units sold	900	1,000	100*
Selling price per unit	$ 204	$ 200	$ 4
Cost per unit	156	150	6

Using the foregoing data, we can show the causes of the decreases in sales, cost of goods sold, and gross profit as follows:

COMPANY *B*

Statement Accounting for Changes in Sales,
Cost of Goods Sold, and Gross Profit
For the Years Ended December 31, 1965 and 1964

	Sales	Cost of Sales	Gross Profit
Amounts:			
1965	$183,600	$140,400	$43,200
1964	200,000	150,000	50,000
Decreases*	$ 16,400*	$ 9,600*	$ 6,800*
Increases (decreases*) due to:			
Quantity factor—Amounts by which decreased volume would have affected sales and cost of sales if there had been no change in unit sale price or cost:			
100* (decrease in units sold) multiplied by:			
$200 (1964 sale price)	$ 20,000*		$20,000*
$150 (1964 unit cost)		$ 15,000*	15,000
Price factor—Amount by which change in unit price would have affected sales if there had been no change in quantity:			
$4 (increase in unit sale price) multiplied by 1,000 (units sold in 1964)	4,000		4,000
Cost factor—Amount by which change in unit cost would have affected cost of sales if there had been no change in quantity:			
$6 (increase in unit cost) multiplied by 1,000 (units sold in 1964)		6,000	6,000*
Quantity-price factor:			
$4 (increase in sale price) multiplied by 100* (decrease in units sold)	400*		400*
Quantity-cost factor:			
$6 (increase in unit cost) multiplied by 100* (decrease in units sold)		600*	600
Totals	$ 16,400*	$ 9,600*	$ 6,800*

A condensed statement may be prepared as follows:

COMPANY *B*

Statement Accounting for Changes in Sales,
Cost of Goods Sold, and Gross Profit
For the Years Ended December 31, 1965 and 1964

	Sales	Cost of Sales	Gross Profit
Amounts:			
1965	$183,600	$140,400	$43,200
1964	200,000	150,000	50,000
Decreases*	$ 16,400*	$ 9,600*	$ 6,800*
Increases (decreases*) caused by:			
Quantity factor	$ 20,000*	$ 15,000*	$ 5,000*
Price factor	4,000		4,000
Cost factor		6,000	6,000*
Quantity-price factor	400*		400*
Quantity-cost factor		600*	600
Totals	$ 16,400*	$ 9,600*	$ 6,800*

Procedure using quantity records. The preceding illustrations made use of detailed statistics relative to quantity volume of sales, unit selling prices, and unit costs. Such data can be developed if there are good inventory and purchase or production records stated in quantities. To illustrate, in the preceding Company *A* illustration, it was assumed that we had the following information:

		1965	1964
Sales	(a)	$253,000.00	$200,000.00
Cost of goods sold	(b)	181,125.00	150,000.00
Unit selling price	(c)	220.00	200.00
Unit cost	(d)	157.50	150.00
Units sold	(e)	1,150	1,000

Let us now assume that we are given only items (a) and (b), but that (using records of inventories and of purchases or production) we can determine the quantities sold, thus:

		Units	
		1965	1964
Inventory at beginning of year		750	675
Purchased or produced		1,300	1,075
Total		2,050	1,750
Inventory at end of year		900	750
Sold	(u)	1,150	1,000

We can then determine average unit selling prices and costs.

		1965	1964
Sales:			
Total	(a)	$253,000.00	$200,000.00
Price per unit (a ÷ u)		220.00	200.00
Cost of goods sold:			
Total	(b)	181,125.00	150,000.00
Cost per unit (b ÷ u)		157.50	150.00

The analysis to disclose the effects of changes in quantities, selling prices, and unit costs can then proceed in the manner illustrated on pages 433 to 436.

Procedures using per cents. If, in addition to the dollar amounts of sales and cost of goods sold, we know the per cent of change in any one of the three factors—quantity, selling price, and unit cost of goods sold—we can compute the per cent of change in each of the other two factors. To illustrate, we shall use the following data, which appeared in the preceding Company *A* illustration:

	1965	1964	Increase
Sales	$253,000	$200,000	$53,000
Cost of goods sold	181,125	150,000	31,125
Gross profit	$ 71,875	$ 50,000	$21,875

In each of the following three cases it is assumed that we know *one* of the three ratios of change, and we shall compute the other two ratios.

	Sales	Cost of Goods Sold
1964	(a) $200,000	(A) $150,000
1965	(b) 253,000	(B) 181,125
Case 1—Volume increase known—15%:		
Price ratio:		
1965 volume on 1964 sales price basis (a × 1.15)	(c) $230,000	
Price ratio (b ÷ c)	1.10	
Cost ratio:		
1965 volume on 1964 cost basis (A × 1.15)		(C) $172,500
Cost ratio (B ÷ C)		1.05
Case 2—Price increase known—10%:		
Volume ratio:		
1965 volume on 1964 sales price basis (b ÷ 1.10)	(c) $230,000	
Volume ratio (c ÷ a)	1.15	
Cost ratio:		
1965 volume on 1964 cost basis (A × 1.15)		(C) $172,500
Cost ratio (B ÷ C)		1.05
Case 3—Cost increase known—5%:		
Volume ratio:		
1965 volume on 1964 cost basis (B ÷ 1.05)		(C) $172,500
Volume ratio (C ÷ A)		1.15
Price ratio:		
1965 volume on 1964 price basis (a × 1.15)	(c) $230,000	
Price ratio (b ÷ c)	1.10	

Statements. When the per cents of change in volume, price, and cost are known, we can determine the effects of the changes in quantity volume, sales price, and unit cost in the manner shown below.

COMPANY *A*

Statement Accounting for Changes in Sales, Cost of Goods Sold, and Gross Profit For the Years Ended December 31, 1965 and 1964

	Sales	Cost of Sales	Gross Profit
Amounts:			
1965	$253,000	$181,125	$71,875
1964	200,000	150,000	50,000
Increases	$ 53,000	$ 31,125	$21,875
Increases (decreases*) due to:			
Quantity factor—Amounts by which increased volume would have affected sales and cost of sales if there had been no change in unit price or cost:			
15% of $200,000 (1964 sales)	$ 30,000		$30,000
15% of $150,000 (1964 cost of sales)		$ 22,500	22,500*
Price factor—Amount by which change in unit price would have affected sales if there had been no change in quantity:			
10% of $200,000 (1964 sales)	20,000		20,000
Cost factor—Amount by which change in unit cost would have affected cost of sales if there had been no change in quantity:			
5% of $150,000 (1964 cost of sales)		7,500	7,500*
Quantity-price factor:			
15% (quantity increase) × 10% (price increase) of $200,000 (1964 sales)	3,000		3,000
Quantity-cost factor:			
15% (quantity increase) × 5% (cost increase) of $150,000 (1964 cost of sales)		1,125	1,125*
Totals	$ 53,000	$ 31,125	$21,875

The condensed statement would be the same as the one on page 435.

Analysis by commodities. In the Company *A* illustration on page 436 and the Company *B* illustration on page 437, it was assumed that each company dealt in one commodity. To show how information relative to changes in sales, cost of goods sold, and gross profit can be assembled if a company deals in more than one commodity, let us assume that the data relative to Company *A* apply to Commodity A, and that the data relative to Company *B* apply to Commodity B, both sold by one company. The combined data are shown below.

Data for *A B* Company

	Sales	Cost of Goods Sold	Gross Profit
1965:			
Commodity A	$253,000	$181,125	$ 71,875
Commodity B	183,600	140,400	43,200
Total	$436,600	$321,525	$115,075
1964:			
Commodity A	$200,000	$150,000	$ 50,000
Commodity B	200,000	150,000	50,000
Total	$400,000	$300,000	$100,000
Increase-decrease*:			
Commodity A	$ 53,000	$ 31,125	$ 21,875
Commodity B	16,400*	9,600*	6,800*
Total	$ 36,600	$ 21,525	$ 15,075

Using the analyses previously made for Company *A* and Company *B*, and regarding them as now applicable to Commodities A and B, respectively, we can account for the changes in sales, cost of goods sold, and gross profit by commodities and in total as follows:

***A B* COMPANY**

Statement Accounting for Changes in Sales, Cost of Goods Sold, and Gross Profit—By Commodities and in Total
For the Years Ended December 31, 1965 and 1964

	Commodities		
	A	B	Total
Increase-decrease*:			
In sales:			
Quantity factor	$30,000	$20,000*	$10,000
Price factor	20,000	4,000	24,000
Quantity-price factor	3,000	400*	2,600
Total	$53,000	$16,400*	$36,600
In cost of goods sold:			
Quantity factor	$22,500	$15,000*	$ 7,500
Cost factor	7,500	6,000	13,500
Quantity-cost factor	1,125	600*	525
Total	$31,125	$ 9,600*	$21,525
In gross profit	$21,875	$ 6,800*	$15,075

UNIT COST AND PROFIT STATEMENTS

Statement of cost of goods manufactured and sold. If the goods in process inventories can be analyzed into their components of material, labor, and overhead, statements can be prepared, similar to those below, showing the total and the per-unit costs of goods manufactured and sold during 1964 and 1965.

THE *ABC* COMPANY
Statements of Cost of Goods Manufactured and Sold
in Total and Per Unit
For the Years Ended December 31, 1965 and 1964

	Year Ended December 31, 1964				
	Units	Material	Direct Labor	Manufacturing Overhead	Total
In process, January 1	50	$ 1,050	$ 940	$ 360	$ 2,350
Put into process during year	5,000				
Manufacturing costs during the year		140,900	176,750	67,620	385,270
Total	5,050	$141,950	$177,690	$67,980	$387,620
In process, December 31	40	800	740	310	1,850
Manufactured during year	5,010	$141,150	$176,950	$67,670	$385,770
Manufacturing cost per unit		$ 28.17	$ 35.32	$13.51	($ 77.00)
Finished goods inventory, January 1	850 at	$ 75.00	(1963 cost)		63,750
Total	5,860				$449,520
Finished goods inventory, December 31	900 at	$ 77.00			69,300
Sold	4,960 at	$ 76.66			$380,220

	Year Ended December 31, 1965				
	Units	Material	Direct Labor	Manufacturing Overhead	Total
In process, January 1	40	$ 800	$ 740	$ 310	$ 1,850
Put into process during year	4,000				
Manufacturing costs during the year		108,975	149,500	61,525	320,000
Total	4,040	$109,775	$150,240	$61,835	$321,850
In process, December 31	45	920	780	550	2,250
Manufactured during year	3,995	$108,855	$149,460	$61,285	$319,600
Manufacturing cost per unit		$ 27.25	$ 37.41	$15.34	($ 80.00)
Finished goods inventory, January 1	900 at	$ 77.00			69,300
Total	4,895				$388,900
Finished goods inventory, December 31	825 at	$ 80.00			66,000
Sold	4,070 at	$ 79.34			$322,900

Note: It is assumed that the work in process inventories at the beginning and end of the year were in the same stage of completion.

If a company manufactures and sells only one commodity, such a statement may be prepared for the business as a whole. If several commodities are dealt in, a separate statement may be prepared for each commodity.

To determine the unit cost of goods sold, we must take into consideration the opening and closing inventories of finished goods. For instance, in the year 1965,

The 3,995 units manufactured cost	$319,600 or $80 per unit
The 900 units in the opening inventory cost	69,300 or $77 per unit
The 4,895 units available for sale cost	$388,900
The 825 units on hand at the end of the year are assumed to be part of those manufactured during the year for	66,000 or $80 per unit
Hence, the 4,070 units sold cost	$322,900 or $79.34 per unit

Income statements. The following statements illustrate a total and per-unit income statement and expense schedule.

THE *ABC* COMPANY

Comparative Income Statement in Total and Per Unit Sold
For the Years Ended December 31, 1965 and 1964

	1965		1964		Increase-Decrease*
	Total	Per Unit	Total	Per Unit	Per Unit
Number of units sold		4,070		4,960	
Gross sales	$468,050	$115.00	$620,000	$125.00	$10.00*
Less sales allowances	5,700	1.40	6,800	1.37	.03
Net sales	$462,350	$113.60	$613,200	$123.63	$10.03*
Cost of goods sold	322,900	79.34	380,220	76.66	2.68
Gross profit on sales	$139,450	$ 34.26	$232,980	$ 46.97	$12.71*
Deduct:					
Selling expenses	$ 62,635	$ 15.39	$ 76,200	$ 15.36	$ .03
General expenses	49,785	12.23	68,750	13.86	1.63*
Total	$112,420	$ 27.62	$144,950	$ 29.22	$ 1.60*
Net income	$ 27,030	$ 6.64	$ 88,030	$ 17.75	$11.11*

THE *ABC* COMPANY

Comparative Statement of Selling Expenses in Total and Per Unit Sold
For the Years Ended December 31, 1965 and 1964

	1965		1964		Increase-Decrease*
	Total	Per Unit	Total	Per Unit	Per Unit
Number of units sold		4,070		4,960	
Advertising	$20,000	$ 4.92	$30,000	$ 6.05	$1.13*
Salesmen's salaries	25,000	6.14	25,000	5.04	1.10
Salesmen's expenses	9,130	2.24	10,300	2.08	.16
Freight and cartage out	5,670	1.39	6,400	1.29	.10
Miscellaneous selling expense	2,835	.70	4,500	.90	.20*
Total	$62,635	$15.39	$76,200	$15.36	$ .03

DEPARTMENTAL OPERATIONS

Income statement by departments. An attempt is sometimes made to prepare a statement showing the net income by departments, in the manner illustrated below.

THE TWO DEPARTMENT STORE
Income Statement
For the Year Ended December 31, 1965

	Department A	Department B	Total
Net sales	$300,000	$500,000	$800,000
Cost of goods sold	256,500	352,800	609,300
Gross profit on sales	$ 43,500	$147,200	$190,700
Operating expenses:			
Selling expenses:			
Store rent	$ 9,600	$ 14,400	$ 24,000
Advertising	6,400	9,600	16,000
Salesmen's salaries	24,000	28,000	52,000
Delivery expense	6,000	10,000	16,000
Total selling expenses	$ 46,000	$ 62,000	$108,000
General expenses:			
Office salaries	$ 3,600	$ 6,000	$ 9,600
Officers' salaries	15,000	25,000	40,000
Insurance	800	1,600	2,400
Bad debts	400	1,200	1,600
Miscellaneous	1,800	3,000	4,800
Total general expenses	$ 21,600	$ 36,800	$ 58,400
Total operating expenses	$ 67,600	$ 98,800	$166,400
Net operating income (loss*)	$ 24,100*	$ 48,400	$ 24,300
Interest earned	1,950	3,250	5,200
Total	$ 22,150*	$ 51,650	$ 29,500
Interest expense	2,400	4,000	6,400
Net income (loss*) before income tax	$ 24,550*	$ 47,650	$ 23,100

Although such a statement may have the superficial appearance of great accuracy, it usually is based on so many assumptions, estimates, and approximations that the results it shows are not worthy of absolute credence. It may be possible to determine, for each department, the sales, cost of goods sold, and certain expenses, such as salesmen's salaries, if each salesman works in only one department. Also, some joint expenses may be apportioned with a reasonable degree of accuracy. For instance, store rent may be apportioned on the basis of floor space occupied, with adjustments in recognition of the relative desirability of the space; advertising may be apportioned on the basis of space, with adjustments for differences in costs of planning, layout, and artwork; and other costs may be apportionable on similarly logical bases, with reasonably accurate results. But many apportionments are arbitrarily made on the basis of sales for want of a better basis.

Significance of the departmental statement. Because the apportionments of expenses in the above statement were largely estimates, many of which were arbitrarily based on sales, complete reliance should not be placed on the amounts shown as net loss for Department A and net income for Department B.

Moreover, even if no estimates had been necessary in the apportionment of overhead expenses, the fact that Department A shows a loss should not be accepted as a conclusive reason for discontinuing it. The discontinuance of Department A would result in eliminating all of the gross profit resulting from its operations, but it would not result in eliminating all of the expenses which were charged to it. Before reaching any decision with respect to the advisability of discontinuing Department A, the management should make a study of the expenses and items of miscellaneous income for the purpose of determining the probable reductions which would result from such a discontinuance. The following statement is assumed to be the result of such a study:

Probable Reduction in Expenses and Miscellaneous Income Which Would Result from Discontinuance of Department A

	Amounts Allocated to Department A	Effect of Discontinuance of Department A	
		Eliminated	Not Eliminated
Selling expenses:			
Store rent	$ 9,600		$ 9,600
Advertising	6,400	$ 6,400	
Salesmen's salaries	24,000	24,000	
Delivery expense	6,000		6,000
Total	$46,000	$30,400	$15,600
General expenses:			
Office salaries	$ 3,600		$ 3,600
Officers' salaries	15,000		15,000
Insurance	800	$ 800	
Bad debts	400	400	
Miscellaneous	1,800	600	1,200
Total	$21,600	$ 1,800	$19,800
Interest earned (customers' notes)	$ 1,950	$ 1,950	$ –
Interest expense	$ 2,400	$ 2,400	$ –

The store rent charged to Department A would not be eliminated, because the entire space would have to be retained under the lease and there is no possibility of subleasing it. The advertising and salesmen's salary charges could be eliminated. The delivery equipment and driver would have to be retained to make deliveries for Department B. The office employees would be retained. The officers' salaries would not be reduced. The cost of insurance on Department A inventories would be eliminated. With the elimination of sales by Department A, its bad debt losses would disappear. It is estimated that one-third of the miscellaneous general expenses apportioned to Department A could be eliminated. The interest income was earned on notes received from customers, and the interest expense was incurred to carry inventories.

The consequences of discontinuing Department A can now be estimated, as follows:

Net income before income tax of Departments A and B			$23,100
Net income which would be lost by discontinuing Department A:			
Income lost:			
Gross profit on sales		$43,500	
Interest earned		1,950	
Total income lost		$45,450	
Expense reductions:			
Selling expenses	$30,400		
General expenses	1,800		
Interest expense	2,400		
Total expense reduction		34,600	
Net income lost			10,850
Resulting net income before income tax			$12,250

Surprising as it may at first seem, this statement shows that, although the departmental statement on page 443 shows that Department A's operations resulted in a net loss of $24,550, the elimination of that department would not cause a $24,550 increase in the net income of the business as a whole, but probably would reduce it by $10,850.

Statement showing contribution to overhead. Some accountants now prepare a statement similar to the following:

THE TWO DEPARTMENT STORE

Statement of Income and Expense
For the Year Ended December 31, 1965

	Department A	Department B	Total
Departmental income:			
Net sales	$300,000	$500,000	$800,000
Cost of goods sold	256,500	352,800	609,300
Gross profit on sales	$ 43,500	$147,200	$190,700
Interest earned	1,950	3,250	5,200
Total	$ 45,450	$150,450	$195,900
Direct departmental overhead—per schedule on page 446	34,600	45,400	80,000
Contribution to nondepartmental overhead	$ 10,850	$105,050	$115,900
Deduct nondepartmental overhead—per schedule on page 446			92,800
Net income before income tax			$ 23,100

It will be observed that no attempt is made to show the net income by departments. Instead, the statement shows, for each department, the income and expenses which, in the opinion of the management, would disappear if the department were discontinued. The excess represents the contribution of the department to what may be called the nondepartmental overhead, or the expenses not specifically allocable to any department.

The amounts of "direct departmental overhead" are those which the management believes would disappear following the discontinuance of either department, as indicated in the following schedule.

Schedule of Expenses

	Total	Direct Departmental Overhead: Department A	Department B	Nondepartmental Overhead
Selling expenses:				
Store rent	$ 24,000			$24,000
Advertising	16,000	$ 6,400	$ 9,600	
Salesmen's salaries	52,000	24,000	28,000	
Delivery expense	16,000			16,000
Total selling expenses	$108,000	$30,400	$37,600	$40,000
General expenses:				
Office salaries	$ 9,600			$ 9,600
Officers' salaries	40,000			40,000
Insurance	2,400	$ 800	$ 1,600	
Bad debts	1,600	400	1,200	
Miscellaneous	4,800	600	1,000	3,200
Total general expenses	$ 58,400	$ 1,800	$ 3,800	$52,800
Interest expense	$ 6,400	$ 2,400	$ 4,000	$ —
Total expenses	$172,800	$34,600	$45,400	$92,800

Analysis of departmental gross profit. When a business consists of several departments with different gross profit rates, the gross profit of the business as a whole will depend on:

The total sales,
The distribution of sales among the departments, and
The gross profit rates of the departments;

and changes in the amount and rate of gross profit of the business as a whole will depend upon changes in these factors. Therefore, an analysis of the causes of the change in the amount and rate of gross profit of a business as a whole requires consideration of the three factors mentioned above.

Basis of illustration. Assume that the statements of a business for three years showed the facts presented below.

	1965	1964	1963
Net sales	$412,250	$380,600	$390,550
Cost of goods sold	207,662	223,166	212,675
Gross profit on sales	$204,588	$157,434	$177,875
Increase (decrease*) in sales from preceding year:			
Amount	$ 31,650	$ 9,950*	
Per cent	8.32%	2.55%*	
Increase (decrease*) in gross profit:			
Amount	$ 47,154	$ 20,441*	
Per cent	29.95%	11.49%*	
Rate of gross profit	49.63%	41.36%	45.55%

How could a decrease of only $9,950 (2.55%) in sales in 1964 have caused a decrease of $20,441 (11.49%) in the gross profit? The answer is obvious: The average rate of gross profit decreased—from 45.55% in 1963 to 41.36% in 1964.

Again, how could an increase of $31,650 (8.32%) in sales in 1965 have caused an increase of $47,154 (29.95%) in gross profit? The answer is of the same nature: The average rate of gross profit increased from 41.36% in 1964 to 49.63% in 1965.

A change in the average rate of gross profit of a business with departments depends upon:

(1) The rate of gross profit of each department.
 (a) Its relation to the rates of other departments.
 (b) Its change since the preceding period.
(2) Any change in the distribution of sales among departments with different gross profit rates.

Departmental gross profit rates. The relation of the gross profit rate of each department to the gross profit rates of the other departments, and the changes in the departmental rates, are shown in the following summary.

	1965	1964	1963
Department A:			
Sales	$285,600	$119,375	$204,370
Cost of goods sold	121,740	53,370	94,725
Gross profit	$163,860	$ 66,005	$109,645
Rate of gross profit	57.37%	55.29%	53.65%
Department B:			
Sales	$ 76,350	$185,325	$125,900
Cost of goods sold	51,190	117,460	76,132
Gross profit	$ 25,160	$ 67,865	$ 49,768
Rate of gross profit	32.95%	36.62%	39.53%
Department C:			
Sales	$ 50,300	$ 75,900	$ 60,280
Cost of goods sold	34,732	52,336	41,818
Gross profit	$ 15,568	$ 23,564	$ 18,462
Rate of gross profit	30.95%	31.05%	30.63%

This summary shows that the gross profit rate in Department A is relatively high, and increasing; the rates in Departments B and C are relatively low; the rate for Department B is decreasing; and the rate for Department C has remained fairly constant throughout the three years.

Distribution of sales among departments. From the foregoing summary of departmental gross profit rates, it is obvious that the average gross profit rate of the business as a whole will increase if the sales of Department A become an increasing percentage of the total sales, and the average rate will decrease if the sales of Department A become a decreasing percentage of the total sales. Therefore, it is of interest to note the per cent of sales in each department each year, as shown on the next page.

Department	Amount of Sales 1965	1964	1963	Per Cent of Total 1965	1964	1963
A	$285,600	$119,375	$204,370	69.28%	31.36%	52.33%
B	76,350	185,325	125,900	18.52	48.69	32.24
C	50,300	75,900	60,280	12.20	19.95	15.43
Total	$412,250	$380,600	$390,550	100.00%	100.00%	100.00%

It is obvious that the decrease in the average rate of gross profit from 45.55% in 1963 to 41.36% in 1964 was largely due to the decrease in the percentage of business done by Department A, the high gross-profit-rate department. And the increase in the average rate from 41.36% in 1964 to 49.63% in 1965 was largely due to the fact that the sales in Department A increased from 31% to 69% of the total.

Departmental rates and sales distribution. The combined effect on the average gross profit rate of the business as a whole of changes in the departmental rates and changes in the distribution of sales among departments operating at different gross profit levels may be shown by a computation in the following form:

	Per Cent of Total Sales		Departmental Rate of Gross Profit		Components of the Average Rate of Gross Profit 1965	1964	1963
Department A	69.28%	×	57.37%	=	39.75%		
	31.36%	×	55.29%	=		17.34%	
	52.33%	×	53.65%	=			28.08%
Department B	18.52%	×	32.95%	=	6.10%		
	48.69%	×	36.62%	=		17.83%	
	32.24%	×	39.53%	=			12.74%
Department C	12.20%	×	30.95%	=	3.78%		
	19.95%	×	31.05%	=		6.19%	
	15.43%	×	30.63%	=			4.73%
Average gross profit rate of the business					49.63%	41.36%	45.55%

A similar analysis could be made by commodities—a fact which becomes obvious if we merely assume that the data, instead of applying to Departments A, B, and C, apply to Commodities A, B, and C.

Departmental merchandise turnovers. The foregoing statements show that the gross profit rate of the business as a whole was very adversely affected in 1964 by the large decrease in sales in Department A, where the highest rate of gross profit is earned. The following statement shows that the turnover in Department A also suffered in 1964.

The foregoing statements also show that Departments B and C are relatively less valuable than Department A from the standpoint of volume of sales and rate of gross profit. The following statement shows that Departments B and C are losing ground in the matter of inventory turnovers.

Departmental Finished Goods Inventory Turnovers

		Department A	Department B	Department C	Total
Finished goods inventories—December 31:					
1965		$ 37,570	$ 15,655	$ 9,395	$ 62,620
1964		36,850	17,210	4,490	58,550
1963		29,360	14,450	2,885	46,695
1962		34,975	20,300	3,355	58,630
Average inventories:					
1965	(a)	$ 37,210	$ 16,433	$ 6,942	$ 60,585
1964	(b)	33,105	15,830	3,688	52,623
1963	(c)	32,168	17,375	3,120	52,663
Cost of sales:					
1965	(d)	$121,740	$ 51,190	$34,732	$207,662
1964	(e)	53,370	117,460	52,336	223,166
1963	(f)	94,725	76,132	41,818	212,675
Turnovers:					
1965 (d ÷ a)		3.27	3.12	5.00	3.43
1964 (e ÷ b)		1.61	7.42	14.19	4.24
1963 (f ÷ c)		2.94	4.38	13.40	4.04

FIXED AND VARIABLE EXPENSES

The break-even point. Assume that a company's income statement may be summarized as follows:

Sales	$500,000
Less cost of sales and expenses	475,000
Net income	$ 25,000

To what extent can the sales decrease before the company begins to lose money? The costs and expenses, amounting to $475,000, are 95% of the sales. If the costs and expenses remained in that proportion to sales, regardless of increases or decreases in sales, the company would always make some profit, no matter how small the sales might be.

But some of the expenses are fixed in amount, regardless of the amount of sales, whereas others vary more or less directly in proportion to sales. The so-called "break-even point" computations are based on the assumption that the expenses can be divided into two classes:

(1) Fixed expenses, which are not affected by changes in the amount of sales.

(2) Variable expenses, which vary in direct proportion to the sales.

If we assume that the $475,000 of costs and expenses are divisible as follows:

Fixed expenses	$200,000
Variable expenses	275,000

the break-even point can be computed as follows:

Let S = the sales at the break-even point.

The variable expenses incurred in making \$500,000 of sales are \$275,000, or 55% of the sales. Because the variable expenses, by definition, always vary in proportion to sales, they will be 55% of any sales volume.

Because the sales at the break-even point will exactly equal the fixed and variable expenses,

$$S = \$200{,}000 \text{ (fixed expenses)} + .55S \text{ (variable expenses)}$$
$$S - .55S = \$200{,}000$$
$$.45S = \$200{,}000$$
S = \$444,444.44, the break-even point; if the sales fall below this amount, the company will incur losses.

Relation of fixed expenses to break-even point. It is obvious that, if any portion of the fixed expense can be converted to variable expense, the break-even point will be lowered. To illustrate, assume the following division of the \$475,000 total of costs and expenses:

Fixed expenses	\$100,000
Variable expenses (75% of net sales)	375,000

Let S = the sales at the break-even point.

Then $S = \$100{,}000$ (fixed expenses) $+ .75S$ (variable expenses).

$$S - .75S = \$100{,}000$$
$$.25S = \$100{,}000$$
S = \$400,000, the break-even point.

Use of break-even computations in management. Guidance in the solution of management problems may often be obtained by the use of the break-even computation. One problem will be presented as an illustration. Assume a company has the following income statement.

Net sales	\$1,000,000
Costs and expenses:	
Fixed	\$ 300,000
Variable (64% of sales)	640,000
Total	\$ 940,000
Net income	\$ 60,000

The company is considering increasing its investment in fixed assets; if it does so, the fixed expenses will be increased from \$300,000 to \$400,000 per year; the variable expenses will continue to be 64% of sales. Is the increase in fixed assets expedient?

In the first place, let us determine what will happen to the break-even point.

Under present conditions:

$$S = \$300{,}000 \text{ (fixed)} + .64S \text{ (variable)}$$
$$.36S = \$300{,}000$$
$$S = \$833{,}333.33$$

Under the proposed conditions:

$$S = \$400{,}000 \text{ (fixed)} + .64S \text{ (variable)}$$
$$.36S = \$400{,}000$$
$$S = \$1{,}111{,}111.11$$

It thus becomes apparent that the sales must be increased $111,111.11 from their present level of $1,000,000 before the company will have any net income.

In the second place, let us determine what sales must be made to produce the same net income, $60,000, as at the present time. Because the sales must provide for the fixed expenses, the variable expenses, and the $60,000 net income,

$$S = \$400{,}000 \text{ (fixed)} + .64S \text{ (variable)} + \$60{,}000$$
$$.36S = \$460{,}000$$
$$S = \$1{,}277{,}777.77$$

In the third place, let us consider the probable limits of net income under the two conditions. With the present plant facilities, the maximum production is estimated at an amount which would enable the company to make sales of $1,200,000. The increased production with the additional facilities would permit the company to make sales of $1,600,000. The probable limits of net income may therefore be estimated as follows:

	Without Plant Additions	With Plant Additions
Sales	$1,200,000	$1,600,000
Fixed expenses	$ 300,000	$ 400,000
Variable expenses—64% of sales	768,000	1,024,000
Total expenses	$1,068,000	$1,424,000
Limits of net income	$ 132,000	$ 176,000

These findings may be summarized as follows:

	Present	Prospective	Difference
Break-even point	$ 833,333.33	$1,111,111.11	$277,777.77
Sales to make the same net income as at present	1,000,000.00	1,277,777.77	277,777.77
Limits of net income	132,000.00	176,000.00	44,000.00
Sales for limits of net income	1,200,000.00	1,600,000.00	400,000.00

The management should now estimate the sales possibilities to determine the wisdom of the proposed expenditures. If the company makes the expenditures, but the sales remain at the present level of $1,000,000, it will lose $40,000 instead of making $60,000, because it will have increased its fixed expenses $100,000 without changing its variable expenses. With the additional plant, the break-even point will be advanced $277,777.77, and the sales must be increased the same amount to make the $60,000 net income now earned. Against these disadvantages may be set off the possibility of making $44,000 more net income than is possible under present conditions, but the earning of this additional net income will depend upon the company's ability to obtain sales of $1,600,000.

Classification of expenses. Break-even computations are predicated on the assumption that all expenses can be grouped into two classes: Those which are absolutely fixed in amount, regardless of sales; and those which vary in direct proportion to the sales.

Such an assumption is not always justified. Some expenses may be fixed to the extent that they will not vary up to a certain sales limit; if the sales are increased above that limit, these expenses will increase, but may remain fixed at the higher amount up to a new sales limit. Moreover, although some expenses may vary in exact proportion to sales, the increases and decreases in other expenses will not be in exact proportion to the increases and decreases in sales.

The rudiments of the break-even computation have been discussed because the computation is becoming of increasing interest to accountants and executives. The practical application of the theory requires a recognition of the fact that expenses cannot be rigidly classified as *fixed* and *variable.*

CHAPTER

24

Funds Statements

Opinion of Accounting Principles Board. In October, 1963, the Accounting Principles Board of the American Institute published an Opinion dealing with "The Statement of Source and Application of Funds." The following is quoted from the Introduction:

> Accountants have long prepared statements of source and application of funds for management. . . . The concept of "funds" used in these statements has varied somewhat in practice, and variations in the concept have resulted in variations in the nature of the statements. For example, "funds" has sometimes been interpreted to mean cash or its equivalent; in such cases the resulting statement of source and application of funds is a statement of cash receipts and disbursements. The most common concept of "funds" has, however, been that of working capital, i.e., current assets less current liabilities. If the definition is applied literally, the resulting statement includes only those transactions which affect the current assets or the current liabilities. A broader interpretation identifies "funds" as all financial resources arising from transactions with parties external to the business enterprise.

In this chapter we shall deal with statements prepared in accordance with the second and third concepts mentioned above.

CONCEPT OF FUNDS AS WORKING CAPITAL

Statement of sources and uses of working capital. The statement showing sources and uses of working capital has long been known as the *statement of application of funds*. This is not an ideal title for two reasons: it does not clearly indicate that the statement deals, not with funds in general, but only with working capital; and it implies that the statement deals only with the uses of working capital. For these reasons, the substitute title used in this text seems desirable.

Change in working capital. The working capital of a company and the change therein between two dates are matters of interest to management, bankers, other grantors of credit, investors, investment analysts, investment counselors, and others interested in the financial health of the company. Such information is furnished by a statement in the following form:

THE *A* COMPANY
Schedule of Working Capital
December 31, 1965 and 1964

	December 31,		Changes in Working Capital	
	1965	1964	Increase	Decrease
Current assets:				
Cash	$ 20,000	$17,000	$ 3,000	
Accounts receivable	35,000	37,500		$ 2,500
Inventory	50,000	45,000	5,000	
Total current assets	$105,000	$99,500		
Current liabilities:				
Notes payable	$ 10,000	$15,000	5,000	
Accounts payable	30,000	38,000	8,000	
Total current liabilities	$ 40,000	$53,000		
Working capital	$ 65,000	$46,500		
Working capital ratio	2.63	1.88		
Total increases and decreases			$21,000	$ 2,500
Increase in working capital				18,500
			$21,000	$21,000

Causes of increase in working capital. The foregoing schedule of working capital would create a favorable impression: the working capital has increased $18,500; the working capital ratio has increased from 1.88 to 2.63.

A person interested in the working capital of a company should not rely on this statement alone. He should find out what caused the increase.

Suppose that The *A* Company reported that the increase was caused as follows:

Working capital sources:	
Operations	$24,500
Working capital uses:	
Dividends paid	6,000
Increase in working capital	$18,500

This information would increase the favorable impression created by the schedule of working capital.

But suppose that The *A* Company furnished the following information:

Working capital sources:	
Operations	$10,000
Sale of long-term investments	14,500
Total	$24,500
Working capital uses:	
Dividends paid	6,000
Increase in working capital	$18,500

A much less favorable impression would be created. The change from the rather unsatisfactory working capital position at the end of 1964 was caused more by the sale of investments than by operations; the sale of the investments increased the working capital at the cost of depriving the company of the income from them.

Or assume that The *A* Company furnished the following information:

Working capital sources:	
Operations	$ 4,500
Issuance of three-year notes	20,000
Total	$24,500
Working capital uses:	
Dividends paid	6,000
Increase in working capital	$18,500

A very unfavorable impression would be created. Paying dividends in excess of the working capital provided by operations and at the same time borrowing money would probably be regarded as questionable financial management; and, if the working capital provided by operations remains at its 1965 level, a continuance of the dividend policy and the payment of the notes at their maturity will leave the company in a seriously depleted working capital position unless long-term funds can be obtained from other sources.

Causes of change in working capital. The *causes* of a change in working capital are shown by a statement of sources and uses of working capital; but, before the statement is illustrated, it will be helpful to look at the comparative balance sheet on page 456 in which the changes in account balances are classified in two pairs of columns:

A pair of columns showing changes in the balances of current asset and current liability (working capital) accounts. The $55,000 net debit in this pair of columns is the amount of the increase in working capital.

A pair of columns showing changes in the balances of other (noncurrent) accounts. The $55,000 net credit in this pair of columns is also the amount of the increase in working capital.

The net debits in the working capital accounts are equal to the net credits in the noncurrent accounts. By referring to the noncurrent accounts and determining what caused the changes in them, we shall at the same time ascertain the causes of the change in the amount of working capital.

The causes of the changes in the noncurrent accounts and the related effects on working capital are shown in an analysis at the top of page 457. Following the analysis are the statement of sources and uses of working capital and a supporting schedule.

THE *B* COMPANY
Comparative Balance Sheet
With Classification of Changes in Account Balances
December 31, 1965 and 1964

	Account Balances December 31,		Changes in Account Balances: In Noncurrent Accounts		Changes in Account Balances: In Working Capital Accounts	
	1965	1964	Debits	Credits	Debits	Credits
Assets						
Cash	$ 75,000	$ 35,000			$40,000	
Accounts receivable	90,000	98,000				$ 8,000
Merchandise inventory	120,000	87,000			33,000	
Long-term investments	10,000	15,000		$ 5,000		
Land	30,000	20,000	$10,000			
	$325,000	$255,000				
Liabilities and Stockholders' Equity						
Accounts payable	$ 45,000	$ 50,000			5,000	
Notes payable (short-term)	35,000	20,000				15,000
Notes payable (due November 30, 1968)	20,000			20,000		
Capital stock	150,000	125,000		25,000		
Retained earnings	75,000	60,000		15,000		
	$325,000	$255,000	$10,000	$65,000	$78,000	$23,000
Net credits in noncurrent accounts			55,000			
Net debits in working capital accounts						55,000
			$65,000	$65,000	$78,000	$78,000

THE *B* COMPANY	Changes in Noncurrent Account Balances		Effect on Working Capital	
	Debit	Credit	Increase	Decrease
Long-term investments:				
Cause of change—Investments sold		$ 5,000		
Effect on working capital—Increase			$ 5,000	
Land:				
Cause of change—Land purchased	$10,000			
Effect on working capital—Decrease				$10,000
Three-year notes payable:				
Cause of change—Notes issued		20,000		
Effect on working capital—Increase			20,000	
Capital stock:				
Cause of change—Stock issued		25,000		
Effect on working capital—Increase			25,000	
Retained earnings:				
Cause of change—Net income		15,000		
Effect on working capital—Increase			15,000	
Totals	$10,000	$65,000	$65,000	$10,000
Net credits to noncurrent accounts and increase in working capital	55,000			55,000
	$65,000	$65,000	$65,000	$65,000

THE *B* COMPANY

Statement of Sources and Uses of Working Capital
For the Year Ended December 31, 1965

Working capital sources:		
Sale of long-term investments	$ 5,000	
Issuance of three-year notes payable	20,000	
Issuance of capital stock	25,000	
Operations	15,000	$65,000
Working capital uses:		
Purchase of land		10,000
Increase in working capital—per schedule		$55,000

THE *B* COMPANY

Schedule of Working Capital
December 31, 1965 and 1964

	December 31,		Changes in Working Capital	
	1965	1964	Increase	Decrease
Current assets:				
Cash	$ 75,000	$ 35,000	$40,000	
Accounts receivable	90,000	98,000		$ 8,000
Merchandise inventory	120,000	87,000	33,000	
Total current assets	$285,000	$220,000		
Current liabilities:				
Accounts payable	$ 45,000	$ 50,000	5,000	
Notes payable	35,000	20,000		15,000
Total current liabilities	$ 80,000	$ 70,000		
Working capital	$205,000	$150,000		
Total increases and decreases			$78,000	$23,000
Increase in working capital				55,000
			$78,000	$78,000

Working papers. The working papers below show a convenient device for assembling the information required for the preparation of a statement of sources and uses of working capital. Because the working capital schedule can be prepared before the statement of sources and uses of working capital, details of current assets and current liabilities may be omitted from the working papers and only the net change in working capital need be shown.

The statement of sources and uses of working capital does not show the noncurrent account balances at the beginning and end of the year, but only the changes therein. Therefore, only the changes in the balances need be accounted for in the working papers.

THE *B* COMPANY

Working Papers for Statement of Sources and Uses of Working Capital
For the Year Ended December 31, 1965

	Year's Changes Detailed		Working Capital	
	Debits	Credits	Uses	Sources
Increase in working capital	55,000			
Noncurrent accounts:				
Long-term investments:				
Sale		5,000		5,000
Land:				
Purchase	10,000		10,000	
Three-year notes payable:				
Issued		20,000		20,000
Capital stock:				
Issued		25,000		25,000
Retained earnings:				
Net income from operations		15,000		15,000
	65,000	65,000		
Working capital from all sources				65,000
Working capital uses			10,000	10,000
Increase in working capital				55,000

The working papers were prepared in the following manner:

The change in working capital was entered in one of the first two columns (debit column for increase; credit column for decrease).

Changes in the noncurrent accounts were entered in the first pair of columns, the causes of the changes being stated in the stub.

As each change in a noncurrent account was entered in one of the first pair of columns, its amount was extended to the appropriate Working Capital Uses or Working Capital Sources column.

The first two columns were totaled to be sure that everything that should be included was included.

The Working Capital Sources column was footed.

The Working Capital Uses column was footed and its total was extended to the Working Capital Sources column.

The total of the Working Capital Uses column was deducted from the total of the Working Capital Sources column to determine the increase in working capital; the amount should agree with the increase shown by the schedule of working capital and with the first item shown in the working papers.

More than one cause of change in noncurrent account balances. The working papers below show that there were two causes of the change in the balance of the Long-Term Investments account, and two causes of change in the balance of the Retained Earnings account.

THE *C* COMPANY

Working Papers for Statement of Sources and Uses of Working Capital
For the Year Ended December 31, 1965

	Year's Changes Detailed		Working Capital	
	Debits	Credits	Uses	Sources
Increase in working capital	26,000			
Noncurrent accounts:				
Long-term investments:				
Purchase	10,000		10,000	
Sale		2,000		2,000
Land:				
Purchase	5,000		5,000	
Long-term notes payable:				
Issuance		15,000		15,000
Capital stock:				
Issuance		10,000		10,000
Retained earnings:				
Net income		20,000		20,000
Dividends	6,000		6,000	
	47,000	47,000		
Working capital from all sources				47,000
Working capital uses			21,000	21,000
Increase in working capital				26,000

Grouping Transfers columns. A pair of Grouping Transfers columns in the working papers is a convenient device for dealing with a situation in which working capital is increased by the disposal of a noncurrent asset at a gain or a loss.

Observe, in the working papers on page 460, the treatment of the sale of investments at a gain. The $300 gain is transferred (entry A) from the Retained Earnings section of the working papers to the Sale line under Investments. The $10,000 and the $300 are added and the $10,300 total is extended to the Working Capital Sources column.

Observe also how the $200 loss on the sale of land is transferred (entry B) from the Retained Earnings section to the line for the land sale; it is deducted from the $5,000 change in the Land account, and the net amount, $4,800, is entered in the Working Capital Sources column.

Sometimes a change in a noncurrent account must be combined with a change in another noncurrent account (other than Retained Earnings) to show the gross or net effect of a transaction on working capital.

Observe in the working papers how the $1,000 issuance discount (entry C) is transferred to the Bonds Payable Issued line to show the $24,000 increase in working capital resulting from the issuance of the bonds.

Observe also how the $500 credit to Capital in Excess of Par Value—Common Stock Issuances is transferred (entry D) to the Common Stock—Issued line to show the $10,500 increase in working capital resulting from the issuance of the stock.

THE *D* COMPANY

Working Papers for Statement of Sources and Uses of Working Capital
For the Year Ended December 31, 1965

	Year's Changes Detailed		Grouping Transfers		Working Capital	
	Debits	Credits	Debits	Credits	Uses	Sources
Increase in working capital	48,300					
Noncurrent accounts:						
Investments:						
Sale		10,000		A 300		10,300
Purchase	6,000				6,000	
Land:						
Sale		5,000	B 200			4,800
Discount on bonds payable:						
Issuance discount	1,000			C 1,000		
Bonds payable:						
Issued		25,000	C 1,000			24,000
Capital stock:						
Issued		10,000		D 500		10,500
Capital in excess of par value—Common stock issuances		500	D 500			
Retained earnings:						
Dividends	2,000				2,000	
Net income		6,800				
Grouping transfers:						
Gain on sale of investments			A 300			
Loss on sale of land				B 200		
Net income from operations						6,700
	57,300	57,300	2,000	2,000		
Working capital from all sources						56,300
Working capital uses					8,000	8,000
Increase in working capital						48,300

Noncurrent account changes not affecting working capital. If a debit to one noncurrent account is offset by a credit to another noncurrent account, the working capital is not affected, and the changes should not appear in the statement of sources and uses of working capital. Therefore, the debit and credit should be reversed in the working papers to clearly indicate that they have no effect on working capital.

A separate pair of columns headed "Reversal of Entries Having No Effect on Working Capital" *could be* provided in the working papers; however, it probably is better to simplify the working papers by using the column provided for Grouping Transfers, changing the heading to:

Grouping Transfers and No-Effect Reversals	
Debits	Credits

The two classes of entries can be distinguished by some device such as using letters for grouping transfers and numbers for no-effect reversals.

Working papers illustrating both grouping transfers and reversals of entries having no effect on working capital are shown below.

THE *E* COMPANY

Working Papers for Statement of Sources and Uses of Working Capital
For the Year Ended December 31, 1965

	Year's Changes Detailed		Grouping Transfers and No-Effect Reversals		Working Capital	
	Debits	Credits	Debits	Credits	Uses	Sources
Increase in working capital	58,200					
Noncurrent accounts:						
Investments:						
Sale		4,000		A 300		4,300
Goodwill:						
Written off to Retained Earnings		10,000	(1) 10,000			
Capital stock—Preferred:						
Converted into common stock . . .	20,000			(2) 20,000		
Capital stock—Common:						
Issued in retirement of preferred .		20,000	(2) 20,000			
Issued for cash		30,000				30,000
Retained earnings:						
Goodwill written off	10,000			(1) 10,000		
Dividends paid:						
Preferred	1,800				1,800	
Common	9,000				9,000	
Net income		35,000				
Grouping transfer:						
Gain on sale of investments .			A 300			
Net operating income						34,700
	99,000	99,000	30,300	30,300		
Working capital from all sources						69,000
Working capital uses					10,800	10,800
Increase in working capital						58,200

Income and expense items not affecting working capital. The income statement may contain items which affected the net income without affecting the working capital. For instance, consider the following:

Depreciation and amortization of fixed assets, and amortization of long-term deferred charges. These reduce the net income without reducing the working capital. Therefore, they must be added to the net income to determine the increase in working capital attributable to operations.

Amortization of long-term deferred credits. These amortizations increase the net income without increasing the working capital. Therefore, they must be deducted from the net income to determine the increase in working capital attributable to operations.

To deal with such items in the working papers, it is advisable to have a separate column in the Working Capital Sources section of the working papers in which to assemble the items used in the computation of the working capital produced by operations. Working papers containing such a column appear on page 463. The illustration is based on the following condensed balance sheet.

THE *F* COMPANY

Condensed Comparative Balance Sheet
December 31, 1965 and 1964

	December 31,		Net Change	
Assets	1965	1964	Debit	Credit
Working capital	$33,550	$29,300	$4,250	
Furniture	8,750	8,000	750	
Less accumulated depreciation	2,400*	1,600*		$ 800
Leasehold improvements	4,500	5,000		500
	$44,400	$40,700		
Liabilities and Stockholders' Equity				
Bonds payable	$20,000	$20,000		
Premium on bonds payable	900	1,000	100	
Capital stock	17,000	15,000		2,000
Retained earnings	6,500	4,700		1,800
	$44,400	$40,700	$5,100	$5,100

* Deduction.

The net income for the year was $2,800; dividends in the amount of $1,000 were paid.

The items affecting net income but not affecting working capital were:

Depreciation of furniture, $800.
Amortization of leasehold improvements, $500.
Amortization of premium on bonds payable, $100.

Observe how the total of the Working Capital Sources—Operations column is extended to the Other sources column so that the working capital provided from all sources may be determined.

Following is the statement.

THE *F* COMPANY

Statement of Sources and Uses of Working Capital
For the Year Ended December 31, 1965

Working capital sources:			
Operations:			
Net income for the year	$2,800		
Add charges (deduct credits*) to operations not affecting working capital:			
Depreciation of furniture	800		
Amortization of leasehold improvements	500		
Amortization of premium on bonds payable	100*	$4,000	
Issuance of capital stock		2,000	$6,000
Working capital uses:			
Purchase of furniture		$ 750	
Payment of a dividend		1,000	1,750
Increase in working capital			$4,250

THE *F* COMPANY

Working Papers for Statement of Sources and Uses of Working Capital
For the Year Ended December 31, 1965

	Year's Changes Detailed		Grouping Transfers and No-Effect Reversals		Working Capital		
						Sources	
	Debits	Credits	Debits	Credits	Uses	Operations	Other
Increase in working capital	4,250						
Noncurrent accounts:							
Furniture:							
Purchase	750				750		
Accumulated depreciation—Furniture:							
Depreciation for year		800				800	
Leasehold improvements:							
Amortization for the year		500				500	
Premium on bonds payable:							
Amortization for the year	100					100*	
Capital stock:							
Issued		2,000					2,000
Retained earnings:							
Net income		2,800				2,800	
Dividends paid	1,000				1,000		
	6,100	6,100					
Working capital provided by operations						4,000	4,000
Working capital from all sources							6,000
Working capital uses					1,750		1,750
Increase in working capital							4,250

* Deduction.

Cash flow. As we have just seen, the net income for a period is not necessarily the amount by which operations have increased the working capital. Some charges against income, such as depreciation of tangible fixed assets and amortization of intangibles, reduce the net income but do not require expenditures during the year; therefore, they must be added to net income to determine the amount of working capital produced by operations.

It should be, but often is not, understood that, in themselves, depreciation and amortization are not sources of working capital; they are merely additions to net income to determine the working capital increase caused by operations.

Some credits to income, such as amortization of deferred credits (premium on bond issuances, for example), increase the net income without increasing the working capital.

"Cash flow" has come into use as a term to denote the working capital produced by operations during a period. It is normally the same as the similarly computed amount shown in a statement of sources and uses of working capital.

Cash flow, computed in total or per share, has come to be regarded by analysts as an informative supplement to net income in measuring the effectiveness of operations as a source of current funds to meet requirements for debt retirements, expenditures for plant replacements and expansion, cash dividends, et cetera. In the comparison of the operating results of two companies whose charges against income include widely varying amounts of expenses for depreciation, amortization, and other items not affecting working capital, cash flow is regarded by many analysts as enhancing comparability.

Without intending to detract from the usefulness of cash flow as an analytical tool, some words of caution seem desirable. The term is a misnomer and therefore misleading. It is too easy to assume that cash flow means the amount of cash brought into, and remaining in, the business as a result of operations. But the mere addition of such items as depreciation to the stated net income does not completely convert a net income computed on an accrual basis to a cash-basis net income. Many other matters, such as increases and decreases in accruals and in trade receivables and payables during the accounting period, must also be considered. Moreover, the cash flow does not necessarily remain in the business at the end of the period as funds available for expansion, dividends, or other discretionary use. Some uses of the cash flow, such as the payment of serial installments of long-term liabilities, may be beyond management's control.

The terms *cash earnings* and *cash income* have sometimes been used as substitutes for *cash flow*. Such terms are even more likely to be misunderstood.

Net loss—Working capital provided. Operations may be a source of working capital even though a loss is incurred, because the operating charges not affecting the working capital, such as depreciation, may be greater than the net loss. The *G* Company statement on page 466 illustrates such a case. The working papers are on page 465.

THE *G* COMPANY

Working Papers for Statement of Sources and Uses of Working Capital
For the Year Ended December 31, 1965

	Year's Changes Detailed		Grouping Transfers and No-Effect Reversals		Working Capital		
						Sources	
	Debits	Credits	Debits	Credits	Uses	Operations	Other
Increase in working capital	5,400						
Noncurrent accounts:							
Investment securities:							
Purchase	2,000				2,000		
Buildings	—	—					
Accumulated depreciation—Buildings:							
Depreciation for the year		1,000				1,000	
Capital stock:							
Issued		7,500					7,500
Retained earnings:							
Net loss	600					600*	
Dividends	500				500		
	8,500	8,500					
Working capital provided by operations						400	400
Working capital from all sources							7,900
Working capital uses					2,500		2,500
Increase in working capital							5,400

* Deduction.

THE *G* COMPANY
Statement of Sources and Uses of Working Capital
For the Year Ended December 31, 1965

Working capital sources:			
Operations:			
Net loss for the year	$ 600*		
Charges to operations not affecting working capital:			
Depreciation—Buildings	1,000	$ 400	
Issuance of capital stock		7,500	$7,900
Working capital uses:			
Purchase of securities		$2,000	
Payment of dividends		500	2,500
Increase in working capital			$5,400

* Red.

Working capital lost in operations. If the income charges not affecting working capital were less than the net loss, working capital was lost in operations. The working capital so lost is sometimes shown in the statement of sources and uses of working capital under the "Working Capital Uses" caption; it is preferable, when possible, to show the amount as a deduction from the working capital from other sources, as in the statement of The *H* Company. The supporting working papers are on page 467.

THE *H* COMPANY
Statement of Sources and Uses of Working Capital
For the Year Ended December 31, 1965

Working capital sources:			
Issuance of capital stock		$6,000	
Deduct working capital lost in operations:			
Net loss for the year	$900*		
Charges to operations not affecting working capital:			
Depreciation—Buildings	600	300	$5,700
Working capital uses:			
Purchase of investment securities		$2,000	
Payment of dividends		1,000	3,000
Increase in working capital			$2,700

* Red.

Decrease in working capital. A decrease in working capital is best shown in the statement of sources and uses of working capital by reversing the usual sequence of the statement, as illustrated in the following statement of The *I* Company.

THE *I* COMPANY
Statement of Sources and Uses of Working Capital
For the Year Ended December 31, 1965

Working capital uses:			
Purchase of office furniture		$7,500	
Payment of dividends		500	$8,000
Working capital sources:			
Operations:			
Net income for the year	$1,500		
Charges to operations not affecting working capital:			
Depreciation—Furniture	1,300	$2,800	
Issuance of capital stock		2,500	5,300
Decrease in working capital			$2,700

THE *H* COMPANY

Working Papers for Statement of Sources and Uses of Working Capital
For the Year Ended December 31, 1965

	Year's Changes Detailed		Grouping Transfers and No-Effect Reversals		Working Capital		
						Sources	
	Debits	Credits	Debits	Credits	Uses	Operations	Other
Increase in working capital	2,700						
Noncurrent accounts:							
Investment securities:							
Purchase	2,000				2,000		
Land	—	—					
Buildings	—	—					
Accumulated depreciation—Buildings:							
Depreciation for the year		600				600	
Capital stock:							
Issued		6,000					6,000
Retained earnings:							
Net loss	900					900*	
Dividends	1,000				1,000		
	6,600	6,600					
Working capital from sources other than operations							6,000
Working capital lost—Operations						300*	300*
Net							5,700
Working capital uses					3,000		3,000
Increase in working capital							2,700

* Deduction.

In the working papers, the total sources would be deducted from the total uses to determine the decrease in working capital.

Extended illustration. The next illustration is based on the following comparative statement.

THE *J* COMPANY
Comparative Balance Sheet
December 31, 1965 and 1964

	December 31,		Net Change	
Assets	1965	1964	Debit	Credit
Cash	$ 3,500	$ 2,000	$ 1,500	
Accounts receivable	14,500	14,000	500	
Allowance for doubtful accounts	1,200*	1,350*	150	
Notes receivable	10,000	5,000	5,000	
Accrued interest on notes receivable	160	100	60	
Finished goods	19,000	13,500	5,500	
Goods in process	8,500	8,200	300	
Materials	21,900	22,600		$ 700
Unexpired insurance	470	420	50	
Manufacturing supplies	580	675		95
Investment in stock of *X* Company		15,000		15,000
Sinking fund	2,000		2,000	
Land	17,000	10,000	7,000	
Buildings	60,000	60,000		
Accumulated depreciation—Buildings	6,300*	8,000*	1,700	
Machinery	43,000	32,000	11,000	
Accumulated depreciation—Machinery	9,000*	7,500*		1,500
Delivery equipment	9,500	9,500		
Patents	16,000	17,000		1,000
Goodwill		10,000		10,000
Organization costs	3,000	4,500		1,500
Discount on 5% bonds payable		50		50
	$212,610	$207,695		
Liabilities and Stockholders' Equity				
Accounts payable	$ 4,500	$ 3,200		1,300
Notes payable—Trade	6,000	5,000		1,000
Accrued wages	210	170		40
Bonds payable—5%		50,000	50,000	
Sinking fund bonds payable—4½%	40,000			40,000
Premium on 4½% bonds payable	900			900
Long-term, unsecured notes payable:				
Current installment	5,000			5,000
Noncurrent portion	20,000	25,000	5,000	
Capital stock—Preferred	10,000	25,000	15,000	
Capital stock—Common	95,000	60,000		35,000
Capital in excess of par value—Common stock issuances	600			600
Reserve for contingencies	2,000			2,000
Retained earnings	28,400	39,325	10,925	
	$212,610	$207,695	$115,685	$115,685

* Deduction.

The first step in the solution is the preparation of the following schedule of working capital.

THE *J* COMPANY
Schedule of Working Capital
December 31, 1965 and 1964

	December 31,		Changes in Working Capital	
	1965	1964	Increase	Decrease
Current assets:				
Cash	$ 3,500	$ 2,000	$ 1,500	
Accounts receivable	14,500	14,000	500	
Allowance for doubtful accounts	1,200*	1,350*	150	
Notes receivable	10,000	5,000	5,000	
Accrued interest receivable	160	100	60	
Finished goods	19,000	13,500	5,500	
Goods in process	8,500	8,200	300	
Materials	21,900	22,600		$ 700
Unexpired insurance	470	420	50	
Manufacturing supplies	580	675		95
Total current assets	$77,410	$65,145		
Current liabilities:				
Accounts payable	$ 4,500	$ 3,200		1,300
Notes payable—Trade	6,000	5,000		1,000
Accrued wages	210	170		40
Current installment of long-term note	5,000			5,000
Total current liabilities	$15,710	$ 8,370		
Working capital	$61,700	$56,775		
Total increases and decreases			$13,060	$ 8,135
Increase in working capital				4,925
			$13,060	$13,060

* Deduction.

The information relative to the changes in the noncurrent accounts is given below. Observe the treatment in the working papers on pages 470 and 471.

Adjustment	
(A)	The $15,000 investment in *X* Company stock was sold at a gain of $750, which was included in the net income for the year.
—	The Sinking Fund account was debited $2,000 during the year. Problems frequently do not give information about all of the changes in the noncurrent accounts, leaving the student to form his own conclusions. The cause of the $2,000 increase in the sinking fund is not stated; presumably the increase was caused by a deposit in the fund.
(B)	Land was purchased at a cost of $10,000. Land carried at $3,000 was sold for $4,500; the gain was included in the net income for the year.
—	Buildings—the balance in the account has not changed; however, a line is devoted to the account in the working papers to indicate that it has not been ignored, and because there may have

(*Continued on page 472.*)

THE *J* COMPANY

Working Papers for Statement of Sources and Uses of Working Capital
For the Year Ended December 31, 1965

	Year's Changes Detailed		Grouping Transfers and No-Effect Reversals		Working Capital		
						Sources	
	Debits	Credits	Debits	Credits	Uses	Operations	Other
Increase in working capital	4,925						
Noncurrent accounts:							
Investment in *X* Company stock:							
Sale		15,000		A 750			15,750
Sinking fund:							
Deposit	2,000				2,000		
Land:							
Purchase	10,000				10,000		
Sale		3,000		B 1,500			4,500
Buildings	—	—					
Accumulated depreciation—Buildings:							
Extraordinary repairs	3,700				3,700		
Depreciation for the year		2,000				2,000	
Machinery:							
Sale		2,000	C 375 D 625				1,000
Purchase	13,000				13,000		
Accumulated depreciation—Machinery:							
On machinery sold	375			C 375			
Depreciation for the year		1,875				1,875	
Delivery equipment:							
Purchase	2,000				2,000		
Depreciation for the year		2,000				2,000	
Patents:							
Amortization for the year		1,000				1,000	
Goodwill:							
Write-off to Retained Earnings		10,000	(1) 10,000				
Organization costs:							
Write-down to Retained Earnings		1,500	(2) 1,500				
Discount on 5% bonds payable:							
Amortization for the year		50				50	
Bonds payable—5%:							
Retired at face value	50,000				50,000		
Sinking fund bonds payable—4½%:							
Issued		40,000		E 1,000			41,000
Premium on 4½% bonds payable:							
Issuance premium		1,000	E 1,000				
Amortization for the year	100					100*	
Totals forward	86,100	79,425	13,500	3,625	80,700	6,825	62,250

THE *J* COMPANY

Working Papers for Statement of Sources and Uses of Working Capital (Concluded)
For the Year Ended December 31, 1965

	Year's Changes Detailed		Grouping Transfers and No-Effect Reversals		Working Capital		
						Sources	
	Debits	Credits	Debits	Credits	Uses	Operations	Other
Totals brought forward	86,100	79,425	13,500	3,625	80,700	6,825	62,250
Long-term unsecured notes payable:							
Portion becoming current during year	5,000				5,000		
Preferred stock:							
Converted into common stock	10,000			(3) 10,000			
Retired	5,000		F 350		5,350		
Common stock:							
Issued in conversion of preferred stock		10,000	(3) 10,000				
Issued as a dividend		15,000	(4) 15,000				
Issued for cash		10,000		G 600			10,600
Capital in excess of par value—Common stock issuances		600	G 600				
Reserve for contingencies:							
Transfer from Retained Earnings		2,000	(5) 2,000				
Retained earnings:							
Net income		22,425					
Grouping transfers:							
Gain on sale of investment			A 750				
Gain on sale of land			B 1,500				
Loss on sale of machinery				D 625			
Net income from operations						20,800	
Write-off of Goodwill	10,000			(1) 10,000			
Write-down of Organization Costs	1,500			(2) 1,500			
Premium on preferred stock retired	350			F 350			
Common stock issued as a dividend	15,000			(4) 15,000			
Transfer to Reserve for Contingencies	2,000			(5) 2,000			
Cash dividend on preferred stock	1,500				1,500		
Cash dividend on common stock	3,000				3,000		
	139,450	139,450	43,700	43,700			
Working capital provided by operations						27,625	27,625
Working capital from all sources							100,475
Working capital uses					95,550		95,550
Increase in working capital							4,925

* Deduction.

Adjustment	
	been offsetting debit and credit entries. Observe the treatment of the Delivery Equipment account.
–	Extraordinary building repairs costing $3,700 were charged to the Accumulated Depreciation–Buildings account.
–	Building depreciation for the year was $2,000.
(C)-(D)	Machinery carried at its $2,000 cost, less $375 depreciation, was sold for $1,000. The $625 loss was reported in the income statement.
–	New machinery was purchased at a cost of $13,000.
–	Machinery depreciation for the year was $1,875.
–	Delivery equipment was purchased at a cost of $2,000.
–	Depreciation of delivery equipment, $2,000, was credited to the asset account.
–	Operations were charged $1,000 for amortization of patents.
(1)	Goodwill was written off by debit to Retained Earnings.
(2)	The Organization Costs account was written down $1,500 by debit to Retained Earnings.
–	The $50 of discount on the 5% bonds was amortized by charge to income.
–	The 5% bonds were retired at face value.
(E)	New sinking fund 4½% bonds of $40,000 face value were issued at a premium of $1,000.
–	Bond premium in the amount of $100 was amortized.
–	A portion, $5,000, of the long-term unsecured notes payable became current during the year.
(3)	Preferred stock of $10,000 par value was converted into common stock of an equal par value.
(F)	Preferred stock of $5,000 par value was retired at a premium of $350, which was charged to Retained Earnings.
(4)	Common stock of $15,000 par value was issued as a dividend.
(G)	Common stock of $10,000 par value was issued for cash at 106. The premium was credited to Capital in Excess of Par Value–Common Stock Issuances.
(5)	A reserve for contingencies, in the amount of $2,000, was created by transfer from Retained Earnings.
–	Cash dividends of $1,500 were paid on the preferred stock.
–	Cash dividends of $3,000 were paid on the common stock.
–	The net income, including items mentioned above, amounted to $22,425.

The working papers appear on pages 470 and 471. They were prepared as follows:

Headings were entered.
The increase in working capital was entered in the first column.
The changes in each noncurrent account were detailed.
Grouping transfers and no-effect reversals were applied.
The working capital effect of each element of change in the noncurrent accounts was extended to the appropriate Working Capital column.
The first four columns were footed. The agreement of the totals in each pair of columns is a test of the accuracy of the work so far done.
The Sources—Operations column was footed and its total was extended to the Sources—Other column.
The Sources—Other column was footed.
The Uses column was footed and its total was extended to the Sources—Other column, where it was deducted to determine the increase in working capital.

In a statement of sources and uses of working capital containing numerous items, it may be desirable to classify the items under side captions, such as the following:

Working capital sources:
  Operations
  Capital sources:
    Issuances of stock
  Issuance of long-term obligations:
    Bonds
  Disposal of assets:
    Sales of investments
    Sales of fixed assets
  Other

Working capital uses:
  Payments to stockholders:
    Retirement of stock
    Payment of dividends
  Retirement of long-term debt:
    Payment of mortgage
    Deposits in sinking fund for bonds
  Expenditures for fixed assets
  Other

Increase in working capital

The statement below, which is based on the working papers on pages 470 and 471, illustrates such classifications.

THE *J* COMPANY
Statement of Sources and Uses of Working Capital
For the Year Ended December 31, 1965

Working capital sources:			
Operations:			
Net income from operations		$20,800	
Add net depreciation and amortization, which reduced net income without affecting working capital		6,825	$ 27,625
Issuance of $10,000 par value of common stock at a premium			10,600
Issuance of $40,000 face value of bonds at a premium			41,000
Sale of assets:			
Stock of *X* Company		$15,750	
Land		4,500	
Machinery		1,000	21,250
Total			$100,475
Working capital uses:			
Payments to stockholders:			
Retirement of $5,000 par value of preferred stock at a premium		$ 5,350	
Cash dividends:			
On preferred stock	$ 1,500		
On common stock	3,000	4,500	
Reduction of long-term debt or provision therefor:			
Retirement of 5% bonds	$50,000		
Sinking fund deposit for 4½% bonds	2,000		
Installment of long-term unsecured notes payable which became a current liability during the year	5,000	57,000	
Expenditures for fixed assets:			
Purchase of land	$10,000		
Purchase of machinery	13,000		
Purchase of delivery equipment	2,000		
Extraordinary building repairs	3,700	28,700	
Total			95,550
Increase in working capital			$ 4,925

CONCEPT OF FUNDS AS ALL FINANCIAL RESOURCES

Statement of sources and uses of funds. In its Opinion published in October 1963, and mentioned at the beginning of this chapter, the Accounting Principles Board stated that:

> In the case of statements prepared for presentation in annual reports, a concept broader than that of working capital should be used which can be characterized or defined as "all financial resources," so that the statement will include the financial aspects of all significant transactions. . . .

In addition to accounting for the change in working capital, the statement should give a comprehensive picture of other changes in financial condition by including the items mentioned below:

Under the Funds Sources caption:

All credits to noncurrent accounts resulting from transactions (but not mere book entries) regardless of whether the offsetting debit was to a working capital account or to some other noncurrent account.

Under the Funds Uses caption:

All debits to noncurrent accounts resulting from transactions (but not mere book entries) regardless of whether the offsetting credit was to a working capital account or to some other noncurrent account.

Illustration. An illustrative statement prepared in accordance with this concept is presented on page 476. It is based on the following condensed comparative balance sheet.

THE *K* COMPANY

Condensed Comparative Balance Sheet
December 31, 1965 and 1964

	December 31,		Net Change	
Assets	1965	1964	Debit	Credit
Working capital	$24,000	$20,000	$ 4,000	
Investment securities		5,000		$ 5,000
Land	8,000	5,000	3,000	
Buildings	50,000	30,000	20,000	
Accumulated depreciation—Buildings	4,000*	3,000*		1,000
Equipment	22,000	15,000	7,000	
Accumulated depreciation—Equipment	3,000*	2,250*		750
Goodwill		5,000		5,000
	$97,000	$74,750		
Liabilities and Stockholders' Equity				
Long-term unsecured notes payable		$10,000	10,000	
Mortgage payable	$15,000			15,000
Capital stock	65,000	50,000		15,000
Retained earnings	17,000	14,750		2,250
	$97,000	$74,750	$44,000	$44,000

* Deduction.

The causes of the changes in the noncurrent accounts are stated below:

Depreciation of buildings during the year was $1,000; depreciation of equipment was $750.

The $5,000 Goodwill account was written off. This was a mere book entry which will not be reflected in the statement.

Capital stock of $10,000 par value was issued to retire the long-term notes payable.

Capital stock of $5,000 par value was issued for cash.

A dividend of $3,500 was paid.

The net income for the year was $10,750.

A purchase of fixed assets was made as follows:

Acquired from seller:	
Land	$ 3,000
Buildings	20,000
Equipment	7,000
Total	$30,000
Given to seller:	
Investment securities	$ 5,000
Mortgage payable	15,000
Cash	10,000
Total	$30,000

THE *K* COMPANY

Statement of Sources and Uses of Funds
For the Year Ended December 31, 1965

Funds sources:			
Operations:			
Net income for the year		$10,750	
Depreciation of buildings		1,000	
Depreciation of equipment		750	$12,500
Issuance of capital stock			15,000
Issuance of mortgage			15,000
Disposal of investment securities			5,000
Total funds from all sources			$47,500
Funds uses:			
Acquisitions of fixed assets:			
Land	$ 3,000		
Buildings	20,000		
Equipment	7,000	$30,000	
Retirement of long-term unsecured notes payable		10,000	
Payment of dividend		3,500	
Total funds uses			43,500
Increase in working capital			$ 4,000

Some other suggested titles for the statement are:

Statement of Resources Provided and Applied, with side captions: Resources provided and Resources applied

Statement of Source and Application of Funds, with side captions: Source of funds and Funds applied

THE *K* COMPANY
Working Papers for Statement of Sources and Uses of Funds
For the Year Ended December 31, 1965

	Year's Changes Detailed		Grouping Transfers and No-Effect Reversals		Funds		
						Sources	
	Debits	Credits	Debits	Credits	Uses	Operations	Other
Increase in working capital	4,000						
Changes in noncurrent accounts:							
Investment securities:							
Part of consideration for plant assets		5,000					5,000
Land:							
Purchase	3,000				3,000		
Buildings:							
Purchase	20,000				20,000		
Accumulated depreciation—Buildings:							
Depreciation for the year		1,000				1,000	
Equipment:							
Purchase	7,000				7,000		
Accumulated depreciation—Equipment:							
Depreciation for the year		750				750	
Goodwill:							
Write-off against Retained Earnings		5,000	A 5,000				
Long-term unsecured notes payable:							
Retired	10,000				10,000		
Mortgage payable:							
Issued for plant assets		15,000					15,000
Capital stock:							
Issued to retire long-term notes		10,000					10,000
Issued for cash		5,000					5,000
Retained earnings:							
Dividend	3,500				3,500		
Net income		10,750				10,750	
Write-off of Goodwill	5,000			A 5,000			
	52,500	52,500	5,000	5,000			
Funds provided by operations						12,500	12,500
Funds from all sources							47,500
Funds uses					43,500		43,500
Increase in working capital							4,000

CHAPTER

25

Statements from Incomplete Records

In this chapter we shall deal with the preparation of statements for businesses which do not keep complete double-entry books. We shall deal first with the so-called single-entry method of computing net income, and then with procedures for developing an income statement in the form that would be used if complete double-entry records were maintained.

SINGLE-ENTRY INCOME STATEMENT

Single-entry bookkeeping. The minimum essentials of a single-entry bookkeeping system consist of accounts with debtors and creditors and a record of cash receipts and disbursements. Other accounts, records, and memoranda may be maintained, but a bookkeeping system short of a complete set of double-entry accounts is still regarded as a single-entry system.

Single-entry income statement. The single-entry method of determining the net income for a period is as follows:

(1) Prepare a statement of assets and liabilities as of the beginning of the period, and a similar statement as of the end of the period. From these statements, the owner's equity at the beginning and end of the period can be determined.

Information regarding accounts receivable, accounts payable, and cash, required for these statements, can be obtained from the ledger and cash records. Information concerning other assets and liabilities must be obtained from any available information.

(2) Add the owner's equity at the beginning of the period and the additional investments during the period; the total represents the proprietor's gross contribution to the business for the period.

(3) Add the owner's equity at the end of the period and the owner's withdrawals during the period; the total represents the amount made available to the owner as the result of contributions and business operations.
(4) Compute the difference between the totals determined in (2) and (3); this difference is accepted as the net income or loss for the period.

First illustration:

Owner's equity, end of period		$12,000
Add drawings		1,000
Total		$13,000
Deduct:		
Owner's equity, beginning of period	$10,000	
Additional investments	500	10,500
Net income		$ 2,500

Second illustration:

Owner's equity, beginning of period		$10,000
Additional investments		1,800
Total		$11,800
Deduct:		
Owner's equity, end of period	$11,000	
Drawings	300	11,300
Net loss		$ 500

STATEMENTS IN DOUBLE-ENTRY FORM

Sources of data. If there is a record of cash receipts and disbursements,

An analysis of the cash receipts will show:
- Cash sales
- Collections from customers
- Receipts from other sources

An analysis of the cash disbursements will show:
- Cash purchases
- Payments to creditors
- Payments for expenses
- Other disbursements

With this information and with information concerning accounts receivable, accounts payable, inventories, and such other matters as accrued and deferred items at the beginning and end of the period, data for the preparation of an income statement in double-entry form can be assembled.

Computation of sales. Several illustrations are presented on the next page showing the computation of sales by the use of data shown by the cash and receivable records.

Basic illustration. This first illustration shows the basic procedure.

Cash sales		$ 75,000
Sales on account:		
Collections from customers	$80,000	
Less accounts receivable, beginning of period	8,100	
Collections from sales for the period	$71,900	
Add accounts receivable, end of period	8,000	79,900
Total sales		$154,900

The computation can be somewhat simplified as follows:

Cash sales	$ 75,000
Add collections from customers	80,000
Total	$155,000
Less decrease in accounts receivable	100
Sales	$154,900

This chapter will show how a systematic set of working papers can be prepared to assemble all of the data required for an income statement in double-entry form. Such working papers consist of three sections:

Comparative balance sheet data.
Cash receipts and disbursements data.
Income statement data.

The balance sheet and cash data are first entered in the working papers in the manner shown below.

Income Statement Working Papers
For the Year Ended December 31, 1965

	Comparative Balance Sheet			
	December 31,		Year's Changes—Net	
	1965	1964	Debit	Credit
Balance sheets:				
Assets:				
Accounts receivable	8,000	8,100		100
			Cash	
			Debit	Credit
Cash:				
Cash sales			75,000	
Collections on accounts receivable			80,000	
			Income Statement	
			Debit	Credit
Income statement:				

The $154,900 credit offsetting the amounts shown in the last two columns of the working papers is then entered in the Income Statement section of the papers, in the manner shown at the top of the next page. Observe that the amounts are given a cross-reference letter (A) so that the items entering into the computation of the $154,900 can be traced.

Income Statement Working Papers
For the Year Ended December 31, 1965

	Comparative Balance Sheet			
	December 31,		Year's Changes—Net	
	1965	1964	Debit	Credit
Balance sheets:				
Assets:				
Accounts receivable	8,000	8,100		100 A
			Cash	
			Debit	Credit
Cash:				
Cash sales			75,000 A	
Collections on accounts receivable			80,000 A	
			Income Statement	
			Debit	Credit
Income statement:				
Sales				154,900 A

Notes received from customers. If notes are taken from customers, the difference between the notes receivable at the beginning and end of the period, as well as the change in the accounts receivable, must be taken into the computation of sales.

Income Statement Working Papers
For the Year Ended December 31, 1965

	Comparative Balance Sheet			
	December 31,		Year's Changes—Net	
	1965	1964	Debit	Credit
Balance sheets:				
Assets:				
Accounts receivable	5,000	5,600		600 A
Notes receivable	3,000	2,500	500 A	
			Cash	
			Debit	Credit
Cash:				
Cash sales			75,000 A	
Collections on accounts receivable			60,000 A	
Collections on notes receivable			20,000 A	
			Income Statement	
			Debit	Credit
Income statement:				
Sales				154,900 A

Returns and allowances. Assume the same facts as in the preceding illustration except that an analysis of the accounts receivable showed credits of $350 for returns and allowances.

Income Statement Working Papers
For the Year Ended December 31, 1965

	Comparative Balance Sheet			
	December 31,		Year's Changes—Net	
	1965	1964	Debit	Credit
Balance sheets:				
Assets:				
Accounts receivable	5,000	5,600		600 A
Notes receivable	3,000	2,500	500 A	
			Cash	
			Debit	Credit
Cash:				
Cash sales			75,000 A	
Collections on accounts receivable			60,000 A	
Collections on notes receivable			20,000 A	
			Income Statement	
			Debit	Credit
Income statement:				
Sales returns and allowances			350 A	
Sales				155,250 A

The $350 debit was entered in the Income Statement debit column, and the $155,250 entered in the credit column was the amount necessary to balance the debits and credits.

Cash discounts on sales. Assume the same facts as in the immediately preceding illustration; in addition, there were cash discounts on sales amounting to $450.

Income Statement Working Papers
For the Year Ended December 31, 1965

	Comparative Balance Sheet			
	December 31,		Year's Changes—Net	
	1965	1964	Debit	Credit
Balance sheets:				
Assets:				
Accounts receivable	5,000	5,600		600 A
Notes receivable	3,000	2,500	500 A	
			Cash	
			Debit	Credit
Cash:				
Cash sales			75,000 A	
Collections on accounts receivable			60,000 A	
Collections on notes receivable			20,000 A	
			Income Statement	
			Debit	Credit
Income statement:				
Sales returns and allowances			350 A	
Sales discounts			450 A	
Sales				155,700 A

Bad debts. Assume the same facts as in the preceding illustration; also assume that $1,200 of accounts had been removed from the ledger as uncollectible. This removal, of course, affected the change in the accounts receivable during the year. If no consideration is given to this matter, the sales will be understated and the loss from bad debts will be ignored.

Income Statement Working Papers
For the Year Ended December 31, 1965

	Comparative Balance Sheet			
	December 31,		Year's Changes—Net	
	1965	1964	Debit	Credit
Balance sheets:				
Assets:				
Accounts receivable	5,000	5,600		600 A
Notes receivable	3,000	2,500	500 A	
			Cash	
			Debit	Credit
Cash:				
Cash sales			75,000 A	
Collections on accounts receivable			60,000 A	
Collections on notes receivable			20,000 A	
			Income Statement	
			Debit	Credit
Income statement:				
Sales returns and allowances			350 A	
Sales discounts			450 A	
Bad debts			1,200 A	
Sales				156,900 A

Computation of purchases. Two illustrations are presented below showing the computation of purchases.

Basic illustration. The first illustration shows the basic procedure.

Cash purchases		$ 3,600
Purchases on account:		
Payments to trade creditors	$92,700	
Less accounts payable, beginning of period	5,900	
Payments for purchases during the period	$86,800	
Add accounts payable, end of period	5,500	92,300
Total purchases		$95,900

The computation can, of course, be simplified by merely deducting the decrease in accounts payable during the year, thus:

Cash purchases	$ 3,600
Add payments to trade creditors	92,700
Total	$96,300
Less decrease in accounts payable	400
Purchases	$95,900

The working-paper treatment is shown below.

Income Statement Working Papers
For the Year Ended December 31, 1965

	Comparative Balance Sheet			
	December 31,		Year's Changes—Net	
	1965	1964	Debit	Credit
Balance sheets:				
Liabilities:				
Accounts payable—Trade	5,500	5,900	400 B	
			Cash	
			Debit	Credit
Cash:				
Cash purchases				3,600 B
Payments to trade creditors				92,700 B
			Income Statement	
			Debit	Credit
Income statement:				
Purchases			95,900 B	

Notes, returns and allowances, and cash discounts. This illustration is based on the same facts as the preceding one, with the following additions:

Notes were given to trade creditors.
Purchase returns and allowances amounted to $1,400.
Purchase discounts amounted to $1,675.

Income Statement Working Papers
For the Year Ended December 31, 1965

	Comparative Balance Sheet			
	December 31,		Year's Changes—Net	
	1965	1964	Debit	Credit
Balance sheets:				
Liabilities:				
Accounts payable—Trade	3,000	3,900	900 B	
Notes payable—Trade	2,500	2,000		500 B
			Cash	
			Debit	Credit
Cash:				
Cash purchases				3,600 B
Payments on accounts payable—Trade				79,800 B
Payments on notes payable—Trade				12,900 B
			Income Statement	
			Debit	Credit
Income statement:				
Purchase returns and allowances				1,400 B
Purchase discounts				1,675 B
Purchases			98,975 B	

Inventories. The working-paper treatment of the inventories at the beginning and end of the period is illustrated below.

Income Statement Working Papers
For the Year Ended December 31, 1965

	Comparative Balance Sheet			
	December 31,		Year's Changes—Net	
	1965	1964	Debit	Credit
Balance sheets:				
Assets:				
Merchandise inventory	16,000	15,460	540 C	
			Cash	
			Debit	Credit
Cash:				
			Income Statement	
			Debit	Credit
Income statement:				
Inventory, December 31, 1964			15,460 C	
Inventory, December 31, 1965				16,000 C

Completed illustration. The working papers on the following page combine those in the last illustrations of the computation of sales and purchases and the illustration of the treatment of inventories. It is now also assumed that the expenses for the year were $50,000—all paid in cash.

H. W. BROWN
Income Statement Working Papers
For the Year Ended December 31, 1965

	Comparative Balance Sheet			
	December 31,		Year's Changes—Net	
	1965	1964	Debit	Credit
Balance sheets:				
Assets:				
Cash	12,740	4,040	8,700	
Accounts receivable	5,000	5,600		600 A
Notes receivable—Trade	3,000	2,500	500 A	
Inventory	16,000	15,460	540 C	
	36,740	27,600		
Liabilities and owner's equity:				
Accounts payable	3,000	3,900	900 B	
Notes payable—Trade	2,500	2,000		500 B
Owner's equity	31,240	21,700		9,540
	36,740	27,600	10,640	10,640

	Cash	
	Debit	Credit
Cash:		
Cash sales	75,000 A	
Collections on accounts receivable	60,000 A	
Collections on notes receivable—Trade	20,000 A	
Cash purchases		3,600 B
Payments on accounts payable		79,800 B
Payments on notes payable—Trade		12,900 B
Expenses		50,000 D
Increase in cash		8,700
	155,000	155,000

	Income Statement	
	Debit	Credit
Income statement:		
Sales returns and allowances	350 A	
Sales discounts	450 A	
Bad debts	1,200 A	
Sales		156,900 A
Purchase returns and allowances		1,400 B
Purchase discounts		1,675 B
Purchases	98,975 B	
Inventory, December 31, 1964	15,460 C	
Inventory, December 31, 1965		16,000 C
Expenses	50,000 D	
Net income	9,540	
	175,975	175,975

Accrued revenue and expense. The illustration on the following page shows the working-paper treatment of accruals.

Income Statement Working Papers
For the Year Ended December 31, 1965

	Comparative Balance Sheet			
	December 31,		Year's Changes—Net	
	1965	1964	Debit	Credit
Balance sheets:				
Assets:				
Accrued interest receivable	85	60	25 E	
Liabilities:				
Accrued wages payable	700	625		75 F
Accrued interest payable	45	58	13 G	

	Cash	
	Debit	Credit
Cash:		
Interest on notes receivable	330 E	
Wages		9,500 F
Interest on notes payable		625 G

	Income Statement	
	Debit	Credit
Income statement:		
Interest earned		355 E
Wages	9,575 F	
Interest on notes payable	612 G	

Revenue and cost apportionments. The following illustration shows the treatment of revenues collected in advance and expenses paid in advance.

Income Statement Working Papers
For the Year Ended December 31, 1965

	Comparative Balance Sheet			
	December 31,		Year's Changes—Net	
	1965	1964	Debit	Credit
Balance sheets:				
Assets:				
Unexpired insurance	650	435	215 H	
Liabilities:				
Rent collected in advance	300	400	100 I	

	Cash	
	Debit	Credit
Cash:		
Insurance policy purchased		400 H

	Income Statement	
	Debit	Credit
Income statement:		
Insurance expense	185 H	
Rent earned		100 I

Depreciation. The best procedure for dealing with depreciation expense is to include in the Comparative Balance Sheet columns the accumulated depreciation at the beginning and end of the year.

Income Statement Working Papers
For the Year Ended December 31, 1965

	Comparative Balance Sheet			
	December 31,		Year's Changes—Net	
	1965	1964	Debit	Credit
Balance sheets:				
Assets:				
Store equipment	35,000	30,000	5,000	
Accumulated depreciation—Store equipment	6,300*	4,800*		1,500 J
* Deduction.				
			Cash	
			Debit	Credit
Cash:				
			Income Statement	
			Debit	Credit
Income statement:				
Depreciation—Store equipment			1,500 J	

Allowance for doubtful accounts. A preceding illustration (page 483) showed the treatment of bad debts when no Allowance for Doubtful Accounts was included in the Comparative Balance Sheet columns, and accounts determined to be uncollectible were simply removed from the ledger. The following illustration shows the procedure if the Comparative Balance Sheet columns contain an allowance account. The illustration assumes that:

Accounts receivable in the amount of $1,000 were removed from the ledger as uncollectible.

It was believed that the allowance required for the remaining accounts should be $1,500. This is $300 more than was believed necessary a year ago.

The $1,000 must be included in the computation of the sales, as explained on page 483. The bad debts expense is the sum of the $1,000 of accounts found to be worthless and the $300 increase in the allowance account.

Income Statement Working Papers
For the Year Ended December 31, 1965

	Comparative Balance Sheet			
	December 31,		Year's Changes—Net	
	1965	1964	Debit	Credit
Balance sheets:				
Assets:				
Accounts receivable	30,000	25,000	5,000 K	
Allowance for doubtful accounts	1,500*	1,200*		300 L

* Deduction.

	Cash	
	Debit	Credit
Cash:		
Collections on accounts receivable	95,000 K	

	Income Statement	
	Debit	Credit
Income statement:		
Bad debts	{300 L 1,000 K	
Sales		101,000 K

Statement of proprietor's capital or retained earnings. If it is desired to prepare a statement of the proprietor's capital, the working papers may be expanded in the manner illustrated below.

HENRY BARTON
Income and Proprietor's Capital Statements Working Papers
For the Year Ended December 31, 1965

	Comparative Balance Sheet			
	December 31,		Year's Changes—Net	
	1965	1964	Debit	Credit
Balance sheets:				
Assets:				
Cash	7,600	3,600	4,000	
Accounts receivable	25,000	21,000	4,000 A	
Inventory	40,000	38,000	2,000 C	
	72,600	62,600		
Liabilities and proprietor's equity:				
Accounts payable	15,000	20,000	5,000 B	
Henry Barton, capital	57,600	42,600		15,000
	72,600	62,600	15,000	15,000

	Cash	
	Debit	Credit
Cash:		
Collections on accounts receivable	125,000 A	
Payments on accounts payable		70,000 B
Expenses		45,000 D
Drawings		6,000 E
Increase in cash		4,000
	125,000	125,000

	Income Statement	
	Debit	Credit
Income statement:		
Sales		129,000 A
Purchases	65,000 B	
Inventory, December 31, 1964	38,000 C	
Inventory, December 31, 1965		40,000 C
Expenses	45,000 D	
Net income—down	21,000	
	169,000	169,000

	Statement of Proprietor's Capital	
	Debit	Credit
Statement of proprietor's capital:		
Balance, December 31, 1964—per balance sheet		42,600
Net income		21,000
Drawings	6,000 E	
Balance, December 31, 1965	57,600	
	63,600	63,600

If the business is a corporation and it is desired to prepare a statement of retained earnings, the working papers may be prepared in the manner shown below.

THE BARTON COMPANY

Income and Retained Earnings Statements Working Papers
For the Year Ended December 31, 1965

	Comparative Balance Sheet			
	December 31,		Year's Changes—Net	
	1965	1964	Debit	Credit
Balance sheets:				
Assets:				
Cash	7,600	3,600	4,000	
Accounts receivable	25,000	21,000	4,000 A	
Inventory	40,000	38,000	2,000 C	
	72,600	62,600		
Liabilities and stockholders' equity:				
Accounts payable	15,000	20,000	5,000 B	
Capital stock	30,000	30,000		
Retained earnings	27,600	12,600		15,000
	72,600	62,600	15,000	15,000

	Cash	
	Debit	Credit
Cash:		
Collections on accounts receivable	125,000 A	
Payments on accounts payable		70,000 B
Expenses		45,000 D
Dividends		6,000 E
Increase in cash		4,000
	125,000	125,000

	Income Statement	
	Debit	Credit
Income statement:		
Sales		129,000 A
Purchases	65,000 B	
Inventory, December 31, 1964	38,000 C	
Inventory, December 31, 1965		40,000 C
Expenses	45,000 D	
Net income—down	21,000	
	169,000	169,000

	Retained Earnings	
	Debit	Credit
Retained earnings statement:		
Balance, December 31, 1964—per balance sheet		12,600
Net income		21,000
Dividends	6,000 E	
Balance, December 31, 1965	27,600	
	33,600	33,600

CHAPTER

26

Quasi-Reorganizations Business Combinations Divisive Reorganizations

The preceding chapters supply ample evidence of the importance of the cost basis and the going-concern assumption within the structure of generally accepted accounting. These contribute to a continuity of accountability in the accounts and financial statements. Thus, fixed assets are recorded at cost, and the cost basis is carried forward year after year, generally without regard to current values because current values are not of particular interest in accounting for a going concern. Granted the importance and usefulness of these two features of present-day accounting, it would be misleading to create an impression that the application of these concepts produces no difficulties. To develop this point, consider the following questions:

Must a business entity always remain on the cost basis, or are there conditions or circumstances that justify or require a departure from the cost basis?

Is it ever desirable to permit a company to make a fresh start, as far as its basis of accounting is concerned?

Is an accounting basis something that is identified with a particular asset or with a business entity? For example, if assets are transferred from the ownership of Company *A* to the ownership of Company *B*, should the accounting basis ever be carried forward or transferred with the asset?

These are important and complex questions. Essentially they deal with the broad question of when, if ever, and under what circumstances, if any, there may be a break in the historical continuity of account balances. The first two questions are particularly relevant during and after periods of significant change in the level of prices, as occurred after World War I, during the depression years of the 1930's, and again following World War II. Under such conditions, there is the possibility of serious erosion in the meaningfulness of financial statements because some of the amounts in the accounts are stated in "old" dollars not reasonably comparable with present-day dollars. Thus, a cost of $100,000 incurred in 1945 and still carried in the accounts certainly conveys different connotations from a cost of $100,000 incurred in the current year. Yet the accounting process does not distinguish between two such amounts. In the preparation of financial statements, the fact that the two $100,000 amounts consist of dollars of unequal size is ignored. This matter is discussed in some detail in Chapter 28.

Justification for a break in the historical continuity of account balances may also arise during a time of business depression. Suppose that a corporation has been operating unprofitably and that it is unable to utilize the capacity of its productive facilities. Under such circumstances, the board of directors might order a number of significant changes, possibly including the removal or reassignment of managerial personnel, the abandonment of certain products or marketing areas, and the adjustment of the company's capital structure, in an attempt to regain business health. Why not establish a new basis of accountability along with the fresh start toward profit?

The third question is particularly relevant in those cases where properties are transferred from one company to another and the transaction *in substance* results in no new conditions, either as to the control over or the underlying stockholder interest in the properties. This sort of situation arises in mergers and similar devices, often induced by income tax considerations, through which new corporate entities may be created and old ones discarded, and through which assets may be shifted among companies without altering, in any significant degree, the underlying proprietary interests.

The accounting matters associated with the questions raised here will be discussed under the headings of "Quasi-Reorganizations," "Business Combinations," and "Divisive Reorganizations." All involve, fundamentally, the matter of continuity of an accounting basis.

QUASI-REORGANIZATIONS

The situation during depressed business conditions. If business conditions are depressed, declining prices and operating losses are often evident. Those businesses adversely affected often undertake drastic actions to reduce expenses. A number of the assets of an unprofitable business, acquired during more prosperous times, may no longer be worth their cost or carrying value. Reasonable men may believe that there is only a remote chance for a depressed business to recover, through future operations, the past outlays made for fixed assets.

Under such conditions, the question arises as to whether financial statements prepared in accordance with generally accepted principles of accounting will always result in meaningful reports. What is the merit of continuing to charge depreciation or amortization on cost if it is likely that a share of such cost outlays has in fact become a "lost" cost? If this is the case, should not the loss be taken now, instead of being taken gradually by continuing the depreciation or amortization charges on the basis of the old costs? Will not future operating results be misstated by a failure to give recognition now to any lost costs? Also, if a corporation has a sizable deficit (debit balance in the Retained Earnings account), is there any merit in a requirement that such deficit be carried forward under all circumstances? Instead of carrying forward in the accounts the handicaps associated with the past, why not, in conjunction with a plan of action to alter the business to conform with its new environment, permit a fresh start in the accounts? If a business is in fact making a fresh start in its operating affairs, it seems desirable that the basis of accountability for its assets and stockholders' equity be similarly adjusted to coincide with the new conditions.

To bring some of the above questions into sharper focus, assume that a corporation's books show the condition summarized below:

Fixed assets, after deducting depreciation and amortization	$2,000,000
Other assets	700,000
Less liabilities	1,000,000*
Net assets	$1,700,000
Capital stock	$1,500,000
Capital in excess of par (or stated) value	500,000
Less debit balance in Retained Earnings account	300,000*
Stockholders' equity	$1,700,000

* Deduction.

It is also assumed that it is unlikely that the investment in fixed assets (the $2,000,000 carrying value above) can be recovered from future operations. In short, the present management would not invest $2,000,000 to acquire the existing fixed assets because of the unlikelihood that such an outlay would be recovered from the use of those facilities.

Consider first the matter of the deficit. To eliminate the deficit, the company *could* transfer its net assets to a newly organized corporation in exchange for the capital stock of the new company, which might begin its corporate existence with the following account balances:

Fixed assets	$2,000,000
Other assets	700,000
Less liabilities	1,000,000*
Net assets	$1,700,000

Capital stock	$1,500,000
Capital in excess of par (or stated) value	200,000
Stockholders' equity	$1,700,000

* Deduction.

One thing would be accomplished: the deficit would be eliminated. But what about the reduction of the carrying value of the fixed assets to more realistic amounts? The transfer of assets to a new corporate entity obviously sanctions a change in asset valuations; but should accounting rules insist upon the creation of a new corporate entity before the historical continuity of any of the account balances can be interrupted?

Quasi-reorganization described. In general, the answer to the above question is no. Within the framework of generally accepted accounting, there is a procedure known as a *quasi-reorganization,* by which a fresh start in an accounting sense may be obtained without the expense and other disadvantages incident to the creation of a new corporate entity. It has the following characteristics:

(1) The existing corporate entity is not disturbed.
(2) Recorded asset values may be readjusted (downward) to conform to present conditions.
(3) Typically, a deficit is eliminated.
(4) A quasi-reorganization requires complete disclosure of the effects it has had on the accounts.

As the above characteristics imply, a quasi-reorganization is something less formal than a legal reorganization. The accounting result of a quasi-reorganization is in substance the same *as though* or *as if* a legal reorganization *had* occurred.

What formalities, if any, are required to effect a quasi-reorganization? *Accounting Series Release* No. 25 of the Securities and Exchange Commission states that "It has been the Commission's view for some time that a quasi-reorganization may not be considered to have been effected unless ... the entire procedure is made known to all persons entitled to vote on matters of general corporate policy and the appropriate consents to the particular transactions are obtained in advance in accordance with the applicable law and charter provisions." However, a Commission ruling must be distinguished from a law of general applicability.

A quasi-reorganization is often effected without legal formalities of any kind. If the company has capital in excess of par (or stated) value which is legally available for dividends, the offsetting of the operating deficit against such "excess" does not affect the net amount legally available for dividends. On the other hand, the change in the capital structure may be such as to necessitate obtaining an amendment of the corporate charter.

As indicated above, a quasi-reorganization enables a company to eliminate a deficit. The deficit may be attributable to operating losses or to the recognition of other losses. A deficit need not exist in the accounts before a quasi-reorganization is effected; the deficit may develop as a result of asset write-downs recorded as part of the quasi-reorganization entries. In other words, if assets are overvalued in the accounts, a write-down of such assets to current values should be a part of the quasi-reorganization. It is a part of the fresh start. The write-down establishes a new and current measure of management's accountability; it gives recognition to a loss which occurred prior to the quasi-reorganization; it enables the company to compute its operating charges for depreciation and amortization on the basis of values as of the date of the fresh start; and such a write-down may produce a debit balance in the Retained Earnings account.

To illustrate asset write-downs in connection with a quasi-reorganization, let us return to the preceding illustration and assume that the fixed assets carried at $2,000,000 would be more properly valued at $1,600,000, considering the new conditions. Assume that, in order to create an amount of capital in excess of par (or stated) value sufficient to provide for writing down the fixed assets to current values and for eliminating the operating deficit, the capital stock is reduced from $1,500,000 to $1,000,000. If the stock has a par value, the reduction can be accomplished by reducing the number or the par value of the shares outstanding, or by changing from a par to a no-par basis and assigning to the no-par shares an aggregate stated value less than the aggregate par value of the shares formerly outstanding. If the stock is without par value, the number of outstanding shares or the stated value per share may be reduced.

Entries to record the quasi-reorganization are shown below:

Capital stock	500,000	
Capital in excess of par (or stated) value		500,000
To record the capital stock reduction from $1,500,000 to $1,000,000.		
Retained earnings	400,000	
Fixed assets		400,000
To record the reduction in the book value of the fixed assets from $2,000,000 to $1,600,000.		
Capital in excess of par (or stated) value	700,000	
Retained earnings		700,000
To write off the debit balance in Retained Earnings against the capital-in-excess account.		

These entries produce the following account balances:

Fixed assets	$1,600,000
Other assets	700,000
Less liabilities	1,000,000*
Net assets	$1,300,000
Capital stock	$1,000,000
Capital in excess of par (or stated) value	300,000
Stockholders' equity	$1,300,000

* Deduction.

Any reduction in the book valuation of fixed or other assets which is made in connection with a quasi-reorganization should represent a real loss incurred prior thereto; any write-down in excess of such an incurred loss would have the unjustifiable result of relieving subsequent operations of proper charges for depreciation, amortization, or other costs and thus would result in an overstatement of earnings subsequent to the reorganization. In other words, an unjustifiable debit to Capital in Excess of Par (or Stated) Value at the time of the quasi-reorganization would ultimately result in an unjustifiable addition to Retained Earnings. However, it is considered proper to create reserves for losses and expenses which can reasonably be assumed to have been incurred in the past although the amounts thereof may not be definitely determinable at the date of the quasi-reorganization. Unrequired balances in such reserves should ultimately be transferred to a capital-in-excess account.

If, subsequent to a quasi-reorganization, it is desired to make additional write-downs in the valuation of assets owned at the time of the reorganization, is it permissible to make such write-downs against the "capital in excess"? The general opinion seems to be that the results of operations may be misstated unless caution is exercised, and that such subsequent write-downs should be charged to a capital-in-excess account only in case they can be definitely established as representing decreases in value which occurred prior to the quasi-reorganization but were not recognized or measurable at that time.

On the other hand, suppose that an asset, written down to its estimated realizable value as a part of a quasi-reorganization, is subsequently sold for more than its new carrying value. Is such excess of sales proceeds over the new carrying value a gain, or does it represent a correction of the quasi-reorganization write-down? If the sale occurs soon after the quasi, the selling price may be a better indication of what the asset was worth at the time of the quasi than the estimate used, in which case the sale should be viewed as providing a basis for a correction of the quasi entries. If the accountant had known the future sale value at the time of the quasi, he probably would have used that amount for the write-down. Then there would have been no "gain" when the asset was sold. In those cases in which a deficit was eliminated by the quasi-reorganization, it would be logical to carry the net credit from the sale to a capital-in-excess account. (Using older terminology, the accountant would state that the net credit should be carried to paid-in surplus.) Of course, if it can be established that the asset increased in value since the quasi-reorganization, then the excess should be accounted for as an extraneous gain.

In the statements rendered at the close of the period in which a quasi-reorganization was effected, there should be disclosure of all facts relative to the quasi—particularly the amount of the operating deficit eliminated. In the statements for that period and subsequent periods, the retained earnings should be "dated": the statements should show that the retained earnings have been accumulated since the date as of which a quasi-reorganization took place with a deficit eliminated from the accounts. The disclosure may be made as follows:

Retained earnings—Accumulated since December 31, 1961, the date of a quasi-reorganization .... $xxxx

How long such dating should be continued has not been determined, but a maximum period of ten years has been mentioned. It has also been suggested that the dating should be continued until the company has established a new earnings record.

As noted earlier, a quasi-reorganization is comparable to a new start. If a deficit in the Retained Earnings account is eliminated at that time, the historical distinction maintained in the accounts between paid-in capital and stockholders' equity resulting from earnings is disrupted. The date of the quasi-reorganization is the starting point for a new record of retained earnings. Should it also be the date of a fresh start in the capital in excess of par (or stated) value accounts? Prior to a quasi, there might have been several capital-in-excess accounts which classified the paid-in elements of the stockholders' equity according to source; it appears to be acceptable to show any capital in excess remaining after the quasi in a single account, indicating in the title of this account that its balance is the aggregate capital in excess of par (or stated) value remaining at the date of the fresh start. Any capital in excess arising after the quasi should be classified by source in new accounts.

What about charges to any capital in excess carried forward after a quasi-reorganization? As a general rule, the source of capital-in-excess accounts is an important criterion in establishing the kinds of charges that can be made to such accounts. For example, prior to a quasi-reorganization a premium paid on the retirement of preferred stock could be charged against any capital in excess traceable to preferred stockholders, under the theory that it would be equitable to consider the retirement premium as a return of capital originally invested by the preferred stockholders. But in the opinion of the authors, if charges have been made to capital-in-excess accounts during a quasi, that destroys the classification according to source and no attempt should subsequently be made to identify any capital-in-excess residue according to source. Some justification other than source would have to be found. When confronted with this problem, accountants should recognize the desirability of seeking and being guided by legal opinion. Neither the Institute nor the Securities and Exchange Commission appears to have expressed an opinion on this matter.

Because the stockholders' authorization of the quasi-reorganization may not occur at a year end (or other date when the books are closed), it is regarded as permissible for the management to choose some other date as the one at which the quasi becomes effective and from which subsequent retained earnings should be dated. The Securities and Exchange Commission appears to have declined to sanction the adoption, for this purpose, of a date prior to the last closing preceding the authorization of the quasi. The adoption of such an earlier date is not sanctioned because that would give the management the opportunity arbitrarily to select a date when losses stopped and earnings began.

Quasi-reorganizations are sometimes effected when a company has some retained earnings. If, in such cases, the asset write-downs do not exhaust the retained earnings, subsequent balance sheets should indicate that such remaining retained earnings arose prior to the date of the quasi-reorganization, and it should be clearly distinguished from retained earnings accumulated after that date.

Status of upward quasi-reorganizations. Can assets be written up in connection with a quasi-reorganization? Accounting sanction of quasi-reorganizations has been based on a recognition of the desirability of allowing corporations to make a fresh start if they have incurred substantial losses of if their assets are materially overstated. Although there seems to be some tendency to sanction write-ups of some assets so long as the adjustments as a whole result in a net write-down, no approval, up to the time of this writing, has been given to a net write-up.

However, financial statements based on historical cost can become just as misleading from the impact of a significant general price increase as from the opposite condition of declining prices and operating losses, which currently is the only situation that may justify a quasi-reorganization. Therefore, it seems reasonable to expect that, in time, the accounting profession may approve upward quasi-reorganizations, provided, of course, that such procedures are surrounded by strict tests and requirements to eliminate the chance of the procedure being abused by the management of companies in a weak position or with a poor showing who might want to use the device as a "smoke screen."

BUSINESS COMBINATIONS

Historical background. Conditions during the period following World War II have been conducive to the combining of businesses. The urge to expand, the appeal of diversification, the interest in improving competitive position, the desire to acquire managerial talent, income tax considerations, and the prospect of economies of larger-scale operations are some of the incentives leading to the bringing together of two or more businesses. These arrangements have included the formation of new corporations, the exchange of corporate shares, and the merger of several corporations, to mention only a few of the procedures used.

Accountants' services in combinations. When businesses are exploring the desirability of combining, the books of account provide information of importance in the negotiations; the book values of assets and the past earnings serve as a logical starting point in forecasting the contributions the several companies will make to the combination.

It is at this point that the services of an accountant are often required to give assurance that generally accepted accounting principles have been applied and that the data for the several companies are on a reasonably uniform basis. Adjustments of recorded data may be necessary. Errors may have been made. The necessity for some adjustments may arise because of differences in accounting policies. Other adjustments may be needed in order to avoid the possibility that misleading impressions may be produced by unusual transactions.

For these reasons, certain accounts should be analyzed in considerable detail. For example, the accountant should analyze the depreciation accounts of the several companies to determine whether the depreciation policies are acceptable and comparable. If differences are revealed, the effect of these differences on book values and reported earnings must be computed in order to place the accounting data on a reasonably comparable basis. Similarly, the stockholders' equity accounts should be analyzed for unusual or nonrecurring items and for evidence of any entries reflecting appraisals or write-downs.

The following list suggests some of the areas where differences are most likely to be discovered:

(1) Depreciation and maintenance policies.
(2) Provision for uncollectible accounts.
(3) Inventory-pricing policy.
(4) Accounting for intangibles.
(5) Valuation of investments.
(6) Provisions for contingencies or losses.
(7) Officers' salaries.
(8) Differences in accounting policy—such as capitalizing or expensing certain expenditures.
(9) Fixed asset valuations in the accounts—cost or appraisal.
(10) Accrual and prepayment policies.
(11) Accounting for unusual and nonrecurring items.

It should be recognized that differences in the above areas may not be an indication of incorrect or improper accounting. There are many areas where generally accepted accounting principles permit alternative accounting procedures. In other words, books of account may lack comparability because of clerical mistakes, incorrect accounting, or the application of equally acceptable alternatives. In any event, comparability of accounting data is the objective when a combination is being developed.

After reasonable comparability of accounting data has been achieved, as a general rule the interested parties endeavor to use the data relative to assets, liabilities, and earning power in an intelligent fashion in arriving at a program for effecting the combination. Accountants and business management recognize that book values, even when determined on a comparable basis, are not the only matters to be given consideration. Technological changes and the decline in purchasing power of money, to mention only two matters, may substantially impair the significance of recorded amounts. The earning power of a business may warrant a total valuation for the business in excess of that shown by the books. The value of an individual asset may be estimated by considering such matters as its condition, its remaining use-life, its replacement cost, and its resale value. But considering the business as a whole, an estimate of earning power is particularly relevant in determining value, and, in most cases, such estimates are feasible.

If the accountant is asked to review estimates of earning power, the following list is illustrative of the possible considerations:

(1) Will any items of expense be higher or lower after the combination is effected?
(2) Will key personnel continue with the new or continuing company?
(3) What is the trend of earnings? Of sales? Of selling prices? Of unit costs?
(4) Will any products or productive capacity be discontinued? If so, what will be the effect on earnings?

Pooling of interests versus purchase. In its Bulletin 43, issued in 1953, the Institute's Committee on Accounting Procedure stated that a business combination may be classified as a pooling of interests or a purchase, and that the accounting basis for recording a pooling differs, and properly so, from the basis for recording a purchase. In its Bulletin 48, issued in 1957, the Committee expanded its pronouncement without materially changing the position originally taken.

We shall now deal with the tests promulgated for differentiating between a pooling and a purchase, and shall then deal with the accounting bases recommended.

Characteristics of poolings. Many business combinations result in no substantive change. Although assets may be transferred, corporations dissolved, and new corporations organized in a plan leading to a combination of two or more businesses, the combination may be more a matter of *form* than of *substance.*

The following conditions, or some combination of them, have been suggested as necessary to justify classifying a combination as a pooling of interests:

Continuance of the former ownership.
Continuity of voting rights and consequent control over management.
Continuity of management.
Businesses being combined are engaged in activities that are either similar or complementary.
Businesses being combined are of about the same relative size.

Characteristics of purchases. If a combination does not meet the qualifications mentioned above as justifying its classification as a pooling of interests, it is regarded as a purchase. Bulletin 48 makes the following specific statements relative to purchases:

> When the shares of stock that are received by the several owners of one of the predecessor corporations are not substantially in proportion to their respective interests in such predecessor, a new ownership or purchase of the predecessor is presumed to result.
>
> Similarly, if relative voting rights, as between the constituents, are materially altered through the issuance of senior equity or debt securities having limited or no voting rights, a purchase may be indicated.
>
> Likewise, a plan or firm intention and understanding to retire a substantial part of the capital stock issued to the owners of one or more of the constituent corporations, or substantial changes in ownership occurring shortly before or planned to occur shortly after the combination, tends to indicate that the combination is a purchase.

Accounting basis—Purchases. If a given combination is classifiable as a purchase, accountants agree that the assets purchased should be recorded on the books of the acquiring corporation at cost to the acquiring corporation. In all probability, this will result in a change in the recorded valuation of the assets being transferred, for there is no reason to expect that the assets would be transferred at their book values.

Accounting basis—Poolings. A discussion of the accounting basis for a pooling of interests requires consideration of the basis applicable to assets, and the basis applicable to retained earnings.

Assets. If a combination is a mere pooling of interests, with no substantive change in ownership or control, there seems to be no reason, assuming that the assets in question have been accounted for in accordance with generally accepted principles, for changing the accounting basis of the assets merely because a change has occurred in the *form* of the business organization.

The Committee on Accounting Procedure took a position on this matter in Bulletin No. 48. The following quotation states the Committee's position: "When a combination is deemed to be a pooling of interests, a new basis of accountability does not arise. The carrying amounts of the assets of the constituent corporations, if stated in conformity with generally accepted accounting principles and appropriately adjusted when deemed necessary to place them on a uniform accounting basis, should be carried forward . . . ."

Retained earnings. The same type of question arises in connection with retained earnings. If a combination represents a mere pooling of interests, and asset and liability account balances can be transferred to the new or surviving corporation at existing carrying values, why is it not equally acceptable to transfer undistributed earnings? Bulletin No. 48, mentioned above, approves of such transfers.

However, permitting such transfers means that a new corporation can start with some retained earnings, or that an existing corporation can increase its retained earnings as a result of asset acquisitions. Traditionally, such results did not have the support of generally accepted accounting principles. A corporation's retained earnings represented *its* undistributed earnings, exclusively. But such transferability seems well established in present-day practice.

With the transfer of retained earnings being permitted in connection with a pooling of interests, it should be recognized that the retained earnings of the new or surviving corporation may be less, but never more, than the sum of the retained earnings amounts of the combined corporations. The combined retained earnings will be less if the stated capital of the new or surviving corporation is larger than the aggregate of the capital stock and capital-in-excess accounts of the combined corporations. For example, assume the following facts:

	Corporations			
	R	*S*	*T*	Total
Common stock (at stated value)	$100,000	$125,000	$150,000	$375,000
Capital in excess of stated value	20,000		30,000	50,000
Retained earnings	80,000	100,000	70,000	250,000
				$675,000

Assume further that the stockholders of Corporations *R*, *S*, and *T* decide to pool their interests by combining the three corporations into one new corporation having a stated capital of $500,000. After the necessary transfers, the stockholders' equity of the new corporation would appear as follows:

Common stock (at stated value)	$500,000
Retained earnings	175,000
	$675,000

If the stated capital of the new corporation is established at an amount less than $375,000, the aggregate stated capital of the old corporations, such reduction is added to the capital in excess of stated value. For example, assume that the stated capital of the new corporation is $300,000. The stockholders' equity will appear as follows:

Common stock (at stated value)	$300,000
Capital in excess of stated value	125,000
Retained earnings	250,000
	$675,000

Income statement. When a combination is being treated as a pooling of interests, the income statement issued by the surviving corporation for the year during which the combination occurred should normally include the combined operating results of the several entities for the entire year. As noted in Bulletin 48, "if combined statements are not furnished, statements for the constituent corporations prior to the date of combination should be furnished separately or in appropriate groups."

Present status of business-combination accounting. According to a recent accounting research study,* there has been some departure from compliance with the tests mentioned above for distinguishing between a pooling and a purchase; and also there appears to be a tendency, in management circles, to sincerely believe that most business combinations can be accounted for at the present time "either under the purchase concept or under the pooling concept, and either treatment would be held to be in accordance with generally accepted accounting principles." This is hardly a desirable state of affairs. Although such latitude does not favor one approach over the other, statistical data show that justification for the pooling approach is being found in an increasing number of combination situations. In fact, in recent years some combinations accounted for initially as purchases have been retroactively adjusted to conform to a pooling. A brief consideration of some of the reasons for this trend in favor of the pooling concept seems warranted.

Income tax rules and the fact that businessmen tend to favor having their books conform to such rules have some influence in this matter. Many combinations are designed to qualify as being tax-free; that is, if certain provisions in the tax law are met, any tax normally arising from the exchange of assets is postponed until the recipients dispose of the assets acquired as a result of the combination. Thus, the tax basis is not affected by a transfer in a tax-free combination. To illustrate, assume that a depreciable asset owned by Company *B*, which cost $100,000 when new and which is one-half depreciated for income tax purposes, is transferred to Company *A* in connection with the tax-free combining of Companies *A* and *B*. Company *A* will be permitted for tax purposes depreciation of $50,000 over the remaining useful life of the fixed asset, no matter how much the asset is worth or the value of the consideration given by Company *A* at the time of the combination. Suppose that the consideration given up by Company *A* was clearly worth $75,000. Although it is being assumed that the exchange is tax-free, that circumstance does not force the accountant to record the fixed asset on the books of Company *A* at its tax basis. Tax status does not determine the nature of a transaction for accounting purposes. If the tax-free exchange is viewed by the accountant as a purchase, the fixed asset should be recorded at its cost to Company *A*, which is $75,000. The $25,000 difference between the tax basis and the cost to Company *A* would result in future charges to expense that would not be allowed for income tax purposes. However, if a pooling approach can be justified, the recorded amounts will conform to the tax basis and, as noted above, businessmen tend to favor having the books conform to income tax rules. Also observe that if a pooling approach can be justified in this instance, future charges not deductible for tax purposes are avoided. Thus, the decision by the ac-

---

* Arthur R. Wyatt, *A Critical Study of Accounting for Business Combinations* (New York: American Institute of Certified Public Accountants, 1963).

countant whether a given combination is a purchase or a pooling can have some effect on the future earnings reported by the newly combined businesses.

In a period of inflation or business prosperity, one of the by-products of recording a business combination as a purchase instead of as a pooling is that subsequent reported earnings will usually be less than if a pooling treatment could have been used. This condition exists because, as a general rule, the assets being transferred and combined are worth more than their carrying value. Thus, future charges for depreciation and/or amortization will be larger if a purchase has occurred than if a pooling has occurred. If given a choice, the parties to a business combination would no doubt prefer to account for the combination by the method that would have the least unfavorable impact on future earnings per share. The importance placed on the maintenance or improvement of earnings per share by those managing the combined businesses has probably had some influence on the trend favoring the pooling approach.

Another consideration favoring a pooling treatment when either a pooling or a purchase can be justified according to generally accepted accounting principles is the practical difficulty in many cases of establishing a new cost assignable to the several assets transferred in connection with a business combination. When a combination of two or more businesses is consummated by the exchange of shares of stock having different rights and for which there may be no clear indication of current value, greater reliance must be placed on opinion in the determination of amounts that would be acceptable for assignment to the several assets. Under such circumstances, the continuation of existing book values in place of reliance on opinion about current values has some appeal. Also, some weight is given to a company's goodwill in working out the settlement plan. However, accountants are reluctant to record goodwill. They are conservative and generally prefer that the balance sheet show a nominal value or no value for goodwill. It is widely known that goodwill amounts are "distrusted" by many users of financial statements. Hence, companies readily adopt amortization policies leading to an early disappearance of goodwill. At the time of a business combination, management might understandably raise the following question: "Why record goodwill if such action is promptly followed by another action designed to eliminate it from the accounts as soon as possible?" Of course, the matter of future income determination for the combined businesses is directly related to this question. Because most goodwill-amortization programs are arbitrary, it is not entirely clear that the recording of goodwill and its subsequent amortization result in more meaningful income data. This whole matter is avoided if a pooling treatment is justified.

What is the nature of a business combination? The accounting research study referred to earlier makes the point that accountants apparently are not in agreement about the basic nature of a business combination. Professor Arthur R. Wyatt, the author of the research study, reasons that a business combination is essentially a particular type of business transaction. A business combination involves an *exchange,* although often shares of stock rather than business assets are exchanged. The transfer of assets may occur after there has been an exchange of "equity" interests. For instance, in an agreement to combine Companies *A* and *B*, the stockholders of Company *B* may exchange their shares for shares of Company *A*. Company *A* thus becomes the owner of Company *B* and, as the owner, may order the transfer of the assets of Company *B* to Company *A* in exchange for the shares of Company *B*. Company *B* thus ceases to exist as an operating entity. Admittedly, it is generally more difficult to assign prices or values to assets when there has been an "indirect" exchange rather than a purchase of assets for cash. But the issue is whether a combination effected through an exchange of capital stock is fundamentally different from a combination effected through an exchange of assets. If there is no fundamental difference, then most combinations would qualify as purchases. It is Professor Wyatt's position that, if the combination has resulted from arm's-length bargaining between independent parties, "the entities involved should give effect to the transaction in a manner consistent with the treatment accorded other transactions in which the economic assets of an entity change. If, however, the transaction is lacking in substance, as when two formerly related companies combine their interests in what amounts merely to a change in legal form, no significant accounting action is required or desirable."

The following quotation from the comments of Robert C. Holsen, appended to the accounting research study, presents an alternative approach:

> Arthur Wyatt states that "a business combination occurs when one company acquires, assumes, or otherwise gains control over the assets . . . of another company by an exchange of assets or equities . . . ." Instead of being a definition of all business combinations, this is a definition of a purchase, a particular kind of business combination. In a purchase one company does acquire control over the assets of another, but that does not hold true in a pooling of interests. In a pooling, one company does not acquire the assets or control of another; rather the shareholders who controlled one company join with the shareholders who controlled the other company to form the combined group of shareholders who control the combined companies.
>
> From these comments are drawn the following conclusions:
>
> 1. A purchase occurs when consideration other than equity shares is exchanged and one group of shareholders gives up its ownership interest in the assets it formerly controlled.
>
> 2. A pooling of interests occurs when equity shares are exchanged and both groups of shareholders continue their ownership interests in the combined companies.

Regrettably, the accounting for business combinations is an unsettled, highly controversial issue. Based on a look at practice, the authors have concluded that the pooling approach will prevail and that a purchase will be found to have occurred only when cash, notes, or bonds have been given in exchange for assets.

DIVISIVE REORGANIZATIONS

Nature of divisive reorganizations. In the preceding paragraphs, the question of continuity of accounting basis was explored in those cases where two or more businesses are combined under an arrangement called a *pooling of interests*. Similar accounting questions arise in the opposite kind of case, namely, where one business is divided into two or more business entities. Under such an arrangement, it is possible to find a continuity of ownership and control, and, accordingly, questions arise as to whether the transfer of assets should be achieved without disturbing their carrying values, and whether some portion of the retained earnings of the original corporation may be transferred to one or more of the new corporations.

Divisive reorganizations may be classified as follows:

"Spin-offs"

A spin-off involves the transfer of a portion of the assets of an existing corporation to a new corporation in exchange for stock of the new corporation, and the subsequent distribution of the stock in the new corporation to the stockholders of the old corporation without surrender by them of any of their stock in the old company.

"Split-offs"

A split-off is like a spin-off except that the stock of the new corporation is distributed to the stockholders of the old corporation in exchange for part of their stock in the old corporation; thus, there is a reduction in the outstanding shares of the old corporation.

"Split-ups"

A split-up involves a transfer of all of the assets of the old corporation to two or more new corporations in exchange for stock in the new corporations. The stock in the new corporations is distributed to the stockholders of the old corporation in exchange for their stock in the old corporation, and the old corporation goes out of existence.

There are detailed and complex income tax regulations applicable to these divisive reorganizations, which influence such plans considerably because, if these reorganizations comply with the tax rules, the consequences are tax-free.

Position of accounting theory regarding divisive reorganizations. The traditional view is that a new corporation starts its affairs showing assets at the cost in money to the new corporation, or, if other consideration is given, at the fair value of such other consideration, or at the fair value of the property acquired, whichever is more clearly evident. Also, the new corporation commences with no retained earnings. If two or more businesses are combined with no real break in the continuity of ownership and control, the recent emphasis has been on making distinctions between form and substance. In cases of no substantive change, the combined business entity is permitted to carry forward the accounting basis and retained earnings of the predecessor entities.

This raises the question of whether matters of form and substance should not be applied in divisive or break-up cases in a fashion paralleling that applied to the combining case. There would seem to be as much justification.

However, the problem of transferring retained earnings is more difficult in the divisive case. In the combining case, all surpluses and deficits of the constituent corporations are combined. But how does the accountant determine how much or what share of the retained earnings goes to the new corporation when the old corporation continues in existence, or how to divide the retained earnings of the old corporation between or among the new corporations when the old corporation is to be discontinued? Any method or basis used would seem to be arbitrary. This complication may make it difficult to apply, to the divisive situation, the retained earnings carry-over concepts developed for combining situations.

The same difficulty does not exist in connection with the transfers of assets and liabilities; therefore, it is likely that, to an increasing extent, prior carrying values will be used for the assets and liabilities transferred in divisive reorganizations. However, there is not a well-established body of doctrine on this general matter, and it will take further experience with it to develop criteria and customs.

CHAPTER

27

Income Tax Allocation

Background. This chapter is not concerned with the preparation of income tax returns or with the computation of the amount to be shown *in the balance sheet as the liability* for taxes currently payable under federal and state income tax laws. Rather, it considers the question of the amount to be shown *in the income statement as expense.*

It has long been considered proper to show the same amount in both statements, but in recent years the acceptability of this procedure has been seriously and increasingly questioned. The questioning arises from the fact that net income before taxes reported in the income statement may be radically different from taxable net income, with the result that the tax liability may bear no normal relationship to the reported net income before taxes. The fact that tax rates are high augments the distortion.

Differences between net income per books before taxes and taxable net income arise from many causes, among which may be mentioned the following:

Items affecting taxes may be shown in the statement of retained earnings instead of in the income statement.

For example, an extraneous gain of a material amount may be shown in the statement of retained earnings instead of in the income statement.

Accounting principles regarding revenue and expense do not agree in all instances with income tax rules.

For example, provisions for losses under product guaranty agreements are not deductible for income tax purposes; only payments arising from such obligations are deductible. However, it is considered desirable accounting to make an expense provision for such losses in the year that the product is sold.

A corporation may adopt one accounting method for income tax purposes and another method in its books and financial statements.

For example, a corporation may adopt the completed-contract method for income tax purposes and use the percentage-of-completion method for accounting purposes.

Income tax allocation consists of procedures (discussed at some length in this chapter) intended to cause the tax expense shown in the income statement (but not the tax liability shown in the balance sheet) to bear a more normal relation to the net income before tax reported in the income statement. Tax allocation is intended to reduce or eliminate distortion when:

(a) Material amounts entering into the computation of the income tax liability are not shown in the income statement, or
(b) Material amounts included in the income statement do not enter into the computation of the income tax liability.

An important event in the historical development of this matter occurred in 1944, when the Committee on Accounting Procedure issued *A.R.B.* No. 23, which stated that: "Income taxes are an expense which should be allocated, when necessary and practicable, to income and other accounts, as other expenses are allocated." In other words, the amount shown in the income statement for income taxes should be the income tax expense properly allocable to the income included in the income statement for the year and not necessarily the amount currently payable for income taxes.

This bulletin stirred up considerable interest and controversy (which has not subsided noticeably in the intervening years). A significant contrary view was expressed in 1945 by the Securities and Exchange Commission. In its *Accounting Series Release* No. 53 it held that: "The amount shown as provision for taxes should reflect only actual taxes believed to be payable under the applicable tax laws." Subsequently, the Committee on Accounting Procedure issued additional releases on this matter, generally expanding the applicability of the thesis set forth in its Bulletin No. 23; the effectiveness of these releases can be judged by the fact that there have been instances where firms of certified public accountants have qualified their opinion because the client did not use the income tax-allocation procedures. In spite of its initial statement in opposition to tax allocation, the S.E.C. has gone along with the accounting profession. Recently it gave some support to income tax allocation in *Accounting Series Releases* 85 and 86, although no suggestion was made that tax allocation should be mandatory.

Purpose and nature of the chapter. Although income tax allocation, if generally adopted, would have a bearing on some matters discussed in preceding chapters, it seems desirable to isolate the topic in a separate chapter. For one reason, it is complex. For another, tax allocation, as yet, has not quite attained the status of a generally accepted accounting principle.

For purposes of this chapter, it is useful to divide the broad issue as follows:

(A) Matters dealing with the location of the income tax charge in the financial statements.
(B) Matters dealing with the allocation of income taxes through time—or, determining the proper income tax expense for the period, which may differ from the current income tax liability.

At the time of this writing, the federal income tax rates applicable to corporate income are:

22% on the first $25,000 of taxable income.
48% on amounts above $25,000 of taxable income.

For convenience, a 50% rate will be used in the following illustrations.

MATTERS DEALING WITH THE LOCATION OF THE INCOME TAX CHARGE IN THE FINANCIAL STATEMENTS

Material charges to retained earnings that reduce the amount of the income tax liability. Assume that the summary below was prepared by *A* Company in connection with the computation of its income tax.

Sales		$800,000
Cost of goods sold	$500,000	
Selling and administrative expenses	200,000	
Unusual loss (which is deductible for income tax)	60,000	760,000
Amount subject to income tax		$ 40,000
Income tax—50%		$ 20,000

Also assume that the accountant, properly, decided that the unusual loss should not be included in the income statement, because it might cause some statement users to draw misleading inferences, and that it should be charged directly to retained earnings. This leads to the question of the proper statement presentation of the income tax. Consider the following financial statements, in which the income tax actually payable is shown in the income statement and the unusual loss is shown in the statement of retained earnings.

A COMPANY
Income Statement
For the Year ___

Sales		$800,000
Deduct:		
Cost of goods sold	$500,000	
Selling and administrative expenses	200,000	700,000
Net income before income tax		$100,000
Income tax		20,000
Net income		$ 80,000

A COMPANY

Statement of Retained Earnings

For the Year ___

Retained earnings—beginning of year	$480,000
Net income	80,000
Total	$560,000
Deduct unusual loss	60,000
Retained earnings—end of year	$500,000

A statement user might wonder why the income tax on $100,000 of net income before income tax is only $20,000, in view of the common knowledge that income tax rates on corporations are near the 50% level. The apparent discrepancy is attributable to the fact that the $60,000 unusual loss, not shown in the income statement, is deductible and has reduced the income tax by $30,000.

Actually, the unusual transaction in this case resulted in a loss of $30,000 to the company, after considering the tax reduction attributable to the loss. Accountants and businessmen often describe the consequences of isolated transactions in terms of their net-of-tax result. Thus, the unusual loss of *A* Company might be referred to as amounting to $30,000, net of tax.

It was the suggestion of the Committee on Accounting Procedure in its release on this topic that, when an item resulting in a material reduction in income taxes is charged to retained earnings, the tax consequences should also be assigned to retained earnings, thus in effect reducing the charge to surplus and showing the loss on a net-of-tax basis. This suggestion was followed when the net-of-tax procedure was briefly discussed on page 64. In journal form, the entry for the income tax and its allocation would be as follows:

Income tax expense	50,000	
Income tax payable		20,000
Retained earnings		30,000

The income statement and statement of retained earnings of *A* Company, prepared in conformance with tax-allocation procedures, are presented below. Note that the effects of income tax-allocation procedures are disclosed in the financial statements. Disclosure should always be made when tax-allocation procedures are used.

A COMPANY

Income Statement

For the Year ___

Sales		$800,000
Deduct:		
Cost of goods sold	$500,000	
Selling and administrative expenses	200,000	700,000
Net income before income tax		$100,000
Income tax expense		50,000
(The estimated tax liability is $20,000 by reason of a reduction of $30,000 in taxes resulting from an unusual loss. This loss has been charged to retained earnings and the related tax reduction has been treated as an offset thereto.)		
Net income		$ 50,000

A COMPANY
Statement of Retained Earnings
For the Year ___

Retained earnings—beginning of year		$480,000
Net income		50,000
Total		$530,000
Deduct:		
Unusual loss	$60,000	
Less tax effect thereof	30,000	30,000
Retained earnings—end of year		$500,000

With or without tax allocation, the balance sheet shows the income tax liability as $20,000.

Material credits to retained earnings that increase the amount of the income tax liability. Assume that *A* Company, instead of suffering a $60,000 unusual loss, had experienced an unusual, taxable gain of $100,000 in addition to the net operating income of $100,000. Under these circumstances, the income tax liability would amount to $100,000, again assuming a 50% tax rate. The income statement and statement of retained earnings, prepared without allocating the income tax, are shown below. The accountant has treated the unusual gain as a direct credit to retained earnings.

A COMPANY
Income Statement
For the Year ___

Sales		$800,000
Deduct:		
Cost of goods sold	$500,000	
Selling and administrative expenses	200,000	700,000
Net income before income tax		$100,000
Income tax		100,000
Net income		$ -0-

A COMPANY
Statement of Retained Earnings
For the Year ___

Retained earnings—beginning of year	$480,000
Unusual gain	100,000
Retained earnings—end of year	$580,000

If the income tax is allocated, the statements will be:

A COMPANY
Income Statement
For the Year ___

Sales		$800,000
Deduct:		
Cost of goods sold	$500,000	
Selling and administrative expenses	200,000	700,000
Net income before income tax		$100,000
Income tax expense	$100,000	
Less portion thereof allocated to taxable gain shown in statement of retained earnings	50,000	50,000
Net income		$ 50,000

A COMPANY
Statement of Retained Earnings
For the Year ___

Retained earnings—beginning of year		$480,000
Net income		50,000
Add unusual gain	$100,000	
Less income tax thereon	50,000	50,000
Retained earnings—end of year		$580,000

Evaluation of preceding illustrations. The two preceding illustrations demonstrate the distortion that develops when

A company charges or credits Retained Earnings with losses or gains of material amount;
Such gains or losses are includible in the determination of the income tax liability;
The income statement shows as the tax expense the amount payable; in other words, when income taxes are not allocated.

In the first illustration, in which the unusual transaction was adverse in character, nonallocation resulted in increasing the stated net income, as shown below:

Reported net income without tax allocation (See page 511)	$80,000
Reported net income with tax allocation (See page 512)	50,000

In the second illustration, in which the unusual transaction was favorable, nonallocation resulted in decreasing the stated net income.

Reported net income without tax allocation (See page 513)	$ 0
Reported net income with tax allocation (See page 513)	50,000

Considering consequences like those shown above, the Committee on Accounting Procedure commented as follows: "Such results ordinarily detract from the significance or usefulness of the financial statements." The authors concur and believe that if the accountant encounters extraordinary items that in his judgment should be excluded from the determination of net income because including them would impair the significance of net income so that misleading inferences might be drawn, then the tax consequences, if any, should also be removed from the income statement. In other words, the tax should follow the extraordinary item.

Income tax allocation within the income statement. If extraordinary items are shown in the income statement, and they have tax consequences, there is merit in allocating the income tax expense within the income statement. The objective would be to associate the tax effect with the unusual items causing the tax change. Such an allocation procedure can be illustrated by returning to the unusual-gain situation of *A* Company.

A COMPANY
Income Statement
For the Year ___

Sales		$800,000
Deduct:		
Cost of goods sold	$500,000	
Selling and administrative expenses	200,000	700,000
Net operating income before income tax		$100,000
Income tax expense thereon		50,000
Net operating income after income tax		$ 50,000
Add unusual gain	$100,000	
Less income tax thereon	50,000	50,000
Net income		$100,000

MATTERS DEALING WITH THE ALLOCATION OF INCOME TAX THROUGH TIME

Nature of problem. In the preceding section, the problem was merely one of statement location. This section deals with the more difficult problem that arises when the year for tax recognition differs from the year of accounting recognition. The problem will occur under either of the following conditions:

For a given period of time:

(1) The income per books exceeds the income per tax return.
(2) The income per tax return exceeds the income per books.

Deferred income tax liability. To illustrate the consequences of a situation in which the income per books exceeds the income per tax return, assume that *B* Company, engaged in the construction business, uses the percentage-of-completion method of accounting in its financial statements and the completed-contract method for its income tax return. Assume, also, the facts presented in the table on page 516.

A review of the data will reveal the potential distortion of some of the amounts shown in the financial statements if *B* Company should follow the practice of reporting as tax expense only the tax actually payable currently. For example, no income tax expense or liability would be shown in the 1965 financial statements. By the end of 1967, the company would have reported accumulated earnings before income taxes of $310,000 ($40,000 + $100,000 + $170,000) on the three contracts, but only $40,000 of income tax thereon would have been charged. Furthermore, the 1967 balance sheet would show no income tax liability, although the company is subject to future tax on $230,000 of income already reported in its income statements. The $230,000 amount is the difference between the aggregate net income before income taxes for the years 1965, 1966, and 1967 ($310,000) and the income reported in the 1966 income tax return ($80,000).

***B* COMPANY**

	Contract	Year Started	Year Completed	Estimated (and Actual) Total Profit
Construction contracts:				
	I	1965	1966	$ 80,000
	II	1966	1968	200,000
	III	1967	1968	120,000

	1965	1966	1967	1968
Per cent of completion during year:				
I	50%	50%		
II		30	40%	30%
III			75	25
Net income before income tax, reported in the financial statements (total estimated profit multiplied by per cent of completion during year):				
I	$40,000	$ 40,000		
II		60,000	$ 80,000	$ 60,000
III			90,000	30,000
	$40,000	$100,000	$170,000	$ 90,000
Income reported in income tax returns (total profit on contracts completed during the year):				
I		$ 80,000		
II				$200,000
III				120,000
	—	$ 80,000	—	$320,000
Income tax actually payable—50% rate	—	$ 40,000	—	$160,000

Accountants in favor of income tax allocation believe that, on the accrual basis of accounting, a proper matching of revenue and expense requires that the income tax should follow the income. Income that ultimately will be taxable should not be reported in the financial statements as though it were tax-free. The inevitable (or, at least, the reasonably expected) tax liability should be included in the financial statements. They would allocate the income tax on an accrual basis as follows:

	1965	1966	1967	1968
Income statement:				
Net income before income tax	$40,000	$100,000	$170,000	$ 90,000
Income tax expense	20,000	50,000	85,000	45,000
Net income	$20,000	$ 50,000	$ 85,000	$ 45,000
Balance sheet:				
Income tax payable		$ 40,000		$160,000
Deferred income tax liability	$20,000	30,000	$115,000	
	$20,000	$ 70,000	$115,000	$160,000

To acquire an impression of the potential distortion involved in this matter, compare the net income figures above with the amounts that would be reported without the application of income tax-allocation procedures.

	1965	1966	1967	1968
Income statement:				
Net income before income tax	$40,000	$100,000	$170,000	$ 90,000
Income tax actually payable	-0-	40,000	-0-	160,000
Net income (loss*)	$40,000	$ 60,000	$170,000	$ 70,000*
Balance sheet:				
Income tax payable	-0-	$ 40,000	-0-	$160,000

If *B* Company uses income tax-allocation procedures, the journal entries for the income tax charges and payments would appear as shown below.

1965 tax expense:

Income tax expense	20,000	
Deferred income tax liability		20,000

1966 tax expense:

Income tax expense	50,000	
Income tax payable		40,000
Deferred income tax liability		10,000

Income tax for 1966 paid:

Income tax payable	40,000	
Cash		40,000

1967 tax expense:

Income tax expense	85,000	
Deferred income tax liability		85,000

1968 tax expense:

Income tax expense	45,000	
Deferred income tax liability	115,000	
Income tax payable		160,000

Income tax for 1968 paid:

Income tax payable	160,000	
Cash		160,000

Observe the following with respect to the income tax-allocation procedures just described:

In each year, the tax expense to be shown in the income statement is the amount that would be payable if the accounting procedures used in the books were also applied in the tax return.

In each year in which the tax expense shown in the income statement exceeds the tax liability for the year, the excess is credited to a Deferred Income Tax Liability account.

In each year in which the tax liability exceeds the tax expense shown in the income statement, the excess is debited to the Deferred Income Tax Liability account.

Two other common examples of situations that cause the same type of tax-allocation question to arise are:

A corporation uses a form of accelerated depreciation for income tax purposes and the straight-line method for its books.

A corporation adopts the installment sales method for income tax purposes only.

Deferred income tax expense. In the *B* Company case, the net income before tax per books exceeded initially the taxable net income. We now turn to the opposite case, in which the taxable income initially exceeds the net income before tax per books.

In such a case, the tax payable in the initial years will be greater than it would have been if it had been computed on the per-books basis; in later years, the reverse can be expected. The tax-allocation procedure to be applied is:

In each year, the tax expense to be shown in the income statement is the amount that would be payable if the accounting procedures used in the books were applied in the tax return.

In each year in which the tax liability exceeds the tax expense shown in the income statement, the excess is debited to a Deferred Income Tax Expense account.

In each year in which the tax expense shown in the income statement exceeds the tax liability, the excess is credited to the Deferred Income Tax Expense account.

To illustrate, assume that *C* Company purchases a fixed asset for $1,500,000. The asset has an estimated use-life of five years, and the company adopts the sum-of-years'-digits depreciation method for its books and the straight-line method for income tax purposes. Data regarding depreciation are presented below:

	Books		Tax Return
Year	Amount	Over-Under* Amount for Taxes	Amount
1	$ 500,000	$200,000	$ 300,000
2	400,000	100,000	300,000
3	300,000	-0-	300,000
4	200,000	100,000*	300,000
5	100,000	200,000*	300,000
Total	$1,500,000	-0-	$1,500,000

The tax-allocation entries for the five years are indicated below:

	Year 1	2	3	4	5
Assume that the amounts of net income per books before income tax were	$700,000	$600,000	$800,000	$700,000	$900,000
Then the income amounts for tax purposes would be	900,000	700,000	800,000	600,000	700,000
The entries would be:					
Credit Income Tax Payable—for amounts actually payable	$450,000	$350,000	$400,000	$300,000	$350,000
Debit Income Tax Expense—for tax that would be payable on income per books	350,000	300,000	400,000	350,000	450,000
Debit (Credit*) Deferred Income Tax Expense—for difference	$100,000	$ 50,000	-0-	$ 50,000*	$100,000*

Nature of accounts. When income taxes are allocated through time, it is likely that the balance sheet will include either a Deferred Income Tax Liability account (credit balance) or a Deferred Income Tax Expense account (debit balance). It seems relevant to inquire about the nature of such balance sheet accounts.

It is difficult to fit these accounts into the standard definitions of assets and liabilities. The deferred liability account arises because the income tax amount charged in the income statement exceeds the tax currently payable. There is no existing tax obligation to the government for this excess amount. The deferred liability account is the result of a concept of net income which in effect holds that accrual accounting, in its most complete sense, requires in any given period an income tax charge that would exist if there were no timing differences between the tax return and the books. In short, the objective is to show in the income statement the tax applicable to the income reported in the statement. This theory is in contrast to a concept of net income that holds that the proper measure of tax expense for a period is the amount of the current legal liability arising as a result of current operations.

A similar analysis fits the case of the Deferred Income Tax Expense account. This account arises when the tax actually payable exceeds the tax applicable, on an accrual basis, to the income before taxes shown in the income statement. In no sense is the tax prepaid from the point of view of the government. It is the result of a procedure of net income measurement.

Thus, these balance sheet accounts are justified, so to speak, through a net income concept. For example, the credit balance account arises because of a charge in the income statement believed necessary to properly measure net income. To generalize, a debit or credit balance account resulting from placing in the income statement a necessary amount for revenue or expense is a suitable balance sheet asset or liability. Although these amounts do not represent assets or liabilities in the conventional sense of being things of value owned or legal obligations, it is well established that they should not be included under the Stockholders' Equity caption.

In many cases the deferred tax accounts are properly included under the Current Assets or Current Liabilities captions. In those instances in which the deferment is expected to extend beyond a period approximating the operating cycle, a current classification would be unacceptable.

Continuing divergence. In the cases presented thus far, it was reasonable to expect that accounting income and taxable income would, in time, accumulate to an identical sum. In other words, the divergence between accounting income and taxable income was a temporary phenomenon, the result of a matter of timing and not the result of any items of revenue and expense being permanently excludible for one or the other income-determination purpose.

However, there are some items of revenue that are nontaxable (interest on tax-exempt bonds) and of expense that are not deductible for tax purposes (life insurance premiums). Thus, the divergence will not cancel out but will continue indefinitely and regularly. The reasons favoring the allocation of income taxes do not apply in such cases.

Assumptions and practical difficulties. There are several assumptions and practical difficulties that deserve attention.

Future tax rates. The most obvious practical difficulty concerns the matter of income tax rates. If an item is properly included currently in the determination of net income and will at some later date be includible in the determination of taxable income, what rate should be used for the computation of the deferred income tax liability? Should it be the rate currently prevailing or the rate that may be expected to prevail when the item will be taken for tax purposes? The following quotation from A.R.B. No. 43 is relevant: "The estimated rate should be based upon normal and surtax rates in effect during the period covered by the income statement with such changes therein as can be reasonably anticipated at the time the estimate is made." The problem of rate estimation is particularly vexatious in cases where current earnings are running near the $25,000-per-year level. This fact is attributable to the prevailing rate structure which taxes corporate income above $25,000 at substantially higher rates.

Balancing-out assumption. It is sometimes asserted that justification for tax allocation rests on the fact that dollar differences resulting from timing differences between the books and the tax return tend to balance out. To illustrate, consider the case of a real estate company organized to build and operate an apartment costing $150,000. Assume that the company adopts a form of accelerated depreciation for tax purposes and straight-line depreciation for its books. This is the situation depicted in Table A. For convenience, a five-year use-life is assumed.

Table A. Depreciation and Deferred Tax—for One Asset

	Depreciation Per				
	Tax Return	Books			
Year	Years'-Digits Method	Straight-Line Method	Difference	Tax Effect—50% Rate	Cumulative Tax Saving
1	$50,000	$30,000	$20,000	$10,000	$10,000
2	40,000	30,000	10,000	5,000	15,000
3	30,000	30,000	-0-	-0-	15,000
4	20,000	30,000	10,000*	5,000*	10,000
5	10,000	30,000	20,000*	10,000*	-0-

Because the aggregate depreciation taken on the apartment, or any asset for that matter, cannot exceed cost for either tax or book purposes, it can be expected that the periodic differences will cancel out in time. Thus, the tax deferment is temporary, as indicated by the column in Table A showing the cumulative tax saving; there is no ultimate tax saving or tax disadvantage unless there is a change of tax rates before the asset is fully depreciated or disposed of. Incidentally, if there is no change in tax rates, any taxes postponed by the adoption of a different accounting method for tax purposes amount to an interest-free loan to the business.

Whether a balancing-out with no cumulative tax saving is likely to occur can be questioned in the case of many businesses. The reason for this is that many businesses own a number of assets of varying ages, with the result that replacements are made more or less regularly. Thus, a gradual turnover occurs among the assets, in contrast to the single-asset case just discussed, and the cumulative tax saving does not show any tendency to return to zero. Such a situation is illustrated in Table B, in which it is assumed that a company replaces one fully depreciated asset on the first of each year and as a result always has five assets in use. The assets cost $150,000 each; a five-year use-life is assumed. Also, the sum-of-years'-digits method of depreciation is adopted for tax purposes in 1965; the straight-line method is continued in the books. The tax policy thus applies to all assets acquired after December 31, 1964. Details of the tax-return depreciation for the years 1965-1969 are shown on the partial lapsing schedule below Table B.

Table B. Depreciation and Deferred Tax—A Group of Assets

Year	Number of Assets Owned	Aggregate Cost of Assets in Use	Depreciation Per Tax Return	Depreciation Per Books	Difference	Tax Effect—50% Rate	Cumulative Tax Saving
1963	5	$750,000	$150,000	$150,000	$ -0-	$ -0-	$ -0-
1964	5	750,000	150,000	150,000	-0-	-0-	-0-
1965#	5	750,000	170,000#	150,000#	20,000	10,000	10,000
1966	5	750,000	180,000	150,000	30,000	15,000	25,000
1967	5	750,000	180,000	150,000	30,000	15,000	40,000
1968	5	750,000	170,000	150,000	20,000	10,000	50,000
1969	5	750,000	150,000	150,000	-0-	-0-	50,000
1970	5	750,000	150,000	150,000	-0-	-0-	50,000
1971	5	750,000	150,000	150,000	-0-	-0-	50,000
							etc.

#Sum-of-years'-digits method adopted for tax purposes in 1965.

Partial Lapsing Schedule
Tax Return Depreciation—Sum-of-Years'-Digits Method Starting in 1965

Year Asset Acquired	Cost	Depreciation 1965	1966	1967	1968	1969
1961	$150,000	$ 30,000				
1962	150,000	30,000	$ 30,000			
1963	150,000	30,000	30,000	$ 30,000		
1964	150,000	30,000	30,000	30,000	$ 30,000	
1965	150,000	50,000	40,000	30,000	20,000	$ 10,000
1966	150,000		50,000	40,000	30,000	20,000
1967	150,000			50,000	40,000	30,000
1968	150,000				50,000	40,000
1969	150,000					50,000
		$170,000	$180,000	$180,000	$170,000	$150,000

When dealing with a group of assets and staggered replacements thereof, tax and accounting differences, although existing for individual assets, tend to cancel out (see the "Difference" column in Table B). Thus, although there is no tax saving from depreciating a single asset on one basis for tax purposes and on another basis for book purposes but only tax postponement (see Table A), it can work out for a group of assets that a postponed tax is in fact a tax saving from the point of view of a going concern (see the "Cumulative Tax Saving" column in Table B).

The situation shown in Table B tends to approximate that of a stable business; there is no expansion in the investment in depreciable assets. The following generalization relating to a stable business seems appropriate: When accelerated depreciation is adopted for tax purposes only, the deferred tax tends to build up rather rapidly and then level off. When a business is growing and increasing its investment in depreciable assets, the adoption of such a tax policy is even more likely to result in a tax saving, because the cumulative deferred tax will not level off but will continue to increase.

The advocates of tax allocation contend that the question of whether a tax deferment is temporary or more or less permanent is not the controlling point. Tax allocation is favored in either case to avoid the distortion of net income that is likely to occur initially whenever a difference in timing develops between the books and the tax return.

Because it is unlikely that amounts treated as tax deferments will be precisely balanced off by opposite differences in the future between the books and the tax return, there is a strong probability that the balance sheet will include, more or less permanently, residuals from the effects of tax-allocation procedures. In time, such deferred tax amounts will tend to become meaningless and the accountant will probably consider some plan by which to reclassify these balances as a part of stockholders' equity, possibly by making a correction of prior years' earnings.

This particular problem apparently did not greatly concern the Committee on Accounting Procedure, for in Bulletin 43 it made the following comment: "The difficulties encountered in allocation of the tax are not greater than those met with in many other allocations of expenses."

Loss years. When a corporation that has adopted tax-allocation procedures has an unprofitable year, what is the correct approach to the determination of the net loss for the year to be shown in the income statement? The loss-carryback privilege (illustrated on page 82) and the operation of the deferred tax account must be given consideration.

In the illustration set forth in Table C, years 2 and 5 are unprofitable. The loss-carryback privilege will enable the corporation to obtain a $10,000 tax refund for the loss in year 2 and a $5,000 tax refund for the loss in year 5.

The operation of the Deferred Income Tax Liability account is not affected by losses. Thus, in years when more depreciation is taken for tax purposes than is recorded in the accounts, the deferred tax account should be credited whether the year is profitable or unprofitable. In years when more depreciation is recorded in the accounts than is taken for tax purposes, as in years 4 and 5 in the illustration, the deferred tax account should be debited.

Table C. Deferred Tax in Loss Years

	Year 1	Year 2	Year 3	Year 4	Year 5
Depreciation per:					
Tax return–Sum of years' digits	$50,000	$40,000	$30,000	$20,000	$10,000
Books–Straight-line	30,000	30,000	30,000	30,000	30,000
Taxable income (loss*)	20,000	20,000*	40,000	50,000	10,000*
Income tax payable (refundable*)	10,000	10,000*	20,000	25,000	5,000*
Income statement:					
Net income (loss*) before income tax	40,000	10,000*	40,000	40,000	30,000*
Income tax expense	20,000	—	20,000	20,000	—
Income tax adjustment–credit		5,000			15,000
Net income (loss*)	20,000	5,000*	20,000	20,000	15,000*
Deferred income tax liability:					
Addition (reduction*) to account	10,000	5,000	—	5,000*	10,000*
Cumulative balance	10,000	15,000	15,000	10,000	—

The following journal entries, relating to the tax refund and the deferred tax liability, are appropriate in the loss years.

Year 2:

	Debit	Credit
Tax refund claim (asset)	10,000	
Income tax adjustment (special credit in income statement)		5,000
Deferred income tax liability		5,000

The income statement for year 2 will show a net loss of $5,000.

Year 5:

	Debit	Credit
Tax refund claim	5,000	
Deferred income tax liability	10,000	
Income tax adjustment		15,000

The income statement for year 5 will show a net loss of $15,000.

Changes in tax rates. When a significant change occurs in the tax rates, a business that has adopted a different method of accounting for tax purposes only may have gained, or lost, as a result of its earlier tax-policy decision. A correction to the deferred tax account is justified under such circumstances. The correction should be handled in a manner consistent with the company's established policy of accounting for unusual and nonrecurring items.

Let us again return to Table A and assume that the tax rate is reduced from 50% to 40% in year 5. Data assumed for year 5 are shown below.

	Tax Return		Books	
Revenue		$100,000		$100,000
Expenses:				
Depreciation	$10,000		$30,000	
Other	50,000	60,000	50,000	80,000
Taxable income		$ 40,000		
Net income before income tax				$ 20,000

The entry to record the tax charge for the year and the correction resulting from the rate reduction is shown below.

Income tax expense (40% of $20,000)	8,000	
Deferred income tax liability	10,000	
Income tax payable (40% of $40,000)		16,000
Correction of prior years' earnings		2,000

Other tax-allocation applications. The question of income tax allocation also arises in connection with asset write-offs when the book and tax-return treatment differ. Two cases are illustrated below.

Asset write-off for tax purposes only. Assume that a company determines that there is an advantage in refunding a bond issue five years before maturity. The unamortized discount on the bonds refunded is deductible, for tax purposes, only in the year of refunding. But suppose that, in its books and financial statements, the company decides to continue amortizing the discount over the remaining original life of the bonds refunded. As a result, the income reported in the tax return for the year of refunding will be less than the income per books. During the succeeding five years (remaining original life of refunded bonds), the reverse will prevail, because the books will show a charge for the amortization of bond discount that will not appear in the tax return.

To illustrate this particular matter, assume that the data below show in summary form information from the books and tax return for the year during which the refunding occurred. (For convenience it is assumed that the refunding occurred at the end of the year.)

	Corporate Books	Income Tax Return
Sales	$600,000	$600,000
Cost of sales and expenses, except regular annual amortization of bond discount	390,000*	390,000*
Regular annual amortization of bond discount	10,000*	10,000*
Net income before income tax	$200,000	
Write-off of unamortized bond discount		50,000*
Income subject to tax		$150,000
Income tax actually payable—50%		$ 75,000

* Deduction.

If income taxes are not allocated and the tax expense shown in the income statement is the amount of tax currently payable, the net income reported in the financial statements for the year of refunding will be distorted (overstated) by $25,000. This amount equals the immediate tax reduction resulting from the refunding.

Under income tax-allocation procedures, the income tax entry for the year during which the refunding occurred is as follows:

Income tax expense	100,000	
Income tax payable		75,000
Deferred income tax liability		25,000

As noted above, during the next five years the taxable income will exceed the book income because the company will have used, for tax purposes, its periodic deduction of the discount on the refunded bond issue. In the books the company will continue to take the regular annual amortization of $10,000 per year. Thus, the tax expense on an allocation basis will differ from the tax actually payable by $5,000 for each of the next five years. This difference is charged each year to Deferred Income Tax Liability. For example, assume that, in the year following the bond refunding, the net income before income tax per books was $100,000. The income per tax return would be $110,000. The entry for the income tax would be as follows:

Income tax expense	50,000	
Deferred income tax liability	5,000	
Income tax payable		55,000

Asset write-off for book purposes only. In the above case the tax recognition preceded the accounting recognition. To illustrate an opposite case, that is, where the accounting recognition precedes the tax recognition, assume that the accountant for *D* Company concludes, justifiably, that an intangible asset, with a book value of $100,000 after the current year's amortization of $20,000 has been recorded, is worthless and writes it off the books. However, it is known that such a write-off will not be permitted for income tax purposes, although continued annual amortization charges of $20,000 will be accepted for tax purposes. This means that the income per books and per tax return will differ as follows:

Year of write-off of asset: Tax-return income will be larger by $100,000.
Succeeding five years: Each year the tax-return income will be smaller by $20,000.

Two comparative income statements of *D* Company are presented. The first comparative statement shows the results of operations without income tax allocation. The second shows the results of operations with income tax allocation.

D COMPANY

Condensed Comparative Income Statement
(Without Income Tax Allocation)
For Two Years

	Year of Write-off	Succeeding Year
Sales	$500,000	$500,000
Cost of sales and expenses, except amortization	$380,000*	$380,000*
Regular annual amortization of intangible	20,000*	-0-
Total	$400,000*	$380,000*
Net income before income tax	$100,000	$120,000
Income tax (actually payable)	50,000*	50,000*
Net income (before unusual item in one year)	$ 50,000	$ 70,000
Write-off of intangible asset	100,000*	
Net loss	($ 50,000)	

* Deduction.

In the preceding comparative income statement, note that the income tax actually payable is the same for both years, because for income tax purposes the regular amortization program is continued.

D COMPANY

Condensed Comparative Income Statement
(With Income Tax Allocation)
For Two Years

	Year of Write-off	Succeeding Year
Sales	$500,000	$500,000
Cost of sales and expenses, except amortization	$380,000*	$380,000*
Regular annual amortization of intangible	20,000*	-0-
Total	$400,000*	$380,000*
Net income before income tax		$120,000
Net income before write-off	$100,000	
Write-off of intangible asset	100,000*	
Income tax expense		60,000*
Net income	$ -0-	$ 60,000

* Deduction.

Income tax entries following income tax-allocation procedures are set forth below:

Year of write-off of asset:

Deferred income tax expense	50,000	
Income tax payable		50,000

Succeeding year:

Income tax expense	60,000	
Deferred income tax expense		10,000
Income tax payable		50,000

Over the years, the aggregate net income will be the same under either approach. If tax-allocation procedures are used, the write-off produces significantly less distortion of the net income in the year of write-off. In effect, the write-off is handled on a net-of-tax basis by the use of tax-allocation procedures. Because the $100,000 balance in the intangible asset account is deductible for future tax purposes, and will afford a potential tax reduction of $50,000, those accountants favoring allocation procedures argue that $50,000 is the correct measure of the loss when it is determined that the intangible is worthless.

Loss provisions and corrections. As noted earlier, income tax-allocation procedures in effect treat the results of unusual transactions on a net-of-tax basis. One such case was the $100,000 write-off of the intangible asset, which, under tax-allocation procedures, resulted in a $50,000 reduction in the net income for the current year. The question arises as to how far the net-of-tax concept should be extended. Specifically, should net-of-tax reasoning apply in the case of loss provisions and asset reinstatements?

For instance, assume that, shortly before year end, a company receives a number of claims for refund from customers asserting that merchandise recently received was not of standard quality. Investigation shows such claims to be valid and that one batch of the company's product shipped during the year was defective, although it was not known to be defective until the customers' claims initiated the investigation. The company's accountant estimates that a loss of $200,000 will result from the defective batch, although only a small portion of refund claims have been received by the company by year end. Such losses are not deductible for tax purposes until the claims are settled. However, generally accepted accounting holds that provision should be made for all known losses, provided, of course, that the amount can be determined with reasonable precision. Under these circumstances, should the accountant report the loss as $200,000, or, because it will be deductible for tax purposes in some future period, on a net-of-tax basis of $100,000, assuming an income tax rate of 50%?

Although no authoritative answer can be given to this question, there is increasing evidence that accountants are taking the net-of-tax approach into consideration when determining the adequacy of loss provisions not yet deductible for income tax purposes. In other words, when a provision is made in the income statement for an estimated liability which is deductible for income tax purposes in future periods, and such amount is material, the future tax reduction is being anticipated more often than was formerly the case. This is particularly true where the earnings record and prospects indicate that the chances are reasonably good for the prospective deduction to result in a future tax reduction. And, as noted earlier, the present carryback-carryforward provisions in the tax law help in providing such an assurance of ultimate tax benefit.

To illustrate the application of net-of-tax reasoning to loss provisions, let us return to the assumed facts relating to the $200,000 of prospective claims for refund for defective merchandise.

Year of loss provision:

Estimated loss from defective merchandise	100,000	
Estimated liability for damage claims		100,000
Provision for $200,000 of damage claims on a net-of-tax basis.		

Year claims are settled:

(Assume that the net income before income tax equals $300,000, exclusive of claims paid; because the claims paid are deductible for tax purposes, the tax return would show income of $100,000.)

Claims paid	200,000	
Cash		200,000
Summary entry for claims paid.		
Income tax expense	150,000	
Income tax payable		150,000
Income tax expense for year.		
Estimated liability for damage claims	100,000	
Income tax payable	100,000	
Claims paid		200,000
To close Claims Paid and Estimated Liability for Damage Claims accounts and adjust the Income Tax Payable account to amount payable.		

Another problem in this general area that may be mentioned concerns the reinstatement of asset amounts that have no further tax deductibility. For instance, assume that a company has fully depreciated certain of its fixed assets. It now discovers that the facilities are of further use and proposes to reinstate some portion of their cost in the accounts (in effect, to correct prior depreciation). Because such costs have been deducted for tax purposes in earlier years and will offer no further deduction benefit, there are those who urge that the lack-of-deductibility feature be one of the elements considered in determining the amount to be reinstated. The reasoning is that an asset with a limited-term existence that cannot be depreciated or amortized in the future for income tax purposes is not as "valuable" as an identical asset whose depreciation or amortization is deductible for income tax purposes. In other words, tax deductibility, in and of itself, has value to a profitable enterprise; in those cases in which such deductibility privilege can be transferred, it has market value.

The following hypothetical facts and journal entries may be helpful in pointing up some of the aspects of this question.

Data:			
	Asset cost	$600,000	
	Original use-life	10 years	
	Present book value	-0-	(fully depreciated)

Present evidence indicates that the asset will last another five years.

Depreciation correction, $200,000—but after taxes are considered, the prior years' earnings are understated by only $100,000.

Correction entry:

Accumulated depreciation	100,000	
Correction of prior years' earnings		100,000

Annual depreciation entry—next five years:

Depreciation expense	40,000	
Income tax payable		20,000
Accumulated depreciation		20,000

Entry for income tax expense:

(Assuming that the books show net income before income tax of $100,000, then the tax return would show income of $140,000, because the $40,000 of depreciation charges shown above are not deductible for income tax purposes.)

Income tax expense	50,000	
Income tax payable		50,000

Note. The income tax expense per income statement is $20,000 less than the tax liability. In the above case, the tax liability is $70,000.

The influence of distortion. A review of the releases by the Committee on Accounting Procedure and a study of some of the applications in published financial statements have led the authors to conclude that an important factor in the development of support for income tax allocation is the accountant's concern with net income distortion. The accountant does not like to see net income made different by a procedure adopted only for tax purposes. The fairly common case arises when a company makes a substantial investment in new equipment and depreciates it on an accelerated plan for tax purposes only. This reduces significantly the current income tax payments. If the tax expense is reported for accounting purposes without tax allocation, the stated net income has been made higher merely by the adoption of a procedure for tax purposes. Such distorted net income figures are often widely publicized, generally in the form of earnings per share or per cent of return on investment. That the apparently favorable showing is really the result of a tax device is not disclosed. To repeat, it is believed that potential distortion is a strong motive in this area of accounting.

Present status. The matter of tax allocation is far from settled. The record to date has been one of continued expansion of the applicability of allocation procedures. However, it is clear that not all accountants favor tax allocation. This is evident from the position taken by the 1957 revision committee of the American Accounting Association, as follows:

> In any given period, some differences may be attributable to the inclusion or exclusion for tax computation of revenue or expired cost recognized under accounting principles as net income determinants in earlier or later periods. Since such differences are often significant, and since they may give rise to expectations of wholly or partially offsetting differences in later periods, they should be disclosed.
>
> Disclosure is sometimes accomplished by recording the differences as prepayments (given an expectation of future tax savings) or accruals (given the opposing prospect). However, these items do not present the usual characteristics of assets or liabilities; the possible future offsets are often subject to unusual uncertainties; and treatment on an accrual basis is in many cases unduly complicated. Consequently, disclosure by accrual may be more confusing than enlightening and is therefore undesirable.

The accounting student sooner or later will encounter this matter in its practical setting and find it necessary to weigh the merits of tax-allocation procedures. The problem has numerous ramifications, is extremely important in its effect on net income measurement, and probably will not be completely settled for years. Of course, any requirement, whether the result of legislation or of voluntary action by accountants, that would minimize or eliminate the differences between the books and tax return would likewise minimize or eliminate the problem that has led to the development of tax-allocation procedures.

CHAPTER

28

Price-Level Impact on Financial Statements

A basic assumption of accounting. The accounting process uses the dollar as its unit of measurement, and assumes that fluctuations in the dollar's purchasing power will be so insignificant as not to undermine its usefulness as a unit of measurement. As noted in an earlier chapter, during certain periods this assumption has squared substantially with reality. But it is also true that during other periods the purchasing power of the dollar has changed significantly. For instance, in the 1940–1948 period, the general level of prices in the United States increased 71%. If the size of the dollar is measured by its purchasing power, the size of the dollar shrank during this period by 42%. During the decade of the 1950's, the dollar shrank by 22%. Nevertheless, during these periods accounting regarded all dollars as though they were the same size, and it continues to regard all dollars as identical.

If a unit of measurement is to serve its function properly, it should be stable. The dollar is not stable. The accounting process adds, subtracts, and compares account balances without making any allowance for the instability of the dollar.

Although financial statements show dollars of "mixed and varying dimensions," it is doubtful whether statement users make any allowances therefor. The consequences and repercussions flowing from the use of an unstable dollar are not fully known or understood. This potentially dangerous situation, dangerous because financial statements may prove to be misleading or of little value, may have contributed to the concern of the

Accounting Principles Board when it went on record in 1961 stating "that the assumption in accounting that fluctuations in the value of the dollar may be ignored is unrealistic" and directed that research be undertaken to study the problem.*

Fundamental questions. Before proceeding further with a re-examination of the assumption regarding the stability of the unit of measurement used in accounting, it seems fundamental to inquire about some of the implications arising from the known fact that the purchasing power of the dollar varies. For instance, we know that the dimensions of the unit of measurement vary through time, but what effect, if any, does this have on the data shown in the financial statements?

As a means of clarifying the point just raised, consider the following case:

In 1940 *X* purchases some land for $10,000.
In 1957 *X* sells the land for $20,000.

First, assume that the purchasing power of the dollar did not change during the period of time that the land was owned by *X*. Did *X* make a gain? The answer, clearly, is yes. Because the dollars spent and those received had the same purchasing power, *X* now has twice as much purchasing power.

Second, analyze the transaction in terms of the conditions that actually prevailed—namely, that the purchasing power of the dollar declined 50% between 1940 and 1957. Did *X* make a gain? Under such circumstances, it is apparent that *X* has not increased his purchasing power. But it is a fact that *X* has 10,000 more dollars after the sale of the land than he invested in the land in 1940. In a "monetary" sense, there has been a gain of $10,000; in an "economic" sense, there has been no gain. (Of course, with a stable price level, monetary and economic results would coincide.)

Under prevailing accounting practices, a gain of $10,000 would be reported as a result of the purchase and sale of the land; no consideration would be given to the change in the dimensions of the unit of measurement. The following question seems to be pertinent: Which definition of "gain" should be used in accounting?

As a further case, assume that a service business is organized to operate on a "cash basis," that is, no credit is extended to customers, and the business needs only one fixed asset in its business operations. The fixed asset is purchased for $16,000 and is depreciated over its eight-year useful life. Condensed income statements and dividends data covering the eight-year period since organization are presented on the next page. For convenience, the results of each year are identical.

---

* This resulted in the publication of *Reporting the Effects of Price-level Changes,* by the Staff of the Accounting Research Division (New York: American Institute of Certified Public Accountants, 1963).

	Year								Aggregate for
	1	2	3	4	5	6	7	8	8-Year Period
Revenue from services	$42,000							$42,000	$336,000
Salaries and wages	$30,000							$30,000	$240,000
Depreciation	2,000	Each year is identical.						2,000	16,000
All other expenses	8,000							8,000	64,000
Net operating income	$ 2,000							$ 2,000	$ 16,000
Income tax	600							600	4,800
Net income	$ 1,400							$ 1,400	$ 11,200
Dividends	$ 1,400							$ 1,400	$ 11,200

A condensed statement of sources and uses of working capital for the company for the eight-year period would appear as follows:

Working capital sources:		
Operations:		
Net income	$11,200	
Add depreciation charges	16,000	$27,200
Working capital uses:		
Dividends		11,200
Increase in working capital (in this case, cash)		$16,000

The income statements report that the company earned $11,200 in the eight-year period. An identical amount was distributed to the owners as dividends. But suppose that during the eight-year period the price level increased 70%, as it did during the 1940–1948 period, and that the company found that $27,200 was needed to replace the fully depreciated and worn-out fixed asset. This price represents a 70% increase in the number of dollars needed to replace the fixed asset. Thus, in order to replace the fully depreciated asset, the company would have to borrow $11,200 or raise additional capital from stockholders in that amount. Management and stockholders might justifiably inquire whether the eight-year period had, in reality, been profitable. Was the aggregate net income $11,200, or $–0–? (Could it be rightfully contended that the "income" tax was in reality a tax on capital?)

Here, also, it is apparent that accounting procedures are based on a "monetary" concept of income. Such accounting is sometimes described as "dollar" accounting. This appears to satisfy some accountants (and some nonaccountants) and to disturb some accountants (and some nonaccountants). Some of the considerations advanced by both groups are submitted in the following paragraphs. In the final analysis, the issue involves the unit of measurement and the way it is used in the accounting process.

Comments supporting conventional accounting. The point is made that the prevailing concepts and practices have worked well over the years. As a consequence, conventional financial statements are widely used and respected. During most periods, the change in the value of money has been so gradual as to have had no discernible effect on financial statements.

It is also noted that many legal rules and agreements have been established within the framework of generally accepted accounting. There is some question whether significant revisions could be made in the way the dollar is used in accounting without the revision of numerous statutes and a multitude of contracts, primarily because the level of earnings would be affected by the change. Income bonds, which provide for the payment of interest only if earned, and profit-sharing agreements are illustrative of contractual arrangements that would need reconsideration.

Some accountants make a point of the fact that, relatively speaking, there are not many "old" dollars in the account balances shown in a current year's financial statements. Therefore, the fact that the dimensions of the dollar have changed does not necessarily lead to a conclusion that financial statements are significantly affected. Old dollars are most likely to be found in the account balances related to the fixed asset group. But, even in this group, the tendency of business management to adopt conservative estimates of useful life removes a considerable portion of the outlays from account balances within ten years. Amounts invested in fixed assets not subject to depreciation or amortization are of slight concern in this matter because they do not enter into the determination of periodic net income.

The point is made by some accountants that price-level changes make it necessary to interpret the results of operations and financial position with greater discrimination, but that users of accounting reports must assume the responsibility for interpreting accounting data. They believe it is the function of accounting to record expenditures and their assignment to expense in cost dollars, which amounts can be adjusted and modified by statement users if desired to serve their objectives and needs.

In this connection, it seems relevant to restate the definition of accounting offered in Chapter 1:

> Accounting is the art of recording, classifying, and summarizing in a significant manner and in terms of money, transactions and events which are, in part at least, of a financial character, and interpreting the results thereof.

This definition by the Committee on Terminology is widely quoted and apparently is quite specific in including the responsibility for interpreting the results of the accounting process. But it does not state that the accounting process should include any built-in "interpretive" techniques to give recognition to purchasing-power changes.

There is the accountability function to consider. An important share of the nation's business is conducted by corporations. Decisions covering most aspects of business, including the purchase of additional fixed assets, the revision of product prices, and the curtailment of output, are made by the management group, acting for and in the interests of the owners. In a sense, the relationship between the managers of a corporate enterprise and the owners is one of stewardship. The management group has been entrusted with certain assets, and it is management's responsibility to use the assets in a way advantageous to the stockholders. One of the basic reasons for accounting to exist is to provide a mechanism through which the results of the stewardship may be reported. The consequences of management's decisions must be revealed by the accounting process and discernible in the financial statements; otherwise, an evaluation of managerial effectiveness would be difficult to obtain. If the accounting process prescribed periodic revisions of account balances based on price levels or current values, then the results of decisions, price-level fluctuations, and value judgments could become so commingled as to blur the consequences of management's decisions. It might not be clear whether management was effective or ineffective.

An example typical of those used to stress the importance of the accountability function may be cited as follows: Suppose that the management of Company *A* reached a decision that it would be good business to expand capacity, and therefore built a new factory costing $500,000, having a daily capacity of 1,000 units. Suppose also that the management of Company *B*, a competing corporation, reached the same decision three years later and built a plant of identical capacity. However, assume that prices had risen in the intervening period, with the result that Company *B*'s new factory cost $600,000. If accounting procedures prescribed that Company *A*'s accounts and financial statements should show its three-year-old plant at the current cost of $600,000 (before accumulated depreciation) and that depreciation should be computed on the $600,000 amount, thus making the plants identical for accounting purposes, it would be more difficult for the statement users to discern the relative effectiveness of the two managements. There is a basic notion that, if all else were identical, Company *A* would be more profitable, and that such a condition should be revealed by the accounting process.

Another reason listed in favor of the conventional approach is that cost is a determinable fact, whereas if the accounting process attempted to give recognition to current values or price-level changes, financial statements would become more subjective in character. No attempt is made to deny the generally held opinion that changes in value are important considerations in measuring economic progress. In fact, a common definition of income is stated in terms of the difference between the value of the owners' equity at the beginning and end of the period, after making allowances for withdrawals and additional capital investments. Of course, the value referred to is not book value, but real value. However, there appear to be no suitable tools to facilitate this approach. How is value determined for specialized plant and equipment? Would the use of index numbers solve the problem? Which index is pertinent? Is an index of wholesale prices more relevant than an index of construction costs? Some accountants assert that "there is no basis in economic theory for believing price level adjustments applied to accounting data would result in an adjusted accounting income which would closely approximate economic income."*

---

* Raymond C. Dein, "Price-Level Adjustments: Fetish in Accounting," *The Accounting Review*, January, 1955, page 5.

Comments critical of conventional accounting. The known instability of the dollar undermines the accounting process, because it is primarily concerned with numbers of dollars and treats all dollars as identical. When dollars of differing dimensions are added and subtracted without regard to such dissimilarity, the resulting net income amounts and account balances are subject to misunderstanding. It is obvious that it would be improper to add dollars and francs, yards and meters, or 2,000-pound tons (short tons) and 2,240-pound tons (long tons). Yet this, in effect, is precisely what is done in accounting. The balance of the following account is considered to be $500,000 for all accounting purposes. But each $100,000 debit therein represents a different amount of purchasing power invested in land.

Land		
1929	100,000	
1936	100,000	
1943	100,000	
1949	100,000	
1955	100,000	

Assume that it is 1962. If the amounts were converted to the equivalent of 1962 dollars, the account would appear as follows:

Land		
1929	181,200	
1936	223,980	
1943	179,487	
1949	130,471	
1955	116,000	

Thus, it is made clear that management did not invest the same amount of purchasing power in each parcel of land.

As noted earlier, although financial statements show dollars of "mixed or varying dimensions," it is doubtful whether statement users so interpret the dollars. It is natural to regard all dollars as present or current dollars. Thus, the $500,000 balance in the first Land account presented above would be thought of in terms of present-day dollars. The same interpretation would probably apply to the fixed asset category generally. Similarly, dollar amounts shown in income statements most likely are interpreted by statement users as dollars of uniform size, although the depreciation charge, as a general rule, is based on dollars expended in earlier years—often under a price structure not typical of the present period.

The following quotation from a monograph by Sidney S. Alexander points to another possible weakness of conventional accounting.

> The accountant . . . has tried to eliminate the element of subjective judgment from the determination of income. He has tried to establish as nearly as possible hard and fast rules of calculation in order to eliminate the guesswork and to introduce precise measurements. But in a dynamic world subject to unforeseen changes of prices and business conditions, it is not possible to avoid guesswork in the determination of income. To the extent that the accountant can eliminate guesses, he is substituting something else for income. That something else will be a good approximation to income in a fairly static situation when prices and business prospects do not change very much; the approximation will be very poor

in a highly dynamic situation when prices and business prospects are fluctuating violently.*

It is probably true that potential income recipients as a group are more interested in knowing how much spending power has been produced by business operations than in an estimate of the current value of the owners' equity. This emphasizes disposability as a test for income. The income for a period is that which a business entity can distribute to owners and still remain in the same position it was in at the beginning of the period. Those critical of conventional accounting assert that during the years following World War II the amounts reported as income did not meet the disposable test, and that spendable income was significantly below reported income. If price-level changes make it necessary for a business to reinvest a significant portion of reported income to replace fixed assets and maintain productive capacity, the question is raised whether such reported amounts are, in fact, income. Conventional accounting can report as income amounts that must be reinvested in the business in order to maintain capacity.

To most accountants, the matching of revenue and expense is the most important part of the entire accounting process. They point out that revenue is automatically stated in current dollars and that logic requires that expense matched against such revenue should be stated in current dollars. Under conventional procedures, some expenses, like wages and rent, are stated in current dollars, whereas other expenses, like depreciation and, to a lesser extent, cost of sales, are stated in old (or less current) dollars. It is pointed out that one of the principal justifications for *lifo* is that it improves the matching process as a result of its assumption that the "last dollars in" are the "first dollars out." Thus, under *lifo,* the cost of sales is stated in more recent dollars than is the case with *fifo* inventory procedures. There are some critics of conventional accounting who advocate extending the essence of the *lifo* method to other cost elements as a means of curing the flaw of matching dissimilar dollars. This objective could be achieved by basing depreciation charges on current prices for fixed assets and by applying the *lifo* method to supplies and similar expense items.

Reason for criticism. It is apparent that there is a lack of unanimity about the objectives to be achieved by the accounting process. There is criticism because:

Depreciation does not provide for the replacement of assets.
Income taxes are paid on "fictitious" incomes.
Historical dollars are not comparable to present-day dollars.
The balance sheet does not reveal current values.
In the matching of revenue and expense, some of the expenses are stated in old dollars.

* Study Group on Business Income, *Five Monographs on Business Income* (New York: American Institute of Certified Public Accountants, 1950), pp. 6–7.

Although such criticism implies that there may be fundamental defects in some of accounting's basic concepts, there appears to be an increasingly vocal group of accountants who contend that the fault is not with accounting's definitions of such concepts as cost, revenue, and expense, but with the imbedded belief that no major consequences result from ignoring fluctuations in the value of money. According to these accountants, the weakness of accounting is its treatment of all dollars in the accounts as identical dollars. The cure is to restate all "old" dollars in terms of their present-day dimensions by the use of a suitable index indicative of changes in the purchasing power of the dollar. These accountants recognize that this procedure would not result in account balances expressive of present-day *asset values* or *replacement costs,* but they maintain that such results would not be feasible objectives of the accounting process.

To pinpoint the basic difference of this approach, consider the following data.

A business purchases a given quantity of shipping supplies for $1,000 when the index of the general price level is stated at 100.

The supplies are used by the business when the index of the general price level is stated at 105 and when their replacement cost is $1,100. (In other words, the price of shipping supplies has risen more than the general level of prices.)

Generally accepted accounting prescribes that assets and expenses should be measured in terms of costs incurred, thus ruling out the $1,100 amount, which is a "could have been" amount. But does it follow that cost should be stated in measurement units (dollars) of the size prevailing at the time goods or services are purchased as opposed to the size prevailing when they are shown in the financial statements? Given unstable dollars, can cost measurements have meaning unless either the date of cost incurrence is known or present-day dollars are used to convey such financial information?

Those advocating the use of index numbers to adjust recorded dollars to a "common dollar" basis assert that they are not seeking to destroy the cost basis of accounting or the well-established definitions of revenue and expense, but are merely seeking to eliminate the misleading consequences of commingling dollars of several sizes. They argue that cost, as a concept, represents an amount of purchasing power that was committed, but if the unit of measure has changed in size, then the purchasing power committed should be stated in terms of currently prevailing dimensions of the dollar. When the accounting process reports that something consumed (an expense) cost $1,000, that fact will be taken to mean 1,000 present-day dollars. If the $1,000 reported is not stated in terms of present-day dollars, then the user of financial data will likely misinterpret such information. The seriousness of such potential misinterpretation depends upon the extent of the fluctuation in the purchasing power of the dollar and the extent to which "old" dollars are used in the preparation of accounting reports.

The aim of this group is to adjust dollar amounts so that amounts compared and interpreted by the statement user will be stated in dollars of uniform size.

Comparative statements. Many of the dollar amounts shown in comparative financial statements are "old" dollars. Thus, comparative statements provide an example of accounting data which are relatively more susceptible to misunderstanding as a consequence of variations in the dollar's purchasing power.

An increasing number of businesses regularly present partial or complete comparative financial statements covering a considerable number of years. Comparative financial statements for a 10-year period are fairly common. Some companies regularly report selected accounting data for a period exceeding 30 years. There are instances where selected yearly data, such as sales, are shown in each annual report for the entire life of the corporation.

When there have been significant movements in the price level, it is obvious that annual data covering several years lose much of their comparability. Consider the following hypothetical data:

	19–	19+1	19+2	19+3	19+4	19+5
Sales	$100,000	$120,000	$140,000	$160,000	$180,000	$200,000

They imply that sales have doubled in five years. But if the size of the dollar has changed significantly during the period, the data are misleading.

This suggests that during periods of change in the price level, consideration might properly be given to

(1) Discontinuing the presentation of noncomparable data—in effect, abandoning the practice of publishing comparative statements for such long periods as five or ten years, or

(2) Expressing the comparative data in the form of ratios or percentages, thus eliminating the showing of dollar amounts. For example, in place of showing total current assets and total current liabilities for a series of years, show the ratio of current assets to current liabilities for each of the years. Or, in place of showing sales and net income data for a series of years, show the per cent of net income to sales, or

(3) Adjusting the data of earlier years by the use of index numbers in such a way as to present dollars of "equal dimensions." Thus, if the index representing the general price level has increased 50% in five years, the sales figure for five years ago would be converted as follows: $\$100,000 \times 150\% = \$150,000$.

Note the different impression that is gained by using adjusted amounts in the following schedule.

	19+5 (Current Year)	19– (Five Years Ago)
Unadjusted Data		
Sales	$200,000	$100,000
Adjusted Data		
Sales	$200,000	$150,000

In a study undertaken by Professor Ralph C. Jones, published by the American Accounting Association, the historical dollars shown in comparative financial statements of four companies were adjusted to a uniform dollar basis.* The effects of such a procedure on the comparative statements can be judged by referring to page 540 and noting the items taken from the comparative earnings statement of Armstrong Cork Company, one of the four companies studied.

Observe that the unadjusted comparative data for net sales report an increase of 156% for the 1941–1951 period, whereas the adjusted data show the increase as 45%.

At the time of this writing there is no evidence to suggest that showing comparative statements in uniform dollars will become the practice of even a small minority of companies. There is no rule of accounting that requires such adjustments. However, it is true that comparative statements showing historical dollars can be misleading, and further fluctuations in the purchasing power of the dollar may stimulate further consideration of uniform-dollar comparative statements.

Current financial statements. Depreciation charges and fixed assets are the amounts most likely to be stated in "old" dollars in the current financial statements. The consequences of this seem less serious for the balance sheet than for the income statement. It is generally agreed that balance sheet usefulness is primarily centered in the reporting of the current position of a business. Under the going-concern assumption, fixed asset balances are residuals and it is not expected that they will be stated in terms of current values or current dollars. Furthermore, the balance sheet is regarded as a statement of secondary importance.

On the other hand, considering the importance attached to net income results, the fact that depreciation is stated in the income statement as a hodgepodge of historical dollars poses a question of considerable significance. As a general rule, the revenues of a business are collectible in reasonably current dollars. And most expenses, other than depreciation, require the disbursement of reasonably current dollars. Such income-statement amounts, although not stated in precisely uniform dollars, are reasonably uniform and reasonably current. This is not the case with depreciation charges; they are based on historical dollars. Thus, if several assets acquired at different dates are being depreciated, the depreciation charge will be a conglomerate of various-size dollars, perhaps bearing only slight semblance to current dollars.

Here is a prime example of accounting's practice of adding nonadditive amounts; depreciation is combined (added) with other expense amounts stated in different kinds of dollars, the extent of the difference being determined by the instability of the dollar. Those accountants who believe that

---

* Ralph Coughenour Jones, *Price Level Changes and Financial Statements—Case Studies of Four Companies* (American Accounting Association, 1955), pp. 86–87 and 92–93.

Unadjusted Data—Historical Dollars in Millions
Adjusted Data—Uniform Dollars in Millions—December 1951 Dollar = $1.00

		1941	1942	1943	1944	1945	1946	1947	1948	1949	1950	1951
Net sales	Unadjusted	$ 78.6	$ 82.7	$111.7	$124.5	$108.8	$104.8	$144.0	$173.1	$163.3	$186.8	$201.1
	Adjusted	141.4	134.1	170.7	187.4	160.0	142.0	170.6	190.4	181.5	205.5	204.9
Cost of goods sold	Unadjusted	55.6	66.0	91.7	98.8	87.3	82.0	108.4	131.6	121.4	137.2	152.7
	Adjusted	101.7	109.2	141.8	149.1	129.3	114.3	129.9	146.4	134.6	152.2	157.3
Depreciation and amortization	Unadjusted	2.2	2.0	2.1	2.3	3.0	2.7	3.0	3.9	4.6	5.0	5.4
	Adjusted	4.4	3.9	4.0	4.4	5.7	4.9	5.4	6.4	7.1	7.5	7.9
Net earnings	Unadjusted	4.2	3.0	3.7	4.2	3.1	4.2	9.6	11.6	10.2	12.4	8.5
	Adjusted	5.4	1.9	2.9	5.0	2.2	1.3	8.1	8.9	9.6	9.9	4.2

Net Sales—Unadjusted and Adjusted Per Cents of Change
1941—Base Year

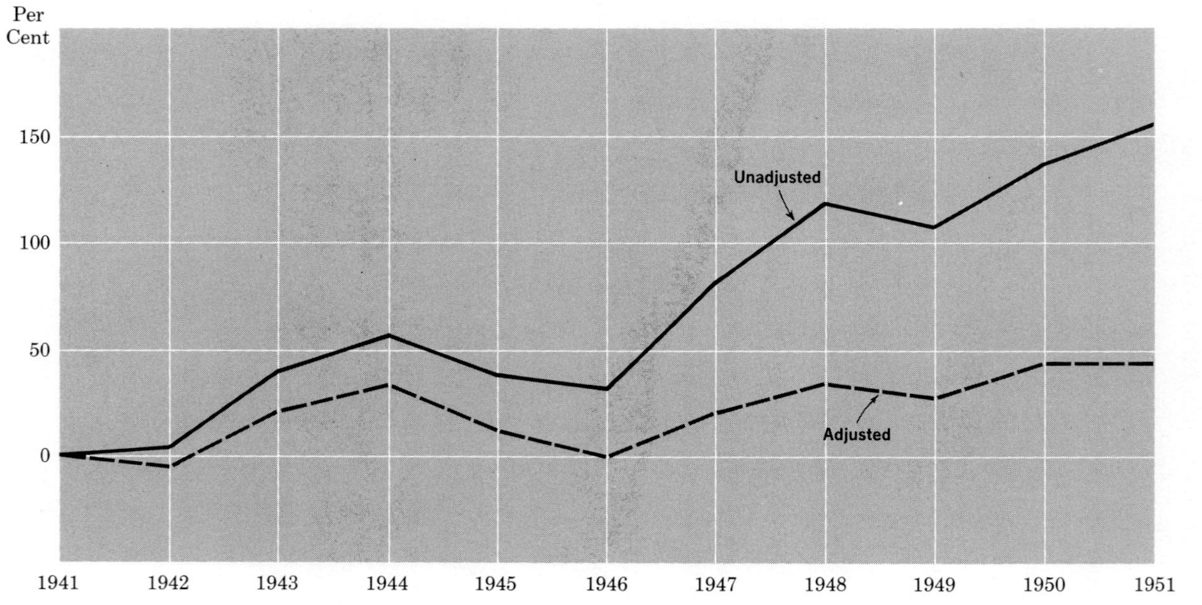

the basic cause of misleading income data is related to the failure to adjust dollar amounts to a uniform basis see merit in applying index numbers in the determination of the depreciation charge. Such a conversion procedure would, in their opinion, eliminate most of the source of potential misunderstanding of the net income data.

To illustrate a procedure of converting depreciation charges to current dollars, assume that assets of a certain class have an estimated life of 20 years, and that they have no salvage value. The asset account has a balance of $50,000. A schedule is prepared breaking down the balance of the asset account by year of acquisition and showing the index number applicable to the year, thus:

Elements of Account Balance by Year of Acquisition	Index Number Applicable to the Year of Acquisition
$20,000	100
8,000	120
9,000	125
6,000	130
7,000	145

We shall assume that depreciation is being computed for a year in which the index number is 150. The depreciation on recorded cost would be $2,500, but the depreciation charges adjusted by the index numbers would be $3,248.22, as computed below:

Recorded Cost	Depreciation at 5%	Conversion Ratio	Depreciation Adjusted by Index Number
$20,000	$1,000	150/100	$1,500.00
8,000	400	150/120	500.00
9,000	450	150/125	540.00
6,000	300	150/130	346.15
7,000	350	150/145	362.07
$50,000	$2,500		$3,248.22

A piecemeal or partial approach which would adjust one or two items in the financial statements and leave all others unadjusted was not viewed with favor by the AICPA research study cited earlier. Nor was a partial approach favored by the Committee on Concepts and Standards Underlying Corporate Financial Statements of the American Accounting Association. In a 1951 release it stated: "The measurement of price level changes should be all-inclusive; all statement items affected should be adjusted in a consistent manner."

Supplementary financial statements. One possible progressive step that has the support of the AICPA research study as well as the AAA committee is the preparation of supplementary statements in which historical dollars are converted to current dollars by the use of a general price index. The supplementary statements would serve as companions to the conventional financial statements, which would continue to be prepared in the usual fashion.

Such supplementary statements are technically feasible. Enough research studies have been made to support this conclusion. It is generally agreed that the index used for conversion purposes should be a general price index designed to measure the over-all purchasing power of the dollar. According to the accounting research study, which investigated this matter in considerable depth, at least one such index is now available.

The use of supplementary statements would

- leave the conventional financial statements and accounting principles undisturbed;
- disclose the effects of changes in the price level on the financial position and results of operations of business enterprises.

The use of supplementary statements would *not*

- provide information on replacement costs or current values;
- resolve any questions, at least for some time, about the need for a revision of some of accounting's basic concepts because of the instability of the dollar;
- represent a departure from the cost basis of accounting (costs would continue to be used but would be stated in dollars of uniform size).

Preparation of supplementary statements demonstrated. Pertinent data about Vision Company and the period since its incorporation are presented below.

Year	Events	Price Index
19–	Company organized and facilities rented	100
19+1	$21,000 of equipment purchased and $6,000 bank loan negotiated	105
19+2		108
19+3	Ending inventory was $5,500	110
19+4	$3,000 of additional equipment purchased	120
19+5	Bank loan reduced on December 31, by special permission of the bank	126

Some conventional financial statements for the company are shown below.

VISION COMPANY

Comparative Income Statement
For 19+4 and 19+5

	19+4		19+5	
Sales		$48,000		$50,000
Cost of sales	$30,000		$32,000	
Depreciation (10% per year)	2,400		2,400	
Other expenses (including interest and taxes)	12,000	44,400	12,600	47,000
Net income		$ 3,600		$ 3,000

VISION COMPANY

Comparative Balance Sheet
For 19+4 and 19+5

Assets	19+4		19+5	
Current assets:				
Cash	$ 5,000		$ 4,000	
Current receivables	12,600		15,000	
Inventory (at cost on *fifo* basis)	6,000	$23,600	8,000	$27,000
Fixed assets:				
Equipment	$24,000		$24,000	
Less accumulated depreciation	8,700	15,300	11,100	12,900
		$38,900		$39,900
Liabilities and Stockholders' Equity				
Current liabilities:				
Current payables		$ 4,000		$ 5,000
Long-term liabilities:				
Bank loan		6,000		4,000
Stockholders' equity:				
Capital stock	$20,000		$20,000	
Retained earnings	8,900	28,900	10,900	30,900
		$38,900		$39,900

VISION COMPANY

Statement of Retained Earnings
For the Year Ended December 31, 19+5

Retained earnings, December 31, 19+4	$ 8,900
Net income	3,000
Total	$11,900
Dividends	1,000
Retained earnings, December 31, 19+5	$10,900

The following schedules show the conversions required for supplementary statements in order that all balances shown thereon will be stated in uniform, 19+5, dollars. In order to convert old dollars into current dollars, a conversion ratio is used; the index number for the current year is the numerator and the index number for the year with which the dollars being converted are identified is the denominator.

19+5 Account Balances
Converted to Current Dollars

		Conversion Ratio	19+5 Dollars
Balances stated in 19— dollars:			
Capital stock	$20,000	126/100	$25,200
Balances stated in 19+1 dollars:			
Equipment—Original acquisition	$21,000	126/105	25,200
Accumulated depreciation—5 years	10,500	126/105	12,600
Depreciation for 19+5 (10%)	2,100	126/105	2,520

Although the bank loan originated in 19+1, no conversion is required for the balance outstanding at the end of the current period. Because the loan is a fixed dollar obligation, its account balance automatically shows the number of current dollars required to satisfy the debt.

(*Continued on next page.*)

			Conversion Ratio	19+5 Dollars
Balances stated in 19+4 dollars:				
Equipment—Additional acquisition		$ 3,000	126/120	3,150
Accumulated depreciation thereon—2 years		600		630
Depreciation on addition for 19+5 (10%)		300		315
Beginning inventory portion of cost of sales		6,000		6,300
Balances stated in 19+5 (current) dollars— No conversion required:				
Cash				4,000
Current receivables				15,000
Inventory				8,000
Current payables				5,000
Bank loan				4,000
Sales				50,000
Cost of sales	$32,000			
Less beginning inventory element converted above	6,000			
Balance, from 19+5 purchases				26,000
Other expenses				12,600
Dividends				1,000

19+4 Account Balances
Converted to Current Dollars

			Conversion Ratio	19+5 Dollars
Balances stated in 19— dollars:				
Capital stock		$20,000	126/100	$25,200
Balances stated in 19+1 dollars:				
Equipment—Original acquisition		$21,000	126/105	25,200
Accumulated depreciation—4 years		8,400		10,080
Depreciation for 19+4		2,100		2,520
Balances stated in 19+3 dollars:				
Beginning inventory portion of cost of sales		$ 5,500	126/110	6,300
Balances stated in 19+4 dollars:				
Cash		$ 5,000	126/120	5,250
Current receivables		12,600		13,230
Inventory		6,000		6,300
Equipment—Additional acquisition		3,000		3,150
Accumulated depreciation thereon—1 year		300		315
Depreciation on addition for 19+4 (10%)		300		315
Current payables		4,000		4,200
Bank loan		6,000		6,300
Sales		48,000		50,400
Cost of sales	$30,000			
Less beginning inventory element converted above	5,500			
Balance, from 19+4 purchases		24,500		25,725
Other expenses		12,000		12,600

The dollars in several of the accounts originated in more than one year, and must be combined as indicated by the following groupings.

	Dollars		
	19+1	19+4	19+5
Equipment:			
Original acquisition	$21,000		$25,200
Addition		$ 3,000	3,150
Total			$28,350
Accumulated depreciation—19+4:			
On original acquisition	$ 8,400		$10,080
On addition		$ 300	315
Total			$10,395
Accumulated depreciation—19+5:			
On original acquisition	$10,500		$12,600
On addition		$ 600	630
Total			$13,230
Depreciation expense:			
On original acquisition	$ 2,100		$ 2,520
On addition		$ 300	315
Total			$ 2,835
Cost of sales—19+4:			
From beginning inventory	$ 5,500		$ 6,300
From purchases		$24,500	25,725
Total			$32,025
Cost of sales—19+5:			
From beginning inventory		$ 6,000	$ 6,300
From purchases			26,000
Total			$32,300

The data in the 19+5 Dollars column of the above conversion schedules have been used to prepare the following supplementary financial statements. The retained earnings, renamed "balance of stockholders' equity" in the supplementary statements, is the balancing figure for the supplementary balance sheet. Note also that the phrase "capital invested by stockholders" has been substituted for "capital stock" in the supplementary balance sheet.

VISION COMPANY
Supplementary Comparative Income Statement
In Current Dollars
For 19+4 and 19+5

	19+4		19+5	
Sales		$50,400		$50,000
Cost of sales	$32,025		$32,300	
Depreciation	2,835		2,835	
Other expenses	12,600	47,460	12,600	47,735
Net income		$ 2,940		$ 2,265

VISION COMPANY
Supplementary Comparative Balance Sheet
In Current Dollars
December 31, 19+4 and 19+5

	19+4		19+5	
Assets				
Current assets:				
Cash	$ 5,250		$ 4,000	
Current receivables	13,230		15,000	
Inventory	6,300	$24,780	8,000	$27,000
Fixed assets:				
Equipment	$28,350		$28,350	
Less accumulated depreciation	10,395	17,955	13,230	15,120
		$42,735		$42,120
Liabilities and Stockholders' Equity				
Current liabilities:				
Current payables		$ 4,200		$ 5,000
Long-term liabilities:				
Bank loan		6,300		4,000
Stockholders' equity:				
Capital invested by stockholders	$25,200		$25,200	
Balance of stockholders' equity	7,035	32,235	7,920	33,120
		$42,735		$42,120

VISION COMPANY
Statement of Changes in Balance of Stockholders' Equity
In Current Dollars
For the Year Ended December 31, 19+5

Balance of stockholders' equity, December 31, 19+4, per above		$7,035
Net income for 19+5—per supplementary statement		2,265
Total		$9,300
Deduct:		
Dividends	$1,000	
Price-level adjustment for monetary items	380	1,380
Balance of stockholders' equity, December 31, 19+5, per above		$7,920

In the preparation of the supplementary financial statements, greater refinement is possible by the use of quarterly or monthly index numbers. However, such refinement would hardly be required under conditions of "creeping" inflation, which typified the decade preceding the time of this writing.

Price-level adjustment of monetary items. Monetary items consist of cash, receivables, and liabilities. When monetary assets are held during a period of rising prices, the holder suffers a loss in purchasing power. A gain in purchasing power is experienced when monetary assets are held during a period of declining prices. Last year Vision Company had a cash balance of $5,000 when the general price index was 120. During the current year (19+5), the price level increased five per cent, which carried the index to 126. A cash balance of $5,000 × 1.05, or $5,250, is required in 19+5 to equal the purchasing power of last year's cash balance of $5,000. By holding cash, the company incurred a loss in purchasing power in the amount of 250 current dollars. Similarly, a purchasing power loss of $630 has resulted from the $12,600 of current receivables held by the company.

Purchasing power gains and losses can also arise from liabilities. Less purchasing power is required to settle a liability incurred when the price level was lower. In the case of Vision Company, less purchasing power is required in 19+5 to settle the liabilities carried over from 19+4.

In the Vision Company illustration, a net purchasing power loss of $380 has resulted from the five per cent increase in the price level during the current year (19+5). This was shown in the supplementary statement reporting the changes that have occurred in the stockholders' equity during the current year. The $380 amount is the difference between the prior-year book balances of the monetary items and their converted balances, as shown below.

	19+4 Book Balances		Conversion	19+5	
	Debit	Credit	Ratio	Dollars	Difference
Monetary items:					
Cash	$ 5,000		126/120	$ 5,250	$250 loss
Current receivables	12,600		126/120	13,230	630 loss
Current payables		$4,000	126/120	4,200	200 gain
Bank loan		6,000	126/120	6,300	300 gain
Net loss					$380

Accountants agree that gains and losses on monetary items should be disclosed if supplementary statements are prepared, but differences of opinion exist concerning the proper method of disclosure. Those accountants who view the primary purpose of supplementary statements as being to set forth all amounts in the conventional statements in dollars of uniform size in order to offset the unreality of the assumption regarding the stability of the dollar see no reason to include gains or losses in purchasing power as elements in arriving at net income. Such inclusion would bring a new factor into the income-measurement process, one not now included among those accounting concepts concerned with income measurement.

On the other hand, if the purpose to be achieved by supplementary statements is something more than to compensate for the unreality of the stable-dollar assumption and is in fact an effort to give effect to additional considerations in the measurement of net income, then a re-examination of some of the accountants' basic concepts is required.

Because what is considered generally acceptable accounting is not static, it is conceivable that in time it may become generally held that all or some part of the gain or loss on monetary items should be included in the computation of net income as shown by uniform-dollar, supplementary statements. Pending this development, the authors favor disclosure of gains or losses on monetary items by showing them in the statement accounting for the changes that have occurred in the balance of the stockholders' equity, as illustrated.

Concluding note. The treatment of all dollars in the accounts as identical dollars is an inherent weakness in the accounting process. The consequences flowing from an unstable dollar are not disclosed by the conventional financial statements. Supplementary companion statements in which the dollars are stated in terms of their current general purchasing power might help to cure this situation. Some of the advocates of such supplementary statements do not view them as representing a departure from the cost basis of accounting. Costs are merely stated in current-sized dollars. It follows from this approach that no changes are needed or advocated for accounting's basic concepts. Other accountants, equally anxious to remedy this inherent weakness, believe that revisions of some of accounting's basic concepts are required. In short, they advocate accounting for purchasing power rather than for dollars stated in uniform size.

The following paragraph, taken from the authors' *Introductory* volume, seems worth repeating: "The advisability of the publication of supplementary price-level-adjusted statements has been questioned in some quarters on the ground that they would be of little usefulness because the public is generally unaware of the fact that financial statements based on the stable-dollar assumption may be conducive to misleading inferences. It also is contended that the concurrent publication of conventional and supplementary statements showing differing results of operations and differing financial position might result in more confusion than enlightenment, and might undermine the public confidence in certified statements prepared in accordance with generally accepted accounting principles. Possibly as a starter, the disclosure of price-level-adjusted information should be limited to selected data, such as sales, net income, and earnings per share. This kind of approach should minimize the chance for confusion which might arise initially from the presentation of two complete sets of statements."

Assignment Material for Chapter 1

QUESTIONS

1. Define *accounting.*
2. Give the sequence of procedures for the accounting cycle.
3. Give general rules for debiting and crediting:

Asset accounts;	Revenue accounts;
Liability accounts;	Expense accounts.
Owners' equity accounts;	

4. What is the function of books of original entry?
5. Describe the relationship between a controlling account and a subsidiary ledger.
6. What objectives are achieved by the use of special columns in books of original entry?
7. Give a brief description of the operation of the voucher system.
8. Comment on the validity of the following statement: If there is to be a correct cut-off at the end of the accounting period, no entries relating to the period just ended should be recorded in the journals after the last business day of the period.
9. (a) What is the function of the trial balance?
   (b) Does a trial balance furnish conclusive evidence of the absence of errors?
10. List the six steps that should be followed to discover errors which have caused the trial balance to be out of balance, and after each operation indicate the general type of error which will be discovered by that operation.
11. If the sales for one month are posted as a debit to the Sales account, state what procedures might be necessary at month end before the error would be discovered.
12. Do accountants have any responsibility to interpret the end product (the financial statements) of the accounting process?
13. As the chief accountant of a medium-sized business, why would you choose to use several specialized journals rather than one general journal for recording the company's transactions?
14. Contrast the cash and accrual bases of accounting.
15. Explain why you agree or disagree with the following statement: In any set of books, the adjusting entry to give recognition to office supplies on hand will always involve a credit to an expense account.
16. Give examples of some typical adjusting entries that might be found in the accounts of a business on a pure cash basis of accounting.

PROBLEMS

Problem 1-1. Record the following transactions of Diamond Top Corporation in a two-column general journal.

19—
March 2—Merchandise was sold on account to Timber Company for $300; terms, 2/10; n/30.
3—Office equipment was purchased from Thrifty Office Supply Company at a cost of $600. Check No. 30 for $300 was given, the balance being payable in 30 days.
6—Merchandise with an invoice price of $100 was returned by Timber Company. Credit memorandum No. 412 was issued.
10—Merchandise was purchased on account from Selby Supply Company for $850; terms, n/30.
12—Cash was received from Timber Company in the amount of $196.
15—A dividend of 10 cents per share on the 10,000 shares of outstanding common stock was declared, payable April 15 to stockholders of record April 1.
16—A $1,200 loan was obtained from the Second National Bank. A 60-day, 6% note was given to the bank.
18—Short-term notes with a face amount of $10,000 were purchased as a temporary investment for $10,212, which included $12 accrued interest to date. A check was issued.
20—The merchandise purchased on March 10 was paid for.
24—A $500 premium was paid by check to the Fidelity Fire Insurance Company covering a one-year fire insurance policy for $20,000 on furniture and equipment. The policy was dated April 1, 19—.
31—Depreciation of furniture and equipment for the month was $20.
31—Accrued interest amounted to $25 as of March 31 on the short-term notes acquired on March 18.
31—The interest accrued on the bank loan was $3.

Problem 1-2. Continuing Corporation has authorized common stock of 40,000 shares with a par value of $50. On March 15, 19—, 8,000 of these shares are outstanding. The chart of accounts used by the corporation is presented below.

Cash
Petty Cash
Accounts Receivable
Allowance for Doubtful Accounts
Notes Receivable
Merchandise Inventory
Land
Buildings
Accumulated Depreciation—Buildings
Equipment
Accumulated Depreciation—Equipment
Accounts Payable
Notes Payable
Accrued Interest Payable
Bonds Payable
Capital Stock
Capital in Excess of Par Value
Retained Earnings
Sales
Sales Returns and Allowances
Sales Discounts
Purchases
Transportation In
Purchase Returns and Allowances
Purchase Discounts
Depreciation Expense—Buildings
Depreciation Expense—Equipment
Selling Expense
Transportation Out
Office Expense
Office Salaries
Miscellaneous General Expense
Interest Earned
Interest Expense
Bond Interest Expense

For each of the following transactions, state:

(1) The book of original entry in which the transaction would be recorded if the following journals were used:

Sales	Accounts payable
Sales returns and allowances	Cash disbursements
Cash receipts	General

(2) The general ledger accounts which would be debited and credited.

19—
March 16—The corporation issued 1,500 shares of capital stock for cash at par.
17—2,000 shares of capital stock were issued for the following assets and liabilities of a going business:

Accounts receivable	$30,610
Merchandise inventory	35,302
Land	15,000
Buildings	60,000
Accounts payable	40,912

17—Purchased merchandise from Boyle and Company, $410. Signed a 30-day, 6% note for $410 in settlement of this purchase.
17—Set up a petty cash fund of $100 by drawing a check for this amount.
18—Sold merchandise to R. A. Stevens, $580; terms, 2/10; n/30.
20—Discounted our 60-day note payable for $4,000 at Merchants Bank. The discount rate was 5% and the proceeds of $3,966.67 were added to our account at the bank.
20—Purchased equipment on account with a list price of $6,800.
22—Paid $120 for freight on the equipment purchased on March 20.
25—Purchased merchandise on account from Jackson Enterprises, $890; terms, 2/10; n/30.
27—R. A. Stevens returned merchandise of $60 invoice value which we sold him on March 18.
28—R. A. Stevens paid the balance due on his purchase of March 18.
30—Paid monthly expenses as follows: telephone, $79.64; office salaries, $342.80.
April 10—Returned merchandise costing $60 to Jackson Enterprises, and paid the balance due on this account.
15—Reimbursed the petty cash fund for expenditures made as follows:

Office supplies	$40.80
Transportation in	32.80

16—Paid note of March 17 to Boyle and Company.

Problem 1-3. The monthly column totals of the special journals and the complete general journal of Flashing Company for the month of March are given below. By using T-accounts, show how the entries would appear in the general ledger after the monthly postings had been completed.

Journal **(Page 1)**

Accounts Payable	General Ledger	Date		L.F.		General Ledger	Accounts Receivable
		1965					
	6,200	Mar.	1		Purchases		
	3,800				Store fixtures		
					Capital stock	10,000	
					Payment with merchandise and store fixtures.		
99			10		McGregor Brothers		
					Purchase returns and allowances	99	
					Merchandise billed at $100.		
	50		17		Sales returns and allowances		
					The English Shop		50
					Allowance on damaged merchandise. Credit memo No. 1.		
	750		19		Notes receivable		
					The English Shop		750
					5% 60-day note in payment of account.		
	25		26		Sales returns and allowances		
					Brady, Inc.		25
					Credit memo No. 2.		

Sales Journal:		
Column total		$ 2,950
Accounts Payable Journal:		
Column totals:		
Accounts Payable		$ 5,225
Purchases		5,050
Sundry		175
Store fixtures	$ 175	
Cash Disbursements Journal:		
Column totals:		
Cash		$ 5,139
Purchase Discounts		37
Accounts Payable		4,376
Purchases		150
Sundry		650
Store rent	$ 200	
Salaries	450	
Cash Receipts Journal:		
Column totals:		
Cash		$12,101
Sales Discounts		29
Accounts Receivable		1,450
Sales		680
Sundry		10,000
Capital stock	$10,000	

Problem 1-4. The following information is gathered from the records of Carey Company at the close of the fiscal year, January 31, 1965.

(1) The balance of Accounts Receivable is $50,000; the balance of Allowance for Doubtful Accounts is $300. It is estimated that approximately 2% of the accounts receivable may prove uncollectible.
(2) Of the office supplies purchased for $6,000 and charged to expense, approximately one-fourth remain unused on January 31, 1965.
(3) Machinery and equipment is being depreciated at 10%. The balance of the asset account on January 31, 1965, is $172,800, including $12,800 additions during the fiscal year which are to be depreciated at half the annual rate.
(4) Small Tools account has a balance of $15,000, but the inventory count showed $11,000 of small tools on hand on January 31, 1965.
(5) Salaries and wages accrued on January 31, 1965, are $3,200.
(6) A 10-year 6% bond issue of $100,000 was sold at 97 on September 1, 1963. Interest is payable March 1 and September 1.

Prepare January 31, 1965 adjusting entries.

Problem 1-5. Auto Instant Clean Company is engaged in the auto-washing business. Except for a few business firms who are billed monthly for the frequent washing of their fleets of cars and trucks, all service is performed on a cash basis. All purchases are made for cash. Wages are paid weekly and rent is paid monthly. Washing supplies are purchased frequently. The company owns the washing equipment outright, but pays a monthly royalty equal to 5% of its gross revenue to Instant Clean Corporation for the use of the name "Instant Clean" and the use of a special patented cleaning agent in its washing operations.

(a) Suggest a practical set of journals, naming the columnar headings and the arrangement thereof, that can be employed by Auto Instant Clean Company.
(b) Describe the method for posting from these journals.

Problem 1-6. From the trial balance on page 554 and additional information prepare the necessary adjusting journal entries.

(1) The bank reconciliation on September 30, 1965, appeared as follows:

Balance per books	$2,817
Less collection and exchange	8
	$2,809
Add outstanding checks	186
Balance per bank statement	$2,995

(2) The United States bonds bear interest at 3%, payable April 1 and October 1.
(3) An uncollectible account receivable with a balance of $300 has not been written off.
(4) It was estimated that 5% of the outstanding accounts receivable [after the write-off in (3)] on September 30 will be uncollectible.
(5) The balance of the Notes Receivable account is the face of a 4%, 6-month note acquired July 1, 1965.
(6) Depreciation of furniture and fixtures is to be recorded at a rate of 10% per annum. The only change in the Furniture and Fixtures account during the year ended September 30, 1965, was the purchase of a display case on April 1, 1965, for $500.
(7) Delivery equipment is estimated to have a service life of 4 years, without scrap value. No acquisitions or disposals of delivery equipment occurred during the current year.

HUDSON ENTERPRISES
Trial Balance
September 30, 1965

Account	Debit	Credit
Cash	2,817	
Petty cash	100	
United States Government bonds	10,000	
Notes receivable	1,000	
Accounts receivable	12,060	
Allowance for doubtful accounts		200
Merchandise inventory	6,424	
Unexpired insurance	693	
Furniture and fixtures	12,620	
Accumulated depreciation—Furniture and fixtures		4,130
Delivery equipment	6,200	
Accumulated depreciation—Delivery equipment		1,910
Notes payable		3,000
Accounts payable		8,407
Capital stock		50,000
Retained earnings (September 30, 1964)		15,032
Sales		114,714
Sales returns and allowances	2,175	
Purchases	104,793	
Sales salaries	12,620	
Advertising expense	8,410	
Delivery expense	4,700	
Rent expense	6,450	
Office supplies expense	712	
Office salaries	7,610	
Collection and exchange	50	
Purchase discounts		1,916
Interest income		125
	199,434	199,434

(8) The insurance in force on September 30, 1965, was represented by the following policies:

Policy	Period Covered	Total Premium
A	1- 1-65 to 1- 1-66	$ 60
B	6-30-64 to 6-30-67	360
C	10- 1-62 to 10- 1-67	480

(9) The only note payable outstanding on September 30, 1965, was dated June 30, 1965, and bore interest at 6%.

(10) A schedule of the accounts payable on September 30 showed a total of $8,488. It was determined that the difference between the controlling account and the subsidiary ledger was due to an error in recording a purchase. The correct amount of the purchase was posted to the creditor's account from the duplicate invoice.

(11) $800 of the balance in the advertising account represents the payment to Superior Advertising Agency for advertising to be released in November and December, 1965.

(12) Rent for October, 1965, had been paid in September, in the amount of $500.
(13) It was estimated that office supplies costing $206 were unused on September 30, 1965.

Problem 1-7. Following are data from the accounts of Bay Sights Company.

Purchases on account	$49,900
Sales on account	39,100
Notes received to settle accounts	6,500
Accounts receivable determined to be worthless	1,200
Payments to creditors	34,000
Discounts allowed by creditors	1,600
Merchandise returned by customers	810
Collections received to settle accounts	22,700
Notes given to creditors in settlement of accounts	1,500
Provision for doubtful accounts	1,900
Interest paid on notes payable	130
Merchandise returned to suppliers	450
Payments made on notes	1,000
Collections received in settlement of notes	3,000
Uncollected matured notes receivable returned to customers' accounts	2,000
Interest received on notes receivable	180

Set up controlling accounts for accounts receivable and accounts payable and enter therein the proper amounts as selected from the above information.

Problem 1-8. Selected transactions taken from the accounts of Sports Corporation during 1965 are presented below. Prepare entries for these transactions in general journal form.

(1) Paid final installment on last year's income tax, $4,820.
(2) The bank returned an N.S.F. check of John Doe, a customer, previously deposited. The check amounted to $101.
(3) A building with a cost of $24,000 and accumulated depreciation of $17,900, and on which there was a mortgage of $4,000, was sold on account for $8,500. The purchaser, New Developers, Inc., agreed to assume the mortgage and pay the $4,500 balance of the sale price within 60 days.
(4) The Goodwill account had a balance of $10,000. During the year the account was written off.
(5) Two years ago a $410 account with Smith Brothers was regarded as worthless and was written off. During the current year the customer informed the company that he would be able to pay $300 on the bill, and sent an accompanying payment of $200.
(6) A vacant plot of land was converted to an employees' parking lot. The total cost of this improvement was $5,500.
(7) Semiannual bond interest in the amount of $1,500 was paid. $75 of bond discount was applicable to this period.
(8) 3,000 shares of par value treasury stock, carried at a cost of $29,000, were sold for $30,500.
(9) It was discovered that a previous payment of $175 on account to Dual Suppliers had been charged to accounts receivable.
(10) The authorized issue of common stock was increased from 10,000 shares to 15,000 shares. This stock has a $10 par value.

(11) Subscriptions were received for 100 shares of $10 par value common stock at par.
(12) The petty cash fund was increased from $100 to $150.
(13) 1,500 shares of $10 par value common stock were issued for land which had a value of $15,000.
(14) Merchandise costing $320 was received to replace goods of an equal cost returned to the supplier last month and recorded as a purchase return.
(15) $7,500 was received from the bank as a result of a mortgage placed on the machinery.
(16) A dividend of $9,000 was paid to satisfy the dividend declaration made one month earlier.
(17) A check for $1,960 was issued in payment for equipment purchased 26 days ago with terms of 2/30; n/60.
(18) A $245 collection was made from G. Wently to cover a 2% discount improperly taken after the expiration of the discount period.
(19) $10 was paid out of the petty cash fund for postage stamps.
(20) Proceeds received from discounting a $500 noninterest-bearing note payable at the bank were $485.
(21) Freight charge of $12 was paid on a shipment to Sam Stover. The sale had been made f.o.b. shipping point.
(22) A check for $260 was sent to Don Fixler to cover the cost of damaged merchandise sold to him.
(23) A cash sale of $150 was made and the $3 sales tax was collected from the customer.
(24) A collection of $490 was made on Sam Lee's account. The $500 sale had been made to him f.o.b. destination and the customer paid the $10 shipping charges.
(25) Fully depreciated machinery costing $1,150 was scrapped.

Problem 1-9. The recently employed bookkeeper for Monarch Company prepared the year-end financial statements from the following unadjusted trial balance.

MONARCH COMPANY
Unadjusted Trial Balance
December 31, 1965

Cash	7,160	
Accounts receivable	18,400	
Merchandise inventory, December 31, 1964	6,600	
Unexpired insurance, December 31, 1964	300	
Equipment	14,800	
Accumulated depreciation		4,920
Accounts payable		3,180
5% Bonds payable, due January 1, 1969		10,000
Bond premium		400
Capital stock		20,000
Retained earnings		9,960
Sales		50,000
Purchases	30,000	
Salaries and commissions	14,000	
Rent expense	3,600	
Insurance expense	240	
Advertising	1,360	
Miscellaneous expense	2,000	
	98,460	98,460

The income statement prepared by the bookkeeper showed a net loss of $1,200 for 1965. He assumed that there was no change in the merchandise inventory, although actually the December 31, 1965 merchandise inventory amounted to $6,100. He also overlooked the accrual of bond interest; $500 is payable on January 1, 1966. Depreciation for 1965 of $740 was ignored. The December 31, 1964 balance of $300 in Unexpired Insurance was the unexpired premium on a policy which expires December 31, 1966. On April 1, 1965, the company took out an additional insurance policy for a three-year term and paid a $240 premium therefor. All receivables appear to be collectible.

Prepare a schedule showing the correct net income (or loss) for 1965.

Problem 1-10. Dunbarton Corporation began operations on July 1, 1965. During the six months ended December 31, 1965, the accounting records have been maintained on a double-entry basis, but the cash basis of accounting has been employed. The trial balance prepared from these records on December 31, 1965, appeared as follows:

DUNBARTON CORPORATION
Trial Balance
December 31, 1965

Cash	7,680	
Purchases	25,120	
Operating expenses	13,600	
Notes payable		5,000
Sales		26,400
Capital stock		15,000
	46,400	46,400

It was decided to convert the accounting records to the accrual basis on December 31, 1965. In this connection, the following information was made available by the bookkeeper:

(1) Outstanding bills on December 31, 1965:

Merchandise purchases	$1,650
Operating expenses	940
Total	$2,590

(2) $3,150 was receivable from customers for sales made in 1965.
(3) Included in operating expenses were:
   (a) $2,500 for the purchase of furniture and equipment on July 1, 1965. It was estimated that the furniture and equipment would have a service life of 10 years, without scrap value.
   (b) $240 for a three-year premium on a fire insurance policy on furniture and equipment, dated July 1, 1965.
(4) Included in sales was $500 deposited by a customer for merchandise to be delivered in 1966.
(5) The Notes Payable account represents a 6%, three-month note issued on December 1, 1965.
(6) Merchandise on hand on December 31, 1965, amounted to $10,520.

Required:

(a) The necessary adjusting journal entries to place the records on an accrual basis on December 31, 1965.
(b) A schedule showing the net income before income taxes for the six months ended December 31, 1965.

Problem 1-11. The trial balance and adjusted trial balance of Olson Togs Company on December 31, 1965, are presented below. Analyze these trial balances and present the December 31, 1965 adjusting entries in general journal form.

	Trial Balance December 31, 1965		Adjusted Trial Balance December 31, 1965	
Cash	4,702		4,702	
Short-term investments	10,000		10,000	
Accounts receivable	21,400		21,200	
Allowance for doubtful accounts (1% of receivables)		300		212
Accrued interest receivable			100	
Advances to suppliers			550	
Inventory	8,900		8,900	
Prepaid rent	1,800		600	
Unexpired insurance			218	
Furniture and equipment	50,000		50,000	
Accumulated depreciation		7,500		10,000
Accounts payable		13,440		13,990
Accrued interest payable				225
Estimated liability for income taxes				4,900
Bonds payable		15,000		15,000
Premium on bonds		1,800		1,725
Common stock		30,000		30,000
Retained earnings		2,818		2,818
Sales		220,000		220,000
Cost of goods sold	140,000		140,000	
Selling expenses	28,800		30,000	
Administrative expenses	25,106		25,000	
Depreciation expense			2,500	
Interest income		300		400
Interest expense	450		600	
Income taxes			4,900	
	291,158	291,158	299,270	299,270

Problem 1-12. Watson Corporation had been in business for one month when the bookkeeper presented the following trial balance and schedules of accounts receivable and payable on July 31, 1965. Several errors apparently have been made.

Using the journals and ledger accounts which appear after the trial balance and schedules, prepare a list of the errors. (See suggested solution form at end of problem.)

Prepare corrected trial balance and schedules of accounts receivable and accounts payable as of July 31, 1965.

WATSON CORPORATION

Trial Balance

July 31, 1965

Cash	7,451	
Accounts receivable	2,838	
Equipment	3,000	
Accounts payable		3,676
Notes payable		5,000

Capital stock		4,000
Sales		5,442
Sales returns and allowances	182	
Sales discounts	33	
Purchases	5,599	
Purchase returns and allowances		245
Purchase discounts		34
Transportation in	28	
Store rent	250	
Transportation out	25	
Salesmen's salaries	650	
	19,856	18,397

Schedule of Accounts Receivable
July 31, 1965

E. J. Waters	—
Sam Fields	900
Wm. Reed	320
	1,220

Schedule of Accounts Payable
July 31, 1965

Cross Corp.	722
C. N. Oliver	3,000
	3,722

Sales Journal **(Page 1)**

Date		√	Name	Invoice No.	Amount
1965					
July	2	√	E. J. Waters	1	300
	8	√	E. J. Waters	2	800
	9	√	Sam Fields	3	1,700
	11	√	Wm. Reed	4	450
	13	√	Sam Fields	5	900
	17	√	E. J. Waters	6	670
	19	√	Wm. Reed	7	320
					5,120
					(2) (8)

Sales Returns and Allowances Journal (Page 1)

Date		√	Name	Credit Memo No.	Amount
1965					
July	5	√	E. J. Waters	1	50
	15	√	Sam Fields	2	62
	22	√	E. J. Waters	3	70
					182
					(9) (2)

Purchase Returns and Allowances Journal (Page 1)

Date		√	Name	Credit Memo No.	Amount
1965					
July	9	√	C. N. Oliver	K14	95
	13	√	Cross Corp.	71	150
					245
					(5) (12)

General Journal (Page 1)

Date			L.F.	Debit	Credit
1965					
July	8	Accounts payable (C. N. Oliver)	√/5	1,050	
		Notes payable	6		1,050
		Gave 20-day note for purchase today from C. N. Oliver .			
	11	Notes receivable	3	450	
		Accounts receivable (Wm. Reed)	√/2		450
		Received a 10-day note for sale today to Wm. Reed.			

Cash Disbursements Journal (Page 1)

Date	Explanation	Cash	Purchase Discounts	Sundry Name	Sundry L.F.	Sundry Amount	Account Debited	Accounts Payable √	Accounts Payable Amount	Purchases	Sundry L.F.	Sundry Amount
		Credits						Debits				
1965												
July 1	Invoice S1211	1,500								1,500		
1	July rent	250					Store rent				15	250
12	Invoice XX101	27								27		
13	July 3 invoice less return	1,519	31				Cross Corp.	√	1,550			
15	Half-month	325					Salesmen's salaries				17	325
25	Freight bills	79					Motor Freight Co.	√	79			
25	July 16 invoice	600	12				Cross Corp.	√	600			
26	C. N. Oliver note	1,050					Notes payable				6	1,050
31	Last half of month	325					Salesmen's salaries				17	325
		5,675	43						2,229	1,527		1,950
		(1)	(13)						(5)	(11)		

Cash Receipts Journal (Page 1)

Date	Explanation	Cash	Sales Discounts	Sundry Name	Sundry L.F.	Sundry Amount	Account Credited	Accounts Receivable √	Accounts Receivable Amount	Sales	Sundry L.F.	Sundry Amount
		Debits						Credits				
1965												
July 1	Stock issued	4,000					Capital stock				7	4,000
2		250								250		
9	Sale of July 2	245	5				E. J. Waters	√	250			
10	First National Bank—60-day	5,000					Notes payable				6	5,000
12		82								82		
16	Sale of July 8	784	16				E. J. Waters	√	800			
21	Reed note dated July 11	450					Notes receivable				3	450
26	Sale of July 17	582	12	Transportation out	16	6	E. J. Waters	√	600			
27	To cover credit memo K14	95					Accounts payable (C. N. Oliver)				5/√	95
29	Sale of July 9	1,638					Sam Fields	√				1,638
		13,126	33			6			1,650	332		11,183
		(1)	(10)						(2)	(8)		

Accounts Payable Journal **(Page 1)**

Date		Subsidiary Ledger Account Credited	Invoice Date		GENERAL LEDGER						
					Credits		Debits				
					√	Accounts Payable	Purchases	Transportation In	Sundry Name	Sundry L.F.	Sundry Amount
1965											
July	3	Cross Corp.	July	2	√	1,700	1,700				
	3	Motor Freight Co.		3	√	26		26			
	8	C. N. Oliver		6	√	1,050	1,050				
	16	Cross Corp.		15	√	600	600				
	23	Cross Corp.		23	√	722	722				
	24	Motor Freight Co.		23	√	53		22	Transportation out	16	31
	30	C. N. Oliver		24	√	3,000			Equipment	4	3,000
						7,151	4,072	28			3,031
						(5)	(11)	(14)			

GENERAL LEDGER

Cash (1)

Date		Explanation	Ref.	Debit	Date		Explanation	Ref.	Credit
1965					1965				
July	31	7,451	CR 1	13,126	July	31		CD 1	5,675

Accounts Receivable (2)

Date		Explanation	Ref.	Debit	Date		Explanation	Ref.	Credit
1965					1965				
July	31	2,838	S 1	5,120	July	11		J 1	450
						31		SR 1	182
						31		CR 1	1,650
									2,282

Notes Receivable (3)

Date		Explanation	Ref.	Debit	Date		Explanation	Ref.	Credit
1965					1965				
July	11		J 1	450	July	21		CR 1	450

Equipment (4)

Date		Explanation	Ref.	Debit	Date		Explanation	Ref.	Credit
1965									
July	30		AP 1	3,000					

Accounts Payable (5)

Date		Explanation	Ref.	Debit	Date		Explanation	Ref.	Credit
1965					1965				
July	8		J 1	1,050	July	27		CR 1	95
	31		PR 1	245		31	3,676	AP 1	7,115
	31		CD 1	2,229					7,200
				3,524					

Notes Payable (6)

Date		Explanation	Ref.	Debit	Date		Explanation	Ref.	Credit
1965					1965				
July	26		CD 1	1,050	July	8		J 1	1,050
						10	5,000	CR 1	5,000

Capital Stock (7)

Date		Explanation	Ref.	Debit	Date		Explanation	Ref.	Credit
					1965				
					July	1		CR 1	4,000

Sales (8)

Date		Explanation	Ref.	Debit	Date		Explanation	Ref.	Credit
					1965				
					July	31		S 1	5,120
						31		CR 1	322
									5,442

Sales Returns and Allowances (9)

Date		Explanation	Ref.	Debit	Date		Explanation	Ref.	Credit
1965									
July	31		SR 1	182					

Sales Discounts (10)

1965									
July	31		CR 1	33					

Purchases (11)

1965									
July	31		AP 1	4,072					
	31		CD 1	1,527					
				5,599					

Purchase Returns and Allowances (12)

					1965				
					July	31		PR 1	245

Purchase Discounts (13)

					1965				
					July	31		CD 1	43

Transportation In (14)

1965									
July	31		AP 1	28					

Store Rent (15)

1965									
July	1		CD 1	250					

Transportation Out (16)

1965					1965				
July	31	25	AP 1	31	July	31		CR 1	6

Salesmen's Salaries (17)

1965									
July	15		CD 1	325					
	31		CD 1	325					
				650					

ACCOUNTS RECEIVABLE LEDGER

E. J. Waters

1965					1965				
July	2		S 1	300	July	5		SR 1	50
	8		S 1	800		10		CR 1	250
	17		S 1	670		16		CR 1	800
				1,770		22		SR 1	70
						26		CR 1	600
									1,770

Sam Fields

1965					1965				
July	9		S 1	1,700	July	15		SR 1	62
	13	900	S 1	900		29		CR 1	1,638
				2,600					1,700

Wm. Reed

1965					1965				
July	11		S 1	450	July	11		J 1	450
	19	320	S 1	320					
				770					

ACCOUNTS PAYABLE LEDGER

Cross Corp.

1965					1965				
July	13		CD 1	1,550	July	3		AP 1	1,700
	13		PR 1	150		16		AP 1	600
	25		CD 1	600		23	722	AP 1	722
				2,300					3,022

Motor Freight Co.

1965					1965				
July	25		CD 1	79	July	3		AP 1	26
						24		AP 1	53
									79

C. N. Oliver

1965					1965				
July	8		J 1	1,050	July	8		AP 1	1,050
	9		PR 1	95		27		CR 1	95
				1,145		30	3,000	AP 1	3,000
									4,145

Suggested Solution Form

Schedule of Errors

	General Ledger Trial Balance		Accounts Receivable		Accounts Payable	
	Debit	Credit	Control	Subsidiary	Control	Subsidiary
General ledger trial balance totals	19,856	18,397				
Controlling account balances			2,838		3,676	
Subsidiary ledger schedule totals .				1,220		3,722
Step #1—Refoot trial balance.						
(a) Debit column is underfooted	+ 200					
	20,056	18,397				

Problem 1-13. Following is a summary of the ledger account postings for 1965, for Central Pacific Company. It was prepared from the books at the end of the company's first year of operations. By analyzing the account balances and assuming typical interrelationships among the accounts, prepare entries in general journal form summarizing the transactions for the year. For example, the $205,060 credited to Sales can be related to the $205,060 debited to Accounts Receivable.

The summary entry would be:

Accounts receivable	205,060	
Sales		205,060

After this process is completed, post to T-accounts in order to compare your account data with the following summary.

	Debit	Credit
Cash	295,605	258,687
Petty cash	500	
Accounts receivable	205,060	165,555
U. S. Government bonds	10,000	
Inventory	175,354	145,346
Fixed assets	62,500	
Accumulated depreciation		2,900
Bank loan	10,000	30,000
Accounts payable	238,187	260,076
Capital stock		100,000
Sales		205,060
Cost of sales	145,346	
Expenses (including depreciation of $2,900)	25,122	
Interest income		50
	1,167,674	1,167,674

Assignment Material for Chapter 2

QUESTIONS

1. What is the purpose of working papers?

2. Under what circumstances, if any, is it acceptable not to enter the adjusting entries in the books of account?

3. Identify the kinds of accounts that should have zero balances after the books have been closed.

4. Which inventory, beginning or ending, is shown in the unadjusted trial balance when the company has adopted the perpetual inventory method?

5. What is the difference between adjusting entries and closing entries?

6. List the items that are used in the computation of the cost of goods sold when the business has adopted the periodical inventory method.

7. In what ways are working papers for a proprietorship different from those for a corporation?

8. Describe in detail two methods of handling an expense account in separate working papers when 80% of the amount is assignable to manufacturing, 15% to selling expense, and 5% to administrative expense.

9. When is it appropriate to use reversing entries, and why do you consider it desirable to use them?

10. "Working papers require an unnecessary duplication of effort at year end." Give the reasons why you agree or disagree with this statement.

11. Explain why in some circumstances an adjusting journal entry could be made one way at one year end and another way at the next year end.

12. The accounts shown below do not appear in the trial balance of *ZYX* Company.

Bad Debts Expense	Interest Expense
Unexpired Insurance	Rent Received in Advance
Accrued Rent Receivable	

For each of the following adjusting entries, state whether you would or would not make a reversing entry, and give your reason why.

(a) To provide for doubtful accounts.
(b) To record accrued rent receivable.
(c) To record the portion of the prepaid interest on a short-term note payable applicable to the current year.
(d) To record the amount of unexpired insurance premiums at year end.
(e) To record the portion of rent received in advance which has not been earned.

PROBLEMS

Problem 2-1. The following data relate to Blue Horizon Company.

Required:

(a) Working papers.
(b) Closing entries, using the closing procedure you prefer.

BLUE HORIZON COMPANY
Trial Balance
December 31, 1965

Cash	20,400	
Accounts receivable	18,000	
Allowance for doubtful accounts		150
Inventory	35,000	
Prepaid interest (on note payable)	200	
Equipment	25,000	
Accumulated depreciation		9,100
Accounts payable		17,750
Note payable		20,000
Customers' advances		600
Capital stock		25,000
Retained earnings		19,180
Dividends	1,250	
Sales		300,000
Sales returns and allowances	3,200	
Purchases	185,450	
Purchase discounts		2,220
Selling expenses	62,300	
Administrative expenses	43,200	
	394,000	394,000

Supplementary data:

(A) The inventory on December 31, 1965, amounted to $37,000.
(B) Uncollectible accounts are expected to equal 2% of the accounts receivable.
(C) The note payable was signed on December 1, 1965, and was for a 60-day term.
(D) Accrued selling expenses amounted to $320 as of December 31, 1965.
(E) A $600 shipment of merchandise was made late in December to the customers from whom advances had been received. No entry was recorded for the shipment.
(F) Depreciation, which is chargeable to Administrative Expenses, has not been recorded for 1965. The rate is 5%.
(G) The first $25,000 of income is taxed at a rate of 20%.

Problem 2-2. The trial balance of a proprietorship is presented below.

A. B. ZEE
Trial Balance
December 31, 1965

Cash	55,488	
Accounts receivable	22,600	
Allowance for doubtful accounts		1,208
Inventory, December 31, 1965	28,300	
Long-term investments	75,000	
Land	5,000	
Buildings	28,000	
Accumulated depreciation—Buildings		12,600
Accounts payable		14,300
Mortgage payable		5,000
A. B. Zee, capital		176,800
Drawings	6,000	
Sales		96,110
Sales returns and allowances	1,980	
Cost of goods sold	49,470	
Salaries and wages	19,900	
Advertising	2,500	
Transportation out	4,520	
Office expense	3,200	
Supplies expense	4,000	
Interest earned		310
Interest expense	370	
	306,328	306,328

Additional information:

(A) It is estimated that 8% of the outstanding accounts receivable will be uncollectible.
(B) When the buildings were purchased nine years ago, it was estimated that they would have a life of 20 years.
(C) $350 of salaries and wages have accrued on December 31, 1965.
(D) Interest accrued on the long-term investments is $500.

Required:

(a) Working papers.
(b) Closing entries, using the procedure you prefer.

Problem 2-3. Using the trial balance and supplementary data below, prepare separate working papers for each statement. All of the accounts required are included in the trial balance.

THE TWIN *R* COMPANY

Trial Balance

June 30, 1965

Account	Debit	Credit
Cash	18,685	
Securities	30,000	
Accounts receivable	8,300	
Allowance for doubtful accounts		330
Accrued interest receivable		
Inventory	17,150	
Prepaid rent	2,000	
Unexpired insurance		
Land	5,000	
Buildings	40,000	
Accumulated depreciation—Buildings		20,000
Equipment	75,000	
Accumulated depreciation—Equipment		15,000
Accounts payable		21,587
Accrued salaries payable		
Accrued bond interest payable		
Income tax payable		
Bonds payable		50,000
Capital stock		50,000
Capital in excess of stated value		5,000
Retained earnings, June 30, 1964		16,725
Dividends	1,500	
Sales		99,070
Cost of goods sold	41,100	
Sales salaries	19,909	
Advertising expense	6,500	
Office salaries	11,988	
Insurance expense	580	
Depreciation—Buildings		
Depreciation—Equipment		
Bad debts expense		
Rent expense		
Interest earned		
Interest expense		
Federal income tax		
	277,712	277,712

Additional information:

(A) Buildings and machinery are to be depreciated at 8% and 10% per annum, respectively.

(B) The rent is paid on January 1 each year for one year in advance.

(C) The securities held pay interest at 3% per annum on March 1 and September 1. They were acquired on their issuance date, which was March 1, 1965.

(D) Of the balance in the insurance account, $420 is the amount of the premium for a two-year policy purchased on March 1, 1965.

(E) Salaries accrued on June 30, 1965, are as follows: Sales salaries, $325; Office salaries, $480.

(F) The company's bank reconciliation prepared on June 30, 1965, is presented below:

Balance per books		$18,685.57
Deduct:		
N.S.F. check of customer	$500.00	
Deposit not taken up by bank	375.00	875.00
Balance per bank statement		$17,810.57

(G) The bonds payable were issued on May 1, 1965, and bear interest at 6% per annum, payable May 1 and November 1.
(H) It is estimated that 6% of the outstanding accounts receivable will be uncollectible.
(I) The applicable income tax rate is 20%.

Problem 2-4. Prepare separate working papers for each statement for Short Manufacturing Company. Only two adjustments are required:

(A) Accrued rent of $4,000, apportioned as follows:

Manufacturing	75%
Selling	12½%
Administration	12½%

(B) Federal income tax at a rate of 20%.

SHORT MANUFACTURING COMPANY
Trial Balance
December 31, 1965

Cash	30,300	
Inventories:		
Finished goods	6,200	
Goods in process	4,060	
Materials	3,160	
Land	30,000	
Accounts payable		8,720
Capital stock		50,000
Retained earnings, December 31, 1964		12,300
Dividends	5,000	
Sales		119,330
Purchases	27,320	
Transportation in	600	
Direct labor	33,410	
Manufacturing overhead	15,770	
Selling expenses	21,210	
Administrative expenses	13,320	
	190,350	190,350

December 31, 1965 inventories:

Finished goods	$7,200
Goods in process	3,860
Materials	4,010

Problem 2-5. Following is the December 31, 1965 trial balance of John S. Green:

JOHN S. GREEN
Trial Balance
December 31, 1965

Cash	8,000	
Accounts receivable	12,000	
Allowance for doubtful accounts		400
Notes receivable	2,000	
Inventory (December 31, 1964)	20,000	
Unexpired insurance	300	
Office supplies	700	
Land	15,000	
Building	50,000	
Accumulated depreciation—Building		15,000
Furniture and fixtures	30,000	
Accumulated depreciation—Furniture and fixtures		8,000
Accounts payable		12,000
Bank loans		10,000
John S. Green, capital		83,300
John S. Green, drawings	7,200	
Sales		150,000
Sales returns and allowances	900	
Sales discounts	2,000	
Purchases	110,600	
Purchase returns and allowances		1,200
Purchase discounts		1,200
Salesmen's salaries	9,000	
Advertising	4,000	
Miscellaneous selling expense	800	
Taxes	1,000	
Office salaries	6,000	
Office expense	1,200	
Interest income		100
Interest expense	500	
	281,200	281,200

Supplementary information:

(A) The Allowance for Doubtful Accounts should be increased to $800.
(B) Provision for depreciation (no additions to the assets during the year): Building, 3%; Furniture and fixtures, 10%.
(C) Salesmen's salaries accrued to December 31, 1965, $300.
(D) Accrued interest receivable on December 31, 1965, $25.
(E) Of the balance of the Interest Expense account, the prepaid portion is $100.
(F) Of the balance of the Unexpired Insurance account, two-thirds has expired.
(G) Inventory, December 31, 1965, $22,000.

Prepare working papers for the year ended December 31, 1965. You may omit the Adjusted Trial Balance columns. Identify the adjusting entries which could properly be reversed.

Problem 2-6. The following trial balance was taken from the books of Stern and Clark on December 31, 1965:

STERN AND CLARK
Trial Balance
December 31, 1965

Cash	6,645	
Petty cash	100	
Accounts receivable	17,675	
Allowance for doubtful accounts		400
Notes receivable	3,000	
Inventory (December 31, 1964)	25,500	
Advertising supplies	1,200	
Prepaid interest	125	
Furniture and fixtures	8,500	
Accumulated depreciation—Furniture and fixtures		2,150
Delivery equipment	8,200	
Accumulated depreciation—Delivery equipment		3,500
Accounts payable		7,855
Bank loans		10,000
Delivery income collected in advance		220
D. H. Stern, capital		12,750
D. H. Stern, drawings	4,200	
K. B. Clark, capital		9,200
K. B. Clark, drawings	3,000	
Sales		151,440
Sales returns and allowances	735	
Sales discounts	1,290	
Purchases	95,300	
Purchase returns and allowances		995
Purchase discounts		715
Advertising	10,700	
Delivery expense	3,125	
Miscellaneous selling expense	960	
Rent expense	4,800	
Taxes	210	
Office salaries	3,150	
Office expense	660	
Interest income		300
Interest expense	450	
	199,525	199,525

Supplementary data:

(A) $120 of delivery income collected in advance applies to 1966.
(B) Depreciation to be provided for 1965:

10% of furniture and fixtures
20% of delivery equipment

(C) It is estimated that $775 of the accounts receivable will probably prove uncollectible.
(D) Advertising supplies of $800 remain unused.
(E) Office expense includes $120 for a two-year insurance policy to May 1, 1967.
(F) No interest for 1966 has been prepaid.

(G) Inventory, December 31, 1965, $25,200.

(H) The partnership agreement provides for the division of earnings in the ratio of two-thirds to Stern and one-third to Clark.

Prepare working papers for the year, omitting the use of Adjusted Trial Balance columns.

Problem 2-7. The trial balance presented below was taken from the ledger of Arch Company on December 31, 1965, before adjusting entries were posted.

ARCH COMPANY
Trial Balance
December 31, 1965

Cash	46,834	
Accounts receivable	19,110	
Allowance for doubtful accounts		816
Inventories, December 31, 1964:		
Finished goods	12,090	
Goods in process	12,663	
Materials	18,901	
Unexpired insurance	420	
Land	55,000	
Buildings	94,600	
Accumulated depreciation—Buildings		12,510
Machinery and equipment	106,640	
Accumulated depreciation—Machinery and equipment		29,810
Office equipment	4,600	
Accumulated depreciation—Office equipment		1,030
Accounts payable		9,610
Bonds payable		50,000
Capital stock		200,000
Retained earnings		24,714
Dividends	10,000	
Sales		447,371
Purchases—Materials	128,126	
Purchase discounts		2,410
Transportation in	4,090	
Direct labor	183,200	
Indirect labor	12,640	
Factory supplies	2,100	
Heat, light, and power	16,900	
Tools expense	10,500	
Repairs—Machinery	1,060	
Taxes—Property	3,640	
Sales salaries and expense	14,641	
Advertising	3,938	
Miscellaneous selling expense	1,014	
Office salaries	9,525	
Office supplies expense	1,816	
Bank charges	75	
Telephone and telegraph	948	
Postage	400	
Interest expense	2,800	
	778,271	778,271

Additional information:

(1) Inventories on December 31, 1965:

Finished goods	$13,115
Goods in process	11,981
Materials	19,110

(2) Data for adjusting entries:

(a) It was estimated that $1,956 of the accounts receivable outstanding on December 31, 1965, would be uncollectible.

(b) Depreciation for 1965:

Buildings	$2,400
Machinery and equipment	4,600
Office equipment	850

(c) Insurance premiums expired during the year amounted to $200.

(d) Office salaries of $650 were accrued on December 31, 1965.

(e) The corporation was liable for $200 of interest expense on December 31, 1965.

(3) The following costs are to be allocated as indicated:

	Manufacturing	Selling Expense	General Expense
Heat, light, and power	75%	10%	15%
Taxes—Property	70	10	20
Insurance expense	75	10	15
Depreciation—Buildings	80	5	15

(4) The corporation was liable for federal income tax in the amount of 50% of its net income before income tax.

Prepare:

(a) Separate working papers for each statement.

(b) Closing entries, using a Manufacturing and a Revenue and Expense account.

Problem 2-8. Using the trial balance on page 576 and supplementary data below, prepare separate working papers for each statement.

Supplementary data:

(A) $100 of delivery income applies to 1966.

(B) Depreciation to be provided for 1965: 10% of furniture and fixtures; 20% of delivery equipment.

(C) It is estimated that $795 of the accounts receivable will probably prove uncollectible.

(D) Advertising supplies of $400 remain unused.

(E) Office expense includes $120 for a two-year insurance policy to May 1, 1967.

(F) No interest for 1966 has been prepaid.

(G) The following expenses are to be apportioned as indicated:

	Selling	General
Rent	80%	20%
Property taxes	70	30

(H) Federal income tax liability—$14,350.

SUPPLY COMPANY
Trial Balance
December 31, 1965

Cash	12,056	
Accounts receivable	17,775	
Allowance for doubtful accounts		400
Notes receivable	3,000	
Inventory, December 31, 1965	25,500	
Advertising supplies	1,200	
Prepaid interest	125	
Furniture and fixtures	8,500	
Accumulated depreciation—Furniture and fixtures		2,150
Delivery equipment	8,200	
Accumulated depreciation—Delivery equipment		3,500
Accounts payable		7,855
Bank loans—Short-term		10,000
Capital stock		15,000
Retained earnings		7,921
Dividends	3,000	
Sales		151,440
Sales discounts	1,290	
Sales returns and allowances	735	
Cost of goods sold	95,300	
Advertising expense	10,700	
Delivery expense	3,125	
Miscellaneous selling expense	960	
Rent expense	4,800	
Property taxes	210	
Office salaries	3,150	
Office expense	660	
Delivery income		220
Commissions earned		1,950
Interest income		300
Interest expense	450	
	200,736	200,736

Problem 2-9. The adjusted and unadjusted trial balances of Charter Corporation follow.

Required:

(a) Closing entries, using the procedure you prefer.

(b) Reversing entries as of February 1, 1965.

CHARTER CORPORATION

	January 31, 1965			
	Adjusted Trial Balance		Unadjusted Trial Balance	
Cash	6,840		6,840	
Petty cash	200		200	
Accounts receivable	11,100		11,100	
Allowance for doubtful accounts		1,400		600
Inventory	21,500		19,000	
Prepaid insurance	300			
Land	4,400		4,400	
Building	30,000		30,000	
Accumulated depreciation—Building		12,500		10,500
Delivery equipment	14,000		14,000	
Accumulated depreciation—Delivery equipment		5,600		4,600
Accounts payable		8,150		8,150
Notes payable		2,900		2,900
Federal income tax liability		990		
Accrued salaries		400		
Accrued interest payable		140		
Capital stock		50,000		50,000
Retained earnings		4,230		4,230
Dividends	1,500		1,500	
Sales—For the year ended January 31, 1965		136,400		136,400
Sales returns and allowances	1,810		1,810	
Purchases			109,300	
Purchase returns and allowances				1,300
Cost of goods sold	105,500			
Salesmen's salaries	8,300		8,000	
Advertising	1,200		1,200	
Delivery expense	2,500		2,500	
Depreciation—Delivery equipment	1,000			
Rent—Store fixtures	2,200		2,200	
Office salaries	6,200		6,100	
Depreciation—Building	2,000			
Insurance expense	150		450	
Bad debts expense	800			
Interest expense	220		80	
Income tax	990			
	222,710	222,710	218,680	218,680

Problem 2-10. From the following trial balance, taken from the books of Light Company as of June 30, 1965, prepare working papers, using a pair of columns for the manufacturing accounts.

LIGHT COMPANY

Trial Balance—June 30, 1965

Account	Debit	Credit
Cash in bank	46,210	
Petty cash	500	
Accounts receivable	231,312	
Allowance for doubtful accounts		10,800
Notes receivable	3,000	
Inventories, July 1, 1964:		
Finished goods	27,600	
Goods in process	36,000	
Materials	18,500	
Land	26,100	
Buildings	60,000	
Accumulated depreciation—Buildings		9,480
Machinery	40,510	
Accumulated depreciation—Machinery		9,900
Office furniture	6,150	
Accumulated depreciation—Office furniture		3,050
Tools	10,500	
Dies and jigs	3,000	
Patents	34,000	
Accumulated amortization—Patents		7,000
Accounts payable		40,100
Notes payable		82,400
Bonds payable		100,000
Capital stock		150,000
Retained earnings		53,937
Sales		1,275,025
Sales returns and allowances	40,260	
Sales discounts	10,900	
Materials purchased	512,600	
Purchase discounts		8,160
Transportation on materials	20,200	
Direct labor	408,160	
Indirect labor	47,600	
Repairs—Machinery	2,160	
Insurance—Buildings	500	
Factory expense	3,910	
Insurance—Machinery	920	
Power, heat, and light	26,100	
Taxes—Land and buildings	4,800	
Repairs—Buildings	700	
Salesmen's salaries	44,100	
Travel—Salesmen	16,900	
Transportation out	5,100	
Insurance—Merchandise	1,200	
Payroll—Office	21,200	
Officers' salaries	23,000	
Telephone and telegraph	1,850	
Bank charges	910	
Office employees' surety bonds	320	
Postage	3,800	
Stationery and printing	2,490	
Interest expense	7,200	
Interest income		410
	1,750,262	1,750,262

Additional information:

(A) Inventories on June 30, 1965, were:

Tools	$ 8,000
Dies and jigs	2,600
Finished goods	25,900
Goods in process	23,200
Materials	28,100
Postage	650

(B) Accounts receivable aggregating $4,162 were determined to be uncollectible. It was estimated that 8% of the remaining outstanding accounts would become uncollectible.

(C) Accrued property taxes on June 30, 1965, were as follows:

Land and buildings	$1,200
Machinery	800
Office furniture	100

(D) Wages had been earned, but not paid on June 30, 1965, in the following amounts:

Salesmen	$2,100
Officers	2,000
Office	1,260
Factory:	
Direct labor	8,900
Indirect labor	1,120

(E) The bonds payable bear interest at 4%, payable April 1 and October 1. Interest had been paid to June 30, 1965, on all notes payable with the exception of one 5% note for $8,000, which was issued on April 1, 1965.

(F) Unexpired insurance premiums on June 30, 1965, were as follows:

Buildings	$350
Merchandise	760
Office employees' surety bonds	180
Machinery	640

Allocate the merchandise insurance as follows: 70% to manufacturing and 30% to selling.

(G) Depreciation is provided at the following rates (applied to ending asset account balances):

Buildings	3%
Machinery	10%
Office furniture	12%

(H) Patents are amortized over the legal life of 17 years.

(I) Interest accrued on notes receivable amounted to $60 on June 30, 1965.

(J) All costs associated with the ownership and use of the land and buildings (including power, heat, and light) are allocated as follows:

Manufacturing	80%
Selling	6%
General	14%

(K) The declaration of a 5% cash dividend on June 28, 1965, payable on July 15, 1965, was not recorded.

(L) The federal income tax for the fiscal year ended June 30, 1965, was estimated to be $7,200.

Problem 2-11. Sunset Dairy Company closes its books semiannually on June 30 and December 31. On March 1, 1965, the company borrowed $12,000 at the bank, giving a six-month 6% note. The note was paid at maturity and the interest payment thereon was charged to Interest Expense. The company had no other interest-bearing indebtedness during 1965. On August 1, 1965, the company rented out some storage space, receiving the $900 annual rental in advance. The company's accountant credited the receipt to Rent Received in Advance. On July 16, 1965, a premium of $192 was paid for a two-year fire insurance policy effective that date. This was a renewal of an identical policy and is the only insurance carried. A debit of $192 was made to Insurance Expense, which was consistent with the entry made two years earlier for the insurance premium.

Considering this information, you are requested to prepare adjusting and all possible reversing entries related to interest, rent, and insurance as indicated below.

(1) Adjusting entries on June 30, 1965.
(2) Reversing entries on July 1, 1965.
(3) Adjusting entries on December 31, 1965.
(4) Reversing entries on January 1, 1966.

Problem 2-12. The following selected account balances were taken from the unadjusted trial balance of Duplex Manufacturing Company on December 31, 1965:

Inventories, December 31, 1964:	
Materials	$ 16,000
Goods in process	34,980
Factory supplies	3,900
Buildings	330,000
Machinery and equipment	500,000
Tools	36,000
Patents	70,000
Accumulated depreciation—Buildings	104,000
Accumulated depreciation—Machinery and equipment	308,000
Unexpired insurance	4,800
Light, heat, and power	8,350
Maintenance and repairs—Factory	6,400
Miscellaneous factory expense	4,302
Direct labor	72,850
Material purchases	83,470
Transportation in	930
Indirect labor	12,632
Property taxes	9,760
Factory supplies expense	8,645
Accrued factory payroll	8,430
Accrued property taxes	8,210

Following are data for adjusting and closing entries; it has not been the practice of the corporation to make reversing entries.

(1) The buildings were acquired on January 1, 1952. It is estimated that they will have a salvage value of $10,000. Office space takes up about 10% of the area of the buildings and shipping space requires another 10%.
(2) Three-fourths of the cost of machinery and equipment was incurred at the time the building was acquired. The balance was purchased on December 31, 1959. It is estimated that 16% of the cost of machinery will remain as scrap value. All units of machinery and equipment are depreciated over the same useful life.

(3) An inventory of tools on December 31, 1965, showed that $33,000 remained on hand.
(4) All of the company's unamortized patent costs are applicable to patents issued on January 2, 1958. The company credits patent amortization (based on the legal life of 17 years) each year directly to the asset account.
(5) Unexpired insurance on December 31, 1965, amounted to $1,300. Insurance expense is allocated 80% to manufacturing, 15% to selling, and 5% to administration.
(6) Accrued factory payroll on December 31, 1964, consisted of direct labor, $6,290, and indirect labor, $2,140. On December 31, 1965, the accruals were: direct labor, $8,420; indirect labor, $1,960.
(7) Property taxes accrued on December 31, 1965, amounted to $8,590. This account is allocated on the same basis as is insurance expense.
(8) Inventories on December 31, 1965, were:

Materials	$23,290
Goods in process	29,400
Factory supplies	4,260

Prepare working papers showing the cost of goods manufactured.

Problem 2-13. Using the financial statements of The Brooks Company, determine the total of the debit column of (a) the December 31, 1965 unadjusted trial balance and (b) the post-closing trial balance after reversing entries had been made and posted.

THE BROOKS COMPANY
Balance Sheet
December 31, 1965

Assets

Current assets:			
Cash		$30,500	
Temporary investments		8,000	
Accounts receivable	$14,320		
Less allowance for doubtful accounts	580	13,740	
Accrued interest receivable		200	
Inventory		21,600	$ 74,040
Fixed assets:			
Delivery equipment		$39,600	
Less accumulated depreciation		10,800	28,800
			$102,840

Liabilities and Stockholders' Equity

Current liabilities:		
Accounts payable	$ 5,905	
Notes payable	6,300	
Accrued salaries	215	
Accrued income tax payable	700	$ 13,120
Stockholders' equity:		
Capital stock	$80,000	
Retained earnings	9,720	89,720
		$102,840

THE BROOKS COMPANY
Income Statement
For the Year Ended December 31, 1965

Gross sales				$56,100
Sales returns and allowances			$ 1,200	
Sales discounts			1,630	2,830
Net sales				$53,270
Cost of goods sold:				
Inventory			$19,200	
Purchases		$38,000		
Purchase returns and allowances	$ 900			
Purchase discounts	1,180	2,080		
Net purchases		$35,920		
Transportation in		740	36,660	
Cost of goods available for sale			$55,860	
Inventory			21,600	34,260
Gross profit on sales				$19,010
Selling expenses:				
Store rent		$ 3,000		
Advertising		2,200		
Depreciation—Delivery equipment		1,800	$ 7,000	
General expenses:				
Office expenses		$ 3,800		
Salaries		4,150		
Bad debts expense		340	8,290	15,290
Net operating income				$ 3,720
Other revenue:				
Interest earned			$ 580	
Other expense:				
Interest expense			370	210
Net income before income tax				$ 3,930
Income tax				700
Net income				$ 3,230

THE BROOKS COMPANY
Statement of Retained Earnings
For the Year Ended December 31, 1965

Retained earnings, December 31, 1964	$ 8,990
Net income for the year	3,230
Total	$12,220
Deduct dividends	2,500
Retained earnings, December 31, 1965	$ 9,720

Problem 2-14. The unadjusted trial balance of Crater Company is presented below.

CRATER COMPANY
Unadjusted Trial Balance
December 31, 1965

Cash	3,120	
Merchandise inventory	9,000	
Office supplies inventory	360	
Unexpired insurance	270	
Land	15,000	
Store fixtures	5,000	
Accumulated depreciation		1,500
Accounts payable		7,170
Accrued interest payable		30
Accrued salaries		1,000
Rent received in advance		4,800
Long-term bank loan—6%		6,000
Common stock		10,000
Retained earnings	3,790	
Sales		80,000
Cost of goods sold	50,000	
Store rent expense	3,000	
Salaries expense	18,000	
Advertising	140	
Insurance expense	45	
Office supplies expense	415	
Interest expense	360	
Land rent income	2,000	
	110,500	110,500

The company pays salaries of $1,500 per month.

On March 1, 1964, the company signed a seven-year lease agreement relating to a portion of the land owned by the company. The $2,400 yearly rental is payable in advance and the $2,400 amounts received on March 1, 1964 and 1965 were credited to Rent Received in Advance.

The company carries only one insurance policy. The $270 premium for the three-year renewal policy dated July 1, 1965, was charged to Unexpired Insurance.

The company spent $415 on office supplies during 1965.

On the first business day of 1965, two adjusting entries dated December 31, 1964, were reversed. After analyzing the unadjusted trial balance, list the reversing entries that could have been made as of the beginning of 1965, and also show the reversing entries that were made.

Assignment Material for Chapter 3

QUESTIONS

1. In the typical balance sheet, are all of the asset accounts stated on the same valuation basis?
2. What elements make up the difference between cost of goods manufactured and cost of goods sold in the case of a manufacturing business?
3. What are deferred credits?
4. Mention several matters which require disclosure in the financial statements.
5. What kinds of assets are properly shown under the Sundry Assets caption?
6. What is the purpose of the income statement? Do you consider that the conventional form of the income statement is satisfactory to meet this purpose? Give reasons for your answer.
7. What is a company's operating cycle? What use is made of a company's operating cycle?
8. Must the precise amount be known and the identity of the creditor definitely established for a liability to be classed as a current liability?
9. Is the accountant under any obligation to disclose matters occurring after the balance sheet date but before the year-end statements are completed and released? Give reasons for your answer.
10. Does the disclosure requirement relating to departures from consistency in the application of accounting principles apply to all departures?
11. Criticize the following definition: Current assets consist of cash and other assets which presumably can be converted into cash within one year without interference with the regular operations.
12. State and explain fully the theory under which certain prepaid expenses may be classified as current assets and others as noncurrent assets.
13. The price received for a business as an entity often differs from the amount shown on the records for the owners' equity. Explain fully why the sale price of a going business may differ from the book value even where acceptable accounting conventions have been followed in keeping the business records.
14. In the preparation of a balance sheet of a dealer in office furniture, to be used for credit purposes, you ascertain that for the past 20 years his stock in trade has had an average turnover of once every three years. Would you include the said stock in trade among the current assets? Would it make any difference in your method of handling the inventory if you were told that the balance sheet was not to be used for credit purposes?

PROBLEMS

Problem 3-1. Using the data given for Problem 2-9, prepare the financial statements for Charter Corporation. The income statement may be presented in condensed form with a supporting schedule for the operating expenses. The corporation carries its fixed assets at cost and its inventory at the lower of cost or market. There are 10,000 shares of $5 par value stock outstanding.

Problem 3-2. Prepare the financial statements for S. E. Cook and Company.

S. E. COOK AND COMPANY
Adjusted Trial Balance
December 31, 1965

Cash	27,700	
Accounts receivable	42,260	
Allowance for doubtful accounts		2,200
Accrued interest receivable	110	
Inventory, December 31, 1964	21,600	
Unexpired insurance	400	
Long-term investments—at cost	5,000	
Delivery equipment	25,000	
Accumulated depreciation—Delivery equipment		10,000
Accounts payable		18,390
Notes payable		4,500
Commissions collected in advance		1,400
Accrued rent payable		800
Capital stock		75,000
Retained earnings		7,860
Dividends	3,000	
Sales		111,700
Sales returns and allowances	4,810	
Sales discounts	5,600	
Purchases	78,000	
Purchase returns and allowances		2,800
Purchase discounts		4,050
Transportation in	1,400	
Salesmen's salaries	19,370	
Depreciation—Delivery equipment	2,500	
Insurance	200	
Rent	3,200	
Office supplies expense	2,940	
Bad debts	1,200	
Interest earned		450
Commissions earned		5,400
Interest expense	260	
	244,550	244,550

The inventory on December 31, 1965, was $23,400. The company uses the last-in, first-out method.

The company's liability for federal income tax for 1965 was $1,500.

The delivery equipment was recorded at cost.

The December 31, 1965 market value of the long-term investments was $5,800.

The company's authorized stock consisted of 100,000 shares of $1 par value.

In January of 1966, the company was advised that its lease would not be renewed.

(*Continued on next page.*)

On February 1, 1966, the company purchased a suitable building for $100,000; the purchase was financed in part by a $70,000 mortgage.

Problem 3-3. An income statement in the form presented below has been included for a number of years in the company's annual report.

THE WESTERN CORPORATION
Income Statement
Year Ended December 31, 1965

Gross income (other than interest and dividends) after provision for cost of products sold and expenses (including depreciation, obsolescence, repairs and renewals, interest, and all state and local taxes)		$2,146,900
Other income:		
Dividends	$183,812	
Interest	49,606	233,418
Gross income before provision for federal income tax		$2,380,318
Federal income tax		1,150,000
Net income		$1,230,318

It is the desire of the vice-president in charge of public and industrial relations to present a more detailed and informative income statement in the annual report for the year ended December 31, 1965. In this connection he has made available to you, in addition to the above statement, the following information relating to operations for the year ended December 31, 1965:

Cost of products sold	$12,088,319
Interest on bonds payable	180,000
Interest on notes payable	51,212
Contribution to employees' pension fund	612,000
State and local taxes	590,308
Selling expenses	984,209
Administrative and general expenses	1,111,612

Prepare an income statement in single-step form.

Problem 3-4. The following account balances were selected from the unadjusted June 30, 1965 trial balance of Central Manufacturing Company:

Inventories, June 30, 1964:	
Finished goods	$18,910
Goods in process	12,356
Materials	8,612
Purchases—Materials	62,850
Purchase returns and allowances	918
Purchase discounts	614
Transportation in	2,420
Direct labor	82,309
Indirect labor	16,350
Heat, light, and power	9,800
Maintenance and repairs—Factory	2,056
Property taxes	4,500
Factory supplies expense	2,800
Miscellaneous factory expense	6,290
Freight out	4,012
Bad debts	1,080
Insurance expense	1,400

Adjustments are to be made as follows:

Accrued wages:	
Direct labor	$2,100
Indirect labor	640
Depreciation:	
Buildings	$4,200
Machinery	9,650
Tools	1,800

Expense allocations are to be made as follows:

	Manufacturing	Selling	Administration
Heat, light, and power	90%	5%	5%
Property taxes	90	2	8
Depreciation—Buildings	80	10	10
Insurance	90	2	8

Inventories on June 30, 1965, were:

Finished goods	$25,610
Goods in process	8,400
Materials	10,250

Required:

(a) A statement of cost of goods manufactured.
(b) A computation showing the cost of goods sold.

Problem 3-5. The trial balance on page 588 was taken after the recording of adjusting entries on December 31, 1965.

The inventories, at cost, on December 31, 1965, were as follows:

Finished goods—last-in, first-out	$42,100
Goods in process	18,850
Materials	58,900
Factory supplies	2,410

Supplementary data:

(1) In January, 1965, it was decided to adopt the last-in, first-out method for the finished goods inventory. The December 31, 1965 finished goods inventory on a first-in, first-out method, the method previously used, would have amounted to $46,600.
(2) The outstanding accounts receivable include $4,000 of short-term loans to members of the corporation's board of directors.
(3) The corporation was involved in litigation, as of December 31, 1965, arising from a negligence claim of $20,000 for injuries which a customer allegedly received from the use of the corporation's product.
(4) As of December 31, 1965, the corporation had outstanding purchase commitments of $60,000.
(5) The capital stock has a par value of $5 per share; one-half of the authorized shares were issued and outstanding as of December 31, 1965.
(6) Federal income tax for 1965 was estimated at $41,600.

Required:

Computation of cost of goods sold.
Combined statement of income and retained earnings.
Balance sheet.

ROYAL CORPORATION
Adjusted Trial Balance
December 31, 1965

Cash	32,400	
Accounts receivable	29,350	
Allowance for doubtful accounts		1,110
Inventories, December 31, 1964—at cost:		
Finished goods	38,600	
Goods in process	19,300	
Materials	46,800	
Factory supplies	2,190	
Unexpired insurance	2,160	
Prepaid general expenses	1,000	
Plant and equipment—at cost	356,200	
Accumulated depreciation		49,400
Accounts payable		27,000
Accrued interest payable		500
Bonds payable, 4%, 1985		150,000
Premium on bonds		1,360
Capital stock		200,000
Retained earnings		25,420
Dividends paid	4,000	
Sales		1,128,670
Sales returns and allowances	12,600	
Sales discounts	8,600	
Material purchases	481,800	
Purchase discounts		9,030
Freight on materials	12,600	
Direct labor	318,060	
Superintendence	26,900	
Factory supplies purchased	14,090	
Power and heat	21,620	
Depreciation—Plant and equipment	32,020	
Factory insurance	2,060	
Other factory costs	4,910	
Sales salaries	28,300	
Sales travel	9,900	
Advertising expense	14,610	
Postage—Selling	7,080	
Other selling expenses	3,900	
Officers' salaries	24,000	
Office salaries	20,250	
Office supplies used	7,340	
Insurance—General	800	
Telephone and telegraph	2,900	
Bad debts expense	1,650	
General expenses	3,000	
Interest expense	1,500	
	1,592,490	1,592,490

Problem 3-6. Prepare financial statements for Miracle Manufacturing Corporation. Include a separate statement of cost of goods sold.

MIRACLE MANUFACTURING CORPORATION
Adjusted Trial Balance
December 31, 1965

Cash	2,744	
Accounts receivable	19,110	
Allowance for doubtful accounts		816
Inventories, December 31, 1964—at cost:		
Finished goods	2,090	
Goods in process	12,663	
Materials	18,901	
Unexpired insurance	420	
Cash surrender value of life insurance	9,000	
Land—at cost	20,000	
Building—at cost	94,600	
Accumulated depreciation—Building		12,510
Machinery and equipment—at cost	106,640	
Accumulated depreciation—Machinery and equipment		29,810
Office equipment—at cost	4,600	
Accumulated depreciation—Office equipment		1,030
Bond issuance costs	950	
Accounts payable		9,610
Withholding and F.I.C.A. tax liabilities		300
Advances from customers		1,700
Bonds payable, 6%, 1975		50,000
Capital stock—$10 stated value		200,000
Retained earnings		33,824
Sales		367,371
Purchases—Materials	128,126	
Purchase discounts		2,410
Transportation in	4,090	
Direct labor	183,200	
Indirect labor	12,640	
Depreciation—Building	2,100	
Heat, light, and power	16,900	
Depreciation—Machinery and equipment	10,500	
Insurance	1,060	
Taxes—Property	3,640	
Sales salaries and expense	24,641	
Advertising	3,938	
Miscellaneous selling expense	1,014	
Office salaries	19,400	
Office supplies	1,816	
Bad debts expense	200	
Telephone and telegraph	948	
Depreciation—Office equipment	400	
Interest expense	3,050	
	709,381	709,381

Additional information:

(1) Inventories on December 31, 1965—at cost:

Finished goods	$ 3,115
Goods in process	11,981
Materials	19,110

(2) The following costs are to be allocated as indicated:

	Manufacturing	Selling Expense	Administrative Expense
Heat, light, and power	80%	5%	15%
Insurance	75	10	15
Taxes—Property	80	10	10
Depreciation—Building	80	5	15

Problem 3-7. Total debits and total credits in selected accounts of Contrail Manufacturing Corporation, after closing entries were posted on December 31, 1965, are given below. Prepare a statement of cost of goods sold for the year ended December 31, 1965.

	Debits	Credits
Materials	$ 46,512	$ 21,902
Goods in process	32,852	17,656
Material purchases	216,604	216,604
Purchase discounts	2,500	2,500
Transportation in	4,910	4,910
Direct labor	248,616	248,616
Manufacturing overhead	342,412	342,412
Finished goods	18,766	8,656
Selling expenses	126,200	126,200
Administrative expenses	114,200	114,200
Sales	652,100	652,100
Revenue and expense	924,318	924,318

Problem 3-8. An employee of Fabricant Fabricating Company has attempted to prepare the 1965 financial statements without making use of working papers. The balance sheet will not balance.

You are called in to review the financial statements in the hope that you will be able to locate any errors made by the employee. In this connection, you are given the following income statement.

FABRICANT FABRICATING COMPANY
Income Statement
For the Year Ended December 31, 1965

Gross sales			$560,600
Sales returns and allowances			3,400
Net sales			$557,200
Cost of goods sold:			
Cost of goods fabricated:			
Materials inventory, December 31, 1964		$ 36,400	
Purchases	$122,500		
Purchase returns and allowances	2,500	120,000	
Total		$156,400	
Materials inventory, December 31, 1965		20,000	
Materials used		$136,400	
Direct labor		129,300	
Freight on purchases of materials		12,000	
Indirect labor		8,400	
Other fabricating costs		40,300	
Cost of goods fabricated		$326,400	
Increase in finished goods:			
December 31, 1965	$ 30,800		
December 31, 1964	22,600	8,200	334,600
Gross profit			$222,600

Selling expenses:			
Sales salaries	$ 54,200		
Bad debts expense	4,200		
Other selling expenses	21,080	$ 79,480	
Administrative expenses:			
Office salaries	$ 38,600		
Advertising	18,300		
Freight out	16,300		
Other office expenses	29,620		
Rent expense—Office	14,800		
Income tax	4,070	121,690	201,170
Net operating income			$ 21,430
Net financial expense:			
Bond interest expense	$ 3,000		
Purchase discounts	6,400	$ 9,400	
Deduct sales discounts		2,400	7,000
Net income			$ 14,430

Compute the correct net income. Also make a list of classification changes you would recommend.

Applicable income tax rates are:

22% for the first $25,000 of earnings.
48% for earnings in excess of $25,000.

There was no work in process at the beginning or end of the year.

Problem 3-9. Seamless Company reported a net income of $83,412 for the year ended December 31, 1965. During this period the company made two changes in the accounting treatment of certain transactions, as follows:

(1) In preceding years the company had followed the practice of considering all expenditures under $200 for items of machinery and equipment as current expense, and all expenditures in excess of that amount as additions to appropriate property accounts. As of January 1, 1965, the $200 amount was increased to $500. During 1965, a total of $17,500 was expended for equipment items costing between $200 and $500. The company has consistently followed the practice of depreciating machinery and equipment at a rate of 8% of the ending account balance.
(2) During 1965, Seamless Company adopted the practice of capitalizing expenditures for research and development activities, and amortizing the intangible asset thus created at a rate of 25% applied to the balance of the account at the close of each year. In prior periods all expenditures of this type had been considered as operating expense when incurred. The December 31, 1965 balance sheet showed $37,200 as Unamortized Research and Development Costs.

Assuming that you are preparing the financial statements of the company for the year ended December 31, 1965, show exactly how you would disclose the effect of the above changes in accounting procedure. Seamless Company is subject to federal income tax rates of 22% on the first $25,000 of taxable income and 48% on amounts in excess of $25,000. It has reason to believe that the changes in accounting procedure will be approved by the Internal Revenue Service in the determination of taxable income.

Problem 3-10. On January 1, 1965, Wagner Corporation, which produces a single product, adopted the policy of treating the proceeds from the sale of scrap metal as a reduction in the cost of materials used in manufacturing operations. Inventories on December 31, 1965, were valued in accordance with this policy. In prior years receipts from scrap sales were credited to Other Income.

During the year ended December 31, 1965, the corporation received $32,200 from the sale of scrap metal. Inventory accounts reveal that on December 31, 1965, 8% of the product started in process during 1965 was still uncompleted and 5% was finished but unsold.

On January 10, 1966, the stockholders of Wagner Corporation approved a contract with Shawnee Products Company for the purchase of a plant building and related equipment owned by that company. The purchase price was $650,000, payment to consist of 5,000 shares of authorized but unissued $100 par value, 5½% cumulative preferred stock of Wagner Corporation, and $200,000 in cash which the corporation expects to obtain from a five-year loan from an insurance company.

Illustrate the disclosure of the effect of the preceding items which you feel would be appropriate in connection with the financial statements for the year ended December 31, 1965. For income tax purposes the corporation will continue to report scrap sales as other income.

Problem 3-11. The cost of materials used by Graybond Manufacturing Company during 1964 and 1965 is presented below. The company has maintained a policy of computing the year-end materials inventory in a manner consistent with its statement presentation of the data relating to materials. In 1965, the company has followed alternative procedures for presentation of certain items related to materials.

	1964			1965	
Materials:					
Inventory, January 1			$ 22,080		$ 27,625
Cost of net purchases:					
Gross purchases		$206,000		$185,000	
Returns	$6,000			5,000	
Discounts	4,000	10,000			
Balance		$196,000			180,000
Transportation in		25,000	221,000		
Total			$243,080		$207,625
Inventory, December 31			27,625		* 30,000
Materials used			$215,455		$177,625

* At gross invoice price.

The company regularly takes advantage of a 2% discount which is offered by all of its materials suppliers.

The transportation in for 1965 is shown as part of the manufacturing overhead in the amount of $24,000.

(1) You are asked to prepare a statement of the cost of materials used in 1965 on a basis consistent with the method of presentation used in 1964.

(2) The management also asks you to draw up a statement for 1965 prepared in the manner shown above for that year, except that it is desired to show the beginning inventory for 1965 and the ending inventory consistently at gross invoice price.

Problem 3-12. For the fiscal year ended September 30, 1965, the bookkeeper for Manhattan Company presented a statement to the directors prepared in the following form:

Sales	$334,000	
Increase of inventories	18,000	$352,000

Cost of goods sold:			
Sundry manufacturing costs, materials, factory supplies		$257,850	
Depreciation of factory buildings		14,000	
Freight on purchases		10,400	282,250
Manufacturing profit			$ 69,750
Other income:			
Purchase discounts		$ 680	
Interest on sales contracts		8,432	
		$ 9,112	
Less:			
Sales discounts	$3,012		
Sales returns and allowances	4,200	7,212	1,900
Net plant profit			$ 71,650
Less:			
General administrative expenses		$ 16,200	
Selling expenses		12,050	
Income tax		11,930	40,180
Net income			$ 31,470

Prepare, in good form, statements of income and cost of goods manufactured for the fiscal year ended September 30, 1965, using such of the above data as may be necessary, together with the following:

Inventories, September 30, 1964:		
Materials	$56,000	
Factory supplies	33,400	
Goods in process	18,300	
Finished goods	21,900	$129,600
Inventories, September 30, 1965:		
Materials	$78,000	
Factory supplies	27,400	
Goods in process	16,000	
Finished goods	26,200	147,600
Cost of materials used during the year, computed without consideration of freight and purchase discounts		48,000
Direct labor		101,300
Heat, light, and power		6,200
Repairs and maintenance		4,900
Indirect labor		14,400
Other manufacturing overhead (excluding depreciation, freight, and supplies)		56,850

Problem 3-13. From the data below, which summarize in part the results of operations for 1965 of Adler Company, prepare the statement of cost of goods sold.

Of the total cost of goods manufactured for 1965, 38% was for materials used, 30% for direct labor, and 30% for manufacturing overhead.

During 1965, the company paid for 90% of the materials purchased, leaving $29,300 of unpaid invoices for materials at year end. The company commenced 1965 operations with a materials inventory of $42,100. All materials were purchased f.o.b. company's plant.

The company disbursed $210,600 for direct labor during 1965. As of December 31, 1965, the accrued liability for direct labor amounted to $14,400, which was twice as much as last year's accrual.

The inventory of finished goods on December 31, 1965, was 10% of the cost of the units finished during the year, and goods in process on that date were one-half the finished goods inventory. This year's finished goods inventory was 150% of last year's.

The manufacturing overhead, except for depreciation of factory buildings and equipment, is detailed below:

Indirect labor	$ 67,200
Heat, light, and power	22,620
Maintenance and repairs	48,830
Insurance—Factory	1,810
Property taxes	6,440
Factory payroll taxes	9,700
Miscellaneous factory costs	27,640
	$184,240

Problem 3-14. New Products, Incorporated, employed an inexperienced bookkeeper during 1965. Given the task of preparing financial statements at the year end, the bookkeeper produced the following income statement for 1965:

Sales	$236,912	
Purchase returns and allowances	460	
Purchase discounts	842	
Total		$238,214
Sundry manufacturing costs	$158,270	
Decline in inventories	690	
Depreciation	7,200	
Freight in	1,400	
Sales returns	2,002	
Sales discounts	3,907	173,469
Profit from manufacturing		$ 64,745
Selling expenses	$ 20,960	
Administrative expenses, including income tax of $9,532	22,582	43,542
Profit from operations		$ 21,203
Patents income	$ 3,090	
Interest expense	425	2,665
Net income		$ 23,868

The management gives you the following additional information:

Inventories, December 31, 1965:	
Materials	$ 9,660
Tools	12,250
Finished goods	8,300
Materials used, 1965, including freight but excluding purchase discounts	64,680
Tools write-off, 1965	1,120
Direct labor	58,930
Indirect labor	8,965
Other manufacturing costs not specifically set forth above	22,025
Material purchases during 1965	64,290
Tools purchased during 1965	4,060

Prepare a condensed income statement for 1965, using the single-step form.

Assignment Material for Chapter 4

QUESTIONS

1. State briefly what is meant by:

(a) The current operating concept of net income.
(b) The all-inclusive or clean surplus theory.

2. Name five items that would be dealt with differently in the statements, depending on which concept of net income governed.

3. Mention some arguments in favor of the current operating concept.

4. Mention some arguments in favor of the clean surplus theory.

5. On which concept of net income is the combined statement of income and retained earnings based?

6. Give an illustration of an error in computing the net income of one year that will be offset by a counterbalancing error in the following year, thus correcting the retained earnings but leaving the net income incorrectly stated by years.

7. What is meant by the phrase "net of tax"?

8. What will be the effect upon the income statement of the present and future periods if:

Prepaid expenses are ignored?	Accrued expenses are ignored?
Income collected in advance is ignored?	Accrued income is ignored?

9. For three years Confusion Company charged to machinery expenditures that should have been charged to machinery repairs. The company applied a 5% depreciation rate to the ending balance in the asset account. Items incorrectly charged were as follows:

1962	$12,000
1963	15,000
1964	16,000

Submit journal entries to correct the accounts as of December 31, 1964, assuming that 1964 depreciation on the uncorrected balance of the Machinery account has been recorded but that the books have not been closed.

10. State four ways of dealing with errors affecting the net income of prior years.

11. Explain how the occurrence of an unusual loss could result in the improvement of the net income for the period in which the loss occurred.

PROBLEMS

Problem 4-1. The following statement conforms to generally accepted accounting principles with one exception.

CANAL COMPANY

Statement of Retained Earnings
For the Year Ended December 31, 1965

Retained earnings, December 31, 1964		$151,680
Add:		
Net income		78,410
Gain on sale of machinery		12,150
Income tax reduction in current year attributable to loss carryforward		8,230
Total		$250,470
Deduct:		
Dividends paid	$30,000	
Payment of additional federal income tax for 1960	12,300	42,300
Retained earnings, December 31, 1965		$208,170

The dividends paid include a dividend of $5,000 declared on December 20, 1964. No record has been made of a dividend of $12,000 declared on December 20, 1965, payable January 10, 1966.

The company suffered a large operating loss in 1964.

Make the necessary correction and recast the above statement applying the clean surplus theory.

Problem 4-2. Net income (loss*) before income tax data for Swell Corporation are presented below.

1960	$100,000	1964	$ 90,000*
1961	80,000	1965	160,000*
1962	20,000	1966	60,000
1963	30,000*	1967	120,000

For purposes of this problem, assume that the income tax rate is 40% for each of the above years and that the corporation is permitted to carry losses back three years and forward five years.

Compute the net income that would be shown for each year under the following conditions:

(a) The corporation uses the all-inclusive income concept.
(b) The corporation uses the current operating concept.
(c) The corporation prepares revised statements for the eight-year period and sets up a noncurrent asset for the loss-carryforward benefit.

Problem 4-3. The following account balances were taken from the ledger of Rover Company at the close of its fiscal year on June 30, 1965:

Loss on sale of short-term investments	$ 31,200
Net sales	398,400
Merchandise inventory, June 30, 1965	38,530
Selling expenses	42,600
Dividends received	2,000
Administrative and general expenses	32,400

Cost of goods sold	242,600
Dividends—Preferred stock	14,000
Dividends—Common stock	6,000
Assessment of state taxes—prior years	9,150
State taxes—current year	4,500
Retained earnings, June 30, 1964	120,800

Inventory of merchandise, June 30, 1964—$41,200.

The state taxes, for both current and prior years, and the loss on sale of short-term securities are deductible for federal income tax purposes.

The following federal income tax rates are applicable:

22%: On the first $25,000
50%: On amounts over $25,000

Prepare the statement of retained earnings, applying the current operating concept and net-of-tax procedures.

Problem 4-4. An audit of the records of Gill Company disclosed the following:

(1) Inventory overstated (understated):	
December 31, 1963	$(22,200)
December 31, 1964	11,600
(2) Accrued interest receivable ignored at year end:	
December 31, 1963	$ 1,230
December 31, 1964	2,330
December 31, 1965	850
(3) Depreciation overstated (understated):	
Year ended December 31, 1964	$ 3,500
Year ended December 31, 1965	(8,900)
(4) Prepaid travel expense overstated (understated):	
December 31, 1963	$ 1,400
December 31, 1964	(700)

Prepare a work sheet to determine the effect of the above errors on the income statements for the years 1963, 1964, and 1965 and on the December 31, 1965 balance sheet. Ignore income taxes.

Problem 4-5. Atherton Company reported net income for the calendar years 1963-1965, inclusive, as follows:

1963	$318,200
1964	401,000
1965	386,500

An audit of the records of Atherton Company disclosed the following:

(1) Inventory overstated (understated):	
December 31, 1962	$ 12,600
December 31, 1964	(21,200)
(2) Accounts payable for operating expenses overstated (understated):	
December 31, 1962	$ (4,800)
December 31, 1964	9,200
(3) Depreciation overstated (understated):	
Year ended December 31, 1963	$(18,200)
Year ended December 31, 1964	3,500

(4) Prepaid interest expense overstated (understated):

December 31, 1963	$ 1,200
December 31, 1964	(3,600)

Required:

(a) A schedule showing the necessary adjustments to reported net income and the corrected net income for the years 1963-1965, inclusive. Ignore income tax considerations.

(b) The necessary correcting journal entry or entries as of December 31, 1965, assuming that the statements for prior years are to be revised and that the books have been closed for 1965.

Problem 4-6. Terminal Corporation, organized in 1963, has employed the cash basis of accounting for operating expenses. Income statements based on the use of this method are presented below:

	Year Ended December 31,		
	1963	1964	1965
Net sales	$592,174	$714,104	$748,898
Cost of goods sold	389,810	477,713	501,893
Gross profit on sales	$202,364	$236,391	$247,005
Operating expenses	134,214	163,491	176,705
Net income before taxes on income	$ 68,150	$ 72,900	$ 70,300
Federal income taxes	34,075	34,992	31,635
Net income	$ 34,075	$ 37,908	$ 38,665

A member of the board of directors has questioned the effect of the use of the cash basis of accounting for operating expenses on the liability for federal income taxes. In this connection, the bookkeeper for Terminal Corporation makes the following information available:

	December 31,		
	1963	1964	1965
Accrued expenses	$12,140	$7,090	$9,312
Prepaid expenses	6,240	5,190	4,472

Required:

(a) Revised income statements for the years 1963, 1964, and 1965, giving effect to the recognition of accrued and prepaid expenses. (Assume the same rate for federal income taxes as was employed in the original income statements.)

(b) Show for each of the three years the effect on federal income taxes of the change in method of accounting for operating expenses.

Problem 4-7. The trial balance presented on page 599 was taken from the ledger of Corl Sales Company after regular adjusting journal entries had been recorded on September 30, 1965.

Additional data:

(1) The company had a loss carryforward of $15,000 at the end of fiscal 1964.

(2) A dividend of $1,000 declared on September 20, 1964, payable on October 15, 1964, was not recorded until paid.

(3) Accrued interest payable of $150 was not recorded on September 30, 1963.

(4) Commissions earned, $830, had been recorded as income in September, 1963, although the related sale was not completed until October 16, 1963.

(5) Assume that 25% is the proper income tax rate.

CORL SALES COMPANY
Adjusted Trial Balance
September 30, 1965

Cash	38,110	
Marketable securities	20,000	
Commissions receivable	14,130	
Automotive equipment	12,600	
Accumulated depreciation		3,150
Unexpired insurance	680	
Accounts payable		1,130
Notes payable		2,000
Accrued interest payable		150
Capital stock		20,000
Retained earnings, September 30, 1964		9,930
Dividends paid	3,000	
Commissions earned		184,200
Gain on sale of securities		30,000
Salaries	140,200	
Rent	12,000	
Depreciation—Automotive equipment	2,700	
Insurance	300	
Taxes—Local	1,130	
Utilities	1,850	
Supplies expense	650	
Gas and oil	3,160	
Interest expense	300	
Interest income		250
	250,810	250,810

Prepare the income statement and statement of retained earnings for the year ended September 30, 1965, using the current operating concept.

Problem 4-8. From the following data taken from the books of Rosshill Company, prepare:

(a) Corrected statements of retained earnings for the years ended December 31, 1964 and 1965.
(b) Journal entries necessary to correct the books in 1966.

	Year Ended December 31,		
	1964	1965	1966
Net income per books	$18,320	$26,190	
Uncollectible accounts written off, arising from sales of preceding year, for which no provision for uncollectible accounts was made	930	1,420	
Payment of liabilities existing but not recorded at close of preceding year:			
Heat and light	410	360	$ 520
Merchandise (goods on hand but not included in inventory)	1,200	1,080	940
Merchandise (goods on hand and included in inventory)	910	560	830
Dividends paid, declared in previous year	5,000	6,000	7,000

Retained earnings, December 31, 1963, per books, $41,320.

(*Continued on page 600.*)

The following information should also be considered:

	December 31, 1963	December 31, 1965
Estimate of uncollectible accounts arising from 1965 sales for which no provision has been made		$2,300
Depreciation not provided	$5,100	

The company uses the periodical inventory method.

Problem 4-9. The trial balance presented below was taken from the ledger of Local Sales Company after adjusting journal entries had been recorded on June 30, 1965.

LOCAL SALES COMPANY
Adjusted Trial Balance
June 30, 1965

Cash	16,255	
Inventory, end of year	15,200	
Office supplies on hand	300	
Automotive equipment	27,300	
Accumulated depreciation		11,305
Accounts payable		10,390
Accrued wages payable		350
Common stock		30,000
Retained earnings		5,450
Dividends	3,000	
Sales		123,000
Cost of goods sold	88,935	
Wages	14,280	
Office supplies expense	1,475	
Depreciation	5,460	
Other expense	8,290	
	180,495	180,495

An examination of the accounts indicates that certain errors were made during prior periods, and possibly the current period, and that these errors were never corrected. The errors are described below:

(a) The June 30, 1964 and June 30, 1965 inventories were overstated by $1,200.

(b) No adjustment has been made to the Office Supplies on Hand account since June 30, 1963. The inventory sheets show the following:

Office supplies on hand—per count:	
June 30, 1963	$300
June 30, 1964	360
June 30, 1965	200

(c) On July 10, 1964, a delivery truck which cost $4,500 was wrecked in an accident. The truck was a total loss. The entry made to give recognition to the accident was as follows:

Accumulated depreciation	3,600	
Automotive equipment		3,600
Accumulated depreciation on truck purchased July 1, 1960, removed from the accounts.		

The company has adopted a five-year useful life for its automotive equipment and computes its annual depreciation by applying the rate of 20% to the balance of the asset account.

(d) During the three-year period ending June 30, 1965, the company had understated accrued wages by an amount aggregating $1,000. The details are as follows:

	Amount	
	Booked	Ignored
Accrued wages, June 30, 1963	$100	$ 350
Accrued wages, June 30, 1964	150	150
Accrued wages, June 30, 1965	350	500
		$1,000

Required:

Working papers for the year ended June 30, 1965, assuming that errors affecting prior years' earnings are to be disclosed in the statement of retained earnings and that the company follows the current operating concept.

Problem 4-10. The following condensed income statement was prepared before giving consideration to the errors and omissions noted below the income statement.

MOLINE COMPANY

Income Statement

For the Year Ended December 31, 1965

Sales		$110,770
Cost of goods sold	$62,000	
Operating expenses	41,000	103,000
Net income		$ 7,770

Accrued wages:

No adjusting entries for accrued wages were made at the end of 1963, 1964, and 1965.

The accruals were:

December 31, 1963	$175
December 31, 1964	215
December 31, 1965	230

Bad debts:

No provisions for doubtful accounts were made. Instead, the Bad Debts account was charged when accounts were written off, as follows:

1963	$365
1964	415
1965	505

If an Allowance for Doubtful Accounts had been used, the following year-end balances for that account would have been acceptable:

December 31, 1962	$370
December 31, 1963	425
December 31, 1964	525
December 31, 1965	600

Depreciation:

In computing depreciation for 1963, one asset was overlooked; as a consequence, the depreciation for 1963 was understated $160. This asset was sold during 1964, and a loss of $300 was shown as resulting from the sale.

Inventories:

Year-end inventories were overstated and understated as follows:

December 31, 1963—understated	$390
December 31, 1964—overstated	610

The 1965 ending inventory was correctly stated.

Prepare the corrected 1965 income statement under each of the following methods of dealing with errors in statements of prior years:

(a) Errors absorbed in current income statement without disclosure.
(b) Errors disclosed in current income statement.
(c) Errors disclosed in current statement of retained earnings.
(d) Statements for prior years revised.

Problem 4-11. Diamond Company presented the following statement of retained earnings:

DIAMOND COMPANY

Statement of Retained Earnings
For the Year Ended December 31, 1965

Retained earnings, December 31, 1964	$500,000
Add net income for the year	46,405
Total	$546,405
Deduct dividends	25,000
Retained earnings, December 31, 1965	$521,405

In the course of your review of the company's accounts and records you discover the following:

(1) On December 31, 1964, merchandise costing $12,140 was on hand, but had not been included in the inventory on that date, although the liability therefor had been recorded. In addition, merchandise costing $1,216 had been omitted from the inventory, and the liability was omitted from accounts payable.
(2) Accrued expenses on December 31, 1964, amounting to $2,184, were not reflected in the adjusting journal entries made on that date.
(3) The December 31, 1965 inventory included merchandise sold in 1965 for $4,480 and returned on December 15, 1965. No entry had been made for the return, and the goods were included in inventory at selling price, which was 140% of cost.
(4) Operating expenses of $2,160 included in the 1965 income statement relate to 1966 operations.

Prepare the corrected 1965 statement of retained earnings under each of the following methods of dealing with errors in financial statements:

(a) Errors absorbed in current income statement without disclosure.
(b) Errors disclosed in current income statement.
(c) Errors disclosed in current statement of retained earnings.
(d) Statements for prior years revised.

Ignore income taxes.

Problem 4-12. The following financial statements have been prepared by *M* and *O* Company as a part of an application for a bank loan.

M AND *O* COMPANY
Income Statements
For the Years Ended October 31, 1964 and 1965

	Year Ended October 31, 1964	Year Ended October 31, 1965
Net sales	$67,120	$81,315
Cost of goods sold	48,234	60,926
Gross profit	$18,886	$20,389
Expenses:		
Wages and salaries	$ 6,500	$ 7,838
Insurance	1,192	12
Taxes	602	905
Repairs	419	753
Rent of building	1,200	1,200
Depreciation	700	830
Other expenses	1,170	1,610
Total expenses	$11,783	$13,148
Net income	$ 7,103	$ 7,241

M AND *O* COMPANY
Statements of Retained Earnings
For the Years Ended October 31, 1964 and 1965

	Year Ended October 31, 1964	Year Ended October 31, 1965
Balance at beginning of year	$ 9,130	$12,233
Net income for the year	7,103	7,241
Total	$16,233	$19,474
Dividends	4,000	5,000
Balance at end of year	$12,233	$14,474

M AND *O* COMPANY
Balance Sheets
October 31, 1964 and 1965

Assets	October 31, 1964	October 31, 1965
Cash	$ 3,110	$ 4,230
Accounts receivable	9,098	11,930
Merchandise inventory	12,014	13,100
Unexpired insurance		710
Furniture and equipment	7,112	8,040
Accumulated depreciation	2,080*	2,910*
	$29,254	$35,100
Liabilities and Stockholders' Equity		
Accounts payable	$ 6,730	$10,190
Taxes payable	291	436
Capital stock	10,000	10,000
Retained earnings	12,233	14,474
	$29,254	$35,100

* Deduction.

The bank has requested that *M* and *O* Company have its financial statements for the years ended October 31, 1964 and 1965, audited by an independent public accountant, and you have been retained by *M* and *O* Company for this purpose.

In the course of your audit, you discover the following errors which affect the financial statements for the two years:

(a) The inventory of merchandise on October 31, 1963, was understated by $474. The difference was caused by clerical errors in the physical inventory count sheets.

(b) The inventory of merchandise on October 31, 1964, was overstated by $703, owing to the erroneous inclusion of obsolete and unsalable merchandise at full value.

(c) An inventory of repair supplies in the amount of $418, on hand on October 31, 1965, was ignored.

(d) Unexpired insurance was not considered when adjusting entries were made on October 31, 1964. The amount of insurance premiums unexpired on that date was $680.

(e) An invoice in the amount of $1,012 for the purchase of a special lot of merchandise which was received and sold in October, 1964, was not recorded until November 12, 1964.

(f) $500 was received from a customer on October 14, 1964, and was recorded as a sale on that date although the merchandise was purchased and shipped to the customer in December, 1964.

(g) There were accrued wages and salaries on October 31, 1964, in the amount of $312, which were not reflected in the adjusting entries made on that date.

Required:

Working papers for revised financial statements for the years ending October 31, 1964 and 1965.

Problem 4-13. Castle Stores Corporation is contemplating the purchase of the entire outstanding capital stock of Cooke Department Store. In this connection, the directors of Castle Stores Corporation have engaged you to examine the financial statements of Cooke Department Store for the three-year period ended January 31, 1966. The condensed statements for this period, as prepared by the controller of Cooke Department Store, are presented below.

COOKE DEPARTMENT STORE

Income Statements

For the Years Ended January 31, 1964, 1965, and 1966

	Year Ended January 31,		
	1964	1965	1966
Net sales	$523,500	$521,000	$555,250
Cost of goods sold	342,082	353,169	394,392
Gross profit	$181,418	$167,831	$160,858
Expenses:			
Selling and delivery	$ 47,012	$ 58,016	$ 60,646
Buying	16,918	20,311	20,003
Building occupancy	20,903	25,902	22,908
General and administrative	33,326	38,806	37,311
Total	$118,159	$143,035	$140,868
Net income from operations	$ 63,259	$ 24,796	$ 19,990
Other income (expense) net	2,301	1,806	2,312
Net income before income tax	$ 65,560	$ 26,602	$ 22,302
Income tax	25,010	8,900	6,840
Net income	$ 40,550	$ 17,702	$ 15,462

COOKE DEPARTMENT STORE

Statements of Earned Surplus

For the Years Ended January 31, 1964, 1965, and 1966

	Year Ended January 31,		
	1964	1965	1966
Balance beginning of year	$ 73,675	$ 94,225	$101,927
Net income for the year	40,550	17,702	15,462
Total	$114,225	$111,927	$117,389
Dividends	20,000	10,000	5,000
Balance end of year	$ 94,225	$101,927	$112,389

COOKE DEPARTMENT STORE

Balance Sheets

January 31, 1964, 1965, and 1966

	January 31,		
Assets	1964	1965	1966
Cash	$ 33,022	$ 25,534	$ 27,862
Accounts receivable	40,316	36,811	44,906
Allowance for bad debts	3,200*	3,200*	3,200*
Merchandise	89,600	94,302	101,311
Prepaid expenses	7,916	9,964	8,043
Building and fixtures	325,947	395,585	411,543
Delivery equipment	39,014	43,012	41,906
Reserve for depreciation	151,956*	172,788*	194,842*
	$380,659	$429,220	$437,529
Liabilities and Stockholders' Equity			
Accounts payable	$ 9,918	$ 12,016	$ 14,316
Accrued expenses	1,506	6,377	3,984
Income tax payable	25,010	8,900	6,840
Bank loans	50,000		
Capital stock—$100 par	200,000	300,000	300,000
Earned surplus	94,225	101,927	112,389
	$380,659	$429,220	$437,529

* Deduction.

In the course of your examination of the accounts of Cooke Department Store for the three years ended January 31, 1966, you discover the following facts:

(a) The inventories of merchandise on January 31, 1964 and 1965, were priced at selling price. You determine that the inventories on these dates, priced at cost, were:

January 31, 1964	$63,300
January 31, 1965	65,106

(b) The Allowance for Bad Debts should have been increased from $3,200 to the following amounts:

January 31, 1964	$ 3,800
January 31, 1965	4,100
January 31, 1966	4,700

(c) Invoices from merchandise suppliers were not recorded until the goods had been inspected and marked, although merchandise in the receiving and marking departments was included in the inventory at the end of each fiscal year. The amounts of merchandise (at cost) in this category were:

January 31, 1963	$ 3,018
January 31, 1964	1,916
January 31, 1965	1,820

(d) 1,000 shares of capital stock were issued on April 15, 1964, for $105 per share. The amount received in excess of the par value of the shares issued was credited to Sales.

(e) The annual provision for depreciation had been computed since January 31, 1963, by applying a rate of 4% to the net sales for each fiscal year and allocating the resulting amount 70% to building and fixtures and 30% to delivery equipment.

You determine that the proper charges for depreciation, based upon cost and estimated service life of the depreciable property, were as follows:

	Building and Fixtures	Delivery Equipment
Year ended January 31,		
1964	$12,800	$5,250
1965	13,700	5,400
1966	14,650	5,970

(f) Unexpired insurance totaling $1,100 was overlooked in making adjusting entries on January 31, 1964. This total applied to insurance coverage on:

Buildings and fixtures	50%
Delivery equipment	20
Merchandise*	30

* Insurance on merchandise is included in general and administrative expenses.

Required:

(1) Working papers for revised financial statements for the fiscal years ended January 31, 1965 and 1966. No change should be made in the provision for income tax.

(2) The necessary adjusting entries on January 31, 1966, assuming that the books have been closed.

Assignment Material for Chapter 5

QUESTIONS

1. What is the main objective in accounting for the stockholders' equity?
2. What are the four basic rights inherent in capital stock? In what two general ways may stock be preferred?
3. If a company has $100,000 common stock and $50,000 preferred, the preferred to have 6% dividends, and if the company has a net income of $2,000 the first year, $10,000 the second year, and $12,000 the third year, what annual dividends will be paid to each class if the preferred is:

   (a) Noncumulative and nonparticipating?
   (b) Cumulative and nonparticipating?
   (c) Cumulative and fully participating?

   It must be understood that the directors declare dividends equal to the net income each year.
4. Under what circumstances might a holder of convertible preferred stock wish to exercise the conversion privilege and exchange the preferred shares for common shares?
5. If preferred stock is callable, can the holder of such preferred shares call upon the issuing corporation to redeem the stock?
6. How should unissued shares be shown in the ledger? How may such unissued shares be shown in the balance sheet?
7. The terms of issuance of preferred stocks frequently contain provisions intended to safeguard the interests of the preferred stockholders. The most customary restrictive provisions have to do with the payment of cash dividends on common stock or the retirement of common shares or their acquisition as treasury shares. List several ways by which such restrictions might be provided.
8. Explain what is meant by "limited liability" as it relates to corporate stockholders.
9. State the usual way in which stated capital is measured.
10. *X* subscribed for 10 shares of the common stock of New Corporation at par of $100. He paid $200 at the time of the subscription; subsequent efforts to collect on the subscription proved futile. *X* demands the return of the $200. New Corporation points out that the state law provides for the payment of losses on resale and expenses incident thereto from the amount paid by the defaulting subscriber, the remainder to be returned. The stock was sold for $920 and expenses amounting to $20 were paid by the corporation. Give journal entries reflecting the proper procedure and payment.
11. State in a single sentence the acceptable basis for the valuation of property acquired by the issuance of stock.
12. Give two reasons why par value stock is rarely issued for less than its par value.
13. What should the balance sheet show with respect to each class of stock?

14. Where should uncollected subscriptions receivable be shown in the balance sheet?

15. On December 26, 1965, *L* Company issued, to the holders of its 5,000 shares of common stock, rights permitting them to acquire, for each 10 shares held, one additional share of common stock ($100 stated value) at 90. The rights were to expire on May 1, 1966, and payment was to accompany the subscription. Prior to the close of 1965, 55 shares had been issued in accordance with the terms of the rights; prior to the completion of your audit field work (March 31, 1966), 322 additional shares had been issued.

Should any of these facts be shown in the December 31, 1965 balance sheet?

16. State two general rules which guide the accountant when recording conversions.

PROBLEMS

Problem 5-1. Cold Steel Products Corporation was organized on January 20, 1966, with capital stock authorized as follows:

Cumulative 5% preferred, $10 par value; 300,000 shares.
Common, no par value; stated value, $5; 1,000,000 shares.

The corporation issues stock certificates when subscriptions are fully paid.

Journalize, in general journal form, the transactions listed below. You may omit explanations.

(1) 40,000 shares of common stock were issued for cash at $6 per share.
(2) 10,000 shares of 5% preferred stock were issued at par for cash.
(3) 50,000 shares of 5% preferred stock were subscribed at par value.
(4) $200,000 was received on the above subscription to 5% preferred stock.
(5) 400 shares of 5% preferred stock were issued in payment of attorneys' fees of $4,000 in connection with organizing the corporation.
(6) 200,000 shares of common stock were issued for plant and equipment which had a fair market value of $1,300,000.
(7) 30,000 shares of 5% preferred stock were issued for cash at a 2% premium.
(8) 80,000 shares of common stock were subscribed for at $544,000.
(9) Fifty per cent of the above common stock subscription was collected.
(10) The balance owing on the subscription described in (3) and (4) was collected and the preferred shares were issued.

Problem 5-2. The following selected account balances appeared in the June 30, 1966 balance sheet of Marvel Corporation:

Current assets:		
Subscriptions receivable—Preferred stock		$ 8,000
Capital stock:		
Preferred—5% cumulative, $20 par; authorized, 8,000 shares; issued and outstanding, 2,600 shares	$52,000	
Subscribed, but not issued, 600 shares	12,000	64,000
Common—No par value; authorized, 10,000 shares; issued and outstanding, 4,000 shares—no stated value		17,000
Capital in excess of par value—Preferred stock issuances		5,000

Marvel Corporation issues stock certificates only upon full payment of subscriptions. Subscriptions were received for the preferred shares as follows:

2,200 shares at par;
1,000 shares at $25 per share.

The common shares outstanding were issued for cash.

Prepare summary entries for the transactions which are indicated by the foregoing data.

Problem 5-3. Prepare the Stockholders' Equity section of the December 31, 1966 balance sheet to show the information presented in each of the following separate situations:

(1) *A* Corporation is authorized to issue 5,000 shares of $100 par value, 6% cumulative, nonparticipating preferred stock and 10,000 shares of no-par common stock with a stated value (established by the board of directors) of $5 per share.

4,000 shares of the preferred stock were issued for cash at $104 per share on January 1, 1962, and the remaining authorized preferred shares were subscribed for at par but were unissued as of December 31, 1966.

6,000 shares of common stock were issued for cash at $12 per share in 1961.

From the date of organization to December 31, 1966, the company had total net income of $212,000 and had declared and paid dividends as follows:

Preferred	$96,000
Common	42,000

(2) *B* Corporation has authorized $100 par value, 4½% cumulative preferred stock in the amount of 10,000 shares. This stock is preferred as to assets in the event of liquidation in an amount equal to par value plus dividends in arrears. The corporation is also authorized to issue 10,000 shares of no par value common stock.

All of the authorized preferred stock has been issued at par; however, there are uncollected subscriptions receivable on the preferred shares in the amount of $20,000, but it seems unlikely that the preferred stockholders will be called upon to pay in the uncollected subscriptions. 8,000 shares of common stock have been issued for cash at $48 per share.

On December 31, 1966, *B* Corporation had a deficit of $6,400, and preferred dividends in arrears amounted to $67,500.

Problem 5-4. (a) Prepare entries, in general journal form, to record the following transactions on the books of Venture Company.

(b) Compute the stated or legal capital of Venture Company. Show the details of your computation.

The company has authorized capital stock as follows:

Class	Par Value	Shares Authorized
$2 dividend cumulative preferred	$30	10,000
Common	No par	50,000

The law of the state in which Venture Company is incorporated requires that stated or legal capital shall include the par value of shares having par value and the total subscription or issue price of no-par shares.

Stock certificates are issued when subscriptions are received.

(1) Subscriptions are received for 4,000 shares of preferred stock at $32 per share and for 26,000 shares of common stock at $20 per share.

(2) Cash is collected from subscribers as follows:

Preferred stock	$ 88,000
Common stock	400,000

(3) Subscriptions are received for 5,000 shares of preferred stock at $30 per share.

(4) The remaining shares of authorized preferred stock are subscribed at $29 per share.
(5) Cash of $132,000 is received from subscribers to preferred stock.
(6) Land with an appraised value of $19,000 is purchased for 1,000 shares of common stock.
(7) Subscriptions are received for 15,000 shares of common stock at $18 per share.
(8) Collections on common stock subscriptions are made in the amount of $285,000.

Problem 5-5. Prepare the necessary journal entries to record the change in authorized (and outstanding) common stock of Stacey Corporation from 500 shares with $50 par value to 1,000 shares of no par value, in each of the following cases:

(a) The corporation issued the 500 shares of $50 par value stock at par. The directors have assigned a stated value of $25 per share to the no-par stock.
(b) The $50 par value stock was issued at a premium of $10 per share. The directors have assigned a stated value of $25 per share to the no-par stock.
(c) The $50 par value stock was issued at a premium of $15 per share. The directors have assigned a stated value of $30 per share to the no-par stock.
(d) The $50 par value stock was issued at par. The directors have assigned a stated value of $40 per share to the no-par stock. On the date of the change to no-par stock, the corporation had retained earnings of $31,410.
(e) The $50 par value stock was issued for $40 per share. The directors have assigned a stated value of $18 per share to the no-par stock.

Problem 5-6. Leverage Company has an issue of convertible bonds outstanding. According to the bond agreement, bondholders are entitled to receive 30 shares of the company's $25 stated value common stock in exchange for each $1,000 bond. This privilege became effective on September 1, 1966.

On October 15, 1966, holders of $500,000 of bonds elected to convert their holdings into common stock.

Another conversion was effected on April 1, 1967, when $200,000 of bonds were exchanged for common stock.

On each of the exchange dates the following balances were taken from the ledger:

	October 15	April 1
Bonds payable	$2,500,000	$2,000,000
Discount on bonds	60,000	45,000

Prepare journal entries on October 15, 1966, and April 1, 1967, to record the conversions.

Problem 5-7. Thorobred Baking Company was incorporated with 10,000 shares of preferred stock with a par value of $100 per share and 80,000 shares of $20 par value common stock. Capital stock was issued on three different dates during the first year of operations. The dates and issues are stated below.

January 2, 1966	Issued for cash, 4,000 shares of preferred stock at par, giving a bonus of one share of common stock with each ten shares of preferred stock.
	Issued 20,000 shares of common stock for $500,000 cash.
July 12, 1966	Issued for cash, 2,000 shares of preferred stock at par, giving a bonus of one share of common stock with each five shares of preferred stock.
	Issued 30,000 shares of common stock for $600,000 cash.

December 18, 1966 Issued for $309,000 cash, 3,000 shares of preferred stock, giving a bonus of one share of common stock with each ten shares of preferred stock.

Issued 15,000 shares of common stock at par for cash.

Required:

(1) Journal entries to record the above stock issues.
(2) The Stockholders' Equity section of the company's balance sheet on December 31, 1966. Earnings for the year amounted to $236,000; no dividends were declared.

Problem 5-8. The accounts of Plastics Company show an operating deficit of $293,000. Dividends are in arrears on the company's preferred stock for a four-year period. The management of the company believes that it must seek foreign markets to return to "black ink." In anticipation of the need for additional financing, permission has been obtained for the following:

To reduce the stated value of the common stock to $10 per share.
To increase the authorized number of common shares to 100,000.
To eliminate the deficit.
To eliminate the claim for cumulative dividends in arrears by issuing shares of common stock to the preferred shareholders on the following basis:
1 share of common for each $20 of dividends in arrears.

Selected data from the company's records before carrying out the above changes are set forth below:

5% cumulative preferred stock—$100 par value; 5,000 shares authorized; 3,600 outstanding shares issued for $103 per share.
Common stock—$20 stated value; 50,000 shares authorized; 42,600 shares outstanding issued for a total of $880,000.

Show how the Stockholders' Equity section will appear as of December 31, 1966, after giving effect to the approved changes.

Problem 5-9. Exotic Products Corporation's stockholders' equity as of December 31, 1965, appears below:

EXOTIC PRODUCTS CORPORATION
Partial Balance Sheet
December 31, 1965

Stockholders' equity:	
Capital stock, $30 par value; 500,000 shares authorized; 80,000 shares issued and outstanding	$2,400,000
Capital in excess of par value	120,000
Retained earnings	268,400

On January 1, 1966, the corporation gave to the old shareholders 20,000 rights, each one permitting the purchase of one $30 par value share at $35. The rights were void after 60 days. The market price of the stock at this time was $42 per share.

All but 260 of the above rights were exercised by March 1, 1966.

On July 1, 1966, the corporation sold to the public a $100,000 4½% bond issue at par. One detachable stock purchase warrant was given for each $100 face value of bonds purchased. These warrants entitled the holder to acquire a share of the corporation's capital stock at $45 per share, any time within five years. The stock was selling at $43 on this date.

By January 2, 1967, the corporation's earnings had increased the retained earnings to $402,600 and the common stock was selling at $48. 230 warrants were exercised on this date.

On December 31, 1967, with retained earnings up to $580,200, the corporation's stock rose to $52, and 720 warrants were exercised on this date.

In the ensuing year the market price of the corporation's stock fell below $45, and the price did not again go above this figure within the five-year period. The remaining warrants were never used by bondholders.

(1) Give appropriate entries in general journal form to record the above transactions.
(2) Present the Stockholders' Equity section of the corporation's balance sheet on December 31, 1967.

Problem 5-10. Square Corporation was organized on January 2, 1966, with an authorized capital consisting of 15,000 shares of preferred stock of $100 par value, and 50,000 shares of common stock of no par value, with a stated value of $10 per share.

Transactions during 1966, relative to capital stock, are:

(1) 4,000 shares of preferred are subscribed at par under the following conditions:
  (a) One share of common stock is to be given as a bonus with each share of fully paid preferred stock. Shares are issued when paid in full.
  (b) Payment may be made at the subscribers' convenience, but final settlement must be made within six months of subscription.
  (c) Any amounts paid in on subscriptions not fully paid will be returned, after deducting any expenses incurred in the re-subscription of the shares.
(2) Payments on these subscriptions are outlined below:
  (a) Subscriptions to 3,600 shares were collected in full within six months and the shares were issued.
  (b) Subscribers to 400 shares paid in a total of $23,700. The costs of re-subscription at $90 per share without the bonus offer were $3,250. These subscribers paid in full within six months.
(3) 40,000 shares of common stock were issued for cash at $10 per share.
(4) 3,000 additional shares of preferred stock were subscribed at $105 on the same terms set forth under (1).
(5) When the year ended, four months after the subscriptions described in (4) were accepted, payment in full had been received on 1,800 shares. $62,800 had been received on 900 of the remaining shares, and the corporation had reason to believe that subscribers to the other 300 shares would not complete their payments within six months.

Required:

(a) Journal entries to record all transactions related to capital stock during 1966.
(b) The Stockholders' Equity section of the corporation's balance sheet at December 31, 1966. A deficit from operations amounting to $76,800 was incurred during 1966.

Problem 5-11. Northeastern Transmission Corporation was organized on May 1, 1966, to acquire facilities and contracts for the transmission of natural gas from producers to local utilities. Capital stock authorized consisted of $20,000,000 in $50 par value common, and $15,000,000 in 5% first preferred of $100 par value.

On May 5, forty per cent of the common stock was subscribed at a 6% premium. Payment was to be made one-half at the date the subscriptions were received and the balance on May 25, 1966. The balance was collected in full.

On May 6, 1,000 shares of common stock were issued to the law firm of Bell and Osmundson in payment of their bill for $50,000 for services in organizing the corporation.

On May 26, the corporation completed arrangements for the purchase of the assets and the assumption of the liabilities of Hudson Public Service Corporation, agreeing to pay for the same $5,000,000 in preferred stock and the balance one-half in common stock (at par) and one-half in cash. The balance sheet of Hudson Public Service Corporation is presented below:

HUDSON PUBLIC SERVICE CORPORATION

Balance Sheet
May 26, 1966

Assets			Liabilities and Net Worth	
Cash		$ 750,000	Accounts payable	$ 3,700,000
Accounts receivable		2,450,000	Accrued expenses	850,000
Sundry assets		3,200,000	5% debenture bonds payable	15,000,000
Plant and equipment	$25,820,000		Capital stock	8,000,000
Less accumulated depreciation	6,870,000	18,950,000	Retained earnings	1,800,000
Goodwill		4,000,000		
		$29,350,000		$29,350,000

By agreement:

An allowance for bad debts of $450,000 is to be set up.
Sundry assets are valued at $4,000,000.
Plant and equipment are valued at $24,000,000.
Goodwill is to be removed from the accounts.

Required:

(1) Journal entries to adjust and close the books of Hudson Public Service Corporation.
(2) Journal entries to record all transactions of Northeastern Transmission Corporation through May 26, when the acquisition of Hudson Public Service Corporation was consummated.
(3) The balance sheet of Northeastern Transmission Corporation at the close of business, May 26, 1966.

Problem 5-12. Surfside Corporation had the following stockholders' equity as of December 31, 1965:

Stockholders' equity:		
Capital stock:		
Preferred—6% cumulative, nonparticipating, convertible; par value, $50; authorized and issued, 10,000 shares	$500,000	
Class A common—$20 stated value, with a cumulative dividend of $1 and full participation with class B common; authorized, 60,000 shares; issued and outstanding, 25,000 shares.	500,000	
Class B common—No par value; authorized, 100,000 shares; issued and outstanding, 30,000 shares	425,000	$1,425,000
Capital in excess of par or stated value:		
From preferred stock issuances	$ 10,000	
From class A common stock issuances	87,000	97,000
Total		$1,522,000
Deficit		62,000
		$1,460,000

The corporation was organized as of January 2, 1959, when the following shares were issued:

	Shares
Preferred	10,000
Class A common	20,000
Class B common	30,000

5,000 shares of class A common were issued as of January 2, 1961.

The corporation has paid the following dividends:

1959	$40,000	1963	—
1960	60,000	1964	—
1961	30,000	1965	—
1962	20,000		

In order to eliminate the deficit and make up the arrearage in cumulative dividends, the corporation obtained the necessary permission from the state and its stockholders to do the following as of January 2, 1966:

Assign a $5 stated value to the class B common stock.
Exchange new class B shares for the old class B shares on a one-for-one basis.
Issue one share of the new class B stock to the preferred and class A stockholders for each $10 of dividends in arrears as of December 31, 1965.

In 1966, the corporation earned $300,000 and declared a 6% dividend on the preferred stock and a $1-per-share dividend on the class A common.

On January 2, 1967, one-half of the preferred shares were converted to class A common; 3 shares of class A were issued for each share of preferred.

Required:

(a) The Stockholders' Equity section of the December 31, 1966 balance sheet of Surfside Corporation.
(b) The January 2, 1967 journal entry for the conversion.

Problem 5-13. The balance sheet of Harmony Corporation on December 31, 1965, is presented in condensed form below:

HARMONY CORPORATION
Balance Sheet
December 31, 1965

Assets

Cash	$ 13,460
Note receivable from officer	4,000
Other current assets	40,870
Fixed assets—net	85,520
	$143,850

Liabilities and Stockholders' Equity

Payable to officer	$ 12,000
Other current liabilities	13,210
Mortgage payable	35,000
Capital stock—$100 par value	60,000
Retained earnings	23,640
	$143,850

Dale Harmon and members of his family own $40,000 of the capital stock and Richard Wiley owns the remainder. Harmon buys Wiley's stock for $22,000 on January 2, 1966. Payment is made by $6,500 of Harmon's personal cash, $10,000 cash from the corporation's bank account, the cancellation of Wiley's note held by the corporation, and the balance being covered by permitting Wiley to have certain equipment which he had originally invested in the business. These assets were recorded at $3,000, with depreciation of $1,500 to December 31, 1965.

On January 5, 1966, Harmon wished to obtain money for the corporation and, to facilitate borrowing, canceled the corporation's liability to him and issued to himself stock having a par value of $10,000. He found the bank unwilling to lend money to the corporation, but accepted the bank's offer to loan him personally $20,000 at 6% for 90 days. Of this sum he placed $15,000 in the corporation's bank account and kept $5,000 for personal use. The note was paid when due from corporate funds.

Give the journal entries to be made on the corporation's books in connection with the above transactions.

Problem 5-14. The following account balances were taken from the accounts of Upper Company as of December 1, 1966.

Bonds payable (Interest dates, June 1 and December 1)	$ 300,000
Premium on bonds	3,300
Preferred stock subscribed	200,000
Preferred stock (par value, $50)	1,500,000
Subscriptions receivable—Preferred	100,000
Subscriptions receivable—Common	165,000
Common stock subscribed	400,000
Common stock (stated value, $25)	250,000
Capital in excess of par value—Preferred stock issuances	50,000
Capital in excess of stated value—Common stock issuances	37,500
Retained earnings (as of December 31, 1965)	300,000
Capital in excess of stated value—Forfeited subscriptions to common stock	500
Common stock warrants outstanding	5,000

The bonds are convertible into preferred stock on any interest date on the initiative of the bondholders. Each $1,000 bond may be converted for 19 shares of preferred stock.

The common stock warrants were issued in connection with the subscription of preferred shares. A holder of one warrant may acquire one share of common stock at stated value. Common stock warrants will not be issued in connection with any future subscriptions to preferred shares.

During December 1966, the following stock transactions occurred:

December 2—Bonds with a face value of $30,000 were converted into preferred stock. (Ignore December interest.)

6—Final installment on 10,000 common shares subscribed for at $26 per share was received; the certificates were issued. The subscriptions were collected in four equal installments.

13—Cash subscriptions of $106,000 were received for the issuance of 2,000 shares of preferred stock; the cash was received and the shares were issued.

14—Land was acquired in exchange for 2,500 shares of preferred stock.

20—Half of the outstanding stock warrants were exercised, $31,250 was collected, and the common shares were issued.

Net income for 1966 was $125,000. Dividends of $95,000 were declared and paid on the preferred shares during the first 11 months of 1966.

At year end it was determined that $10,000 of common stock subscriptions might not be collectible.

The stock authorization is as follows:

6% Preferred....................	100,000 shares
Common	200,000 shares

Required:

(a) All necessary journal entries during December 1966, based on the above information.

(b) Stockholders' Equity section of the December 31, 1966 balance sheet.

Assignment Material for Chapter 6

QUESTIONS

1. List four principal sources of paid-in surplus.
2. Do the classifications of surplus made by accountants indicate which portions of surplus are available for dividends?
3. Can any amount received upon the issuance of no-par stock be returned to the stockholders in the form of dividends?
4. What, if any, charges can with propriety be made against paid-in surplus?
5. May retained earnings be transferred to other accounts within the stockholders' equity group?
6. If an unrealized increment in value is recorded in the accounts, what disposition should be made of the resulting credit-balance account when the written-up assets have been fully depreciated or sold?
7. Is a surplus reserve always the best means of disclosing a restriction on, or an appropriation of, retained earnings?
8. Cite two examples of dividend restrictions that can result from the voluntary action of the directors.
9. Distinguish between a split-up and a stock dividend.
10. Describe the alternative methods of accounting for a reserve for self-insurance.
11. Is it possible for a corporation to declare a dividend without reducing the stockholders' equity?
12. Is it illegal to declare a dividend in excess of the corporation's cash balance?
13. What is the proper amount of retained earnings to capitalize when a stock dividend is declared?

PROBLEMS

Problem 6-1. On December 22, 1966, when the fair value of the stock of Famous Corporation was $28 per share, a 10% stock dividend was declared and issued on the $25 par value common stock. Immediately prior to the stock dividend, the corporation had an authorization of 10,000 shares, of which 7,000 were issued and outstanding; a paid-in surplus—premium on stock—of $26,000; and retained earnings of $50,990.

(a) Prepare the journal entry to record the declaration and the issuance of this dividend.

(b) If the stock dividend was not to be issued until January 5, 1967, state how it should be disclosed in the corporation's balance sheet on December 31, 1966.

Problem 6-2. (A) From the following list of account balances as of December 31, 1965, compute the total stockholders' equity of Mansfield Corporation.

Common stock, stated value $10	$800,000
Retained earnings	500,000
Dividends payable	100,000
Common stock subscribed	250,000
Capital in excess of stated value—From stock dividends	200,000
Subscriptions receivable—Common (fully collectible)	80,000
Preferred stock, par $50	700,000
Fractional-share certificates—Common	20,000
Reserve for contingencies	90,000
Bonds payable	350,000
Reserve for self-insurance (by charges to expense)	52,000
Unrealized increment in valuation of assets	100,000

(B) The following occurred during January 1966. Compute the amount of free retained earnings as of January 31, 1966.

January 5—Stock certificates for 1,600 full shares were issued in exchange for outstanding fractional shares.
7—Payment of $100,000 was made for the previously declared dividends.
10—The right to exchange the remaining fractional shares expired. (Under the law of the state of incorporation, the declaration of a dividend cannot be in part rescinded.)
15—The board of directors ordered the capitalization of the Unrealized Increment in Valuation of Assets by the issuance of 5,000 shares of common stock as a stock dividend.
18—An uninsured loss of $18,000 occurred as a result of a small fire.
20—The company acquired 10,000 shares of its preferred stock at its liquidation price of $65 per share. The shares were cancelled.
31—The controller reported January net income of $100,000.

Problem 6-3. The authorized and issued shares of the three classes of stock of Loon Company as of December 31, 1966, are set forth below.

	Shares	
Description	Authorized	Issued
5% cumulative, fully participating preferred; par value, $25	100,000	60,000
6% cumulative, nonparticipating preferred, par value, $10	100,000	40,000
6% common stock; par value, $5	200,000	150,000

The 5% preferred was issued at $26 per share.

The company has been profitable since the date of its organization, January 2, 1963, when the 250,000 shares of stock now outstanding were issued. However, all of the company's earnings were transferred to a Reserve for Contingencies at the end of each year because of uncertainty in connection with a patent infringement suit brought against the company in 1963. Early in 1967, the suit was finally resolved in favor of Loon Company, and the board of directors took the following actions:

Ordered the elimination of the Reserve for Contingencies.

Declared the necessary dividends to satisfy all arrearage claims through December 31, 1966.

Directed that one-half of the cumulative net income after making allowance for the preferred dividends be reserved for the retirement of the 5% preferred stock.

The earnings for the first four years are set forth below:

Year	Net Income
1963	$ 80,000
1964	120,000
1965	200,000
1966	220,000

Prepare the journal entries to give effect to the above actions by the board of directors.

Also prepare the Stockholders' Equity section of the December 31, 1967 balance sheet. The net income for 1967 was $280,000. Dividends were declared on the preferred shares plus an 8% dividend on the common stock. The directors ordered that $40,000 from the 1967 earnings be added to the reserve for the retirement of the 5% preferred stock.

Problem 6-4. Carbon Steel Company adopted a self-insurance program as of January 1, 1963. The company debited Insurance Expense for 5% of the net income before insurance expense. The Reserve for Self-Insurance account is analyzed below.

Reserve for Self-Insurance

1963 Losses	7,000	1963 Provision	10,000
1964 Losses	4,000	1964 Provision	18,000
1965 Losses	9,000	1965 Provision	4,000
1966 Losses	8,000	1966 Provision	15,000
1967 Losses	16,000	1967 Provision	400

Compute the net income for the years 1963-1967, inclusive, assuming that a Reserve for Self-Insurance account had not been used in connection with the self-insurance program.

Problem 6-5. The balances in the stockholders' equity accounts of Montana Manufacturing Corporation on December 31, 1965, were as follows:

Capital stock—$10 par value; authorized, 100,000 shares; issued and outstanding, 60,000 shares	$600,000
Capital in excess of par value—From stock issuances	30,000
Retained earnings	183,420

As of January 2, 1966, an appraisal of the company's landholdings revealed that the current value thereof exceeded recorded cost by $210,000. The board of directors ordered that the appraised value of the land be taken up in the accounting records and, as permitted by the law of the state of incorporation, that 10,000 shares of unissued capital stock be issued as a stock dividend to capitalize the appraisal increment. Both actions were taken and recorded as of the date of the appraisal.

During the year ended December 31, 1966, the company had net income of $42,180 and paid a cash dividend of 30 cents per share. A Reserve for Contingencies was set up for $25,000.

On January 2, 1967, when the fair value of the company's stock was $26 per share, the company declared a 2% stock dividend. The shares were to be issued January 15, 1967.

Required:

The Stockholders' Equity section of the balance sheet on January 2, 1967. Show any necessary supporting computations.

Problem 6-6. Cliffs Corporation presented the following condensed statement as of the close of the fiscal year.

CLIFFS CORPORATION
Balance Sheet
August 31, 1966

Assets		Liabilities and Stockholders' Equity	
Cash	$ 92,800	Current liabilities	$ 462,400
Other current assets	285,400	5% First preferred stock	300,000
Fixed assets, net	1,265,100	6% Second preferred stock	200,000
		Common stock	400,000
		Paid-in surplus	102,000
		Retained earnings	178,900
	$1,643,300		$1,643,300

Details of the capital stock and paid-in surplus of Cliffs Corporation are as follows:

The common stock has no par value, with a stated value of $20 per share; 50,000 shares are authorized; 20,000 shares are issued and outstanding.

The first preferred stock is cumulative; the stock has a par value of $100 per share; 3,000 shares are authorized, issued, and outstanding. Dividends have not been paid for the last two years. In the fiscal year ended August 31, 1964, dividends were paid on the first preferred in the amount of $5,000.

The second preferred stock is cumulative; the stock has a par value of $50 per share; 5,000 shares are authorized; 4,000 shares are issued and outstanding. Dividends have not been paid for the last three years.

The paid-in surplus consists of the following:

Excess of issue price over stated value of common stock	$100,000
Proceeds from the sale of donated common treasury stock	40,000
Total	$140,000
Deduct operating losses during start-up period	38,000
Net paid-in surplus	$102,000

As of September 1, 1966, the board of directors of the corporation reached an agreement with the representatives of each class of stock to the effect that the dividend arrearages on the preferred stock should be satisfied by the issuance of common stock on the basis of one share of common stock for each $25 of dividends in arrears. The necessary common shares were issued on September 10, 1966.

As of September 30, 1966, a stock dividend was declared to common stockholders on the basis of 1/10 of a share of common for each share of common outstanding. The shares were to be issued October 15, 1966. The directors ordered that the retained earnings to be capitalized should be determined on a basis consistent with the $26 current market value of the stock.

Net income for the month of September was $12,600.

Required:

(a) The journal entries to record the above dividends.

(b) The Stockholders' Equity section of the corporation's balance sheet as of September 30, 1966.

Problem 6-7. The following accounts appear in the December 31, 1966 trial balance of Brothers Company.

Common stock—$10 stated value; 32,900 shares outstanding....	$374,000
Fractional-share certificates—100 shares	1,000
Capital in excess of par value—From preferred stock issuances ..	4,000
Retained earnings	93,000
Reserve for retirement of preferred stock	50,000

Submit whatever journal entries you believe are necessary in view of the following information:

When the company was organized, 30,000 shares of common stock were issued for $330,000.

Recently a 10% stock dividend was declared when the market value of the company's stock was $15 per share.

The fractional-share certificates, issued in connection with the stock dividend, have expired. The directors cannot rescind, in part, a stock dividend.

The preferred stock was retired as of July 1, 1966, for a total cash outlay $9,000 greater than the amount received when the stock was originally issued.

Problem 6-8. The management of Princess Company is giving consideration to the adoption of a self-insurance program. The records show the following for the last five years:

	1961	1962	1963	1964	1965
Insurance premiums paid	$ 4,000	$ 4,000	$ 4,000	$ 4,000	$ 4,000
Loss recoveries from insurance companies.	1,200	800	1,100	10,000	900
Net income before insurance expense and before income taxes..................	30,000	32,000	28,000	29,000	33,000
Net income..........................	18,000	19,000	16,800	17,500	19,500

When insurance is carried with insurance companies, the premiums are deductible for income tax purposes and, because they are recoverable, the losses are not deductible. When no insurance is carried, the losses are deductible when incurred; amounts debited to expense under a "self-insurance" program are not deductible.

In order to assist management in making a decision whether to discontinue carrying insurance, you are asked to refigure the net income for each of the five preceding years under the following methods:

(a) A self-insurance reserve is created by annual charges of $4,000 to Retained Earnings.

(b) A self-insurance reserve is created by annual charges of $4,000 to expense.

Use the following income tax rates:

30% on first $25,000 of taxable income.
50% on income above $25,000.

Problem 6-9. Eastern Company presented the Stockholders' Equity section of its June 30, 1966 balance sheet in the following form:

Stockholders' equity:		
Capital stock—Par value, $20; authorized, 100,000 shares; issued and outstanding, 24,900 shares...	$498,000	
Surplus	559,500	$1,057,500

Restate the Stockholders' Equity section of the balance sheet, making any changes required to comply with generally accepted accounting principles.

Capital stock in the amount of 5,000 shares was issued and outstanding at the time of a 5-for-1 stock split.

An analysis of the company's records disclosed that the surplus resulted from the following:

Nonoperating losses	$ 50,000
Recognition of increased value of land	220,000
Excess of fair value ($105) over par ($100) when stock was split 5 for 1	25,000
Par value of new shares held awaiting presentation of old $100 par value certificates	2,000
Net operating income	500,000
Cash dividends declared and paid	150,000
Cash dividends declared but unpaid	12,500
Premium on sale of $100 par value capital stock (since replaced with $20 par value stock)	50,000
Credits to Reserve for Contingencies	75,000
Debits to Reserve for Contingencies	25,000
Credits to Reserve for Self-insurance	25,000

Problem 6-10. Prepare journal entries to record the transactions for 1966 indicated by the following information:

(A) Liquid Malt Company had the following stockholders' equity account balances on July 1, 1966:

6% preferred stock—$100 par value; 1,000 shares authorized, issued, and outstanding (issued, when the company was organized, at 108 for some factory equipment)	$100,000
Capital in excess of par value—From preferred stock issuances	8,000
Common stock—No par value; 100,000 shares authorized; 60,000 shares issued and outstanding	547,000
Donated surplus—Unimproved land donated by city subject to certain conditions	50,000
Retained earnings	195,000

On July 5, 1966, the factory equipment acquired for the preferred stock was sold for $82,000; at the time of the sale, the factory equipment had a book value of $87,000.

On August 11, 1966, one-half of the preferred stock was acquired for $56,000 and cancelled.

On September 15, 1966, $15,000 was paid to the city to remove the conditions attaching to the earlier gift of unimproved land.

(B) Regional Corporation had authorized capital of $500,000, represented by 20,000 shares of $25 par value capital stock, 15,000 shares of which were issued for $27 per share on October 1, 1964, when the corporation was organized.

On July 1, 1966, when the corporation had retained earnings of $132,400, and when the stock was selling for $28 per share, the board of directors declared a 10% stock dividend on the 15,000 shares outstanding on that date. The distribution of the outstanding shares indicated that certificates for 1,300 full shares would be issued and that fractional-share certificates for the remaining shares would be necessary.

On August 1, 1966, the dividend shares and fractional-share certificates were issued.

As of August 10, 1966, fractional-share certificates equivalent to 160 shares were presented and certificates were issued. No additional fractional-share certificates were presented.

The fractional-share certificates expired on December 1, 1966. The law of the state in which Regional Corporation was incorporated did not permit the directors to rescind any part of a declared dividend.

Problem 6-11. Streamliner Corporation had outstanding on January 1, 1965, 30,000 of its 50,000 authorized shares of common stock, par value $5 per share.

Retained earnings, unappropriated, on the above date amounted to $72,300, premium on common stock was $30,000, other paid-in surplus was $25,000, and reserve for self-insurance was $10,000.

During the year 1965, the corporation declared, December 1, and paid, December 8, an 8% dividend, the net income was $34,800, and $5,000 was added to the self-insurance reserve.

On January 2, 1966, the corporation took title to a tract of unimproved real estate worth $40,000, received as a gift from the City of Y.

In order to conserve cash for building needs, a 10% stock dividend was declared as of December 1, 1966, and issued on December 15, 1966. It was necessary to issue fractional-share certificates for 120 shares. During the latter part of November and the early part of December, the corporation's stock was worth $8 per share.

The net income for 1966 was $38,800. The self-insurance reserve was discontinued and a plant expansion reserve was set up for $30,000.

By December 31, 1966, fractional-share certificates had been presented and full-share certificates issued for 90 shares. On June 15, 1967, the remaining fractional-share certificates expired and the board of directors took appropriate action (in conformity with state law) to give recognition to this fact in the accounts of the corporation. By law, the board of directors is empowered to rescind any part of a stock dividend.

Required:

(a) Journal entries to record all activity affecting the stockholders' equity accounts of the corporation from January 1, 1965 through June 15, 1967. (Debit Other Assets when recording net income.)

(b) The Stockholders' Equity section of the corporation's balance sheet on December 31, 1966.

Problem 6-12. Dexter Scooter Company leases 75 retail outlets. It owns the store equipment in the leased stores. A decision was reached, at the beginning of 1964, to cancel the existing fire insurance coverage on the store equipment and to adopt a policy of self-insurance, thus "saving" annual insurance premiums of $5,000.

The company's accountant decided to set up a Reserve for Self-insurance by annual charges to Retained Earnings equal to the premium savings, less any uninsured losses. No addition to the reserve would be made in those years when the uninsured losses exceeded the premium savings.

During 1964, the uninsured fire losses amounted to $930.

As of January 1, 1965, all fire insurance rates increased 7%.

During 1965, the uninsured fire losses amounted to $1,110.

During 1966, the uninsured losses amounted to $12,000, and the company's accountant decided to charge the losses to Retained Earnings, net of tax, to avoid any distortion of the net income.

Other Data

	1964	1965	1966
Retained earnings, December 31, 1963—$47,800.			
Net income before uninsured losses and income taxes	$18,280	$17,660	$15,200
Dividends	6,000	6,000	4,000
Applicable income tax rate	22%	22%	22%

Prepare a comparative statement of retained earnings for the three-year period ended December 31, 1966.

Problem 6-13. The condensed balance sheet of Midwest File Company on December 31, 1965, was as follows:

MIDWEST FILE COMPANY
Balance Sheet
December 31, 1965

Assets

Cash		$ 89,400
Accounts receivable		188,600
Inventories		218,300
Unexpired insurance		12,000
Property, plant, and equipment	$324,300	
Less accumulated depreciation	173,300	151,000
		$659,300

Liabilities and Stockholders' Equity

Accounts payable		$ 28,400
Accrued expenses		9,100
4% preferred stock—$100 par value	$420,000	
Common stock—No par value—Stated value, $10 per share	120,000	
Capital in excess of par value—Preferred stock issuances	13,600	
Capital in excess of stated value—Common stock issuances	24,000	
Retained earnings	24,200	
Reserve for contingencies	20,000	621,800
		$659,300

Details of the capital stock of the corporation are as follows:

	Authorized	Issued to December 31, 1965
4% noncumulative preferred	5,000 shares	4,200 shares
Common	20,000 shares	12,000 shares

The following transactions affecting the corporation's stockholders' equity accounts occurred during 1966:

January 10—Dividends were declared, payable February 10, as follows:
- (a) The regular quarterly dividend on preferred stock.
- (b) A 5% stock dividend on the common stock, payable in common stock. The current market price is $12 per share.

February 10—Dividends were settled.

April 10—The quarterly dividend on preferred stock was declared, payable May 10.

April 30—Subscriptions were received for 500 shares of preferred stock at $104 per share. Cash of $70 per share was received. The shares are to be issued when the subscription price is received in full.

May 10—Dividend was settled.

June 15—Necessary authorization was obtained to change the authorized preferred stock to 10,000 shares of $2 noncumulative, no-par preferred stock with a stated value of $50 per share. The change was effective on this date and two new shares were issued for each share of outstanding preferred.

June 30—The balance receivable from subscribers to preferred stock was received.

July 10—The quarterly dividend on the preferred stock was declared, payable August 10.

August 10—Dividend was settled.

October 10—The quarterly dividend on the preferred stock was declared, payable November 10.

November 10—Dividend was settled.

December 31—The directors authorized the return of the remaining balance of $5,000 in the Reserve for Contingencies account to Retained Earnings. During 1966, a cash disbursement of $15,000 in settlement of a claim for damages was charged to Reserve for Contingencies. The disbursement was deductible for income tax purposes and resulted in a reduction in the company's income tax obligation from $37,200 to $30,000.

December 31—Net income from regular operations for 1966 was $52,000, resulting in the following increases in asset and liability accounts:

Cash	$24,000
Accounts receivable	17,000
Inventories	9,000
Unexpired insurance	1,000
Property, plant, and equipment	46,000
Accumulated depreciation	9,000
Accounts payable	4,000
Accrued expenses	2,000
Liability for income taxes	30,000

After giving consideration to the other cash transactions during the year, including the $15,000 payment for damages, the ending cash balance is $132,600.

December 31—The directors authorized the establishment of a $40,000 reserve to disclose the board's approval of an expansion of the company's physical facilities.

(a) Prepare journal entries to record all transactions indicated by the foregoing information, including any necessary correction entries.

(b) Prepare a balance sheet as of December 31, 1966, and a statement of retained earnings for the year ended on that date, following the current operating concept of earnings and net-of-tax procedures.

Assignment Material for Chapter 7

QUESTIONS

1. State the three elements of the definition of treasury stock.
2. The *A* Company, whose stock is listed on an exchange, has purchased about 5% of its outstanding stock at current market price (which is nearly three times the original issuance price) for distribution to employees under a bonus plan. It is estimated that not more than 20% of the present holdings will be distributed during the current year. It has been the practice of the company to show the stock as an asset in its balance sheet and, in its income statement, to show dividends applicable to such stock as miscellaneous income. Do you approve? If not, how would you deal with these items?
3. What is meant by the "surplus rule" in connection with the acquisition of treasury stock?
4. (a) The Zenith Process Company is incorporated with a capital stock of 100,000 shares with no par value. It issues 10,000 shares at $50 per share and issues the remaining 90,000 shares to the same stockholders for property consisting for the most part of a quartz gold mine and its equipment, which it records at a valuation of $4,500,000. The declared paid-in capital is $10 per share. After five years' operations, the company's surplus of all classes was $1,000,000, no dividends having been paid. To get rid of a disgruntled stockholder, the company buys his 5,000 shares at $55 per share. The company debits the purchase price of the stock, $275,000, to Treasury Stock. Would you, as auditor, approve this entry? Give your reason.
   (b) Assume that the company's operations had resulted in a deficit of $100,000, and that the 5,000 shares of treasury stock were acquired at $35 per share. The entry for the purchased stock debited Treasury Stock with $250,000 (the amount entered in the books at the time of issuance) and credited a paid-in surplus account with $75,000, the amount by which the issuance price exceeded the amount paid for the treasury stock. Would you approve this entry?
5. List three methods by which the surplus restriction created by the acquisition of treasury shares may be disclosed.
6. On the published balance sheet of a well-known industrial company appears this caption for earned surplus:

   "Earned surplus, of which $2,058,500 is restricted by reason of purchase of treasury stock until such stock is sold or cancelled, $3,286,491.03."

   Explain the significance of this caption.
7. When a corporation issues stock for land, a valuation problem may arise. If the corporation pays for the land with treasury stock, which has a definitely ascertainable cost, is the valuation problem altered?
8. May retained earnings increase as a result of a cancellation of shares of a company's stock? May retained earnings decrease as a result of a cancellation of shares of a company's stock?

9. *A* owns 10,000 shares of stock in Hammond Manufacturing Company and donates 5,000 shares of said stock to the corporation. Would this donation affect the book value of the capital stock? If so, explain.

10. A company whose stock is widely distributed and much dealt in increases its capital stock of $400,000 by a 100% stock dividend. Some years later an original stockholder brings suit for elimination of what he claims to be water in the stock resulting from the stock dividend.

    Do you believe that the stock dividend necessarily watered the stock? If it did, how can the water be eliminated?

11. What sequence is followed when assigning treasury stock losses to the stockholders' equity accounts?

12. State the basic objectives that govern the accounting for treasury stock transactions.

13. Who benefits from the reissuance of treasury stock at more than its cost? The corporation? The shareholders?

PROBLEMS

Problem 7-1. The stockholders' equity of *XYZ* Company, as of June 30, 1966, was composed of the following elements:

Capital stock, $10 par value, 20,000 shares outstanding	$200,000
Capital in excess of par value—From issuance of shares at $11	20,000
Retained earnings	60,000
	$280,000

The company's management has been negotiating for the purchase of a parcel of unimproved land. The owner has agreed to sell the land for 2,000 shares of *XYZ* Company stock.

Management is considering the following alternatives:

Acquisition and transfer of 2,000 shares of treasury stock. The treasury stock can be acquired for $16 per share.

Issuance of 2,000 shares of unissued stock.

You are asked to show the consequences of the above alternatives by preparing a schedule, similar to that above, of the stockholders' equity as it would appear after the purchase of land under each of the following conditions:

(a) Treasury shares are used and accounted for by the cost method.

(b) Treasury shares are used and accounted for by the method recommended by the American Accounting Association.

(c) Unissued shares are used.

Problem 7-2. Hermanson Golf Equipment Co. had authorized, issued, and outstanding on December 31, 1965, 10,000 shares of $100 par value 6% preferred stock. This stock was issued at a 5% premium, which was the only paid-in surplus on the records of the corporation; the retained earnings on this date were $150,000. The corporation had 30,000 shares of $40 par value common stock authorized, issued, and outstanding.

Prepare journal entries to record the following assumed 1966 transactions on the cost basis.

January 2—Acquired 1,000 shares of preferred stock at $80 per share.
February 1—Reissued the above shares at $105 per share.
February 10—Acquired 1,000 shares of preferred stock at $95 per share.

March 1—Reissued these shares at $91 per share.
July 1—Acquired 1,000 shares of preferred stock at $100 per share.
August 1—Reissued these shares at $85 per share.
October 20—Acquired 1,000 shares of preferred stock at $92 per share.

Also prepare the Stockholders' Equity section of the corporation's balance sheet on December 31, 1966. The net income for 1966 was $180,000; dividends declared amounted to $150,000. State law imposes a restriction on retained earnings equal in amount to the cost of treasury shares.

Problem 7-3. From the Stockholders' Equity section of the balance sheet of General Defense Industries presented below, prepare a computation of the book value per share of the preferred stock and the common stock.

GENERAL DEFENSE INDUSTRIES
Partial Balance Sheet
December 31, 1966

Stockholders' equity:		
Capital stock:		
Preferred, cumulative 4%; $100 par value; liquidation preference, $105 per share; 2,000 shares authorized; 1,600 shares issued and outstanding	$160,000	
Common, $30 par value; 10,000 shares authorized; 7,000 shares issued, of which 600 shares are in the treasury	210,000	$370,000
Capital in excess of par value:		
From preferred stock issuances	$ 12,800	
From common stock issuances	24,000	
Proceeds from sale of donated common treasury stock	11,600	48,400
Retained earnings:		
Appropriated:		
Reserve for redemption of preferred stock	$ 20,000	
Reserve for higher replacement cost of fixed equipment	130,000	
Total	$150,000	
Free (Note 1)	8,000	158,000
Total		$576,400
Deduct cost of common treasury stock		22,800
		$553,600

Note 1. Dividends and future treasury stock acquisitions are restricted to the total of retained earnings less the cost of treasury stock amounting to $22,800; cumulative preferred stock dividends are in arrears in the amount of $12,800.

Problem 7-4. In each of the following cases:

(1) Prepare journal entries to record the transactions.
(2) Prepare the Stockholders' Equity section of the balance sheet, giving effect to the transactions recorded in (1). Assume that dividends are restricted by holdings of treasury stock.
(A) Dubuque Corporation was authorized to issue 5,000 shares of no-par capital stock. 4,000 shares were issued for cash at $64 per share, of which $60 was credited to Capital Stock in accordance with action by the board of directors. However, state law provides that legal capital is equal to the amount received for issued shares. 500 shares were reacquired at a price

of $60 per share, and 300 of these shares were subsequently reissued, for cash, at $54 per share. Dubuque Corporation had net income of $64,000 and paid no dividends during the period in which the preceding transactions occurred.

(B) Dakota Company was authorized to issue 20,000 shares of $25 par value 4% preferred stock and 100,000 shares of no-par common stock with a stated value of $5 per share. Shares were issued, for cash, as follows:

Preferred—12,000 shares for $30 per share
Common—70,000 shares for $8 per share

Outstanding shares were reacquired, for cash, as follows:

Preferred—1,000 shares for $32 per share
Common—1,600 shares for $6 per share

800 of the preferred treasury shares were subsequently reissued for $28 per share. By the end of the period covered by the preceding transactions, the corporation had earned $84,120 from operations.

Dakota Company desires to employ the procedure recommended by the American Accounting Association in handling treasury stock transactions.

Problem 7-5. Watsonia Corporation issued 400,000 shares of no-par value stock for $6,800,000 on January 2, 1963. The directors established a stated value of $12 per share. During the next four years, the company earned $1,346,210 and, on December 15 of each year, declared dividends of 40¢ per share. On December 31, 1963, the corporation acquired 200 shares by donation. On January 2, 1965, 14,670 shares were acquired by the corporation for $15 per share. On December 31, 1965, 10,000 shares were reissued for $19 per share. On January 2, 1966, 400 shares were accepted by the corporation in settlement of an account with a customer whose balance was $7,824. As of December 31, 1966, the 400 shares acquired in settlement of the account were canceled by order of the board of directors.

Prepare the Stockholders' Equity section of the corporation's balance sheet as of December 31, 1966, using the cost basis for the valuation of the treasury stock. Dividends and future stock acquisitions are restricted to the amount of the retained earnings less the cost of treasury stock held. There were no unissued shares as of December 31, 1966.

Problem 7-6. On January 2, 1964, Grayson Petroleum Company issued 30,000 of the 50,000 authorized shares of $20 par value stock for $26 per share. The company was incorporated in a state which permits dividends to be paid from paid-in surplus after retained earnings are exhausted. Earnings and dividends for the next three years follow.

	Net Income	Dividends
1964	$ 8,000	$12,000
1965	60,000	18,000
1966	66,000	30,000

On July 1, 1965, the company acquired 800 shares of its stock at $23 per share; on October 10, 1965, 100 of these shares were reissued at $21 per share. On July 3, 1966, 400 of these shares were reissued at $32 per share. The remaining shares were still on hand on December 31, 1966.

A reserve for plant expansion was established in 1965 and it was decided to add $25,000 each year to this account.

Prepare the Stockholders' Equity section of the company's balance sheet as of December 31, 1965, and December 31, 1966. Assume that treasury stock acquisitions place a restriction on retained earnings.

Problem 7-7. On December 31, 1965, the Stockholders' Equity section of the balance sheet of Density Corporation was as follows:

DENSITY CORPORATION
Partial Balance Sheet
December 31, 1965

Stockholders' equity:		
Capital stock:		
6% Preferred, $50 par value, noncumulative:		
8,000 shares authorized	$400,000	
2,000 shares unissued	100,000	
6,000 shares issued	$300,000	
1,000 shares in the treasury (at cost)	45,000	
5,000 shares outstanding		$ 255,000
Common, no par value (stated value, $10 per share):		
60,000 shares authorized	$600,000	
10,000 shares unissued	100,000	
50,000 shares issued and outstanding		500,000
Total		$ 755,000
Surplus		600,000
Total stockholders' equity		$1,355,000

The following data pertain to stockholders' equity account balances as of December 31, 1965, and to recorded transactions affecting these accounts during 1966:

(1) On February 10, 2,000 shares of common stock were acquired by the corporation from an estate for $12 per share, and recorded at cost.

(2) On May 1, 400 of the preferred treasury shares were reissued for $44 per share and the proceeds were credited to the Treasury Stock—Preferred account.

(3) Surplus as shown in the December 31, 1965 balance sheet included a write-up in 1962 to the Land account of $60,000; gains of $8,000 from transactions in treasury stock, common, in 1964; and $50,000 excess of issue price over stated value on issue of common stock when the corporation was organized.

(4) Reserves created from Surplus, which appeared in a special section of the balance sheet on December 31, 1965, were:

Plant expansion	$300,000
Contingencies	80,000

No entries were made in these accounts during 1966.

Required:

(a) Adjusting journal entries which should be made to correct the ledger accounts of the corporation as of December 31, 1966.

(b) The Stockholders' Equity section of the corporation's balance sheet as it should appear on December 31, 1966, if the cost basis of recording treasury stock was followed, and if the 1966 net income was $130,000. There is no restriction on dividends from treasury stock acquisitions.

Problem 7-8. Using the December 31, 1966 Stockholders' Equity section of the Towers Corporation balance sheet, compute the book value per share for each class of stock. All outstanding shares were issued on the date of organization, January 2, 1950.

TOWERS CORPORATION
Partial Balance Sheet
December 31, 1966

Stockholders' equity:			
Capital stock:			
First preferred stock—5% cumulative, fully participating; par value, $100; liquidation value, $105 plus unpaid dividends in arrears; authorized, 10,000 shares; issued and outstanding, 8,000 shares (Note 1)		$800,000	
Second preferred stock—6% cumulative, nonparticipating; par value, $50; liquidation value, par plus unpaid dividends in arrears; authorized, 12,000 shares; issued and outstanding, 6,000 shares (Note 2)		300,000	
Common stock—No par value; authorized and issued, 7,000 shares, of which 500 shares are in the treasury	$350,000		
Deduct treasury stock	25,000	325,000	$1,425,000
Capital in excess of par or stated value:			
Premium on second preferred stock		$130,000	
Forfeited subscriptions—First preferred		5,000	
From treasury stock transactions—Common		10,000	145,000
Retained earnings:			
Appropriated:			
Reserve for contingencies		$ 30,000	
Reserve for retirement of first preferred stock		50,000	
Total		$ 80,000	
Free		60,000	140,000
			$1,710,000

Note 1. Shares of this stock may be called at $102.
Note 2. Dividends have not been paid on this class of stock since 1963, when $9,000 was declared and paid. These shares are not callable.

Problem 7-9. Valiant Corporation had authorized capital of $225,000 represented by 3,000 shares of capital stock with a par value of $75 per share. At the date of organization 1,200 shares had been issued for $85 per share. The remaining authorized shares were unissued on September 30, 1966, at which date the balance of Retained Earnings was $192,000. The outstanding shares were closely held. In spite of the sizable retained earnings, the corporation found itself in need of working capital because earnings had been invested in fixed assets. Therefore, the stockholders voted to declare and issue a 100% stock dividend, each stockholder agreeing to donate, after the stock dividend, one-fourth of his holdings to the company. The donated shares were to be reissued to provide working capital.

The actions described above were carried out as of October 15, 1966. Retained earnings equal to $85 per share were capitalized by the stock dividend. The donated shares were reissued at 60% of their September 30 book value, for cash, on October 30, 1966.

On November 15, 1966, the corporation acquired for cash 400 shares of its capital stock at a premium of 90% of its par value. On December 31, 1966, one-half of these shares were reissued for 95% of their cost.

Net income for the three months ended December 31, 1966, was $24,400, and no cash dividends were declared.

Required:

(1) Journal entries to record the transactions for 1966 described above (except for net income).

(2) The Stockholders' Equity section of the balance sheet on December 31, 1966.

Problem 7-10. The December 31, 1966 balance sheet of Research Products Corporation, as prepared by the treasurer of the corporation, was as follows:

RESEARCH PRODUCTS CORPORATION

Balance Sheet

December 31, 1966

Assets

Cash		$ 28,620
Accounts receivable—after deducting reserve for bad debts of $4,000		65,470
Inventories		132,400
Prepaid expenses		2,130
Treasury stock		16,500
Plant and equipment	$168,200	
Less reserve for depreciation	18,930	149,270
		$394,390

Liabilities and Net Worth

Accounts payable	$ 12,910
Dividends payable	1,000
Accrued expenses	4,180
Reserve for contingencies	10,000
Capital stock	300,000
Surplus	66,300
	$394,390

Recast the above balance sheet, making any changes you feel are appropriate in view of the information presented below, including revisions in terminology.

The corporation has authorized capital stock as follows:

4% cumulative preferred—$100 par value—callable at 105 and accrued dividends	1,000 shares
Common—no par value—stated value, $5 per share	50,000 shares

The entire authorized issue of preferred stock was issued on July 1, 1965, to the president of the corporation in exchange for a plant building which was recorded on the corporation's books at the par value of the shares issued therefor and which has been depreciated since the date of acquisition at an annual rate of 8%.

On the same date as the transaction described above, the president donated 200 shares of the preferred stock to the corporation. These shares were immediately reissued for cash of $80 per share, which was credited to Surplus.

Common stock in the amount of 40,000 shares was issued on July 1, 1965, for cash aggregating $216,000, the amount in excess of the stated value of the shares being credited to Surplus.

On June 30, 1966, the corporation acquired 4,000 shares of its common stock for $5.50 per share. On September 30, 1966, 1,000 of these shares were reissued for $5,000.

The corporation had the following earnings:

Six months ended December 31, 1965	$12,600
Year ended December 31, 1966	38,200

Dividends on preferred stock have been declared as required. The preferred stock contract requires the appropriation from earnings of $5,000 per year for a reserve for preferred stock redemption.

Dividends and future treasury stock acquisitions are restricted to the amount of unappropriated earned surplus less the cost of treasury stock held.

Problem 7-11. On December 31, 1966, the adjusted trial balance of New York Consumers Corporation was as follows:

NEW YORK CONSUMERS CORPORATION
Adjusted Trial Balance
December 31, 1966

Cash in bank	54,000	
Accounts receivable	30,000	
Allowance for bad debts		300
Treasury stock, at cost	19,600	
Inventories	70,000	
Equipment	240,000	
Accumulated depreciation		50,000
Accounts payable		10,000
Capital stock		319,000
Surplus		34,300
	413,600	413,600

Considering the following information, prepare necessary correcting entries as of December 31, 1966, and compute the book value per share for each class of stock as of December 31, 1966.

The corporation was organized on January 2, 1964, with authorizations of 10,000 preferred shares and 50,000 no-par common shares. The preferred stock had the following features: 5% cumulative, $10 par value, with a liquidation value of $12 per share plus dividends in arrears. No stated value was given to the common shares.

On the date of organization, 7,000 preferred shares were issued at $13 per share, cash. On the same day 12,000 common shares were issued, also for cash. The proceeds were credited to Capital Stock.

In 1965 600 preferred shares were acquired for $14 per share; 400 of these shares were reissued for $15 per share. During 1966 1,000 common shares were acquired; 200 of these shares were reissued for $18 per share.

Subsequently during 1966, a stockholder donated 400 common shares, of which 200 were reissued for $20 per share and 200 were canceled. The cancellation has not been recorded.

Earnings for the three years totaled $40,000.

Dividends were declared and paid in 1964, including $.50 per share on common.

Problem 7-12. The accounts showing the stockholders' equity in Worthmore Corporation, as of December 31, 1965, are shown on page 634.

Required:

(a) A statement of retained earnings for the year 1966.

(b) The Stockholders' Equity section of the December 31, 1966 balance sheet.

Preferred stock, 6% cumulative; par value, $100 per share; redeemable at $110 per share:		
Authorized, 10,000 shares; issued and outstanding, 9,640 shares	$ 964,000	
Common stock, without par value:		
Authorized, 200,000 shares; issued and outstanding, 200,000 shares	2,000,000	$2,964,000
Reserve for tax contingencies		20,000
Retained earnings		827,220
Total stockholders' equity		$3,811,220

The following data relate to transactions which occurred during 1966:

(1) Net income from operations amounted to $266,416. Dividends of $6 per share were paid on the preferred stock and $1 per share on the common stock, each being paid in quarterly amounts.

(2) Additional income taxes for 1962 of $12,400 were paid as provided in a compromise agreement dated May 6, 1966.

(3) Treasury stock was acquired on July 1, 1966, as follows:

Preferred stock—420 shares	$ 40,810
Common stock—12,140 shares	182,100

(4) On December 1, 1966, the necessary action was taken to reduce stated capital by the cancellation of 10,000 shares of common stock acquired on July 1, 1966.

(5) On December 31, 1966, the necessary action was taken to close the tax reserve account.

Problem 7-13. The stockholders' equity of June Company amounted to $480,000 as of December 31, 1965, as shown below.

Capital stock—$20 stated value	$400,000
Capital in excess of stated value—From the issuance of 20,000 shares at $21.20	24,000
Retained earnings	56,000
	$480,000

Summary of 1966 Transactions Relating to Stockholders' Equity

Sequence

(1) 4,000 treasury shares were acquired for $88,000.
(2) 800 treasury shares were donated to the company when the market price was $24 per share.
(3) 600 of the treasury shares acquired in (1) were reissued for $23 per share.
(4) Dividend declared—$1 per share.
(5) 400 of the donated treasury shares were exchanged for assets worth $9,000.
(6) 700 of the treasury shares acquired in (1) were reissued for $25 per share.
(7) Net income for 1966—$30,000.

Prepare schedules similar to that above showing the stockholders' equity as of December 31, 1966:

(a) if the treasury stock is accounted for on a cost basis;
(b) if the treasury stock is accounted for following the recommendation of the American Accounting Association.

Assignment Material for Chapter 8

QUESTIONS

1. Why do accountants place such importance on consistency?
2. Why are accountants reluctant to abandon the stable-dollar assumption?
3. Do the income statement and the balance sheet show facts or opinions? Give reasons for your answer.
4. Mention some of the considerations that cause accountants to question the merits of replacement values for balance sheet purposes.
5. Why may balance sheet conservatism result in unconservative income statements?
6. Give a concise definition of revenue.
7. The following have been suggested as possible bases for the recognition of profits:

   (a) Upon signing of the contract of sale.
   (b) Upon purchase of materials to fill the contract.
   (c) In proportion to work completed.
   (d) Upon completion of the manufacturing process.
   (e) Upon segregation of the goods for the purchaser.
   (f) Upon delivery to the purchaser.
   (g) Upon collection of the account in fu'l.
   (h) In proportion to collections made.

   When, if ever, could each of the above bases appropriately be used?
8. A long-term investment which cost $50,000 is sold for $60,000. How much revenue resulted from this transaction? Give a reason for your answer.
9. List the criteria used by the accountant for the determination of the propriety of making a provision for a loss.
10. The text states that, if the current operating concept of income determination is applied, the reported net income is more affected by judgment decisions than is the case if the all-inclusive concept is applied. Why?
11. The text notes that after the date of sale, events may occur which will modify the amounts of revenue and income on the sale transaction. Cite three examples of such events. When are they given recognition in the accounts?
12. On January 2, 1966, Doe paid $3,000 for a three-year fire insurance policy, effective January 1, 1966. As of December 31, 1967, a question has arisen as to the amount of prepaid insurance that should be shown on Doe's balance sheet.

    One proposal is to show prepaid insurance at $600, which is the short-rate cancellation value of the policy on December 31, 1967.

    A second proposal is to show prepaid insurance at $1,000, representing one-third of the original premium cost.

    A third proposal is to show prepaid insurance at $1,200, which is the one-year premium cost for a policy for the same amount as the policy in force.

    You are to discuss each of the proposals as to acceptability, as to the general principle underlying it, and as to its effect on reported income.

13. Is unrealized appreciation revenue? Give reasons in support of your answer.
14. When merchandise is purchased at a special price below the normal market price, has income been earned?

PROBLEMS

Problem 8-1. The following data are taken from the accounts of Slope Company. They show the debits to all of the company's asset accounts during 1966.

Cash	
Collections on accounts receivable	$141,000
Advances from customers (Note 1)	3,000
Bank loan	6,000
Cash sales	7,500
Collection of employee loans	1,800
Proceeds from sale of short-term investment	10,000
Accounts Receivable	
Sales on account	145,000
Short-term Investments (no beginning balance or ending balance)	
Cost of investment	8,000
Inventory	
Purchases	84,000
Land	
Property received in exchange for capital stock	25,000
Equipment	
Cost of equipment constructed by company	45,000
Amount of saving as a result of construction of equipment	5,000

Note 1. Shipments of merchandise during the latter part of 1966, which cost $900, covered one-half of the advances. Shipments planned for the early part of 1967 will cover the remaining part of the advances from customers.

Prepare a schedule showing the amount of revenue earned by the company in 1966.

Problem 8-2. From the following data, compute the revenue earned by Uphill Company for each of the years 1964, 1965, and 1966.

Analysis of Cash Receipts

	1964	1965	1966
Cash sales	$ 7,500	$12,000	$ 14,600
Cash from reissuance of treasury shares acquired for $6,000		6,500	
Cash from sale of land costing $27,000			30,000
Cash from bank loan	5,000		
Cash received on account:			
Current year's sales	74,400	80,900	104,400
Last year's sales	6,700	7,500	8,400
Sales of two years ago	300	200	1,000
Dividends received	250	250	250
From purchase returns		75	
From service calls	3,100	3,300	3,125
From supplier for overpayment of purchase invoice	35		
Advance from customer equal to the 10% profit potential on contract negotiated in December of 1966 to sell damaged merchandise			700

An aging schedule of the accounts receivable disclosed the following:

	December 31, 1963	December 31, 1966
Less than 1 year old	$7,700	$14,100
1 to 2 years old	600	900
2 to 3 years old		225
Over 3 years old		750
Total accounts receivable	$8,300	$15,975

Schedule of Accounts Written Off

Year of Origin	1964	1965	1966
1962	$100		
1963		$200	$ 50
1964			175

Problem 8-3. The Shady Acres Corporation was organized on January 1, 1965, to develop and sell building lots. The authorized capital consisted of 1,000 shares of $50 par value capital stock, all of which was issued at par for cash. The following transactions took place during 1965.

There was purchased for account of the corporation a plot of 10 acres of land. The sum of $8,000 was paid for the land in cash and a mortgage was given for $12,000. A total of $5,000 cash was spent for filling and grading and $10,000 for streets and sidewalks. Payments were made for assessments for improvements, amounting in all to $5,000.

The property was divided into lots and offered for sale at prices as follows:

12 A lots at $3,000 per lot.
24 B lots at $2,000 per lot.
24 C lots at $1,500 per lot.

Five of the A lots, 6 of the B lots, and 11 of the C lots were sold for cash at prices as stated. The mortgage was paid; the total interest cost was $500. Expenses for the year, paid in cash, consisted of: sales commissions amounting to $4,700; other sales expenses, $3,200; and telephone, telegraph, stationery, and other general expenses, $4,100.

Prepare a balance sheet as of December 31, 1965.

Problem 8-4. The income statements for three years are set forth below in comparative form.

NEW DEVICES COMPANY
Income Statements
For the Years Ended December 31, 1964, 1965, and 1966

	1964	1965	1966
Sales	$210,000	$242,000	$251,000
Miscellaneous income	6,500	9,100	14,300
Total revenue	$216,500	$251,100	$265,300
Deduct:			
Cost of sales	$175,000	$190,000	$196,000
Selling expenses	30,400	38,600	35,200
Administrative expenses	27,100	29,500	25,100
Total costs and expenses	$232,500	$258,100	$256,300
Net income (loss)	$(16,000)	$ (7,000)	$ 9,000

The company had no income tax liability for 1966 as a result of operations for 1964 and 1965.

A number of changes in accounting and business policies were made as of January 1, 1965. The changes are described below.

(1) The company discontinued its practice of writing up its investment in land for the annual increment in value. The last write-up, recorded as of December 31, 1964, amounted to $4,000 and was credited to Miscellaneous Income.

(2) Starting on January 1, 1965, all customers were required to make a 20% cash deposit with each sales order. Such deposits were credited to Sales when received. When delivery was made, Sales was credited for the remaining 80%. Undelivered sales orders, at gross sales price, amounted to $18,000 at the end of 1965; the amount was $23,000 at the end of 1966.

(3) Starting in 1965, the company wrote down its inventory at each year end for losses believed possible should new products come on the market during the next 12 months. The inventory was written down $4,000 at the end of 1965 and $2,500 at the end of 1966. Cost of Sales was debited for the write-downs.

(4) In order to avoid showing accrued salaries for administrative employees in the balance sheet, the employees were paid on December 31, 1965 and 1966 for the partial payroll periods. The amounts paid were $3,200 and $3,700, respectively. The accrual, which was recorded as of December 31, 1964, was for $2,950.

(5) The investment in securities was written up to market value as of December 31, 1965 and 1966. As a result, Miscellaneous Income was credited $7,000 and $12,400, respectively.

(6) As of January 1, 1965, the company adopted a policy of leasing all delivery trucks required by its volume of business. The lease period is three years and the company pays monthly rental charges. The company has the privilege of painting its name and colors on the leased trucks. However, if the trucks are so painted, the lease agreement states that the company must, at the end of the three-year period, repaint all of the leased trucks black. The company painted the trucks in 1965 and charged the cost ($1,800) to selling expense. It is estimated that the same amount will be required to repaint the trucks at the end of the lease period.

(7) Starting in 1965, the company doubled its advertising budget. As a result, $8,000 was spent annually in 1965 and 1966.

Present revised income statements in columnar form to comply with the requirements of generally accepted accounting principles.

Problem 8-5. Palm Company presented the following statement for the calendar year 1966, its first year of operations.

Sales			$501,950
Sales discounts			12,400
Net sales			$489,550
Cost of sales:			
Purchases		$201,275	
Direct labor		134,225	
Factory overhead		98,500	
Total		$434,000	
Deduct closing inventories:			
Materials	$21,700		
Finished goods	61,845	83,545	350,455
Gross profit on sales			$139,095

Deduct:		
Selling expenses	$ 87,000	
General expenses	54,000	141,000
Net loss from operations		$ 1,905
Other income:		
Appreciation of factory site	$ 50,000	
Saving from manufacture of office equipment	10,000	
Interest on plant investment	6,000	
Rental of factory building	30,000	96,000
Net income		$ 94,095

Although interest and rental were charged to factory overhead, neither represented an actual cash outlay. The new office equipment which the company manufactured for its own use at a saving of $10,000 was put in service on July 1, 1966. The equipment has an expected useful life of 20 years.

Recast this statement into a more acceptable form and make such changes as you think necessary. You may ignore income taxes.

Problem 8-6. Airlift Company became operational at the beginning of 1966. Its principal asset, a helicopter, is used as follows:

(1) For morning and evening passenger-carrying round trips to a major air terminal located 80 miles from the company's base of operations.

As a source of working capital and as a new business promotion, the company sold "commuter bird" booklets to local businesses for $360 each, which included $20 for transportation tax. Each booklet contained 20 one-way tickets. Fifty booklets were sold. In the first year, the holders of "commuter bird" booklets used 560 of their tickets.

(2) For passenger charter flights.

A deposit equal to 25% of the charter fee is required when the charter is booked. The deposit is not refundable. As of December 31, 1966, such deposits on scheduled charter flights amounted to $970.

(3) For construction material and equipment transportation.

Contractors may rent the "chopper" for $150 an hour to move material and equipment to and from otherwise inaccessible locations.

The company had gross earnings of $28,000 from this source during 1966. Although $3,500 of this amount had not been collected at year end, collections in full were made in January of 1967.

The cash receipts for 1966 are summarized below.

Source	Amount
Stockholders	$100,000
Loan	80,000
"Commuter bird" booklets	18,000
Contractors	24,500
Charter flights	11,700
Passengers on scheduled flights	79,200
Transportation tax collected from passengers	3,960
Hangar rentals	1,200

A preliminary draft of the income statement for 1966, as prepared by the company, is presented below.

AIRLIFT COMPANY
Income Statement
For the Year Ended December 31, 1966

Revenue		$133,400
Expenses:		
Salaries	$30,000	
Fuel	34,050	
Maintenance	12,000	
Depreciation—Helicopter	40,000	
Advertising	1,800	
Amortization	1,000	
License fees	550	119,400
Net income before income tax		$ 14,000
Charge for federal income tax—22%		3,680
Net income		$ 10,320

When the company was organized, it purchased a new hangar from the city. The city built the hangar for $80,000, but as an incentive to the formation of a business to provide local helicopter service, offered to sell it for $50,000; the offer was accepted by Airlift Company. The hangar will be useful for 25 years. The company expects to recover its investment in the hangar by renting storage space to private pilots; therefore, no depreciation was taken on the hangar, and hangar rentals were credited to the hangar asset account.

The organizer and principal stockholder of Airlift Company received his training while in the armed forces. He reasoned that his training to be a helicopter pilot cost the government at least $30,000. Accordingly, he has set this amount up on the company's books as an intangible asset and has planned to amortize it over a 30-year period, which should approximate his active flying career.

Prepare a revised income statement. Show details of revenue according to source.

Problem 8-7. Leased Structures, Inc., was organized in 1965. Its business was to lease small buildings which the company assembled from prefabricated sections. At the end of a lease period, the structure was dismantled and the prefabricated sections were returned to the premises of Leased Structures, Inc., pending their use on subsequent leases.

The standard leasing agreement specified that the lessee was required to pay, on the effective date of the lease, the monthly rental for the first month and the last three months of the lease. The other monthly rentals were payable at the beginning of each month. The lessor agreed to make monthly inspections of the structure and to remove the structure within 10 days after the termination of the lease.

No leases were negotiated during 1965. During 1966, the following leases became effective.

Lease	Date	Term	Monthly Rental	Total Rental	Cash Collections During 1966
A	1/1/66	3 years	$500	$18,000	$7,500
B	7/1/66	4 years	400	19,200	3,600
C	12/1/66	3 years	600	21,600	2,400

Costs to assemble each structure were as follows:

	Lease A	Lease B	Lease C
Labor	$900	$800	$1,000
Transportation—Rented trucks	240	350	235
Supplies (nonrecoverable)	120	100	130
Overhead	450	400	500

It will require as much labor, transportation, and overhead to dismantle the structures and return the prefabricated sections to the company's premises at the termination of each lease.

The company has $40,000 invested in prefabricated sections, acquired as follows:

December 20, 1965	$18,000
January 2, 1966	16,000
June 30, 1966	6,000

The company expects that the prefabricated sections will last for 10 years, whether or not used.

The company's bookkeeper has prepared the following list of account balances as of December 31, 1966:

Cash	9,815	
Accounts receivable	45,300	
Small tools	800	
Prefabricated sections	18,000	
Unpaid bills		740
Capital stock		50,000
Deficit	4,100	
Sales		58,800
Purchases—Prefabricated sections	22,000	
Labor—Including monthly inspection labor	6,300	
Overhead	2,000	
Transportation—Rented trucks	825	
Supplies purchased	400	
	109,540	109,540

An inventory of small tools as of December 31, 1966, showed $750 worth remained in usable condition.

Compute the company's net income (or loss) for 1966. If necessary, assume that the income tax rate is 20%, subject to the operation of a loss-carryforward provision.

Problem 8-8. The unaudited trial balance of Blundy Company is presented on page 642.

You are to assume that you are a member of the audit staff of a firm of certified public accountants. Your firm was first appointed as auditor of Blundy Company in 1965. Your firm completed the audit for 1965 and prepared audited financial statements directly from the audit working papers.

You have returned to make the 1966 audit, and discover that, inadvertently, the client's bookkeeper failed to record the adjusting entries made in the 1965 audit working papers. Your 1965 audit uncovered the following, for which adjustments were made in the audit working papers:

(a) The December 31, 1965 inventory was overstated $3,000.
(b) No adjusting entry was made for accrued administrative salaries of $2,530, as of December 31, 1965.

(c) Ordinary building repairs of $1,200 were charged to the accumulated depreciation account during 1965.
(d) The company had made no provision for uncollectible accounts. You established, with the approval of the client, a policy of providing for bad debts by a charge to expense equal to ½% of sales, which amounted to $1,620 in 1965.

BLUNDY COMPANY
Trial Balance
December 31, 1966

Cash	17,000	
Accounts receivable	29,000	
Inventory	85,400	
Unexpired insurance	810	
Investment in stocks	20,120	
Land	11,000	
Building	130,000	
Accumulated depreciation—Building		32,400
Furniture and fixtures	44,400	
Accumulated depreciation—Furniture and fixtures		23,200
Intangible—Additional cost to replace building	19,000	
Accounts payable		5,000
Bank loans		20,000
Capital stock		200,000
Retained earnings		32,870
Sales		375,400
Cost of goods sold	201,200	
Selling expenses, except depreciation	62,200	
Administrative expenses, except depreciation	58,100	
Depreciation—Building, 4%	5,200	
Depreciation—Furniture and fixtures, 10%	4,440	
Amortization of intangible asset	1,000	
	688,870	688,870

Your examination of the 1966 entries in the accounts disclosed the following:

(A) An expenditure of $1,400 for repairs to office furniture had been charged to Furniture and Fixtures.
(B) A 1965 account receivable in the amount of $810 had been written off as uncollectible by a charge to Selling Expenses.
(C) Salesmen's commissions of $575 had been paid on undelivered customers' orders.
(D) The Investment in Stocks account had increased $5,470 as a result of a trade with a customer for merchandise. The transaction was recorded by debiting Investment in Stocks and crediting Inventory. You note the following:

Cost of merchandise exchanged	$5,470
Advertised selling price of merchandise	6,800
Market value of shares of stock received in trade (based on closing price on stock exchange on day of trade)	6,400

(E) The company's bookkeeper made a study of construction costs and concluded that, as of January 1, 1966, when the building had a remaining useful life of 20 years, it would cost an additional $20,000 to replace the building. The additional replacement cost was recorded as a credit to Retained Earnings.

(F) The December 31, 1966 inventory was correctly set forth at $85,400.

Required:

(1) A computation of the December 31, 1965 retained earnings as it was shown in the 1965 (last year's) audited financial statements. Ignore income taxes.

(2) A computation of the net income before income taxes for 1966 as it would be shown in the 1966 audited financial statements.

Problem 8-9. From the following post-closing trial balance, prepared by the accounting department of Alexander Company from its records on September 30, 1966, and the supplementary information outlined below, prepare:

(a) Working papers, setting forth the necessary adjustments to the company's accounts; and

(b) A corrected balance sheet as of September 30, 1966.

Carry computations to the nearest dollar.

ALEXANDER COMPANY
Post-Closing Trial Balance
September 30, 1966

Accounts payable		183,000
Accounts receivable	380,000	
Accumulated depreciation		100,000
Allowance for losses (receivables)		62,500
Bonds payable—4%—1975		200,000
Capital stock		400,000
Cash	198,333	
Deferred income (discounts receivable)		37,500
Fixed assets	400,000	
Goodwill	80,000	
Installment notes receivable	321,667	
Note payable		100,000
Retained earnings:		
Balance, September 30, 1965		263,500
Net income for the year ended September 30, 1966		43,500
Treasury stock (at cost, which equals par value)	10,000	
	1,390,000	1,390,000

It has been determined that the following transactions or circumstances have not been adequately considered by the company's accountants in the preparation of the above trial balance:

(1) Installment notes receivable represent the uncollected balances of a considerable number of notes receivable, acquired on a discount basis, in the aggregate original amount of $375,000. The discount rate was 10%, and the deferred income of $37,500 is the full amount of the discount at the dates of acquisition, which were as follows:

Date	Aggregate Amount
June 15, 1966	$200,000
July 21, 1966	90,000
September 10, 1966	85,000

By their terms, the notes are collectible in equal monthly installments over a period of 15 months. The management is of the opinion that the aggregate discount on the notes acquired should be regarded as earned over the life of the notes, but that no discount will be transferred to income in the month of acquisition.

(2) The company executed a lease agreement in July, 1966, for a five-year period beginning September 1, 1966, which stipulated an annual rental of $10,000. Under the lease provisions, the annual rental is due on the first day of each lease year, but no rent had been paid or recorded as an accrual on September 30, 1966.

(3) The $100,000 note payable is a two-year note due June 30, 1967. The interest, at 4% per year, is not payable until maturity.

(4) A 2% dividend was declared on September 30, 1966, to holders of record on October 15, 1966. The dividend is payable on November 1, 1966.

(5) Under a contract with an advertising agency, payments of $11,000 were made during the year in connection with a direct-mail campaign. The payments represented a deposit ($2,500) and services and expenses through August 31 ($8,500). A bill for services and expenses for the month of September has been received in the amount of $6,000. All payments have been charged to expense; no accruals are reflected in the records.

The contract was entered into and the program was commenced on June 1, 1966. The campaign is to continue until May 31, 1967, but benefits are expected to accrue over a three-year period. The deposit is intended to serve as a working fund for the payment of day-to-day expenses by the advertising agency; it will be deducted from the agency's final billing.

Total expenditures under this contract are estimated at $40,000. The company engages in more or less similar campaigns almost continuously.

(6) Cash for the payment of the semiannual bond interest, due October 15, 1966, was deposited in advance with the trustee in September. The transfer of cash was treated as a charge against income.

Problem 8-10. You are asked to audit the books of The Norris Company as of December 31, 1966, and to prepare a balance sheet, statement of retained earnings, and income statement for the year 1966.

The trial balance before closing follows:

Accounts payable		13,350
Accounts receivable	27,900	
Bank loans—1967		7,500
Capital stock		35,000
Cash	2,805	
Dividends	3,750	
Furniture and fixtures—at cost	2,000	
Other expenses	9,500	
Building—at cost	18,000	
Merchandise	11,700	
Retained earnings, December 31, 1965		20,780
Taxes	600	
Interest paid	375	
	76,630	76,630

The following facts are disclosed by your examination:

The furniture and fixtures were acquired late in March 1965, and the building late in December 1965. Furniture and fixtures and buildings of the kind owned by the company are generally considered to last 10 and 50 years, respectively.

The analysis of the Merchandise account shows that it is made up of: Sales, $101,200; purchases, $64,000; inventory on December 31, 1965, $48,900.

Unexpired insurance amounted to $200 on December 31, 1966, and $350 on December 31, 1965; the latter item was not taken into consideration when the books were closed at the end of 1965.

The taxes paid during the year were for the year 1965. The taxes for 1966 are estimated to be 30% higher than the 1965 taxes.

Uncollectible accounts are to be written off as follows: Philo Co., $1,350, due since February, 1965, and Hart Co., $900, due since February, 1966.

Unrecorded liabilities for expenses total $500.

Debit balances in the accounts payable ledger total $540, and credit balances in the accounts receivable ledger total $600.

The inventory on December 31, 1966, amounts to $28,500.

Interest has been paid on the bank loans, at the rate of 5%, to April 30, 1967.

Make adjustments of prior years' income in Retained Earnings. Ignore income taxes.

Problem 8-11. The accounts of Sandusky Manufacturing Corporation have never been audited by outside accountants. The corporation wishes to renew the $300,000 of notes payable which mature in January of 1967. The note holders have indicated a willingness to renew the notes, provided that the following conditions are satisfied as of December 31, 1966: (a) the accounts are audited by outside auditors; (b) the ratio of current assets to current liabilities, including the notes, is at least 2 to 1; and (c) the retained earnings exceed $200,000.

As outside auditor, make the determinations required of (b) and (c) above.

SANDUSKY MANUFACTURING CORPORATION
Adjusted Trial Balance
December 31, 1966

Cash	100,000	
Investments	300,000	
Accounts receivable	100,000	
Inventories	600,000	
Prepaid expenses	20,000	
Fixed assets	5,000,000	
Treasury stock—at stated value	1,000,000	
Notes payable		300,000
Accounts payable		50,000
Accrued expenses		40,000
Allowance for doubtful accounts		30,000
Accumulated depreciation and amortization		1,600,000
Estimated federal income tax		71,600
Capital stock—shares authorized at stated value		5,000,000
Surplus		257,200
Dividends—$8 per share	320,000	
Sales		3,300,000
Cost of sales	2,240,000	
Selling and administrative expenses	900,000	
Interest expense	18,000	
Other income—From investments		20,800
Federal income tax	71,600	
	10,669,600	10,669,600

As a result of your examination, the following information is available:

The sales include $300,000 proceeds from the sale of patents. They were acquired for $250,000, which amount, less the amortization of $80,000 properly accumulated thereagainst, is included in cost of sales.

In order to record as many transactions as possible which were applicable to 1966, the company kept open some of its journals until the middle of January, 1967. As a result, checks for $200,000, received in January in payment of customers' November and December purchases, were included in the December cash receipts journal; checks for $150,000, issued in January in payment of vendors' December invoices, were recorded as December transactions, as were $80,000 of vendors' invoices received in January for goods and services delivered in December. Of the latter amount, $50,000 represented goods included in the closing materials inventory and $30,000 was for expense items.

The investments consist of:

The cost of a tract of land acquired on January 10, 1966, to be used as a site for future plant expansion—$80,000.

The cost of 2,600 shares of capital stock of Sandusky Manufacturing Company—$220,000. This stock was purchased in 1962 because the price was considered cheap. The company now intends to retire these shares.

The inventories consist of:

Materials and supplies	$200,000
Finished product	400,000

Materials and supplies are carried at cost, which is below current replacement value. For simplicity the company carried its finished-product inventory at 50% of the selling price. Former inventories have always been carried at cost, and upon your advice it has been decided to continue this practice. The officials point out, and you have verified, that the gross profit margin on products is uniform and has remained the same for the past two years.

The treasury stock represents 10,000 shares authorized by the corporation's charter but not yet issued.

The Accumulated Depreciation and Amortization has been analyzed for the year as follows:

	Buildings	Machinery and Equipment	Patents
Balance, December 31, 1965	$150,000	$ 930,000	$355,000
Provision for the year 1966	20,000	150,000	75,000
	$170,000	$1,080,000	$430,000
Less amount accumulated on patents sold			80,000
Balance, December 31, 1966	$170,000	$1,080,000	$350,000

When the capital stock was issued, the $100,000 excess over stated value was credited to Surplus to be used as a partial offset to the deficit that was anticipated from the first year's operations.

You may assume that the following income tax rates are applicable:

First $25,000	22%
Over $25,000	48%

Assignment Material for Chapter 9

QUESTIONS

1. How should the following items be shown in the balance sheet?

(a) Currency held by salesmen as a result of advances for traveling expenses.
(b) Postage stamps.
(c) I.O.U.'s from employees.
(d) Cash deposited with state highway department in connection with a contract bid.

2. Postdated checks from customers totaling $12,500 appear as part of the cash on hand of a company you are auditing. These checks were ultimately deposited and collected in full. Would you object to their inclusion as cash?

3. In an audit as of December 31, 1966, you find that the books show a $10,000 overdraft on the bank. Where should this item be shown in the balance sheet? Would you make any adjustment if you discovered that checks totaling $12,000 had been drawn and dated in December but were not mailed until January 5, 1967?

4. Describe a procedure for safeguarding cash receipts and cash disbursements.

5. Using your own figures, prepare an illustration of the operation of an imprest cash fund.

6. Using your own figures, prepare an illustration of lapping of cash receipts.

7. A corporation which uses the calendar year as its accounting period held its cash receipts journal open until the 15th of January, during which time $20,000 was collected on customers' accounts and recorded as of December 31; $15,000 of this amount was used to pay liabilities recorded in the accounts prior to December 31. The cash disbursement entries were properly dated. What adjustments would you make, if any?

8. What internal control procedure should be applied to minimize the danger of covering a defalcation by making entries for noncash credits to accounts receivable?

9. What circumstances cause a company's cash balance per books to differ from the bank balance?

PROBLEMS

Problem 9-1. Prepare entries in general journal form to record the following transactions, and any necessary adjusting entries, in the books of Lewis Company, which closes its books annually on December 31.

November 15, 1965—The company established an imprest cash fund of $100.
November 30, 1965—An examination of the imprest cash fund disclosed the following composition:

Currency and coin	$ 6
Memoranda showing expenditures for:	
Office supplies expense	28
Telephone and telegraph	18
Postage	42
Sundry general expense	6

Owing to the rapid exhaustion of the fund, a check was drawn to replenish the fund and to increase its amount to $200.

December 31, 1965—The composition of the imprest cash fund was as follows:

Currency and coin	$86
Check of the president of the company dated January 10, 1966	75
Postage stamps	5
Memoranda showing expenditures for:	
Telephone and telegraph	19
Postage	20

The fund was not replenished.

January 10, 1966—The president's check was deposited in the company's regular checking account.

January 31, 1966—A check was drawn to replenish the fund. The composition of the fund was as follows:

Currency and coin	$10
Postage stamps	9
Memoranda showing expenditures since November 30, 1965, for:	
Telephone and telegraph	32
Postage	52
Office supplies expense	15
Contributions	10
Sundry general expense	5

Problem 9-2. In your audit of the accounts of National Box Corporation, you find the following facts:

Balance of Cash in Bank account July 31, 1965	$7,056
Balance of Cash on Hand account July 31, 1965	-0-
Balance on bank statement July 31, 1965	4,210

Outstanding checks, July 31, 1965:

Date	Number	Amount
6/10/64	412	$ 12
1/ 6/65	553	62
7/31/65	804	80
	805	40
	806	65
	807	120
Total		$379

Receipts of July 31, 1965, deposited August 1, 1965	3,200

Payment has been stopped on check number 412, which was for wages; the payee cannot be located.

The bank statement shows the following charges:

(1) Service charges for July	$ 3
(2) N.S.F. check received from a customer on July 10, deposited on July 11, but charged back by the bank on July 17 as uncollectible	22

There was a cash shortage of $421 which had been concealed by "lapping" collections from customers. This shortage is covered by a surety bond.

The stub for check number 807 and the invoice relating thereto show that it was for $102. It was recorded incorrectly in the cash disbursements journal as $120. This check was drawn in payment of an account payable.

Required:

(a) Bank reconciliation, using a form that sets forth the adjusted balance of cash in bank for the balance sheet on July 31, 1965.

(b) Necessary adjusting journal entries in view of the preceding information.

Problem 9-3. The following data are to be used in reconciling the May 31, 1966 bank balance of Burton Envelope Company:

	1966	
	April	May
Cash in Bank balance—at month end	$3,561.00	$ 4,629.72
Bank statement balance—at month end	7,403.50	3,862.20
Bank service charges for the month	6.00	6.80
Checks marked "N.S.F."	815.00	118.00
Deposits in transit—at month end	950.00	925.40
Drafts collected by the bank (unrecorded by the company until the month following collection)	1,500.00	202.00
Outstanding checks at month end	4,463.00	140.68
Checks of Barton Engine Corporation charged to the company's account in error	349.50	60.00
Check number 6129 erroneously recorded in the check register as $78; the correct amount is (This check is outstanding on May 31, 1966.)		87.00
Receipts during the month		42,700.17
Total credits to Cash in Bank		41,631.45
Total charges on bank statement		45,317.57

Prepare a reconciliation of receipts, disbursements, and bank account for the month of May, 1966.

Problem 9-4. Moonbeam Company, whose fiscal year ends on June 30, held open its cash journals in 1966, recording $27,015.10 received in July under the date of June 30. Of this amount $18,771.83 was received from credit customers who took cash discounts of $340.20. The balance represented the proceeds from cash sales on which an average gross profit of 30% of gross selling price was realized and which were subject to a 2% cash discount. With the amounts so collected, accounts payable of $15,214.70 were paid, with cash discounts of $226.10 being taken. A bank loan of $8,000.00 was paid with interest of $120.00, of which $12.00 accrued subsequent to June 30.

The current position as shown in the company's June 30, 1966 balance sheet was as follows:

Current assets:		
Cash	$18,015.15	
Accounts receivable—net of allowance for bad debts	31,497.10	
Inventory	23,311.20	
Prepaid expenses	2,118.00	$74,941.45
Current liabilities:		
Accounts payable	$26,211.60	
Income taxes payable	8,200.00	34,411.60

Prepare corrected current asset and current liability sections of the June 30, 1966 balance sheet and compute the change in the amount of working capital and working capital ratio caused by your corrections.

Problem 9-5. The bank statement received by Hayes Supply Company showed a balance of $13,673 on June 30, 1965. You have been asked to determine if the cash balance (cash on hand and in bank) of $15,397, as shown by the company's books on July 15, 1965, was correct. In the course of your examination, you obtain the following information:

(1) The bank reconciliation on June 30, 1965, showed outstanding checks of $1,640 and a deposit in transit of $565.

(2) The bank reported that during the period July 1, 1965 to July 15, 1965 inclusive, it had credited the account of Hayes Supply Company with deposits of $18,510, and that charges to the account during the same period totaled $21,015, including service charges of $12 and a charge of $1,200 in reduction of a loan.

(3) Checks drawn during the period July 1, 1965 to July 15, 1965, aggregated $19,411. Cash received during the same period, as shown by the cash receipts journal, amounted to $22,210, of which $1,425 was on hand on July 15, 1965.

(4) There were no irregularities in the handling of cash or recording of cash transactions.

Problem 9-6. As accountant for Brandon Company, you obtain from the company's bank the bank statement, canceled checks, and other memoranda which relate to the company's bank account for December, 1965. In reconciling the bank balance on December 31, 1965 with that shown on the company's books, you observe the facts set forth below.

(1) Balance per bank statement, 12/31/65		$88,489.12
(2) Balance per books, 12/31/65		58,983.46
(3) Outstanding checks, 12/31/65		32,108.42
(4) Receipts of 12/31/65; deposit mailed 12/31/65		5,317.20
(5) Service charge for November, 1965, per bank memo of 12/15/65		3.85
(6) Proceeds of bank loan, 12/15/65, discounted for 3 months at 5% per annum, omitted from company books		9,875.00
(7) Deposit of 12/23/65 omitted from bank statement		2,892.41
(8) Check of Larue Block Company charged back on 12/22/65 for absence of countersignature and redeposited with complete signature on 1/5/66, no entry on the books having been made for the chargeback or the redeposit		417.50
(9) Error on bank statement in entering deposit of 12/16/65:		
Correct amount	$3,182.40	
Entered in statement	3,181.40	1.00

(10) Check No. 469 of Brandau Production Corporation, charged by bank in error to company's account		2,690.00
(11) Proceeds of note of Connor Shade Company collected by the bank, 12/10/65, not entered in cash journal:		
Principal	$2,000.00	
Interest	20.00	
	$2,020.00	
Less collection charge	5.00	2,015.00
(12) Erroneous debit memo of 12/26/65, to charge company's account with settlement of bank loan, which was paid by check No. 3682 on same date		5,000.00
(13) Error on bank statement in entering deposit of 12/11/65:		
Entered as	$4,817.10	
Correct amount	4,807.10	10.00
(14) Deposit of Brandau Production Corporation of 12/15/65 credited in error to this company		1,819.20

(a) Prepare a reconciliation of Brandon Company's bank account as of December 31, 1965.

(b) Prepare one or more journal entries to adjust Brandon Company's books to reflect the correct bank balance as of December 31, 1965.

Problem 9-7. The bookkeeper-cashier of Austin Mercantile Company absconded on the evening of April 16, 1965, apparently with a large portion of the company's cash, and has taken with him certain accounting records, including the cash journals and the general ledger. You are called upon to ascertain, if possible, the shortage with which the missing employee may be charged.

From available subsidiary journals and ledgers and other data you obtain the following information:

Balances at close of business, April 16, 1965:	
Accounts receivable	$ 44,255.50
Accounts payable—Merchandise	20,730.27
Other debtors or creditors	None
Cash in bank, less checks outstanding	9,883.43
Transactions January 1—April 16, 1965:	
Sales, per receivables clerk	587,617.48
Cash sales	None made
Sales allowances in customers' accounts	1,833.63
Cash purchase of furniture, per invoice	300.00
Depreciation provision—3½ months	380.15
Merchandise purchase record total	361,526.42
Expenses paid, supported by paid invoices and payrolls	186,583.68
Cash dividend declared, $5,000, of which $1,000 remains unpaid	4,000.00
Changes in capital stock	None

Cash credits posted to customers' accounts, less deposits reported on statements from the bank during January, February, March, and April (through the sixteenth), amounted to $4,383.42.

A check for $10,000 had been cashed by the bookkeeper shortly before his departure. Although the signatures on the check had been obviously forged, it was paid by the bank and returned with other canceled checks.

In addition to obtaining the amount of the possible shortage, you are asked to prepare a balance sheet as of April 16, 1965 and income statement for the period January 1, 1965 through April 16, 1965. The merchandise inventory at that date has been estimated as having a cost of $41,211.15, which is less than market. Use 20% to make provision for income taxes. A balance sheet prepared from the books as of December 31, 1964, and discovered in the files follows:

AUSTIN MERCANTILE COMPANY
Balance Sheet
December 31, 1964

Assets

Cash		$ 3,267.49
Accounts receivable		22,623.45
Inventory (cost)		44,035.78
Fixtures	$7,456.26	
Less accumulated depreciation	3,180.42	4,275.84
		$74,202.56

Liabilities and Stockholders' Equity

Accounts payable	$11,472.61
Capital stock	50,000.00
Retained earnings	12,729.95
	$74,202.56

Problem 9-8. The bookkeeper for Specialty Products Company does not usually prepare the monthly bank reconciliations. However, because the employee regularly assigned to the task of preparing the monthly reconciliation was on vacation, the bookkeeper prepared the August, 1966, reconciliation shown below.

Balance per bank statement—August 31		$24,513.70
Add:		
Checks drawn but not paid by bank (see detailed list below)	$3,871.09	
Credit memo for proceeds of a note receivable which had been left at the bank for collection but which has not been recorded as collected	400.00	
Check for an account payable entered on the books as $468.13 but drawn, and paid by bank, as $706.11	237.98	4,309.07
Total		$28,822.77
Deduct:		
Collections received on the last day of August and debited to Cash in Bank on books but not deposited	$3,859.83	
Debit memo for customer's check returned unpaid (check is on hand but no entry has been made in the books)	200.00	
Debit memo for bank service charge for August	11.26	4,071.09
Balance per ledger—August 31		$24,751.68

Checks Drawn But Not Paid by Bank

No. 5480	$475.00	No. 5514	$ 316.79
5493	137.39	5515	423.23
5511	600.28	5516	542.55
5513	757.98	5517	417.87
			$3,871.09

Required:

(a) A corrected bank reconciliation.

(b) Journal entries for items which should be adjusted prior to closing the books on August 31.

Problem 9-9. The following information concerning the cash accounts of Penetration Company is available.

CORRECTED CASH FIGURE

1. Balance per bank:
   - November 30, 1965 .... $ 18,570
   - December 31, 1965 19,362
2. Balance per books:
   - November 30, 1965 .... $ 12,368
   - December 31, 1965 18,808
3. Outstanding checks:
   - November 30, 1965 .... $ 6,352
   - December 31, 1965 7,504
4. December deposits, per bank statement $135,040
5. December cash receipts, per cash receipts journal $170,510

N.S.F. checks returned by the bank are recorded as a reduction in the cash receipts journal. Those redeposited are recorded as regular cash receipts. Data regarding N.S.F. checks:

Returned by bank in November and recorded by company as a reduction in cash receipts in December, $150.

Returned by bank in December and recorded by company as a reduction in cash receipts in December, $1,350.

Returned by the bank in December and recorded by company as a reduction in cash receipts in January, $230.

Redeposited by company during December, $800.

6. According to the repayment terms of a large loan with the bank, the bank credits the company's checking account with 80% of amount presented for deposit. The remaining 20% is applied to reduce the unpaid balance of the loan. The following summary entries for December indicate the company's treatment of the deposits and resulting loan reductions:

Cash in bank	172,010	
Cash on hand		172,010
Recorded in cash receipts journal.		
Bank loan	34,402	
Cash in bank		34,402
Recorded in cash disbursements journal.		

The above summary entries include one deposit in transit on December 31, in the amount of $3,210.

There were no deposits in transit on November 30, 1965.
There was no undeposited cash on hand on December 31, 1965.

7. Interest on the bank loan for the month of December charged by bank against the checking account, $1,829.
8. On December 31, 1965, a $2,323 check of Precision Company was charged to the company's account in error.

Required:

(a) A reconciliation of receipts, disbursements, and bank account for December 31, 1965.
(b) December 31, 1965 adjusting entries relating to the cash accounts of Penetration Company.

Problem 9-10. Your client, John Doe, is contemplating going into business on January 1, 1966. He plans to sell product X on the installment plan. He will carry no inventory and will pay for the units of X and all associated expenses at the time of sale. Collections will be made in 10 equal installments, the first being made at the date of sale.

Mr. Doe has prepared the following estimate of sales volume:

Month	Units	Month	Units
January	50 units	July	300 units
February	95	August	275
March	115	September	250
April	245	October	250
May	460	November	200
June	450	December	150

You are given the following additional information:

Selling price of X	$180
Monthly installment	18
Cost of X	125
Selling expense per unit	35
Net profit per unit	20

Because Mr. Doe must pay all the costs connected with the sale at the time the sale is made, and because collections are deferred over 10 months, he is aware of the need for a considerable amount of cash to finance the business until it has been established long enough for receipts to exceed disbursements.

A bank has agreed to loan the new business any amount required during the first year up to 50% of the outstanding installment receivables.

Mr. Doe has $80,000 he can use in his business and needs to know whether this amount will be sufficient. He asks you to prepare a schedule covering the first 12 months which shows the following:

(a) His potential borrowing capacity at the end of each month.
(b) The prospective amount of bank indebtedness at the end of each month, assuming that borrowings and repayments may be made monthly.

Problem 9-11. Convey Corporation, a newly organized company, is planning to build a continuous-belt conveyor facility for the movement of coal from a coal mine to a nearby public utility electricity generating plant. The conveyor facility is designed in such fashion as to permit partial utilization before construction is completed.

The public utility has signed an agreement with Convey Corporation for the following tonnage to be moved by the conveyor facility:

1966	5,000,000 Tons
1967	5,300,000 Tons
1968	6,000,000 Tons

On or before January 1, 1966, the stockholders will invest $100,000 in the company's capital stock to provide the working capital. To finance the construction of the conveyor facility, the company has arranged for a mortgage loan of $2,000,000, which equals the contract cost. Interest of 4% per year will be charged on the unpaid balance. The principal amount of the loan is to be repaid in equal semiannual installments of $100,000 beginning June 30, 1967.

The amounts borrowed under the loan agreement are scheduled to coincide with the schedule of payments in the construction contract, as follows:

January 1, 1966	$100,000
April 1, 1966	800,000
July 1, 1966	600,000
January 1, 1967	300,000
April 1, 1967	200,000

Based on the estimates of the company's accountant, an operating profit, before depreciation, interest, and income taxes (use a rate of 25% if needed), of 4 cents per ton is expected. Depreciation has been set at 3 cents per ton.

Prepare a cash budget, by year, for the years 1966, 1967, and 1968. You may assume that the applicable income tax law has a loss carryback-carryforward provision.

Problem 9-12. Some investors are considering the formation of a company to market anti-smog devices which are designed and packaged in such a way that purchasers may readily affix them to their automobiles. Thus, the new company will not need to provide any installation services or invest in any installation equipment.

The articles will cost the company $125 and will sell for $200. It is expected that 25% of the sales will be for cash, with the balance on a monthly installment plan. The installment plan requires a 10% down payment and 10 monthly payments of $20 each, which will include the finance and carrying charges.

Salesmen will be paid a commission of $20 per unit. The commission will be paid in full in the month of sale.

The manufacturer of the product has agreed to sell to the company on the following terms:

20% cash down payment
80% balance payable at end of month unit is sold

A local bank has agreed to make a revolving loan under the following terms:

An amount equal to 50% of the installment receivables acquired during the month will be advanced to the company each month.
50% of the installment collections must be applied to reduce the bank loan.
The company must maintain a minimum bank balance of $12,000.
Interest expense will be charged monthly at 6% per annum on the unpaid balance as of the end of the preceding month.

Estimated sales by month:

January	200 units
February	320
March	360
April	440
May	760
June	720

The company plans to make an initial purchase of 400 units and to make monthly purchases equal to the number of units sold during the month. (You may assume no time lag between purchase order and delivery.)

Variable expenses, in addition to interest and salesmen's commissions, should approximate $30 per unit sold. Fixed cash expenses should approximate $2,400 per month.

From the above information prepare a cash budget by months, with suitable supporting schedules, which will show the cash receipts, the cash disbursements, and the cumulative cash investment required of the investors.

Carry computations to the nearest dollar.

Assignment Material for Chapter 10

QUESTIONS

1. Describe three customary procedures for computing the periodical provisions for uncollectible accounts.
2. May debit balances in accounts with consignees for goods shipped on consignment be shown as accounts receivable?
3. In the December 31, 1966 trial balance of a corporation, there is a debit of $55,000 against John Doe for a payment to him on account of material purchased from him to be delivered after said date. How should this item be classified in the balance sheet?
4. You find the following items included among the accounts composing the Accounts Receivable controlling account balance of a concern you are auditing. State how you would show each item in the balance sheet.

    Accounts receivable from employees.
    Interest receivable on notes.
    Rebates receivable on returned merchandise purchases.
    Prepaid interest on notes payable.
    Advances to salesmen.
    Federal tax refunds receivable.

5. Should amounts owed a parent company by a subsidiary be shown as accounts receivable in the parent company's balance sheet?
6. If sales payable in installments are made, is it permissible to show under the Current Assets caption any installments not due within one year from the balance sheet date?
7. When an account that has been charged off as uncollectible is eventually collected in whole or in part, why should the collection be passed through the customer's account? By what entries is this accomplished?
8. In the trial balance prepared toward the close of a corporation's fiscal year there is a debit balance in the account Allowance for Doubtful Accounts. Explain how the debit balance probably arose. Does the debit balance indicate that the allowance at the close of the prior fiscal year was inadequate?
9. State one advantage of basing bad debt provisions on aging schedules. Also give a weakness of this approach.
10. Should a contra account be set up to provide for the probable allowances to be credited to customers on accounts open at the end of the period?
11. Assume that Bailey Company obtains funds by open accounts receivable financing. Using figures of your own, compute the amount of the resulting contingent liability to be shown by Bailey Company as a balance sheet footnote.
12. State two reasons why a bank may prefer to have a borrower discount its customers' trade acceptances rather than its own notes payable.

PROBLEMS

Problem 10-1. Data from the accounts receivable subsidiary ledger of Trade Winds Company as it appeared on December 31, 1965, are presented below.

Eiteman Corporation			Dean Corporation			David Company		
Debits:								
9/ 3	a	$ 378	7/29	a	$ 398	8/ 1	a	$ 898
10/20	b	345	8/ 6	b	280	9/14	b	714
11/ 1	c	271				10/18	c	1,206
11/25	d	846						
Credits:								
10/ 8	a	$ 378	9/16	a	$ 300	9/ 2	a	$ 898
11/18	b	345				12/15	b	500
12/ 1	c	271						

Sylvia Company			Margaret Co.			Wilfred Company		
Debits:								
9/16	a	$ 413	7/ 5	a	$ 660	8/ 2	a	$ 247
9/20	b	216	9/15	b	1,020	9/17	b	202
10/29	c	1,105	12/ 1	c	849			
11/30	d	904	12/20	d	580			
			12/30	e	386			
Credits:								
10/15	a	$ 200	8/ 7	a	$ 660	9/16	a	$ 100
10/30	a	200	10/15	b	1,020			
11/30		200						

(a) Prepare an aging schedule of the accounts receivable, making use of the following categories: Not Due; Past Due Less Than 2 Months; Past Due More Than 2 Months. Accounts are considered past due 60 days after date of sale.

Data from the allowance account of the company as it appeared on December 31, 1965, are presented below:

Allowance for Doubtful Accounts				
Debits:	5/ 6	$125	Credits: 1/1	Balance $566
	8/11	401		
	12/20	80		

The company establishes an allowance account for uncollectible receivables equal to:

10% of accounts less than 2 months past due;
30 % of accounts more than 2 months past due.

(b) Prepare the journal entry for the December 31, 1965 provision for uncollectible accounts.

Problem 10-2. The balances of selected accounts taken from the September 30, 1965 balance sheet of Diamond Sports Company were as follows:

Accounts receivable	$ 273,200
Allowance for doubtful accounts	8,196

The following transactions (in summary) affecting accounts receivable occurred during the year ended September 30, 1966:

Sales—all on account	$1,311,416
Cash received from customers	1,428,980

The corporation's credit terms were 2/10; n/30; and customers paying $1,004,921 of the above-stated cash took advantage of the discount.
Cash received included $2,450 recovered on accounts receivable written off as uncollectible in prior periods.

Accounts receivable written off as worthless	$ 9,330
Credit memoranda issued for returned sales and allowances . . .	18,435

Required:

(a) Journal entries to record the transactions summarized for the year ended September 30, 1966.

(b) Adjusting journal entry for estimated bad debts on September 30, 1966, omitting pennies. The corporation adjusts its allowance account to a percentage of outstanding accounts receivable. The credit experience of the corporation during the year ended September 30, 1966, indicates that the percentage rate to be used on September 30, 1966, should be two-thirds of that used on September 30, 1965.

Problem 10-3. The following transactions are from among those experienced by Gusty Company during 1966.

1966

August 14—Sale of $9,050 to Quality Company; f.o.b. destination; 2/10; n/30.
September 7—Receipt of 60-day, 4% note dated September 5 from Quality Company. The face of the note was the amount of the invoice minus transportation charges of $50 paid in connection with the August 14 sale.
September 20—Quality Company note discounted at bank at 6% discount rate.
November 5—Receipt of notification from bank of Quality Company default. Bank paid today, including $9 protest fee.
December 4—Receipt of cash from Quality Company for the full amount of its indebtedness, including interest at 4% to date on amount paid to bank.

(a) Journalize the above transactions.

(b) Journalize the September 20th transaction following an alternative approach.

Problem 10-4. The following T-accounts summarize the debit-credit activity found in the books of Middle East Company during 1966.

Accounts Receivable (Control)

	Debit		Credit	
1/1	Balance, after deducting credit balances of $1,100	27,400	Collections from customers, including overpayments of $700	311,250
	Charge sales	317,410	Write-offs	555
	Memo entry for goods shipped on consignment	4,290	Merchandise returns	2,210
	Subscriptions receivable for capital stock	10,500	Allowances to customers for shipping damages	810
	Bad debts recovered	220	Collections on carrier claims . . .	670
	Cash disbursed to customers for 1/1 credit balances.	900	Memo entry for consignment sales	2,070
	Goods shipped to cover balance of 1/1 credit balances	200		
	Cash disbursed for recoverable contract bids	9,000		
	Claims against carriers for shipping damages	810		

Allowance for Doubtful Accounts

Write-offs	555	1/1	Balance	770
			Recoveries	220
			Provision	614

Notes Receivable

Notes Receivable Discounted

	Proceeds from customer's $600 note received on account and discounted at bank upon receipt	598

Compute the amount at which the accounts receivable should be shown in the year-end balance sheet.

Problem 10-5. American Plan Company was organized in 1961. All of its sales are on an installment-plan basis which calls for 24 equal monthly installments.

The company has not made any provision for uncollectible accounts. The company's policy has been to write off at year end those accounts on which no collections had been received for two months. The company's sales and bad debt record are shown below:

Year	Installment Sales	Accounts Written Off (Year of Sale)			Recoveries (Year of Sale)
1961	$200,000	$1,100 (1961)			
1962	500,000	3,000 (1961)	$ 2,000 (1962)		$ 200 (1961)
1963	600,000	1,000 (1961)	8,000 (1962)	$2,600 (1963)	800 (1962)
1964	650,000	2,400 (1962)	9,000 (1963)	3,000 (1964)	1,000 (1963)
1965	550,000	5,400 (1963)	10,000 (1964)	2,800 (1965)	1,200 (1964)

Accounts receivable as of December 31, 1965:

1964 sales	$120,000	
1965 sales	334,000	$454,000

The company wishes to change its accounting for uncollectible accounts to an allowance basis and to have the change made effective for its 1965 financial statements.

Prepare the necessary entry (or entries) as of December 31, 1965, to effect the change. Ignore income tax matters.

Problem 10-6. On May 31, 1966, the Notes Receivable account of Speedway Corporation has a balance of $15,980.

Analysis of the account disclosed that $42,250 of notes were received from customers during the fiscal year ended May 31, 1966, and that $20,800 of these notes were collected from the makers at maturity and $11,050 of the notes were discounted at the bank. Of the notes discounted, $5,200 have been paid by the makers and one note for $1,560, given by Foreman Axle Company, was not paid when due. As endorser, the company paid $1,580 to the bank. A three-month 6% note for $4,000 was received from an officer of the corporation. The note was dated December 1, 1965. No interest had been recorded.

Partial payments in the amount of $1,650 have been received on notes not yet due, and these collections have been credited to Partial Collections on Notes Receivable, which is shown as a liability on the balance sheet. Such partial collections included $32 of interest.

A customer's note for $2,500 was pledged as collateral for the payment of a bank loan.

Required:

(a) Journal entries necessary to correct the accounts of Speedway Corporation.

(b) Show how the facts regarding all notes discussed above should be disclosed on a balance sheet to be used for credit purposes.

Problem 10-7. You have just been hired by Machinery Products Company to be its chief accountant. The company is three years old and has never been audited. All transactions for 1966 have been recorded, but closing entries have not been prepared.

In your preliminary review of the company's accounting system you note the following:

A. A relatively small number of machines has been shipped on consignment. These transactions have been recorded as ordinary sales and billed as such. On December 31 of each year, machines billed and in the hands of consignees amounted to:

1964	$6,110
1965	None
1966	5,343

Sales price was determined by adding 30% to cost.

B. Advances to suppliers have been charged to Accounts Receivable. On December 31 of each year, such advances amounted to:

1964	$2,000
1965	1,500
1966	3,800

C. Uncollectible accounts have been recorded on a direct write-off basis. Experience of similar businesses indicates that losses will approximate 1/4 of one per cent of sales. Accounts written off were:

	Year of Sales		
	1964	1965	1966
1964	$670		
1965	720	$ 480	
1966	200	1,700	$1,500

During 1966, Miscellaneous Income was credited $175 for the recovery of an account previously written off. The customer had refused to pay for the February 5, 1966 sale, alleging that the item ordered had not been delivered. Later the customer discovered that his accountant had made an error, and he mailed a check for $175.

You have decided to adopt the allowance method for uncollectible accounts for all receivables originating subsequent to December 31, 1965. Thus, uncollectible accounts traceable to 1964 and 1965 sales will not be charged to the allowance account.

D. It has been the practice of the company to sell some of its prime accounts receivable to Finance Factors, Inc. The difference between the amount received and the face amount of the receivables sold has been charged to Financial Expense. Financial Expense has been credited whenever "holdback" amounts were subsequently released by Finance Factors, Inc. All withheld amounts are expected to be recovered.

A review of the factoring transactions indicates the following:

Holdback on accounts sold in:

1964	$3,800
1965	4,450
1966	5,100

Holdback released by Finance Factors, Inc.:

1964	$2,100
1965	3,850
1966	4,700

E. Sales, as shown in the accounts, were as follows:

1964	$ 844,710
1965	905,032
1966	1,609,343

Required:

The journal entries suggested by the above data.

Problem 10-8. On April 1, 1966, State Finance Company made an agreement with Comstock Company to advance 80% of the accounts assigned by Comstock. The agreement provided for interest of 1/30 of 1% per day on the advances for the period during which the assigned account was uncollected. The agreement also provided that Comstock Company was to pay all accounts which became 20 days past due.

On April 1, 1966, the following accounts were assigned under the agreement: Acme, $7,000; Bell, $10,000; Grey, $13,000; Don, $8,000; Evers, $2,000. The finance company advanced $32,000 to Comstock Company on this date.

On April 6, Bell's account was collected in full, less 2% discount. The collection was transmitted to the finance company. The finance company acknowledged that the collection was received on April 7, and remitted $1,800 on this account.

On April 9, Comstock Company notified the finance company that Grey had been permitted a $600 allowance for damaged merchandise.

On April 12, Grey paid his account, less 2% discount. The collection reached the finance company on April 13, and the appropriate balance was remitted to Comstock Company.

The Acme account was collected on April 20, without discount. According to the advice with the cash returned by State Finance Company, the collection was received on April 21.

On April 26, the finance company reported that the Evers account was 20 days past due. The 80% advance was returned to the finance company; it reached the finance company today.

On April 28, the following accounts were assigned under the agreement: Moon, $3,000; Noon, $5,000. The finance company advanced $6,400 to Comstock Company on this date.

On May 1, the interest for April was paid. (Carry interest computation on each account to the nearest dollar.)

(a) Prepare necessary entries on the books of Comstock Company.
(b) Compute the contingent liability as of April 30, 1966.

Problem 10-9. Modern Credit Corporation has agreed to purchase selected accounts receivable from Gull Lake Company. The agreed commission was 1% and interest on advances was set at 6% per annum. The holdback was established at 20% of the account minus cash discount and commission. The commission is subject to reduction for returns or allowances in excess of 10% of the net amount of the invoice.

Prepare journal entries on the books of Gull Lake Company for the following:

(a) On March 26, 1966, the following accounts were sold under the above agreement:

Customer	Gross Amount	Terms	Invoice Date
Alpha	$5,200	2/10; n/30	March 25
Beta	8,200	2/10; n/30	March 26
Chi	3,900	2/10; n/30	March 23
Delta	4,400	2/10; n/30	March 21
Epsilon	3,100	2/10; n/30	March 26

In addition to the above instructions, compute the average "due date," using March 28 as the focal date.

(b) On June 23, 1966, an account receivable from Omega was transferred under the agreement. The gross amount of the invoice was $1,650; the terms were 2/10; n/30; and the date of the invoice was June 22.

Gull Lake Company drew an advance of $1,200 on June 24. On June 28, Omega was allowed a $200 credit for damaged merchandise.

Omega remitted in full to Modern Credit Corporation on July 2, 1966, and the factor settled this account with Gull Lake Company on the due date.

Problem 10-10. The outside auditor of a small company noticed an increase in uncollectible accounts and returns and allowances during the latter part of the current year. Because the client, Rodger Company, had engaged a new bookkeeper-cashier during the current year, the auditor decided to expand his review of the company's cash and receivables transactions. Accordingly, he accumulated the following information from the company's records for the period since the employment of the new bookkeeper-cashier.

A. Accounts receivable beginning balances: A, $290; B, $185; C, $145; D, $300; and E, $320.

B. Summary of journal entries per books, with supporting detail:

	Debit	Credit
Cash on hand	10,750	
Sales		10,750
Cash sales; no checks are accepted.		
Accounts receivable	1,940	
Sales		1,940
Sales on account: A, $180; B, $90 and $120; C, $75 and $55; E, $210 and $295; F, $175 and $240; and G, $65, $200, and $235.		
Cash on hand	1,290	
Accounts receivable		1,290
Collections on account: A, $290; B, $185; C, $130; E, $320 and $190; and F, $175.		
Sales returns and allowances	190	
Accounts receivable		190
Returns: B, $90; C, $15; E, $20; G, $65.		
Allowance for doubtful accounts	315	
Accounts receivable		315
C, $75 and F, $240.		
Notes receivable	300	
Accounts receivable		300
60-day, 6% note from D.		

Cash in bank	12,690	
Cash on hand		12,690

Currency: $10,427.
Checks: A, $290; B, $185 and $90; C, $130 and $75; D, $303; E, $320 and $190; F, $175 and $240; G, $65 and $200.

Accounts receivable	300	
Notes receivable		300

D dishonored note.

C. Weekly cash register readings—per informal record maintained by sales manager:

$1,100	$ 910
980	1,250
1,110	1,020
1,330	1,130
1,070	1,050

Prepare any correction entries that seem to be justified.

Problem 10-11. Prepare journal entries on the books of Windy Company for the following transactions.

1966

March 14—Sold merchandise to Arne Corp. for $4,360, f.o.b. shipping point. Invoice dated today; 2/10; n/30.

15—The Arne Corp. account was assigned, in return for a 75% advance, to Regional Finance Company. Interest was set at 1/30 of 1% per day on the cash advanced.

17—Credit approved for sales returns by Arne Corp. of $460.

Sold merchandise to Colorado Company for $3,220, f.o.b. shipping point. Invoice dated today; 2/10; n/30. Transportation charges of $90 will be paid by the buyer.

20—Sold merchandise to Alto Corporation for $5,420, f.o.b. destination. The invoice date was March 19, and Alto Corporation will pay transportation charges of $150. Terms, n/10.

22—Sold merchandise to Hatters Stores for $13,100. Invoice dated today. Terms, n/10; f.o.b. shipping point. Transportation charges of $80 will be paid by the buyer.

23—Received a check from Arne Corp. in satisfaction of sale of March 14. The check was forwarded to Regional Finance Company.

24—Regional Finance Company confirmed receipt of Arne Corp. check on this date. Interest charges terminated March 24.

25—Received a check from Regional Finance Company in final settlement of Arne Corp. assignment.

26—Sold merchandise to Diamond Mfg. Co. for $8,000, f.o.b. destination. Invoice was dated today and the transportation charges of $138 will be paid by the buyer. Terms, 2/10; n/30. The account was immediately sold, without guarantee, to Stout Factoring Company. The agreed commission was 1% of "net" after all deductions by the buyer, and the holdback was established at 20%. Interest of 6% per annum was agreed upon for advances. An advance of $4,000 was requested and received from the balance of $6,099.98 against which such advances could be drawn.

March 29—Received a 60-day, $4,000 note from Alto Corporation and a check in satisfaction of the remainder of the sale of March 20. The note was dated March 29 and carried interest at 5%.

31—Received a 30-day, 6% note from Hatters Stores for $13,100. The note was dated April 1.

April 4—Learned that Diamond Mfg. Co. had paid its account in full to Stout Factoring Company.

11—Discounted the note from Hatters Stores at the Second City Bank. Bank discount rate was 5%.

15—Received a check from Stout Factoring Company in settlement of the factoring arrangement.

May 1—Issued check to Second City Bank upon learning that Hatters Stores had dishonored its note. A $4 protest fee was included in the check.

Assignment Material for Chapter 11

QUESTIONS

1. In preparing your worksheet at the close of the year, how would you treat the following invoices, dated December 28, for materials shipped to your client but not received?

   (a) Invoice for $25,000; terms, 30 days net; f.o.b. destination.
   (b) Invoice for $10,000; terms, 2/10; 30 days net; f.o.b. point of origin.

2. If purchases are received during the last part of the accounting period, why is it incorrect to postpone the recording of the purchase transaction until the next accounting period if the goods are also omitted from the ending inventory?
3. Do you favor classifying under the Inventories caption of the balance sheet any advances made to vendors against purchase commitments? State your reason.
4. Under what circumstances should purchased goods in transit at the end of the period be included in the inventory?
5. Before whiskey can be "bottled in bond," it must be at least four years old. Original cost includes materials, labor, overhead, and certain taxes. Additional costs for carrying the whiskey four years include insurance, taxes, depreciation (on warehouses), warehousing labor, light and heat, and recoopering costs. The distillery may have bank loans on which interest must be paid. It has a substantial investment in warehouses, on which it believes that it is entitled to a reasonable earning.

   You are asked for an opinion about how to value the whiskey inventory at the end of the first full year after production.
6. What should be included in the inventory, and what should be excluded therefrom?
7. What is direct costing? Give some arguments for and against its use.
8. A standard cost system was installed by a company several years ago as a result of which the company has been distributing its factory overhead on a basis equivalent to approximately 200% of direct labor. For 1966, however, the actual ratio of factory overhead to direct labor was 400%, as compared with 450% for 1965. Work in process and finished stock at the end of each of these years were valued as follows:

	December 31, 1965	December 31, 1966
Material	$120,000	$150,000
Direct labor	40,000	54,000
Factory overhead	80,000	108,000
	$240,000	$312,000

Because of the poor showing in 1966, it has been suggested that the closing inventory be valued on the basis of the actual overhead rate for 1966, it having been determined that the closing inventory contained no items that were on hand January 1.

What position would you take regarding the above suggestion?

9. Under what conditions might the valuation of an inventory on a cost basis be less than actual cost?

10. Give the reason why you believe the following statement is proper or defective: If the incidental costs are immaterial, the accountant will consent to either their inclusion or their exclusion for inventory-pricing purposes.

11. Under what circumstances, if any, may standard costs be used for inventory-pricing purposes?

12. Give a brief description of the two generally accepted methods of accounting for long-term contracts.

PROBLEMS

Problem 11-1. Data relative to a commodity purchased and sold by Chevron Company are presented below.

Inventories:

	Quantity	Amount
December 31, 1965	6,000	$2,880
December 31, 1966	9,000	

Purchases during 1966:

	Quantity	Cost
February 10	4,000	$2,240
March 20	5,000	2,400
July 22	7,500	3,000
September 9	3,000	1,800
December 18	6,000	3,240

Required:

The December 31, 1966 inventory by each of the following methods:

(a) Simple average;
(b) Weighted average;
(c) First-in, first-out.

Problem 11-2. A partial perpetual inventory record of Flower Company for the month of June, 1966, is presented below.

	Quantity			Cost		
Date	Into Stock	Out of Stock	Balance	Into Stock	Out of Stock	Balance
June 1	800		800	$ 960		$960
5	400		1,200	500		
8		200	1,000			
11	600		1,600	690		
15		400	1,200			
17		500	700			
21	1,000		1,700	1,200		
25		800	900			
28	600		1,500	780		
30		350	1,150			

Compute the dollar balance that would be shown on the above perpetual inventory record as of June 30th under each of the following methods:

(a) Moving-average method;
(b) First-in, first-out method.

Problem 11-3. Martin Sales Corporation was organized January 1, 1965. The corporation lost most of its inventory in a fire on December 31, 1966, before the year-end inventory was taken. The corporation's books disclose the following:

	Year Ended December 31,	
	1965	1966
Inventory, beginning of year		$ 51,000
Purchases during year	$215,000	173,000
Purchase returns	11,530	16,150
Sales	197,000	209,000
Sales returns	4,000	5,000

At the beginning of 1966, the corporation changed its pricing policy to produce a gross profit rate three percentage points higher than the gross profit rate earned in 1965.

Undamaged merchandise salvaged was marked to sell at $6,000. Damaged merchandise marked to sell at $4,000 had an estimated realizable value of $900.

Estimate the amount of loss to the corporation's inventory arising from the fire on December 31, 1966.

Problem 11-4. A tract of land was purchased by Suburban Planning Company on January 2, 1966, for $1,100,000. Costs of leveling, platting, and staking of lots were $112,000.

Subdivision of lots was as follows:

300 lots to sell for $3,000 each
400 lots to sell for $2,000 each
200 lots to sell for $1,600 each

On December 31, 1966, the unsold lots consisted of 180 $3,000 lots, 60 $2,000 lots, and 25 $1,600 lots.

Prepare a computation of the cost of the unsold lots on December 31, 1966.

Problem 11-5. Accounts of Lewers Manufacturing Company on December 31, 1966, showed total manufacturing costs for the year to be $672,000. During 1966, 150,000 units of the single product manufactured were finished and delivered to the shipping department. On December 31, 1966, 30,000 units were in the process of manufacture; these units were, on the average, one-third completed. There were no inventories at the beginning of the year.

(a) Assuming that all manufacturing costs were incurred proportionately throughout the manufacturing process, compute the following:
  (1) The unit cost of finished goods.
  (2) The cost of the work in process inventory on December 31, 1966.
(b) Assume that the manufacturing costs for 1966 were as follows: materials, $216,000; direct labor, $336,000; and manufacturing overhead, $120,000. Assuming that all the materials for each unit were put into process when work was started, compute the cost of the work in process inventory, December 31, 1966.

Problem 11-6. During the course of the annual audit of Booming Products Company, the auditor noted the following:

(a) Merchandise on hand purchased for $1,794 was properly charged to Purchases in the records maintained by the accounting department, but it was not included in the June 30, 1966 physical inventory because no receiving slip could be found for the merchandise.

(b) Merchandise costing $1,124 was received on July 2, 1966, but it was recorded on the books as of June 30, 1966, and was included in the physical inventory on that date. The goods were shipped June 29, f.o.b. shipping point.

(c) Merchandise with a cost of $2,186 was received on June 30, 1966, as evidenced by a receiving slip, and it was included in the physical inventory as of that date. However, no entry was made for the purchase.

(d) Merchandise which cost $678 was on hand and was included in the physical inventory on June 30, 1966. It was sold and billed to a customer on June 30, 1966, for $1,084.

(e) Merchandise with a cost of $697 was in the shipping department on June 30, 1966, but was not included in the physical inventory because it had been billed to customers on June 30, 1966, for $1,120. The goods were shipped and title thereto passed on July 5, 1966.

All revenue and expense accounts have been closed as of June 30, 1966. However, the Revenue and Expense summary account has been held open awaiting any auditor's adjustments before closing to Retained Earnings.

Prepare the journal entries that the auditor should make as of June 30, 1966, in connection with the above disclosures.

Problem 11-7. The following account balances were taken from the December 31, 1966 trial balance of Crescent Production Company:

Work in process, December 31, 1965	$ 90,000
Materials used	540,000
Direct labor	450,000
Manufacturing overhead	180,000

At the beginning of the year there were 36,000 units in the work in process inventory; each unit was one-fourth completed.

The December 31, 1966 inventory of work in process contained 81,000 units one-third completed. During the year 981,000 units were started in the manufacturing process. All the materials were put into process at the start of production.

There were 135,000 finished units on hand at the end of the year; all were units started in production during 1966.

Required:

(a) A determination of the cost of the work in process inventory of December 31, 1966.

(b) A determination of the cost of the finished goods inventory of December 31, 1966.

Carry unit cost computations to the nearest cent.

Problem 11-8. Whiting Company, which does not maintain perpetual inventory records, was in the process of moving to a new location at the close of its fiscal year, January 31, 1966. As a consequence, some confusion prevailed in relation to the inventory cut-off, as indicated by the following:

(1) One lot of merchandise with a cost of $4,306 was counted twice.

(2) Merchandise on hand costing $1,640 was included in the inventory although the invoice was not recorded until February 10, 1966.

(3) Merchandise in transit, shipped to the company f.o.b. shipping point, was

recorded as a purchase as of January 31, 1966, at its cost of $8,200, but was not included in the inventory.

(4) Merchandise shipped on January 31, 1966, f.o.b. destination and received by the customer on February 4, 1966, was not included in the inventory. The cost of this merchandise was $1,750; the sale was recorded at $2,410 on January 31, 1966.

(5) Merchandise costing $4,390 was included in the inventory, although it was shipped to a customer on January 31, 1966, f.o.b. shipping point, and the company recorded the sale ($5,800) on that date.

Required:

(a) On the assumption that the company's books were closed January 31, 1966, without discovery of these errors, a computation of the amount of overstatement or understatement of cost of goods sold which would appear in the income statements for the fiscal years ended January 31, 1966 and 1967.

(b) On the same assumption as in (a), a computation of the overstatement or understatement of Retained Earnings as of January 31, 1966 and 1967.

(c) On the assumption that the errors were not discovered until the latter part of the fiscal year ending on January 31, 1967, the journal entry (or entries) necessary to correct the books at that time.

Ignore income taxes.

Problem 11-9. Celebrity Company included the following items under Inventories on its December 31, 1966 balance sheet:

Materials	$34,918
Advances for materials ordered for February, 1967 delivery	1,802
Work in process	16,804
Unexpired insurance on inventories	516
Advertising catalogs	1,710
Shipping cartons	892
Finished goods in factory	41,305
Finished goods in company-owned retail store, at 120% of cost	9,168
Finished goods in hands of consignees (at 180% of cost)	6,300
Finished goods in transit to customers (shipped f.o.b. point of shipment)	6,820
Finished goods out on approval, at cost (selling price, $1,500)	950
Unsalable finished goods, at cost	580
Office supplies	904
Samples held by distributors, at selling price (cost, $2,400)	4,320
Materials in transit (shipped f.o.b. shipping point), plus estimated freight of $340	2,850
Merchandise held on consignment from Ajax Novelty Company, at sales price (sales commission, 30% of selling price)	7,917

Prepare a partial balance sheet for the company on December 31, 1966, giving appropriate disclosure of the above items.

Problem 11-10. During 1966, Plaid Fabrics Company produced 718,400 square yards of floor-covering materials. The product was priced on the basis of uniformity of texture and appearance as follows:

Grade	Price in cents per square yard
A	80
B	75
C	65
D	60
E	50

Total cost of goods manufactured for 1966 amounted to $360,000. Inventories and sales were as follows:

	Inventories in Square Yards		
Grade	January 1, 1966	December 31, 1966	Sales—at List Prices
A	31,000	14,720	$109,024
B	41,200	42,800	114,000
C	30,000	22,000	130,000
D	27,000	18,340	110,796
E	12,400	10,200	39,500
Totals	141,600	108,060	$503,320

Compute the cost of the December 31, 1966 inventory, showing your computations in detail.

Problem 11-11. Topper Manufacturing Company during 1966, its first year of operation, finished 45,000 units of a single product, for which all production costs are incurred evenly as processing occurs. The factory manager has questioned the valuation of his inventories and engaged you to make a verification of these items. The inventories are:

Materials		$ 22,000
Goods in process (2/3 completed):		
Materials	$16,000	
Direct labor	20,000	
Overhead	14,000	50,000
Finished goods (9,000 units)		225,000

The cost sheets show materials issuances of $376,000 and direct labor charges of $470,000. Analysis of factory overhead for the year, which is prorated over the product on a basis of direct labor cost, is as follows:

Indirect labor	$131,500
Freight in on materials	39,800
Heat, light, and power	21,000
Factory supplies	16,800
Advertising	27,400
Repairs	29,500
Depreciation—Plant and equipment	36,200
Shipping expenses	26,800
Total	$329,000

The freight in on materials shown above is the total paid for this item of expense; all materials are purchased from the same source and shipped in the same manner.

Required:

Computations showing the correct cost of materials, goods in process, and finished goods inventories on December 31, 1966.

Problem 11-12. Gifts Unlimited, Inc., lost a significant portion of its inventory to thieves late in December of 1966. The company determined that the inventory immediately after the theft amounted to $22,105. The following information was taken from the records of the company.

	1966 to Date of Theft	1965
Purchases	$129,045	$134,433
Purchase returns and allowances	6,021	7,017
Sales	196,677	203,317
Sales returns and allowances	2,402	2,167
Wages	17,743	18,356
Salaries	8,000	9,000
Taxes other than income	3,732	3,648
Rent	5,400	5,400
Insurance	967	982
Light, heat, and water	1,134	1,271
Advertising	4,250	2,680
Interest expense	2,755	3,020
Depreciation expense	1,255	1,280
Furniture and fixtures, net of depreciation	10,065	10,570
Miscellaneous expenses	6,634	6,897
Beginning inventory	47,880	49,200

From the above information, estimate the cost of the inventory stolen.

Problem 11-13. The data given are from the records of Status Company. Using first-in, first-out procedures, (a) determine the inventory balances under direct costing and conventional costing.

(b) Would the net income before income taxes for 1966 be higher or lower, and by how much, if direct costing had been adopted in place of conventional costing when the company was organized in 1964?

	Year		
Units	1964	1965	1966
Completed	30,000	42,000	51,000
Completed, but unsold:			
Beginning of year	-0-	3,000	5,000
End of year	3,000	5,000	10,000
In process:			
Beginning of year	-0-	9,000	8,000
End of year (2/3 complete)	9,000		
End of year (1/2 complete)		8,000	
End of year (1/4 complete)			12,000
Dollars			
Manufacturing costs:			
Fixed	$ 72,000	$ 72,000	$ 72,000
Variable	108,000	120,000	150,000
Selling expenses:			
Fixed	12,000	12,000	12,000
Variable	27,000	37,000	46,000
Administrative expenses:			
Fixed	18,000	18,000	18,000
Variable	40,500	55,500	69,000

Problem 11-14. Tall Construction Company signed a long-term construction contract in 1963. The contract price was $590,000, and the company expected to earn $90,000 on the contract, before income taxes.

Prepare a schedule showing the income earned each year under the percentage-of-completion method. Ignore income taxes.

Year Ended December 31,	Actual Costs	Estimated Cost to Complete Contract
1963	$ 50,000	$450,000
1964	147,600	322,400
1965	208,000	114,400
1966	112,000	-0-
Total actual costs	$517,600	

Problem 11-15. The Pontiac Corporation has followed the practice of inventorying its finished goods at selling prices and has prepared the following statement on this basis.

THE PONTIAC CORPORATION
Income Statement
For the Year Ended December 31, 1966

Sales			$478,150
Cost of goods sold:			
Materials used (at cost)		$110,681	
Direct labor		152,081	
Manufacturing overhead		51,954	
Total manufacturing costs		$314,716	
Work in process (at cost):			
December 31, 1965	$188,114		
December 31, 1966	128,205	59,909	
Goods manufactured		$374,625	
Finished goods (at selling prices):			
December 31, 1965	$ 79,850		
December 31, 1966	226,075	146,225	228,400
Gross profit			$249,750
Selling and administrative expenses			209,300
Net income			$ 40,450

Prepare a corrected statement, assuming that the per cent of markup for the current year is normal. Show supporting computations.

Problem 11-16. Johnson Construction Company was engaged, on January 1, 1966, to erect a city-county building under a contract which called for a total price of $840,000 to be paid to Johnson Construction Company in five payments. One-fifth of the price was to be paid upon the completion of each quarter of the work (as defined in detail by the terms of the contract), the final payment being due within 30 days after the company had entirely executed its obligations under the contract.

On December 28, 1966, three-fourths of the building was completed, whereupon the third billing was made in accordance with the contract. Previously, cash was received for the first two billings.

During 1966, a total of $425,000 had been disbursed by the company for costs incurred under the contract, and the outstanding accounts payable for materials purchased for this construction amounted to $125,000 at year end. It was estimated that an additional $150,000 would be required to complete the contract.

Prepare a schedule showing the December 31, 1966 balances in the following accounts: Cost of Contract Work, Revenue from Contract Work, Contract Value of Work in Process Unbilled, and Accounts Receivable.

Problem 11-17. Diversified Construction Company was organized on January 2, 1966. The following cash transactions occurred during 1966.

Cash receipts:	
Proceeds from issuance of capital stock	$ 50,000
Received on contracts	470,000
Cash disbursements:	
Contract costs	$420,600
Construction equipment	45,000
Administrative expenses	22,400

During 1966, six contracts were signed. Data about the contracts are presented below.

Contract No.	Contract Price	Estimated Cost	Cash Costs to Date	Unpaid Bills 12/31/66	1966 Billings	1966 Collections
1	$100,000	$ 85,000	$ 85,500		$100,000	$100,000
2	140,000	120,000	82,000	$ 8,000	105,000	97,500
3	127,500	109,750	108,000		127,500	125,000
4	250,000	225,000	100,000	12,500	110,000	90,000
5	45,000	35,000	29,000	2,500	40,500	37,500
6	170,000	150,000	16,100	6,400	25,000	20,000

Other data:

Billings are made on a percentage-of-completion basis.

A suitable depreciation rate for the construction equipment is 20%. The use made of the construction equipment is in proportion to the other construction costs.

Contracts 1 and 3 were completed during 1966.

Administrative expenses are considered as period costs.

Prepare the December 31, 1966 balance sheet following the completed-contract method. If a provision for income taxes is required, use a rate of 20%.

Assignment Material for Chapter 12

QUESTIONS

1. The following data relate to an inventory item on hand at the year end: cost, $75; market value, $50; selling price less estimated cost to complete and sell, $68; selling price less estimated cost to complete and sell at a normal profit margin, $52. At what price should this item be inventoried at the year end in conformity with A.R.B. 43? What objection can you see to this inventory procedure?
2. Give an evaluation of the cost-or-market basis of inventory valuation.
3. What are the advantages to the use of inventory loss and inventory contra accounts in conjunction with the cost-or-market inventory method?
4. Why is the propriety of the old cost-or-market rule now being subjected to some questioning?
5. Whenever work in process reaches a stage of completion at which there is an established market for such partially finished goods, can such market-price data be used in valuing the work in process inventory?
6. On what basis should merchandise repossessed in a damaged condition be valued for inventory purposes?
7. Mention two conditions under which it might be proper to value inventories on the basis of selling prices. Does "on the basis of selling prices" mean the same thing as "at selling prices"?
8. The variety of methods of inventory pricing regarded as acceptable may affect the comparability of: (a) the income statements of a company for successive periods, and (b) the income statements of two or more companies for the same year. What accounting principle minimizes the hazards of noncomparability? Does the minimization apply equally to (a) and (b)?
9. A trading concern valued its inventory on December 31, 1965, at market value, which was less than cost. The valuation on this basis was $60,000. Believing that there might be further declines in market value after the first of the year, the directors decided to set up a reserve of $5,000 to provide for possible losses resulting from such declines. During 1966, the market value did further decline, and it was estimated that the goods on hand on December 31, 1965, could have been purchased in 1966 for $57,000. At what value should the inventory on December 31, 1965, be shown in the income statements for the years 1965 and 1966? How should the $5,000 reserve have been set up on December 31, 1965? What disposition should finally be made of it?
10. Indicate two ways in which the accountant can make use of the retail inventory method.

PROBLEMS

Problem 12-1. State, for each of the items listed below, the unit value which would be employed for inventory-pricing purposes, using lower of cost or market as defined by Bulletin 43 of the Committee on Accounting Procedure of the American Institute of Certified Public Accountants.

Item	Original Cost	Replacement Cost	Selling Price	Estimated Cost to Complete and Sell	Normal Profit Margin
a	$1.16	$1.22	$1.50	$.18	$.06
b	.42	.40	.44	.05	.02
c	4.06	4.00	4.50	.33	.18
d	.91	.85	.95	.05	.04
e	.20	.18	.22	.03	.01
f	1.46	1.50	1.70	.12	.06
g	2.18	2.10	2.20	.12	.08
h	.65	.60	.70	.04	.03

Problem 12-2. The warehouse inventory of Modern Furniture Company on December 31, 1966, was prepared as shown below:

	Classification	Count	Unit Cost	Unit market to replace on December 31, 1966	Unit sale price less cost to complete and sell	Unit sale price less cost to complete and sell and normal profit margin
Living room suites:	A-1	5	$80	$85	$150	$110
	A-2	2	70	68	135	102
	A-3	4	50	46	88	63
Bedroom suites:	B-1	6	60	58	84	66
	B-2	1	55	56	82	60
	B-3	3	30	35	50	34
	B-4	2	35	33	57	34
Dining room suites:	C-1	4	85	82	81	78
	C-2	2	90	94	124	102
Dinette sets:	C-11	6	40	37	64	51
	C-12	7	30	26	25	22
Tables:	D-1	11	30	35	48	40
	D-2	14	22	24	28	23
	D-3	6	10	9	16	12
	D-4	5	14	15	20	16
Chairs:	E-1	22	45	42	66	48
	E-2	12	50	35	49	37
Lamps:	F-1	17	9	11	14	12
	F-2	6	10	9	15	13
	F-3	14	7	8	10	6

Some items are shipped to the company unassembled and must be assembled and finished at the warehouse. Effect is given to this in the computations above.

Compute the December 31, 1966 inventory using the lower-of-cost-or-market (item-by-item) method as set forth in Accounting Research Bulletin 43 of the American Institute of Certified Public Accountants.

Problem 12-3. The data presented at the top of page 677 were taken from the October 31, 1966 inventory records of Valley Hardware Company.

Item	Quantity	Unit Price Cost	Unit Price Market
Garden tools:			
Wheelbarrows	28	$ 16.50	$ 16.00
Rakes	79	4.10	4.30
Shovels	106	2.90	2.80
Appliances:			
Stoves	24	161.10	156.00
Refrigerators	18	204.00	210.00
Washing machines	12	147.00	144.00
Building supplies:			
Nails—lbs.	284	.18	.16
Screws—lbs.	187	.37	.40
Bolts and nuts—lbs.	140	.78	.70

Price the above inventory, using the lower-of-cost-or-market method, applied:

(1) Item by item.
(2) To categories of inventory.
(3) To total inventory.

Problem 12-4. Triangle Sales Corporation presents the following data to be used in pricing its inventory on December 31, 1966.

The corporation prices its inventory on the first-in, first-out basis and does not use a perpetual inventory system.

The last three purchases for the year 1966, of the commodities sold by the corporation, are shown below:

Commodity	Quantity	Invoice Unit Price	Per Unit Transportation In
1	800	$ 7.00	$ .40
1	1,100	7.40	.40
1 (most recent)	600	7.70	.44
2	200	12.00	1.20
2	400	11.00	1.20
2 (most recent)	300	10.50	1.32
3	500	24.00	1.60
3	450	23.00	1.76
3 (most recent)	400	21.00	1.76
4	700	30.00	2.20
4	2,000	30.00	2.20
4 (most recent)	800	30.00	2.42

Additional information indicates inventories and market prices (f.o.b. shipping point) to be:

Commodity	December 31, 1966 Inventory Quantities	December 31, 1966 Market Price
1	700	$ 7.50
2	800	11.00
3	1,000	20.00
4	900	30.00

Commodity 4 was purchased on a contract to buy all units purchased during the year at this price, and if purchases for the year exceeded 25,000 units, a refund of $3.00 per unit was to be given. It is found that the corporation has made net purchases of 25,600 units in this year and has filed a claim for rebate.

Compute the company's inventory as of December 31, 1966, using the lower of cost or market as determined by:

(a) Item-by-item method.
(b) Total-inventory method.

Problem 12-5. From the data below, taken from the departmental records of Community Discounters, compute the January 31, 1966 inventory, using the retail inventory method. Carry per cents to two decimal places.

Inventory, January 31, 1965:	
Cost	$ 55,620
Selling price	87,020
Purchases:	
Cost	285,982
Selling price	436,880
Transportation in	7,660
Returns:	
Purchases:	
Cost	2,620
Selling price	4,920
Sales	8,280
Purchase discounts	4,820
Markups	10,620
Markdowns	16,240
Cancellations of markups	3,720
Sales	442,420

Problem 12-6. Fashion Wholesale Company experiences a substantial variation in the rate of markon applicable to its spring- and fall-season merchandise. In the past, this has been ignored and the December 31 inventories have been computed by the use of the retail inventory method applied on an annual basis.

During 1966, the difference in ratio of cost to selling price as between the first and last half of the year was larger than in the past, and the treasurer decided that this variation should be given recognition in the computation of the December 31, 1966 inventory.

A summary of the retail records for the year ended December 31, 1966, appeared as follows:

Inventory, December 31, 1965:	
Cost	$ 485,600
Selling price	694,300
Purchases:	
Cost	3,062,700
Selling price	4,311,500
Inward freight	33,400
Costs of altering merchandise before showing	14,800
Markdowns—net	36,600
Sales	4,512,300

Further analysis of the retail records shows the following amounts to be applicable to the six months ended June 30, 1966:

Purchases:	
Cost	$1,490,200
Selling price	1,816,500
Inward freight	14,600
Costs of altering merchandise before showing	6,900
Markdowns—net	19,200
Sales	1,948,500

Compute the December 31, 1966 inventory:

(a) On the basis of an annual calculation.

(b) Giving recognition to the variation in markon between the first and last half of the year.

Carry per cents to two decimal places and amounts to the nearest dollar.

Problem 12-7. Round Top Corporation has followed the practice of showing cash discounts in its income statement as financial income and expense, and of valuing its inventory at cost without deduction for cash discounts on purchases. It desires to change, for the year 1966, to a basis of reporting discounts in its income statement as deductions from sales and purchases and of valuing its inventory net of purchase discounts. As the company's auditor, you are concerned as to whether the change in procedure will affect the net income enough to make it necessary for you to include in your opinion a qualification relative to consistency.

The following account balances were taken from the company's December 31, 1966 trial balance:

Sales	$1,147,000
Sales returns	37,000
Sales discounts	22,200
Purchases	790,000
Transportation inward	24,000
Purchase returns	14,000
Purchase discounts	15,520
Merchandise inventory, December 31, 1965	148,000
Selling expense	81,400
Administrative expense	165,200

The December 31, 1966 inventory has not been completed, but it is known that the average gross profit rate for the preceding three years was 30% of net sales, and there is no reason to believe that there was any change in the rate in 1966.

Make the estimate of the effect of the change on the net income before income taxes.

Problem 12-8. Western Bank, which holds promissory notes of Liberty Stores Corporation, was not satisfied with the amount at which the corporation stated its merchandise inventory in its January 31, 1966 balance sheet. As a result of this feeling, the bank suggested that the corporation engage an independent accountant to examine its inventory accounting and pricing procedures. You have been retained by Liberty Stores Corporation for this purpose, and in the course of your examination you discover the following:

(1) The corporation has employed the retail method in the computation of merchandise inventory for several years, using the cost ratio thus computed to reduce the physical inventory, taken at selling price, approximately to lower of cost or market.

(2) The following calculations were made in the computation of the January 31, 1966 inventory:

	Cost	Selling Price
Inventory, January 31, 1965	$ 59,190	$ 83,120
Purchases—net	284,090	401,050
Markups—net of markup cancellations		6,230
Total	$343,280	$490,400

Cost ratio—70%.

Inventory, January 31, 1966:	
Selling price	$ 90,400
Cost ($90,400 × 70%)	63,280

(3) You find that the merchandise handled by the corporation is of two classes, Type A and Type B, with sharply differing ratios of cost to selling price. A review of the merchandise records for the year ended January 31, 1966, discloses that Type A merchandise accounted for the following amounts:

	Cost	Selling Price
Inventory, January 31, 1965	$ 43,600	$ 52,350
Purchases—net	226,850	278,420
Markups—net		4,640
Inventory, January 31, 1966		46,240

(4) During the year ended January 31, 1966, several lots of special-sale merchandise were purchased, and the following amounts are included in the data for Type A merchandise presented above, representing special-sale goods:

	Cost	Selling Price
Purchases—net	$ 22,350	$ 24,300
Inventory, January 31, 1966		2,200

Compute the January 31, 1966 merchandise inventory which you would report to Western Bank.

Show calculations and carry per cents to two decimal places—for example, 45.85%—and amounts to the nearest dollar.

Problem 12-9. On December 31, 1966, Stanton Products, Incorporated, had an inventory of merchandise in the amount of $72,000, at cost, and $67,500 at the lower of cost or market. It was believed that a further decline of $7,500 would be experienced before the merchandise could be sold. Accordingly, the company made two journal entries to disclose the above situation.

(a) Give the two journal entries.
(b) What entries should be made if the expected decline in market value occurs in 1967?
(c) State how both balance sheet accounts created in (a) should have appeared in the December 31, 1966 balance sheet.
(d) How should the inventory have appeared in the income statement for 1966?
(e) Give the entries that would be made on December 31, 1967, if cost and lower of cost or market of the inventory on that date were equal and no future price declines were anticipated.

Problem 12-10. Central Variety Store, which uses the retail inventory method, has prepared the following summary of merchandise transactions covering the six-month period ended June 30, 1966:

	Cost	Retail
Inventory, December 31, 1965	$ 82,420	$119,800
Net purchases	621,300	884,600
Markups		28,100
Markdowns		14,150
Net sales		902,340
Markup cancellations		6,100
Markdown cancellations		3,950
Physical inventory, June 30, 1966, at marked selling prices		108,450

Required:

(Carry per cents to two decimal places and amounts to the nearest dollar.)

(1) The June 30, 1966 inventory, stated at approximate lower of cost or market.
(2) The loss from inventory shortages.
(3) The cost of goods sold, assuming that 50% of the loss from inventory shortage is considered abnormal and should be separately reported.

Problem 12-11. The account balances listed below were taken from the ledger of Modesto Corporation on June 30, 1966, before any year-end adjusting or closing entries were made.

Sales	$481,200
Inventory, June 30, 1965—at cost	31,200
Reduction of inventory to lower of cost or market—June 30, 1965	4,650
Purchases	369,100
Purchase returns and allowances	2,340
Transportation in	1,010
Selling expenses	39,200
Administrative expenses	41,250
Retained earnings, June 30, 1965	88,130
Dividends	15,000

On June 30, 1966, the corporation had outstanding purchase commitments, at firm prices, aggregating $22,000. Management is concerned about these commitments because recent market reports predict price declines. Should the price declines materialize, the corporation would stand to lose about $4,000 on the goods on order. Management desires to establish a reserve for such possible loss.

The June 30, 1966 inventory sheets of Modesto Corporation showed the following:

Inventory at cost	$37,150
Inventory at the lower of cost or market	35,900

Prepare the income statement and the statement of retained earnings for the year ended June 30, 1966. Ignore income taxes.

Problem 12-12. Olin Corporation was organized and began operations on July 1, 1965, for the purpose of manufacturing a single product. The manufacturing operations were organized into two departments. The first department manufactured parts which were assembled into the finished product in the second department. The condensed income statement for the year ended June 30, 1966, was as follows:

OLIN CORPORATION
Income Statement
Year Ended June 30, 1966

Sales			$181,600
Cost of goods sold:			
Materials used—Cost	$68,200		
Direct labor	91,400		
Manufacturing overhead	24,600		
Total manufacturing costs		$184,200	
Deduct work in process		10,200	
Cost of goods manufactured		$174,000	
Deduct finished goods		15,520	
Cost of goods sold			158,480
Gross profit on sales			$ 23,120
Operating expenses			42,500
Net loss			$ 19,380

An examination of the accounts of the corporation disclosed the following:

(1) Olin Corporation did not use perpetual inventories, but computed June 30, 1966 inventories on the basis of a physical count of work in process and finished goods.

(2) The inventory of work in process on June 30, 1966, consisted entirely of finished parts ready for assembly in the second department. These parts had been priced at the amount for which they could be purchased from an outside supplier. Manufacturing records showed that the cost of producing these parts in the first department was $8,600.

(3) The June 30, 1966 balance sheet showed an inventory of scrap parts of $3,200, representing the estimated realizable value as scrap metal of finished parts spoiled in the assembly process. This inventory was recorded by a debit to Scrap Inventory and a credit which was reflected in the income statement as a reduction in operating expenses.

A summary of manufacturing operations in the second department showed the following:

Finished units started and completed	1,000
Finished units on hand on June 30, 1966	80
Finished units sold	920

The manufacturing cost data used in pricing the June 30, 1966 inventory of finished goods were as follows:

Finished parts used—at price at which available from outside suppliers (cost in first department, $92,100)	$110,500
Other materials used	6,500
Direct labor	60,700
Manufacturing overhead	16,300
Total	$194,000

Prepare a revised income statement for Olin Corporation taking into account the information presented above. Show computations supporting any adjustments of the original figures.

Problem 12-13. Regal Company was organized in January of 1965. The lower-of-cost-or-market inventory method was adopted and it was to be applied by comparing the total cost and market for the entire inventory. A contra account was to be used to disclose market losses. Because of market losses, the following entry was made as of December 31, 1965:

Loss on reduction of inventory to lower of cost or market.......	850	
Reduction of inventory to lower of cost or market		850

During 1966, the following procedures were applied to the Inventory account:

(1) Purchases were charged to the Inventory account at cost.
(2) The Inventory account was reduced for goods sold by the use of the unit costs applicable to the December 31, 1965 inventory.

During 1966, the prices of all categories of goods purchased for resale gradually and steadily increased. Nevertheless, December 31, 1965 unit cost data were used throughout the year in making the daily computation for the cost of goods sold entry.

By the end of 1966, costs had increased to such an extent that the accountant for Regal Company became concerned about the prospect of inventory price declines in the near future. He could not believe that the market prices prevailing at year end, the highest for many years, would continue for long. Accordingly, he used the same unit cost data used in pricing the December 31, 1965 inventory to price the December 31, 1966 inventory. The inventory dollar amount was thus more conservative and less vulnerable to losses from future price declines.

The December 31, 1966 inventory priced at December 31, 1965 costs amounted to $10,000. Because this was lower than the balance in the Inventory account at year end, he increased the contra account, set up last year to disclose market losses, by the following journal entry dated December 31, 1966:

Cost of goods sold......................................	6,950	
Reduction of inventory to lower of cost or market......		6,950

The following T-accounts show, in summary form in some instances, the entries made in compliance with the policies and decisions mentioned above.

Inventory

12/31/65	Inventory, at cost ..	9,700	1966	Cost of goods sold, priced at 12/31/65 unit costs	119,700
1966	Purchases, at cost ..	127,800			

Reduction of Inventory to Lower of Cost or Market

			12/31/65	Disclosure of market losses	850
			12/31/66	Special adjustment .	6,950

Cost of Goods Sold

1966	Cost of goods sold ..	119,700			
12/31/66	Special adjustment .	6,950			

Prepare a more acceptable estimate of the December 31, 1966 inventory for use in the 1966 financial statements. Also adjust the cost of goods sold to conform to your estimate of the December 31, 1966 inventory. You may assume that the merchandise flow follows a first-in, first-out sequence and that the business is not subject to seasonal volume changes.

Assignment Material for Chapter 13

QUESTIONS

1. What are the major arguments advanced by the proponents of the *lifo* method of inventory valuation?
2. What is the major argument advanced by the opponents of the *lifo* method?
3. Under what circumstances might a strict application of the *lifo* method result in matching some old costs as well as some current costs against current revenues?
4. In the statements prepared at the close of the period in which *lifo* is adopted, an accounting principle requires that a certain disclosure be made. What should be disclosed, and what principle requires the disclosure?
5. Assume that the end-of-year inventory quantity of a certain article exceeded the beginning-of-year quantity. State three bases for determining the *lifo* cost of the incremental quantity. Which basis is consistent with *lifo* theory?
6. The January 1, 1965 inventory in a department of a retail store was $30,000 at cost and $48,000 at retail on the *lifo* basis. The December 31, 1965 inventory in this department was $45,000 at retail. Retail prices at this time were 110% of retail prices on January 1, 1965. Markon for the year 1965 was 40%. Compute the December 31, 1965 inventory at cost on the *lifo* basis.
7. If you were on a corporate policy committee, and prices were rising, would you favor the adoption of *lifo* for income tax considerations? State your reason.
8. Describe the application of the dollar-value *lifo* inventory method.
9. A company uses the retail inventory procedure and prices inventories by the *lifo* method. In recent years, selling prices have increased considerably from year to year for the same inventory items. If these changes in selling price are ignored in the inventory computations, what will be the effect on the inventory figure? State how you would correct for the above situation in the computation of the inventory under the *lifo* retail method.
10. Describe the modifications to the retail inventory method when the *lifo* concept is applied to that method.

PROBLEMS

Problem 13-1. Trailway Company decided to drop the first-in, first-out inventory method and adopt the last-in, first-out inventory method as of December 31, 1966. The company also decided that in the application of the *lifo* method, it would assume that incremental quantities related to the earliest acquisitions of the given period.

Using the following data, compute the December 31, 1966 inventory, following the *lifo* method. Also determine the effect of the change in inventory method on the 1966 net income before income taxes.

December 31, 1965 inventory (*fifo*):

Item	Quantity	Unit Cost	Total
WW	200	$5.09	$1,018
	100	5.06	506
	300	5.00	1,500
Total			$3,024

1966 purchases of WW:

Date	Quantity	Unit Cost	Total
January 20	200	$5.08	$1,016
April 1	320	5.10	1,632
June 5	400	5.07	2,028
August 25	500	5.08	2,540
October 10	300	5.10	1,530
December 22	100	5.12	512

December 31, 1966 inventory: 900 units of WW

Problem 13-2. Riverside Sales Corporation adopted the last-in, first-out inventory method at the end of 1964.

Inventories on December 31, 1963 and 1964, for the single product sold by the corporation, were computed as follows:

	1963		1964	
12,000 units at $1.30	$15,600			
9,000 units at $1.40	12,600			
3,000 units at $1.50	4,500	$32,700		
24,000 units at $1.3625			$32,700	
2,000 units at $1.60 (from the earliest acquisition in 1964)			3,200	$35,900

Purchases for the years 1965 and 1966 are detailed below:

1965		
January	27	3,000 units at $1.90
March	5	4,000 units at $2.00
April	12	11,000 units at $2.10
May	29	20,000 units at $2.30
June	28	16,000 units at $2.40
August	10	12,000 units at $2.50
October	1	5,000 units at $2.60
December	14	4,000 units at $2.65
1966		
January	10	2,000 units at $2.70
February	23	4,000 units at $2.68
May	3	7,000 units at $2.55
June	17	12,000 units at $2.40
August	3	11,000 units at $2.10
September	30	8,000 units at $1.90
November	8	5,000 units at $1.65
December	26	12,000 units at $1.20

Inventories on December 31, 1965 and 1966, were 19,000 units and 28,000 units, respectively. Compute the cost of these inventories on the last-in, first-out basis.

Problem 13-3. Artic Company has been using the first-in, first-out method of inventory valuation, but in 1966 the company decides to price its year-end inventories on the last-in, first-out basis. It plans to price any layers by reference to the last acquisitions of the current year.

The company gives you the following pertinent information and requests that you compute the December 31, 1966 inventory on the new basis and also prepare an appropriate footnote, covering the above change, to accompany the financial statements in the company's published annual report for the year 1966.

	Quantity			Unit purchase price		
	X	Y	Z	X	Y	Z
1965 purchases						
February 20	2,000	4,000		$12.40	$17.00	
April 29		9,000	1,000		17.00	$23.00
June 14	7,000		3,000	12.60		23.00
September 4		13,000	5,000		17.60	24.00
October 19	15,000	4,000	2,000	12.80	17.80	26.00
November 23	3,000			13.00		
December 15	2,000	3,000	1,000	13.20	18.00	26.80
1966 purchases						
January 25			500			27.00
March 10	6,000	2,500	1,000	13.40	18.20	27.05
May 16	5,000	4,000		13.50	18.40	
August 8		8,000	2,000		18.50	27.20
October 21	1,000	10,000	6,000	13.52	18.54	27.28
December 12		3,000			18.60	
Inventory quantities						
December 31:						
1965	2,500	2,500	2,000			
1966	3,700	2,400	2,200			

Problem 13-4. *XYZ* Corporation has been using a modified retail inventory method designed to approximate the cost method. The corporation wishes to change to the last-in, first-out retail method beginning with the year ending December 31, 1966.

The corporation's records provide the following information:

	At Cost	At Retail
Inventory, December 31, 1965	$ 5,190	$ 15,000
Purchases—1966	47,250	100,000
Markups		7,000
Markdowns		2,000
Sales—1966		95,000

Compute the December 31, 1966 inventory following the *lifo* method. Also determine the effect of the change in inventory method on the 1966 net income before income taxes. Prices remained relatively stable during 1966.

Problem 13-5. Rugged Corporation deals in one commodity. The following amounts were received and sold during 1966:

Period	Purchases: Units	Purchases: Unit Price	Units Sold
First quarter	20,000	$2.10	
Second quarter	30,000	2.20	
Third quarter	28,000	2.30	
Fourth quarter	10,000	2.40	
Total sales for year			80,000

The company expects to pay $2.50 per unit for purchases in the next year.

All purchases were made on the first day of the quarter; the inventory on January 1, 1966, consisted of 12,000 units priced at cost, at $2.00 each.

The company is contemplating changing its inventory method and has requested its accountant to prepare a statement showing the results of several inventory methods on the income statement for 1966. The directors inform the accountant that an inventory of 10,000 units would be the minimum that the company should have. The accountant prepared the following statement:

	Method			
	A	B	C	D
Sales	$286,500	$286,500	$286,500	$286,500
Cost of goods sold	176,400	173,400	176,320	179,600
Gross profit	$110,100	$113,100	$110,180	$106,900

Identify the inventory methods used, showing computations required to establish the identity of each method.

Problem 13-6. During 1966, Golden Company experienced a 33⅓ per cent gross profit rate, compared with the 30 per cent rate it had averaged in recent years. You are asked to determine the most likely cause of this improvement and to compute the extent of its effect.

The following data are from the records of the company:

1966 sales (at an average price of $15.90 per unit)	$817,260
1966 purchases (at an average cost of $11.13 per unit)	470,799
Inventory method—Last-in, first-out, since 1960.	

Problem 13-7. Given the following data, compute the inventory for December 31, 1964, 1965, 1966, and 1967, using the dollar-value *lifo* method. The company adopted *lifo* as of January 1, 1961. The inventory shown in the December 31, 1963 balance sheet amounted to $18,000, which was less than the inventory when *lifo* was adopted.

Inventory Data

	Inventory Computed by Using Average Costs of	
	Current Year	Base Year
December 31, 1964	$19,982	$19,400
December 31, 1965	21,000	20,000
December 31, 1966	21,600	20,000
December 31, 1967	21,780	19,800

Problem 13-8. Fargo Company adopted the last-in, first-out method of inventory pricing in connection with its use of the retail inventory method during 1964. The inventory on December 31, 1963, was $46,400 at retail and $27,840 at *lifo* cost. The retail records for the years 1964, 1965, and 1966 show the following:

Year ended December 31:	Cost	Retail
1964:		
Opening inventory	$ 27,840	$ 46,400
Purchases	228,800	351,400
Markups—net		2,100
Markdowns—net		1,500
Sales		345,800

1965:		
Purchases	$238,000	$340,600
Markups—net		2,800
Markdowns—net		3,400
Sales		330,400
1966:		
Purchases	257,950	382,500
Markups—net		5,100
Markdowns—net		2,600
Sales		408,200

Compute the inventories on December 31, 1964, 1965, and 1966, in accordance with the last-in, first-out concept used in conjunction with the retail method. (Assume that selling prices did not change during the three years ended December 31, 1966.)

Problem 13-9. Family Retail Store had been using the retail inventory method. Early in 1961 a decision was reached to modify the retail method to last-in first-out. Using the following data, compute the year-end inventories for the years 1961 through 1966. You may assume that prices remained stable during this period until 1966. In 1966, prices increased 5%.

	Year Ended December 31,			
	1960		1961	
	Cost	Retail	Cost	Retail
Inventory, beginning of year	$ 22,540	$ 32,200	?	$ 37,100
Purchases	142,094	211,000	$153,318	217,440
Transportation in	8,674		9,132	
Markups		2,100		2,220
Markdowns		3,700		3,060
Sales		204,500		211,500

Year Ended December 31,	Cost Ratio For Year	Inventory at Retail
1962	77%	$39,600
1963	74	42,200
1964	76	40,000
1965	78	36,000
1966	80	39,900

Problem 13-10. The management of Specialty Products Company has been looking for opportunities to diversify its line of products. As of December 31, 1965, the company took advantage of an opportunity and purchased the manufacturing facilities and inventories of Tubular Manufacturing Company at 66⅔% of their book values. A separate division was set up, identified as Tubular Products Division, to conduct this new line of business for Specialty Products Company.

The inventories thus acquired, for a price of $513,200, were shown in the records of Tubular Manufacturing Company as follows:

December 31, 1965 inventories—at cost:

Materials—22,000 units	$3 per unit
Work in process:	
Department A—None.	
Department B—5,400 units 50% complete.	
Finished goods—24,600 units.	
Purchased parts	$180,000

One unit of material is required for one unit of finished goods. The purchased parts are optional accessories shipped with the finished goods if ordered by the customer.

According to the 1965 cost records of Tubular Manufacturing Company, it took $9 of labor and overhead to process one unit through Department A and $6 to process one unit through Department B.

At the end of its first year of operations, the new division reported the following:

1966 purchases of materials—114,800 units	$ 367,360
Department A labor and overhead	1,140,000
Department B labor and overhead	822,500
Materials inventory—16,800 units.	
Work in process:	
In Department A—None.	
Through Department A awaiting transfer to Department B —3,000 units.	
In Department B—50% complete—4,400 units.	
Finished goods—26,600 units.	
Purchased parts—at current costs	210,000

In order to avoid taking into the 1966 operating income all of the discount on the "bargain purchases," the management of Specialty Products Company adopted the last-in, first-out method for the material content and purchased parts segments of the inventories. The first-in, first-out basis was adopted for the other segments of the inventories.

Prepare a schedule of inventories for the Tubular Products Division as of December 31, 1965 and 1966. Prices paid for purchased parts have increased 5% during 1966. You may assume that no losses were suffered during production from spoilage or breakage. Also assume that any increments to the *lifo* inventories relate to the most recent acquisitions.

Problem 13-11. Headway Company has adopted the dollar-value *lifo* inventory method. Compute the inventories for years 1, 2, and 3. (Carry index-number computations to two decimal places and dollar amounts to the nearest dollar.)

Inventory Quantities

	Year			
Item	Base	1	2	3
A	1,820	2,000	2,200	2,210
B	2,200	2,400	2,500	2,450
C	3,200	3,220	3,400	3,330

Inventory Prices—Per Unit

	Year			
Item	Base	1	2	3
A	$ 8.00	$ 8.08	$ 8.50	$ 8.82
B	9.20	9.30	9.70	10.10
C	10.00	10.31	10.60	11.00

Problem 13-12. United Company had used the retail inventory method for a number of years. In January of 1962, the company decided to change to the last-in, first-out modification of the retail inventory method. Using the following data, compute the year-end inventories for the years 1962 through 1966.

	Year Ended December 31,			
	1961		1962	
	Cost	Retail	Cost	Retail
Inventory, beginning of year	$ 20,160	$ 28,800	?	$ 31,500
Purchases	114,126	171,600	$114,822	170,200
Transportation in	3,588		3,772	
Markups		1,870		1,780
Markdowns		2,870		2,560
Sales		168,900		166,260

Year Ended December 31,	Cost Ratio For Year	Inventory at Retail	Price Index*
1962	—	—	102
1963	72%	$37,800	105
1964	71	36,850	110
1965	74	31,320	108
1966	75	36,960	112

* 1961 = 100.

Problem 13-13. Bargain Shoe Store sells all of its shoes at a uniform retail price. The sales price is revised whenever there is a change in the wholesale cost of shoes. It maintains perpetual inventory records and applies the last-in, first-out concept in the computation of cost of shoes sold and inventories.

On June 30, 1964, the shoe inventory included 3,800 pairs at an average cost of $2.80 per pair. On June 30, 1965, the inventory was 4,020 pairs. The inventory records showed that 1,800 of these were carried at $2.80 and the remainder at $4.00, which was also the average price of shoes purchased during the year ended June 30, 1965.

The operating accounts for the year ended June 30, 1965, included the following:

Sales	$81,000
Cost of goods sold	46,200

On October 15, 1965, the store was badly damaged by fire. The perpetual inventory records were destroyed, but the following figures were obtained from other records:

Sales to October 15	$21,000
Purchases to October 15	15,330
Salvage value of damaged shoes	1,150

The purchase cost of shoes was $4.20 for the period July 1 to October 15, 1965.

Compute the amount of the loss, in terms of current purchase cost of shoes, caused by fire damage to the shoe inventory.

Problem 13-14. Enterprise Company has priced its inventory at the lower of cost or market, using the retail inventory method for the purpose of computing income subject to federal income tax. The inventories resulting from the use of this method were as follows:

December 31,	
1963	$28,430
1964	29,832
1965	35,983
1966	22,153

The management of Enterprise Company is considering the advisability of adopting the last-in, first-out method of inventory pricing for the purpose of computing income subject to federal income tax.

All merchandise handled by the company has the same rate of markon.

You have been engaged to determine the change in taxable income for the calendar years 1964 to 1966, inclusive, which the adoption of the *lifo* method on January 1, 1964, would have caused. In this connection, you obtain the following information from the records of the company:

Year Ended December 31,	Cost	Retail
1963:		
Beginning inventory	$ 23,920	$ 46,000
Purchases	108,000	185,000
Transportation in	6,080	
Markups—net		2,000
Markdowns—net		3,000
Sales		182,000
1964:		
Purchases	124,000	230,000
Transportation in	9,110	
Markups—net		3,600
Markdowns—net		4,100
Sales		225,500
1965:		
Purchases	134,800	259,800
Transportation in	10,800	
Markups—net		4,100
Markdowns—net		3,900
Sales		247,200
1966:		
Purchases	148,200	270,400
Transportation in	11,100	
Markups—net		4,200
Markdowns—net		4,600
Sales		296,300

Indexes of selling prices on December 31 were:

1963	100
1964	104
1965	108
1966	110

Compute the amount of change in taxable income for the calendar years 1964 to 1966, inclusive, which the adoption of *lifo* as of January 1, 1964 would cause. Show computations supporting your results.

Assignment Material for Chapter 14

QUESTIONS

1. If securities are being purchased on an installment contract, how should they be valued in the accounts?
2. In reorganizations and mergers in which an exchange of securities is not made at the option of the holder, under what conditions should a gain or loss be recorded at the time of exchange?
3. How does a debenture bond differ from a mortgage bond?
4. Describe the proper accounting for the conversion of one class of securities into another class of securities of the same company when no market-value data are available for either class of securities.
5. *A* Company invests its surplus cash, which will be needed in six months, in marketable bonds. Assume that the balance sheet date is one month before the bonds will be sold. Assume that the market quotation of the bonds at the balance sheet date is (a) 10 points below purchase price; (b) 10 points above purchase price. At what valuation should the bonds be stated in the balance sheet in each case?
6. Following is a transcript of all the items in the Investments account of Company *A*:

April 10, 1966—100 shares of Apex Foundries common stock purchased	$4,826.25	
June 25, 1966—1,180 shares of Southern Sugar preferred stock purchased	4,748.50	
Nov. 26, 1966—100 shares of Apex Foundries common stock sold		$2,960.00

The fair market value of Southern Sugar preferred stock on December 31, 1966, the date of your audit, as reflected by stock exchange quotations, was $6 per share; in view of this fact, the president of the company recommends that the book balance of the account be allowed to stand, because it is less than the market value of the stock remaining. The president explains that the account represented a temporary investment of cash, and that, in view of this single purpose, appreciation logically offset depreciation.

Explain what valuation should be placed on the account for balance sheet purposes.

7. If cost has been reduced to give recognition to a decline in the market value of securities, may cost be reinstated if the market value of the securities returns to cost?
8. During the course of an audit, you find the accounts shown on the next page.

Stock in *A* Company ($100 par per share)

1966			1966		
Jan. 2	Cost of 100 shares	18,000	July 1	25 shares of dividend stock sold	3,125
Feb. 1	50 shares received as stock dividend	5,000			

Revenue and Expense

			1966		
			Feb. 1	Cash dividend on *A* Company stock	3,125
			1	Stock dividend on *A* Company stock, 50% . . .	5,000

What accounting errors were made?

9. Dividends are usually declared on one day, payable on a subsequent day, to stockholders of record at some intermediate date. At which of these dates should the dividends be recorded as income to the stockholder?

10. What is the proper classification of the account "Cost of Stock Warrants"? What typical events cause the account to be credited?

11. If a bond, which is redeemable at a premium at the option of the issuer, is acquired at a premium greater than the premium at which it can be retired at the next optional retirement date, what plan of amortization should be adopted?

12. When an investment is made in bonds with interest in default, how should subsequent collections of defaulted interest be recorded?

PROBLEMS

Problem 14-1. An analysis of the Temporary Investments account on the books of Crafty Company disclosed the following debits and credits.

Debits

12/31/65	Balance:		
	100 shares *X* Co. common—cost, which equaled market value	$ 9,000	
	200 shares *Y* Co. preferred—market value, which was $2,000 below cost	16,000	
6/2/66	100 shares of *A* Co. preferred—cost	8,000	
8/8/66	200 shares of *B* Co. common—cost	18,000	
9/20/66	150 shares of *C* Co. common—cost	6,000	
12/1/66	50 shares of *A* Co. common from involuntary exchange of 100 preferred shares	8,000	$65,000

Credits

1/25/66	200 shares of *Y* Co. preferred sold	$ 9,000	
2/2/66	100 shares of *X* Co. common sold	16,000	
12/1/66	100 shares of *A* Co. preferred exchanged	8,000	
12/20/66	Regular semiannual dividend of $1 per share declared by *B* Co. 12/1/66, to stockholders of record 12/20/66, payable 1/5/67	200	33,200
	12/31/66 balance		$31,800

Adhering to general practice, determine the amount at which the temporary investments should be shown in the December 31, 1966 balance sheet, if the per-share market values on that date were as follows:

A Co. common	$62*
B Co. common	88
C Co. common	45

* On December 1, 1966, when the preferred shares of *A* Co. were exchanged according to the terms of a reorganization plan, the market value of the common stock was $60 per share.

Problem 14-2. Aluminum Assembly Company bought five per cent of the 10,000 outstanding common shares of Mountain Mining Corporation at 52. Brokerage fees paid by the company in connection with this transaction amounted to $320. Mountain Mining Corporation has followed the policy of paying the maximum legal amount of cash dividends to stockholders, which amount includes depletion provisions.

During the first year following the purchase of the shares mentioned above, Mountain Mining Corporation reported net income of $248,400, after deduction of depletion of mine property of $62,200. A cash dividend was declared and paid consistent with the corporation's established dividend policy.

Shortly after the receipt of this dividend, Aluminum Assembly Company sold one-half of its investment in Mountain Mining Corporation for $49 per share. Brokerage fees on the sale amounted to $155.

Compute the gain or loss on the sale of stock. Show all computations.

Problem 14-3. Cooper Company acquired common stock of Midland Products Company as follows:

Date	Shares	Total Cost
July 1, 1963	80	$2,400
March 15, 1964	110	3,960
January 10, 1965	60	5,040

On March 15, 1965, Midland Products Company issued a 20% stock dividend. On September 30, 1965, Cooper Company sold 126 shares of the stock for $4,032.

Compute the gain or loss on the sale, calculating the cost of shares sold on the basis of:

(a) First-in, first-out cost.
(b) Average cost.

Problem 14-4. On September 1, 1963, Wheel Company purchased $6,000 face value of the 4% first-mortgage bonds of The United Corporation at 103 and accrued interest.

These bonds mature on May 1, 1970, and interest is payable on May 1 and November 1. On July 1, 1966, Wheel Company sold $3,000 face value of these bonds for 105 and accrued interest.

Prepare journal entries to record:

(a) All transactions during 1963 and 1964 relating to the bond investment (including closing-date adjustments on the basis of a calendar-year accounting period).
(b) The sale transaction on July 1, 1966.

Problem 14-5. A schedule showing the investments made by Globe Circling Company is presented on the following page.

	Date	Number of Shares	Face Value of Bonds	Maturity Date	Interest	Brokerage	Accrued Interest	Total Cash Payment	Market Price 5/31/66
(L)	7/1/65		$300,000	10/1/74	5% Oct. 1 Apr. 1	$400	$3,750	$300,420	100½
(T)	9/1/65	3,000				600		54,300	15
(T)	12/1/65		70,000	11/1/84	6% May 1 Nov. 1	100	350	67,830	98
(L)	4/10/66	2,000				450		38,950	19⅛

The character of each investment is indicated by "T" (for temporary investment) or "L" (for long-term investment).

All interest due on the bonds has been collected. The following dividends have been received:

No. of Shares	Date Declared	Date of Record	Date of Payment	Dividend per Share
3,000	12/10/65	12/20/65	12/30/65	15 cents
2,000	4/ 1/66	4/15/66	4/30/66	20 cents

Prepare all journal entries required for the fiscal year ended May 31, 1966, in connection with the above investments. Use the following account titles for the investment accounts: Temporary Investments; Long-term Investments.

Problem 14-6. Ohio Company purchased common stock of Round Corporation as follows:

January 10, 1964 .... 50 shares at $66 per share
March 8, 1965 .... 100 shares at $84 per share

Round Corporation issued a 10% common stock dividend on December 8, 1964, and issued common stock rights on December 6, 1965. Each right entitled the holder to subscribe for 1/5 share at $50 per share. At the date of issue of the rights, market values were: per right, $10; per share ex-rights, $110.

On January 8, 1966, Ohio Company sold 50 of the rights, which had been received on the stock purchase of March 8, 1965, at $12 each. The remaining rights were exercised on this date.

Required:

(a) Computation of gain or loss on the sale of rights.
(b) Computation of the number of shares in each lot, and the cost basis of each lot on January 9, 1966.

Problem 14-7. Kentucky Company purchased as a temporary investment $10,000 face value of 20-year, 6% bonds for cash on August 1, 1964, at 90 and accrued interest. The bonds were issued on April 1, 1961; interest is paid semiannually on April 1 and October 1.

On December 31, 1964, the close of the company's annual accounting period, the market value of the bonds was 86.

On December 31, 1965, before adjusting and closing entries were made, the officers of Kentucky Company decided that the above bonds would be held to maturity. The bonds on this date had a market value of 92.

Required:

(a) Journal entries to record the purchase of these bonds, the adjustments on December 31, 1964 and 1965, and the receipt of interest from August 1, 1964 through April 1, 1966.
(b) Balance sheet presentation of this account on December 31, 1964 and 1965.

Problem 14-8. Round Top Corporation owned $40,000 face value of the 40-year, 4% convertible bonds of Tantalus Manufacturing Company, which it acquired at 98 on the date of issue, January 1, 1960. These bonds were convertible into common stock during the first five years of their life at the rate of 5 shares of stock for each $1,000 face value of bonds. Any interest accrued on the date of conversion was to be paid in cash by Tantalus Manufacturing Company. On December 31, 1964, when interest for one-half year was accrued (but had not been recorded on the books of Round Top Corporation), the bonds were converted into common stock. On December 31, 1965, Tantalus Manufacturing Company declared and issued a 20% stock dividend. As part of a reorganization on June 30, 1966, Tantalus Manufacturing Company called in all common shares and replaced them with new no-par shares and paid $3.75 per share to the stockholders as part of the exchange consideration.

On January 30, 1967, Round Top Corporation sold 80 shares of the new stock for $150 cash per share.

Prepare journal entries to record all of the transactions described above.

Problem 14-9. The books of Quality Manufacturing Company have been closed as of December 31, 1966, as is indicated by the post-closing trial balance shown below. However, the 1966 financial statements have not been prepared.

QUALITY MANUFACTURING COMPANY
Post-Closing Trial Balance
December 31, 1966

Cash	58,330	
Accounts receivable	176,910	
Allowance for doubtful accounts		6,100
Inventories:		
Finished product	48,411	
Work in process	36,916	
Materials	58,414	
Prepaid expenses	12,640	
Investments	95,139	
Land	40,000	
Building	168,016	
Accumulated depreciation—Building		42,100
Machinery and equipment	224,416	
Accumulated depreciation—Machinery and equipment		108,912
Accounts payable		116,140
Estimated liability for profit-sharing bonus*		20,200
Accrued expenses		28,610
Capital stock—$10 stated value		400,000
Retained earnings		197,130
	919,192	919,192

* Profit-sharing bonus is equal to 25% of net operating income.

An examination of the accounts disclosed that asset and liability accounts are correctly stated with the exception of the Investments and related accounts. Details of the composition of this account are presented below:

Common stock of Comfort, Inc.—1,500 shares $22,500
2,000 shares were acquired in 1962 at a total cost of $30 per share. In 1964 Comfort, Inc., split its stock 3 for 2. On April 10, 1966, 1,500 shares were sold for $25 per share. Comfort, Inc., declared a cash dividend of $2 per share on December 18,

1966, payable on January 10, 1967, to stockholders of record on December 28, 1966.	
7% Debenture bonds of Maxwell Industries—$5,000 face value . . .	3,400
These bonds were acquired on August 1, 1961, at a cost of $3,400. On this date interest totaling $1,400 was in arrears. Interest of $350 was received by Quality Manufacturing Company on November 30, 1966.	
5% First-mortgage bonds of The Universal Coupling Corporation —$8,000 face value	8,864
These bonds were acquired on October 1, 1962, at a total cost of $8,864, ex-interest. This issue matures on October 1, 1974, and interest is paid on April 1 and October 1.	
State of *X* 2½% bonds—$60,000 face value	60,375
These bonds were acquired on November 30, 1966, at face plus accrued interest as an investment of seasonally excess cash. It is the intention of the company to dispose of this investment early in 1967. These bonds are dated September 1, 1966, and interest is paid on March 1 and September 1.	
Total	$95,139

Required:

(a) Any journal entries required to correct the accounts as of December 31, 1966. Ignore income taxes.

(b) The December 31, 1966 balance sheet of Quality Manufacturing Company.

Problem 14-10. From the following information of the stock dealings of Richard Roe, you are asked to determine: (a) the gain or loss on the sale of stock; (b) the cost of remaining stock held; and (c) the gain or loss on the sale of rights. Use the first-in, first-out method.

On October 1, 1963, he purchased 800 shares of *A* Company stock for $41,040 and 600 shares of *B* Corporation stock for $6,000. On December 1, 1963, a 5% stock dividend was received on *A* Company stock, and Roe purchased an additional 200 shares of *A* Company stock for $12,960. A stock dividend of 20% and a cash dividend of 10% were received on the *B* Corporation stock on June 1, 1964.

Roe engaged in no other transactions for over a year; on July 1, 1965, he received a 4% cash dividend on his holdings in both the *A* Company and the *B* Corporation.

Roe received rights on January 15, 1966, from *A* Company, entitling him to purchase 1 additional share of stock for $50 for every 10 shares held, the rights expiring February 3, 1966. On the same date (January 15), Roe sold 560 rights for $2 each and 90 shares of *A* Company stock for $6,300.

He exercised his option on the remaining rights on February 1, 1966.

Problem 14-11. Allison Company made certain purchases of stock in Mills Corporation, an important supplier. When Allison Company needed cash, sales of this stock were made in the open market.

A transcript of Allison Company's "Investment in Mills Corporation" account appears below:

Investment in Mills Corporation

1960			1960			
April 8	Purchased 250 sh at 35 . .	8,750	June 28	Sold 400 sh at 17	6,800
June 12	Purchased 500 sh at 16 . .	8,000	1966		
July 20	Purchased 275 sh at 15 . .	4,125	Dec. 20	Sold 750 sh at 4	3,000

Officers of Allison Company want to know the cost basis of the stock sold in 1966 in order that they may determine, for income tax purposes, the gain or loss on the sale. They inform you that the cost of individual shares has been changed since their acquisition by events which are not reflected in the accounts. These are:

(a) On May 1, 1960, 3 new shares were received in exchange for each old share.
(b) On June 25, 1960, a 20% stock dividend was issued to holders of record as of June 15, 1960.
(c) On July 15, 1960, rights were issued entitling stockholders to subscribe to 1 share at $15 for each 4 shares held. On this date, rights were selling for $.50. The stock ex-rights was selling for $18 per share.
(d) On June 30, 1964, a large paid-in surplus was created by a reduction of par value of the stock, and a cash dividend of $2 per share was paid on July 20, 1964, to holders of record as of July 10, 1964, from this paid-in surplus.

Required:

(a) Detailed computations to indicate the adjusted cost per share of the shares on hand. Use the first-in, first-out assumption.
(b) Adjusting journal entries on December 31, 1966, to correctly state the balance in the above account. You find 625 shares of Mills Corporation stock to be on hand on that date.

Problem 14-12. The Investment in Bonds account of Dale Corporation on December 31, 1966, is presented below.

Investment in Bonds—4% (1981)

Jan. 16, 1961	62,064	Aug. 31, 1963	16,650
		Oct. 31, 1966	31,400

The bonds acquired on January 16, 1961, for a total cash outlay of $62,064 had a face value of $60,000. Interest is paid semiannually on January 1 and July 1. The bonds mature on July 1, 1981.

Interest payments have been made regularly. The bonds sold on August 31, 1963, had a face value of $15,000; the bonds sold on October 31, 1966, had a face value of $30,000. The amounts credited to the investment account represent the proceeds from the sale of bonds, including accrued interest.

Prepare adjusting journal entries as of December 31, 1966. The corporation uses a calendar-year accounting period. The corporation has failed to make any adjusting entries for accrued interest since the bonds were acquired.

Assignment Material for Chapter 15

QUESTIONS

1. Booth Corporation organized a subsidiary, The Booth Company, investing $500,000 on January 2, 1965, for 5,000 shares of the subsidiary's stock with a par value of $100 per share. During 1965, the subsidiary's net income was $60,000 and it paid a dividend of $25,000 at the end of the year. During 1966, the subsidiary lost $15,000 and paid a dividend of $10,000. Give the entries to be made by the parent company by: (a) the legal-basis method; (b) the economic-basis method.

What was the stockholders' equity as shown by the books of the subsidiary at the end of 1966, and at what amount would the stock investment be shown on the parent's books at the end of that year by each of the accounting procedures mentioned above?

2. How should a parent company record a dividend from a subsidiary which was paid from surplus created prior to the time when the investment was made in the subsidiary?

3. Distinguish between funds and reserves.

4. Under what circumstances may a fund be classified as a current asset?

5. Is it considered acceptable accounting to credit the sinking fund reserve account for interest earned on sinking fund investments?

6. A company has established a fund for the retirement of a bond issue. Investments have been made in bonds of other companies; their present market value is somewhat below cost. Would you value them in the balance sheet at market?

7. Must a reserve account which is related to a fund account have a balance equal to the balance of the fund account?

8. What entries should be made to record the following sinking fund transactions? Reserve entries are not desired.

(a) Deposit of cash in the sinking fund.
(b) Purchase of sinking fund securities at an interest date.
(c) Purchase of sinking fund securities between interest dates.
(d) Collection of income on bonds in the fund purchased at par.
(e) Collection of income on bonds in the fund purchased at a discount.
(f) Collection of income on bonds in the fund purchased at a premium.
(g) Payment of expenses.
(h) Disposal of the sinking fund securities and cancellation of the liability at its maturity.

9. When some of a company's own bonds have been acquired and held alive in the sinking fund being accumulated to retire the bonds at maturity, should such bonds be shown as an asset in the company's balance sheet or as a deduction from the bond liability?

10. Discuss the legality of a provision in a preferred stock issue requiring the redemption of a stipulated amount of stock annually.

11. List six purposes for which an industrial company might establish funds. Three of these should be current asset funds and three noncurrent asset funds. What is the essential difference between the two types of funds mentioned above?

PROBLEMS

Problem 15-1. In order to acquire a marketing organization to handle its products in the Western states, Diversified Manufacturing Company acquired 80 per cent of the outstanding shares of Western Company for $250,000. The earnings and dividend record of the subsidiary since the stock acquisition by the parent company is set forth below.

Year	Net Income	Cash Dividends Paid
1964	$20,000	$25,000
1965	30,000	25,000
1966	50,000	25,000
1967	8,000*	10,000

* Loss.

Required:

All journal entries affecting the Investment in Stock of Western Company account on the books of Diversified Manufacturing Company, assuming that the parent company, in accounting for its investment in the subsidiary, employs:

(a) The legal-basis method.
(b) The economic-basis method.

Problem 15-2. Downdraft Company had been accumulating a sinking fund which was scheduled to amount to $100,000 in ten years. At the beginning of the tenth year, the fund consisted of $88,300 in securities and $426 of cash. During the tenth year, investments in this fund earned 3%; and, at the end of the tenth year, the regular contribution of $8,112 was made to the trustee. This amount was not invested, as it was to be used to retire the bonds about to mature. The investments in the sinking fund were sold and, after brokerage fees, netted $87,624. The company contributed enough cash to cover the deficiency, and the trustee retired the bonds.

Give the journal entries for all transactions relating to the sinking fund during the tenth year and the retirement of the bonds.

Problem 15-3. Seaside Company has set up a sinking fund with a trustee. Equal annual contributions are made to the fund on December 31 of each year, which earn a constant annual rate of return guaranteed by the trustee. The Reserve for Sinking Fund also is increased by equal amounts each year.

Use the following information taken from the company's trial balances and present journal entries accounting for all changes in the sinking fund and related reserve account during the years 1965 and 1966.

Data from Trial Balances

	December 31,		
	1964	1965	1966
Sinking fund	385,000	442,400	—
Sinking fund income	13,195	15,400	17,696
Bonds payable—12/31/66	500,000	500,000	—
Reserve for sinking fund	400,000	450,000	—

Problem 15-4. Northern Mining Corporation was required to accumulate a sinking fund for the retirement of bonded debt by the deposit of 25 cents for each ton of ore mined. It was also a requirement of the bond indenture that the accumulated fund, inclusive of earnings on fund investments, at the end of any calendar year, must be at least $20,000 times the number of years which have elapsed. The fund earned 5% a year.

The record of tonnage mined during the first five years of the operation of the sinking fund was as follows:

Year	Tons Mined
1	64,240
2	78,400
3	102,680
4	70,400

Assume that the contributions to the sinking fund were made as of the close of each year for the purpose of computing earnings on the fund.

Required:

(a) A table showing annual contributions to the fund, fund earnings, and the balance in the fund as of the close of each year.

(b) Journal entries to record the changes in the fund during the second and fourth years.

Problem 15-5. On April 1, 1964, Stanford Company acquired 18,000 of the 20,000 outstanding shares of stock of Electronic Supply Corporation for $20 per share. On this date the stockholders' equity of Electronic Supply Corporation included common stock of $100,000 and retained earnings of $64,500.

On April 25, 1964, Stanford Company received a cash dividend of 50 cents per share which had been declared by Electronic Supply Corporation on March 20, 1964, payable to stockholders of record on April 10, 1964.

Electronic Supply Corporation reported net income of $36,000 for the year ended December 31, 1964, earned evenly during the year. No additional dividends were declared during the year 1964.

During 1965, net income of Electronic Supply Corporation amounted to $34,000, and dividends for 1965 were as follows:

April 25—10% stock dividend.
October 25—Cash dividend of 80 cents per share.

Set up a T-account for the investment in the subsidiary and show the 1964 and 1965 entries therein under the legal-basis method. Then set up another T-account for the investment in the subsidiary and show the 1964 and 1965 entries therein under the economic-basis method.

Problem 15-6. Wente Corporation issued 10,000 shares of $100 par value 5% preferred stock at a premium of $5 per share. The corporation is required by the terms of the indenture relating to its preferred stock to create a fund for the redemption thereof. Contributions to the fund must be made on March 31 of each year in an amount equal to 25% of the net income for the preceding calendar year. The fund is to be used to acquire preferred stock whenever it can be purchased at or below a price of $100 per share. The portion of the fund not used to acquire preferred stock is temporarily invested to yield 2% per annum.

The net income and preferred stock purchases during the first five years of operation of the fund were:

Year	Net Income	Preferred Stock Purchased
1961	$416,000	
1962	380,000	940 shares at $ 98
1963	488,000	1,010 shares at $ 96
1964	520,000	1,050 shares at $ 99
1965	564,000	1,460 shares at $100
1966		1,210 shares at $ 97

Assuming that purchases of preferred stock are made on April 1 of each year, prepare a table showing all additions to and deductions from the fund during the five-year period ended December 31, 1966. Also give the journal entry for the redemption of the 1,210 shares purchased on April 1, 1966.

Problem 15-7. Briggs Company organized Southern Company on July 1, 1963. The parent company paid $100,000 for the entire issue of 10,000 shares of the subsidiary's $10 stated value common stock.

On January 2, 1966, Briggs Company sold 500 shares of its investment in Southern Company for $12 per share.

The earnings and dividend record of Southern Company subsequent to July 1, 1963, was as follows:

Year ended December 31:	Net Income* (Loss)	Cash Dividends Date Paid	Cash Dividends Amount Per Share
1963 (six months)	$ 6,000	December 10	$ .50
1964	12,800	July 1	1.00
1965	26,400	September 10	1.20
1966	(1,000)	September 10	.50

* Assume that net income and loss accrue evenly throughout the year.

Give the journal entries on the books of the parent company to record the data presented, except closing entries, using the economic-basis method of accounting for the investment in the subsidiary.

Problem 15-8. Blue Company suffered the loss of a warehouse as a result of a fire during December of 1962. As a temporary measure, Friendly Company agreed to cooperate with Blue Company by leasing one of its storage buildings under the following terms:

Term of lease: Five years ending December 31, 1967.
Rental: $5,000 for the five-year term, payable in advance.
Restoration fund: $3,000 to be paid by Blue Company at the end of the first and second years; $2,000 to be paid at the end of the third and fourth years. If the cost of restoring the building is less than $10,000, the difference is to be returned to Blue Company. The lessor is required to establish a building restoration fund with such receipts.

The lessor received the following amounts from Blue Company:

Date	Amount
January 2, 1963	$5,000
December 31, 1963	3,000
December 31, 1964	3,000
December 31, 1965	2,000
December 31, 1966	2,000

Friendly Company paid a contractor $9,940 on March 15, 1968, for work completed to restore the building to its condition as of January 1, 1963.

Give all of the entries on the books of Blue Company associated with the above lease for the years 1963, 1966, and 1968. The company closes its books on December 31. Also show how the accounts associated with the lease will appear in the December 31, 1963 balance sheet of Friendly Company. You may assume that both companies have operating cycles of less than a year.

Problem 15-9. International Company's export building was completely destroyed in December of 1963 by a severe earthquake. In order to give the company adequate time to plan and build a new structure, Local Corporation agreed to lease one of its buildings to International Company under the following terms and conditions:

Term of lease: Three years ending December 31, 1966.

Rental: $6,000 for the three-year term, payable as follows: $4,000 on January 2, 1964, and $2,000 on January 2, 1965.

Building restoration fund: To be deposited with City Bank as trustee, $6,000 on December 31, 1964, $4,000 on December 31, 1965, and $2,000 on December 31, 1966. The bank has agreed to pay interest on the fund at 3% per annum. The interest is to be transferred annually on each January 2 to the general account maintained at City Bank by International Company. On January 2, 1967, City Bank will transfer the fund balance ($12,000) to Local Corporation.

Restoration fund reserve: To be established on the books of International Company at the rate of $4,000 per year.

Show how the accounts set up to comply with the terms and conditions of the lease would be set forth in the December 31, 1964, 1965, and 1966 balance sheets of International Company. You may assume that the operating cycle of International Company is 18 months.

Problem 15-10. Cramer Corporation issued $150,000 of 5%, 20-year bonds on November 1, 1964, realizing $151,875, including accrued interest. The bonds were dated August 1, 1964, and interest was payable August 1 and February 1. The bond indenture required the deposit of $7,500 with a trustee on June 30 of each year, beginning in 1965. The trustee had the power to purchase the corporation's bonds whenever they could be acquired below the call price of 104. The trustee was required to present for retirement at face value immediately following the next interest date any bonds acquired by the fund, along with evidence showing the price paid for the bonds.

The trustee agreed to credit the fund on June 30 of each year with interest at 2/10 of 1% per month on uninvested cash in the fund at the end of each month. Cash interest received on any of the corporation's bonds while held by the trustee was to be added to the fund.

The trustee was able to acquire $6,000 of the corporation's bonds on November 1, 1965, at 102¼ and accrued interest.

Give all journal entries affecting the sinking fund from June 30, 1965 through June 30, 1966. You should maintain detailed sinking fund accounts and assume that the trustee advises the corporation promptly of all bond acquisitions.

Problem 15-11. Mainland Company issued $200,000, 4½%, 10-year bonds dated January 1, 1964, to be retired by means of a sinking fund accumulated by the deposit of 10 annual sinking fund installments. The company is to maintain a sinking fund reserve, the year-end balance of which is to equal the balance in the related fund. On December 31, 1964, the first installment of $20,000 is deposited with the designated trustee.

The report of the trustee received on December 31, 1965, showed the following transactions for the year 1965:

(1) The purchase of investments on April 1, as follows:
  (a) $10,000 face value of 6% mortgage bonds, due July 1, 1976 (interest payable on January 1 and July 1), at 109 and accrued interest.
  (b) $6,000 face value of 4% debenture bonds, due December 1, 1971 (interest payable June 1 and December 1), at 98 and accrued interest.
(2) The regular collection of all interest.

On December 31, 1965, Mainland Company remitted to the sinking fund trustee the second installment, $20,000 less earnings on the fund investments during 1965.

On December 31, 1966, the trustee reported the transactions for the year 1966 as follows:

(1) The purchase of investments on February 1, as follows:
  $19,000 face value of the company's own bonds (interest payable on January 1 and July 1), at 97½ and accrued interest.
(2) The sale of the 4% debenture bonds on April 1, at face plus accrued interest.
(3) The regular collection of all interest.

On December 31, 1966, Mainland Company remitted to the sinking fund trustee the third installment, $20,000 less earnings on the fund investments during 1966.

Prepare journal entries to record the transactions relating to the sinking fund, maintaining separate accounts for sinking fund cash and sinking fund investments.

Problem 15-12. Barnum Company issued $100,000 of 5%, 20-year bonds on May 1, 1964, at 102.37 and accrued interest. The bonds were dated February 1, 1964, and interest was payable on February 1 and August 1. The indenture required the deposit of $5,000 with a trustee on January 31 of each year beginning in 1965, to be used for the purchase and cancellation of the 5% bonds when they could be acquired below the call price of 105. The trustee agreed to credit Barnum Company on January 31 of each year with 2% of any funds from previous years on hand at that date not used to purchase bonds. The amount credited was to be applied as a reduction of the contribution to the trustee on the following January 31.

A summary of the transactions affecting the bond redemption fund during the years ended January 31, 1965, 1966, and 1967, showed the following:

(1) Contributions were made to the trustee as required.
(2) The trustee reported the following purchases of the 5% bonds:

Date	Face Value	Price
April 1, 1965	$4,000	104 and accrued interest
March 1, 1966	5,000	103.5 and accrued interest

Interest on the 5% bonds was paid when due. The company operates on a calendar-year basis.

Required:

Present journal entries, including closing entries, from the issue date of the 5% bonds to January 31, 1967. Use the following accounts:

(1) Cash;
(2) Bond Redemption Fund;
(3) Accrued Bond Interest Payable;
(4) Bonds Payable;
(5) Premium on Bonds Payable;
(6) Earnings on Bond Redemption Fund;
(7) Bond Interest Expense;
(8) Loss on Redemption of Bonds Payable;
(9) Revenue and Expense.

Assignment Material for Chapter 16

QUESTIONS

1. What distinction, if any, should be made in the books and in the balance sheet between land held for speculation or plant enlargement and land used as a factory site?

2. The Jordan Development Company purchases a plant which has been in use for 15 years for $75,000. This plant is in a run-down condition and it is necessary to spend $15,000 to put it into shape for use.

   This expenditure is principally for repairs, painting, and similar work that would have been considered an operating charge had the plant been properly maintained by the previous owner. As auditor of The Jordan Development Company, what treatment of the $15,000 expenditure would you be prepared to approve?

3. The Alpha Company purchased a store building for $100,000. Immediately thereafter $10,000 was spent to remodel the store front. In the opinion of competent real estate firms, the expenditure of this additional $10,000 did not add to the resale value of the building—that is, this building, which was purchased for $100,000, could not be resold for more than that amount even though the additional $10,000 was spent in improving the store front.

   What is your advice regarding the accounting treatment of this $10,000 expenditure?

4. Distinguish between an addition and an improvement or betterment.

5. State two ways of accounting for ordinary repairs.

6. A contract for construction of a corporation's plant and machinery completely installed is executed. The cost in the aggregate is $200,000, and the payment is to be made in one sum within ten days after completion by the contractor and acceptance by the corporation. During the course of construction, the contractor finds that he will need funds at periodic intervals before the date set in the contract for the one and final payment. In consideration of the corporation's making such advance payments, it is mutually agreed that the total expenditure by the corporation shall be reduced to $190,000. Where should this unexpected saving of $10,000 be reflected in the books of account? Explain your reasoning.

7. On January 2, 1965, *ABC* Company purchased display equipment for its store under the following terms: $2,000 to be paid upon installation, plus five annual payments of $1,000, the first installment note to be payable on December 31, 1965. Title to the display equipment was retained by the seller until the final payment was made. It is estimated that the display equipment will be used for ten years, with no residual value.

   This same display equipment was available at a cash price of $6,600.

   You are required to make all accounting entries relating to the display equipment as of January 2 and December 31, 1965, and as of December 31, 1966. For each entry, you are to give your supporting reasons. Do not consider income tax aspects of the transaction.

8. A concern engaged in building locomotives wishes to equip its machine shop with some new machinery of standard types, and decides to have it made in its own plant by its own workmen from materials which are in stock. By this means the machinery will cost much less than if bought from outsiders. The company desires to charge its Machinery account with the current market prices of the machinery so produced, on the ground that the workmen, while making it, have been detached from other profitable employment.

Discuss this question pro and con, and state what you would advise.

9. State clearly, but not at too great length, the proper manner of recording assets on the books of account in instances where payment has been made in stock, the face value of the stock being greatly in excess of the actual value of the assets acquired.

10. Describe a theoretically ideal method of accounting for extraordinary repairs.

11. In 1965 Enterprise Electric Company built a new plant, chiefly with its own labor and under the direct supervision of its own engineers. Pursuant to instructions from the board of directors, a percentage of direct labor costs incident to this project was included in the cost of the new plant. Also, a portion of the salaries of the president, the general manager, and the controller were capitalized and included in the cost of the new plant.

(a) Discuss briefly the theoretical soundness of the procedure of including in the cost of construction any part of the salaries of such officials as are identified above.
(b) Indicate on what basis, if at all, any portion of such salaries should be charged to the cost of the new plant.

12. The *M* Company buys the land, building, and machinery of *L* Company for a total price of $30,000. The building and machinery are in bad condition. It is expected that the building will be torn down and replaced, and that, before the machinery is used, an expenditure of $10,000 will be necessary, after which it will be worth $25,000. The books of *L* Company show the land to have cost $2,000, the building to have cost $16,000 and to have an 80% depreciation credit, and the machinery to have cost $60,000, against which there was a $35,000 depreciation credit.

(a) How should the purchase price be recorded in the accounts of The *M* Company? Give reasons for your answer.
(b) How should the $10,000 cost of repairing the machinery be recorded in the accounts? Give the justification for your answer.

13. Is the entire cost of acquiring a natural resource subject to depletion?

14. Bonds amounting to $100,000 and bearing interest at 6% were issued to finance the purchase of a plant site and the construction of a suitable building. The land cost $20,000 and the building $180,000. Exactly a year elapsed from the date the bonds were issued until the building was ready for occupancy. How should the interest charge be journalized? Should any depreciation have been allowed during this period? If so, how should it have been journalized?

15. *A* Company received a gift of several acres of land adjoining its present plant site. The assessed value of the property is $30,000. The day after the property had been transferred to it, *A* Company refused a firm offer of $100,000 for it. The donor had paid $150 for the land 30 years before.

Draft a journal entry to record the foregoing transaction in the accounts of *A* Company, indicating the reason for selecting whatever value, if any, you use for recording the gift.

Facts as to the valuation to be stated, other than those included in the question, may be assumed and stated, if necessary, to develop what you consider an appropriate accounting procedure and to provide adequate supporting reasons for that procedure.

16. What is the position taken by accountants on the question of whether or not depreciation should be taken on donated fixed assets?

17. *A* acquired a building, subject to the rights of the tenants in the property, who could continue to occupy the building for six months. *A* intended to demolish the building as soon as he could obtain possession thereof, and to erect a building to be used in an entirely new enterprise. He proceeded to do this as soon as the tenants vacated the property. Is the rent collected from the tenants properly creditable to income, or should it be treated as a deduction from the cost of acquiring the old and erecting the new building?

PROBLEMS

Problem 16-1. Chapman Company purchased some new machinery in July of 1966. From the following data prepare a schedule showing the proper amount to be capitalized as the cost of the new machinery.

List price of machinery	$10,000
Cash discount taken on purchase	200
Freight on new machine	125
Cost of moving old machinery to a new location	235
Installation costs of new machine	305
Testing costs before machine was put into regular operation	65
Operating costs during first month of regular use	175
Estimated cost of manufacturing a similar machine in company's own plant, excluding overhead	7,500
(Overhead would add 20 per cent to the cost.)	

Problem 16-2. Wellington Company was organized on January 2, 1965, at which time 10,000 shares of its $5 stated value common stock were issued for a total of $60,000. Shortly thereafter, the company purchased a tract of land with an old building on it for 5,000 shares of the company's $5 stated value common stock. The company assumed a liability of $1,600 for back taxes on the property. The old building was torn down at a cost of $3,200. Materials salvaged from the building were sold for $630. Excavation was completed at a cost of $2,800 and a new building was built. The construction began on July 1, 1965, and was financed in part by the sale, on the same date, of $50,000 of 6% bonds at face value. The contractors estimated that the building would cost $82,000, but it was completed, on December 31, 1966, at a cost of $90,000. In order to make settlement with the contractor, $8,000, the amount of the additional cost, was borrowed from a bank on a one-year 7% note dated December 31, 1966.

The company began doing business on January 2, 1967. Property taxes from the date of purchase to December 31, 1966, were $600. The new building was not assessed for property-tax purposes until January of 1967.

What amounts should be assigned to the land and the building as of January 2, 1967?

Problem 16-3. Thurston Company made the following individual purchases:

From *A*:	
Land and buildings	$40,000

From *B*:	
Machinery and office equipment	$18,000
From *C*:	
Delivery equipment	6,000

The question of apportioning the cost of the purchases between the assets arose; so an appraisal was made, which disclosed the following values:

Land	$10,000
Buildings	40,000
Machinery	10,000
Office equipment	5,000
Delivery equipment	7,000
Total	$72,000

State the values properly assignable to each asset; explain the method used in making the assignments.

Problem 16-4. Allied Tool Corporation acquired a crane on July 1, 1964, at an invoice price of $32,400, which was paid in cash. Freight and installation costs paid amounted to $1,800. It was estimated that ordinary repairs would amount to $8,000 over the 20-year life of the crane. Ordinary repairs paid were as follows:

October 1, 1964	$280
August 15, 1965	310
September 10, 1966	460

Prepare dated journal entries to record the information presented above, through December 31, 1966, using the reserve method of accounting for ordinary repairs. Depreciation entries are not required. The corporation uses a calendar-year accounting period.

Problem 16-5. Service Enterprises, Inc., was the successful bidder on a contract to "sweep" the runways of a large airport twice daily to minimize the risk of debris ingestion into aircraft turbines. The following debit-credit data indicate the entries recorded in the accounts of Service Enterprises, Inc., relating to the mobile sweeper acquired to perform the services required by the contract.

1963				
July	1	Machinery	36,000	
		Accounts payable		36,000
		Purchase of mobile sweeper. Terms: 2/30; n/90.		
	5	Transportation in	200	
		Cash		200
		Transportation cost of the mobile sweeper.		
	30	Accounts payable	36,000	
		Notes payable		30,000
		Cash		5,880
		Purchase discounts		120
		Renegotiated settlement terms: one-year, 6% note; balance in cash, less discount.		
Dec.	31	Depreciation expense—Machinery	1,800	
		Accumulated depreciation—Machinery		1,800
		Depreciation for six months. Useful life, 10 years.		

Date		Account	Debit	Credit
1964				
Jan.	2	Miscellaneous expense	400	
		Cash		400
		Installation of two-way radio on mobile sweeper.		
July	1	Maintenance expense	120	
		Cash		120
		Installation of rotating warning light on mobile sweeper.		
	30	Notes payable	30,000	
		Machinery	1,800	
		Cash		31,800
		Paid 6% note at maturity.		
Dec.	31	Depreciation expense—Machinery	1,980	
		Accumulated depreciation—Machinery		1,980
		Annual depreciation.		
1965				
Sept.	1	Machinery	900	
		Cash		900
		Replaced suction motor with more powerful unit to increase efficiency of mobile sweeper. New motor, which cost about 50% more than the smaller, discarded motor, will not extend useful life of the mobile sweeper.		
Dec.	31	Depreciation expense—Machinery	2,050	
		Accumulated depreciation—Machinery		2,050
		Annual depreciation.		

Prepare a schedule showing the debits and credits that should appear in the Machinery account and the related Accumulated Depreciation—Machinery account to account for the above transactions. For purposes of depreciation computations, consider any changes in the asset as occurring on the first of the nearest month, and compute depreciation for fractional periods by months.

Problem 16-6. Valley Development Commission made a contract with Electronics Corporation whereby it agreed to donate a vacant factory to the corporation provided that the corporation employed an average of 200 people a day for two years. If the corporation failed to meet this requirement, it could purchase the land and building at their appraised value minus any expense, not to exceed $7,500, incurred by the company in connection with the contract. This proposal was made by the Commission because it recognized that, even if the conditions were not fully met, the community would benefit by the increased employment.

At the time of the agreement, January 2, 1965, the land was appraised at $18,000 and the factory at $84,000. The estimated life of the building was 20 years.

Required:

(a) Journalize the following transactions:
  (1) Acceptance of the property at the beginning of the contract.
  (2) Payment of $5,000 in legal and other fees in connection with the contract on February 8, 1965.
  (3) Provision for depreciation for the year 1965.
  (4) Transfer of title upon completion of the contract.

(*Continued on next page.*)

(b) The journal entry made at the end of the second year if the company failed to meet the requirements of the contract and purchased the property, paying cash.

Problem 16-7. Custom Corporation acquired a new processing machine on June 30, 1966. Details of the acquisition are as follows:

Invoice cost	$40,000
Terms, 1% discount if payment is made in 30 days in cash. The company paid on July 21, 1966.	
Cost of transportation of the machine to the corporation's factory, paid on July 8, 1966	1,260
Cost of installation on July 10, 1966:	
Labor paid	350
Materials issued	80
Payment on July 3, 1966, for strengthening the floor to support the weight of the new machine	2,000
The corporation's chief engineer spent two-thirds of his time during July on trial runs of the new machine. His monthly salary is $1,800.	
On August 1 the corporation requested an allowance from the supplier because the machine proved to be of less than standard performance capabilities. The supplier granted a cash allowance of $5,500 for this reason, which was received on August 6, 1966.	
The $400 cost of removing the machine used before the new machine was acquired was paid on June 30, 1966. (The old machine was sold for less than its book value.)	

Present entries in general journal form for the facts stated above.

Problem 16-8. The Industrial Development Commission of New City made the following proposition to Space Age Corporation, a newly organized corporation, to induce it to locate in New City and build a factory facility there.

A contingent gift of a factory site appraised at $40,000, the contingency to be removed when the corporation completed a factory facility on the site.

Ninety per cent of the contract cost of the factory facility would be financed by a mortgage loan from the Commission. The mortgage would mature in 15 years from the completion of construction. The interest would be at 2% per annum, payable December 31.

As of January 1 following, each year in which the corporation's plant payroll exceeded $1,000,000, one-tenth of the original mortgage principal indebtedness would be forgiven.

The corporation accepted the proposition of the Commission on July 1, 1963. The factory facility was completed and placed in operation on January 1, 1965; its useful life was estimated at 25 years. The contract cost was $400,000.

The corporation received the following sums under the mortgage agreement and paid interest on the advances as shown.

Mortgage Loan		Interest at 2%	
Date	Amount	Date Paid	Amount
October 1, 1963	$ 60,000	December 31, 1963	$ 300
January 1, 1964	100,000		
July 1, 1964	100,000		
December 31, 1964	100,000	December 31, 1964	4,200

The sums received from the Commission were immediately remitted to the contractor. The construction contract specified that the final 10% would be due 60 days after the factory was completed. The corporation made this payment on the due date with its own funds.

Give all entries arising from the acceptance of the proposal through December 31, 1967, including entries for annual depreciation.

The plant payroll exceeded $1,000,000 in 1966 and 1967, but not in 1965.

Problem 16-9. Symons Company used its plant for construction of fixed assets during 1966. The results are partially set out below.

	Total	Finished Goods	Fixed Assets
Direct labor	$120,000	$90,000	$30,000
Materials	100,000	60,000	40,000
Overhead	80,000	?	?
Total	$300,000	?	?

Compute the total cost of both finished goods and fixed assets manufactured by each of the following methods:

(a) No overhead is to be assigned to the fixed assets.
(b) Normal production of finished goods amounts to 25,000 units. Because of the construction of fixed assets, finished goods production totaled only 17,500 units in 1966. The fixed assets are to be charged with the overhead which would have been charged to the 7,500 units which were not produced.
(c) Overhead is to be apportioned in the ratio of direct labor.

Problem 16-10. Master Company sells product *X* in returnable containers, one container being required for each unit of *X*. One unit of *X* sells for $10. The containers cost the company 50 cents each and are billed separately. The company commenced operations on January 1, 1965. The following summarizes the company's transactions for 1965:

(1) Purchased 1,600 containers.
(2) Sold 6,500 units of *X*.
(3) 5,800 containers were returned.
(4) 600 containers were paid for by customers.
(5) An inspection resulted in an estimate that the containers still owned by the company on December 31 were worth an average of 45 cents each.

Submit entries in journal form to record the above transactions:
(a) Assuming that the containers were billed at cost.
(b) Assuming that the containers were billed at 75 cents each.

Problem 16-11. Triumph Company effected a program of expansion and improvement of its plant during the year 1966. The following information, related to this program, is given to you.

(1) On October 31, 1966, a 30-foot extension to the present factory building was completed at a contract cost of $46,000.
(2) During the course of construction, the following costs were incurred for the removal of the end wall of the plant where the extension was being constructed:
    (a) Payroll costs during the month of April arising from employees' time spent in removal of the wall, $2,816.
    (b) Payments to a salvage company for removing unusable debris were $430.
    The cost of the original structure allocable to the end wall was estimated to be $16,800, with recorded depreciation thereon of $7,040.

$3,620 was received by Triumph Company from the construction company for windows and other assorted materials salvaged from the old wall.

(3) The old flooring was covered with a new-type long-lasting floor covering at a cost of $2,860.

(4) The interior of the plant was painted in new, bright colors for a contract price of $3,790.

(5) New and improved pencil sharpeners were installed at a cost of $178.

(6) Old electrical wiring was replaced at a cost of $6,812 and new electrical fixtures using fluorescent bulbs were installed. The new fixtures were purchased on the installment plan; the schedule of monthly payments showed total payments of $6,200, which included interest and carrying charges of $480. Cost of the old wiring was determined to be $3,100 with depreciation recorded to date of $1,370. The old fixtures were carried at a cost of $1,860, with depreciation to date of $796. The old fixtures had no scrap value.

Prepare a schedule showing the proper disposition of the above items in the accounts.

Problem 16-12. Industrial Liquids Company delivers its principal product in containers which are returnable by customers. These containers cost $7 each, but are charged to customers at $10 each when shipped. The customer is allowed a credit of $8 for each container returned. It is the experience of the company that customers return approximately 90% of the containers shipped.

Data for the two years ended December 31, 1966, are as follows:

	Year Ended December 31,	
	1965	1966
Containers:		
Purchased during year	300	3,000
Shipped during year	15,870	19,200
Returned during year	13,800	15,900
Scrapped during year after return by customers	None	201
Collections:		
For container use	$26,410	$39,180
For unreturned containers	6,480	8,064

3,702 containers were owned on January 1, 1965, all of which were on hand on that date.

Required:

(a) Journal entries summarizing all transactions related to containers in the two-year period, including year-end adjusting entries. Use the following accounts:

Container Inventory
Receivable—Containers
Allowance for Returnable Containers
Income from Containers Sold
Income from Container Use Charges
Container Expense
Receivable—Container Use Charges

(b) Disclosure of facts relative to containers in the December 31, 1966 balance sheet.

Problem 16-13. Sunrise Company was organized on November 1, 1965. It commenced production of its single product on July 1, 1966, when the company's new factory was completed.

An analysis of the recorded entries associated with the building of the new factory is set forth below:

Reference	Date	Item	Land	Building	Expense
(1)	12/1/65	Land and old building	$ 83,000		
(2)	12/20/65	Removal of old building		$ 3,750	
	3/1/66	Partial payment to contractor		70,000	
(3)	4/1/66	Legal fees paid			$2,000
	5/15/66	Second partial payment to contractor		60,000	
(4)	6/1/66	Insurance premium			2,700
(5)	6/30/66	Salaries		24,000	
	7/15/66	Final payment to contractor		70,000	
(6)	8/15/66	Cost to place fence around property	8,000		
(7)	12/1/66	Financing cost during construction period		1,750	
(8)	12/31/66	Value of gift from city	20,000		
				$229,500	
(9)	12/31/66	Depreciation—1%		2,295	
	12/31/66	Balance	$111,000	$227,205	$4,700

Supplementary Information

(1) 600 shares of 5%, cumulative preferred stock plus $23,000 cash.
(2) Cost of removing old building; $5,000 less $1,250, the value of salvaged materials retained by contractor.
(3) The legal fees were for the following services:

Incorporation	$800
Title examination.......................	700
Construction contract	500

(4) Insurance policy on building for three-year term starting March 1, 1966.
(5) President's salary—7 months ended June 30, 1966 .... $14,000
Company's engineer—For time spent on inspection of construction 4,000
Office salaries—50% of such salaries for period preceding the start of production... 6,000
(6) The fence has an expected useful life of 40 years.
(7) Preferred dividends during period of construction:
7/12 of 5% dividend on 600 preferred shares.
(8) The city paid for the cost of a water system as an incentive for the company to locate in an area adjoining the city's industrial park. The system is expected to last for the life of the factory.
(9) Estimated life of new factory—50 years.

Prepare a revised and expanded analysis; however, a single column for items properly chargeable to expense will suffice.

Problem 16-14. Double Company owns its own building. It maintains a Building Expense and Income account which is charged with actual costs of maintaining the building and is credited with theoretical departmental rentals. A transcript of the account for 1966 (which was the first year the company used this system) is presented on the following page.

Building Expense and Income

Depreciation	4,000	Department A—Manufacturing	24,000
Heat	8,000	Department B—Manufacturing	18,000
Power and light	3,000	Sales department	6,000
Taxes	2,500	Administrative department	12,000
Insurance	4,500		
Maintenance	3,000		
Balance—to Revenue and Expense	35,000		
	60,000		60,000

The ending inventory contains 15% of Department A's and 12% of Department B's total 1966 production (all completed). What is the amount of the error, if any, in the net income reported for 1966? Ignore income taxes.

Problem 16-15. Lately Corporation was organized as of January 1, 1964. In connection with the use and occupancy of its building, the corporation maintained the accounts shown below. As revealed by these accounts, the corporation rents a small portion of the building to outsiders. In 1965, the rent charged per square foot was increased 10% and the space thus rented was doubled. The space was taken away from Department B, and as a result its space was reduced by one-third in 1965.

Costs Incurred in Lieu of Rent

1964			1964		
Dec. 31	Insurance	900	Dec. 31	To Building Occupancy	8,400
31	Taxes	3,600			
31	Depreciation	3,900			
		8,400			8,400
1965			1965		
Dec. 31	Insurance	900	Dec. 31	To Building Occupancy	8,450
31	Taxes	3,650			
31	Depreciation	3,900			
		8,450			8,450

Building Occupancy

1964			1964		
Dec. 31	Heat and light	5,200	Dec. 31	To Rental Activities	3,260
31	Maintenance	8,000	31	To Building Expense and Income	29,340
31	Housekeeping	11,000			
31	Transfer	8,400			
		32,600			32,600
1965			1965		
Dec. 31	Heat and light	5,310	Dec. 31	To Rental Activities	6,930
31	Maintenance	8,780	31	To Building Expense and Income	27,720
31	Housekeeping	12,110			
31	Transfer	8,450			
		34,650			34,650

Rental Activities

1964			1964		
Dec. 31	Transfer	3,260	Jan. 2	Rental income	1,000
31	To Revenue and Expense	740	April 1	Rental income	1,000
			July 1	Rental income	1,000
			Oct. 1	Rental income	1,000
		4,000			4,000
1965			1965		
Dec. 31	Transfer	6,930	Jan. 2	Rental income	2,200
31	To Revenue and Expense	1,870	April 1	Rental income	2,200
			July 1	Rental income	2,200
			Oct. 1	Rental income	2,200
		8,800			8,800

Building Expense and Income

1964			1964		
Dec. 31	Transfer	29,340	Dec. 31	Dept. A—Manufacturing	18,000
31	To Revenue and Expense	10,660	31	Dept. B—Manufacturing	12,000
			31	Selling and administrative	10,000
		40,000			40,000
1965			1965		
Dec. 31	Transfer	27,720	Dec. 31	Dept. A—Manufacturing	18,000
31	To Revenue and Expense	12,280	31	Dept. B—Manufacturing	12,000
			31	Selling and administrative	10,000
		40,000			40,000

The December 31, 1964 ending inventory of finished goods contained 8% of Department A's and 10% of Department B's total 1964 production. The December 31, 1965 ending inventory of finished goods contained 10% of Department A's and 15% of Department B's total 1965 production. There was no work in process at either year end.

What was the amount of error (if any) in the net income before income taxes reported for 1964 and 1965?

Assignment Material for Chapter 17

QUESTIONS

1. Should the depreciation amounts accumulated in the accounts be made to agree approximately with the physical depreciation of the assets?
2. When fixed assets, such as buildings and machinery, are used in connection with the operation of a wasting asset, should the depreciation be based on the life of the fixed assets or on the life of the wasting asset?
3. An electric lamp manufacturing company has charged to cost of manufacturing lamps, as "depreciation," one-fourth of the value of the filament-filtering machinery acquired a little more than one year ago. The life of the machinery is estimated to be 10 years; but, owing to discovery by a competitor of a new process of metal pulling which, although still imperfect, promises to revolutionize the lamp industry, the machinery in question will probably be obsolete within a period of three years. State what you would say concerning the propriety of making such a charge to cost of manufacturing.
4. The chief engineer of a manufacturing firm suggested in a conference of the company's executives that the accountants should speed up depreciation on the machinery in Department 3 because improvements are making those machines obsolete very rapidly, and it is desirable to have a depreciation fund big enough to cover their replacement. Discuss the issues raised by the chief engineer.
5. The management of a corporation suggests the reduction or elimination of depreciation charges on plant and machinery on these grounds:

   (a) Nothing need be written off, because the plant is actually more valuable than it was when acquired, owing to a rise in the cost of similar machinery.
   (b) Repairs have been fully maintained, and the plant is as good as ever.
   (c) To charge depreciation to the same extent in a poor year as in a good year will prevent a dividend in the poor year, with a consequent objection from stockholders and a fall in the price of the shares.

   Combat these arguments.
6. When a physical-inventory approach to depreciation is justified, is it considered acceptable to put some reliance on market values, second-hand values, or replacement costs in the application of this method? Explain your answer.
7. The owner of a new office building estimates the life of the building to be 50 years if it is adequately maintained and repaired. The owner objects to the use of straight-line depreciation because, he says, his maintenance and repair costs are lowest in the early years and his rental income will be largest during this period; whereas in the late period of the building's life, the maintenance and repair costs will increase and rents will decrease. Outline in detail the features of two depreciation methods which might possibly avoid his objections to the usual depreciation method. State carefully how these methods might overcome the owner's objections, and also state any objections to the use of the depreciation procedures proposed.

8. In determining the results of the operations of a company whose business requires the use of a large number of perishable tools, how would you proceed in making the assignment of the cost of such equipment to the periods benefited?

9. Because of its large volume of business, Hall Company is operating its plant 70 hours a week instead of the 35 hours a week which it usually operates. The company computes depreciation on a straight-line basis. Because of the increased rate of operation, the treasurer has suggested that depreciation rates should be doubled.

Discuss the suggestion of the treasurer, including a full discussion of the factors that should be considered by the company. Do not give consideration to income tax effects.

10. Why are income taxes a factor in the selection of depreciation methods?

11. What do you understand by the retirement system of fixed asset accounting, particularly as applied by public utilities? Do you approve of such a system? State your reasons.

12. A small manufacturing company owned in 1961 one factory building with a net depreciated cost of $90,000. Equipment was carried at $120,000. Because of expanding business in 1962, a new building was constructed at a cost of $150,000 and $210,000 of equipment was installed in it. In the period from 1962 to the end of 1965, some new equipment was put into the old building and the company continued to operate both plants. Depreciation has been computed on a straight-line basis.

In 1966 the directors of the company order the old plant shut down because of lack of orders. They propose that they should quit taking depreciation on the old building and equipment. They suggest that, although the old plant is useful, it is not in use and is not wearing out. They also suggest that to take depreciation on it increases their cost, overvalues inventory, and places them in a poor competitive position to bid for business because their costs are high.

You are to give a full discussion of their proposal and of their arguments.

13. What is the position taken by accountants regarding the writing up of wasting assets above cost?

PROBLEMS

Problem 17-1. Disc Company acquired a machine at a cost of $42,500. It was estimated that it would have a scrap value of $1,250 at the end of its useful life. Prepare depreciation tables for five years and submit journal entries to record depreciation for the third year under each of the following methods:

(a) Working hours; estimated life in working hours—16,500.
(b) Production; estimated life in units of product—82,500.
(c) Declining-balance method, using double the straight-line rate for the first three years and shifting to the straight-line method for the last two years of its five-year estimated life. Follow the approach permitted for income tax purposes.

Additional data:

Year	Working Hours	Units of Product
1	3,080	16,250
2	3,420	17,550
3	3,360	16,900
4	3,090	15,700
5	3,550	16,100

Problem 17-2. Vital Company has depreciated machinery and equipment on a composite-life basis for four years, using a single accumulated depreciation account. It now desires to maintain a separate accumulation account for each type of machinery and equipment, and to employ a separate depreciation rate for each type. You are asked to prepare the journal entry necessary to give effect to this plan, using the data presented below:

Type	Cost	Salvage Value	Estimated Life
1	$33,400	$1,400	16 years
2	86,800	6,000	10 years
3	43,250	2,000	15 years
4	18,500	1,700	8 years

Problem 17-3. Leonard Lamp Corporation acquired a machine in the first week of July, 1965, and paid the following bills:

Invoice price	$42,000
Freight in	1,710
Installation cost	2,040

Estimated life of the machine was 7½ years; estimated scrap value was $750.

State what the accumulated depreciation will be for this machine on December 31, 1965, and December 31, 1966, under each of the following methods:

(a) Straight-line method.
(b) Working-hours method:

Estimated total hours	90,000
Operating hours to December 31, 1965	2,200
Operating hours—1966	6,250

(c) Production method:

Estimated total units of production	180,000
Production to December 31, 1965	4,400
Production—1966	12,800

(d) Constant rate of 30% of diminishing balance.
(e) The sum-of-years'-digits method.

Problem 17-4. Using the following data, prepare a lapsing schedule covering the first eight years of the business life of Clinton Corporation. The corporation was organized as of January 1, 1965.

Asset						
Acquisitions					Disposals	
Date	Description	Use-Life	Cost	Scrap	Identity	Date
1/1/65	I	4 years	$7,600	—	I	12/31/68
7/1/65	II	5 years	4,000	—	II	7/1/69
4/1/66	III	6 years	5,000	$200	III	10/1/70
7/1/67	IV	10 years	8,000	500		
1/1/69	V	4 years	4,200	—		
10/1/70	VI	5 years	6,000	500		

Problem 17-5. Northeast Company received an invoice for $17,814 covering a specially designed machine. The invoice included shipping charges of $614 and $600 for spare parts. According to the manufacturer, the spare parts accompanying the machine should supply all of the parts needed as a result of breakage during the useful life of the machine.

When the invoice was paid, the company deducted a purchase discount of $344, which was available according to the terms of the purchase agreement. It cost the company $830 to install the machine. The estimated scrap value of the machine, including any remaining spare parts, was $300 and the estimated useful life was 15 years.

At the end of the second year, accessories costing $830 were added to the machine. They did not prolong the estimated useful life of the machine, but they did increase the efficiency of the machine and increase the expected scrap value to $350.

State what the depreciation will be for the third year under each of the following methods of computing depreciation:

(a) Straight-line method.

(b) Working-hours method. Total estimated hours, 36,000. Used the first year, 2,500; the second year, 2,200; the third year, 2,750.

(c) Production method. Total estimated units of production, 67,500. Produced the first year, 4,700; the second year, 4,400; the third year, 5,100.

(d) Constant rate on a diminishing-value method.

$$r = 1 - \sqrt[15]{300 \div 18{,}300} = .2397$$
$$r = 1 - \sqrt[15]{300 \div 17{,}470} = .2101$$
$$r = 1 - \sqrt[13]{350 \div 11{,}408.43} = .2429$$
$$r = 1 - \sqrt[13]{1{,}080 \div 17{,}470} = .3018$$

(e) The sum-of-years'-digits method.

Problem 17-6. Island Gravel Company purchased a tract of gravel land in the fall of 1964 for $198,000. The gravel content of the tract was estimated at 600,000 cubic yards. When the gravel has been exhausted, it is estimated that the land will be worth $2,000.

Fixed installations were set up at a cost of $48,000. Equipment was purchased early in January, 1965, for $62,000, and operations were started as soon as the weather permitted.

The following depreciation rates are considered to be reasonable for the classes of fixed assets shown:

Installations—5%
Equipment—12%

At the end of 1965, 60,000 cubic yards had been extracted. This was about one-half of the annual extraction which can be expected following the initial year of operations. In 1966, 126,000 cubic yards were extracted. The fixed installations will be abandoned when the gravel is completely exhausted, but the equipment can be transferred to another location.

Required:

The adjusting entries for depletion and depreciation on December 31, 1965 and 1966.

Problem 17-7. Compute the depreciation for 1965 and 1966 for the following asset, using the depreciation methods indicated below.

Date Acquired: April 1, 1965
Cost: $110,000
Scrap Value: $11,000
Estimated Useful Life: 10 years

(a) Sum-of-years'-digits method.

(b) Declining-balance method, using a depreciation rate twice that of the straight-line rate.

Problem 17-8. Data relating to three pieces of equipment owned by Banner Company are set forth below.

Type	Date Acquired	Cost	Scrap Value	Use-Life	Depreciation Method
A	1/2/60	$130,000	$9,000	10 years	Sum of years' digits
B	1/2/62	60,000	6,000	5 years	Declining balance double straight-line rate
C	7/1/65	80,000	8,000	5 years	

The company uses the calendar year as its accounting period.
Compute the depreciation charge for 1965 and 1966.

Problem 17-9. Since Plymouth Corporation was organized, it has owned and operated a fleet of four special-order trucks. The corporation's experience has been that it can expect to recover, on the average, 10 per cent of the cost of the truck when it is retired from service.

In 1966 the corporation's business expanded to such a degree that a fifth truck was added to the fleet on July 1.

The following summary shows the facts relating to the trucks during 1966:

Truck Number	Date Acquired	Cost	Date Sold	Proceeds
23	1/2/62	$5,000		
24	1/2/62	5,500	1/3/66	$540
25	1/2/63	6,000	10/2/66	625
26	1/2/64	6,000		
27	1/2/66	6,500		
28	7/1/66	6,400		
29	10/1/66	6,800		

Compute the depreciation charge for 1966 under the following methods:

(a) Declining balance, using a rate of 40% (double the typical straight-line rate).
(b) Retirement.
(c) Replacement.

Carry computations to the nearest dollar.

Problem 17-10. Dawson Oil Corporation purchased a lease on potential oil property for $160,000 and spent $144,000 drilling producing wells on the property. It was estimated that the oil potential of the property was 1,800,000 barrels, with the discovery value of $720,000.

During 1966, the first year of operations, 90,000 barrels of oil were produced, of which 81,000 were sold. Cash operating costs for the year associated with the removal of the oil from its underground location to the company's storage facilities were $40,000, and a net income of $30,000 was earned. In the computation of net income, depletion was based on discovery value.

Prepare a partial balance sheet as of December 31, 1966, showing therein the proper amounts and classification of all balance sheet accounts for which the necessary data have been supplied.

Problem 17-11. The management of Lewiston Company has decided against the renewal of its contract with Regional Delivery Service, Inc., and, starting in January of 1966, the company will undertake its own delivery service. In connection with this decision, the following plan of motor truck acquisitions and utilization has been developed.

Planned Acquisitions			Planned Disposals	
Date	Vehicle Identity	Cost	Date	Proceeds
12/30/65	1	$6,000	12/31/70	$-0-
12/30/65	2	6,000	12/31/70	-0-
1/2/67	3	6,000	12/31/71	-0-
7/1/69	4	6,300	6/30/74	-0-
12/31/70	5 (Replacement)	6,300	12/31/75	-0-
12/31/70	6 (Replacement)	6,300	12/31/75	-0-
12/31/71	7 (Replacement)	6,800	12/31/76	200
10/1/73	8	6,800	9/30/78	200
6/30/74	9 (Replacement)	7,800	6/30/79	300

Management is undecided about the depreciation method that it should adopt. To assist in this decision, you are asked to prepare a schedule for the ten-year period ending December 31, 1975, which will show the following data for each of the depreciation methods under consideration:

Depreciation charge per year;
Prospective annual and cumulative income tax "savings" under the accelerated methods. (Use a 50% income tax rate.)

Depreciation methods under consideration:

(a) Straight-line.
(b) Declining balance, double the straight-line rate, converted to straight-line for the last two years.
(c) Sum of years' digits.

Carry computations to the nearest dollar.

Problem 17-12. Bay Coast Corporation acquired sulphur-producing property at a cost of $1,152,000. A geological survey indicated that the property contained approximately 4,200,000 tons of crude sulphur. The total purchase cost included $60,000 for buildings estimated to have a service life of 10 years, with no salvage value. In addition to the original purchase price, the company expended $63,000 on improvements and developments, of which it was estimated that two-thirds would remain in service over the life of the sulphur deposit and the remainder would have an estimated service life of six years, with no salvage value.

Operations commenced on July 1, 1966, and during the six months ended December 31, 1966, 140,000 tons of crude sulphur were extracted, of which 126,000 tons were sold for $4 per ton. Production costs, other than depreciation and depletion, were $248,000, and selling and administrative expenses totaled $119,500.

Required:

Income statement for the six months ended December 31, 1966. Ignore income taxes. (Show supporting computations for depletion, amortization, and depreciation.) Also compute the amount available for dividends.

Problem 17-13. Globe Pottery Company employed a large number of identical dies in its operations. On the date of organization of the company, July 1, 1962, a working complement of these dies was acquired. Subsequent purchases were made to replace dies retired and to adjust the number of dies on hand to current operating needs. The company's annual accounting period ends June 30.

A summary of transactions involving dies during the first five years of the company's operations appears at the top of the next page.

Date	Purchases*		Retirements*		Estimated Use Value of Dies on Hand at End of Year
	Units	Unit Cost	Units	Unit Salvage	
July 1, 1962	3,000	$1.40			
Year ended:					
June 30, 1963	800	1.50	600	$.20	$3,850
June 30, 1964	600	1.60	300	.22	4,100
June 30, 1965	1,000	1.58	850	.24	4,200
June 30, 1966	300	1.50	400	.20	4,000
June 30, 1967	500	1.54	700	.18	3,750

* Assume that purchases and retirements are cash transactions.

Prepare entries in general journal form to record all transactions indicated by the preceding summary, using the following methods of computing depreciation:

(a) Inventory method.
(b) Retirement method.

Problem 17-14. International Ore Company was organized in January, 1966, with authorized capital of $1,000,000, consisting of 10,000 shares of $100 par value capital stock, one-half of which was immediately sold for cash at $105 per share.

In February, 1966, the company acquired a tract of ore-bearing land at a cost of $289,600, which was paid in cash. A few days after exploration activities were begun, it was discovered that the land contained ore deposits substantially in excess of the expectations of International Ore Company when it purchased the land. A geological survey conducted subsequent to this discovery indicated a probable recoverable ore deposit of 1,810,000 tons, with an estimated value of $543,000. After the discovery of the ore deposit, the company leased the required mining equipment and commenced operations.

During the year ended December 31, 1966, the company mined 112,000 tons, of which 89,600 tons were sold for a cash price of $1.70 per ton. Other costs and expenses incurred and paid during this period were as follows:

Direct mining costs	$123,200
Administrative expenses	42,500

Required:

(1) Entries, in general journal form, to record all of the transactions summarized above, including recognition of the "discovery value" of the ore property and the periodic transfer of realized appreciation.
(2) Income statement for the year ended December 31, 1966.
(3) Balance sheet as of December 31, 1966.

Problem 17-15. Mineral Resources Company was organized to take over a lease of property thought to contain beryllium. The company paid $97,200 for the lease and, after an investment of $345,600, a deposit estimated to contain 1,080,000 tons of beryllium ore was discovered. It may be assumed for purposes of this problem that the company has received a report prepared by respected engineers which states that the fair value underground of the deposit is $5 per ton.

In 1964 the company invested $626,400 in the construction of buildings having an estimated useful life of 25 years, arranged for the lease of mining equipment at $50,000 per annum, and commenced mining operations. The management of the company expects that the mining operations will proceed at a fairly even pace until the deposit is exhausted, although some fluctuation in the rate of sales is anticipated.

One of the clauses in the land lease stipulates that, when mining operations cease, all depreciable property must be removed from the premises and the land must be graded to specified standards in order to minimize the risk of damage to adjoining property from improper drainage. The company's engineers have estimated that a future cash outlay of $32,400 will be required to meet these requirements.

Discussions were held within the company about the advisability of recording the discovery value of the beryllium deposit. The company's accountant was reluctant to give recognition in the accounts to the discovery value of the ore prior to the time that the ore was above ground and in the inventory. Therefore, the following accounting policy was adopted: Inventory was to be debited and Realized Discovery Value was to be credited for $5 for each ton of ore mined.

Mine reports and accounting data indicate the following for the first three years of mining operations:

	Tons		Dollars
	Mined	Sold	Year-End Inventory
1964	54,000	50,000	$44,000
1965	60,000	58,000	66,000
1966	61,000	62,000	55,000

Comparative data taken from the company's income statements are set forth below.

	1964	1965	1966
Sales (at $16 per ton)	$ 800,000	$ 928,000	$ 992,000
Cost of ore sold	$ 550,000	$ 638,000	$ 682,000
Depreciation—4%	25,056	25,056	25,056
Depletion—Exploration costs	17,280	19,200	19,520
Amortization of investment in lease	4,860	5,400	5,490
Rent of mining equipment	50,000	50,000	50,000
Direct mining expenses—payroll, supplies, etc.	436,000	442,000	468,500
Administrative expenses—payroll, supplies, etc.	179,804	180,344	181,434
Total	$1,263,000	$1,360,000	$1,432,000
Operating loss	$ 463,000	$ 432,000	$ 440,000
Realized discovery value	594,000	660,000	671,000
Net income before income taxes	$ 131,000	$ 228,000	$ 231,000

Compute the corrected net income before income taxes for the years 1964, 1965, and 1966.

Assignment Material for Chapter 18

QUESTIONS

1. Under what circumstances, if any, do accountants consider assigning gains or losses arising from fixed asset disposals directly to retained earnings?
2. On July 15, 1965, Oldham Products Company sold its factory site and building for $1,000,000 cash, realizing a book gain of $400,000, and erected a more modern plant on the outskirts of the city at a cost of $1,300,000. In view of the fact that the capacity of the new plant is no greater than that of the old, the president of the company suggests that the gain be credited to the cost of the new plant; in this way, future depreciation charges will be reduced and income tax will be avoided.
   Prepare a memorandum to the president, giving your views on the matter.
3. List four depreciation policies that may be applied in connection with additions and disposals of fixed assets.
4. The following information relates to the purchase of an asset which was paid for by a trade-in of an old asset and the balance in cash.

List price of new asset	$10,000
Cash payment	5,800
Cost of old asset	8,000
Depreciation accumulated—old asset	5,000
Second-hand market value—old asset	3,600
Trade-in allowance	4,000

   You are to prepare journal entries to show three different methods of recording the transaction.
5. What is an "involuntary conversion"? Develop an illustration to demonstrate how an involuntary conversion is handled in the accounts.
6. Describe the operation of group-basis depreciation.
7. Under what circumstances would the recording of an appraiser's estimate not be considered a departure from the cost basis of accounting?
8. How do you believe fully depreciated assets should be handled in the accounts?
9. The *G* Corporation carries insurance considerably in excess of the book value of its fixed assets because of the increased cost of replacement. One of its buildings was destroyed by fire and the company collected an amount approximately three times the carrying value of the asset. It then used the entire proceeds from the insurance to construct a similar building. In your examination of the accounts, you find that the company accountant, following instructions from the company president, has charged annual depreciation on the new building at the same amount as previously charged on the old building, although depreciation computed on the cost of the new building would be almost double the previous

depreciation. The president's argument is that the company must be consistent. Discuss the propriety or impropriety of the procedure followed by the company. Do not consider income tax effects.

10. A disagreement between the accumulated depreciation per books and the accumulated depreciation per an appraisal does not necessarily indicate that an adjustment of the accumulated depreciation account should be made. Why is this so?

11. It has been argued that, if the replacement cost of fixed assets is greatly in excess of their cost, depreciation should be computed on the replacement values, so that the accumulated depreciation will be equal to the replacement value when the time arrives for abandoning the old property and acquiring new. It is contended that, if this procedure is followed, the company will have sufficient cash to make replacements without impairing the capital. State your opinion with regard to this matter.

12. State the arguments which have been advanced by proponents of the theory of basing depreciation on replacement costs, and discuss objections which others have expressed to this theory.

PROBLEMS

Problem 18-1. Sideways Manufacturing Company purchased a machine on January 2, 1964, for $20,000. The service life was estimated at five years, with no salvage value. The machine was traded in on a new machine on July 1, 1966. The invoice price of the new machine was $24,000. A trade-in allowance of $6,200 was granted for the old machine, and the balance was paid in cash. The fair market value of the old machine on this date was $6,000. The company closes its accounts on December 31.

Required:

Journal entries on July 1, 1966, assuming that the trade-in is recorded by each of the following methods:

(a) Fair market value of the old machine is to be used in determining the recorded cost of the new machine.
(b) Trade-in allowance on the old machine is to be used in determining the recorded cost of the new machine.
(c) The income tax method is to be used in determining the recorded cost of the new machine.

Problem 18-2. East-West Company purchased a machine on July 1, 1961, for $52,000. It was estimated to have a life of 12 years with a salvage value of $1,000. During 1965, it became apparent that this machine would become uneconomic after January 1, 1970, and that $150 would be a more realistic scrap value. The chief accountant was directed to make allowance for this new determination when making the annual adjustments for 1965. The company closes its books on December 31.

Prepare a schedule showing the depreciation charge for the years 1961, 1962, 1965, and 1966, assuming the following:

(a) Past depreciation is to be corrected in 1965.
(b) Past depreciation is not to be corrected in 1965.

Problem 18-3. Fairfax Manufacturing Company employed a large number of identical hand tools in its operations. When operations were begun on October 1, 1962, 700 of these tools were acquired at a unit cost of $4.40, and an additional 700 were acquired on October 1, 1963, at the same unit cost. On April 1, 1966, 300 were acquired at a unit cost of $4.80. It was estimated that the average service life of these tools would be five years. The history of this group of tools during the first four years of use was as follows:

Year Ended September 30,	Tools Retired	Net Salvage Received From Tools Retired
1963	—	$ —
1964	50	75
1965	100	130
1966	220	240

Assuming that retirements occur at the end of each year and that the salvage from tools retired is received in cash, prepare journal entries, using the group method of depreciation, to record all transactions indicated by the preceding information.

Problem 18-4. General Insurance Agency maintains in its ledger a separate asset account for typewriters. New typewriters cost $200. As a general rule, the agency uses typewriters for four years and each year sells a number of its oldest typewriters when new ones are being purchased. It has been the agency's experience to realize about $44 from the sale of each such old machine.

Purchases and sales of typewriters for a five-year period are summarized below.

Year	Purchases of New Typewriters	Sales of Old Typewriters	Proceeds From Old Typewriters
1962	24	14	$560
1963	18	18	738
1964	20	20	880
1965	25	22	990
1966	22	24	960

You may assume that all purchases and sales of typewriters occur early in January.

As of December 31, 1961, the agency owned 80 typewriters and the balance in the accumulated depreciation account was $6,340.

Prepare a schedule showing the debit-credit activity and the annual balances in the asset account and the related accumulated depreciation account.

Problem 18-5. Channel Company completed construction of a special-purpose machine on January 2, 1961, and capitalized $16,450 as the cost of the fixed asset. Management estimated that this asset would have a scrap value of $500 after a service life of 10 years. The company closes its books on a calendar-year basis and records depreciation on its assets by the sum-of-years'-digits method.

Early in 1965, during an audit in connection with the issuance of securities to the public, it was determined that the company had failed to include $1,100 of overhead when computing the cost of the special-purpose machine. It was also apparent that the original use-life and scrap-value estimates were excessive. On the basis of the information available in 1965, it was evident that the original estimates should have been an eight-year service life and a $90 scrap value.

The chief accounting officer of the company decided that the necessary corrections or revisions should be made when preparing adjusting entries for 1965.

Submit two acceptable sets of journal entries as of December 31, 1965, either of which would comply with the above decision. Include the 1965 entry for depreciation. Also compute the depreciation charge for 1966 under each alternative. Assume that the company has adopted a clean surplus policy.

Problem 18-6. Industrial Corporation acquired land and a building on October 1, 1958, at a cost of $88,000, of which $8,000 was allocated to land. The December 31, 1965 balance sheet showed that depreciation on the building had accumulated to $11,600. On July 1, 1966, the building was completely destroyed by fire.

Show all entries that would appear in the company's books as a result of the fire, the settlement by the insurance company, and the replacement of the building as of December 1, following the income tax regulations relating to involuntary conversions,

(a) if $75,000 is received from the insurance company and $80,000 is invested in the new building;
(b) if $72,000 is received from the insurance company and $68,000 is invested in the new building;
(c) if $70,000 is received from the insurance company and $62,000 is invested in the new building.

Problem 18-7. The Casting Machines account of Tuthill Company for 1966 appears as follows:

1966			Debit	Credit
Jan.	1	Balance—Machines 1, 2, 3, and 4 at $2,000	$ 8,000	
Sept.	1	Machine 5	2,200	
Oct.	1	Machine 6	1,800	
Oct.	1	Machine 3		$ 950
Dec.	1	Machines 7 and 8 at $2,400	4,800	
Dec.	1	Machine 2		1,450
Dec.	31	Balance down		14,400
			$16,800	$16,800

The Accumulated Depreciation—Casting Machines account contained no entries for the year 1966; the balance on January 1, 1966, was $3,500, as follows:

Machine 1	$1,500
Machine 2	500
Machine 3	1,000
Machine 4	500
	$3,500

Upon inquiry, you find the following facts:

(a) Machine 5 was purchased for cash; it replaced machine 1, which was junked on this date, with no net salvage value.
(b) Machine 2 was destroyed by a boiler explosion December 1, 1966, and insurance of $1,450 was recovered. Machine 7 was to replace machine 2.
(c) Machine 3 was traded in on machine 6, at an allowance of $950; the difference was paid in cash. Fair market value of machine 3 at trade-in date was $1,000.
(d) Depreciation rate, 25% per year.

Required:

(a) Journal entries to adjust the accounts on December 31, 1966, before closing, assuming that the company wishes to compute depreciation at the annual rate on the opening balance in the fixed asset account, plus or minus depreciation at one-half the annual rate on the net additions or deductions during the year. Gains or losses are to be computed in the conventional accounting manner. Also compute the account balances for the Casting Machines account and its related accumulated depreciation account.
(b) Do everything as in (a), but assume that the management of the company decides to determine the depreciable basis of fixed assets in the manner required by the Internal Revenue Service for trade-ins and involuntary conversions, and desires this figure to be the one used in the accounting records.

Problem 18-8. Stateside Corporation acquired a warehouse on January 2, 1955, at a cost of $100,000, of which $10,000 was assigned to land. It was estimated that the scrap value of this structure would be $6,000 at the end of a 25-year life. The company closes its books on a calendar-year basis and records depreciation on its assets by the straight-line method.

Late in 1965, an appraisal of the company's property revealed the replacement cost, new, of this warehouse to be $127,500. The appraisers indicated that such a building should have a scrap value of $3,000 and a total estimated life of 30 years.

The directors of the company request that you prepare entries to record the appraisal as of January 1, 1966, using separate appraisal accounts, the depreciation expense for 1966, and the piecemeal realization appraisal increment on December 31, 1966.

Problem 18-9. Circle Corporation purchased certain real estate on January 1, 1959, for cash as follows:

Building	$50,000
Land	10,000
Total	$60,000

An appraisal of the property on the basis of the replacement cost, new, was made late in 1965, and the results of the appraisal were recorded on December 31, 1965, before the books were closed. The appraisal was as follows:

Building	$ 80,000
Land	22,000
Total	$102,000

Depreciation had been recorded in 1959 and through 1964 at 2% of cost annually, but the appraisal stated that the rate should have been 3% annually. The corporation has consistently followed the policy of disclosing any corrections of prior years' depreciation in the statement of retained earnings.

This real estate was sold by the corporation on June 30, 1966, for cash. The price agreed on is indicated below:

Building	$ 90,000
Land	16,000
Total	$106,000

Required:

(a) Journal entry to record depreciation on the above property for the year 1964.
(b) Journal entry to record the 1965 appraisal, maintaining separate accounts for the appraisal increments.
(c) Journal entries to record depreciation on the basis of replacement cost for the year 1965, including amortization of appraisal increment.
(d) Journal entries to be made on June 30, 1966, at the time of the sale of this property.

Problem 18-10. Vilmont Corporation, a family-owned corporation, purchased a building on July 1, 1955, for $180,000, of which $28,000 was assigned to the Land account. The board of directors adopted a policy of straight-line depreciation for the building.

Early in 1965, the board of directors received an appraisal report which showed that the replacement cost, new, of the building would be $243,000 as of January 1, 1965. The report also stated that the building would have a useful life of 20 years from that date. The board of directors ordered that the appraisal be recorded in the accounts as of January 1, 1965. On the recommendation of the chief accountant, the board also voted that past depreciation was not to be corrected.

The December 31, 1964 balance sheet showed that $76,000 of depreciation had been accumulated on the building.

The property was sold on January 2, 1967, for $145,000.

Required:

(a) Journal entries for the following:
   (1) Depreciation on the building for 1964.
   (2) Depreciation on the building for 1965.
   (3) Amortization of appraisal increment as of December 31, 1965.
   (4) Those arising from the sale of the property.

(b) A partial balance sheet, as of December 31, 1965, showing the location and balances of all accounts relating to the property.

Problem 18-11. Spherical Company was organized in 1961. It adopted the sum-of-years'-digits method of depreciation and a four-year use-life with no scrap value in accounting for its investment in heavy, mobile equipment.

The management of Spherical Company has been approached by a representative of a much larger company. He has indicated that the larger company would like to engage in negotiations that could lead to the merger of the two companies. Because the earnings performance of Spherical Company will be an important factor in the negotiations, and because the larger company depreciates similar equipment following the straight-line method over a five-year use-life, the management of the smaller company has been asked to recompute the net income before income taxes for the 1961-1966 period in order to make the earnings data more comparable with those of the larger company. Prepare a schedule showing the recomputation.

Both companies compute depreciation by applying the annual rate to the closing balance in the asset account. And both companies follow the clean surplus theory.

Equipment Data

Acquisitions		Disposals			
During	Cost	During	When Acquired	Cost	Proceeds
1961	$40,000	1964	1961	$20,000	$5,000
1962	50,000	1965	1961	10,000	2,000
1963	60,000	1965	1962	30,000	8,000
1964	20,000	1966	1962	10,000	3,000
1965	40,000				
1966	10,000				

Net Income Before Income Taxes

Year	Amount	Year	Amount
1961	$10,000	1964	$15,000
1962	12,000	1965	20,000
1963	9,000	1966	26,000

Problem 18-12. The balance of the Machinery account kept by Triangle Donut Corporation on December 31, 1966, was $6,418.71. Purchases had been made as follows: On January 1, 1963, two identical machines at $3,125.00 each, designated A and B; on March 1, 1964, Machine C for $3,465.00; on May 1, 1965, Machine D for $4,230.00; and on October 1, 1966, Machine E, for which Machine A was traded in and a cash payment of $2,200.00 made in addition. Machine B was sold for $1,400.00 on April 1, 1966.

The company charged the Machinery account with all cash payments for machines and credited the account with cash received from sales and depreciation computed at 25% on the closing balance.

Revise the accounts, setting up an Accumulated Depreciation—Machinery account in which depreciation is credited at 20% for the actual period of ownership. State the balances in the Machinery account and the Accumulated Depreciation—Machinery account on December 31, 1966. State the change made in the depreciation charge for 1966 by your correction of the accounts. Make the entry to adjust the books, assuming that they have been closed.

Problem 18-13. In the course of the first annual audit of Plastic Boxes, Incorporated, made in January, 1967, the following facts were determined concerning equipment:

Equipment

Date	Item	Debit	Credit
May 1, 1962	Purchase	200,000	
Mar. 15, 1963	Purchase	25,000	
July 1, 1964	Purchase	70,000	
Feb. 20, 1965	Purchase	75,000	
Nov. 1, 1966	Purchase	30,000	

Depreciation Expense

Debit date	Amount	Credit date	Amount
Dec. 31, 1963	22,500	Dec. 31, 1963	22,500
Dec. 31, 1964	29,500	Dec. 31, 1964	29,500
Dec. 31, 1965	37,000	Dec. 31, 1965	37,000
Aug. 1, 1966	1,500		
Dec. 31, 1966	40,000		

Accumulated Depreciation

Debit date	Amount	Credit date	Amount
Apr. 15, 1965	9,000	Dec. 31, 1963	22,500
		Dec. 31, 1964	29,500
		Dec. 31, 1965	37,000
		Dec. 31, 1966	40,000

The entry in the Depreciation Expense account under date of August 1, 1966, represents new equipment purchased to replace items scrapped and sold. The charge in the Accumulated Depreciation account under date of April 15, 1965, represents new equipment purchased to replace items which were scrapped; the latter cost $4,200 on March 15, 1963, and when scrapped were sold for $600, the $600 being received in cash and credited to sundry income.

On August 1, 1966, equipment which was bought May 1, 1962, for $1,200 was sold for $200. New equipment was purchased for $1,500 to replace the old (see above). The $200 was received in cash and was also credited to sundry income.

Prepare adjusting journal entries. State the adjusted balances in the three accounts shown above. Depreciation should be provided on the basis of actual periods of use at a 10% rate. It is the company's policy to follow the current operating concept of income reporting.

Problem 18-14. *ABC* Company moved from the east coast to the west coast. It disposed of all of its east coast fixed assets late in 1961, and put its west coast manufacturing facility into operation early in 1962. The new facility was constructed on leased land. All administrative and sales work is performed in rented space in a downtown office building.

Coincident with the move, the company made several changes in policy, as set forth on the following page.

The straight-line method was dropped in favor of the sum-of-years'-digits method for both the factory building and its equipment.
The use-life of all equipment was reduced from five years to four years. (The use-life of the new building was set at 25 years.)
Equipment installation costs, which typically add 5% to the total of all other acquisition costs of equipment, were to be charged to expense rather than capitalized.

The company manufactures only special-order products. It closes the factory each year during the latter part of December to provide for a vacation period for the factory employees and to facilitate annual maintenance work on the equipment. As a result, there is no work in process and no undelivered or unsold finished product at year end.

Data taken from the company's financial statements are presented below:

Balance Sheet Data
December 31, 1966

Current assets		$150,000
Factory building	$325,000	
Accumulated depreciation—Factory	115,000	210,000
Equipment	$360,000	
Accumulated depreciation—Equipment	224,000	136,000
		$496,000
Current liabilities		$100,000
Capital stock		200,000
Retained earnings		196,000
		$496,000

Income Statement Data

	1962	1963	1964	1965	1966
Net operating income (loss*)— before bonus	$ 40,000*	$ 10,000	$ 30,000	$ 60,000	$ 50,000
Bonus—10% (payable 30 days after close of year)	-0-	1,000	3,000	6,000	5,000
Net income (loss*) before income taxes	$ 40,000*	$ 9,000	$ 27,000	$ 54,000	$ 45,000
Income taxes (a flat rate of 25% is assumed to apply)		2,250	6,750	13,500	11,250
Tax refund (carryback of loss)	10,000				
Net income (loss*)	$ 30,000*	$ 6,750	$ 20,250	$ 40,500	$ 33,750

Statement of Retained Earnings

	1962	1963	1964	1965	1966
Beginning balance	$129,750	$ 99,750	$106,500	$116,750	$137,250
Add:					
Net income (loss*)	30,000*	6,750	20,250	40,500	$ 33,750
Gain on disposal of fully depreciated assets					$ 60,000
Less income tax effect					15,000
Net gain					$ 45,000
Total	$ 99,750	$106,500	$126,750	$157,250	$216,000
Deduct dividends	-0-	-0-	10,000	20,000	20,000
Ending balance	$ 99,750	$106,500	$116,750	$137,250	$196,000

The management of *ABC* Company wants to evaluate the changes in policy that were adopted in 1962 relating to the accounting for fixed assets. To assist in such evaluation, you are asked to show the December 31, 1966 balance sheet data presented on the preceding page as they would have appeared if the policy changes had not been adopted.

Additional Information

No additions have been made to the building.
Equipment additions and disposals were as follows:

Acquisitions		Disposals		
Year	Cost	Year	Cost	
1962	$300,000	1966	$200,000	(from 1962 acquisitions)
1964	40,000			
1966	220,000			

Depreciation is computed annually on the year-end account balances.

Assignment Material for Chapter 19

QUESTIONS

1. State the conditions under which intangible assets for which amortization is not usually required may properly be subject to amortization or complete write-off.
2. Under what circumstances may a partial write-down of an intangible asset be made and charged to retained earnings?
3. A concern owning a patent brings a suit against a competitor for infringement. What entries should be made by the patent holder if the suit is successful? What entries should be made if the suit is lost?
4. Assume that a concern buys a patent on an article that may prove to be a competing product. It does not manufacture this patented article. What should be done with the cost of the patent?
5. Is a practice of arbitrarily writing off intangibles upon, or immediately after, acquisition acceptable? Why?
6. Most companies do not capitalize any portion of research and development costs although future periods will likely benefit from such outlays. What seems to be the reason for this apparent breach of the accounting objective of matching revenue with related expense?
7. If a company operates a research department for the purpose of developing patentable devices, describe three approaches that may be used to determine the amount of such research costs that may be capitalized.
8. A manufacturing corporation occupying a factory under a long lease installs removable and nonremovable property on the premises of the lessor. State fully the basis on which the depreciation incident to such property should be determined.
9. Your client, a small manufacturing concern, occupies rented land and has signed a 25-year lease, which does not contain a renewal clause. The concern has erected on the land, at a cost of $150,000, a building having an estimated life of 40 years. A 4% depreciation rate has been employed, which will fully depreciate the building at the termination of the lease.

   (a) Do you believe that the depreciation rate of 4% is correct?
   (b) If, at the end of the fifteenth year, the lease is canceled and a new one for 35 years is signed, would you at that time recommend any change in the depreciation rate?
   (c) What depreciation rate would you have recommended at the outset if the original lease had contained a clause giving your client the option of renewal for 25 years?

10. Your client, a retailer, has recently taken occupancy of property under the terms of a ten-year renewable lease. In this connection, you note the following items of information:

    (a) Annual rental under the lease is $12,000.
    (b) At a cost of $60,000 your client has made leasehold improvements which have an estimated life of 30 years.

(c) The lease calls for removal of the improvements at the expiration of the lease. It is estimated that this will cost $15,000 net of salvage.

Describe fully the treatment of each of the above items in the financial statements. Justify the treatments you describe.

11. What occurs in a sale-and-leaseback transaction?

12. If a long-term lease were capitalized in the accounts, how would the financial statements differ from those prepared from accounts in which such lease was not capitalized?

13. If expenses are incurred in obtaining a trademark, should they be immediately written off, should they be capitalized and carried indefinitely, or should they be capitalized and gradually written off?

14. When does goodwill exist?

15. *R* Company has agreed to sell its business to *Q* Company for a sum which represents the book value of its assets less its liabilities plus an amount for goodwill. The directors of *R* Company propose as the payment for goodwill the sum of the company's net income after income taxes for the years 1963, 1964, 1965, and 1966. You are asked to comment on the fairness of this proposal and to suggest a basis for determining the goodwill if you feel that the proposal of *R* Company is open to criticism.

16. How can the possible misleading effects from the form of financing used by a business be neutralized when earnings data are being used to determine whether a particular business has goodwill?

17. Two concerns have been in business for five years. They started with the same capital, the average earnings during the five years have been exactly the same, and the dividends have been the same. Does it necessarily follow that the goodwill of one company is the same as that of the other?

PROBLEMS

Problem 19-1. The management of Dobbins Company has reached an agreement with a purchaser that the net tangible assets of the company are worth $670,000. Discussions are in process concerning the value of the company's goodwill. Three formulas are being considered:

(a) Purchase of average excess earnings for five years.
(b) Average excess earnings capitalized at the normal profit rate.
(c) Average excess earnings up to $20,000 capitalized at the normal rate, and those above $20,000 capitalized at 20%.

The negotiators have agreed that five years is a reasonable period in which to evaluate the company's earnings performance, but that consideration should be given to expected increases in sales and expenses. They have also agreed on the following:

Stockholders' equity, December 31, 1966	$740,000
Recorded goodwill on company's books was paid for	50,000
Average earnings for the past five years	112,000
Expected increase in yearly sales attributable to recently completed addition to the company's facilities	140,000
Expected increase in annual expenses from the operation of the new facilities, including income taxes	110,000
Normal rate of earnings for the industry	10%

Compute the goodwill under each of the three alternatives.

Problem 19-2. Stateline Company, organized in 1964, has set up a single account for all intangible assets. The following summary discloses the entries that have been recorded therein during 1964 and 1965.

Intangibles

Debits

7/1/64	10-year franchise; expiration date 6/30/74	$18,000
10/1/64	Advance payment on leasehold (Terms of lease: 5 years; annual rent, $6,000; advance payment, $5,000; annual payment, $5,000)	10,000
12/31/64	Net loss for 1964, after deducting state incorporation fee ($500) and related legal fees ($3,500)	8,000
1/2/65	Patent (expected economic life—8 years)	34,000
10/1/65	Cost of secret formula..	50,000

Credits

None.

Submit a schedule showing the proper total for intangible assets as of December 31, 1965.

Problem 19-3. Advanced Products Corporation is considering an offer for the purchase of its business. The management has decided that a proper goodwill amount to be added to the price agreed upon for the net tangible assets is three times the current year's "normal" earnings.

The net income reported for the current year is $280,000, after additions and deductions for the items listed below:

Gain from revaluation of securities	$12,000
Dividends received on securities to be retained by Advanced Products Corporation	6,200
Gain on sale of land	45,000
Plant rearrangement expense	10,400
Depreciation of fixed assets	40,000
Appropriation of net income for possible expansion of facilities ..	24,000

The depreciable assets are to be valued at 25% above their present carrying value.

Compute the amount of goodwill according to the specifications set forth by management. Ignore the question of income taxes.

Problem 19-4. Companies *A* and *B* are in the same industry, one in which a 10% return on assets is considered normal. After giving consideration to the following data, determine which company apparently has the larger goodwill.

	A	*B*
Net income (after income taxes at 25%):		
1965	$ 24,750	$ 28,050
1966	26,250	29,250
December 31, 1966:		
Current liabilities..............................	$ 30,000	$ 50,000
Bonds payable: A—6%; B—5%	50,000	100,000
Stockholders' equity	170,000	150,000

You may assume that the companies follow the practice of paying out dividends equal to the earnings and that no additional shares were issued by either company during the two-year period ending December 31, 1966.

Problem 19-5. The Monarch Development Company was organized on July 1, 1957, with an authorized capital of 20,000 shares of $5 par value capital stock, all of which were issued for three patents. Patent A had been issued six months earlier and Patents B and C had just been issued. This transaction was recorded as follows:

Patent A	20,000	
Patent B	60,000	
Patent C	80,000	
Capital stock		100,000
Capital in excess of par value		60,000

Amortization, based on the legal lives of the patents, has been recorded on the above values in a contra account at the close of each calendar year.

On January 8, 1966, an agreement was reached with the Internal Revenue Service covering the years 1957-1964, inclusive, under which the I.R.S. agreed to accept $120,000 as the proper cost of the three patents. The directors of The Monarch Development Company have decided that the accounts should be adjusted to reflect the settlement, and that separate asset and contra accounts should be established for each patent.

Prepare the necessary working papers and adjusting journal entries. The books have been closed for 1965.

Problem 19-6. Condensed statements of Process Manufacturing Company, per books, and after auditor's adjustments, are as follows:

PROCESS MANUFACTURING COMPANY
Balance Sheet
December 31, 1966

	Per Books	Adjusted
Assets		
Current assets	$2,325,000	$2,250,000
Pension fund	325,000	335,000
Fixed assets	1,875,000	1,810,000
Goodwill	300,000	300,000
	$4,825,000	$4,695,000
Liabilities and Stockholders' Equity		
Current liabilities	$ 875,000	$ 960,000
Bank loans	600,000	600,000
Capital stock	1,500,000	1,500,000
Retained earnings	1,575,000	1,345,000
Pension fund reserve	275,000	290,000
	$4,825,000	$4,695,000

PROCESS MANUFACTURING COMPANY
Statement of Retained Earnings
For the Period January 1, 1964 to December 31, 1966

	Per Books	Adjusted
Balance, January 1, 1964	$1,003,000	$ 800,680
Net income, 1964	450,600	380,500
Gain on sale of investments	90,800	110,200
Total	$1,544,400	$1,291,380
Deduct: Dividends paid—cash	$ 62,500	$ 62,500
Organization costs written off	25,000	25,000
Total	$ 87,500	$ 87,500

Balance, January 1, 1965	$1,456,900	$1,203,880
Net income, 1965	274,590	262,200
Total	$1,731,490	$1,466,080
Deduct: Goodwill written down	$ 200,000	$ 200,000
Organization costs written off	21,000	21,000
Dividends paid—cash	62,500	62,500
Pension fund reserve provision	125,000	130,000
Total	$ 408,500	$ 413,500
Balance, January 1, 1966	$1,322,990	$1,052,580
Net income, 1966	652,010	702,420
Total	$1,975,000	$1,755,000
Deduct: Stock dividend issued—20%	$ 250,000	$ 250,000
Pension fund reserve provision	150,000	160,000
Total	$ 400,000	$ 410,000
Balance, December 31, 1966	$1,575,000	$1,345,000

An interested party offers to buy out the business as of December 31, 1966, the goodwill to be valued by capitalizing at 25% the average of the net income for each of the past three years in excess of 10% of the net tangible assets at the beginning of each year. There were no changes in the capital stock during the period except for the stock dividend in 1966.

Compute the goodwill on this basis.

Problem 19-7. Companies *K*, *L*, and *M* are in different industries. Data from their 1966 financial statements are set forth below.

	K	*L*	*M*
Long-term debt—6%		$ 50,000	$ 75,000
Capital stock	$100,000	60,000	75,000
Retained earnings (deficit)	(20,000)	20,000	30,000
Total assets	100,000	150,000	200,000

The following additional information may be considered to be reliable.

Dividend policy for next 3 years:

K	No dividends
L	40% of earnings
M	60% of earnings

	K	*L*	*M*
Expected net income (after income taxes at 50%):			
1967	$10,000	$12,500	$24,000
1968	10,800	13,500	25,000
1969	11,664	14,000	25,250
Normal rate of return on assets	8%	10%	12%

Submit computations which indicate the following:

Which companies have goodwill?
Which company has the most goodwill?

Problem 19-8. Some indication of the present financial position and operating performance of Powder Company can be gathered from the following condensed financial statements.

CONDENSED FINANCIAL STATEMENTS OF POWDER COMPANY

Balance sheet
December 31, 1966

Current assets		$200,000
Fixed assets	$400,000	
Accumulated depreciation	180,000	220,000
		$420,000
Liabilities		$100,000
Capital stock	$250,000	
Retained earnings	70,000	320,000
		$420,000

Income Statement
For the Year Ended December 31, 1966

Sales		$800,000
Cost of sales	$450,000	
Selling and administrative expense	260,000	
Depreciation expense	40,000	750,000
Net income before income taxes		$ 50,000
Income taxes—25%		12,500
Net income		$ 37,500

The company has signed a long-term equipment lease which becomes effective on January 1, 1967, and terminates on December 31, 1976. Although no payments have been made under the lease, ten annual payments of $10,000 each are required. The equipment being leased has a useful life of ten years and can be purchased for $78,000, cash. Thus, the company is in effect paying financing costs of $22,000 (the difference between the aggregate rental payments and the cash price of the equipment) by making use of the leasing arrangement.

The management of Powder Company is curious about the effects that a policy of capitalization of the long-term lease would have on the company's financial statements. You are asked to prepare condensed financial statements for the years 1967 and 1971, first assuming that the lease is not capitalized (the conventional treatment) and then assuming that the lease is capitalized (a treatment advocated by some accountants).

Assumptions

A reasonable initial capitalized value for the long-term lease is $78,000.
Each annual payment is considered as including $2,200 of financing cost.
The annual payments are deductible for income tax purposes.
Expected annual dividend payments—$20,000.
Except for the addition of the annual payments under the lease, no other changes in revenue and expense (except for income taxes).
No change in income tax rates.
No acquisitions or dispositions of fixed assets.

Problem 19-9. Prepare a schedule showing the cost, amortization, and net balance of the patents of Stern Manufacturing Company for the period January 1, 1961 to December 31, 1966.

The company spent a total of $58,000 developing a basic patent which was applied for on March 1, 1960.
Additional legal costs incurred in expediting the issue of the patent amounted to $1,500 by December 31, 1960.
The patent was issued on January 2, 1961, and manufacture began on that date.

On April 30, 1962, the corporation paid $25,500 to attorneys for services in connection with an attempted infringement of this patent.

On July 1, 1963, the corporation purchased a patent on a closely related improvement of the original patent for $39,600. The patent purchased had 16½ years to run from July 1, 1963. An opinion was given to the firm by competent counsel that this patent will extend the life of the old patent.

To protect its patent position, the company purchased a competing patent on October 1, 1964. This patent cost the company $32,000 and had 16 years to run from the date of acquisition.

During 1966, the corporation paid a total of $51,000 to perfect and apply for a modification of the company's original patent. The patent on the modification was issued on January 2, 1967. It was understood that this patent would extend the period of protected production of the earlier patents over the life of the new patent.

Problem 19-10. Condensed financial statements of three retail companies are set forth below.

Balance Sheet—December 31, 1966

	Company		
	X	*Y*	*Z*
Cash	$100,000	$110,000	$ 70,000
Receivables—net	100,000	100,000	100,000
Inventories	250,000	250,000	250,000
	$450,000	$460,000	$420,000
Land	$ 50,000		
Building	400,000		
Accumulated depreciation	100,000*		
Equipment	220,000		
Accumulated depreciation	160,000*		
Leasehold interest in fixed assets			$670,000
Accumulated amortization			210,000*
	$410,000		$460,000
	$860,000	$460,000	$880,000
Current payables	$100,000	$100,000	$100,000
Long-term loan	460,000		
Long-term lease rental obligation			460,000
	$560,000	$100,000	$560,000
Capital stock	$200,000	$200,000	$200,000
Retained earnings	100,000	160,000	120,000
	$300,000	$360,000	$320,000
* Deduction.	$860,000	$460,000	$880,000

Income Statement—1966

	X	*Y*	*Z*
Sales	$600,000	$600,000	$600,000
Cost of goods sold	$400,000	$400,000	$400,000
Operating expenses, except depreciation and rent	93,000	93,000	93,000
Rent		72,600	
Depreciation	44,000		42,000
Financing charges	23,000		24,000
	$560,000	$565,600	$559,000
Net income before income tax	$ 40,000	$ 34,400	$ 41,000
Income tax—25%	10,000	8,600	10,250
Net income	$ 30,000	$ 25,800	$ 30,750

The companies were organized at about the same time. They use about the same kinds and quantities of fixed assets in their business operations. For all practical purposes, the fixed assets used by the three companies are identical. However, the companies have used different legal and financing arrangements in connection with their fixed assets. Company *X* owns its fixed assets and has raised some of the capital needed by long-term borrowing. Company *X* depreciates its equipment on the basis of a ten-year useful life, by the sum-of-years'-digits method; however, it depreciates the building, which it has owned for five years, on a straight-line plan. Company *Y* sold its fixed assets at a gain of $60,000, paid off its long-term debt, and leased back the assets for their estimated useful lives. Company *Z* has consistently made use of long-term leases extending for the estimated useful lives of the assets and has followed the practice of capitalizing such leases. Company *Z*'s annual rental payments amount to $66,000.

Make adjustments to the condensed balance sheets to improve their comparability for analytical purposes and, assuming that no dividend payments have ever been made by any of the companies, indicate which company has probably been most profitable to date from the point of view of its stockholders.

Problem 19-11. On the basis of the following information, prepare a schedule as of December 31, 1965, showing the estimated future annual net income which Olson Corporation may expect if it acquires the assets of Johnson Company. The estimated future annual net income will be used as a basis for goodwill determination.

Net income:

1960	$44,000
1961	45,000
1962	40,000
1963	47,000
1964	51,700
1965	55,000

(A 10 per cent reduction in income tax rates took place in 1964, causing the 1964 and 1965 income of the corporation to be taxed at about 45 per cent. No further changes in income tax rates are foreseeable.)

Expected annual increase in executive salaries—$18,000.

Excess of agreed price for building, acquired by Johnson Company on January 1, 1944, over its present book value (a 2 per cent depreciation rate was being used) —$58,800.

In 1962, the company wrote off and junked obsolete inventory which cost $18,000.

On the first business day of 1964, Johnson Company traded in all of its old machines of a certain type for new models. The book value of the old assets amounted to $16,000 and, after deduction of the trade-in allowance on the old machines, $80,000 cash was spent for the new assets. The income tax rules were followed in the accounts, so that neither gain nor loss resulted from the transaction. However, on the basis of the company's recent experience, it seems that an eight-year useful life would be more appropriate than the ten-year useful life being used by the company. Olson Corporation will change to an eight-year useful life for this type of asset as soon as it acquires the assets of Johnson Company.

A patent, the amortized cost of which is $16,000, will be retained by Johnson Company because its remaining legal and economic life is but two years. Johnson Company paid $40,000 for the patent in December, 1962, as an investment. Licensing agreements with other companies were negotiated early in 1963, under which Johnson Company has grossed annual royalties of $14,000 for the last three years.

Problem 19-12. Quality Company is negotiating to purchase all of the assets except cash and receivables of Hickam Company. No great difficulty is anticipated in negotiating prices for specific assets. However, there is some concern on the part of the representatives of Quality Company about the evaluation of Hickam Company's earnings as to whether superior earning power from the assets is indicated, because Hickam Company has followed different accounting policies from those of Quality Company in several instances.

The representatives of Quality Company believe that the best way to evaluate the earnings potential is to analyze the earnings of the three preceding years and to recompute them following the accounting policies of Quality Company. In addition to the adjustments attributable to the differences in accounting policies, adjustments should be made to remove any distortion introduced into the earnings record by unusual or nonrecurring items, and consideration should be given to any known factors which will affect future earnings.

You are asked to make a determination of the average earnings of Hickam Company, based on the earnings for the years 1964, 1965, and 1966, assuming that the policies of Quality Company had been in force, making whatever other revisions seem relevant in view of the objective of using such data for purposes of negotiating a price for goodwill. It is assumed that the charge for income taxes should be recomputed using the rate applicable to the earnings for 1966. Also show what the carrying values of the assets, except cash and receivables, would have been as of December 31, 1966.

Relevant financial information and policy differences are set forth below.

HICKAM COMPANY
Balance Sheet
December 31, 1966

Assets

Cash	$ 30,700
Receivables	180,400
Inventory	273,000
Lease of mineral rights	150,000
Depreciable fixed assets	256,300
Accumulated depreciation (deduct*)	125,400*
	$765,000

Liabilities and Stockholders' Equity

Accounts payable	$ 62,300
Liability for 1966 income taxes	24,000
Bonds payable—5% (issued 7/1/60)	120,000
Common stock	400,000
Retained earnings	158,700
	$765,000

Net Income

1964	$ 49,000
1965	52,500
1966	56,000

Quality Company has used the last-in, first-out cost as a basis for pricing its inventory. Hickam Company has used first-in, first-out. Inventory data for Hickam Company under both methods follow.

	Fifo	*Lifo*
December 31, 1963	$230,000	$210,000
December 31, 1964	246,000	218,000
December 31, 1965	258,000	224,000
December 31, 1966	273,000	229,000

Hickam Company discontinued a small segment of its business at the end of 1963. It is estimated that 1964 expenses included $8,000 of charges relating to the discontinuance.

Quality Company has followed a policy of writing off as current expenses all minor equipment items costing less than $300. This was the practice of Hickam Company prior to 1964. In 1964, Hickam changed its policy and expensed only items costing less than $100. Both companies have charged a full year's depreciation in the year of acquisition, regardless of the purchase date, and have used a 10 per cent depreciation rate. Items costing between $100 and $300, by year of purchase by Hickam Company, were:

1964	$3,000
1965	2,000
1966	5,000

No utilization has as yet been made of the mineral rights held under lease. Development costs incurred in the past two years and charged to expense were: 1965, $10,000; 1966, $14,000. Data thus gathered indicate that the leasehold will, without further cost, generate royalty revenue of $25,000 per year for the next ten years.

Assignment Material for Chapter 20

QUESTIONS

1. Is the deduction of United States Government securities from tax liabilities—which amounts to an offsetting of assets and liabilities—acceptable?

2. A manufacturer of ice cream purchased, on the deferred-payment plan, refrigerator units at a cost of $15,000. All these units were resold to customers at cost. Collections from the customers in payment of the units had been $3,126.18, whereas payments by the manufacturer to the distributor of the units totaled $6,180.31.

You are auditing the books of the manufacturer, who contends that he has no liability to the distributor because he purchased the refrigerator units for his customers and that an asset should appear on his balance sheet as follows:

Advances to customers:	
Payment made for customers' account	$6,180.31
Less cash received from customers	3,126.18
Balance	$3,054.13

Do you believe that your client is correct in his contentions? Why or why not?

3. What entries should be made to record the deposit of cash with a fiscal agent for the payment of bond interest?

4. What is the basic objection to the write-off of bond discount by charge to Retained Earnings at the date of issuance, or shortly thereafter?

5. What would be the proper treatment of unamortized bond discount and expense from time to time as holders of convertible bonds exercised their rights to convert them into capital stock?

6. A company refunds a bond issue of $5,000,000 principal amount of 5% bonds, due five years hence, on which there is still an unamortized debt discount and expense of $250,000, by the issuance of $5,500,000 principal amount of 4% 20-year bonds at 90. The difference between the amount of cash necessary to retire the old bond issue and the amount produced by the refunding bonds is supplied from the general funds of the company. The expenses of the new issue are $50,000. Discuss briefly three procedures which may be followed by the company to dispose of the unamortized debt discount and expense applicable to the old issue, and list them in the order of your preference.

7. The text refers to one possible exception to the rule that reacquired bonds should not be shown as an asset. State the exception and evaluate the reasoning usually given in justification for the exception.

8. The December 31, 1965 balance sheet of a medium-sized manufacturing corporation did not include the following items among the current liabilities: (All are material in amount.)

(a) Notes payable to a group of 12 stockholders, the notes to become due and payable on the demand of at least eight of the group.

(b) A note due March 31, 1966, in settlement of which the holder accepted preferred stock on January 6, 1966.
(c) Rent collected in advance.

For each of the items above, you are to give arguments to justify its exclusion from current liabilities. If your answer involves assumptions as to facts not given in the question, state your assumptions.

9. During the course of an audit as of December 31, 1965, you find that your client in 1959 purchased two acres of land adjacent to its present plant for future expansion, subject to a first mortgage, the maturity of which was May 10, 1963. The mortgage has not been refinanced but has been extended for one year at each May 10th since 1963, the date of the annual 5% interest payment. The bank which owns the mortgage informs you that, subject to the usual interest payment at May 10, 1966, it will grant the customary one-year extension of the mortgage to May 10, 1967. Your client is in a good financial position. How will you show the mortgage liability on the balance sheet?

10. What are the effects on the financial statements of a failure to show the liability for goods in transit shipped f.o.b. shipping point if the goods are not included in the inventory?

11. An intercity bus company, wishing to equalize the expense caused by accidents, adopted the plan of depositing 2% of its gross receipts each month in a local savings bank, charging the funds so set aside to an account called Reserve for Accidents. The deposits in the fund during the year amounted to $4,869.26, and payments were made on account of accidents totaling $950. These payments were debited to Accidents and credited to Reserve for Accidents. The bookkeeper endeavored to close the books at the end of the year by debiting Accidents and crediting Reserve for Accidents with $3,919.26, thus making a total charge for accidents of $4,869.26. But the result was that the company was left with cash assets of $3,919.26 not represented on the books. Wherein did the bookkeeper err, and what entries should have been made to show the facts correctly?

12. Define operating reserves. Cite an example of an operating reserve.

13. Describe the nature of general contingency reserves and state the proper accounting for such reserves.

14. State the debit-credit rules and other considerations that have a bearing on the proper location of reserves in the financial statements.

PROBLEMS

Problem 20-1. Royal Company issued $800,000 of $1,000 bonds on December 31, 1963, at 94. These bonds were to mature as follows:

December 31,	
1965	$100,000
1966	100,000
1967	100,000
1968	100,000
1969	200,000
1970	200,000
Total	$800,000

Prepare a schedule showing the prospective amortization of the bond discount by years.

On December 31, 1968, the company purchased $40,000 (face value) of its bonds maturing on December 31, 1969, at 98 and retired them. Prepare the journal entry to record the purchase.

Problem 20-2. Pierpont Corporation authorized the issuance of $2,000,000 of 4% bonds to be dated May 1, 1965. The bonds were to mature on May 1, 1985, with semiannual interest payments on May 1 and November 1.

Bonds were issued as follows:

Date	Face Value	Issue Price
May 1, 1965	$1,200,000	98
February 1, 1966	400,000	102
July 31, 1967	400,000	106

Interest was paid on the due dates. The corporation operates on a calendar-year basis.

Required:

(a) Journal entries to record the issuance of each lot of bonds.

(b) Balance sheet presentation of all accounts relevant to the above bonds on December 31, 1965, 1966, and 1967. Show all computations.

Problem 20-3. Milan Electrical Corporation issued $600,000 of 5% bonds at 104½ on December 31, 1965. Interest was payable annually on December 31. Costs associated with the issuance of the bonds amounted to $2,700.

Prepare a schedule showing the interest expense by years during the life of the bond issue under the conditions set forth below.

(a) The bonds are to be retired in six equal annual installments beginning on December 31, 1967.

(b) The bonds are to be retired in six equal annual installments beginning on December 31, 1970.

Problem 20-4. Stanford Company issued 6%, 30-year mortgage bonds in the principal amount of $1,200,000 on September 1, 1945, at a discount of $30,000, which it proceeded to amortize over the life of the issue. The indenture securing the issue provided that the bonds could be called for redemption in total but not in part at any time prior to maturity at 103% of the principal amount.

On September 1, 1966, the company issued its 5%, 25-year mortgage bonds in the principal amount of $1,200,000 at 101, and the proceeds were used in the refunding of the 6%, 30-year mortgage bonds on that date. The indenture securing the new issue did not provide for retirement before maturity.

Both bond issues provided for the payment of interest on March 1 and September 1. The company's fiscal year ends on November 30.

Submit all journal entries required during the calendar year 1966 in connection with the above bond issues.

Problem 20-5. Fiftieth Company issued $200,000 of 20-year, 4% bonds, dated June 1, 1958, on September 1, 1958, at 101¼ plus accrued interest. Interest is payable semi-annually. The bonds were convertible into the company's common stock on a rising scale of prices for the stock. (Interest accrued to the date of conversion to be paid in cash.)

The common stock had a par value of $25 per share.

During 1965, conversions were made as follows:

Date	Face Value Converted	Conversion Price	Number of Shares
May 1, 1965	$21,000	$30	700
October 1, 1965	32,000	32	1,000

Prepare the journal entries necessary to record the issuance of the bonds and the above conversions. The company's fiscal year ends on September 30.

Problem 20-6. Mercer Corporation entered into a lease agreement for the use of a warehouse for 12 years from July 1, 1954. The type of materials handled caused more than normal wear of approaches and runways. For this reason, the corporation was required to make payments to a trustee, the fund to be used for resurfacing these areas at the termination of the lease. Under the terms of the lease, Mercer Corporation retained title to the fund assets. Payments were to be made at the end of each lease year as follows: Years 1 through 3, $5,000 per year; years 4 and 5, $4,000 per year; years 6 and 7, $3,500 per year; years 8 through 11, $2,000 per year; and $1,000 in the final year. Any amount not used for the resurfacing was to be returned. The trustee retained all earnings on fund assets as compensation for his services.

The rental was $10,000 per year, payable in advance. The resurfacing work, completed three months after termination of the lease, actually cost $36,600, which was paid by the trustee. The corporation operates on a calendar-year basis.

Prepare all journal entries arising from the above lease in each of the following years: 1954, 1955, 1965, and 1966.

Problem 20-7. After negotiations with employee representatives during 1964, Multiproducts Corporation entered into an agreement to provide pensions at the corporation's expense for its employees when they reach retirement age.

The pension plan is carried with an insurance company. It is to become effective on January 1, 1965. Current pension costs are to be met by quarterly payments to the insurance company, payable within one month after the end of each quarter. Past-service pension cost is to be paid to the insurance company in equal annual installments in the years 1965 through 1974, the payment being due on or before December 31 of each year. Corporate officers estimate that employees covered by the past-service pension cost will continue to serve the corporation for an average of 12 years after the plan is started.

The following facts are determined from past operating records and records of operations in 1965 and 1966:

Past-service pension cost	$1,800,000
Current costs per quarter:	
1965:	
First	26,810
Second	20,930
Third	18,480
Fourth	21,940
1966:	
First	25,370
Second	23,200
Third	17,990
Fourth	20,860

Total payments to the insurance company each year amounted to:

1965	$246,220
1966	268,500

(a) Prepare all journal entries relevant to the corporation's pension program for the years 1965 and 1966, assuming that the following accounts are to be used:

Deferred Past-Service Pension Cost
Past-Service Pension Cost Payable (Entire liability to be recorded at start of program.)

Pension Premiums Payable
Pension Program Expense

The corporation employs a calendar-year accounting period.

(b) Show how the accounts listed above would appear in the December 31, 1965 and 1966 balance sheets.

Problem 20-8. In the course of your examination of the accounts of Exeter, Incorporated, for the three years ended December 31, 1966, you discover the following transactions:

January 1, 1964:
Sold $400,000 face value of 20-year, first-mortgage, 3% bonds, interest payable June 30 and December 31. The bonds were sold at 96 and the discount was charged to Retained Earnings.

During the next three years, all interest payments were made in full when due.

January 1, 1965:
Purchased $40,000 face value of its bonds at 98. The bonds were canceled and the discount was credited to Retained Earnings.

July 1, 1966:
Purchased $60,000 face value of bonds at 102. The bonds were canceled and the premium was charged to Retained Earnings.

Required:

(1) The correct interest expense for the years 1964, 1965, and 1966.
(2) The amount of bond discount which should remain unamortized on December 31, 1966.
(3) The gain or loss on each bond retirement.
(4) The necessary adjusting journal entry on December 31, 1966, assuming that the books have not been closed for 1966.

Problem 20-9. On March 1, 1958, Regal Products Corporation issued $500,000 of 20-year, 5% bonds at 98. The bonds were callable at 104 plus accrued interest. From the issue date to March 1, 1964, $96,000 of these bonds were acquired and canceled by the corporation. During 1964, as interest rates declined, the cost of retiring bonds rose above the call price, and the corporate officers decided to issue refunding bonds at a lower rate of interest. The old bonds were called on September 1, 1964, after payment of interest, and a new 3%, 16-year issue in the amount of $400,000 was disposed of at 97. Interest was payable semiannually on both bond issues.

Required:

(a) Journal entries for the refunding operations.
(b) Journal entries to be made on the first interest-payment date after refunding. The books are closed on November 30.

Problem 20-10. The following accounts are reproduced from the ledger of Carhart Corporation on December 31, 1966.

4% Bonds Payable—Due January 1, 1969

Date	Explanation	Amount	Date	Amount
Jan. 1, 1965	Purchased at face value and retired	15,000	Jan. 1, 1959	300,000
July 1, 1966	$20,000 face value purchased at 90 and retired	18,000		

Discount on 4% Bonds Payable

Jan. 1, 1959	15,000	

Bond Interest Expense

July 1, 1966	5,700	

Required:

(a) Balances of Bonds Payable and Discount on Bonds Payable accounts for the balance sheet on December 31, 1966.
(b) Computation of bond interest expense to be shown in the income statement for the year ended December 31, 1966.
(c) Adjusting journal entries on December 31, 1966.

Problem 20-11. Continuous Process Company closes its processing plant during the first two weeks of July each year in order to give the plant workers their two weeks' paid vacation and to enable the company's maintenance crew to perform annual maintenance on the machinery and equipment.

Management decided to prepare quarterly financial statements starting in 1964, and, in order to minimize distortion to the quarterly statements from the vacation pay and annual maintenance work, decided to establish budgetary reserves for these two expenses. The company closes its books on December 31.

Management also decided to base the operation of the budgetary reserves for the first three years on average costs for the five years preceding 1964. The averages were $47,200 for vacation pay and $128,400 for maintenance work, with the latter showing greater fluctuation than the former. After three years' experience, the amounts used for the provisions would be reviewed and possibly revised for subsequent years.

Actual costs for the first three years following the establishment of the budgetary reserves were:

	Vacation Pay	Maintenance
1964	$46,600	$128,000
1965	47,500	126,500
1966	47,900	130,000

Required:

(a) The entries which would be made quarterly to the budgetary reserves.
(b) The amounts and balance sheet locations of the budgetary reserves on the following dates:

June 30, 1964	June 30, 1965
September 30, 1964	December 31, 1965
December 31, 1964	December 31, 1966

Problem 20-12. The following condensed income statement was prepared from the adjusted trial balance of Comet Company. The company has been following the current operating concept of income reporting.

COMET COMPANY
Income Statement
For the Year Ended December 31, 1966

Sales		$1,800,000
Cost of goods sold	$1,500,000	
Operating expenses	396,000	
Interest expense	4,000	1,900,000
Net loss		$ 100,000

The following accounts were taken from the adjusted trial balances of the company. The trial balances were in balance, although in your analysis of the facts given in the problem you will no doubt discover instances of improper accounting.

	December 31,	
	1965	1966
Reserve for general contingencies	$ 60,000	$100,000
Reserve for advertising	200,000	160,000
Reserve for plant expansion	200,000	60,000
Reserve for bond sinking fund	90,000	-0-
Reserve for patent amortization	129,600	113,400
Reserve for land appreciation	-0-	200,000
Reserve for vacation pay	-0-	1,000
Reserve for capitalized long-term lease	-0-	200,000
Reserve for insurance	100,000	50,000
Reserve for losses on treasury stock transactions	10,000	15,000
Dividends declared (* debit)	50,000*	50,000*

Additional information:

During 1966 the company settled a customer's damage suit out of court by the payment of $10,000, which was charged to Reserve for General Contingencies.

During 1966 the company spent, and charged to Reserve for Advertising, $40,000 in an effort to halt an adverse sales trend. In 1965 the board of directors had appropriated $200,000 from retained earnings for such a purpose.

During 1966 the company spent $140,000 for architect's plans and site preparation, which was charged to the reserve account. The company is awaiting bids from contractors.

On November 1, 1966, the ten-year bond issue of $100,000 was retired.

Early in 1966 it became apparent that the commercial life of the patent would be 12 years instead of 9 years.

During 1966 the company made monthly provisions for vacation pay in the amount of $10,000. The vacation pay disbursement amounted to $119,000.

On December 15, 1966, the company signed a long-term lease. One of the clauses in the lease provided that the company could purchase the property at the termination of the lease for $100. The lease was capitalized.

During 1966 the company increased the amount of insurance carried with insurance companies and thereby reduced the potential loss it might suffer from inadequate insurance.

Dividends applicable to treasury stock are credited to a special reserve account. Only credits of this type are made to the account. There were no treasury stock transactions during 1966, although the company had in its treasury 10,000 shares acquired prior to 1966 at a cost of $88,000.

The retained earnings—free and unappropriated—as of December 31, 1965, as shown by the statement of retained earnings for 1965, amounted to $345,600.

Prepare the statement of retained earnings for the year ended December 31, 1966. You should feel free to revise the net loss of $100,000 if you believe that it has been improperly computed.

Also prepare the Stockholders' Equity section of the December 31, 1966 balance sheet. The capital stock was $10 par value; 100,000 shares were authorized and issued.

Problem 20-13. The following was taken from an improperly classified balance sheet. The account terminology is admittedly poor in some instances.

Current liabilities:			
Accounts payable		$ 98,217	
Reserve for restoration of leased property		6,000	
Reserve for income taxes		114,500	
Accrued operating expenses		17,211	$ 235,928
Reserves:			
Reserve for increased cost of replacement of machinery		$ 160,000	
Reserve for dealer warranties		78,610	
Reserve for self-insurance		68,000	
Reserve for depreciation		218,380	
Reserve for possible future decline in inventory value		312,000	
Reserve for contingencies		80,000	
Reserve for possible additional income taxes		25,000	941,990
Stockholders' equity:			
Common stock, $10 par value; authorized, 200,000 shares; issued and outstanding, 160,000 shares		$1,600,000	
Capital in excess of par value		240,000	
Retained earnings:			
Reserve for repairs and maintenance	$ 32,300		
Reserve for building fund	64,210		
Reserve for past-service pension cost	314,206		
Unappropriated	416,266	826,982	
Reserve for accretion to natural resources		180,000	2,846,982
			$4,024,900

Required:

(a) For each reserve account, list the account that should have been debited when the reserve was credited.
(b) For each reserve account, list the account normally credited to reduce or dispose of the reserve balance.
(c) The correct balance sheet classification for those reserve accounts you believe to be improperly classified.

Problem 20-14. The following account balances were taken from the records of Pudget Company.

	December 31,	
	1965	1966
Reserve for fire losses	$ 32,000	$ 27,000
Reserve for future inventory losses	50,000	45,600
Reduction of inventory to lower of cost or market	9,000	23,000
Reserve for contingencies	55,000	75,000
Allowance for vacation pay	-0-	1,200*
Common stock	500,000	500,000
Retained earnings	125,000	195,000
Capital in excess of stated value	50,000	50,000

* Debit balance.

The company has been applying the following policies:

(1) The "clean surplus" theory.
(2) Each year $6,000 is debited to Insurance Expense and credited to Reserve for Fire Losses. Fire losses are charged to the reserve.

(3) The company values its inventory at cost or market, whichever is lower. Each year $4,000 is debited to Cost of Goods Sold and credited to Reserve for Future Inventory Losses. Whenever the inventory priced at market is below cost, 60 per cent of the decline is debited to Reserve for Future Inventory Losses and the remainder to Cost of Goods Sold.
(4) Each year, before net income is finally determined, a debit or credit is made to the Reserve for Contingencies, a profit-equalization reserve. The amount of the debit or credit is equal to 50 per cent of the difference between the preliminary net income and $100,000. No other entries are made in the reserve account.
(5) The Allowance for Vacation Pay is used as a budgetary reserve.
(6) Each year $50,000 is paid in dividends.

Required:

(a) A schedule showing the net income for 1966, following generally accepted accounting principles.
(b) The Stockholders' Equity section as it should appear in the December 31, 1966 balance sheet.

Problem 20-15. The balance sheet on page 752 was prepared from the records of Phillips Products Company. Before releasing it to several banks for their use in connection with negotiations for additional bank financing, it has been submitted to you for review and possible revision.

Your review discloses the following:

(1) Accounts receivable on the balance sheet date total $247,400, and credit balances in customers' accounts arising from returned merchandise and cash advances amount to $8,800.
(2) The company has followed the policy of maintaining the allowance for doubtful accounts at 1½% of accounts receivable at year end. You observe that a transposition of numbers used in this computation makes the present allowance balance incorrect.
(3) The manufacturing cost records confirm that cost per books was the basis used in stating the inventories. The cost of goods sold was stated at $1,330,000. Any underabsorbed or overabsorbed manufacturing overhead is distributed pro rata to cost of goods sold and the ending inventories of goods in process and finished goods.
(4) The building was constructed during the first half of 1966, at a contract cost of $400,000. It was placed in service on June 30, 1966. Depreciation is being based on a useful life of 50 years. Ninety per cent of the building is used for manufacturing purposes.
(5) The semiannual interest payments on the 3% bonds were made to the interest-payment agent. The report from the agent shows that all interest coupons dated June 30, 1966, were turned in and destroyed. As of December 31, 1966, $460 of the coupons bearing that date had been honored by the agent.
(6) The 3% bonds were dated and issued on December 31, 1965, at 92. The proceeds were used to help pay for the construction of the new building. The discount on the bonds was added to the cost of the building, although the company decided against the capitalization of the $6,000 of interest accrued during construction.
(7) Because of recent court decisions, it is likely that the company will have to pay additional income taxes of $8,700 for the years 1963 and 1964. A charge to expense for this amount was made in 1966.
(8) The company has used a budgetary reserve account for the factory vacation pay to minimize distortion in the monthly financial statements.

(9) The Reserve for Product Warranty is credited for charges to expense and debited for cash disbursements to customers. The account balance seems reasonable.

PHILLIPS PRODUCTS COMPANY

Balance Sheet

December 31, 1966

Assets

Current assets:			
Cash on hand and in banks		$211,136	
Accounts receivable	$238,600		
Less allowance for doubtful accounts	3,552	235,048	
Inventories—at cost:			
Finished goods	$280,000		
Goods in process	140,000		
Materials	76,000		
Factory supplies	17,800	513,800	
Prepaid expenses		34,680	$ 994,664
Fixed assets:			
Land		$ 72,000	
Building	$432,000		
Accumulated depreciation	4,320	427,680	
Machinery and equipment	$998,600		
Accumulated depreciation	317,280	681,320	1,181,000
			$2,175,664

Liabilities and Stockholders' Equity

Current liabilities:			
Accounts payable		$360,830	
Accrued operating expenses		51,110	
Notes payable—Banks		250,000	
Estimated liability for income taxes—Current	$ 75,100		
Less U.S. Government securities	60,000	15,100	$ 677,040
Long-term liability:			
3% bonds payable—December 31, 1981			400,000
Stockholders' equity:			
Capital stock—$10 par value; 80,000 shares authorized and issued		$800,000	
Surplus:			
Reserve for product warranty	$ 62,500		
Reserve for vacation pay—Factory	1,480		
Reserve for prior years' income taxes	8,700		
Retained earnings	225,944	298,624	1,098,624
			$2,175,664

Prepare necessary correcting entries, assuming that the accounts have been closed, and a revised balance sheet. You may assume that the income tax liability accounts do not require revision.

Assignment Material for Chapter 21

QUESTIONS

1. Briefly discuss the advantages of comparative statements as opposed to statements applicable only to the current period.
2. When comparative statements are being prepared, what does the accountant do with footnotes, explanations, and accountants' qualifications which appeared on the statements for the preceding years that are now being used to provide the comparative data?
3. How would you distinguish between horizontal and vertical procedures for comparative statement analysis? What are the advantages of each procedure?
4. If horizontal-analysis per cents are included in a comparative income statement for three years, what base or bases should be used in the computation of the per cents to prevent misleading inferences? Why?
5. In horizontal analysis, is it always possible to determine per cents of increase or decrease for each statement item? Explain.
6. For management purposes, statements are sometimes prepared showing the results of operations for the current month and for the same month of the preceding year. Will such comparisons always be meaningful? Explain.
7. The higher the income tax rate, the greater is the leverage effect of borrowing. Is this statement true?
8. How are income taxes treated in computing the number of times bond interest has been earned?
9. What inference would you draw from the following data relating to a manufacturing corporation?

   A low ratio of stockholders' equity to liabilities.
   A high ratio of liabilities to assets.
   A low ratio of stockholders' equity to assets.

10. How is the operating ratio computed? What is indicated by the operating ratio?
11. Assume that a corporation has significant amounts invested in securities and other properties not closely associated with the principal operating activities of the business. What modification, if any, would you make when computing the ratio of net income to stockholders' equity if you were interested in forming an opinion about the profitability of the company?
12. Comparisons of the ratios of one company with those of another or with composites of numerous companies should be made with great caution. Do you agree with this statement? Why?
13. A stockholder who owns some stock in a listed corporation is concerned because she receives such small dividends. She has reviewed the last stockholders' report and has concluded that there is ample cash available for much larger dividends.

In addition to cash in banks, the corporation's balance sheet shows the following items which, she believes, represent cash funds:

(a) a large "paid-in surplus";
(b) plenty of "undivided profits";
(c) a large "reserve for general contingencies";
(d) a substantial "accumulated depreciation" balance.

The stockholder is further perturbed because the corporation's most recent balance sheet shows Goodwill at only $500,000, whereas a year before it had been shown at $1,000,000. She believes that a corporation which is losing goodwill so rapidly must be poorly managed.

In simple, nontechnical language, write a letter which should clear up the stockholder's misunderstanding.

PROBLEMS

Problem 21-1. Refer to the following account balances taken from the ledger of The Gordon Company on the dates indicated and compute the amounts and per cents of the changes shown therein.

	December 31,	
	1965	1964
Sales	$610,400	$560,000
Officers' salaries	60,000	60,000
Delivery expense	20,220	24,540
Interest expense	920	460
Commissions earned	6,000	4,450
Purchases	276,736	390,400
Sales discounts	14,716	10,400
Purchase returns and allowances	4,434	6,000
Gain (loss*) on disposal of machinery	9,040	6,560*
Freight in	4,536	4,800
Insurance expense	1,200	900
Bad debts	4,270	2,800

Problem 21-2. Copy the following condensed comparative balance sheet and add colums showing:

(a) The per cent that each item in the December 31, 1965 balance sheet is of the balance sheet total.
(b) The amount and per cent of increase or decrease in each item. Note: Carry per cents to two decimal places.

MONTANA CORPORATION
Comparative Balance Sheet
December 31, 1965 and 1964

	December 31,	
	1965	1964
Assets		
Current assets:		
Cash	$ 28,400	$ 22,200
Accounts receivable—net	92,800	104,600
Inventories	83,600	73,200
Prepaid expenses	6,000	5,200
Total current assets	$210,800	$205,200

Fixed assets:		
Machinery and equipment	$193,000	$160,400
Less accumulated depreciation	42,800	28,800
Net	$150,200	$131,600
Deferred charge—Unamortized bond discount	$ 3,000	$ 3,600
	$364,000	$340,400

Liabilities and Stockholders' Equity

Current liabilities:		
Accounts payable	$ 48,600	$ 36,800
Accrued expenses	25,200	26,600
Total current liabilities	$ 73,800	$ 63,400
Bonds payable	100,000	100,000
Total liabilities	$173,800	$163,400
Stockholders' equity:		
Capital stock (15,000 shares)	$150,000	$150,000
Retained earnings	40,200	27,000
Total stockholders' equity	$190,200	$177,000
	$364,000	$340,400

Problem 21-3.

MONTANA CORPORATION

Condensed Comparative Statement of Income and Expense
For the Years Ended December 31, 1965, 1964, and 1963

	Year Ended December 31,		
	1965	1964	1963
Gross sales	$250,800	$165,600	$208,000
Sales allowances	4,800	1,600	6,000
Net sales	$246,000	$164,000	$202,000
Cost of goods sold	155,600	99,600	136,000
Gross profit on sales	$ 90,400	$ 64,400	$ 66,000
Operating expenses:			
Selling expenses	$ 52,800	$ 33,600	$ 40,000
General expenses	19,200	16,000	24,000
Total operating expenses	$ 72,000	$ 49,600	$ 64,000
Net operating income	$ 18,400	$ 14,800	$ 2,000
Net financial expense	4,800	4,800	8,000
Net income (loss*)	$ 13,600	$ 10,000	$ 6,000*

From the above data, prepare:

(a) A comparative statement of income and expense for the three years expressed in terms of per cents of net sales.

(b) A comparative statement of income and expense for the years ended December 31, 1965 and 1964, with columns for amounts and per cents of increase.

(c) A comparative statement of income and expense for the years ended December 31, 1965, 1964, and 1963, with columns showing differences between 1965 and 1964 amounts and between 1964 and 1963 amounts, and columns showing ratios of 1965 and 1964 amounts to 1963 amounts.

Problem 21-4. Use the data of Dunham, Incorporated, set forth on the next page, to compute the required ratios.

(a) Ratio of total liabilities to total assets.
(b) Ratio of security to long-term liabilities. (All of the fixed assets are pledged as security to the long-term liabilities.)
(c) Ratio of net income to stockholders' equity.
(d) Ratio of net income to total assets.

	December 31,	
	1965	1964
Fixed assets	$190,000	$152,750
Total assets	255,000	222,500
Long-term liabilities	37,500	50,000
Total liabilities	75,000	85,000
Stockholders' equity	180,000	137,500
Net income for the year ended on the stated date	19,000	14,750

Problem 21-5. The following information for 1965 and 1964 was gathered from the records of Motor City Company.

	1965	1964
Net sales	$106,000	$101,000
Cost of goods sold	66,036	61,275
Selling and administrative expenses	29,000	30,500
Bond interest expense	600	450
Other interest expense	364	275
Net income	6,000	5,000
Federal income tax	4,000	3,500
Stockholders' equity	56,000	50,000

Compute the following for these years:
(a) Ratio of sales to stockholders' equity.
(b) Operating ratio.
(c) Income available for bond interest and number of times bond interest earned.
(d) Ratio of net income to stockholders' equity.

Problem 21-6. Excell Company presented the following condensed income statements covering three calendar years.

	1966	1965	1964
Net sales	$573,480	$652,424	$853,624
Cost of goods sold	397,125	421,706	569,740
Gross profit on sales	$176,355	$230,718	$283,884
Operating expenses:			
Selling expenses	$131,098	$142,240	$163,300
General expenses	37,120	47,265	72,290
Total operating expenses	$168,218	$189,505	$235,590
Net operating income	$ 8,137	$ 41,213	$ 48,294
Net financial expense	12,652	21,485	18,365
Net income (loss*) before income tax	$ 4,515*	$ 19,728	$ 29,929
Federal income tax		4,340	6,584
Net income (loss*)	$ 4,515*	$ 15,388	$ 23,345

Prepare a comparative income statement, showing the increases and decreases from year to year, with ratios based on amounts for the preceding year.

Problem 21-7. Refer to Problem 21-6. Prepare a comparative income statement for the three-year period showing the increases and decreases in relation to 1964. Also compute ratios based on the amounts for 1964.

Problem 21-8.

(a) The Atlantis Corporation has $800,000 of 3% bonds outstanding secured by a mortgage on its land and buildings. The land had a cost of $1,000,000 and the buildings a cost of $2,200,000. The buildings have a depreciated book value of $1,400,000. Compute the ratio of the security to the bond issue.

(b) Assume the same facts as in (a). In addition, The Atlantis Corporation has a sinking fund for retirement of the bonds. The fund, amounting to $400,000, is invested in securities of *X* Company. Compute the ratio of the security to the funded debt.

(c) Assume the same facts as in (b) except that the sinking fund is invested in the bonds of The Atlantis Corporation. What is the ratio of the security to the bonds outstanding?

(d) In 1965, The Atlantis Corporation had a net income of $79,200, after income taxes of $52,800. What number of times did the company earn its bond interest?

Problem 21-9.

BARBOUR METAL PRODUCTS
Summary Balance Sheet
December 31, 1966

Total assets	$275,000
Total liabilities	$ 75,000
Stockholders' equity:	
Preferred stock—5% (500 shares)	50,000
Common stock (1,000 shares)	100,000
Retained earnings	50,000
Total liabilities and stockholders' equity	$275,000

The net income for 1966 was $20,000.

Compute:

(a) The ratio of net income to stockholders' equity.
(b) The ratio of net income to total assets.
(c) The ratio of stockholders' equity to total liabilities.
(d) The ratio of stockholders' equity to total assets.
(e) The earnings per share of stock, assuming that the preferred stock shares ratably in all earnings after 5% has also been paid to common stockholders.
(f) The earnings per share of common stock, assuming that the preferred stock received only the 5% indicated.
(g) The book value per share of common stock, assuming:
(1) Preferred stock shares in earnings as indicated in (e) above.
(2) Preferred stock is nonparticipating.

Problem 21-10. Refer to the financial statements of Montana Corporation in Problems 21-2 and 21-3 and make the following computations for 1964 and 1965:

(a) The ratio of sales to stockholders' equity.
(b) The ratio of cost of goods manufactured to fixed assets. The finished goods inventories were: December 31, 1963, $18,400; December 31, 1964, $16,300; December 31, 1965, $20,200.
(c) The equity ratios.
(d) The ratio of net sales to fixed assets.
(e) The operating ratio.
(f) The book value per share of stock.
(g) The ratio of stockholders' equity to fixed assets.
(h) The earnings per share of stock.

Problem 21-11. Following are balance sheets of Diagram Company.

	December 31, 1966		December 31, 1965	
Assets				
Current assets:				
Cash		$ 21,365		$ 27,865
Accounts receivable	$67,785		$56,384	
Less allowance for doubtful accounts	2,486	65,299	2,755	53,629
Inventories		41,964		31,465
Total current assets		$128,628		$112,959
Fixed assets:				
Land		$ 12,000		$ 10,000
Buildings	$35,000		$35,000	
Less accumulated depreciation	7,700	27,300	7,000	28,000
Machinery	$37,500		$40,000	
Less accumulated depreciation	17,861	19,639	16,000	24,000
Total fixed assets		$ 58,939		$ 62,000
		$187,567		$174,959
Liabilities and Stockholders' Equity				
Current liabilities:				
Accounts payable		$ 25,365		$ 15,320
Notes payable		26,000		30,000
Total current liabilities		$ 51,365		$ 45,320
Stockholders' equity:				
Capital stock		$ 72,000		$ 60,000
Retained earnings		54,202		69,639
Reserve for contingencies		10,000		
Total stockholders' equity		$136,202		$129,639
		$187,567		$174,959

An examination of the Retained Earnings account showed that a stock dividend of 20% and later a cash dividend of 5% were paid during the year 1966.

Prepare a statement accounting for the increase in stockholders' equity and the resulting increase in net assets during the year 1966, with supporting schedules.

Problem 21-12. Selected information from the accounting records of Buckeye Company and Williams Company is presented below. Using the data presented (admittedly inadequate), compute ratios suitable for use in comparing the companies, briefly interpreting the results shown by the ratios.

	Buckeye Company	Williams Company
Cost of goods manufactured	$142,000	$ 47,500
Fixed assets—less depreciation	620,000	177,500
Retained earnings	100,000	48,000
Total assets	800,000	262,500
Capital stock ($100 par value)	550,000	150,000
Total liabilities	120,000	64,500
Reserve for plant expansion	30,000	-0-

Problem 21-13. Using the data presented in Problems 21-2 and 21-3 and the additional information given, prepare a statement accounting for the change in stockholders'

equity for the year ended December 31, 1965, and the resulting change in net assets, with supporting schedules.

Dividends of $10,000 were declared and paid and a federal income tax refund of $9,600 applicable to 1961 was received.

Problem 21-14. Crescent Company has issued preferred stock under an agreement to maintain net tangible assets (tangible assets being defined as all assets other than goodwill) at an amount not less than 250% of the preferred stock outstanding and also to maintain current assets at not less than 200% of the current liabilities, with the working capital to be maintained at not less than 150% of the preferred stock outstanding. On December 31, 1966, the company submits the following balance sheet.

CRESCENT COMPANY
Balance Sheet
December 31, 1966

Assets

Cash	$ 25,000
Notes and accounts receivable—net	75,000
Inventories	100,000
Total current assets	$200,000
Tangible fixed assets—net	150,000
Goodwill	50,000
	$400,000

Liabilities and Stockholders' Equity

Liabilities:	
Notes payable	$ 20,000
Accounts payable	30,000
Bonds payable	50,000
Total liabilities	$100,000
Stockholders' equity:	
Preferred stock	$100,000
Common stock	100,000
Retained earnings	100,000
Total stockholders' equity	$300,000
	$400,000

As an accountant representing the interests of the preferred stockholders, you ascertain that the $50,000 of bonds were issued on December 31, 1966, that the proceeds were used to liquidate current accounts payable, and that, on December 31, $50,000 additional cash was also paid to trade creditors. Show, by means of ratios, the conditions before and after these transactions occurred. Comment briefly on your findings.

Problem 21-15. Refer to the comparative balance sheet on page 760 and submit:

(a) A statement accounting for the changes in stockholders' equity and resulting changes in net assets for the years ended December 31, 1966 and 1965. Accompany your statement with schedules of working capital and fixed assets on December 31, 1966, 1965, and 1964.

(b) A statement showing the percentage distribution of assets, liabilities, and stockholders' equity on December 31, 1966, 1965, and 1964.

(c) A comparative balance sheet for December 31, 1966, 1965, and 1964, with columns for the amount of change, and the ratios of 1966 and 1965 items to 1964 items.

HOWARD COMPANY
Comparative Balance Sheet
December 31, 1966, 1965, and 1964

Assets	December 31, 1966		December 31, 1965		December 31, 1964	
Current assets:						
Cash		$ 25,000		$ 12,000		$ 18,000
Accounts receivable	$ 52,500		$ 21,000		$ 33,000	
Less estimated uncollectibles	2,500	50,000	1,000	20,000	1,500	31,500
Inventories		115,000		36,000		63,000
Prepaid expenses		10,000		7,000		10,500
Total current assets		$200,000		$ 75,000		$123,000
Fixed assets:						
Land		$125,000		$125,000		$125,000
Buildings	$150,000		$150,000		$150,000	
Less depreciation to date	75,000	75,000	70,000	80,000	65,000	85,000
Machinery and equipment	$200,000		$200,000		$180,000	
Less depreciation to date	100,000	100,000	80,000	120,000	63,000	117,000
Total fixed assets		$300,000		$325,000		$327,000
Total assets		$500,000		$400,000		$450,000

Liabilities and Stockholders' Equity	December 31, 1966	December 31, 1965	December 31, 1964
Current liabilities:			
Accounts payable	$ 80,000	$ 34,000	$ 45,000
Notes payable	45,000	16,000	30,000
Total current liabilities	$125,000	$ 50,000	$ 75,000
Stockholders' equity:			
Capital stock	$250,000	$200,000	$200,000
Retained earnings	125,000	150,000	175,000
Total stockholders' equity	$375,000	$350,000	$375,000
Total liabilities and stockholders' equity	$500,000	$400,000	$450,000

Notes:

1. The net income for 1965 was $25,000. A $50,000 dividend was paid at the end of 1965.
2. The net income for 1966 was $50,000. A cash dividend of $25,000 was paid and a $50,000 stock dividend was distributed.

Assignment Material for Chapter 22

QUESTIONS

1. Describe how to estimate the approximate time required for the collection of receivables.
2. How is merchandise turnover computed? What is the advantage of using monthly inventories in computing turnover?
3. Define *working capital.*
   What is meant by the "current ratio"?
   Which is the more important factor in the analysis of the financial condition of a company: the working capital stated in dollars, or the working capital ratio?
4. (a) How is the acid-test ratio computed?
   (b) What tests are used to determine whether investments may be included in the numerator when computing the acid-test ratio?
5. A statement analyst notes that the working capital and the working capital ratio for two companies being analyzed are identical. Is it safe for him to conclude that the working capital position of the two companies is identical? Explain.
6. There is considerable agitation for the adoption of a natural business year. Are there any reasons why you as an auditor would recommend to some of your clients a change from the calendar-year to a fiscal-year closing? If so, give the reasons.
7. *A* Company and *B* Company are engaged in the same type of merchandising business. For the year 1965, they report substantially the same amounts for sales, cost of goods sold, and gross profit. *A* Company reports a merchandise turnover of 10 while *B* Company reports one of 4.5. Explain, using an illustration if necessary, how such a difference might occur.
8. If merchandise is received during the last part of the accounting period, why is it incorrect to omit the charge to Purchases and the credit to Accounts Payable, and also to omit the goods from the inventory?
9. Prepare an estimate of the outstanding accounts receivable on December 31, 1965, on the basis of the following information:

   Sales are made at an average gross profit of 40%.
   The average inventory is $43,800 and the turnover is 8.
   Terms of sale are 2/10; n/30, and customers take advantage of the discount on 55% of the sales, the remaining 45% being outstanding an average of 45 days.
10. Does it follow that an improvement in the working capital ratio will be accompanied by an improvement in the equity ratios? State why or why not, giving your reasons.
11. The Hunter Corporation manufactures a seasonal product, new models of which are brought out annually early in August. Sales of the old model are continued

through August in outlying territories. Monthly sales to established outlets on net 20-day terms gradually increase until they are highest in the winter months and then taper off so that inventory quantities are lowest on June 30, before material and parts for the new model are purchased. Development of a new model is started in January and involves relatively large expenditures for design, engineering, dies, and tools, culminating in a plant shutdown the last ten days of July to prepare for volume production of the new model starting in August.

The company wishes to change from a calendar-year basis to some other closing date. What date would you suggest they use? Discuss the advantages and disadvantages of the date you suggest, including consideration of the problem of income determination and the presentation of other significant financial information. Do not consider income tax effects.

12. How does the computation of turnovers of materials, finished goods, and receivables help in determining the adequacy of the working capital?

PROBLEMS

Problem 22-1. On the basis of the following data, which of the two companies do you believe to be the better short-term credit risk? Support your conclusion by appropriate computations.

	Company *M*	Company *N*
Current assets:		
Cash	$ 208,031	$156,590
Marketable securities	145,621	70,465
Accounts receivable	339,788	164,421
Finished goods	69,343	148,760
Goods in process	194,162	125,272
Materials	346,718	78,295
Prepaid expenses	83,212	39,147
Total current assets	$1,386,875	$782,950
Current liabilities:		
Accounts payable	$ 277,375	$156,590
Notes payable	118,875	67,110
Total current liabilities	$ 396,250	$223,700
Working capital	$ 990,625	$559,250

Problem 22-2. Refer to Problem 22-1. Using the following additional information, which of the two companies do you believe to be the better credit risk?

	Company *M*	Company *N*
Net sales	$2,427,031	$352,327
Cost of goods sold	1,040,156	297,521
Materials used	693,438	117,442

Problem 22-3. Use the data of Humboldt Company presented at the top of page 763 to make the following computations for the years 1965 and 1964:

(a) Material turnovers and the number of days per turnover.
(b) Finished goods turnovers and the number of days per turnover.
(c) Average number of days' sales uncollected.
(d) Ratio of accounts payable to purchases.

	1965	1964	1963
Net sales	$416,450	$422,850	
Finished goods inventory, December 31	30,000	33,500	$29,500
Materials inventory, December 31	32,500	35,000	33,500
Cost of goods manufactured	262,700	265,800	
Net purchases—Materials	133,000	137,500	
Accounts receivable, December 31	94,350	94,500	
Accounts payable, December 31	26,700	25,750	
Transportation in	2,150	2,250	

Problem 22-4. Determine the relative liquidity of the following companies by means of a table showing the accumulation of the working capital ratio. Comment on the conclusions which may be drawn from this table.

	Squall Company	Sudden Company
Current assets:		
Cash	$118,900	$ 36,800
Marketable securities	28,600	12,400
Receivables	181,040	61,900
Finished goods	92,350	41,620
Goods in process	88,450	55,090
Materials	101,900	44,830
Prepaid expenses	12,600	8,100
Current liabilities	286,125	124,090

Problem 22-5. From the following data:

(a) Prepare a schedule of working capital, with a column showing the ratio of 1965 items to the corresponding 1964 items.
(b) Compute the working capital ratios.
(c) Compute the acid-test ratios.
(d) Prepare a table showing the percentage distribution of current assets.
(e) Prepare a table showing the accumulation of the working capital ratios.

	December 31,	
	1965	1964
Cash	$145,000	$ 90,000
Marketable securities	108,500	140,000
Accounts receivable—net	67,500	40,000
Inventories	107,500	100,000
Prepaid expenses	22,500	20,000
Accounts payable	112,500	150,000
Income tax payable	43,500	38,000

Problem 22-6. You are given the following data on Bailey Company and are asked to report on the efficiency with which the working capital is being managed.

	1965	1964
Current assets at beginning of year	$ 225,000	$ 175,000
Current assets at end of year	275,000	225,000
Current liabilities at beginning of year	100,000	100,000
Current liabilities at end of year	100,000	100,000
Net sales	1,116,837	1,215,630
Cost of sales and expenses	1,087,500	1,170,000

Problem 22-7. The following amounts were taken from the records of Evans Company:

	December 31, 1965	December 31, 1964
Sales	$364,000	$494,400
Cost of goods sold and expenses	350,000	480,000
Net income	$ 14,000	$ 14,400
Total current assets on December 31	$200,000	$150,000

Total current assets on December 31, 1963, were $170,000.

Required:

(1) For the years ended December 31, 1965 and 1964:
  (a) The frequency of current asset turnover.
  (b) The profitability of current asset turnover.
  (c) The rate of profit per turnover.

(2) You are now told that depreciation and amortization charges amounted to $87,500 in 1965 and $80,000 in 1964. Using this information, recompute the above ratios.

Problem 22-8. The Brown and Green Corporation prepared the balance sheet below for presentation at the annual meeting of the stockholders of the corporation.

THE BROWN AND GREEN CORPORATION
Balance Sheet
December 31, 1965

Assets

Current assets:			
Cash		$ 15,300	
Accounts receivable (net of allowance for doubtful accounts of $6,100)		39,200	
Inventories		84,900	
Prepaid expenses		12,200	$151,600
Fixed assets:			
Land		$ 70,000	
Buildings	$ 97,700		
Less accumulated depreciation	31,300	66,400	
Machinery and equipment	$232,800		
Less accumulated depreciation	92,400	140,400	276,800
			$428,400

Liabilities and Stockholders' Equity

Current liabilities:		
Accounts payable	$ 28,600	
Accrued expenses	8,800	$ 37,400
Serial bonds payable		150,000
Stockholders' equity:		
Capital stock	$200,000	
Retained earnings	41,000	241,000
		$428,400

You have been engaged by a group of stockholders to examine the accounts and financial statements of The Brown and Green Corporation, and in the course of your examination you discover the following errors, which affected the December 31, 1965 balance sheet:

(1) A $20,000 note payable to Second State Bank, due on June 30, 1966, was deducted from the balance on deposit in the bank.
(2) The corporation prepared and recorded checks totaling $18,400 in payment of accounts payable on December 31, 1965. These checks were still on hand in the office of the corporation on January 20, 1966.
(3) An advance payment of $5,000 made by a customer for goods to be manufactured and delivered in 1966, was deducted from accounts receivable.
(4) Organization costs of $4,500 were included in prepaid expenses.
(5) The serial bonds mature in annual installments of $25,000, the first payment being due on June 30, 1966.

Required:

(1) Prepare a revised balance sheet as of December 31, 1965, giving effect to any corrections you think necessary.
(2) Prepare or compute the following tabulations or ratios (1) based on the original balance sheet, and (2) based upon your revised balance sheet.
  (a) Working capital ratio.
  (b) Acid-test ratio.
  (c) Percentage distribution of current assets.
  (d) Accumulation of working capital ratio.

Problem 22-9. Refer to the statements of Southwind Company, and

(1) As of December 31, 1965 and 1964, compute:
  (a) Working capital ratio.
  (b) Acid-test ratio.
  (c) Per cent of each current asset to total current assets.
  (d) Accumulation of working capital ratio.
  (e) Current asset turnovers: frequency, profitability, rate of profit per turnover. (Total current assets on January 1, 1963, $240,000.)
  (f) Turnover of finished goods.
  (g) Turnover of materials.
  (h) Accounts receivable conversion period.
  (i) Ratio of accounts payable to purchases.
(2) Comment briefly on the change in current position.

SOUTHWIND COMPANY
Partial Balance Sheet
December 31, 1965 and 1964

	December 31, 1965	December 31, 1964
Current assets:		
Cash	$ 18,100	$ 13,000
Marketable investments	40,000	20,000
Accounts receivable	73,900	90,000
Inventories:		
Finished goods	40,000	57,000
Work in process	21,000	30,000
Materials	32,000	40,000
Total current assets	$225,000	$250,000
Current liabilities:		
Bank loans	$ 40,000	$ 95,000
Accounts payable	38,500	41,000
Accrued expenses	1,500	4,000
Total current liabilities	$ 80,000	$140,000

(*Continued on next page.*)

SOUTHWIND COMPANY

Operating Statements, 1965 and 1964

	1965	1964
Sales—net	$950,000	$800,000
Cost of sales:		
Materials:		
Inventory, January 1	$ 40,000	$ 44,500
Purchases	276,000	253,500
Total	$316,000	$298,000
Inventory, December 31	32,000	40,000
Materials used	$284,000	$258,000
Labor	230,000	210,000
Factory overhead	160,000	148,000
Total	$674,000	$616,000
Add decrease in inventory of work in process	9,000	1,500
Cost of goods manufactured	$683,000	$617,500
Add decrease in inventory of finished goods	17,000	2,500
Cost of sales	$700,000	$620,000
Gross profit on sales	$250,000	$180,000
Expenses (including income taxes)	210,000	165,000
Net income	$ 40,000	$ 15,000
Total depreciation charged	$ 24,000	$ 22,000

Problem 22-10. Comment on the relative current financial position of the two corporations, the condensed balance sheets and certain operating data of which are presented below. Show computations supporting your comments.

FIRST AVENUE COMPANY

Balance Sheet

June 30, 1965

Assets

Cash	$ 142,000
Short-term investments	120,000
Accounts receivable—net	390,000
Inventories	510,000
Prepaid expenses	48,000
Land	80,000
Buildings, machinery, and fixtures—net	450,000
Goodwill	400,000
	$2,140,000

Liabilities and Stockholders' Equity

Accounts payable	$ 289,000
Accrued expenses	67,000
Income tax payable	72,000
Preferred stock	500,000
Common stock	1,000,000
Retained earnings, June 30, 1964	84,000
Net income, year ended June 30, 1965	128,000
	$2,140,000

SECOND STREET CORPORATION
Balance Sheet
June 30, 1965

Assets

Cash	$ 118,000
Accounts receivable—net	420,000
Inventories	620,000
Prepaid expenses	87,000
Land	140,000
Buildings—net	281,000
Machinery and tools—net	564,000
Patents	200,000
	$2,430,000

Liabilities and Stockholders' Equity

Accounts payable and accrued expenses	$ 490,000
Notes payable—due December 1, 1965	200,000
Income tax payable	39,000
Capital stock	1,200,000
Capital in excess of par value	250,000
Retained earnings, June 30, 1964	190,000
Net income, year ended June 30, 1965	61,000
	$2,430,000

Selected Operating Data for the Year Ended June 30, 1965

	First Avenue Company	Second Street Corporation
Sales—net	$1,350,000	$980,000
Cost of sales	950,000	735,000

Problem 22-11. In July, 1965, the loan officer of Security Bank presents to you for analysis the following condensed balance sheet of Anderson Corporation.

The company's operating statements for the 12 months ended June 30, 1965, show sales of $1,490,000, a gross profit of $312,900, and a net income of $62,150.

Anderson Corporation has requested a loan of at least $160,000, the funds to be used to pay past-due trade accounts of $70,000, to pay the current mortgage installment, and to pay the $60,000 note of the retiring president.

ANDERSON CORPORATION
Balance Sheet
June 30, 1965

Assets

Current assets:		
Cash	$ 20,650	
Accounts receivable—net	50,100	
Inventories	329,500	$400,250
Investment in real estate		65,000
Fixed assets:		
Cost	$300,000	
Accumulated depreciation	126,000	174,000
Goodwill		75,000
		$714,250

(*Continued on next page.*)

Liabilities and Stockholders' Equity

Current liabilities:		
Mortgage installment due July 31, 1965	$ 30,000	
Notes payable—Officer	60,000	
Accounts payable	200,000	
Accruals	5,000	$295,000
Mortgage payable—$30,000 due annually on July 31		120,000
Stockholders' equity:		
Preferred stock	$150,000	
Common stock	125,000	
Retained earnings	24,250	299,250
		$714,250

Submit the advice and comments you would present to the loan officer of the bank.

Problem 22-12. The following information was taken from the records of Zan Company:

Acid-test ratio	.92
Average finished goods inventory	$ 52,000
Average number of days' sales uncollected	73
Expenses (including income tax)	$212,000
Finished goods turnovers	12.20
Net sales	$900,000
Total current liabilities	$200,000
Working capital turnover	4.50
Turnover of average total current assets	1.55

The records also revealed that the current assets and current liabilities both decreased by an equal amount during the last fiscal year.

Required:

(a) Working capital ratio.
(b) Total quick assets.
(c) Accounts receivable at end of year.
(d) Ratio of net income to average total current assets.

Problem 22-13. Rambling Corporation is preparing a report for its stockholders as of December 31, 1965. The corporation wishes to include in its report a questionnaire grouping of ratios. Prepare such a questionnaire by using the comparative statements appearing below.

RAMBLING CORPORATION

Comparative Income Statement
For the Years Ended December 31, 1965 and 1964

	1965	1964
Net sales	$591,000	$570,000
Cost of goods sold	445,200	459,240
Gross profit on sales	$145,800	$110,760
Expenses (including income tax)	120,000	101,400
Net income for the year	$ 25,800	$ 9,360

RAMBLING CORPORATION
Comparative Balance Sheet
December 31, 1965 and 1964

	December 31, 1965	December 31, 1964
Assets		
Current assets:		
Cash	$ 17,760	$ 9,000
Accounts receivable—net	76,080	69,120
Inventories	47,400	66,600
Total current assets	$141,240	$144,720
Fixed assets:		
Equipment—net	150,300	157,800
	$291,540	$302,520
Liabilities and Stockholders' Equity		
Current liabilities:		
Bank loans	$ 22,800	$ 48,600
Accounts payable	18,600	30,000
Accrued expenses	1,260	3,720
Total current liabilities	$ 42,660	$ 82,320
Bonds payable	90,000	90,000
Total liabilities	$132,660	$172,320
Stockholders' equity:		
Preferred stock—$100 par value; 5%, nonparticipating	$ 30,000	$ 24,000
Common stock—$100 par value	105,000	90,000
Retained earnings	23,880	16,200
Total stockholders' equity	$158,880	$130,200
	$291,540	$302,520

The bonds are secured by all of the fixed assets.

The current assets on December 31, 1963, totaled $142,020; the inventory on that date was $77,280.

Assignment Material for Chapter 23

QUESTIONS

1. Into what groups can you classify the causes of a change in the net income from one period to another?
2. Identify two possible causes for a change in sales.
3. A company carries an average inventory of $50,000, which it turns three times per year at a gross profit of 40%, and a net income of 10% of sales. If a 10% reduction in selling prices will result in four turnovers per year with a 10% increase in expenses, will the company make more or less net income, and how much?
4. How would you apportion the following expenses among the several departments of a retail store?

Advertising	Salesmen's salaries
Rent	Fire insurance on merchandise

5. How much reliance can be placed on departmental net income figures?
6. Assume that the sporting goods department of a department store shows a net loss. Should that fact be accepted as a conclusive reason for discontinuing the department? Explain.
7. The inventory of a retail shoe store has been increasing each year over a three-year period, but gross profits have been declining. What probable reasons would you advance for that condition, and how would you proceed to determine the real cause?
8. From the following data, extracted from the audited statements of the CBC Company, determine the reason for the increase in gross profit and prepare a statement reflecting such changes.

	Year Ending June 30,	
	1964	1965
Sales	$164,850	$168,147
Cost of sales	118,650	121,023
Gross profit	$ 46,200	$ 47,124

Units sold:

1964	$144,900
1965	147,798

9. Give a possible explanation of how a department store might, during a period of stable prices, show a 30% increase in gross profit over the preceding year while sales increased only 10 per cent.
10. During a period of business prosperity, a company's accountants make a very careful computation of the company's break-even point, using current accounting data. May this computation be used by the management without adjustment as an indication of the point where losses would develop during a period of business depression? Explain.

PROBLEMS

Problem 23-1.

WATSON COMPANY
Comparative Income Statement
For the Years Ended December 31, 1965 and 1964

	1965	1964
Net sales	$500,000	$400,000
Cost of goods sold	325,000	240,000
Gross profit on sales	$175,000	$160,000
Operating expenses:		
Selling expenses	$ 75,000	$ 72,000
General expenses	70,000	64,000
Total	$145,000	$136,000
Net operating income	$ 30,000	$ 24,000
Net financial income	10,000	4,000
Net income	$ 40,000	$ 28,000

Prepare a statement accounting for the increase in net income. Use columns for per cent of net sales, amounts, and ratio of 1965 to 1964.

Problem 23-2.

WAVERLY COMPANY
Comparative Income Statement
For the Years Ended December 31, 1965 and 1964

	1965	1964
Net sales	$268,800	$306,600
Cost of goods sold	203,700	228,200
Gross profit on sales	$ 65,100	$ 78,400
Operating expenses:		
Selling expenses	$ 21,700	$ 32,200
General expenses	23,800	22,400
Total	$ 45,500	$ 54,600
Net operating income	$ 19,600	$ 23,800
Net financial expense	1,400	2,100
Net income	$ 18,200	$ 21,700

Prepare a statement accounting for the decrease in net income. Use columns for per cent of net sales, amounts, and ratio of 1965 to 1964.

Problem 23-3.

WHEEL COMPANY
Condensed Comparative Statement of Gross Profit on Sales

	Year Ended December 31,	
	1965	1964
Net sales	$302,500	$250,000
Cost of goods sold	202,125	175,000
Gross profit on sales	$100,375	$ 75,000

You learn that during 1965:

(a) Volume increased 10%.
(b) Selling price increased 10%.
(c) Costs increased 5%.

Account for the changes in sales, cost of goods sold, and gross profit.

Problem 23-4.

COLORFUL COMPANY

Condensed Comparative Statement of Sales, Cost of Sales, and Gross Profit

	Year Ended December 31,	
	1965	1964
Net sales	$236,250	$250,000
Cost of goods sold	176,400	175,000
Gross profit on sales	$ 59,850	$ 75,000

You learn that during 1965:

(a) Volume increased 5%.
(b) Selling price decreased 10%.
(c) Cost decreased 4%.

Prepare a statement accounting for the changes in sales, cost of goods sold, and gross profit.

Problem 23-5. The records of Special Corporation show:

	1965	1964
Net sales	$77,625	$75,000
Cost of goods sold	53,460	55,000
Gross profit on sales	$24,165	$20,000

During 1965:

(a) Volume decreased 10%.
(b) Selling prices increased 15%.
(c) Costs increased 8%.

Prepare a statement accounting for the changes in sales, cost of goods sold, and gross profit.

Problem 23-6. Assume the following data:

	1965	1964
Sales	$577,500	$500,000
Cost of goods sold	379,500	300,000
Gross profit on sales	$198,000	$200,000

If sales volume increased 10% in 1965, what were the per cents of change in:

(a) Selling prices?
(b) Costs?

Problem 23-7. Assume the following data:

	1965	1964
Sales	$249,984	$240,000
Cost of goods sold	172,329	170,000
Gross profit on sales	$ 77,655	$ 70,000

If volume decreased 7% in 1965, what were the per cents of change in:

(a) Selling price?
(b) Costs?

Problem 23-8. Assume the following data:

	1965	1964
Sales	$445,500	$375,000
Cost of goods sold	257,580	225,000
Gross profit on sales	$187,920	$150,000

If selling prices increased 10% in 1965, what were the per cents of change in:

(a) Volume?
(b) Costs?

Problem 23-9. Assume the following data:

	1965	1964
Sales	$501,584	$580,000
Cost of goods sold	415,104	480,000
Gross profit on sales	$ 86,480	$100,000

If selling prices decreased 6% in 1965, what were the per cents of change in:

(a) Volume?
(b) Costs?

Problem 23-10. Assume the following data:

	1965	1964
Sales	$882,000	$800,000
Cost of goods sold	693,000	600,000
Gross profit on sales	$189,000	$200,000

If costs increased 10%, what were the per cents of change in:

(a) Volume?
(b) Selling price?

Problem 23-11. You are given the following information concerning the operations of Menlo Company during the years 1964 and 1965. Prepare a comparative statement of cost of goods manufactured and sold, showing both total and per-unit costs.

	1965	1964
Materials used	$1,000,000	$1,040,000
Direct labor	1,400,000	1,310,000
Manufacturing overhead	460,000	385,000

Analysis of Inventories

	Number of Units	Material	Labor	Manufacturing Overhead	Total
January 1, 1964:					
Work in process	2,500	$150,000	$190,000	$60,000	$400,000
Finished goods	4,000				560,000
January 1, 1965:					
Work in process	3,000	200,000	240,000	85,000	525,000
Finished goods	5,000				
December 31, 1965:					
Work in process	2,000	100,000	140,000	45,000	285,000
Finished goods	4,500				

18,500 units were put into process in 1964 and 19,000 units were put into process in 1965. Inventories are valued on the first-in, first-out basis.

Problem 23-12. You are given the following additional information relative to the operations of Menlo Company during the years 1964 and 1965. Using this information, plus the information contained in your answer to the preceding problem, prepare a comparative income statement in total and per unit sold.

	1965	1964
Sales	$4,100,000	$3,230,000
Selling expense	440,750	362,950
General and administrative expense	312,625	275,400
Financial expense	44,075	37,400

Problem 23-13. From the following data prepare:

(a) A schedule showing annual gross profit rates by departments and for the business as a whole.
(b) A schedule showing the distribution of sales among departments in dollars and per cents.
(c) A schedule analyzing the departmental components of the annual gross profit rates.

	Total	Department A	Department B	Department C
1965:				
Sales	$252,000	$113,400	$50,400	$88,200
Cost of goods sold	187,362	80,514	32,760	74,088
Gross profit	$ 64,638	$ 32,886	$17,640	$14,112
1964:				
Sales	$194,000	$ 97,000	$58,200	$38,800
Cost of goods sold	146,858	75,660	38,994	32,204
Gross profit	$ 47,142	$ 21,340	$19,206	$ 6,596
1963:				
Sales	$230,000	$ 92,000	$80,500	$57,500
Cost of goods sold	169,855	67,160	55,545	47,150
Gross profit	$ 60,145	$ 24,840	$24,955	$10,350

Problem 23-14.

CARLSON CORPORATION
Income Statement
For the Year Ended December 31, 1965

	Department A	Department B	Total
Gross sales	$90,000	$200,000	$290,000
Sales allowances	2,000	4,000	6,000
Net sales	$88,000	$196,000	$284,000
Cost of goods sold	65,000	95,000	160,000
Gross profit on sales	$23,000	$101,000	$124,000
Selling expenses:			
Advertising	$ 5,000	$ 9,000	$ 14,000
Delivery expense	3,000	6,000	9,000
Salesmen's salaries	10,000	15,000	25,000
Store rent	2,000	2,000	4,000
Total	$20,000	$ 32,000	$ 52,000
General expenses:			
Office salaries	$ 8,000	$ 12,000	$ 20,000
Officers' salaries	15,000	20,000	35,000
Bad debts	1,000	2,000	3,000
Miscellaneous	2,500	4,000	6,500
Total	$26,500	$ 38,000	$ 64,500
Net income (loss*) before income tax	$23,500*	$ 31,000	$ 7,500

The president of Carlson Corporation is considering closing Department *A* because it is operating at a loss. He asks your advice in the matter.

Your investigation discloses that the following expenses, charged to Department *A*, would be eliminated by closing that department:

Completely eliminated: Advertising; Salesmen's salaries; Bad debts.
Partially eliminated: Delivery expense—$2,000 eliminated; Miscellaneous—$1,500 eliminated.

Submit:

(a) A schedule showing the probable reduction in expenses which would result from closing Department *A*.
(b) A statement showing the probable net income before income tax which would result after closing Department *A*.
(c) Your opinion as to the advisability of closing Department *A*.

Problem 23-15. The management of Batten Company asks your advice as to whether or not to close Department *A*, which has been operating at a loss. Your investigation discloses the following additional information:

1. Salesmen are paid a straight commission equal to 20 per cent of their sales.
2. If Department *A* is closed, it will probably be necessary to increase Department *B*'s advertising by 10 per cent to retain its volume of business.
3. Depreciation is apportioned to each department on the basis of use or occupancy. Closing Department *A* will reduce the depreciation charge relating to store fixtures by 40 per cent.
4. Three truck drivers, paid equal annual salaries, operate the two delivery trucks in shifts. By eliminating Department *A*, one truck driver may be dispensed with.

5. One-half of the insurance expense results from policies on the company's inventory. No insurance is carried on the store fixtures.
6. Bad debts are estimated at 2 per cent of net sales.
7. Office and officers' salaries will not be reduced by the proposed change.

Submit:

(a) A schedule showing the probable reduction in expenses which would result from a discontinuance of Department *A*.
(b) A statement showing the probable net income before income tax which would result after discontinuance of Department *A*.
(c) Your opinion as to the advisability of closing Department *A*.

BATTEN COMPANY
Income Statement
For the Year Ended December 31, 1965

	Department *A*	Department *B*	Total
Net sales	$290,000	$650,000	$940,000
Cost of goods sold	250,000	350,000	600,000
Gross profit on sales	$ 40,000	$300,000	$340,000
Operating expenses:			
Selling expenses:			
Salesmen's commissions	$ 58,000	$130,000	$188,000
Delivery truck drivers' salaries	4,320	6,480	10,800
Advertising	6,000	15,000	21,000
Depreciation—Delivery equipment	500	1,000	1,500
Depreciation—Store building	2,500	3,750	6,250
Depreciation—Store fixtures	2,000	3,000	5,000
Total selling expenses	$ 73,320	$159,230	$232,550
General expenses:			
Office salaries	$ 10,000	$ 25,000	$ 35,000
Officers' salaries	10,000	20,000	30,000
Insurance	4,000	10,000	14,000
Bad debts	5,800	13,000	18,800
Total general expenses	$ 29,800	$ 68,000	$ 97,800
Total operating expenses	$103,120	$227,230	$330,350
Net income (loss*) before income tax	$ 63,120*	$ 72,770	$ 9,650

Problem 23-16.

GROWING COMPANY
Condensed Income Statement
For the Year Ended December 31, 1965

Net sales		$200,000
Costs and expenses:		
Fixed	$ 40,000	
Variable (60% of sales)	120,000	
Total costs and expenses		160,000
Net income		$ 40,000

Growing Company is considering making an investment in plant and equipment. This investment will increase the annual fixed costs by $25,000. The sales potential of the present plant is $225,000. With the new investment, the potential would be raised to $400,000.

Assuming that the variable costs will always be 60 per cent of net sales:

(a) What is the break-even point under the conditions prevailing in 1965?
(b) What will the new break-even point be if the investment is made?
(c) What amount of sales would have to be made, after the investment, for the company to earn $40,000?
(d) What are the limits of profit under both the present and the proposed conditions?

Problem 23-17. The president of *Q* Department Store received from the accounting department a statement of net sales, net income, and rates of net income of five departments for 1965 and 1964.

Total sales decreased in 1965. The rate of net income of each department also decreased in 1965. Still the net income in 1965 was higher than it was in 1964.

With the idea that something might possibly be wrong, the president asks you to review the figures and give reasons for the apparent inconsistency.

Prepare your explanation in the form of a report from the statements presented below.

1964

Department	Sales	Net Income	Per Cent of Net Income
A	$ 22,500	$ 2,925	13%
B	45,200	8,136	18
C	33,700	6,740	20
D	101,300	8,104	8
E	22,500	2,700	12
Total	$225,200	$28,605	

1965

Department	Sales	Net Income	Per Cent of Net Income
A	$ 52,600	$ 5,786	11%
B	63,100	9,465	15
C	73,600	13,984	19
D	8,400	588	7
E	12,630	1,263	10
Total	$210,330	$31,086	

Problem 23-18. The president of Haywire Stores hands you the departmental operating statement for the year 1965 shown on the next page.

The president states that Department *B* showed a loss of $30,000 for the year; that price competition was too stiff in this department; and that Departments *A* and *C* were too crowded anyway. For all these reasons he has decided to discontinue Department *B* and to allocate its space as follows: three-fifths to *A* and two-fifths to *C*. Even if sales of *A* and *C* do not increase, he says, there will be a saving of $30,000. Is the president correct?

What sales volume (assuming a proportionate change in each department) will be required to produce the same total net income in 1966 as in 1965?

	Department			
	A	*B*	*C*	Total
Sales	$450,000	$300,000	$350,000	$1,100,000
Cost of sales	300,000	250,000	175,000	725,000
Gross profit	$150,000	$ 50,000	$175,000	$ 375,000
Departmental expenses:				
Direct—Salaries, supplies, advertising, etc.	$ 75,000	$ 30,000	$ 70,000	$ 175,000
Indirect—Building and space costs (spread on basis of floor space)	30,000	25,000	20,000	75,000
Total	$105,000	$ 55,000	$ 90,000	$ 250,000
Operating income (loss*)	$ 45,000	$ 5,000*	$ 85,000	$ 125,000
Administrative expenses—Fixed (divided equally)	25,000	25,000	25,000	75,000
Net income (loss*) before income tax	$ 20,000	$ 30,000*	$ 60,000	$ 50,000
Income tax—25%				12,500
Net income				$ 37,500

Problem 23-19. A client is trying to decide whether to sell his substantial investment in the common stock of Dual Channel Company. The current market price of the stock is $20, which is $8 above the price paid for it in 1962. The stock has been paying a quarterly dividend of 15 cents per share.

Your client has asked you to analyze the following accounting data, recently released by the company, and to prepare a report that will be helpful to him in reaching a decision.

You are assigned the task of developing material, including ratios and comments thereon, suitable for inclusion in the above report. The range of topics might include reference to the company's financial position, efficiency, and prospects, to the extent permitted by the available data.

DUAL CHANNEL COMPANY

Comparative Condensed Income Statement

	1965	1964	1963	1962
Net sales:				
Retail store	$494,750	$499,849	$505,000	$500,000
Mail order	498,960	475,200	440,000	400,000
Totals	$993,710	$975,049	$945,000	$900,000
Cost of goods sold	$610,996	$579,120	$564,000	$540,000
Selling expense:				
Retail store	89,055	79,976	70,700	60,000
Mail order	39,917	38,016	35,200	32,000
Administrative expense	141,742	142,937	141,100	138,000
Federal income tax	49,260	60,500	64,180	62,100
Totals	$930,970	$900,549	$875,180	$832,100
Net income	$ 62,740	$ 74,500	$ 69,820	$ 67,900

DUAL CHANNEL COMPANY

Comparative Balance Sheet

	December 31, 1965	December 31, 1964
Assets		
Current assets:		
Cash	$ 38,200	$ 27,500
Marketable securities	5,000	20,000
Accounts receivable—net of allowance for doubtful accounts:		
Retail store	89,200	76,300
Mail order	45,700	47,200
Inventory—first-in; first-out	289,100	227,200
	$467,200	$398,200
Fixed assets:		
Land, buildings, and equipment	$520,000	$500,000
Less accumulated depreciation	366,500	333,200
	$153,500	$166,800
	$620,700	$565,000
Liabilities and Stockholders' Equity		
Current liabilities:		
Accounts payable	$184,700	$120,500
Bank loan	50,000	-0-
Income tax	49,260	60,500
	$283,960	$181,000
Long-term bank loan—December 1, 1966	-0-	$ 50,000
Stockholders' equity:		
Common stock—$1.50 stated value	$150,000	$150,000
Capital in excess of stated value	50,000	50,000
Retained earnings	136,740	134,000
	$336,740	$334,000
	$620,700	$565,000

Related Information

1. The company sells a single product through two channels: through a retail store and mail order. The selling price of the product through the mail-order division has not changed; the selling price of the product through the retail store has increased 1 per cent each year.

2. In 1962, the rate of gross profit for the retail store was equal to that earned by the mail-order business.

3. There have been no significant acquisitions of fixed assets since 1960. The company uses a declining-balance method of depreciation.

Assignment Material for Chapter 24

QUESTIONS

1. Mention five charges or credits to operations which do not affect working capital, and state how they should be shown in the statement of sources and uses of working capital.
2. If there has been a decrease in working capital, in what sequence should the sources and uses appear in the statement of sources and uses of working capital?
3. How should a net loss (after adjustment for income and expense items not affecting working capital) be shown in the statement of sources and uses of working capital?
4. To what do analysts refer when they use the words *cash flow*?
5. The following accounts appear in a company's ledger. State how the data reflected by the accounts should be shown in the statement of sources and uses of working capital.

Machinery

Jan. 1	Balance	40,000	July 8	Sale	5,000
June 15	Appraisal	10,000			
Sept. 9	Purchase	8,000			

Accumulated Depreciation—Machinery

July 8	Accumulated depreciation on machinery sold	3,000	Jan. 1	Balance	6,000
			June 15	Appraisal	3,000
Oct. 10	Extraordinary repairs	600	Dec. 31	Depreciation for year	2,000

Appraisal Increment

			June 15		7,000

Retained Earnings

July 8	Loss on machinery sale	300	Jan. 1	Balance	12,000
			Dec. 31	Net operating income	10,000

6. During the year a portion of the Goodwill account was written off. Under what circumstances would the amount thus written off be added back to net income in the preparation of a statement of sources and uses of working capital? Under what circumstances would the amount thus written off not be added back to net income, and under such circumstances how would it be handled in the working papers?
7. Comment on the merits of the concept of "cash flow."

8. Company *A* owned all of the stock of Company *B*. At the end of the year it made the following entry:

Investment in stock of Company *B*	15,000	
Income from Company *B*		15,000
To take up the increase in Company *B*'s retained earnings during the year.		

How should this matter be dealt with in the preparation of a statement of sources and uses of working capital?

How should this matter be dealt with in the preparation of a statement of sources and uses of funds?

9. During the year a large short-term obligation was converted into a long-term obligation, no cash being received or disbursed. How would this matter be dealt with in a statement of sources and uses of working capital?

10. Which of the following items would be included in a statement of sources and uses of working capital? Which would be included in a statement of sources and uses of funds?

(a) Fully depreciated machinery scrapped.
(b) Periodic amortization of premium on bonds payable.
(c) Patents written off to Retained Earnings.
(d) Retirement of mortgage payable before maturity.
(e) Land acquired by issuance of capital stock.
(f) Sale of investments at a gain, which was credited to Retained Earnings.

11. Explain the important difference between a statement of sources and uses of working capital and a statement of sources and uses of funds.

PROBLEMS

Problem 24-1. The following data were taken from the books of Baker Company:

	December 31, 1966	December 31, 1965
Debits		
Cash	$ 3,000	$ 2,500
Accounts receivable	7,000	4,500
Land	4,000	
Equipment	11,000	11,000
	$25,000	$18,000
Credits		
Accounts payable	$ 3,000	$ 2,500
Accumulated depreciation—Equipment	1,000	500
Capital stock	15,000	10,000
Retained earnings	6,000	5,000
	$25,000	$18,000

The net income for the year was $1,000. Depreciation of equipment amounted to $500. Capital stock in the amount of $5,000 was sold at par and a tract of land was purchased for $4,000.

Prepare a statement of sources and uses of working capital.

Problem 24-2. Following is the comparative balance sheet of the Sunding Corporation.

	December 31, 1966	December 31, 1965
Assets		
Cash	$ 5,000	$ 7,000
Accounts receivable	17,200	20,100
Land	10,000	10,000
Patents	800	900
Goodwill		2,000
	$33,000	$40,000
Liabilities and Stockholders' Equity		
Accounts payable	$10,000	$12,000
Bonds payable	2,000	
Capital stock	20,000	20,000
Retained earnings	1,000	8,000
	$33,000	$40,000

The net income for the year was $1,000. Amortization of patents was $100. Bonds were issued at par, $2,000. A $6,000 dividend was paid.

Prepare:
(a) Working papers.
(b) A statement of sources and uses of working capital.

Problem 24-3. From the following condensed comparative statement of balance sheet accounts of The Wabash Company and supplementary information, prepare a schedule of working capital, working papers, and a statement of sources and uses of working capital.

	December 31, 1966	December 31, 1965
Debits		
Cash	$ 5,800	$ 8,000
Accounts receivable	9,200	10,000
Equipment	20,000	20,000
Long-term investments	41,000	49,000
	$76,000	$87,000
Credits		
Accounts payable	$ 5,000	$10,000
Notes payable	1,600	3,000
Accumulated depreciation—Equipment	17,000	16,000
Capital stock	50,000	50,000
Retained earnings	2,400	8,000
	$76,000	$87,000

The company had a net loss of $600 in 1966; the charge for depreciation of equipment was $1,000. Long-term investments carried at $8,000 were sold for $7,800. A $5,000 dividend was paid.

Problem 24-4.

JASPER COMPANY
Comparative Statement of Balance Sheet Accounts
December 31, 1966 and 1965

	December 31, 1966	December 31, 1965
Debits		
Cash	$ 20,000	$14,000
Accounts receivable	35,000	36,000
Land	15,000	10,000
Buildings	43,000	35,000
	$113,000	$95,000
Credits		
Accounts payable	$ 17,000	$19,000
Notes payable	13,730	13,000
Accumulated depreciation—Buildings	6,000	5,000
Bonds payable	10,000	
Premium on bonds payable	270	
Capital stock	55,000	50,000
Retained earnings	11,000	8,000
	$113,000	$95,000

The net income for the year was $3,000. Depreciation of buildings amounted to $1,000. An issue of ten-year bonds with a face value of $10,000 was sold on January 2, 1966, at 103. A new garage was constructed at a cost of $8,000. Additional land was acquired in exchange for capital stock.

Prepare a schedule of working capital, working papers, and a statement of sources and uses of funds, applying the concept of funds as comprising all financial resources.

Problem 24-5. During 1966 Clear Air Company acquired control of Turbulence Company in order to assure itself of a supply of raw materials. Details of the transaction are shown below:

Securities acquired:	
Capital stock of a par value of $30,000 acquired at a valuation of	$32,500
Bonds—at face value	25,000
Total Turbulence Company securities acquired	$57,500
Payment:	
Clear Air Company capital stock:	
Preferred—Par	$50,000
Premium	2,500
Total	$52,500
Common—Par	5,000
Total payment	$57,500

The company also issued $5,000 of its common stock for equipment.

Clear Air Company had a net income of $21,900 during 1966; it paid dividends of $6,600 on its common stock and $2,500 on its preferred stock.

Prepare a statement of sources and uses of funds, applying the concept of funds as including all financial resources. (Working papers are not required.)

CLEAR AIR COMPANY
Condensed Comparative Balance Sheet
December 31, 1966 and 1965

	December 31, 1966	December 31, 1965
Assets		
Working capital	$ 93,200	$ 78,000
Land	10,000	8,000
Buildings	50,000	50,000
Accumulated depreciation—Buildings	8,000*	6,000*
Equipment	40,000	35,000
Accumulated depreciation—Equipment	8,700*	6,300*
Stock of Turbulence Company	32,500	
Bonds of Turbulence Company	25,000	
	$234,000	$158,700
Liabilities and Stockholders' Equity		
Mortgage payable	$ 30,000	$ 30,000
Capital stock—Common	110,000	100,000
Capital stock—Preferred	50,000	
Capital in excess of par value—Preferred stock issuance	2,500	
Retained earnings	41,500	28,700
	$234,000	$158,700

* Deduction.

Problem 24-6. The following data were taken from the records of The R S Company.

	December 31, 1966	December 31, 1965
Debits		
Cash	$ 900	$ 1,650
Accounts receivable	5,500	3,785
Notes receivable	400	250
Inventories	8,231	7,852
Prepaid expense	200	250
Furniture and fixtures	400	620
Land	2,100	2,100
Building	9,000	8,000
Patents	500	600
	$27,231	$25,107
Credits		
Accounts payable	$ 1,500	$ 300
Bonds payable	2,000	1,000
Premium on bonds payable	135	150
Accumulated depreciation—Building	900	800
Allowance for bad debts	105	95
Capital stock	18,000	20,000
Capital in excess of par value	600	1,000
Retained earnings	3,991	1,762
	$27,231	$25,107

Depreciation of $50 was credited during the year directly to the Furniture and Fixtures account. The remaining change in this account represents the book value of furniture sold, without gain or loss. A new roof costing $350 was put on the building and charged to Accumulated Depreciation—Building. Bonds in the amount of $1,000 were sold at face value. The $100 amortization of patents was charged to expense. Capital stock of $2,000 par value was retired during the year at a cost of $2,400. No dividends were paid.

Prepare a statement of sources and uses of working capital. (Working papers are not required.)

Problem 24-7.

SAVAGE COMPANY
Trial Balances
December 31, 1966 and 1965

	December 31,			
	1966 Before Closing		1965 After Closing	
	Debit	Credit	Debit	Credit
Cash	10,000		8,000	
Accounts receivable	17,000		15,000	
Allowance for bad debts		1,000		800
Merchandise inventory	30,000		25,000	
Prepaid expenses	3,000		2,000	
Land	10,000		10,000	
Building	80,000		80,000	
Accumulated depreciation—Building		10,000		7,500
Furniture and fixtures	15,000		12,000	
Accumulated depreciation—Furniture and fixtures		4,000		4,000
Organization expense	9,000		10,000	
Accounts payable		21,000		27,200
Current installment due on bonds payable		5,000		
Bonds payable		20,000		25,000
Capital stock		100,000		90,000
Retained earnings		6,500		7,500
Sales		250,000		
Cost of goods sold	200,000			
Selling expense	20,000			
General expense	15,000			
Depreciation of building	2,500			
Depreciation of furniture and fixtures	1,000			
Dividends paid	5,000			
	417,500	417,500	162,000	162,000

Furniture which cost $1,500, and against which there was accumulated depreciation of $1,000, was traded in on new furniture valued at $4,500. The difference of $4,000 was paid in cash. Uncollectible accounts written off in 1966 amounted to $300.

Prepare:

(a) Schedule of working capital.
(b) Working papers.
(c) Statement of sources and uses of working capital.

Problem 24-8. From the following data prepare a statement of sources and uses of funds (with supporting working papers) and a schedule of working capital. Apply the broad concept of funds.

HUDSON COMPANY

Comparative Balance Sheet
December 31, 1966 and 1965

	December 31, 1966	December 31, 1965
Assets		
Cash	$ 14,150	$ 4,500
Accounts receivable	31,600	29,700
Allowance for doubtful accounts	1,500*	1,200*
Finished goods	10,000	12,500
Goods in process	18,320	15,800
Materials	9,700	10,000
Advances to salesmen	1,000	750
Unexpired insurance	250	300
Land	70,000	65,000
Buildings	155,000	110,000
Accumulated depreciation—Buildings	16,000*	10,000*
Machinery	110,000	100,000
Accumulated depreciation—Machinery	13,500*	11,000*
Tools—less depreciation	22,000	25,000
Patents—less amortization	28,000	30,000
Investments in stocks—Noncurrent		25,000
Discount on bonds	1,800	
	$440,820	$406,350
Liabilities and Stockholders' Equity		
Accounts payable	$ 12,000	$ 33,500
Notes payable	5,000	27,000
Long-term loans		20,000
Bonds payable	300,000	200,000
Capital stock	109,000	100,000
Reserve for contingencies		16,000
Retained earnings	14,820	9,850
	$440,820	$406,350

* Deduction.

Analysis of Retained Earnings

Balance, December 31, 1965		$ 9,850
Add:		
Net income—1966		5,970
Return of Reserve for Contingencies		16,000
Total		$31,820
Deduct:		
Dividends paid	$15,000	
Loss on sale of investments	2,000	17,000
Balance, December 31, 1966		$14,820

During the year, machinery which cost $10,000 was sold for $6,000. The accumulated depreciation account was debited $4,000 although depreciation of only $2,500 had been provided.

Bonds of $100,000 face value were issued at 98 at the beginning of 1966.
Depreciation and amortization were charged to operations during the year as follows:

By credit to accumulated depreciation accounts:	
Buildings	$6,000
Machinery	6,500
By credit to fixed asset accounts:	
Tools	$5,000
Patents	2,000
By credit to deferred charge account:	
Discount on bonds	$ 200

Land that cost $4,000 was sold for $4,300 and an additional parcel was purchased by the issuance of capital stock with a par value of $9,000.

Long-term creditors accepted investments that were carried as noncurrent assets at $20,000 in satisfaction of their claims. The remaining $5,000 of noncurrent investments were sold at a loss.

Problem 24-9. From the following information prepare a statement of sources and uses of working capital and supporting working papers.

JEFFERSON COMPANY

Balance Sheets

December 31, 1966 and 1965

	December 31, 1966	December 31, 1965
Assets		
Cash	$ 10,165	$ 24,815
Accounts receivable—net	107,230	128,425
Notes receivable—Officers	22,145	24,200
Accrued interest receivable	725	1,435
Merchandise inventory	156,010	115,300
Fixed assets	600,990	476,240
Accumulated depreciation	112,625*	83,255*
Investment securities		10,000
Organization expense		25,000
	$784,640	$722,160
Liabilities and Stockholders' Equity		
Accounts payable	$ 29,400	$ 20,945
Notes payable	20,000	10,000
Accrued salaries	1,300	1,450
Bonds payable—due December 31, 1969		50,000
Capital stock	525,000	400,000
Unrealized increment per appraisal	100,000	
Retained earnings	108,940	239,765
	$784,640	$722,160

Summary of Retained Earnings

Balance, December 31, 1965		$239,765
Deduct:		
Net loss—1966	$25,825	
Dividends paid—Cash	25,000	
Dividends paid—Stock	50,000	
Discount on capital stock	5,000	
Write-off of organization expense	25,000	130,825
Balance, December 31, 1966		$108,940

JEFFERSON COMPANY
Income Statement
For the Year Ended December 31, 1966

Sales		$311,110
Deduct:		
Sales returns and allowances	$ 2,010	
Sales discounts	4,100	6,110
Net sales		$305,000
Cost of sales		245,000
Gross profit on sales		$ 60,000
Deduct expenses:		
Advertising	$ 3,100	
Sales salaries	24,345	
Bad debts	1,610	
Depreciation	21,170	
Office expense	18,120	
Other expenses	17,000	85,345
Net operating loss		$ 25,345
Interest and miscellaneous nonoperating items:		
Interest expense	$ 2,500	
Interest income	1,520*	
Gain on sale of investment securities	500*	480
Net loss		$ 25,825

* Deduction.

Extraordinary building repairs costing $1,800 were charged to Accumulated Depreciation.

The entry to record the appraisal included a $110,000 debit to Fixed Assets and a $10,000 credit to Accumulated Depreciation.

The company wrote off $1,000 of accounts receivable as uncollectible.

Problem 24-10. The following data have been taken from the financial statements of Bishop Company. Prepare working papers for the statement of sources and uses of working capital.

Debits	December 31, 1966	December 31, 1965	Increase (Decrease)
Accounts receivable	$ 180,000	$ 92,000	$ 88,000
Bond discount	2,100	2,500	(400)
Buildings	810,000	560,000	250,000
Cash in bank	-0-	8,000	(8,000)
Cash on hand	2,000	1,000	1,000
Goodwill	-0-	200,000	(200,000)
Inventories	210,000	218,000	(8,000)
Land	200,000	150,000	50,000
Long-term investments	3,000	15,000	(12,000)
Machinery	330,000	200,000	130,000
Notes receivable—Trade	21,000	27,000	(6,000)
Tools	40,000	70,000	(30,000)
Unexpired insurance	1,200	1,400	(200)
	$1,799,300	$1,544,900	$254,400

Credits			
Accounts payable	$ 58,000	$ 52,000	$ 6,000
Accrued interest	10,000	6,000	4,000
Accrued taxes	5,000	3,000	2,000
Accumulated depreciation	271,200	181,000	90,200
Allowance for doubtful accounts	4,500	2,300	2,200
Bank loans—Short-term	1,500	6,800	(5,300)
Bank overdraft	4,000	-0-	4,000
Bonds payable	150,000	100,000	50,000
Capital stock—$100 par value	700,000	400,000	300,000
Notes payable—Trade	-0-	10,000	(10,000)
Retained earnings	595,100	783,800	(188,700)
	$1,799,300	$1,544,900	$254,400

Net income (current operating concept)—1966	$ 2,500
Depreciation expense—1966	123,500

Additional Information—1966

(1) The holders of the trade notes payable accepted securities carried on the books at $12,000 in satisfaction of their notes, which were noninterest bearing.

(2) Bonds with a face value of $50,000 were issued for machinery costing $50,000.

(3) Old machinery which cost $4,500 was scrapped and written off the books. Accumulated depreciation thereon amounted to $3,300.

(4) A 2% dividend was declared and paid, on the stock outstanding as of the first of the year.

(5) There were no additions to or disposals of tools during the year.

(6) Capital stock was issued during the year at 90; the discount was charged to Goodwill.

Problem 24-11. Prepare a schedule of working capital, working papers, and a statement of sources and uses of working capital.

HYPERSONIC COMPANY
Income Statement
For the Year Ended June 30, 1966

Sales	$210,000	
Cost of goods sold	155,000	
Gross profit on sales	$ 55,000	
Gain on sale of land	1,500	
Interest earned	400	$56,900
Deductions:		
Salesmen's commissions	$ 12,400	
Rent expense	3,600	
Bad debts expense	800	
Depreciation	1,000	
Interest expense	480	
Loss on sale of investments	300	
Other expenses	31,920	50,500
Net income before income tax		$ 6,400
Federal income tax		1,800
Net income		$ 4,600

HYPERSONIC COMPANY
Statement of Retained Earnings
For the Year Ended June 30, 1966

Balance, June 30, 1965		$23,860
Add:		
Net income	$4,600	
Release of Reserve for Contingencies	5,000	9,600
Total		$33,460
Deduct:		
Dividends—Cash	$2,750	
Dividends—Stock	5,500	8,250
Balance, June 30, 1966		$25,210

HYPERSONIC COMPANY
Comparative Balance Sheet
June 30, 1966 and 1965

	June 30,		Net Changes	
	1966	1965	Debit	Credit
Assets				
Cash	$ 28,000	$ 21,810	$ 6,190	
Accounts receivable	24,000	25,900		$ 1,900
Allowance for doubtful accounts	350*	400*	50	
Merchandise inventory	31,450	31,150	300	
Prepaid rent	300		300	
Investments	12,000	15,000		3,000
Furniture and fixtures	18,000	20,000		2,000
Accumulated depreciation	4,600*	5,600*	1,000	
	$108,800	$107,860		
Liabilities and Stockholders' Equity				
Accounts payable—Merchandise	$ 8,400	$ 9,160	760	
Accrued salesmen's commissions	600	800	200	
Dividends payable	2,750	2,500		250
Deposits from customers	420			420
Federal income tax payable	1,800	2,400	600	
Bonds payable—5%	10,000	10,000		
Bond premium	120	140	20	
Common stock	55,000	50,000		5,000
Paid-in surplus	4,500	4,000		500
Reserve for contingencies		5,000	5,000	
Retained earnings	25,210	23,860		1,350
	$108,800	$107,860	$14,420	$14,420

* Deduction.

Additional information:

During the year, the company retired fully depreciated fixtures which had cost $2,000.

On May 1, 1966, the company sold a parcel of land which it had purchased on August 15, 1965, at a cost of $8,000.

On June 15, 1966, the company purchased additional investments at a cost of $1,200.

Problem 24-12. The following data are from the balance sheets of Fore Specialties Corporation as of December 31, 1966 and 1965:

	December 31, 1966	December 31, 1965
Debits		
Cash	$ 327,500	$ 200,000
Certificate of deposit	200,000	-0-
Marketable securities	10,000	172,000
Customers' notes and accounts receivable	290,000	327,000
Inventories	155,000	201,000
Investment in Conway Novelty Company	40,000	90,000
Cash deposited with trustee—Bond redemption fund	-0-	62,000
Deposit on special machine	137,500	-0-
Plant and equipment	2,137,000	1,953,000
Goodwill	-0-	250,000
Discount on bonds payable	-0-	20,000
	$3,297,000	$3,275,000
Credits		
Accounts payable	$ 192,000	$ 147,000
Bank loans	-0-	130,000
Accruals	50,000	72,000
Accumulated depreciation	610,000	400,000
Bonds payable:		
First-mortgage 5% bonds	-0-	350,000
4% serial bonds	100,000	-0-
Capital in excess of stated value	150,000	-0-
Capital stock	1,100,000	900,000
Retained earnings	1,095,000	1,276,000
	$3,297,000	$3,275,000

The first-mortgage bonds were redeemed on January 1, 1966. Dividends were paid as follows: stock dividend, $100,000, which caused the issuance of shares with an aggregate stated value of $60,000; cash dividend, $90,000. The corporation earned $329,000 from its own operations in 1966 and the subsidiary showed a net loss of $50,000. Extraordinary repairs of $5,000 were made to the plant and charged to Accumulated Depreciation.

Prepare a statement showing the sources and uses of working capital supported with a schedule of working capital and working papers.

Problem 24-13. The net change in working capital and the net changes in the balance sheet accounts of United Company for the year ended December 31, 1965, are shown below:

	Debit	Credit
Working capital	$23,400	
Investments		$30,000
Land	3,200	
Buildings	35,000	
Machinery	3,000	
Office equipment		1,500
Accumulated depreciation:		
Buildings		2,000
Machinery	2,100	
Office equipment	600	
Bond discount	1,000	
Bonds payable		20,000
Capital stock—Preferred	10,000	
Capital stock—Common		12,400
Capital in excess of par value—Common		5,600
Retained earnings		6,800
	$78,300	$78,300

Additional information:

(1) The net income for the year, on an all-inclusive basis, was $28,000.

(2) A cash dividend of $18,000 was declared December 15, 1965, payable January 15, 1966. A 2% stock dividend was issued March 31, 1965, when the market value was $12.50 per share.

(3) The investments were sold for $32,500.

(4) A building and the land on which it stood were sold for $54,000. The land cost $4,000 and the building cost $45,000. There was accumulated depreciation on the building of $4,500.

(5) A new machine was purchased during the year on the following terms: $11,000 cash plus the trade-in of an old machine which cost $10,000 and on which there was accumulated depreciation of $8,000. No gain or loss was shown for the transaction.

(6) A fully depreciated office machine which cost $1,500 was written off.

(7) Preferred stock of $10,000 par value was retired for $10,200.

(8) The company issued 1,000 shares of its common stock (par value, $10) on June 15, 1965, for $15 per share. There were 13,240 shares outstanding on December 31, 1965.

Prepare a statement of sources and uses of working capital and supporting working papers.

Problem 24-14. The comparative statement of balance sheet accounts on the next page was prepared from the records of Automated Manufacturing Company. Prepare a statement of sources and uses of working capital with a supporting schedule of working capital and working papers.

	December 31, 1966	December 31, 1965
Debits		
Cash	$ 2,200	$ 3,300
Accounts receivable	12,000	29,000
Notes receivable	8,000	10,000
Advances to employees	600	1,300
Materials	7,000	9,200
Goods in process	10,340	16,200
Finished goods	33,000	22,000
Prepaid expense	200	250
Land	105,000	72,000
Buildings	120,000	114,000
Machinery	110,000	83,000
Tools	25,000	20,000
Patents	18,000	18,000
Discount on bonds payable	3,000	
Investment in bonds—Long-term	19,110	
Goodwill		50,000
	$473,450	$448,250
Credits		
Accounts payable	$ 26,000	$ 21,000
Notes payable		10,000
Bank loans	20,000	
Bonds payable	250,000	200,000
Accumulated depreciation—Buildings and machinery	21,000	26,000
Allowance for doubtful accounts	1,600	1,400
Reserve for construction	18,000	12,000
Capital stock	100,000	100,000
Retained earnings	36,850	77,850
	$473,450	$448,250

Depreciation and amortization were provided during the year as follows:

Buildings and machinery—credited to contra account	$9,000
Tools—asset written down	7,000
Patents—asset written down	5,000

An old patent carried at $2,000 was sold for that amount and a new patent was purchased for $7,000.

Machinery which cost $15,000 and against which depreciation of $14,000 had accumulated, was abandoned and removed from the accounts.

Following is an abstract of the Retained Earnings account:

Balance, January 1, 1966		$ 77,850
Add appraisal increase in land		33,000
Total		$110,850
Deduct:		
Net loss for 1966	$ 3,000	
Credit to Reserve for Construction	6,000	
Dividends paid on December 31, 1966	15,000	
Goodwill charged off	50,000	74,000
Balance, December 31, 1966		$ 36,850

Assignment Material for Chapter 25

QUESTIONS

1. What are the minimum essentials of a single-entry bookkeeping system?
2. Describe the single-entry method of determining the net income for a period.
3. In each of the following cases, determine the net income or loss for the year 1965.

(a)	Proprietorship equity, beginning of period	$23,000
	Additional investments during the period	1,000
	Withdrawals during the period	5,000
	Proprietorship equity, end of period	25,000
(b)	Proprietorship equity, beginning of period	$30,000
	Additional investments during the period	5,000
	Withdrawals during the period	3,000
	Proprietorship equity, end of period	31,000
(c)	Proprietorship equity, beginning of period	$20,000
	Additional investments during the period	1,000
	Withdrawals during the period	6,000
	Proprietorship equity, end of period	18,000
(d)	Proprietorship equity, beginning of period	$14,000
	Additional investments during the period	5,000
	Withdrawals during the period	2,000
	Proprietorship equity, end of period	11,000

4. The accounts receivable of a business at the beginning of a year were $15,000; the accounts receivable at the end of the year were $16,500; the cash collections from charge customers amounted to $95,000; and the cash sales were $15,000. The charge customers deducted $1,800 of cash discounts from their payments. What were the total sales for the year?
5. Cash sales for the year were $23,000; the cash collections from charge customers were $63,200; the accounts receivable regarded as collectible decreased $2,470; one account, in the amount of $650, was determined during the year to be worthless. What were the total sales for the year?
6. Accounts payable at the beginning of the year were $9,500 and at the end of the year were $10,600; payments to trade creditors during the year amounted to $83,000; and cash purchases of merchandise amounted to $55,900. Compute the total cost of purchases during the year.

7. Compute the interest earned, the wages expense, and the interest expense for the year.

	Beginning of Year	End of Year	During Year
Accruals:			
Interest receivable	$200	$240	
Wages payable	475	500	
Interest payable	383	312	
Cash receipts and payments:			
Interest on notes receivable			$ 620
Wages			32,000
Interest on notes payable			465

PROBLEMS

Problem 25-1. The owner of Service Center has compiled the following comparative data:

	December 31, 1966	December 31, 1965
Assets		
Cash in bank	$ 16,000	$ 4,000
Accounts receivable	20,000	30,000
Allowance for doubtful accounts	1,000*	1,500*
Inventory	35,000	60,000
Investment securities	14,000	10,000
Service and delivery equipment	30,000	25,000
Accumulated depreciation	5,000*	6,000*
	$109,000	$121,500
Liabilities		
Accounts payable	$ 12,500	$ 15,000
Mortgage payable		10,000

* Deduction.

Upon inquiry you learn the following:

(1) Cash receipts from customers during 1966 amounted to $185,000. Cash disbursements included drawings of $110 per week.

(2) The investment securities were paid for by the owner's wife with her funds, and the securities are held by the owner and his wife jointly.

(3) The mortgage was on the owner's residence. It was paid by a store check, which included interest for 1966 in the amount of $100.

(4) The increase in fixed assets was accounted for by the acquisition of an additional delivery truck costing $5,000. Only $3,000 of the store's funds were spent for this purpose, because a $2,000 trade-in allowance was granted on a convertible previously used by the owner's son while in college.

Compute the net income or loss for 1966.

Problem 25-2. Joseph George maintains records of cash, accounts receivable, and accounts payable in connection with his operation of a small grocery store. At the end of each calendar year, he prepares a statement of assets and liabilities based upon these records, with estimates of the value of other assets. The statements so prepared at the beginning and end of 1966 appear as follows:

JOSEPH GEORGE
Statements of Assets and Liabilities
December 31, 1966 and 1965

	December 31, 1966	December 31, 1965
Cash	$ 1,115	$ 964
Accounts receivable	1,416	1,212
Merchandise	3,980	4,650
Equipment	4,120	4,110
	$10,631	$10,936
Note payable	$	$ 1,000
Accounts payable	814	1,120
Joseph George, capital	9,817	8,816
	$10,631	$10,936

Compute, on the accrual basis:

(1) Net income or loss for 1966: The cash records show that Mr. George withdrew $400 per month and invested $1,000 in cash on September 30, 1966. In addition, he paid the note payable with interest of $25 from personal funds on June 30, 1966.

(2) Sales: $10,115 was collected in cash from customers, discounts of $240 were allowed, and one account with a balance of $410 was removed from the accounts receivable records as being uncollectible.

(3) Merchandise purchases: $9,160 was paid to merchandise creditors during 1966, merchandise returned to suppliers aggregated $390, and cash discounts of $188 were taken.

Problem 25-3. Comparative balance sheet data for the business of A. B. Cecil are presented below:

	June 30, 1966	June 30, 1965
Balance sheet data:		
Cash	$15,710	$ 7,040
Accounts receivable	6,600	7,200
Notes receivable—Trade	3,900	3,400
Inventory	16,100	15,560
Accounts payable	3,100	4,000
Taxes payable	2,200	1,700
Owner's equity	37,010	27,500

An analysis of the cash journals for the year ended June 30, 1966, reveals the following data, presented in summary form:

Cash receipts:	
Cash sales	$28,000
Collections on accounts receivable	96,000
Collections on notes receivable	4,300
Bank loan	3,000

Cash disbursements:	
Cash purchases	$ 2,400
Payments on accounts payable	81,100
Repayment of bank loan—with interest	3,120
Taxes	1,700
Rent	2,400
Other expenses	27,110
Withdrawals	4,800

Prepare the income statement for the year ended June 30, 1966. Submit working papers.

Problem 25-4. An analysis of the incomplete records of Discount Company produced the following information applicable to 1966.

List of Increases

Accounts receivable	$ 720
Inventory	5,400
Equipment	1,500
Accounts payable	240
Accrued office expense	480

List of Decreases

Cash	$ 7,008
Notes receivable—Trade	2,100
Unexpired insurance	180

Summary of Cash Transactions

Receipts:	
Cash sales	$ 51,000
Collections from customers	156,000
Collections on notes receivable	4,200
Interest	270
Purchase returns	255
Disbursements:	
Cash purchases	2,745
Sales returns	606
Payments on accounts payable	93,312
Insurance premium	900
Salesmen's commissions	27,318
New equipment	9,000
Rent	4,800
Office expense	19,533
Other operating expenses	60,519

The records indicated that a noninterest-bearing note in the amount of $900 proved to be uncollectible during the year. No fixed assets were sold or retired from use. The owners of the business had made no additional investments during the year and no amounts had been withdrawn. Prepare the income statement for 1966. Submit working papers.

Problem 25-5. The owner of Village Center has analyzed the store's records and prepared the data shown on the following page.

Summary of Cash Transactions for 1966

Receipts:	
Cash sales	$33,600
Collections on account, including collection from *A*	12,525
Rent from upstairs apartment	1,320
Proceeds from 90-day, 6% bank loan received December 1	3,000
Disbursements:	
Payments on account	25,108
Wages	8,844
Taxes	800
Advertising	205
Office expense	3,985
Sales returns	72
Insurance premium—Renewal of 3-year policy (no change in premium or coverage)	450
Equipment	2,000
Drawings of owner	6,000

Unpaid Bills

	12/31/66	12/31/65
For merchandise (amounting to 10% of the inventory)	$1,100	$980
For advertising	35	65
For office expense	35	55

Uncollected Accounts

	12/31/66	12/31/65
A		$110
B	$ 44	140
C	181	175
D	214	198
F	44	69
G	42	

A's account was considered to be uncollectible as of July 1, 1966, and was removed from the record of uncollected accounts at that time. Subsequently, $25 was collected from *A*. However, no further collections seem likely.

Depreciation for the year is estimated as $2,800.

Prepare the 1966 income statement. You need not prepare working papers, but show all supporting computations.

Problem 25-6. Using the following data from incomplete records, prepare income statement working papers for the business owned by M. N. Olson.

The changes that occurred between June 30, 1965, and June 30, 1966, in the accounts classified under the Assets and Liabilities captions of the balance sheet are shown below.

Increases:	
Cash	$ 940
Inventory	3,000
Allowance for uncollectible accounts	20
Accrued salaries	150
Decreases:	
Accounts receivable	3,400
Prepaid insurance	110
Store fixtures	800
Accounts payable	3,430

An analysis of the cash transactions for the year ended June 30, 1966, is shown below.

Cash receipts:	
Customers	$143,220
Cash disbursements:	
Merchandise	109,430
Salaries	14,850
Other expenses	18,000

There were no retirements or disposals of store fixtures during the year. It was established during the year that $180 of accounts receivable were uncollectible. There were no additional investments or withdrawals by the owner during the year.

Problem 25-7. Prepare the income statement and the statement of retained earnings for Delta Company for the year ended December 31, 1966.

During the year, $850 of accounts receivable were found to be uncollectible.
During the year, the company retired some fully depreciated fixtures.

DELTA COMPANY

Comparative Balance Sheet

December 31, 1966 and 1965

	December 31,		Net Changes	
	Debit	Credit	1966	1965
Assets				
Cash	$ 26,480	$ 20,290	$ 6,190	
Accounts receivable	24,000	25,900		$ 1,900
Allowance for doubtful accounts	350*	400*	50	
Merchandise inventory	31,450	31,150	300	
Prepaid rent	300		300	
Investments	12,000	15,000		3,000
Furniture and fixtures	18,000	20,000		2,000
Accumulated depreciation	4,600*	5,600*	1,000	
	$107,280	$106,340		
Liabilities and Stockholders' Equity				
Accounts payable—Merchandise	$ 8,400	$ 9,160	760	
Accrued salesmen's commissions	600	800	200	
Dividends payable	2,750	2,500		250
Deposits from customers	420			420
Federal income tax payable	1,800	2,400	600	
Bonds payable—5%	10,000	10,000		
Bond premium	120	140	20	
Common stock	55,000	50,000		5,000
Capital in excess of par value	4,500	4,000		500
Reserve for contingencies		5,000	5,000	
Retained earnings	23,690	22,340		1,350
	$107,280	$106,340	$14,420	$14,420

* Deduction.

Cash receipts:		
From customers	$211,470	
From interest	400	
From sale of land	9,500	
From sale of investments	3,900	$225,270

Cash disbursements:		
For merchandise	$156,060	
For salesmen's commissions	12,600	
For rent	3,900	
For other operating expenses	31,920	
For interest	500	
For federal income tax	2,400	
For purchase of land	8,000	
For purchase of investments	1,200	
For dividends	2,500	219,080
Increase in cash		$ 6,190

Problem 25-8. Q. R. Sharp owns and operates a rifle range. Revenue is from admissions, rifle rentals, and sales of ammunition, some of the latter being sold on credit.

Mr. Sharp does not maintain adequate accounting records. However, the following information is available:

As of December 31, 1966

Assets:	
Cash on hand	$ 55
Accounts receivable	15
Inventory	1,108
Liabilities:	
Accounts payable	149
Taxes payable	178

As of December 31, 1965

Assets:	
Cash on hand and in bank	$ 2,345
Accounts receivable	86
Inventory	1,119
Prepaid insurance	270
Land	500
Building and building improvements	6,800
Rifles	3,000
Accumulated depreciation	(4,120)
	$10,000
Liabilities:	
Accounts payable	$ 882
Taxes payable	113
Accrued interest payable	120
Bank loan	4,000
	$ 5,115

For 1966

Cash receipts:	
Admissions	$11,550
Admissions tax collected (2%)	231
Rifle rentals	1,823
Sales of ammunition	13,196
	$26,800

Cash disbursements:	
Wages paid	$ 4,200
Purchases of ammunition	8,420
Insurance premiums	750
Admissions tax	239
Property tax	74
Utilities	424
Supplies	111
Repairs	216
Miscellaneous expense	2,926
Payment to bank on July 1 for 6% interest and annual installment on principal	1,240
Drawings	6,000
	$24,600

The December 31, 1966 listing shown above is incomplete. A search of the records produces the following details:

	December 31, 1966	December 31, 1965
Accounts payable:		
Ammunition	$ 71	$160
Utilities	43	63
Supplies	14	32
Repairs		116
Miscellaneous	21	511
	$149	$882
Taxes payable:		
Admissions tax	$ 31	$ 39
Property tax	147	74
	$178	$113

A review of the 1966 cash transactions reveals the following:

(1) All insurance policies are for a one-year term.

	Premium
Fire insurance on business building—policy expires 9/1/67	$144
Business liability—policy expires 7/15/67	360
Fire insurance on residence of Q. R. Sharp—policy expires 7/1/67	246
	$750

(2) Miscellaneous expense includes $1,100 in full payment of a city assessment for water lines connecting the rifle range to the city water system.

Assume that the following depreciation rates are appropriate:

Building and building improvements	5%
Rifles	20%

Required:

Income statement for 1966.
December 31, 1966 balance sheet.

Problem 25-9. At the beginning of 1965, Mr. Fred Davis started an unincorporated business known as Davis Company, with the following investment:

Cash	$2,000
Equipment	8,600

Mr. Davis has asked you to prepare an income statement on the accrual basis for the six months ended June 30, 1966. Although the accounting records maintained are inadequate, it has been possible to determine the following information as of December 31, 1965:

Cash	$ 1,650
Accounts receivable	1,300
Inventory	3,170
Prepaid insurance	315
Equipment (No additions or disposals during 1965)	8,600
	$15,035
Accounts payable—Suppliers	$ 1,690
Accrued expenses (miscellaneous)	55
	$ 1,745

Mr. Davis has followed the practice of depositing all cash receipts. An analysis of the 1966 bank statements through June and the canceled checks disclosed the following:

Deposits:	
Collections from customers	$25,025
Proceeds from March 31 sale of equipment costing $1,000	400
Proceeds from bank loan ($2,000, 4-month note due September 30, 1966)	1,960
	$27,385
Canceled checks:	
Payments to suppliers—checks dated 1966	$19,921
Insurance premiums	264
Employee's salary	875
Installment on income tax of Mr. Davis	300
Purchase of equipment on April 1	1,600
Rent (at $100 a month through July, 1966)	700
Miscellaneous expense	736
Drawings	2,400
	$26,796

You may assume that you have prepared the following bank reconciliation.

DAVIS COMPANY
Bank Reconciliation
June 30, 1966

Balance per bank statement	$2,239
Add deposit in transit—customer's check received on June 30	450
Total	$2,689
Deduct outstanding check dated 6/20/66—to a supplier	300
Balance	$2,389

As of June 30, 1966, the accounts receivable, after deducting the $450 collection noted in the bank reconciliation, amounted to $2,300. However, Mr. Davis believes that one account, arising from a March, 1966, sale of $150, is uncollectible.

The equipment has an expected useful life of 10 years, with no salvage value.

The employee was hired on April 1, 1966. His annual salary is $4,200, payable semimonthly. You may ignore payroll taxes.

The insurance policies purchased for the business are listed below:

Policy	Date	Term	Premium
7940-A	January 1, 1965	3 years	$360
X-3842	June 1, 1965	1 year	180
MN-300	April 1, 1966	1 year	72
I-2701	June 1, 1966	1 year	192
			$804

An analysis of goods ordered from suppliers during the six months ended June 30, 1966, disclosed the following:

Goods ordered	$22,329
Goods received	20,431
Orders unfilled as of June 30, 1966	$ 1,898

The June 30, 1966 inventory amounted to $3,940.

As of June 30, 1966, there were accrued miscellaneous expenses of $70.

Your solution should include suitable working papers in support of the income statement for the six months ended June 30, 1966.

Problem 25-10. You have been asked to prepare working papers that will facilitate the preparation of the statements of income and retained earnings of Diminutive Company for 1966. The company does not maintain adequate records, but the following data are available.

Assets as of December 31, 1965	
Cash on hand and in bank	$ 2,972
Accounts receivable—Customers	30,110
Merchandise inventory	16,150
Prepaid expenses	2,890
Land	7,000
Depreciable assets—net of accumulated depreciation of $56,620	73,380
	$132,502

There has been no change in the following items during 1966:

Notes payable—6%	$ 10,000
Mortgage payable	26,000
Capital stock	40,000
Land	7,000

All disbursements are made by check. The results of an analysis of checks written during 1966 are set forth below.

	Cleared the Bank During 1966	Outstanding as of 12/31/66
Checks for 1965 purchases of merchandise	$ 17,200	
Checks for 1966 purchases of merchandise	451,120	$6,620
Loan to officer of company	340	
Travel advance to purchasing agent		250
Expenses—Other than interest and income tax	121,135	1,630
Check for 1965 income tax	1,000	
Interest payments	2,282	

The December 31, 1966 bank statement showed an ending balance of $18,642. Undeposited cash receipts at year end equaled $1,212.

All of the $30,110 of accounts receivable outstanding as of December 31, 1965, were collected during 1966. However, during 1966, $3,090 of accounts arising from 1966 sales were written off as uncollectible. There were no cash sales during 1966. As of December 31, 1966, the accounts receivable amounted to $28,210, all of which were believed to be collectible.

A 4% dividend was declared on December 15, 1966, payable January 15, 1967. This was the first dividend declaration since 1964.

As of December 31, 1966, 120 days' interest was accrued on the notes payable.

The company has been using a rate of 8 per cent for depreciation purposes. There were no additions to or disposals of depreciable assets during 1966.

Unpaid bills for merchandise, as of December 31, 1966, amounted to $18,610.

There were $4,800 of prepaid expenses as of December 31, 1966, exclusive of the travel advance. The merchandise inventory on that date was $21,700.

You may use $800 as a reasonable estimate for the 1966 income tax.

Assignment Material for Chapter 26

QUESTIONS

1. List several conditions, the existence of which has been suggested as being necessary to justify classifying a combination as a pooling of interests.
2. Give three reasons why the books of account may lack comparability when used by businesses exploring the desirability of combining.
3. What is a quasi-reorganization?
4. By means of a reduction during the year in the stated value of its common no-par stock, a company has absorbed a large deficit existing at the beginning of the year. A net income is earned on the year's operations. How would you state these facts in your balance sheet at the close of the year?
5. Is an accounting basis something that is identified with a particular asset or with a business entity? For example, if assets are transferred from the ownership of Company *X* to the ownership of Company *Y*, should the accounting basis ever be carried forward or transferred with the assets?
6. What formalities, if any, are required to effect a quasi-reorganization?
7. When a combination is being treated as a pooling of interests, the income statement issued by the surviving corporation for the year during which the combination occurred should normally include the combined operating results of the several entities for the entire year. What alternative is considered acceptable?
8. Suppose that an asset, written down to its estimated realizable value as a part of a quasi-reorganization, is subsequently sold for more than its new carrying value. Is such excess of sales proceeds over the new carrying value a gain?
9. What is the nature of a divisive reorganization?
10. Distinguish between the following: a spin-off, a split-off, and a split-up.
11. When retained earnings are being transferred in conjunction with a pooling of interests, under what circumstances, if any, may the retained earnings of the new or surviving corporation be less than the sum of the retained earnings amounts of the combined corporations? Under what circumstances, if any, may such retained earnings be larger than the sum of the retained earnings amounts of the combined corporations?
12. During the process of a quasi-reorganization, is it ever permissible to write up an asset?
13. Is it necessary for a deficit to exist in order for a quasi-reorganization to be effected?

PROBLEMS

Problem 26-1. Companies *R*, *S*, *T*, and *U* are being combined. Just prior to combining, their stockholders' equity data were reported as follows:

	Company			
	R	*S*	*T*	*U*
Common stock	$200,000	$100,000	$150,000	$50,000
Capital in excess of par value				15,000
Capital in excess of stated value		50,000	20,000	
Retained earnings	60,000	30,000	90,000	15,000
Total stockholders' equity	$260,000	$180,000	$260,000	$80,000

Determine the amount of retained earnings that will be shown in the balance sheet as of the date when the combination becomes effective under each of the following plans.

(a) Company *R* is the surviving business entity with a stated capital of $600,000, and the plan is a pooling of interests.
(b) Company *S* is the surviving business entity with a stated capital of $350,000, and the plan is a purchase.
(c) Company *T* is the surviving business entity with a stated capital of $450,000, and the plan is a pooling of interests.
(d) Company *U* is the surviving business entity with a stated capital of $650,000, and the plan is a pooling of interests.

Problem 26-2. Green Wing Company had authorized and outstanding 20,000 shares of $50 par value common stock which had been issued at par. On December 31, 1965, the corporation had an operating deficit of $290,000.

The corporation was in need of additional cash, but the directors felt that borrowing or issuing additional stock was impractical because of the appearance of the balance sheet. For this reason, appropriate procedures were followed during January, 1966, to obtain authorization for the quasi-reorganization outlined below:

(1) Change the capitalization to 50,000 shares of no par value with a stated value of $25 per share.
(2) Exchange shares on a one-for-one basis.
(3) Write down the long-term investments by $25,000. The securities involved are not listed on any organized stock exchange.
(4) Remove the deficit by appropriate accounting entry.

The quasi-reorganization was completed and recorded in the corporation's accounts as of January 2, 1966.

On February 15, 1966, the company was able to issue 5,000 shares of stock for $26 per share.

On February 25, 1966, the company was able to sell its long-term investments, now carried at $75,000, for $80,000. There were no significant changes in the level of business activity, or in the prospects of the companies whose securities were sold, during the period since the quasi-reorganization.

Required:

(a) Journal entries to effect the quasi-reorganization as of January 2, 1966, and to record the February transactions.
(b) The Stockholders' Equity section of the company's balance sheet as of December 31, 1966, assuming that the net income for 1966 was $40,000 and that no dividends were declared during the year.

Problem 26-3. A pooling of interests has been negotiated by the officers of Companies *M*, *N*, and *O*. The exchange of shares is to be made on the basis of the market values of the stock, which were as follows: Company *M*, $12 per share; Company *N*, $3 per share; Company *O*, $4 per share. No decision has been reached about which company is to be the surviving company.

The capital structure of each company is set forth below.

	Company		
	M	*N*	*O*
Common stock:			
$10 stated value	$500,000		
$5 stated value		$600,000	
$1 stated value			$240,000
Capital in excess of stated value		50,000	180,000
Retained earnings	480,000	150,000	480,000
	$980,000	$800,000	$900,000

Each company has sufficient authorized, unissued shares to effect the pooling. The following plans are under consideration:

Plan 1. Company *M* to be the surviving company.
Shareholders of Company *N* to receive one share of Company *M* stock for every four shares of Company *N* stock.
Shareholders of Company *O* to receive one share of Company *M* stock for every three shares of Company *O* stock.

Plan 2. Company *O* to be the surviving company.
Shareholders of Company *M* to receive three shares of Company *O* stock for each share of Company *M* stock.
Shareholders of Company *N* to receive three shares of Company *O* stock for every four shares of Company *N* stock.

Show the Stockholders' Equity section for the surviving company under each of the above plans.

Problem 26-4. The condensed balance sheet of McDaniel Company, prior to giving effect to a quasi-reorganization as of September 30, 1965, is presented below.

McDANIEL COMPANY
Balance Sheet
September 30, 1965

Assets		Liabilities and Stockholders' Equity		
Current assets	$324,400	Current liabilities		$180,000
Fixed assets (net)	527,600	Capital stock	$800,000	
		Retained earnings—deficit	128,000	672,000
	$852,000			$852,000

The quasi-reorganization which was approved included the following actions:

(1) The reduction of the par value of the company's stock from $50 to $30 per share. The new stock was exchanged for the old stock on a one-for-one basis.
(2) The provision of additional depreciation of $40,000.
(3) The recognition of an $18,000 loss on obsolete inventory.
(4) The elimination of the deficit.

During the three months ended December 31, 1965, the company earned $22,000, which included a $4,000 gain on the sale of the obsolete inventory on October 16, 1965. Depreciation expense for the three-month period was $12,000.

During the three months, no dividends were declared; no additions to or disposals of the fixed assets were made; no financing was undertaken. As of December 31, 1965, the current liabilities amounted to $155,000.

Prepare the December 31, 1965 balance sheet of McDaniel Company.

Problem 26-5. The balance sheet of Modern Era Company, a closely held corporation, is presented below.

MODERN ERA COMPANY
Balance Sheet
December 31, 1965

Assets		
Current assets:		
Cash		$ 44,400
Trade accounts receivable, less allowance for doubtful accounts of $1,400		88,600
Contract research in progress		25,000
Inventories:		
Finished goods	$ 62,000	
Work in process	30,000	
Materials	21,000	
Research supplies	48,000	161,000
		$319,000
Fixed assets:		
Land	$ 40,000	
Manufacturing facilities, less accumulated depreciation of $63,000	237,000	
Research facilities, less accumulated depreciation of $45,000	155,000	
Research and development—Company research in progress	100,000	532,000
		$851,000

Liabilities and Stockholders' Equity		
Current liabilities:		
Accounts payable—Manufacturing activity		$ 65,000
Accounts payable—Research activity		26,000
		$ 91,000
Long-term liability:		
Bonds payable—Secured by mortgage on the research facilities—Maturity date, July 1, 1975		120,000
Stockholders' equity:		
Capital stock, $5 stated value	$400,000	
Retained earnings	240,000	640,000
		$851,000

The company has been doing an increasing amount of contract research for other companies in addition to research for its own business. The stockholders have voted in favor of a split-off in order to separate the ownership and management of the research facilities from the manufacturing part of the business. A new corporation, Modern Research Company, has been formed and authorized to issue 100,000 shares of $2 stated-value stock.

Modern Research Company will take over all of the assets and liabilities identified with the research activity, and enough cash to satisfy the current liabilities attributable to the research activity. The land thus transferred to the new company cost $16,000.

The stockholders have voted to transfer a portion of the retained earnings to the new company, the portion being based on the net assets transferred. The stockholders will surrender to Modern Era Company one share of its stock for each share of Modern Research Company stock issued to them. Modern Era Company will carry the shares received in exchange as treasury stock.

Prepare the balance sheet of each company after giving effect to the split-off as of December 31, 1965.

Problem 26-6. You are asked by the boards of directors of Single Company and Unit Company to determine the amount of retained earnings that would emerge upon combination of the two businesses under each of the following plans:

(a) Single Company to carry on the combined businesses with sufficient additional shares authorized to exchange shares with the stockholders of Unit Company on the following basis: 1½ shares of Single Company stock for each share of Unit Company stock.

(b) Formation of a new company, The Multiple Company, to carry on the combined businesses with sufficient shares of $1 par value stock authorized to exchange shares with the stockholders of Single Company and Unit Company on the following bases:

One share of stock in the new company for each share of Single Company stock.

Three-fourths share of stock in the new company for each share of Unit Company stock.

(c) Unit Company to increase its authorized shares and to issue the newly authorized shares to its stockholders for $400,000, such proceeds to be used to pay Single Company for the purchase of its net assets.

The balance sheets of the separate companies, just prior to the combining, are presented below in comparative form.

Balance Sheets—December 31, 1966

	Single Company	Unit Company
Cash	$175,000	$ 74,000
Accounts receivable	70,000	60,000
Inventory	130,000	180,000
Prepaid expenses	6,000	
Long-term investment—at cost	64,000	
Fixed assets—net	200,000	130,000
	$645,000	$444,000
Accounts payable	$167,000	$177,000
Accrued expenses	3,000	2,000
Common stock—$2 par value; authorized, issued, and outstanding	400,000	100,000
Capital in excess of par value	40,000	
Retained earnings	35,000	165,000
	$645,000	$444,000

The long-term investment consists of $60,000 face value of bonds, purchased 10 years ago when the 25-year bonds were issued.

(*Continued*)

Unit Company, as a matter of policy, does not record any short-term prepaid expenses. As of December 31, 1965 and December 31, 1966, they were $2,200 and $2,000, respectively.

Problem 26-7. The June 30, 1965 condensed balance sheet of Mound Company is presented below.

MOUND COMPANY
Balance Sheet
June 30, 1965

Assets		
Current assets		$220,000
Long-term investments—at cost		30,000
Property, plant, and equipment	$840,000	
Less accumulated depreciation	320,000	520,000
Patent—at cost less amortization		160,000
		$930,000

Liabilities and Stockholders' Equity	
Accrued bond interest payable	$ 54,000
Other current liabilities	120,000
Bonds payable—1980	300,000
Common stock—$5 stated value	400,000
Capital in excess of stated value	36,000
Retained earnings	20,000
	$930,000

One of the products manufactured and sold by the company—the one covered by the patent—was not well received in the market place. This caused the company to be unprofitable in recent years, which in turn caused the company to postpone the payment of bond interest for the last three years.

Management decided to discontinue the product, to scrap the related manufacturing facilities, and to write off the patent as worthless. Cost and market studies prepared by management indicated that the company would regain a profitable status if it concentrated on its other products, which were well received by the company's customers.

Management obtained the necessary approvals for the following plan, which was made effective as of July 1, 1965:

(1) Common stock was assigned a stated value of $2 per share.
(2) The accrued bond interest liability was settled by the issuance of 9,000 shares of the company's common stock (which had a current market value of $6 per share).
(3) The patent was written off.
(4) A reserve for losses from the disposal of manufacturing facilities and unsold inventory was established in the amount of $100,000.
(5) The deficit was eliminated.

During the year ended June 30, 1966, the company disposed of all of its manufacturing facilities and inventory related to the discarded product at a loss of $85,000. Its net income from operations for the fiscal year ended June 30, 1966, was $32,000. No dividends were declared.

Required:

(a) The journal entries made as of July 1, 1965, for the quasi-reorganization.
(b) The Stockholders' Equity section of the June 30, 1966 balance sheet, including any pertinent disclosures.

Problem 26-8. In the latter part of December, 1965, the stockholders of *A* Company and *Z* Company agreed to a pooling of interests which called for the exchange, as of January 1, 1966, of 4,000 shares of stock by *A* Company for the 6,000 shares of *Z* Company stock outstanding.

The December 31, 1965 balance sheets of the two companies are presented below.

Balance Sheets
December 31, 1965

	A Company	*Z* Company
Cash	$ 46,400	$ 37,200
Accounts receivable	42,900	21,700
Inventories	71,100	49,600
Prepaid expenses	13,000	3,300
Plant and equipment	83,200	43,500
Accumulated depreciation	12,800*	9,300*
	$243,800	$146,000
Accounts payable	$ 66,000	$ 31,600
Dividends payable (Declared 12/20/65, payable 1/20/66, to stockholders of record 1/10/66)		4,500
Capital stock, $20 par value	80,000	
Capital stock, $10 par value		60,000
Capital in excess of par value	28,000	20,000
Retained earnings	91,800	29,900
Treasury stock—1,000 shares, at cost	22,000*	
	$243,800	$146,000

* Deduction.

To effect the pooling, *A* Company transferred to the stockholders of *Z* Company 3,000 previously unissued shares and the 1,000 shares held as treasury stock. All of the assets and liabilities of *Z* Company were transferred to *A* Company in exchange for the *Z* Company stock.

Prepare the balance sheet for *A* Company as of January 1, 1966, after the pooling has been completed.

Problem 26-9. Trend Company is a manufacturer of tools and equipment used in connection with lawn maintenance. As a result of an unwise acquisition of another business, the company has been unprofitable for several years. As indicated by the following partial balance sheet, the company had a deficit of $421,100 as of December 31, 1965.

TREND COMPANY
Partial Balance Sheet
December 31, 1965

Stockholders' equity:	
$3 cumulative preferred stock—$50 par value; outstanding, 48,100 shares (dividends in arrears since January 1, 1958)	$2,405,000
Common stock—$5 stated value; outstanding, 700,000 shares	3,500,000
Retained earnings (Deficit)	(421,100)
Total	$5,483,900

A plan of asset and capital adjustment had been worked out during 1965, which was ratified by the stockholders and made effective as of January 1, 1966. The details of the plan were as follows:

(1) Goodwill of $100,000 was to be written off.

(2) Manufacturing equipment costing $88,000 and on which $54,000 of depreciation had accumulated was to be written off as worthless.

(3) The $3 preferred was to be reduced from $50 par value to $40 par value; it would continue to be preferred for $3-per-share dividends on a cumulative basis; it would be preferred in liquidation at $50 per share and redeemable at the option of the company at $55 per share.

(4) In settlement of the dividends in arrears, the company would pay $192,400 cash and issue 96,200 shares of "B" stock having a par value of $10 per share. The "B" shares are nonvoting and are not entitled to dividends. They are redeemable at $12 per share and entitled to $10 per share after preferred but prior to common in liquidation. The company is required to devote 50% of annual net income in excess of the dividend requirements on the preferred stock to the redemption of the "B" shares.

(5) The stated value of the common was to be reduced to $2 per share. No dividends may be paid on the common stock until the "B" shares are redeemed.

The operations for 1966 resulted in a net income of $276,000; the preferred dividends for 1966 were paid.

Show how the Stockholders' Equity section will be presented in the December 31, 1966 balance sheet.

Problem 26-10. Household Company manufactures a diverse line of chemical-based products for use in the home. Because packaging is such an important part of an effective marketing program, a pooling of interests with a company in the packaging business is being explored.

After a careful search, the company made contact with Consumer Packaging Corporation, and, after negotiations, the following proposal has been drawn up to be submitted to the respective stockholders for approval.

Household Company will take over all of the assets and liabilities of Consumer Packaging Corporation, issuing shares of stock therefor to the packaging corporation, which in turn will distribute such shares to its stockholders. The number of shares of stock to be issued will be governed by the proportionate relationship between the estimated future average annual earnings of the separate companies. Thus, if the estimated future average annual earnings of Consumer Packaging Corporation equal 40% of the estimated future average annual earnings of Household Company, the shares to be issued to the packaging corporation will equal 40% of the outstanding shares of Household Company. Data for the three years ending December 31, 1966, appropriately adjusted to achieve comparability and equity, are to be used in estimating the future average annual earnings for the purpose of determining the proportionate stockholdings.

Data taken from the financial statements follow.

Balance Sheet Data
December 31, 1966

Assets	Household Company	Consumer Packaging Corporation
Cash	$134,720	$ 83,340
Receivables	176,940	34,280
Inventory	258,910	127,300
Plant and equipment	256,300	294,500
Accumulated depreciation (*Deduct)	125,400*	127,400*
Chemical property lease	150,000	
	$851,470	$412,020

Liabilities and Stockholders' Equity	Household Company	Consumer Packaging Corporation
Accounts payable	$146,470	$ 25,960
Accrued expenses	81,800	17,560
Bonds payable—5% (20-year bonds maturing 7/1/77)	120,000	
Common stock—$10 par value	300,000	200,000
Capital in excess of par value		12,000
Retained earnings	203,200	156,500
	$851,470	$412,020

	Income Tax Rate	Net Income	
		Household Company	Consumer Packaging Corporation
1964	50%	$59,100	$43,250
1965	50	58,400	45,000
1966	45	56,550	51,425

(Assume that it is reasonable to expect an income tax rate of 40% for 1967 and subsequent years.)

Household Company has used the dollar-value, *lifo* inventory method since 1954. Inventory data for the company, and estimated inventory data on a first-in, first-out basis, are shown below.

	Lifo	*Fifo*
December 31, 1963	$250,000	$275,000
December 31, 1964	252,100	279,500
December 31, 1965	256,810	287,210
December 31, 1966	258,910	289,310

Consumer Packaging Corporation has used the first-in, first-out inventory method.

Consumer Packaging Corporation has used accelerated depreciation, for both books and income tax purposes, whereas Household Company has used a straight-line method. It is estimated that if Consumer Packaging Corporation had used a straight-line method, $26,400 less depreciation would have been recorded during the three-year period ending December 31, 1966.

No utilization has as yet been made of the resources available to Household Company through its lease agreement, which expires December 31, 1976. However, development costs incurred in 1965 and 1966, which were charged to expense but were not deducted for income tax purposes, have made the resources available for utilization starting in 1967. During the term of the lease, it will no longer be necessary to purchase such materials from outside suppliers. The amounts were: 1965, $4,000; 1966, $10,000. It is estimated that utilization of the resources acquired through the lease during the 10 years ending December 31, 1976, will reduce the outside purchases of such material by $40,000 per year. It will cost about $21,000 a year to take the material from the leased property and deliver it to the company's processing facilities.

Show how the December 31, 1966 balance sheet of Household Company would look after the pooling of interests, applying accepted accounting procedures.

Assignment Material for Chapter 27

QUESTIONS

1. Describe three causes for the existence of a difference between the net income per books, before taxes, and taxable net income. Cite an example under each cause.
2. In essence, what is the objective of income tax-allocation procedures?
3. Describe the point of view adopted by the Securities and Exchange Commission in regard to income tax allocation when the question first became an important issue.
4. Is it likely that the question of income tax allocation would continue to hold its present importance if (1) income tax rates applicable to corporations were cut in half or if (2) accelerated depreciation methods were not permissible for income tax purposes?
5. If income tax-allocation procedures are applied, does it follow that the balance sheet will not show the estimated current tax liability?
6. Under what circumstances, if any, is it possible for a tax saving to result from the adoption of an accelerated depreciation method for tax purposes only?
7. Devise an illustration of income tax-allocation procedures involving the use of a Deferred Income Tax Liability account.
8. Describe the nature of the Deferred Income Tax Liability and Deferred Income Tax Expense accounts.
9. Can a gain ever result from the adoption of an accelerated depreciation method for tax purposes coupled with the continuation of the straight-line method in the books? Explain.
10. Assuming the general acceptability of income tax-allocation procedures, are they applicable in all instances where there is a difference or divergence between book income and tax-return income?
11. Does the matter of income tax allocation arise in connection with the correction of past depreciation?
12. In your opinion, does the tax-deductibility status of an asset affect its value?
13. Present a brief argument against the use of income tax-allocation procedures.

PROBLEMS

Problem 27-1. Transistor Company maintains a perpetual inventory. A physical inventory is taken each December 31 and the book balance is adjusted to conform with the physical inventory.

The trial balance on page 815 is final except for any adjustment to the book inventory which may be necessary upon the completion of the year-end physical inventory, currently being tabulated. The adjustment for income taxes is also delayed pending the completion of the physical inventory.

TRANSISTOR COMPANY
Trial Balance
December 31, 1966

Cash	43,100	
Accounts receivable	212,100	
Allowance for doubtful accounts		2,200
Inventory	374,500	
Accounts payable		65,300
Common stock		300,000
Retained earnings, December 31, 1965		152,200
Dividends	30,000	
Sales		985,500
Cost of goods sold	515,500	
Selling expenses	205,000	
General expenses	125,000	
	1,505,200	1,505,200

Because the board of directors at its December meeting voted to discontinue one of the company's product lines, a sizable inventory write-down is expected. While waiting for the completion of the physical inventory, the president, who is concerned about the impact of the inventory write-down on the financial statements, asks to have a tentative income statement prepared under the assumption that the inventory write-down will amount to $100,000. He wants to see the tentative income statement prepared under each of the following alternatives:

(a) The write-down is shown in the income statement with income tax-allocation procedures.
(b) The write-down is charged to Retained Earnings on a net-of-tax basis.

The company's accountant estimates that the liability for income taxes, should the write-down amount to $100,000, will be $20,000. You may assume that a tax rate of 50 per cent is proper.

Problem 27-2. Clay Construction Company specializes in the building of dams. During the years 1964, 1965, and 1966, three dams were completed. The first dam was started in 1962 and completed in 1964 at a profit before income taxes of $120,000. The second and third dams were started in 1963. The second dam was completed in 1965 at a profit before income taxes of $126,000, and the third dam was completed in 1966 at a profit before income taxes of $150,000.

The company uses the percentage-of-completion method of accounting in its books and the completed-contract method for income tax purposes.

Data relating to the progress toward completion of work on each dam as reported by the company's engineers are set forth below.

Dam	1962	1963	1964	1965	1966
1	20%	60%	20%		
2		30	60	10%	
3		10	30	50	10%

Assuming that the applicable income tax rate is 50%, prepare journal entries for the income tax charges and payments relating to the years 1962 through 1966, following income tax-allocation procedures.

Problem 27-3. Rounder Company has been depreciating its equipment over a five-year useful life by the straight-line method for both book and tax purposes. A partial lapsing schedule, relating to equipment owned on December 31, 1964, is presented below.

Partial Lapsing Schedule—Equipment

Year Acquired	Cost	Depreciation 1965	1966	1967	1968	1969	1970
1961	$100,000	$20,000					
1962	120,000	24,000	$24,000				
1963	120,000	24,000	24,000	$24,000			
1964	125,000	25,000	25,000	25,000	$25,000		

As indicated by the above data, the equipment has no scrap value, and a full year's depreciation is taken in the year of acquisition.

The equipment-acquisition plan of the company is as follows: 1965, $150,000; 1966, $180,000; 1967, $180,000; 1968, $210,000; 1969, $210,000; and 1970, $150,000.

Management has decided to adopt the sum-of-years' digits method for tax purposes only starting in 1965 and applicable to assets acquired after December 31, 1964.

(a) Prepare lapsing schedules for the 1965-1970 period for book depreciation and tax depreciation, assuming that assets are retired and acquired as planned. Also prepare a schedule showing the prospective cumulative deferred tax during this period. Use a 50% income tax rate.

(b) Assuming that the company changed its method of depreciation for tax purposes as planned but failed to apply income tax-allocation procedures, compute the aggregate effect which the failure to adopt income tax-allocation procedures would have on the amount of net income shown in the income statements for the six-year period ending December 31, 1970.

Problem 27-4. Slick Trenching Company purchased five special machines during the first five years of its business life. As shown by the schedule below, it adopted different depreciation methods for books and tax-return purposes. This is the only instance where the company's tax return differs from its books.

	Machine Number 1 — Depreciation Per		2 — Depreciation Per		3 — Depreciation Per	
Year	Tax Return	Books	Tax Return	Books	Tax Return	Books
1962	$25,000	$15,000	$20,000	$12,000		
1963	20,000	15,000	16,000	12,000	$25,000	$15,000
1964	15,000	15,000	12,000	12,000	20,000	15,000
1965	10,000	15,000	8,000	12,000	15,000	15,000
1966	5,000	15,000	4,000	12,000	10,000	15,000

	4 — Depreciation Per		5 — Depreciation Per	
Year	Tax Return	Books	Tax Return	Books
1962				
1963				
1964	$20,000	$12,000		
1965	16,000	12,000		
1966	12,000	12,000	$30,000	$18,000

The net income (loss) before income tax, as shown in the company's books, for each of the five years, is set forth below:

Year	Amount	Tax Rate
1962	$200,000	50%
1963	220,000	50
1964	(140,000)	50
1965	300,000	50
1966	(100,000)	50

Prepare journal entries for the income tax charges, payments, and refunds for the years covered by the above data following income tax-allocation procedures.

Problem 27-5. Coastal Shipbuilding Company has contracts for four motel ships. Data relating to these contracts are presented below.

Contract Identification	Year Started	Year Completed	Profit
I	1962	1964	$ 80,000
II	1963	1965	84,000
III	1963	1966	100,000
IV	1964	1966	60,000

Per cent of completion during year:

	1962	1963	1964	1965	1966
I	30%	50%	20%		
II		20	60	20%	
III		10	30	50	10%
IV			10	40	50

The company uses the percentage-of-completion method of accounting in its books and the completed-contract method for income tax purposes.

Assume that the applicable income tax rate has been 50% for a number of years and that such rate was expected to continue indefinitely. Prepare journal entries for the income tax charges and payments relating to the years 1962 through 1966, following income tax-allocation procedures; however, in 1965, the tax rate for that year, and future years, was reduced to 40%. As was indicated, such reduction was not anticipated.

Problem 27-6. Limo Service Company owns 10 motor coaches which it uses to haul airline passengers to and from the local airport. The company has been depreciating the vehicles on the straight-line method over a five-year useful life for both book purposes and income tax purposes.

The company is considering the adoption of the declining-balance method, at twice the straight-line rate for the first three years, with a change to the straight-line method for the remaining two years of useful life, for income tax purposes only and for new equipment purchased after January 1, 1965.

The depreciation status of its present fleet is set forth below.

Number of Vehicles	Year Acquired	Aggregate Cost	Aggregate Residual Value	Accumulated Depreciation December 31, 1964
3	1961	$ 60,000	$3,000	$45,600
3	1962	60,000	3,000	34,200
4	1964	84,000	4,000	16,000
10		$204,000		$95,800

The company takes a full year's depreciation in the year of acquisition and no depreciation in the year of disposal.

The company has prepared a projection of its motor-equipment needs for the next five years. The plan is submitted below:

	Number of Vehicles to be Purchased		Per Unit		
Year	Replacements	Additions	Cost	Residual Value	Useful Life—Years
1965		2	$22,000	$1,000	5
1966	3		22,000	1,000	5
1967	3		22,000	1,000	5
1968		2	25,000	1,500	5
1969	4		25,000	1,500	5

(a) Prepare a schedule showing the potential cumulative tax savings from the adoption of the declining-balance method of depreciation for tax purposes only for the five-year period ending December 31, 1969. You may assume that neither gain nor loss is realized upon disposal. Also assume an income tax rate of 50%.

(b) Compute the amount of the correction to the deferred tax account, should the income tax rate be lowered to 45% effective for 1970 and subsequent years.

Problem 27-7. The following accounts are among those in the ledger of Shower Company.

Bond Discount

Debit	Credit
1958	1958
Oct. 1 36,000	Dec. 31 900
	1959
	Dec. 31 3,600
	1960
	Dec. 31 3,600
	1961
	Dec. 31 3,600
	1962
	Dec. 31 3,600
	1963
	Dec. 31 3,600
	1964
	Dec. 31 3,600
	1965
	Dec. 31 3,600

Bonds Payable

Debit	Credit
(5% Bonds due	October 1, 1968)
	1958
	Oct. 1 300,000

As of October 1, 1965, the company refunded the above bond issue and took as a deduction in its 1965 income tax return the balance of the Bond Discount account. However, the company continued its bond discount-amortization program in its books.

The following data relating to 1965 are taken from the company's books and tax return.

	Books	Tax Return
Sales	$800,000	$800,000
Cost of sales and expenses, except the annual charge for amortization of bond discount	700,000	700,000
Amortization of bond discount	3,600	2,700
Write-off of unamortized discount		10,800

Assume that the income tax rate is 50% and that the income subject to tax for the years indicated is as shown below:

Year	Loss (Which May Be Carried Back)	Taxable Income
1965		$86,500
1966		80,000
1967		32,000
1968	$10,000	
1969		45,000

Prepare journal entries for the income tax charges, payments, and refunds applicable to the years 1965 through 1969, following income tax-allocation procedures.

Problem 27-8. Seacraft Company, a diversified and profitable builder of ships, developed a prototype "air-cushion" craft at a cost of $4,000,000. In view of the uncertain commercial prospects, management decided to write off the development cost as an unusual deduction in the income statement for 1965, even though the company was advised that for income tax purposes the development costs must be amortized over a four-year period, 1965-1968, at $1,000,000 per year.

Assume that the income tax rate is 50% and that the income tax actually payable for the years indicated is as shown below.

Year	Income Tax Payable
1965	$1,800,000
1966	900,000
1967	800,000
1968	1,000,000

Prepare journal entries for the income tax charges and payments applicable to the years 1965 through 1968, following income tax-allocation procedures.

Problem 27-9. The following data are taken from the adjusted trial balances of Splicer Company.

	December 31,		
	1964	1965	1966
Sales	1,800,000	1,880,000	1,850,000
Cost of goods sold	1,200,000	1,260,000	1,240,000
Operating expenses	380,000	400,000	390,000
Loss—Inventory obsolescence	100,000	50,000	—
Gain on sale of obsolete inventory	—	—	10,000
Income tax	110,000	72,500	77,500
Income tax payable (50% rate)	110,000	72,500	77,500
Obsolete inventory (Asset)	100,000	25,000	—

In the latter part of 1964 it became apparent that inventory costing $200,000 was obsolete. On the basis of the information then available to management, it seemed reasonable to expect that the obsolete inventory could be sold for export for $100,000. The following journal entry was authorized and recorded as of December 31, 1964, although the loss was not deductible for income tax purposes until a sale or other disposal occurred.

December 31, 1964	Obsolete inventory	100,000	
	Loss—Inventory obsolescence	100,000	
	Inventory		200,000

During 1965, one-half of the obsolete inventory was sold for export for $25,000. In view of this experience, management directed that the obsolete inventory still on hand at the end of 1965 be further written down to 25% of its original cost. The loss arising from the sale during 1965 of one-half of the obsolete inventory was deductible for income tax purposes on the 1965 tax return.

During 1966, the remaining one-half of the obsolete inventory was sold for export for $35,000.

The company did not use income tax-allocation procedures; however, it followed the clean surplus theory of reporting.

Required:

(a) A schedule comparing the net income as shown by the company's income statement for each of the three years with the net income that would have been shown if income tax-allocation procedures had been followed.

(b) The 1964 income statement as it would have appeared if the company had followed income tax-allocation procedures.

(c) Journal entries as of December 31, 1964, 1965, and 1966, for the income tax, following income tax-allocation procedures.

Problem 27-10. After Unsinkable Mining Company was organized, it spent $4,200,000 developing an ore deposit believed to contain 6,000,000 tons of ore. The depletion rate was, therefore, set at 70 cents per ton.

The company also constructed a processing plant at a cost of $882,000. Because the processing plant would easily last as long as the ore deposit, but would have no value after the ore deposit was exhausted, depreciation was properly based on the rate of extraction. The depreciation rate set was 14.7 cents per ton.

At the beginning of 1965, several years after the company commenced its profitable mining operations and after 5,000,000 tons of ore had been mined, processed, and sold, it was discovered that the ore deposit contained 2,000,000 tons of available ore. The processing plant was in good condition and could process the remaining ore without any additional capital outlay.

On the basis of this new information, it was evident that the rates should have been 60 cents per ton for depletion and 12.6 cents per ton for depreciation. The company desires to use the revised rates in its future financial statements and to make a correction of prior years' earnings as of January 1, 1965.

Such correction will have no status for income tax purposes. However, the depletion and depreciation rates will have to be changed for tax purposes starting in 1965 in order to spread the remaining book values over the 2,000,000 tons of available ore.

During 1965, 400,000 tons of ore were mined, processed, and sold. The correct income tax liability relating to 1965 operations was $200,000.

Required:

(a) The journal entry for the correction of prior years' earnings, following income tax-allocation procedures.

(b) Journal entries for depreciation and depletion for 1965, also following income tax-allocation procedures.

(c) The journal entry required for the $200,000 of income taxes actually payable, resulting from 1965 operations.

You may assume an income tax rate of 50%.

Assignment Material for Chapter 28

QUESTIONS

1. Distinguish between the terms *economic* and *monetary* as they are used in describing income.
2. Give one reason why accountants believe they are justified in continuing to rely on the assumption that fluctuations in the purchasing power of the dollar will be so insignificant as not to undermine the usefulness of the dollar as a unit of measurement.
3. What is meant by the phrase *dollar accounting?*
4. Why might a profitable business need to borrow money merely to replace some of its fixed assets? Is the need for such borrowing more likely attributable to financial matters or to accounting matters?
5. There has been a good deal of criticism of the traditional "historical" cost records and the data which they reflect, especially during times of inflation or deflation. In order to assist in the interpretation of accounting reports as normally prepared, many accountants have suggested that the recorded cost data be first utilized in the preparation of the conventional financial statements, and then, as a supplementary technique, that these statements be converted into dollars having a uniform purchasing power through the application of price indexes to the recorded dollar amounts. Evaluate this suggestion.
6. List three suggestions that deserve consideration in connection with the practice of disclosing comparative data when there has been a significant change in the price level.
7. List some of the criticisms of conventional accounting.
8. Give some of the comments that are offered in support of conventional accounting.
9. Give two reasons favoring the use of supplementary financial statements.
10. Some items in accounting statements are stated in current dollars, although other items are normally stated in less current dollars. Is this condition influenced in any way by the accounting procedures employed? Explain.
11. What is the effect of changes in the level of prices over a period of time upon comparative financial statements?
12. When might an accountant advise a businessman to reduce the span of years covered by comparative statements? Explain.
13. In considering the merits of using price indexes for the purpose of converting the accounting data as reflected in the conventional historical cost accounts, some people have suggested that these price-level adjustments should be confined to the fixed assets and related depreciation. What can be said in favor of such a proposal? Against it?

14. Data for the current year and the two preceding years are given below:

	Sales	General Price Index
Two years ago	$240,000	150
Last year	300,000	200
Current year	325,000	225

(a) For comparative purposes, you are to state the sales in terms of current-year dollars.
(b) What is revealed by a comparison of the restated amounts?

15. Is the fact that the purchasing power of money varies of equal significance to the balance sheet and the income statement?

16. Answer *yes* or *no* to the following questions:

Would supplementary financial statements prepared by the use of a general price index provide information on replacement costs?
Would such supplementary statements disclose current values?
Would such supplementary statements represent a departure from the cost basis?

17. What are monetary items? When monetary items are held during a period of rising prices, does the holder gain or lose purchasing power?

PROBLEMS

Problem 28-1. Prepare a supplementary comparative income statement for Selfserve Laundry Company in 19+7 (current) dollars.

SELFSERVE LAUNDRY COMPANY
Comparative Income Statement
For 19+6 and 19+7

	19+6	19+7
Revenue from machines	$108,000	$114,000
Expenses:		
Depreciation—Building	$ 7,200	$ 7,200
Depreciation—Machines	3,600	3,600
All other	94,200	99,000
Total expense	$105,000	$109,800
Net income	$ 3,000	$ 4,200

The building was acquired in 19+5. The machines are being depreciated at a rate of 10% per year. The asset account shows that $18,000 was invested in machines in 19+5 and another $18,000 was invested in 19+6.

Year	Price Index
19—	100
19+5	120
19+6	125
19+7	130

Problem 28-2. The conventional income statement of Apartment Supply Company is presented on the next page.

APARTMENT SUPPLY COMPANY
Income Statement
For the Year Ended December 31, 19+4

Sales		$300,000
Cost of sales	$192,000	
Depreciation—Building	32,000	
Depreciation—Equipment	21,000	
All other expenses	41,000	286,000
Net income		$ 14,000

Selected accounts from the company's general ledger are set forth below in T-account form. The company follows a first-in, first-out inventory method.

Inventory

19+3 inventory	26,250	19+4	192,000
19+4 purchases	210,000		

Cost of Sales

19+4	192,000	

Building

19+1	800,000	

Equipment

19+1	80,000	
19+3	25,000	

A general price index covering a recent period of years is set forth below:

19+1	120	19+3	125
19+2	122	19+4	132

Prepare a supplementary income statement in current dollars.

Problem 28-3. State the following account balances in current (19+10) dollars.

ALPHA COMPANY
Trial Balance
December 31, 19+10

Cash	18,630	
Equipment	156,600	
Accumulated depreciation		62,130
Accounts payable		6,300
Capital stock		63,000
Retained earnings		39,300
Revenue		105,000
Depreciation	7,830	
Other expenses	92,670	
	275,730	275,730

Price Index and Historical Data

Year		Price Index
19—	Company organized and capital stock issued	105
19—	Equipment acquired—Cost, $75,600	105
19+5	Equipment acquired—Cost, $66,000	110
19+9		120
19+10	Equipment acquired—Cost, $15,000	126

Problem 28-4. Comparative trial balances are set forth below. State the account balances in 19+10 dollars.

XYZ COMPANY
Trial Balances
December 31, 19+9 and 19+10

	December 31,			
	19+9		19+10	
Cash	83,600		96,000	
Land	44,880		44,880	
Building	210,000		210,000	
Accumulated depreciation		50,400		58,800
Mortgage payable		160,000		160,000
Capital stock		100,000		100,000
Retained earnings		15,230		28,080
Revenue		175,000		160,000
Depreciation expense	8,400		8,400	
Other expenses	153,750		147,600	
	500,630	500,630	506,880	506,880

Other Data

Year		Price Index
19—	Company organized and stock issued	100
19+1	Land acquired	102
19+3	Building constructed	105
19+4	Mortgage obtained	106
19+9	Last year	125
19+10	Current year	120

Problem 28-5. Data taken from the conventional comparative statements of Circular Company appear below and on the following page.

Required:

Supplementary comparative income statement.
Supplementary comparative balance sheet.
Supplementary statement of changes in balance of stockholders' equity for 19+6.

Debit Balances

	19+5	19+6
Cash	7,350	18,150
Accounts receivable	32,340	21,300
Inventory—end of year	17,640	15,800
Land	38,500	48,500
Building	252,000	252,000
Cost of sales	68,250	69,500
Depreciation	12,600	12,600
Salaries	16,170	16,300
Rent expense—Equipment	8,820	9,000
Taxes	2,205	2,400
Other expense	5,145	6,200
Dividends	6,000	6,600
	467,020	478,350

Credit Balances

	19+5	19+6
Accumulated depreciation	50,400	63,000
Accounts payable	19,110	12,400
Accrued expenses	4,998	4,628
Mortgage payable	66,150	66,150
Capital stock	150,000	150,000
Retained earnings—beginning of year	49,942	57,172
Sales	126,420	125,000
	467,020	478,350

Year	Events	Price Index
19–	Company organized and stock issued	100
19+1	Land purchased for cash	110
19+2	Building constructed, occupied, and mortgaged	120
19+4	Year-end inventory was $16,800	140
19+5		147
19+6	Additional land purchased for cash	155

Problem 28-6. The following data were taken from the conventional financial statements of Downtown Building Corporation. The corporation closes its books as of December 31.

	19+5	19+6
Cash	18,000	56,500
Rent receivable	2,400	3,000
Supplies on hand	1,200	900
Land	49,500	59,500
Building	550,000	550,000
Depreciation expense	22,000	22,000
Taxes expense	28,000	30,000
Repairs and maintenance	15,000	15,200
Supplies used	7,410	7,500
Salaries	18,000	18,900
	711,510	763,500
Accumulated depreciation	66,000	88,000
Accrued taxes	8,000	8,400
Mortgage payable	300,000	300,000
Capital stock	200,000	200,000
Retained earnings	17,510	47,100
Rent revenue	120,000	120,000
	711,510	763,500

The corporation was organized and the capital stock was issued when the price level was indicated by an index number of 100. The land was acquired for cash; the first parcel was purchased when the price index was 105. The building was completed and space rented when the price index was 110. The mortgage financing was secured when the index was at 107. The supplies on hand at the end of 19+4 cost $590.

The price index for recent years is set forth below:

19+4	118
19+5	120
19+6	126

Required:

Supplementary comparative income statement in 19+6 dollars.
Supplementary comparative balance sheet in 19+6 dollars.
Statement of changes in "balance of stockholders' equity" for 19+6.

Problem 28-7. Tower Company used the following data to prepare its 19+4 conventional statements.

December 31, 19+4		
Cash	4,040	
Accounts receivable	3,100	
Inventory	9,000	
Equipment	28,860	
Accumulated depreciation		10,494
Long-term investment in common stocks—at cost (Market value, $19,000)	16,200	
Accounts payable		3,900
Accrued expenses		1,306
Capital stock		30,000
Retained earnings		11,200
Dividends	1,500	
Sales		85,000
Cost of goods sold	51,400	
Depreciation expense	2,886	
Salaries	16,400	
Rent expense	4,800	
Other expense	3,714	
	141,900	141,900

Tower Company issued its capital stock in 19—, when the index of general prices was 100. The following accounting policies were adopted with the start of business:

The last-in, first-out inventory method.
Straight-line depreciation on year-end balance of asset account.

Additional Data

	Account Balances				
Year	Inventory	Equipment	Depreciation	Accumulated Depreciation	Index Number
19—	$10,000				100
19 + 1	9,800	$20,400	$2,040	$ 2,040	102
19 + 2	9,500	30,900	3,090	5,130	105
19 + 3	9,200	28,860	2,886	7,608	108
19 + 4	9,000	28,860	2,886	10,494	110

In 19+3, some of the equipment acquired in 19+1 was sold for its book value of $1,632. In the same year, $16,200 was invested in common stocks.

The December 31, 19+3 conventional balance sheet showed the following subtotals:

Current assets	$16,598
Current liabilities	4,158

Prepare the following supplementary financial statements for 19+4, in current dollars:

Income statement; Balance sheet; Statement of changes in balance of stockholders' equity.

Problem 28-8. Data from the conventional, comparative balance sheet of Low Rise Apartment Company are presented below.

Debits	December 31, 19+5	December 31, 19+6
Cash	$ 9,000	$ 17,000
Land	38,500	38,500
Apartment	252,000	252,000
	$299,500	$307,500

Credits	19+5	19+6
Accumulated depreciation	$ 50,400	$ 63,000
Accounts payable	1,500	3,000
Mortgage payable	160,000	150,000
Capital stock	75,000	75,000
Retained earnings	12,600	16,500
	$299,500	$307,500

A cash dividend of $5,000 was declared and paid during 19+6.

Additional Data

Year		Price Index
19—	Company organized and stock issued	100
19+1	Land purchased for cash	110
19+2	Apartment built and occupied; financed in part with a mortgage	120
19+5		140
19+6	Mortgage reduced as of December 31	147

Required:

Statement of changes in balance of stockholders' equity for 19+6, to accompany the supplementary, comparative statements.

Problem 28-9. The conventional statement of retained earnings of Haskins Corporation follows.

HASKINS CORPORATION
Statement of Retained Earnings
For the Year Ended December 31, 19+5

Retained earnings, December 31, 19+4		$40,000
Net income for the year		35,000
Total		$75,000
Deduct dividends:		
Cash—5% (before stock dividend)	$10,000	
Stock—10% (at market value, which equals par value)	20,000	30,000
Retained earnings, December 31, 19+5		$45,000

Data from the December 31, 19+4 conventional balance sheet:

Current assets	$150,000
Fixed assets	260,000
Total assets	$410,000

Data from the 19+5 supplementary financial statements:

Total assets	$495,000
Total liabilities	190,000
Net income	30,000

The general price level has increased 25% since the company was organized. During the most recent year, the price level has increased 5%.

Prepare the statement of changes in balance of stockholders' equity for 19+5, to accompany the supplementary, comparative statements.

Problem 28-10. This problem carries the Vision Company illustration presented in Chapter 28 one year forward. You will need to make use of the illustration in your solution to this problem.

The conventional income statement and balance sheet for the next year are presented below.

VISION COMPANY
Income Statement
For the Year Ended December 31, 19+6

Sales		$51,000
Cost of sales	$33,000	
Depreciation	2,400	
Other expenses	12,800	48,200
Net income		$ 2,800

VISION COMPANY
Balance Sheet
December 31, 19+6

Assets

Current assets:		
Cash	$11,200	
Current receivables	14,000	
Inventory	7,000	$32,200
Fixed assets:		
Equipment	$24,000	
Less accumulated depreciation	13,500	10,500
		$42,700

Liabilities and Stockholders' Equity

Current liabilities:		
Current payables		$ 6,000
Long-term liabilities:		
Bank loan		4,000
Stockholders' equity:		
Capital stock	$20,000	
Retained earnings	12,700	32,700
		$42,700

The general price index for 19+6 indicated a 4% increase over 19+5, which carried the index to 131.04.

Required:

Supplementary comparative income statement for the three-year period ended December 31, 19+6, in current (19+6) dollars.

Supplementary comparative balance sheet for the dates December 31, 19+4, 19+5, and 19+6, in current (19+6) dollars.

Carry computations to the nearest dollar.

Index

A

B

C

D

E

F

G

H

I

J

L

M

N

O

P

Q

R

S